A ONE-OF-A-KIND REFERENCE

- What is the term for grinding your teeth?

- What is the name of that spicy Anglo-Indian vegetable soup?

- What is the Jerusalem house of worship revered by Jews, Christians and Moslems?

- What is the Italian name for Florence?

- Who wrote *The Divine Comedy*?

- What was Cary Grant's real name?

You'll discover the answers to these and thousands of other fascinating and perplexing questions in this compact and completely up-to-date reference. Now you can find all that you're looking for and more, in . . .

ON THE TIP OF YOUR TONGUE
The Word/Name/Place Finder

IRENE M. FRANCK is co-author, with her husband, David M. Brownstone, of *The Self-Publishing Handbook,* which is available in a Plume edition.

ON THE TIP OF YOUR TONGUE
The Word/Name/Place Finder

by
Irene M. Franck

A SIGNET BOOK

SIGNET
Published by the Penguin Group
Penguin Books USA Inc., 375 Hudson Street,
New York, New York 10014, U.S.A.
Penguin Books Ltd, 27 Wrights Lane, London W8 5TZ, England
Penguin Books Australia Ltd, Ringwood, Victoria, Australia
Penguin Books Canada Ltd, 2801 John Street,
Markham, Ontario, Canada L3R 1B4
Penguin Books (N.Z.) Ltd, 182–190 Wairau Road,
Auckland 10, New Zealand

Penguin Books Ltd, Registered Offices:
Harmondsworth, Middlesex, England

First published by Signet, an imprint of Penguin Books USA Inc.

First Printing, November 1990
10 9 8 7 6 5 4 3 2 1

 REGISTERED TRADEMARK—MARCA REGISTRADA

Printed in the United States of America

CONTENTS

PREFACE

What is the word for "fear of the number 13"?
What is the cape at the southern tip of Africa?
What was the name of the family on *Upstairs, Downstairs*?
What is the Italian name for Florence?

How many times have you asked yourself just such questions as these, trying to shake the answer out of your memory? This is the place to find all these answers that hover on the brink of consciousness.

On the Tip of Your Tongue is designed to allow you to answer questions when ordinary reference books don't help. For example, many reference librarians say that the question they are asked most often is: What is the word for "fear of the number 13"? The problem is that unless people already know the word, they cannot look it up. Even people with a substantial reference library at their disposal would have a hard time finding the answer to that question, starting from scratch. Looking up "fear" or "phobia" or even "thirteen" will get them nowhere. But in *On the Tip of Your Tongue*, they would need only to look in the Quick-Finder Index under "fear" or "phobia" to locate the list of common phobias, from which they could easily pick out "triskaidekaphobia" as the word they want.

In essence, *On the Tip of Your Tongue* is a reverse reference book of popular knowledge or—to put it another way—a backward book of lists. The book presents lists of information grouped by themes, around the kinds of. questions people commonly ask. The Quick-Finder Index will direct you to the proper list for your particular question. Trivia games players and puzzle-solvers may find the Quick-Finder Index especially useful. People who are browsing for fun, rather than with a specific question in mind, may turn instead to the Quick-Finder Outline, which shows how the whole book and its sections are organized.

Apart from its unique organization, *On the Tip of Your Tongue* is special in its coverage. Many questions that come up in everyday conversation cannot be answered in standard reference works, because the works focus on classical and traditional facts, often ignoring popular culture and non-political events. While *On the Tip of Your Tongue* includes much classical and traditional information, it also focuses on many areas of popular interest.

It includes palaces and castles, diseases and desserts, parts of speech and parts of the body, favorite movies or players, divinations and invocations, phobias and manias, vitamins and villains, gods and goddesses, stage names and pseudonyms, presidents and kings, artists and scientists, cities and regions, extinct prehistoric animals and geological time periods, islands and capes, mountains and rivers, astronauts and spacecraft, words from foreign languages and special languages from the arts, sciences, law, religion, philosophy—and a great deal more. The Quick-Finder Outline gives an overview of the book's store of information, while the Quick-Finder Index helps you answer specific questions. The following section, How to Use This Book, tells how to find the words, names, and places you want.

HOW TO USE THIS BOOK

In *On the Tip of Your Tongue* names, words, and places are organized by content into meaningful groups, for ease of access. Within each grouped list, items are arranged in the way that best fits the topic, for example:

- chronologically (as in Key Figures in World History or Geological time Periods),
- ascending or descending order (as in Prefixes for Large and Small Numbers),
- from beginning to end (as in the Anatomy and Physiology section of The Digestive System),
- by associative grouping (as in Parts of Speech or Time, Calendars, and Anniversaries).
- alphabetically by the "question" in the left-hand column (as in Fears and Phobias)
- alphabetically by a key word in the left-hand column (as in Mystery Writers and Detectives or Modern Politicians and Public Figures)
- alphabetically by the "answer" in the right-hand column (as in Islands of the World)

The Quick-Finder Outline (on p. 00) will give you a general overview of the book's coverage, showing the 10 main parts of the book and the many sections contained in each. If you're interested in just browsing in a general area—music or international foods, for example—the Quick-Finder Outline will direct you to it.

But if you are starting with a specific question, you should turn to the Quick-Finder Index (on p. 00), which is actually the key to the book. It will let you find that otherwise elusive word with ease. Here are some examples of how to use it to find what you want in *On the Tip of Your Tongue*:

What's the word for fear of the number 13?

1. Look in the Quick-Finder Index under either fears or phobias. You'll find page references to a list called "Fears and Phobias" in the part called *In Sickness and in Health*.

2. You'll find that "Fears and Phobias" is organized alphabetically by the "question" in the left-hand column. Scan down the left-hand column to find "number 13" and you'll have the word you're looking for: triskaidekaphobia or tredecaphobia.

What is the name of Agatha Christie's elderly spinster detective?

1. Look in the Quick-Finder Index under mysteries or detectives. You'll be directed to the list called "Mystery Detectives and Regulars" in the *World of Letters* part.
2. You'll find that the list is organized alphabetically by the author's name in the left-hand column. Go to the "C's" for Christie, and you'll find your answer: Jane Marple.

What is the term for grinding your teeth?

1. Look in the Quick-Finder Index under teeth or dentistry. You'll be directed to a section called "The Teeth" in the *In Sickness and in Health* part.
2. You'll find that the section is organized into three lists—anatomy and physiology (parts of the teeth and mouth), diseases and problem conditions, and treatments, tests, and tools. Scan the second list to find the problem condition you want: bruxism.

Who was Florence's Renaissance leader nicknamed "The Magnificent"?

1. Look in the Quick-Finder Index under historical figures or Italy. You'll find page references to the two sections about Italians in "Key Figures in World History" in the part called *People from the Past*. The first reference is to Roman times; the second reference, from the Middle Ages to the mid-20th century, is the one you want.
2. You'll find that the list of Italian figures is organized chronologically. Scan down the list to find the Renaissance man you want: Lorenzo de' Medici.

What's the name of that spicy Anglo-Indian vegetable soup?

1. Look in the Quick-Finder Index under soups or foods. You'll be directed to an entry on food, where you'll find page references for "Soups, Stews, and One-Dish Meals" in the *Everyday Life* part, with various geographical subdivisions. The one you want is "Asia and the Pacific."

2. You'll find that the list is organized alphabetically by the list of dishes in the right-hand column. If you think you know that the soup you want begins with an "m," go directly to the "m's"; otherwise scan the list to find the description of the soup you want: mulligatawny.

What's the French word for "welcome"?

1. Look in the Quick-Finder Index under foreign languages or France. You'll be directed to the list "Words from the French" in the section called "In other words" in the part called *Everyday Life.* This is divided into sublists of words and phrases grouped by theme; the list you want is called "Hail and Farewell."
2. You'll find the list is organized alphabetically by the left-hand column. Look under the "w's" for "welcome" and find the word you want: bienvenue.

What is the Jerusalem house of worship revered by Jews, Christians, and Moslems?

1. Look in the Quick-Finder Index under churches, sacred places, or religion. You'll be directed to the list called "Churches and Other Sacred Places" in the section *Special Places.* This is further subdivided geographically; the list you want is "In Asia, Africa, Australia, and the Pacific."
2. You'll find that the list is organized alphabetically by the list of churches and sacred sites in the right-hand column. If you have some idea of the beginning of the word, go to the "d's." Otherwise, scan down the list until you find the description that fits the site you are looking for: Dome of the Rock.

Note that *On the Tip of Your Tongue* does not attempt to give a complete definition or description of the word, name, or place listed. The aim is to give you just enough information to identify the term or name you seek. So you will not find, for example, all the major works of Tennessee Williams listed. What you will find is generally one very well-known, characteristic work—*A Streetcar Named Desire*—that should instantly call to mind the playwright's name, even if you started with another of his plays in your mind. And you will have been able to answer that all-important question: Now, what was the name of . . . ?

QUICK-FINDER INDEX

The following Quick-Finder Index is an alphabetical guide to the contents of *On the Tip of Your Tongue.* Since the book covers so very much information, the index is very general, using major topics such as art, music, anthropology, or politics. Under such topics, you will find further breakdowns—under *food,* for example, by type of food (soups, breads, etc.) and region of origin, or under *historical figures,* region of origin and period of prominence (classical, medieval, etc.).

Where geography is involved, you should look generally under these continent-wide designations: Africa, Asia, Americas, Australia, and Europe; only a few countries—the United States, USSR, Canada, Great Britain, France, and Italy—are broken out as separate topics in the index. For an overview of the organization of the whole book, look at the Quick-Finder Outline (p. xxxvii). For some notes on how to reach what you want most quickly, see How to Use This Book (p. ix).

QUICK-FINDER OUTLINE

The following Quick-Finder Outline is a structural guide to the contents of *On the Tip of Your Tongue*. It shows you what information is covered in all of the sections and sub-sections in each of the 10 parts of the book. This outline will be especially useful if you have a general interest in a particular area (rather than a specific question you might look up in the index). If, for example, you are interested in literature, you might look at the *World of Letters*, to see what parts of the book you want to browse in. Similarly, a general curiosity about medical terms might take you to the *In Sickness and in Health* section. For some notes on how to reach what you want most quickly, see How to Use This Book on page ix.

World of the Arts, 74-158

In Sickness and in Health, 159–227

World of Philosophy and Belief, 296–333

Politics and People, 405–450

People From the Past, 451–483

Special Places, 484–555

World of Letters

Classical Authors

(See also Key Figures in Religion and Philosophy in *World of Philosophy and Belief*)

Among authors from Classical Greece and Rome, who wrote . . . ?

Aeneid and *Georgics*	**Vergil (Virgil)**
Anabasis	**Xenophon**
Carmina and *The Epodes*	**Horace**
Clouds and *The Frogs*	**Aristophanes**
De Re Publica and *De Oratore*	**Cicero**
epigrams on Roman life	**Martial**
fables collection in the 5th c. B.C.	**Aesop**
histories of the Roman emperors in the 2nd c. A.D.	**Tacitus**
History of Rome in the 1st c. A.D.	**Livy**
history of Rome through the Punic Wars in the 2nd c. B.C.	**Polybius**
history of the Greco-Persian Wars in the 5th c. B.C.	**Herodotus**
History of the Jewish War in the 1st c. A.D.	**Flavius Josephus**
history of the Peloponnesian Wars in 5th c. B.C.	**Thucydides**
Iliad and *Odyssey*	**Homer**
lyric poetry, from Lesbos	**Sappho**
Medea and *Iphegenia in Aulis*	**Euripides**
Metamorphoses	**Ovid**
Oedipus Rex and *Electra*	**Sophocles**
On Nature	**Heraclitus**
Oresteia trilogy	**Aeschylus**
Parallel Lives	**Plutarch**
satires on Roman habits and morals	**Juvenal**

1

Epics

Among epics and anonymous works, what was or were the . . . ?

Anglo-Saxon epic about killing Grendel	*Beowulf*
Arthurian work by the "Pearl Poet"	*Sir Gawain and the Green Knight*
most famous English morality play	*Everyman*
French epic about the art of love	*Romance of the Rose*
French medieval epic of war with the Moslems	*Chanson de Roland (Song of Roland)*
German epic focusing on Siegfried	*Nibelungenleid*
Hindu epic about the godlike Rama	*Ramayana*
Icelandic collections of Scandinavian myth	*Eddas*
Indian epic including the *Bhagavadgita*	*Mahabharata*
Portuguese epic about Da Gama by Luis de Camões	*Os Lusiadas (The Lusiads)*
Scheherazade stories	*The Arabian Nights' Entertainments*
Spanish epic of El Cid's fight against the Moors	*Poema del Cid* or *Cantar de Mio Cid*

Homer's Characters and Places

In the Greek epics attributed to Homer, who or what was or were . . . ?

In the Iliad

the city besieged by the Greeks	**Troy (Illum)**
the king of Sparta	**Menelaus**
Menelaus's wife	**Helen**
the king of Troy	**Priam**
Priam's son, who abducts Helen	**Paris**
the king of Mycenae and leader of the Greeks	**Agamemnon**
the priest of Apollo, whose daughter Agamemnon refuses to give up	**Chryses**
the Greek hero who argues with Agamemnon and retires from battle	**Achilles**

the leader of the Trojan army, killed in battle	**Hector**
Hector's opponent in single combat	**Ajax**
Achilles's friend, killed wearing his armor	**Patroclus**
Hector's wife, captured when Troy fell	**Andromache**

In the Odyssey

the hero of the *Odyssey*	**Odysseus (Ulysses)**
Odysseus's home	**Ithaca**
the war for which Odysseus left home	**Trojan War**
Odysseus's wife, who weaves while waiting him	**Penelope**
Odysseus's son, who searches for his father	**Telemachus**
Odysseus's father	**Laertes**
Telemachus's guide, inspired by Pallas Athena	**Mentor**
the wise king of Pylos, Odysseus's ally	**Nestor**
the sorceress who changed Odysseus's men to swine	**Circe**
the whirlpool opposite Scylla	**Charybdis**
the race of one-eyed giants	**Cyclops**
the Cyclops giant Odysseus blinded	**Polyphemus**
the sea monster opposite Charybdis	**Scylla**
the sweet-singing tempting bird-women	**Sirens**

Medieval and Renaissance Authors

(See also Key Figures in Religion and Philosophy in *World of Philosophy and Belief*)

Among medieval and Renaissance authors through the 17th century, who wrote . . . ?

All for Love and *Absalom and Achitophel*	**John Dryden**
Anatomy of Melancholy	**Robert Burton**
Astrophel and Stella and *An Apologie for Poetrie*	**Philip Sidney**
Ballade des Pendus and *Grand Testament*	**François Villon**

Canterbury Tales	**Geoffrey Chaucer**
Changeling	**Thomas Middleton**
Chronicles much-used by Shakespeare	**Raphael Holinshed**
Compleat Angler	**Izaak Walton**
Country Wife	**William Wycherley**
"Death Be Not Proud" and "Ask Not for Whom the Bell Tolls"	**John Donne**
Decameron	**Giovanni Boccaccio**
diaries of 17th-c. English life	**Samuel Pepys** and **John Evelyn**
Divine Comedy	**Dante Alighieri**
Don Quixote	**Miguel de Cervantes Saavedra**
Duchess of Malfi	**John Webster**
Fables Choisies, Mises en Vers, French fables	**Jean de La Fontaine**
Faerie Queene and *Epithalamion*	**Edmund Spenser**
Gargantua and Pantagruel	**François Rabelais**
Hamlet, Macbeth, and *King Lear*	**William Shakespeare**
Homer translations that Keats admired	**George Chapman**
Le Cid and *Médée*	**Pierre Corneille**
Le Morte d'Arthur	**Thomas Malory**
letters in 17th-c. France	**Marquise de Sévigné**
lyrics to Laura	**Francesco Petrarch**
Paradise Lost	**John Milton**
Phèdre (Phaedra)	**Jean Racine**
Philaster and *The Maid's Tragedy*	**Francis Beaumont** and **John Fletcher**
Pilgrim's Progress	**John Bunyan**
Puss in Boots	**Charles Perrault**
Religio Medici	**Thomas Browne**
Rover and *Oroonoko,* the 1st professional woman writer	**Aphra Behn**
"Sacrifice" and "Easter Wings"	**George Herbert**
Spanish Tragedy	**Thomas Kyd**
Tamburlaine the Great and *Dr. Faustus*	**Christopher Marlowe**
Tartuffe	**Molière**
"They Are All Gone into the World of Light"	**Henry Vaughn**
'Tis Pity She's a Whore	**John Ford**
"To Althea from Prison" and "To Lucasta . . ."	**Richard Lovelace**
"To His Coy Mistress"	**Andrew Marvell**
"To the Virgins, to Make Much of Time"	**Robert Herrick**
Utopia	**Thomas More**
Volpone and "Drink to Me Only with Thine Eyes"	**Ben Jonson**
Way of the World	**William Congreve**

Shakespeare's Characters

Among the characters in Shakespeare's plays, who was or were . . . ?

In As You Like It

The duke banished to the Forest of Arden	Frederick
Frederick's daughter, who joins him	Rosalind (Ganymede)
Rosalind's friend, who joins her	Celia
Rosalind's love	Orlando

In Hamlet

Hamlet's uncle, who killed King Hamlet	Claudius
Hamlet's mother, now Claudius's wife	Gertrude
Hamlet's love, who commits suicide	Ophelia
Hamlet's friend, Ophelia's brother	Laertes
Laertes's and Ophelia's father, full of advice	Polonius
Hamlet's schoolmates, turned spies on him	Rosencrantz and Guildenstern

In Henry IV, Part I

Prince Hal's fat, riotous companion	Falstaff
hostess of the Eastcheap Inn	Mistress Quickly
the hot-tempered noble soldier, killed in battle	Hotspur (Harry Percy)

In Julius Caesar

Caesar's erstwhile friend, to whom he says "Et tu"	Brutus
the conspirator with "a lean and hungry look"	Cassius
Caesar's friend, who rouses the crowd	Mark Antony

In King Lear

Lear's darling youngest daughter, who dies	Cordelia
Lear's ungrateful, other two daughters	Regan and Goneril
Lear's banished adviser, later blinded	Gloucester
Gloucester's falsely accused son	Edgar
Gloucester's vilely scheming bastard son	Edmund

In Macbeth

the king killed by Macbeth and his lady	**Duncan**
the murdered man who haunts MacBeth	**Banquo**
the man who kills Macbeth at Dunsinane	**Macduff**

In Measure for Measure

the deputy left in charge of Vienna	**Angelo**
the woman who pleads for her brother's life	**Isabel**

In Merchant of Venice

a woman who disguises herself as a lawyer	**Portia**
Portia's husband, who chooses the right casket	**Bassanio**
Bassanio's friend, who loans him money	**Antonio**
the moneylender who wants a pound of flesh	**Shylock**

In Midsummer Night's Dream

the Duke of Athens	**Theseus**
his fiancée, the queen of the Amazons	**Hippolyta**
the king of the fairies	**Oberon**
the queen of the fairies	**Titania**
Titania's mischievous meddler	**Puck**
the woman who rejects her father's choice	**Hermia**
the man Hermia loves	**Lysander**
the man who loves Hermia	**Demetrius**
the woman who loves Demetrius	**Helena**
the weaver who awakes with an ass's head	**Bottom**
the play the workmen perform	***Pyramus*** and ***Thisbe***

In Much Ado About Nothing

the couple who fall in love despite themselves	**Beatrice** and **Benedict**
Beatrice's cousin, wronged by her uncle	**Hero**
the man who rejects Hero at the altar	**Claudio**

In Othello

the wife Othello kills in a jealous rage	**Desdemona**

the man who creates Othello's jealous rage	Iago

In Romeo and Juliet

the family of the young lover Romeo	Montague
the family of the young lover Juliet	Capulet
the cleric who helps them marry	Friar Laurence

In Taming of the Shrew

the shrew, Baptista's willful daughter	Katherine
Katherine's more pliant sister	Bianca
the man who "tames" Katherine	Petruchio

In The Tempest

the man marooned on a desert island	Prospero
Prospero's daughter	Miranda
Miranda's shipwrecked lover	Ferdinand
the island's misshapen inhabitant	Caliban
the sprite freed by Prospero	Ariel

In Twelfth Night

the brother shipwrecked off Illyria	Sebastian
his twin, who dresses as a young man	Viola
the countess who falls in love with Viola	Olivia
the duke who loves Viola	Orsino
Olivia's servant, deluded that she loves him	Malvolio
Olivia's shiftless but lovable uncle	Sir Toby Belch
Olivia's timorous would-be suitor	Sir Andrew Aguecheek
Olivia's maid, who marries Toby	Maria
Olivia's fool	Feste

Early Modern Authors

Among 18th- and 19th-century authors, who wrote . . . ?

Alice's Adventures in Wonderland	Lewis Carroll
American Dictionary of the English Language	Noah Webster
Arabian Nights, as translator	Richard Burton
Around the World in 80 Days	Jules Verne

"Auld Lang Syne"	Robert Burns
Barber of Seville	Beaumarchais
"Battle Hymn of the Republic," as a poem	Julia Ward Howe
"Because I could not stop for Death"	Emily Dickinson
Beggar's Opera	John Gay
Ben-Hur	Lew Wallace
Camille	Alexandre Dumas, fils (the son)
Candide	Voltaire
Cloister and the Hearth	Charles Reade
Confessions of an English Opium Eater	Thomas de Quincey
Consuelo	George Sand
Crime and Punishment and The Brothers Karamazov	Fyodor Dostoevsky
"Crossing the Bar"	Alfred, Lord Tennyson
Cyrano de Bergerac	Edmond Rostand
Dead Souls	Nikolai Gogol
Democracy and Mont St-Michel and Chartres	Henry Adams
Dictionary of the English Language and Rasselas	Samuel (Dr.) Johnson
Doll's House	Henrik Ibsen
Don Juan and Childe Harold	Lord Byron (George Gordon)
"Dover Beach"	Matthew Arnold
Dracula	Bram Stoker
Egoist	George Meredith
"Elegy Written in a Country Churchyard"	Thomas Gray
Ethan Frome	Edith Wharton
Eugene Onegin	Alexander Pushkin
"Evangeline" and "Hiawatha"	Henry Wadsworth Longfellow
"Eve of St. Agnes" and "Ode on a Grecian Urn"	John Keats
Faust and The Sorrows of Young Werther	Johann Wolfgang von Goethe
Frankenstein	Mary Wollstonecraft Shelley
Gil Blas de Santillane	Alain René Lesage
Golden Bowl	Henry James
Gulliver's Travels	Jonathan Swift
Harp Weaver	Edna St. Vincent Millay
Hero of Our Time	Mikhail Lermontov
"How Do I Love Thee?"	Elizabeth Barrett Browning
Huckleberry Finn and Tom Sawyer	Mark Twain
Human Comedy (La Comédie Humaine)	Honoré de Balzac
Importance of Being Earnest	Oscar Wilde
I Promessi Sposi (The Betrothed)	Alessandro Manzoni

Ismaelillo, a Cuban poet	**José Martí**
Ivanhoe	**Sir Walter Scott**
Jane Eyre	**Charlotte Brontë**
Jungle Books, "If," and "Gunga Din"	**Rudyard Kipling**
Kit Carson's Ride	**Joaquin Miller**
L'Après-midi d'un faune (The Afternoon of a Faun)	**Stéphane Mallarmé**
Last Days of Pompeii	**Edward Bulwer-Lytton**
Last of the Mohicans	**James Fenimore Cooper**
Leaves of Grass and "When Lilacs Last . . . "	**Walt Whitman**
"Legend of Sleepy Hollow"	**Washington Irving**
Les Fleurs du Mal (The Flowers of Evil)	**Charles Baudelaire**
Les Liaisons Dangereuses	**Choderlos de Laclos**
Les Miserables	**Victor Hugo**
Liberator, as abolitionist newspaper editor	**William Lloyd Garrison**
Life of Samuel Johnson	**James Boswell**
Little Women	**Louisa May Alcott**
Lorna Doone	**Richard D. Blackmore**
Magnificent Ambersons	**Booth Tarkington**
Mill on the Floss and *Silas Marner*	**George Eliot**
Moby Dick	**Herman Melville**
Month in the Country	**Ivan Turgenev**
"Murders of the Rue Morgue"	**Edgar Allan Poe**
"My Last Duchess"	**Robert Browning**
Nana and the "J'Accuse" letter defending Dreyfus	**Émile Zola**
Nature and other Transcendentalist works	**Ralph Waldo Emerson**
New Colossus ("Give me your tired, your poor")	**Emma Lazarus**
Ode to Freedom	**Friedrich Schiller**
"Ode to the West Wind" and "Ozymandias"	**Percy Bysshe Shelley**
"Old Ironsides"	**Oliver Wendell Holmes**
Old Wives' Tale	**Arnold Bennett**
Oliver Twist	**Charles Dickens**
On War	**Karl von Clausewitz**
Oregon Trail	**Francis Parkman**
"Outcasts of Poker Flats"	**Bret Harte**
Palliser and *Barchester* novels	**Anthony Trollope**
Pamela; or, Virtue Rewarded and *Clarissa*	**Samuel Richardson**
"Peter Grimes"	**George Crabbe**
Poor Richard's Almanack	**Benjamin Franklin**
Prelude and "Ode: Intimations of Immortality"	**William Wordsworth**

Pride and Prejudice	Jane Austen
Ramona	Helen Hunt Jackson
Rape of the Lock	Alexander Pope
Red and the Black	Stendhal
Red Badge of Courage	Stephen Crane
"Rime of the Ancient Mariner"	Samuel Taylor Coleridge
Rivals and *The School for Scandal*	Richard Brinsley Sheridan
Robinson Crusoe	Daniel Defoe
Rubáiyát of Omar Khayyám, as translator	Edward FitzGerald
Madame Bovary	Gustave Flaubert
Sartor Resartus	Thomas Carlyle
Scarlet Letter	Nathaniel Hawthorne
Season in Hell	Arthur Rimbaud
Shakespeare's plays, expurgated versions	Thomas and Henrietta Maria Bowdler
She Stoops to Conquer	Oliver Goldsmith
"Snowbound" and "The Barefoot Boy"	John Greenleaf Whittier
Songs of Innocence	William Blake
"Star-Spangled Banner"	Francis Scott Key
Stones of Venice	John Ruskin
Tales from Shakespeare	Charles and Mary Lamb
Tatler and *The Spectator* essays	Joseph Addison and Richard Steele
Tess of the D'Urbervilles	Thomas Hardy
Three Musketeers	Alexandre Dumas, père (the father)
Tom Jones	Henry Fielding
Treasure Island	Robert Louis Stevenson
Trelawney of the Wells	Arthur Wing Pinero
Trilby	George Du Maurier
Tristram Shandy	Laurence Sterne
Two Years Before the Mast	Richard Henry Dana, Jr.
Uncle Tom's Cabin	Harriet Beecher Stowe
Vanity Fair	William Makepeace Thackeray
"Visit from St. Nicholas" (" 'Twas the night before Christmas . . .")	Clement C. Moore
Walden and "Civil Disobedience"	Henry David Thoreau
War and Peace and *Anna Karenina*	Leo Tolstoy
"Windhover"	Gerard Manley Hopkins
Woman in White	Wilkie Collins
Wuthering Heights	Emily Brontë

Swift's Characters

Among the fictional characters of Jonathan Swift, who were . . . ?

the giants in *Gulliver's Travel*	**Brobdingnaglans**
the tiny people visited by Lemuel Gulliver	**Lilliputians**
the scientific quacks and knaves Gulliver met	**Laputans**
the rational horses Gulliver met	**Houyhnhnms**
the bestial humans ruled by the Houyhnhnms	**Yahoos**

Dickens's Characters

Among the characters in Dickens's novels, who was or were . . . ?

In Bleak House

the heroine	**Esther Summerson**
the family involved in the law suit	**Jarndyce**
the do-gooder who neglected her own family	**Mrs. Jellyby**

In A Christmas Carol

the mean skinflint	**Ebenezer Scrooge**
the crippled boy who wins Scrooge's heart	**Tiny Tim Cratchit**

In David Copperfield

the poor, ever-hopeful man	**Mr. Micawber**
the family that befriends young David	**Peggotty**
David's aunt and guardian	**Betsy Trotwood**
David's ill-suited 1st wife	**Dora Spenlow**
the deceitful, falsely humble blackmailer	**Uriah Heep**
David's true love and 2nd wife	**Agnes Wickfield**

In Great Expectations

the young hero	**Pip (Philip Pirrip)**
Pip's blacksmith brother-in-law	**Joe Gargery**
the convict Pip helps	**Abel Magwitch**
the embittered, once-jilted rich lady	**Miss Havisham**
Miss Havisham's ward and Pip's love	**Estella**

In **Nicholas Nickleby**

the brutal schoolmaster	**Wackford Squeers**
the brothers who help Nicholas	**Cheeryble Brothers**
the boy who follows Nicholas	**Smike**

In **Oliver Twist**

the head of the pickpockets	**Fagin**
Oliver's pickpocket friend, the "Artful Dodger"	**Jack Dawkins**
the violent man who kills Nancy	**Bill Sikes**

In **Tale of Two Cities**

the woman whose father was in the Bastille	**Lucie Manette**
the man Lucie marries	**Charles Darnay**
the fanatic who knitted at the guillotine	**Madame Defarge**
Darnay's double, who dies in his stead	**Sydney Carton**

Trollope's Characters

Among the fictional characters of Anthony Trollope, who was or were . . . ?

In the Barchester novels

the guileless warden	**Septimus Harding**
the Barsetshire bishop and his wife	**Proudle**
the archdeacon	**Grantly**
the schemer who comes up against Mrs. Proudie	**Obadiah Slope**

In the Palliser novels

the badly matched couple at the series's center	**Plantagenet** and **Glencora Palliser**
Plantagenet's interfering uncle	**Duke of Omnium**
the widow who hid her diamonds	**Lizzie Eustace**
the impetuous, impecunious Irish MP	**Phineas Finn**
the rich Austrian widow who rejects the duke	**"Madame Max" Marie Goesler**

Proust's Characters

Among the fictional characters in Proust's *Remembrance of Things Past (Àla recherche du temps perdu)*, who was or were . . . ?

the partly autobiographical narrator	**Marcel**
the aristocratic family	**Guermantes**
the vulgar, nouveau riche family	**Verdurins**
the tortured bourgeois man and his not-quite-proper wife	**Charles** and **Odette Swann**
the Swanns' daughter	**Gilberte**
Marcel's love	**Albertine Simonet**

Galsworthy's Characters

Among the fictional characters in Galsworthy's *The Forsyte Saga*, who was or were . . . ?

the son who left his wife for a governess	**Young Jolyon Forsyte**
Young Jo's daughter	**June Forsyte**
June's fiancé, an architect	**Philip Bosinney**
June's uncle, the "man of property"	**Soames Forsyte**
Soames's wife, Bosinney's lover, and then Young Jo's wife	**Irene Forsyte**
Soames's daughter by a 2nd marriage	**Fleur Forsyte**

Mystery Detectives and Regulars

In the world of mystery novels, who are the following regular characters . . . ?

Catherine Aird's Berebury detective	C. D. Sloan
John Ball's black Philadelphia detective	Virgil Tibbs
Milton Bass's Irish-Jewish San Diego cop	Benny Freedman
Earl Derr Bigger's Chinese detective	Charlie Chan
Nicholas Blake's London sleuth	Nigel Strangeways

Strangeways's lady companion, an artist	Clare Massinger
Michael Bond's gastronomic sleuth	Aristide Pamplemousse
Lilian Jackson Braun's newspaper reporter	Jim Qwilleran
Qwilleran's Siamese cats	Koko and Yum Yum
Simon Brett's 50-ish struggling actor	Charles Paris
John Buchan's hero, as in *The 39 Steps*	Richard Hannay
William Buckley, Jr.'s, American agent	Blackford Oakes
Robert Campbell's Chicago politico/inspector	Jimmy Flannery
John Dickson Carr's favorite detective	Dr. Gideon Fell
Raymond Chandler's hardboiled detective	Philip Marlowe
Leslie Charteris's suave "Saint"	Simon Templar
G. K. Chesterton's clerical sleuth	Father Brown
Agatha Christie's moustachioed Belgian	Hercule Poirot
Christie's ditsy female mystery writer	Ariadne Oliver
Christie's elderly village spinster	Jane Marple
Christie's 1920's detecting couple	Tuppence and Tommy Beresford
Michael Collins's one-armed NYC private eye	Dan Fortune
Edmund Crispin's Oxford don-detective	Gervase Fen
Amanda Cross's female professor-detective	Kate Fansler
E. V. Cunningham's Buddhist Nisei policeman	Masao Masuto
Len Deighton's cool British agent	Bernard Samson
Colin Dexter's lonely Oxford cop	Inspector Morse
Arthur Conan Doyle's sleuth par excellence	Sherlock Holmes
Holmes's medical friend and chronicler	Dr. Watson
Holmes's arch enemy	Professor Moriarty
Doyle's dim police inspector	Inspector Le Strade
Holmes's brother	Mycroft Holmes
the international organization of Holmes fans	Baker Street Irregulars
Loren Estelman's Detroit ex-vet private eye	Amos Walker

Tony Fennelly's gay New Orleans antiques man	Matt Sinclair
Ian Fleming's (and John Gardner's) agent 007	James Bond
Dick Francis's sleuthing steeplechase jockey	Kit Fielding
Nicholas Freeling's French policeman	Henri Castaing
Freeling's Amsterdam detective	Inspector Van der Valk
Erle Stanley Gardner's never-bested lawyer	Perry Mason
Mason's faithful secretary	Della Street
Jonathan Gash's antique dealer–sleuth	Lovejoy
William Campbell Gault's LA ex-football PI	Brock Callahan
Bartholomew Gills's Irish inspector	Peter McGarr
Dorothy Gilman's genteel lady CIA agent	Emily Pollifax
E. X. Giroux's London barrister	Robert Forsythe
Sue Grafton's ex-cop private eye in California	Kinsey Millhone
John Greenwood's impetuous detective	Inspector Mosley
Martha Grimes's handsome police inspector	Richard Jury
Grimes's bachelor friend, the ex-Lord Ardry	Melrose Plant
Dashiell Hammett's hard-boiled detective	Sam Spade
Joseph Hansen's homosexual detective	Dave Brandstetter
Ray Harrison's turn-of-the-20th-c. London cop	Joseph Bragg
Bragg's gentlemanly assistant	James Morton
Morton's lady friend, a reporter	Catherine Marsden
Mark Hebden's French chief inspector	Evariste Clovis Désiré Pel
Reginald Hill's police superintendent	Andrew Dalziel
Dalziel's detective sidekick	Peter Pascoe
Tony Hillerman's Navajo police sergeant	Jim Chee
Hillerman's Navajo police lieutenant	Joe Leaphorn
Chester Himes's Harlem amateur sleuths	Grave Digger and Coffin Ed
John Buxton Hilton's superintendent hero	Simon Kenworthy
Timothy Holme's dapper Venice Commissario	Achille Peroni

Alan Hunter's police inspector	George Gently
Michael Innes's police inspector	John Appleby
Appleby's wife	Judith Raven
P. D. James's police detective and poet	Adam Dalgliesh
James's young woman private eye	Cordelia Gray
James's policewoman/detective	Kate Miskin
Roderic Jeffries's Mallorca inspector	Enrique Alvarez
Stuart Kaminsky's 1940's LA private eye	Toby Peters
H. R. F. Keating's Indian detective	Inspector Ghote
William Kienzle's sleuthing Detroit priest	Father Robert Koesler
Emma Lathen's bank officer-detective	John Putnam Thatcher
John le Carré's paunchy Russian-watcher	George Smiley
Smiley's Russian arch-enemy	Karla
Frances and Richard Lockridge's sleuthing publisher and wife	Gerald and Pamela North
the Norths' Siamese cats	Martini, Gin, and Sherry
the Lockridges' Westchester, NY, state trooper	Merton Heimrich
Heimrich's wife, a fabric designer	Susan Faye
the Heimrichs' Great Dane	Colonel
Peter Lovesey's Victorian cop	Sergeant Cribb
John Lutz's crippled former Florida cop	Fred Carver
J. J. Marric's London policeman	George Gideon
Ed McBain's big city stable of cops	87th Precinct
McBain's amateur Florida sleuth	Matthew Hope
Gregory Macdonald's incorrigible sleuth	Fletch
John D. MacDonald's Florida private eye	Travis McGee
Ross Macdonald's California sleuth	Lew Archer
J. P. Marquand's Japanese sleuth	Mr. Moto
Ngaio Marsh's police inspector	Roderick Alleyn
"Handsome" Alleyn's sidekick	Bre'r Teddy Fox
Alleyn's artist wife	Agatha Troy
John Mortimer's defending barrister	Horace Rumpole
Michael Nava's gay California attorney	Henry Rios
Sister Carol Anne O'Marie's 70ish sleuth	Sister Mary Helen

Sarah Paretsky's Chicago lawyer/sleuth	Victor (V.I.) Warshawski
Robert Parker's literary gourmet sleuth	Spenser
Spenser's lady friend, a psychologist	Susan Silverman
Spenser's ex-football colleague and sidekick	Hawk
Hugh Pentecost's Beaumont Hotel manager	Pierre Chambrun
Anne Perry's Victorian inspector and wife	Thomas and Charlotte Pitt
Ellis Peters's sleuthing medieval monk	Brother Cadfael
Edgar Allan Poe's ratiocinative sleuth	C. Auguste Dupin
Richard S. Prather's LA private eye	Shell Scott
Ellery Queen's eponymous writer	Ellery Queen
Ruth Rendell's suburban policeman	Inspector Wexford
Wexford's partner	Mike Burden
John Rhode's eccentric British detective	Dr. Priestley
Richard Rosen's Boston private eye	Harvey Blissberg
Dorothy L. Sayers's aristocratic sleuth	Lord Peter Wimsey
Wimsey's manservant	Mervyn Bunter
Wimsey's love, a female mystery writer	Harriet Vane
Wimsey's police inspector/brother-in-law	Charles Parker
head of Wimsey's spinster detective bureau	Katharine Climpson
Dell Shannon's Hispanic LA policeman	Luis Mendoza
Georges Simenon's Paris police inspector	Jules Maigret
Roger L. Simon's LA Jewish private eye	Moses Wine
Maj Sjowell and **Per Wahloo's** Stockholm cop	Martin Beck
Mickey Spillane's tough-guy private eye	Mike Hammer
Rex Stout's orchid-loving reclusive sleuth	Nero Wolfe
Wolfe's assistant, who does the leg-work	Archie Goodwin
Martin Sylvester's wine merchant–sleuth	William Warner

Julian Symons's actor-detective	Sherwood Haynes
Leonard Tourney's medieval clothier and wife	Matthew and Joan Stock
Jan Willem Van de Wetering's Amsterdam cop	Inspector Grijpstra
Grijpstra's sidekick in homicide detecting	Sergeant de Gier
S. S. Van Dine's sophisticated interwar sleuth	Philo Vance
Charles Willeford's Miami homicide sergeant	Hoke Moseley
Sara Woods's London barrister	Anthony Maitland
Ted Wood's small-town Canadian cop	Reid Bennett

Other Notable Characters in Fiction

Among other notable characters in fiction, who was or were . . . ?

Anna Karenina's young officer	Count Vronsky
Arabian Nights' most famous characters	Ali Baba and the 40 Thieves and Sinbad the Sailor
Around the World in 80 Days's hero	Phineas Fogg
Caine Mutiny's embattled commander	Captain Queeg
Candide's foolish tutor	Dr. Pangloss
Catcher in the Rye's narrator	Holden Caulfield
Catch-22's anti-hero	Captain Yossarian
Crime and Punishment's murderer	Raskolnikov
Death in Venice's German writer	Gustave Aschenbach
Death of a Salesman's broken hero	Willy Loman
Doll's House's wife who leaves	Nora Helmer
Don Quixote's sidekick	Sancho Panza
Dr. Zhivago's lover, dedicatee of his poems	Lara
Foundation's father of psychohistory	Hari Seldon
Godfather's self-made mafia don	Vito Corleone
Gone With the Wind's self-centered heroine and rakish hero	Scarlett O'Hara and Rhett Butler
Grapes of Wrath's main dispossessed Okie	Tom Joad

Human Comedy's (Balzac's cynical climber)	Eugène de Rastignac
Hunchback of Notre Dame's title character	Quasimodo
Ivanhoe's hero, his Jewish nurse, and his true love	Wilfred, Rebecca, and Rowena
Jane Eyre's tormented hero	Edward Rochester
Leatherstocking Tales' hero	Hawkeye (Natty Bumppo)
Legend of Sleepy Hollow's teacher	Ichabod Crane
Les Miserables' much-pursued hero	Jean Valjean
Little Women's tomboy heroine	Jo March
Lolita's pedophile	Humbert Humbert
Lord of the Rings' questing hobbit	Frodo
Middlemarch's selfish scholar	Rev. Mr. Casaubon
Moby Dick's whale-obsessed captain/and narrator	Ahab/Ishmael
Portrait of the Artist as a Young Man hero	Stephen Dedalus
Pride and Prejudice's spirited heroine and proud suitor	Elizabeth Bennet and Fitzwilliam Darcy
Prisoner of Zenda's fake Ruritanian king	Rudolf Rassendyl
Rebecca's lord of Manderley	Maxim de Winter
Red and the Black's hero	Julien Sorel
Rivals' word mis-user	Mrs. Malaprop
Scarlet Letter's adulteress	Hester Prynne
Sons and Lovers's central figure	Paul Morel
South Pacific's Little Rock ensign and French hero	Nellie Forbush and Émile de Becque
Streetcar Named Desire's young husband and his sister-in-law driven mad	Stanley Kowalski and Blanche Du Bois
Tale of Peter Rabbit's bunny siblings	Flopsy, Mopsy, Cottontail, and Peter
Three Musketeers' swashbuckling hero	D'Artagnan
Three Penny Opera's anti-hero and his ex-lover	Mack the Knife and Pirate Jenny
To Kill a Mockingbird's lawyer-father	Atticus Finch
Treasure Island's pirate-captain	Long John Silver
Trilby's mesmerizer	Svengali
Ulysses' principal Dublin couple	Molly and Leopold Bloom

Uncle Tom's Cabin's brutal slavemaster	Simon Legree
Vanity Fair's cunning climber	Becky Sharp
Wuthering Heights' rough, rejected lover	Heathcliff

Modern Novelists and Short-Story Writers

(See also Mystery Detectives and Regulars)

Among 20th-century novelists and short-story writers, who wrote . . . .?

Above Suspicion	Helen MacInnes
Accidental Tourist	Anne Tyler
Advise and Consent	Allen Drury
Agony and the Ecstasy	Irving Stone
Aleph	José Luis Borges
Alexandria Quartet	Lawrence Durrell
All Quiet on the Western Front	Erich Maria Remarque
All the King's Men	Robert Penn Warren
All We Need of Hell	Harry Crews
American Language	H. L. Mencken
Amerika and *The Metamorphosis*	Franz Kafka
Amityville Horror	Jay Anson
And Ladies of the Club	Helen Hooven Santmyer
Andersonville	MacKinlay Kantor
Andromeda Strain	Michael Crichton
Angle of Repose	Wallace Stegner
Anubis Gates	Tim Powers
archy and mehitabel	Don Marquis
Arrangement	Elia Kazan
At Risk	Alice Hoffman
At the Mountains of Madness	H. P. Lovecraft
Auntie Mame	Patrick Dennis
Avaryan Rising trilogy	Judith Tarr
Bang the Drum Slowly	Mark Harris
Beans of Egypt, Maine	Carolyn Chute
Because I Was Flesh	Edward Dahlberg
Been Down So Long It Looks Like Up to Me	Richard Fariña
Bellefleur	Joyce Carol Oates
Bell Jar	Sylvia Plath
Best of Everything	Rona Jaffe
Beulah Quintet	Mary Lee Settle
Beyond the Bedroom Wall	Larry Woiwode
Black Narcissus	Rumer Godden
Blue Knight	Joseph Wambaugh

Bonfire of the Vanities	**Tom Wolfe**
Bonjour Tristesse	**Françoise Sagan**
Boys of Summer	**Roger Kahn**
Brave New World	**Aldous Huxley**
Bread and Wine	**Ignazio Silone**
Brideshead Revisited	**Evelyn Waugh**
Bridge on the River Kwai	**Pierre Boulle**
Bright Lights, Big City	**Jay McInerney**
Buddenbrooks and *Death in Venice*	**Thomas Mann**
Burger's Daughter	**Nadine Gordimer**
Burr	**Gore Vidal**
By the Waters of Manhattan	**Charles Reznikoff**
Cakes and Ale	**W. Somerset Maugham**
Call of the Wild	**Jack London**
Camberwell Beauty	**V. S. Pritchett**
Canticle for Leibowitz	**Warren Miller**
Cardinal Sins	**Andrew Greeley**
Carpetbaggers	**Harold Robbins**
Case Against Tomorrow	**Frederik Pohl**
Catcher in the Rye	**J. D. Salinger**
Catch-22	**Joseph Heller**
Chamber Music	**Doris Grumbach**
Chaneysville Incident	**David Bradley**
Cheri and *La Chatte*	**Colette**
Childhood of Nivasio Dolcemarie	**Alberto Savinio**
Children of the Arbat	**Anatoli Rybakov**
Chilly Scenes of Winter	**Ann Beattie**
Chosen	**Chaim Potok**
Christ Stopped at Eboli	**Carlo Levi**
Chronicles of Clovis	**Saki**
Chronicles of Narnia and *The Screwtape Letters*	**C. S. Lewis**
Citadel	**A. J. Cronin**
Cities of the Interior series	**Anaïs Nin**
Clan of the Cave Bear	**Jean Auel**
Clockwork Orange	**Anthony Burgess**
Cold Sassy Tree	**Olive Ann Burns**
Color Purple	**Alice Walker**
Coma	**Robin Cook**
Come Love a Stranger	**Kathleen E. Woodiwiss**
Compromising Positions	**Susan Isaacs**
Confessions of Zeno	**Italo Svevo**
Cotton Comes to Harlem	**Chester Himes**
Coup de Grâce and *Memoirs of Hadrian*	**Marguerite Yourcenar**
Cruel Sea	**Nicholas Monsarrat**
Crystal Cave	**Mary Stewart**
Cry, the Beloved Country	**Alan Paton**
Dago Red	**John Fante**
Dance to the Music of Time novels	**Anthony Powell**

Darkness at Noon	**Arthur Koestler**
Day of the Jackal	**Frederick Forsyth**
Day of the Locust	**Nathanael West**
Dear and Glorious Physician	**Taylor Caldwell**
Death in the Family	**James Agee**
Death of the Heart	**Elizabeth Bowen**
Death on the Installment Plan	**Louis-Ferdinand Céline**
Deliverance	**James Dickey**
Deptford trilogy	**Robertson Davies**
Destroyer series, with Warren Murphy	**Richard Sapir**
Diary of a Rapist	**Evan S. Connell, Jr.**
Dictionary of the Khazars: a Lexicon Novel	**Milorad Pavic**
Doctor Zhivago	**Boris Pasternak**
Dog Soldiers	**Robert Stone**
Doña Flor and Her Two Husbands	**Jorge Amado**
DragonLane chronicles	**Margaret Weis** and **Tracy Hickman**
Dragonriders series	**Anne McCaffrey**
Drums Along the Mohawk	**Walter D. Edmonds**
Dune series	**Frank Herbert**
Eagle Has Landed	**Jack Higgins**
Education of H*y*m*a*n K*a*p*l*a*n	**Leo Rosten**
Egyptian	**Mika Waltari**
Ellis Island	**Fred Mustard Stewart**
Elmer Gantry and *Dodsworth*	**Sinclair Lewis**
Eloise	**Kay Thompson**
Empire of the Sun	**J. G. Ballard**
Enormous Changes at the Last Minute	**Grace Paley**
Europa and *The Mothers*	**Robert Briffault**
Evergreen	**Belva Plain**
Exodus	**Leon Uris**
Eye of the Needle	**Ken Follett**
Eye of the Storm	**Patrick White**
Fail-Safe	**Eugene Burdick** and **Harvey Wheeler**
Falconer	**John Cheever**
Fan's Notes	**Frederick Exley**
Far Pavilions	**M. M. Kaye**
Fathers	**Herbert Gold**
Fear of Flying	**Erica Jong**
Fiddler on the Roof–inspiring stories	**Sholem Aleichem**
Final Payments	**Mary Gordon**
Finishing School	**Gail Godwin**
First Among Equals	**Jeffrey Archer**
Fixer and *The Natural*	**Bernard Malamud**

Flight of the Intruder	**Stephen Coonts**
Flight of the Old Dog	**Dale Brown**
Flowers in the Attic	**V. C. Andrews**
For Whom the Bell Tolls	**Ernest Hemingway**
Forsyte Saga	**John Galsworthy**
Fortunes of War	**Olivia Manning**
Foundation, Robot, and Empire series	**Isaac Asimov**
Fountainhead and *Atlas Shrugged*	**Ayn Rand**
Fourth Deadly Sin	**Lawrence Sanders**
Free-Lance Pallbearers	**Ishmael Reed**
Freedom and *New York Times* language column	**William Safire**
French Lieutenant's Woman	**John Fowles**
Friendly Persuasion	**Jessamyn West**
Friends of Eddie Coyle	**George V. Higgins**
From Here to Eternity	**James Jones**
From the Terrace	**John O'Hara**
Gang That Couldn't Shoot Straight	**Jimmy Breslin**
Garden of the Finzi-Continis	**Giorgio Bassani**
"Garden Party" and *"Bliss"*	**Katherine Mansfield**
Ghost Story	**Peter Straub**
"Gift of the Magi" and *"The Last Leaf"*	**O. Henry**
Giles Goat-Boy	**John Barth**
Ginger Man	**J. P. Donleavy**
Glastonbury Romance	**John Cowper Powys**
Godfather	**Mario Puzo**
God Sends Sunday	**Arna Bontemps**
Going After Cacciato	**Tim O'Brien**
Going All the Way	**Dan Wakefield**
Golden Notebook	**Doris Lessing**
Gone With the Wind	**Margaret Mitchell**
Goodbye to Berlin (basis for *Cabaret*)	**Christopher Isherwood**
Goodbye, Mr. Chips and *Lost Horizon*	**James Hilton**
Goodbye, Sweetwater	**Henry Dumas**
Good Companions	**J. B. Priestley**
Good Earth	**Pearl Buck**
Good Man Is Hard to Find	**Flannery O'Connor**
Good Soldier Schweik	**Jaroslav Hasek**
Gorky Park	**Martin Cruz Smith**
Gormenghast Trilogy	**Mervyn Peake**
Grandmaster	**Warren Murphy**
Grapes of Wrath	**John Steinbeck**
Great Gatsby and *Tender Is the Night*	**F. Scott Fitzgerald**
Green Berets	**Robin Moore**
Green Mansions	**W. H. Hudson**

Group	Mary McCarthy
Group Portrait with Lady	Heinrich Böll
Gulag Archipelago	Alexander Solzhenitsyn
Guns of Navarone	Alistair MacLean
Handmaid's Tale	Margaret Atwood
Hanta Yo	Ruth Beebe Hill
Heart of Darkness	Joseph Conrad
Heiress and many other romance novels	Janet Dailey
Herland	Charlotte Perkin Gilman
Holcroft Covenant	Robert Ludlum
Hollywood Wives	Jackie Collins
Hondo and How the West Was Won	Louis L'Amour
Hopscotch	Julio Cortázar
Horatio Hornblower novels	C. S. Forester
Horse's Mouth	Joyce Cary
Hotel Du Lac	Anita Brookner
Hot Rock	Donald Westlake
Hound of the Baskervilles	Arthur Conan Doyle
House and Its Head	Ivy Compton-Burnett
House for Mr. Biswas	V. S. Naipaul
House of the Spirits	Isabel Allende
How Green Was My Valley	Richard Llewellyn
Humboldt's Gift	Saul Bellow
Hunger	Knut Hamsun
Hunt for Red October	Tom Clancy
I Can Get It for You Wholesale	Jerome Weidman
I, Claudius	Robert Graves
If on a Winter's Night a Traveler	Italo Calvino
I Know Why the Caged Bird Sings	Maya Angelou
Immigrants and Freedom Road	Howard Fast
Immoralist and Strait Is the Gate	André Gide
I Never Promised You a Rose Garden	Joanne Greenberg
Informer	Liam O'Flaherty
Inheritance	Judith Michael
In the Heart of the Heart of the Country	William H. Gass
In the Heat of the Night	John Ball
In the Prison of Her Skin and The Bastard	Violette Leduc
In the Skin of a Lion	Michael Ondaatje
Invisible Man and The Time Machine	H. G. Wells
Invisible Man	Ralph Ellison
Invitation to the Waltz	Rosamond Lehmann
In Watermelon Sugar	Richard Brautigan
Irish R. M.	E. Œ. Somerville and Martin Ross

January Tale	**Bryher**
Jaws	**Peter Benchley**
Jeeves and Bertie Wooster novels	**P. G. Wodehouse**
Jerusalem the Golden	**Margaret Drabble**
Jewel in the Crown in the Raj Quartet	**Paul Scott**
Jonathan Livingston Seagull	**Richard Bach**
J R	**William Gaddis**
Judas Kiss	**Victoria Holt**
Jungle and the Lanny Budd novels	**Upton Sinclair**
Just Relations	**Rodney Hall**
Kate Vaiden	**Reynolds Price**
Kinflicks	**Lisa Alther**
King Must Die and *The Persian Boy*	**Mary Renault**
Kiss of the Spider Woman	**Manuel Puig**
Lady Chatterley's Lover	**D. H. Lawrence**
Land of Laughs	**Jonathan Carroll**
Last Picture Show	**Larry McMurtry**
Last Princess	**Cynthia Freeman**
Leopard	**Giuseppe Lampedusa**
Levitation	**Cynthia Ozick**
Life and Loves of a She-Devil	**Fay Weldon**
Little Big Man	**Thomas Berger**
Little Miss Marker	**Damon Runyon**
Lolita and *Pale Fire*	**Vladimir Nabokov**
Lolly Willowes	**Sylvia Townsend Warner**
Looking for Mr. Goodbar	**Judith Rossner**
Lord of the Flies	**William Golding**
Lord of the Rings and *The Hobbit*	**J. R. R. Tolkien**
"*Lottery*"	**Shirley Jackson**
Love for Lydia	**H. E. Bates**
Love in a Cold Climate	**Nancy Mitford**
Love Medicine	**Louise Erdrich**
Lover (L'Amant)	**Marguerite Duras**
Lucky Jim	**Kingsley Amis**
Magician of Lublin	**Isaac Bashevis Singer**
Magic of Xanth and Apprentice Adept series	**Piers Anthony**
Magister Ludi: The Glass-Bead Game	**Hermann Hesse**
Maltese Falcon	**Dashiell Hammett**
Manawaka novels	**Margaret Laurence**
Man in the Gray Flannel Suit	**Sloan Wilson**
Man's Fate and *Man's Hope*	**André Malraux**
Man Who Loved Children	**Christina Stead**
Man with the Golden Arm	**Nelson Algren**
Many-Splendored Thing	**Han Suyin**

Mapp and Lucia	E. F. Benson
Martian Chronicles	Ray Bradbury
Mask of Dimitrios	Eric Ambler
Member of the Wedding	Carson McCullers
Mr. Roberts	Thomas Heggen
Mrs. 'arris Goes to Paris	Paul Gallico
Moon Tiger	Penelope Lively
Mortal Friends	James Carroll
Moviegoer	Walter Percy
Mulata	Miguel Angel Asturias
Murder on the Orient Express	Agatha Christie
My Antonia	Willa Cather
My Left Foot	Christy Brown
My Name Is Aram	William Saroyan
Mysteries of Pittsburgh	Michael Chabon
Mysteries of the Moon	Hortense Calisher
Naked and the Dead	Norman Mailer
Naked Lunch	William Burroughs
Name of the Rose	Umberto Eco
Native Son	Richard Wright
Nausea	Jean-Paul Sartre
Neveryon series	Samuel R. Delany
New Confessions	William Boyd
1984 and *Animal Farm*	George Orwell
Ninety-two in the Shade	Thomas McGuane
Ninja and *Shan*	Eric van Lustbader
North and South	John Jakes
Northwest Passage	Kenneth Roberts
Not Now but Now	M. F. K. Fisher
Once and Future King	T. H. White
Once Is Not Enough	Jacqueline Susann
One Flew over the Cuckoo's Nest	Ken Kesey
One Hundred Years of Solitude	Gabriel García Marquez
Only Apparently Real	Philip K. Dick
On the Road	Jack Kerouac
On the Waterfront	Budd Schulberg
Ordinary People	Judith Guest
Other Voices, Other Rooms and *In Cold Blood*	Truman Capote
Ox-Bow Incident	Walter van Tilburg Clark
Oxford novels, e.g., A Staircase in Surrey	J. I. M. Stewart
Paco's Story	Larry Heinemann
Painted Bird and *Being There*	Jerzy Kozinski
Panic of '89	Paul Erdman
Parable of the Blind	Gert Hofmann
Parade's End tetralogy and *Good Soldier*	Ford Madox Ford
Passage to India and *A Room with a View*	E. M. Forster

People Will Always Be Kind	Wilfred Sheed
Perfume	Patrick Suskind
Peyton Place	Grace Metallous
Phantom of the Opera	Gaston Leroux
Play It As It Lays	Joan Didion
Poldark novels	Winston Grahame
Pollyanna	Eleanor Porter
Portnoy's Complaint	Philip Roth
Portrait in Brownstone	Louis Auchincloss
Postman Always Rings Twice	James M. Cain
Post Office	Charles Bukowski
Precious Bane	Mary Webb
Presumed Innocent	Scott Turow
Prime of Miss Jean Brodie	Muriel Spark
Prince of the City	Robert Daly
Prince of Tides	Pat Conroy
Princess	Jude Devereaux
Princess and the Goblin	George MacDonald
Prisoner of Zenda	Anthony Hope Hawkins
Prize	Irving Wallace
Queenie	Michael Korda
Quo Vadis	Henry Sienkiewicz
Rabbit novels	John Updike
Rage of Angels	Sidney Sheldon
Ragtime	E. L. Doctorow
Rebecca	Daphne du Maurier
Remembrance of Things Past (À la recherche du temps perdu)	Marcel Proust
Richard novels and Great River	Paul Horgan
Rich Man, Poor Man	Irwin Shaw
Riddley Walker	Russell Hoban
Ring of Bright Water	Gavin Maxwell
Ringworld	Larry Niven
Rogue Male	Geoffrey Household
romances, innumerable fluffy British ones	Barbara Cartland
Rosemary's Baby	Ira Levin
Rubyfruit Jungle	Rita Mae Brown
Rumpole stories	John Mortimer
Sailor Who Fell from Grace with the Sea	Yukio Mishima
Salome of the Tenements, the "Hester St. Cinderella"	Anzia Yezierska
Satanic Verses	Salman Rushdie
Saturday Night and Sunday Morning	Alan Sillitoe
Savages	Shirley Conran
Scarlet Pimpernel	Baroness Orczy
Scruples	Judith Krantz
Sea Change	Lois Gould

Sea-Hawk	**Rafael Sabatini**
Sea of Grass	**Conrad Richter**
Sea, The Sea	**Iris Murdoch**
"Secret Life of Walter Mitty"	**James Thurber**
Secret of Santa Vittoria	**Robert Crichton**
Semi-Tough	**Dan Jenkins**
Separate Peace	**John Knowles**
Seven Days in May	**Fletcher Knebel** and **Charles W. Bailey**
Seven Storey Mountain	**Thomas Merton**
Shadow Knows	**Diane Johnson**
She	**H. Rider Haggard**
Shining and *Cujo*	**Stephen King**
Ship of Fools	**Katherine Anne Porter**
Shoes of the Fisherman	**Morris West**
Shogun	**James Clavell**
Shootist	**Glendon Swarthout**
Show Boat and *Giant*	**Edna Ferber**
Silver Chalice	**Thomas B. Costain**
Sister Carrie	**Theodore Dreiser**
Skye O'Malley series	**Blaze Wyndham**
Slaughterhouse Five	**Kurt Vonnegut, Jr.**
Slaves of New York	**Tama Janowitz**
Small Changes	**Marge Piercy**
Someone Is Killing the Great Chefs of Europe	**Nan and Ivan Lyons**
Something of Value	**Robert Ruark**
Sophie's Choice	**William Styron**
Sound and the Fury	**William Faulkner**
Southern Rapture	**Jennifer Blake**
Space Merchants, with Pohl	**C. M. Kornbluth**
Star Diaries	**Stanislaw Lem**
Stick and *Glitz*	**Elmore Leonard**
Story of an African Farm	**Olive Shreiner**
Stranger	**Albert Camus**
Stranger in a Strange Land	**Robert A. Heinlien**
Strangers and Brothers novels	**C. P. Snow**
Strangers on a Train	**Patricia Highsmith**
Studs Lonigan and Danny O'Neill novels	**James T. Farrell**
Summons to Memphis	**Peter Taylor**
Sunlight Dialogues and *Grendel*	**John Gardner**
Sunne in Splendour	**Sharon Kay Penman**
Sweetsir	**Helen Yglesias**
Tale of Genji	**Murasaki Shikibu**
Tales of the South Pacific and *Centennial*	**James Michener**
Tar Baby and *Beloved*	**Toni Morrison**
Tarzan of the Apes	**Edgar Rice Burroughs**
Terra Nostra	**Carlos Fuentes**
Their Eyes Were Watching God	**Zora Neale Hurston**

Third Man	Graham Greene
Thorn Birds	Colleen McCullough
Time in Its Flight	Susan Fromberg Schaeffer
Time Master trilogy	Louise Cooper
Time of the Hero	Mario Vargas Llosa
Time Patrol series	Poul Anderson
Time Trilogy	Madeleine L'Engle
Tin Drum	Günter Grass
Tinker, Tailor, Soldier, Spy	John le Carré
Tobacco Road	Erskine Caldwell
To Kill a Mockingbird	Harper Lee
Too Much, Too Soon	Jacqueline Briskin
To Serve Them All My Days	R. W. Delderfield
To the Land of the Cattails	Aharon Appelfeld
To the Lighthouse	Virginia Woolf
Town Like Alice and *On the Beach*	Nevil Shute
Treasure	Clive Cussler
Treasure of the Sierra Madre	B. Traven
Tree Grows in Brooklyn	Betty Smith
Tropic of Cancer	Henry Miller
True Confessions	John Gregory Dunne
Two Mrs. Grenvilles	Dominick Dunne
Two Solitudes	Hugh MacLennan
2001: A Space Odyssey	Arthur C. Clarke
Ugly American	William J. Lederer and Eugene L. Burdick
Ulysses	James Joyce
Unbearable Lightness of Being	Milan Kundera
Underground Woman	Kay Boyle
Under the Eye of the Clock	Christopher Nolan
Under the Volcano	Malcolm Lowry
Unfinished Business	Maggie Scarf
Universal Baseball Association	Robert Coover
Unspeakable Practices, Unnatural Acts	Donald Barthelme
USA trilogy	John Dos Passos
021V and *Gravity's Rainbow*	Thomas Pynchon
Vampire Chronicles	Anne Rice
Walden II	B. F. Skinner
Wall and *A Bell for Adano*	John Hersey
Wanderlust	Danielle Steel
War Between the Tates	Alison Lurie
Way of All Flesh	Samuel Butler
Watership Down	Richard Adams
Weave-World	Clive Barker
Weep No More, My Lady	Mary Higgins Clark
Well of Loneliness	Radclyffe Hall
Wheels and *Airport*	Arthur Hailey
Where I'm Calling From	Raymond Carver
White Hotel	D. M. Thomas

White Noise	Don DeLillo
"Why I Live at the P.O."	Eudora Welty
Wicked Loving Lies	Rosemary Rogers
Wide Sargasso Sea	Jean Rhys
Winds of War	Herman Wouk
Winesburg, Ohio	Sherwood Anderson
Winter's Tales and *Out of Africa*	Isak Dinesen
Woman of Independent Means	Elizabeth Forsythe Hailey
Woman of Substance	Barbara Taylor Bradford
Women's Room	Marilyn French
World According to Garp	John Irving
World's End	T. Coraghessan Boyle
World Without End	Francine du Plessix Gray
Word for the World Is Forest	Ursula K. Le Guin
Wreck of the Mary Deare	Hammond Innes
Xenogenesis trilogy	Octavia E. Butler
Year of the French	Thomas Flanagan
Yes, Minister diaries	Right Hon. James Hacker
You Can't Go Home Again	Thomas Wolfe
You Know Me, Al	Ring Lardner
Zorba the Greek	Nikos Kazantzakis
Zuleika Dobson	Max Beerbohm

Children's Authors

Among authors of books for children, who wrote . . . ?

Anne of Green Gables	Lucy M. Montgomery
Babar	Jean de Brunhoff
Black Beauty	Anna Sewell
Cat in the Hat	Dr. Seuss
Catfish Bend books	Ben Lucien Burman
Charlie and the Chocolate Factory	Roald Dahl
Curious George	Margaret Rey
Germany fairy tales, as collectors and translators	Jacob and Wilhelm Grimm
Hardy Boys and Nancy Drew series	Carolyn Keene
Hatchet	Gary Paulsen
Little House on the Prairie	Laura Ingalls Wilder
Little Lord Fauntleroy	Frances Hodgson Burnett
Little Prince	Antoine de Saint-Exupéry
Mary Poppins stories	P. L. Travers
My Friend Flicka	Mary O'Hara
National Velvet	Enid Bagnold
"Owl and the Pussycat"	Edward Lear
Paddington Bear books	Michael Bond
Rebecca of Sunnybrook Farm	Kate Douglas Wiggin
Rumble Fish	S. E. Hinton
Tale of Peter Rabbit	Beatrix Potter
Then Again, Maybe I Won't	Judy Blume

Ugly Duckling	**Hans Christian Andersen**
Uncle Remus stories	**Joel Chandler Harris**
Where the Wild Things Are	**Maurice Sendak**
Wind in the Willows	**Kenneth Grahame**
Winnie-the-Pooh	**A. A. Milne**
Wonderful Wizard of Oz	**L. Frank Baum**
Yearling	**Marjorie Kinnan Rawlings**

Modern Poets

Among 20th-century poets, who wrote . . . ?

Algonquin witticisms, as about girls who wear glasses	**Dorothy Parker**
"Anthem for a Doomed Youth"	**Wilfred Owen**
"Anyone Lived in a Pretty How Town"	**e. e. cummings**
Ariel and *The Colossus*	**Sylvia Plath**
Arrow in the Wall	**Andrei Voznesensky**
Astonishing Eye Looks Out of the Air	**Kenneth Patchen**
Awful Rowing Toward God	**Anne Sexton**
Beast in View and *The Gates*	**Muriel Rukeyser**
Bells in Winter and *The Witness of Poetry*	**Czeslaw Milosz**
Black Christ	**Countée Cullen**
Black Magic	**Amiri Baraka (Leroi Jones)**
Book of Nightmares	**Galway Kinnell**
Brothers, I Loved You All	**Hayden Carruth**
Cantos and *Personae*	**Ezra Pound**
Carnival of Animals verses to Saint-Saens music	**Ogden Nash**
"Casey at the Bat"	**Ernest Lawrence Thayer**
Compass Flower	**W. S. Merwin**
Coney Island of the Mind	**Lawrence Ferlinghetti**
Counter-Attack and *The Weald of Youth*	**Siegfried Sassoon**
Cuttlefish Bones	**Eugenio Montale**
Dead Reckoning	**Kenneth Fearing**
Dear Lovely Death	**Langston Hughes**
Death of a Naturalist	**Seamus Heaney**
Dragon and the Unicorn	**Kenneth Rexroth**
"Emperor of Ice Cream"	**Wallace Stevens**
Far Field	**Theodore Roethke**
"Fire and Ice" and "Stopping by Woods . . ."	**Robert Frost**
Gasoline and *Earth Egg*	**Gregory Corso**

"General William Booth Enters into Heaven"	Vachel Lindsay
Grey Is the Color of Hope	Irina Ratushinskaya
Hawk in the Rain	Ted Hughes
"Helen" and *Turning Point*	George Seferis
"Howl" and *Reality Sandwiches*	Allen Ginsberg
Iliad and *Odyssey*'s new translations	Robert Fitzgerald
In Dreams Begin Responsibilities	Delmore Schwartz
"In Flanders Field"	John McRae
"Ithaca" and "Waiting for the Barbarians"	Constantine Cavafy
Jacob's Ladder	Denise Levertov
J.B. and *Conquistador*	Archibald MacLeish
John Brown's Body	Stephen Vincent Benét
"Lake Isle of Innisfree" and "Easter 1916"	William Butler Yeats
Life of the Dead	Laura Riding
"Listeners" and *Come Hither*	Walter de la Mare
Listen to the Warm	Rod McKuen
Little Mariner	Odysseas Elytis
Lord Weary's Castle and *The Dolphin*	Robert Lowell
Losses	Randall Jarrell
Lyrics of Lowly Life	Paul Laurence Dunbar
Maximus Poems and *Projective Verse*	Charles Olson
"Musée de Beaux Arts" and "September 1, 1939"	W. H. Auden
Names of the Lost	Philip Levine
Nights and Days and *Divine Comedies*	James Merrill
No Matter No Fact	Alain Bosquet
"Ode to the Confederate Dead"	Allan Tate
Paterson, a New Jersey physician	William Carlos Williams
"Patterns" and "Lilacs"	Amy Lowell
People, Yes, and *Smoke and Steel*	Carl Sandburg
Person, Place and Thing and "Dome of Sunday"	Karl Shapiro
Pluies (Rains) and *Vents (Winds)*	St-John Perse
Poet in New York	Federico García Lorca
Poet's Alphabet	Louise Bogan
"Poetry" and *Nevertheless*	Marianne Moore
Private Mythology	May Sarton
Residence on Earth	Pablo Neruda
"Roan Stallion"	Robinson Jeffers
Sea-Fever ("I must go down to the sea again")	John Masefield
Sea Garden and *Bid Me to Live*	H.D. (Hilda Doolittle)

Self-Portrait in a Convex Mirror	John Ashbery
"She Passed Through the Fair" and *Wild Earth*	Padraic Colum
"Shooting of Dan McGrew"	Robert W. Service
Shropshire Lad	A. E. Housman
Shuttle in the Crypt	Wole Soyinka
Sitting Here	Robert Creeley
Sleepers Joining Hands	Robert Bly
Snow Poems	A. R. Ammons
Time in the Rock	Conrad Aiken
To Give and to Have (Debit and Credit)	Salvatore Quasimodo
"Trees"	Joyce Kilmer
Turtle Island and *The Back Country*	Gary Snyder
Under Milk Wood and *A Child's Christmas in Wales*	Dylan Thomas
Urania	Joseph Brodsky
Waste Land and *Old Possum's Book of Practical Cats*	T. S. Eliot
Winter Lightning and *Inside the Onion*	Howard Nemerov
Women and the Men	Nikki Giovanni

Modern Playwrights

Among 20th-century writers of plays and scripts, who wrote . . . ?

Abe Lincoln in Illinois	Robert E. Sherwood
Annie Get Your Gun	Irving Berlin
Architect and the Emperor of Assyria	Fernando Arrabal
Bad Seed	Maxwell Anderson
Bell, Book, and Candle	John Van Druten
Blacks	Jean Genet
Blood Wedding	Federico García Lorca
Born Yesterday	Garson Kanin
Brighton Beach Memoirs	Neil Simon
Buried Child	Sam Shepard
Butley	Simon Gray
Chalk Garden	Enid Bagnold
Cherry Orchard	Anton Chekhov
"City on the Edge of Forever" *Star Trek* script	Harlan Ellison
Cloud Nine and *Top Girls*	Caryl Churchill
Corn Is Green	Emlyn Williams
Day in the Death of Joe Egg	Peter Nichols
Death of a Salesman	Arthur Miller

Deathtrap	Ira Levin
Deputy	Rolf Hochhuth
Easy Rider	Terry Southern
Effect of Gamma Rays on Man-in-the-Moon Marigolds	Paul Zindel
Equus	Peter Shaffer
Fantasticks	Harvey Schmidt and Tom Jones
Fences	August Wilson
Four Saints in Three Acts ("Pigeons in the grass, alas")	Gertrude Stein
Front Page	Charles MacArthur and Ben Hecht
Gentlemen Prefer Blondes	Anita Loos
Glengarry Glen Ross	David Mamet
Glittering Prizes	Frederic Raphael
Great White Hope	Howard Sackler
Green Pastures	Marc Connelly
Guys and Dolls	Frank Loesser
Harvey	Mary Chase
Heat and Dust and Merchant-Ivory movies	Ruth Prawer Jhabvala
He Who Gets Slapped	Leonid Andreyev
Hitch Hiker's Guide to the Galaxy	Douglas Adams
Homecoming	Harold Pinter
Hotel Paradiso and other farces	Georges Feydeau
Indians	Arthur Kopit
Inherit the Wind	Robert E. Lee and Jerome Lawrence
Judgment at Nuremberg	Abby Mann
Juno and the Paycock	Sean O'Casey
Kitchen	Arnold Wesker
Lady's Not for Burning	Christopher Fry
Lark and *Antigone*	Jean Anouilh
La Ronde	Arthur Schnitzler
Little Foxes	Lilian Hellman
Little Murders	Jules Feiffer
Long Day's Journey into Night	Eugene O'Neill
Look Back in Anger	John Osborne
Loose Ends	Michael Weller
Loot	Joe Orton
Luv	Murray Schisgal
M*A*S*H and *The Woman of the Year*	Ring Lardner, Jr.
Man for All Seasons	Robert Bolt
Marat/Sade	Peter Weiss
Marty	Paddy Chayevsky
Master Harold and the Boys	Athol Fugard
Memorandum (Vyrozumeni)	Vaclav Havel

Miracle Worker	William Gibson
Miss Julie	August Strindberg
Morning's at Seven	Paul Osborn
Music Man	Meredith Willson
My Fair Lady	Alan Jay Lerner and Frederick Loewe
No Exit	Jean-Paul Sartre
Norman Conquests trilogy	Alan Ayckbourn
Oh! Calcutta	Kenneth Tynan et al.
Old Glory trilogy	Robert Lowell
Our Town	Thornton Wilder
Pelléas and Melisande	Maurice Maeterlinck
Peter Pan	J. M. Barrie
Philadelphia Story	Philip Barry
Philadelphia, Here I come	Brian Friel
Picnic	William Inge
Pins and Needles	Harold Rome
Playboy of the Western World	John Millington Synge
Private Lives	Noël Coward
Pygmalion	George Bernard Shaw
Raisin in the Sun	Lorraine Hansberry
Rhinoceros	Eugene Ionesco
Roberta	Jerome Kern and Otto Harbach
Rosencrantz and Guildenstern Are Dead	Tom Stoppard
R. U. R.	Karel Capek
Separate Tables	Terence Rattigan
Serjeant Musgrave's Dance	John Arden
Six Characters in Search of an Author	Luigi Pirandello
Sleuth	Anthony Shaffer
State of the Union	Howard Lindsay and Russell Crouse
Streamers	David Rabe
Street Scene	Elmer Rice
Streetcar Named Desire	Tennessee Williams
Student Prince	Sigmund Romberg and Dorothy Donnelly
Sunrise at Campobello	Dore Schary
Swan	Ferenc Molnár
Talley family plays	Lanford Wilson
Taste of Honey	Shelagh Delaney
Three-Penny Opera	Bertolt Brecht and Kurt Weill
Tiger at the Gates	Jean Giraudoux
Time of Your Life	William Saroyan
Torch Song Trilogy	Harvey Fierstein
Twelve Angry Men	Reginald Rose
Twilight Zone	Rod Serling
Ubu Roi	Alfred Jarry
Vagabond King	Rudolf Friml and Brian Hooker
Visit	Friedrich Dürrenmatt

Waiting for Godot	**Samuel Beckett**
Waiting for Lefty	**Clifford Odets**
Who's Afraid of Virginia Woolf	**Edward Albee**
Women	**Clare Boothe Luce**
You Can't Take It with You	**George S. Kaufman** and **Moss Hart**

Modern Commentators, Biographers, and Essayists

(See also People of Science and Invention in *World of the Sciences*)

Among 20th-century commentators, biographers, and essayists, who wrote . . . ?

Against Interpretation	**Susan Sontag**
All Creatures Great and Small	**James Herriot**
American Way of Death	**Jessica Mitford**
Anatomy of an Illness	**Norman Cousins**
Arctic Dreams	**Barry Lopez**
Axel's Castle and *Patriotic Gore*	**Edmund Wilson**
Believe It or Not	**Robert L. Ripley**
Best and the Brightest	**David Halberstam**
Between the Woods and the Water	**Patrick Leigh Fermor**
Blue Highways	**William Least Heat Moon**
Born Free	**Joy Adamson**
Born on the Fourth of July	**Ron Kovic**
Borstal Boy	**Brendan Behan**
Bring 'Em Back Alive	**Frank Buck**
Coming into the Country	**John McPhee**
Common Ground: A Turbulent Decade in the Lives of Three American Families	**J. Anthony Lukas**
Communion	**Whitley Strieber**
Culture of Cities	**Lewis Mumford**
Day Christ Died	**Jim Bishop**
Death at an Early Age	**Jonathan Kozol**
Death of a President	**William Manchester**
Desert Year	**Joseph Wood Krutch**
diary of hiding from the Nazis in a Dutch attic	**Anne Frank**
Dictionary of Slang and Unconventional English	**Eric Partridge**
Dragons of Eden	**Carl Sagan**
Egg and I	**Betty MacDonald**
84 Charing Cross Road	**Helene Hanff**
Eleanor and Franklin	**Joseph Lash**

Elements of Style	**William Strunk, Jr.** and **E. B. White**
Eminent Victorians	**Lytton Strachey**
Eros and Civilization	**Herbert Marcuse**
Etiquette, from 1924	**Emily Post**
etiquette guides after Emily Post	**Amy Vanderbilt**
etiquette guides for the 1980s	**Miss Manners**
Fate of the Earth	**Jonathan Schell**
Fear and Loathing on the Campaign Trail	**Hunter S. Thompson**
Fire Next Time	**James Baldwin**
Flame Trees of Thika	**Elspeth Huxley**
Flowering of New England	**Van Wyck Brooks**
Free to Be . . . You and Me	**Marlo Thomas** et al.
Gift from the Sea	**Anne Morrow Lindbergh**
Gödel, Esher, Bach: An Eternal Golden Braid	**Douglas R. Hofstadter**
Great Railway Bazaar	**Paul Theroux**
Greatest Salesman in the World	**Og Mandino**
Great War and Modern Memory	**Paul Fussell**
Growing Up	**Russell Baker**
Growing Up Absurd	**Paul Goodman**
Hard Times	**Studs Terkel**
Hidden Persuaders	**Vance Packard**
House of Intellect	**Jacques Barzun**
If Life Is a Bowl of Cherries— What Am I Doing in the Pits	**Erma Bombeck**
Immense Journey	**Loren Eiseley**
Inside Europe and *Death Be Not Proud*	**John Gunther**
Italian Painters of the Renaissance	**Bernard Berenson**
La Vida	**Oscar Lewis**
Let Us Now Praise Famous Men	**James Agee**
Life with Father	**Clarence Day**
Lonely Crowd	**David Riesman, Jr., Reuel Denney,** and **Nathan Glazer**
Love and Death in the American Novel	**Leslie Fiedler**
Making of the President books	**Theodore H. White**
Manchild in the Promised Land	**Claude Brown**
Medium Is the Message	**Marshall McLuhan**
Medusa and the Snail	**Lewis Thomas**
Merry-Go-Round column	**Drew Pearson**
Middletown	**Robert Lynd** and **Helen Lynd**
My Daddy Was a Pistol and I'm a Son of a Gun	**Lewis Grizzard**
My Ten Years in a Quandary	**Robert Benchley**
Naked Ape	**Desmond Morris**
New Criticism	**John Crowe Ransom**
North With the Spring	**Edwin Way Teale**

Old Glory	Jonathan Raban
On Native Grounds	Alfred Kazin
One, Two, Three . . . Infinity	George Gamow
Only Yesterday	Frederick Lewis Allen
Origins of Totalitarianism	Hannah Arendt
Our Crowd	Stephen Birmingham
Oxford English Dictionary	James Murray
Passages	Gail Sheehy
Periodic Table	Primo Levi
Personal History	Vincent Sheean
Please Don't Eat the Daisies	Jean Kerr
Portrait of a Marriage	Nigel Nicolson
Psychedelic Reader	Timothy Leary
Public Opinion	Walter Lippman
Rats, Lice, and History	Hans Zinsser
Red Star over China	Edgar Snow
Ring of Bright Water	Gavin Maxwell
Rise and Fall of the Third Reich	William L. Shirer
Road Less Traveled	M. Scott Peck
Roots	Alex Haley
Sand County Almanac	Aldo Leopold
Sex and the Single Girl, editor of Cosmopolitan	Helen Gurley Brown
Silent Spring	Rachel Carson
Snow Leopard	Peter Matthiessen
Snow Walker and People of the Deer	Farley Mowat
Soul on Ice	Eldridge Cleaver
Stalking the Wild Asparagus	Euell Gibbons
Strachey and Shaw biographies	Michael Holroyd
Syntactic Structures	Noam Chomsky
Teaching a Stone to Talk	Annie Dillard
Ten Days That Shook the World	John Reed
Testament of Youth	Vera Brittain
Thinking About the Unthinkable	Herman Kahn
Thousand Days	Arthur Schlesinger, Jr.
Thy Neighbor's Wife	Gay Talese
Trial of Socrates and a longtime newsletter	I. F. Stone
Two Cultures	C. P. Snow
View from a Distant Star	Harlow Shapley
Westward, Ha! and Marx Brothers scripts	S. J. Perelman
While Rome Burns	Alexander Woollcott
Whole Earth Catalog	Stewart Brand
Winning Through Intimidation	Robert Ringer
World of Our Fathers	Irving Howe
Worlds in Collision	Immanuel Velikovsky
Wretched of the Earth	Frantz Fanon
You Have Seen Their Faces	Margaret Bourke-White and Erskine Caldwell

Zen and the Art of Motorcycle Maintenance	**Robert W. Pirsig**

Modern Historians

Among modern historians, who wrote . . . ?

Across the Wide Missouri	**Bernard De Voto**
Age of Roosevelt	**Arthur Schlesinger, Jr.**
Centuries of Childhood	**Philippe Aries**
Mediterranean and the Mediterranean World . . .	**Fernand Braudel**
Civilization of the Renaissance in Italy	**Jakob Burckhardt**
Decline of the West	**Oswald Spengler**
English country houses books	**Mark Girouard**
Enlightenment: An Interpretation	**Peter Gay**
European Discovery of America	**Samuel Eliot Morison**
Fatal Shore	**Robert Hughes**
From Slavery to Freedom	**John Hope Franklin**
Frontier in American History	**Frederick Jackson Turner**
Guns of August	**Barbara Tuchman**
History as the Story of Liberty	**Benedetto Croce**
History of Sexuality	**Michel Foucault**
History of the Crusades	**Steven Runciman**
Idea of Progress	**J. B. Bury**
Immigrant in American History	**Marcus Lee Hansen**
In Search of the Trojan War	**Michael Wood**
Longest Day	**Cornelius Ryan**
Ordeal of the Union	**Allan Nevins**
Our Times	**Mark Sullivan**
Outline of History	**H. G. Wells**
Religion and the Rise of Capitalism	**R. H. Tawney**
Rise and Fall of the Great Powers	**Paul Kennedy**
Rise of American Civilization	**Charles Austin Beard**
Rise of the Greeks	**Michael Grant**
Science and Civilization in China	**Joseph Needham**
Stillness at Appomattox	**Bruce Catton**
Study of History	**Arnold Toynbee**
United States and China	**John King Fairbank**
Uprooted	**Oscar Handlin**
Woman in American History	**Gerda Lerner**

Modern Educators

In the world of 19th- and 20th-century education, who . . . ?

invented a system of raised letters for reading by the blind	**Louis Braille**
ruled his New Jersey school with a baseball bat	**Joe Clark**
wrote *Education for a Classless Society*	**James Bryant Conant**
was the guru of progressive education	**John Dewey**
developed the library decimal cataloguing system	**Melvil Dewey**
founded Boston's Perkins School for the Blind	**Samuel Gridley Howe**
reformed US education in the mid-19th c.	**Horace Mann**
wrote the famous *Eclectic Readers*	**William McGuffey**
was Helen Keller's "miracle worker"	**Anne Sullivan**
was the Tennessee biology teacher tried for teaching evolution in the 1925 "Monkey Trial"	**John Scopes**
pioneered in education testing	**Edward Thorndike**
founded the 1st women's college, Troy Female Seminary, in 1821	**Emma Willard**

Pen Names

What were the real names of the following authors?

Beaumarchais	**Pierre Augustin Caron**
Acton Bell	**Anne Brontë**
Currer Bell	**Charlotte Brontë**
Ellis Bell	**Emily Brontë**
Nicholas Blake	**Cecil Day Lewis**
Nellie Bly	**Elizabeth Cochrane Seaman**
Bryher	**Annie Winifred Ellerman Macpherson**
Lewis Carroll	**Charles Lutwidge Dodgson.**
Agatha Christie	**Mary Clarissa Miller**
Colette	**Sidonie Gabrielle Colette**
Joseph Conrad	**Josef Teodor Korzeniowski**

Edmund Crispin	Robert Bruce Montgomery
Amanda Cross	Carolyn Heilbrun
E. V. Cunningham	Howard Fast
George Eliot	Mary Ann (Marian) Evans (Cross)
Jonathan Gash	John Grant
James Hacker	Jonathan Lynn and Antony Jay
O. Henry	William Sydney Porter
James Herriot	James Alfred Wight
Michael Innes	J(ames) I(nnes) M(ichael) Stewart
Carolyn Keene	Edward Stratemeyer and daughter Harriet
Emma Lathen	Mary Jane Latsis and Martha Henissart
John le Carré	David John Moore Cornwell
Ursula K. Le Guin	Ursula Kroeber
Ed McBain	Evan Hunter
Ross Macdonald	Kenneth Millar
J. J. Marric	John Creasey
Judith Michael	Judith Barnard and Michael Fain
Molière	Jean Baptiste Poquelin
Jan Morris	James Morris (before 1972)
Toni Morrison	Chloe Anthony Wofford
Pablo Neruda	Ricardo Naftalí Reyes
Dorothy Parker	Dorothy Rothschild
St-John Perse	Alexis Saint-Léger
Ellery Queen	Frederic Dannay and Manfred B. Lee
Ayn Rand	Alice Rosenbaum
Mary Renault	Mary Challans
Françoise Sagan	Françoise Quoirez
Saki	H. H. Munro
George Sand	Amandine Lucie Aurore Dupin, Baronne Dudevant
Albert Savinio	Andreas de Chirico
Dr. Seuss	Theodore Geisel
Dell Shannon	Elizabeth Linington and Egan O'Neill
Stevie Smith	Florence Margaret Smith
E. Œ. Somerville and Martin Ross	Edith Somerville and Violet Martin
Wole Soyinka	Akinwande Oluwole Soyinka
Stendhal	Marie Henri Beyle
Mark Twain	Samuel Langhorne Clemens
S. S. Van Dine	Willard Huntington Wright
Barbara Vine	Ruth Rendell
Voltaire	François Marie Arouet
Nathanael West	Nathanael Wallenstein Weinstein

Tennessee Williams	**Thomas Lanier Williams**
Tom Wolfe	**Thomas Kennerly, Jr.**
Marguerite Yourcenar	**Marguerite de Crayencour**
Yukio Mishima	**Kimitake Hiraoka**

Specialties of Literary Study

In the world of letters, esp. literature and history, what is or was the special study of . . . ?

analysis and evaluation of literary works	**literary criticism**
arranging events in a time sequence	**chronology**
authenticity of written documents	**bibliotics**
cultural areas such as philosophy, literature, and the fine arts	**humanities**
dialects	**dialectology**
dictionaries, esp. the making of them	**lexicography**
evolutionary development of language	**historical linguistics** or **philology**
general culture, e.g., philosophy or languages, rather than vocational training	**liberal arts**
handwriting, esp. in character analysis	**graphology** or **graphanalysis**
history, comparison, and classification of books	**bibliography**
information about books or groups of books	**bibliography**
language and the structure of speech	**linguistics, glottology,** or **glossology**
languages as they exist, esp. their grammars	**descriptive linguistics**
languages, their likenesses and differences	**comparative linguistics**
law as a formal discipline	**jurisprudence**
libraries as functioning entities	**library science**
names	**onomastics** or **onomatology**
oratory and the qualities of literary prose	**rhetoric**
penmanship	**chirography**
people and events since written records	**history**

regional speech patterns	**geolinguistics** or **linguistic geography**
shorthand	**stenography**
signs or sign language	**semiology**
sound	**phonics** or **acoustics**
speech sounds and representations of them	**phonology**
speech units that are distinct in a language	**phonemics**
standard pronunciation of words	**orthoepy**
standard spelling and handwriting	**orthography**
teaching	**pedagogy**
word histories and derivations	**etymology**

Literary Forms and Genres

Among literary forms and genres, what is or are . . . ?

a biography written by its subject	**autobiography**
the story of a person's life	**biography**
a tale in which the characters and setting stand for general or abstract ideas or qualities	**allegory**
a formal advisory address	**allocution**
a simple, brief retelling of an incident	**anecdote**
a terse statement of truth or opinion	**aphorism, adage,** or **maxim**
a character type or plot common in literature and folklore, and so carrying great resonance	**archetype**
elegant, artistic, literary writings, as opposed to academic or factual writings	**belles-lettres**
a novel about a young person's growth from innocence to experience and maturity	**bildungsroman**
a work that mocks a subject by using an inappropriate style	**burlesque**
a medieval French verse epic about heroes and saints	**chanson de geste**
a discussion meeting or academic seminar	**colloquy**
a work in which the characters are embarrassed or discomfited, but (amusingly) turn out well	**comedy**

shaped verse, with words arranged into forms	**concrete poetry**
a literary attack, in France	**coup de plume**
a critical review or analysis of a work	**critique**
a formal argument on opposing views	**debate**
a recitation; also a vehement speech	**declamation**
a conversation with 2 or more people	**dialogue**
contemporaneous day-to-day accounts of the events in a person's own life	**diaries** or **journals**
a harsh, bitter denunciation	**diatribe** or **tirade**
a work pushing a particular thesis	**didactic**
a poetic form in which a character speaks as if overheard, as in Robert Browning's work	**dramatic monologue**
a poem lamenting a passing, as of a person	**elegy** or **dirge**
a poem written to praise, glorify, or eulogize	**encomium**
a long, serious, narrative poem on a heroic figure	**epic** or **heroic poem**
a brief, terse, pointed poem; also an inscription	**epigram**
a quotation at the start of a book or chapter; also an inscription on a building or statue	**epigraph**
a novel told completely through letters	**epistolary novel**
a poem written to celebrate a marriage	**epithalamion**
a summary or abstract; also a representative	**epitome**
a brief prose work aimed at a general audience	**essay** or **article**
a tale with a moral, with animals acting like humans, as in Aesop's work	**fable**
a short, comic, ribald medieval tale from France	**fabliau**
a form of literary work, such as poetry or romance	**genre**
a modern imitation of a medieval romance, often set in a gloomy be-dungeoned castle	**gothic novel**
a vehement tirade	**harangue**

a formal opening speech, e.g., by a new president	**inaugural address**
a long, drawn-out tale of woe	**jeremiad**
a work of broad, good-humored satire or ridicule	**lampoon**
a short poem focusing on a person's state of mind	**lyric**
an elaborate court entertainment involving dance, drama, and music, including masked players	**masque**
a suspenseful, sensational, romantic drama, often with a happy ending	**melodrama**
medieval, religious verse morality plays	**miracle** or **mystery plays**
a recurrent character, incident, or idea	**motif**
a traditional story, esp. about a culture's gods and heroes	**myth**
a long lyric poem in a serious style, with an elaborate stanza structure	**ode**
a poem retracting sentiments from an earlier poem	**palinode**
a tale told to teach a lesson, as with Christ	**parable**
a work ridiculing another by mimicking it	**parody**
a work dealing with rural life	**pastoral, idyll, eclogue,** or **bucolic**
a long, grandiose speech; also a formal review at the end of a speech	**peroration**
an abusive, caustic, personal verbal attack	**philippic**
an episodic, satirical novel with a roguish hero	**picaresque novel**
a play focusing on a social concern	**problem play**
spoken, public delivery of memorized materials	**recitation**
a fictionalized account of real people and events, literally a novel with a key	**roman à clef**
a medieval narrative focusing on knights, ladies, and love, today primarily a love story	**romance**
a multi-generational, often multi-volume work	**saga** or **roman fleuve**

a welcoming address, e.g., at a graduation	**salutatory address**
a work of literary ridicule, evoking contempt	**satire**
a serious work in which the main character meets disaster, in Aristotle leading to our catharsis	**tragedy**
a serious work in which events turn out well for the main character	**tragicomedy**
a grossly broad parody or burlesque	**travesty**
a closing address, e.g., at a graduation	**valedictory address**

Poetic Rhyme and Meter

Relating to rhyme and meter in poetry, what is or are . . . ?

the heavier elements in poetry's rhythmic units	**accents** or **stresses**
a poetic line with 6 iambic feet	**Alexandrine**
1 or more unstressed syllables before a line's normal meter begins	**anacrusis**
a foot with 2 unstressed, then 1 stressed syllable, in poetry	**anapest**
unrhymed iambic pentameter	**blank verse**
rhyming words at the end of poetic lines	**bouts-rimes**
a pause or break within a poetic line	**caesura**
a pair of rhymed lines in poetry	**couplet**
a foot with 1 stressed, then 2 unstressed syllables	**dactyl**
a poetic line with 2 feet	**dimeter**
the end of a poetic line that coincides with the end of a sentence, clause, or phrase	**end-stopped**
a sentence, clause, or phrase that carries over beyond the end of a poetic line	**enjambement** or **run-on lines**
ending a poetic line with an extra unstressed syllable	**feminine ending**
a poem's recurring rhythmic unit of stressed and unstressed syllables, e.g., iambic	**foot**

poetry without any recurrent foot or stress unit	**free verse (vers libre)**
a poetic line with 7 feet	**heptameter**
a poetic line with 6 feet	**hexameter**
a foot with 1 unstressed, then 1 stressed syllable	**iamb**
rhymes occurring within a line	**internal rhymes**
ending a poetic line with a stressed syllable	**masculine ending**
the regular rhythmic unit of stronger and weaker syllables occurring in a poetic line	**meter**
stressing a word because of poetic rhythm	**metrical accent**
a poetic line with one foot	**monometer**
a group of 8 lines in a sonnet	**octave**
an Italian-inspired 8-line stanza with the rhyme scheme a b a b a b c c	**ottava rima**
a poetic line with 5 feet	**pentameter**
a sonnet with the rhyme scheme a b b a a b b a c d e c d e	**Petrarchan sonnet**
poetic rhythm that depends on the duration or length of syllables, rather than their stresses	**quantitative meter**
a 4-line stanza, e.g., in a ballad	**quatrain**
1 or more lines, repeated, as in a ballad	**refrain**
marking the metrical pattern of a poem	**scansion**
a group of 6 lines in a sonnet	**sestet**
a sonnet with the rhyme scheme a b a b c d c d e f e f g g	**Shakespearean** or **English sonnet**
a lyric poem of 14 lines and a standard rhyme scheme	**sonnet**
a foot with two successive stressed syllables	**spondee**
a mixed meter, with a stressed syllable alone or with 2 or more unstressed syllables, as in Hopkins	**sprung rhythm**
a division within a poem, often with a recurring rhyme scheme and number of lines	**stanza**
a 3-line stanza, usually with a single rhyme	**tercet**
an Italian form of tercets with the rhyme scheme a b a, b c b, c d c, d e d . . .	**terza rima**
a poetic line with 4 feet	**tetrameter**

a poetic line with 3 feet	**trimeter**
a foot with 1 stressed, then 1 unstressed syllable	**trochee**
when rhythm shifts the normal accent of a word	**wrenched accent**

Name Words

Among words about names and names of words, what is the word or phrase for . . . ?

an assumed name	**alias**
a person, esp. a writer, taking another's name	**allonym**
an unknown name, esp. of an author	**anonym**
using a title instead of a name, e. g., "the Boss"	**antonomasia**
words that have opposite meanings	**antonyms**
an antiquated, outdated word	**archaism**
words in different languages from the same root	**cognates**
a secret name	**cryptonym**
a word deriving from a person's name	**eponym**
the earliest known form of a root word	**etymon**
a good name	**euonym**
words that sound and are often spelled the same, but differ in meaning	**homonyms**
a pet name or endearment, e. g., "Cuddles"	**hypocorism** or **-istic**
an example of a more general class, e.g., "dog" as a kind of "animal"	**hyponym**
under a false name to protect one's privacy	**incognito**
a woman's family name at birth	**maiden name**
use of a word to evoke a larger idea, e. g., bat for baseball	**metonymy**
one's family name on the mother's side	**metronymic** or **matro-**
a name given or applied erroneously	**misnomer**
a new word, or a new meaning for an old one	**neologism**

a pseudonym taken on entering the military, in France	**nom de guerre**
a system of names	**nomenclature**
an invalid or insufficient taxonomic name	**nomen nudum**
a word or phrase that reads the same backward and forward, e.g., "Madam, I'm Adam"	**palindrome**
words derived from the same root	**paronym** or **conjugates**
one's family name on the father's side	**patronymic**
a false name assumed by a writer	**pen name** or **nom de plume**
having more than one name	**polyonymy**
2 words packed into 1, to carry the meanings of both, e. g., "slithy" for "lithe and slimy"	**portmanteau word**
one's 1st or given name	**praenomen**
a fictitious name, esp. taken by a writer	**pseudonym** or **anonym**
an amusing nickname or assumed name	**sobriquet**
a family name or last name	**surname** or **cognomen**
words that have the same meaning	**synonyms**
a taxonomic name, esp. in zoology, where the parts of the name are the same, e. g., Gorilla gorilla	**tautonym**
place-names; also names for areas of the body	**toponymy**
a taxonomic name based on type, not description	**typonym**

Words of Literary Criticism

In the world of literary criticism, what is the word or phrase for . . . ?

judging a work by its emotional effect	**affective fallacy**
when a writer, aiming for the sublime, hits the ridiculous	**bathos**
wordy, pretentious, overinflated diction	**bombast**

expurgating supposed indecencies from a work	**bowdlerizing**
a "make-much-of-your-time" motif	**carpe diem**
a mixed metaphor, or use of the wrong word	**catachresis**
a "purging of pity and fear," as in tragedy	**catharsis**
a trite, overused expression, e.g., "my better half"	**cliché**
humorous action to relieve a serious work	**comic relief**
a parallel used to create a striking, often elaborately worked-out figure of speech in poetry	**conceit**
an overused comparison between objects no longer seen as unlike, e.g., "leg of a table"	**dead metaphor**
the final unknotting of a plot's problem	**dénouement**
one's choice of words; also clarity in speech	**diction**
the moral of the tale	**epimythium**
a moment of revelation	**epiphany**
a post-WWI literary movement, distorting time, objects, and events in a work	**expressionism**
a hero's tragic flaw or error of judgment, as in Aristotle	**hamartia**
the tragic flaw of pride or overconfidence	**hubris**
gross exaggeration for serious or comic effect	**hyperbole**
the descriptive passages of a poem, or the pattern of figurative language in a work	**imagery**
an early 20th-c. free-verse movement in poetry akin to impressionism in art	**imagism**
starting at a key point in the middle of the action	**in medias res**
using an author's background and stated intentions in interpreting a work	**intentional fallacy**
expressing one attitude but implying its opposite	**irony**
17th-c. poets who used elaborate imagery and conceits, e.g., Donne	**metaphysical poets**

focusing on characters as largely driven by sociological pressures, rather than individual will	**naturalism**
focus on the text, rather than its biographical or historical context	**New Criticism**
a situation written so as to "objectify" an emotion, causing the reader to feel it, too	**objective correlative**
suffering or passion, to the Greeks	**pathos**
a reversal in the hero's fortunes at the end	**peripety**
using high-sounding substitutes for commonplace terms	**periphrasis** or **circumlocution**
an inanimate object or abstraction given human qualities	**personification, prosopopoeia,** or **pathetic fallacy**
use of redundant words	**pleonasm**
artistic liberty for effect	**poetic license**
the outlook from which a fictional narrative is told	**point of view**
the study of poetic rhythms and forms	**prosody**
focus on everyday people and concerns, rather than romantic, adventurous ones	**realism**
a long, introspective 1st-person passage, describing a character's thoughts and feelings	**stream of consciousness**
an 18th-c. movement focusing on turbulent emotions and heightened sensibility	**Sturm and Drang**

Other Literary Language

In the world of literature, what is the word or phrase for . . . ?

repetition of consonants in stressed words	**alliteration**
a brief reference to a person, place, or event the reader is supposed to recognize	**allusion**
multiple meanings for a word or phrase	**ambiguity**
repeating phrases at the start of successive sentences	**anaphora**

a word used to mean its opposite	**antiphrasis**
a sudden shift to direct address of a person or abstract entity	**apostrophe**
repetition of the same or similar vowel sounds, as in: "In Xanadu did Kubla Khan . . ."	**assonance**
harsh, grating, unpleasant sounds in poetry	**cacophony**
the group of men who danced, sang, and commented on the action in early Greek plays	**chorus**
the associated meanings and ideas that accompany the hard, specific meaning of a word	**connotation**
repetition of consonants, with different intervening vowels, as in "live-love"	**consonance**
the specific meaning a word, as opposed to its associations	**denotation**
having a risqué double meaning	**double-entendre**
an unpleasant word for something pleasant or neutral	**dysphemism**
Welsh poetry and music fair	**eisteddfod**
a term characterizing a person or thing	**epithet**
a pleasant word for something unpleasant	**euphemism**
pleasant, warm, musical sounds in poetry	**euphony**
language that shifts words from their literal meanings, e.g., similes and metaphors	**figurative language** or **tropes**
an anonymous writer for a named author	**ghost writer**
calling on a god or muse for aid in writing	**invocation**
understating for effect, e.g., "I am not unmoved"	**litotes**
understatement for comic effect	**melosis**
the use of one word to stand for another, without the use of "like" or "as", e.g., "He is a lion"	**metaphor**
words sounding like what they describe, e.g., "hiss"	**onomatopoeia**
repetition for emphasis or stylistic effect	**palilogy**
an old document showing remains of earlier writings	**palimpsest**

a statement that appears self-contradictory, yet is sound	**paradox** or **oxymoron**
a play on words similar in sound but varying in meaning	**pun, paranomasia,** or **equivoque**
a verbal contest of wits	**repartée**
stressing a word for its function, not its meter	**rhetorical accent**
a question asked for emphasis, not for a reply	**rhetorical question**
caustic praise that is actually criticism	**sarcasm**
a comparison between two unlike things, using "like" or "as," as in: "He is like a lion"	**simile**
part of something standing for the whole, as in "two hands" for "a craftsman"	**synecdoche**

Parts of Speech

Among parts of speech, what is or are . . . ?

a word modifying a noun or pronoun	**adjective**
a word modifying a verb, adjective, or other adverb	**adverb**
a word part attached to a root, e.g., "un-" or "-ful"	**affix**
"a," "an," or "the," indicating a noun	**article**
an adjective placed next to a noun, e.g., *red* sky"	**attributive**
a noun referring to a group, e.g., "family"	**collective noun**
a noun preceded by an article, referring to one of a class	**common noun**
2 or more words acting as 1, e.g., "first-rate"	**compound word**
a word that connects words, e.g., "and" or "but"	**conjunction**
a word shortened by omission, e.g., "don't"	**contraction**
a conjunction that connects similar elements, e.g., "You *and* I go"	**coordinating conjunction**
a conjunction with related parts, e.g., "either-or"	**correlative conjunction**

"the," indicating a definite noun	**definite article**
a verb that shows person, number, or tense in its form, e.g., "I *sing*" or "You *sang*"	**finite verb**
a verb form used as a noun, e.g., "*Living* is easy"	**gerund**
"a" or "an," indicating a noun, but not a specific one	**indefinite article**
a verb not fixed in person, number, or tense, e.g., a gerund, participle, or infinitive	**infinite verb**
the "to" form of a verb, e.g., "to read"	**infinitive**
a verb that takes no direct object, e.g., "I *think*"	**intransitive**
a word, phrase, or clause that explains, qualifies, or limits another, e.g., an adjective or adverb	**modifier or qualifier**
a word denoting a person, place, thing, or quality, e.g., a subject or object in a sentence	**noun or substantive**
a noun or pronoun and all its modifiers	**noun phrase**
a verb acting as an adjective, e.g., "a *smoking* gun"	**participle**
a word part attached before a root, e.g., "*dis*able"	**prefix**
a word that relates its object to the words in a sentence, e.g., "Wizard *of* Oz"	**preposition**
a word that replaces a noun, e.g., "he" or "it"	**pronoun**
a noun that identifies a specific person, place, or thing with no modifier, usually capitalized	**proper noun**
"who," "which," and "that," in adjective clauses	**relative pronouns**
a word or word part to which other parts may be added to change the meaning, e.g., "*home*less"	**root**
a word that links a dependent clause with another subordinating part of the sentence, e.g., "*When* I think"	**conjunction**
a word part attached after a root, e.g., "help*less*"	**suffix**
a verb that takes a direct object, e.g., "I *hit* it"	**transitive**

a word or words expressing action or being	**verb**
a form of verb that cannot stand alone, e.g., gerunds, participles, and infinitive	**verbal**
a verb plus all its auxiliaries and modifiers	**verb phrase**

Parts of a Sentence

Among parts of a sentence, what is or are . . . ?

a dependent clause modifying a noun or pronoun	**adjective clause**
a dependent clause modifying a verb or verbal	**adverb clause**
the noun to which a pronoun refers	**antecedent**
an explanatory noun, e.g., "George, the *painter*"	**appositive**
a verb that indicates the tense, mood, aspect, or voice of a main verb, e.g., "I *will* go"	**auxiliary verb**
a group of words, with a subject and predicate, e.g., dependent or independent	**clause**
a sentence with 1 independent clause and 1 or more dependent clauses, e.g., "As I see, I do"	**complex sentence**
a sentence with 2 or more independent clauses, e.g., "I see, and I do"	**compound sentence**
an adjective that specifies its noun, e.g., "this"	**demonstrative**
a group of words that cannot stand alone but are linked to another clause by a relative pronoun or subordinating conjunction, e.g., "As I see"	**dependent clause**
the word(s) receiving the action of a transitive verb, e.g., "I broke *it*"	**direct object**
a group of words that can stand alone, but may be linked with other clauses, e.g., "As I see, I *do*"	**independent clause**

an object that receives the verb's action indirectly, e.g., "He gave the book to *me*"	indirect object
a clause supplying information, but not specifically identifying, e.g., "He, *who is an Elk,* is going"	nonrestrictive
a dependent clause acting as a noun, e.g., "*That I left* was a problem"	noun clause
a noun or pronoun affected by an action verb or related to a preposition	object
a noun or pronoun modifying a direct object, e.g., "They made her *mayor*"	objective complement
the sentence part that tells something about the subject, e.g., "He *took the cake*"	predicate
a word that, with a verb, completes a predicate, e.g., "It is *good*"	predicate complement
a noun or pronoun that, with a verb, completes a predicate, e.g., "Jan is the *leader*"	predicate nominative
a verb with the same subject and direct object, e.g., "I *am she*"; also the form of pronoun in "I was *myself* "	reflexive
a clause supplying identifying information, e.g., "All who own cars must register"	restrictive
the doer in an active sentence, or the receiver in a passive one	subject

Grammatical Tenses, Voices, and Moods

Among tenses, voices, and moods in grammar, what is . . . ?

a change in verb form, as to indicate tense, e.g., "sing, sang, sung"	ablaut or gradation
the voice when the subject acts, e.g., "I saw that"	active
the mood of "If I do this . . ."	conditional
the tense of "I *will be*"	future
the tense of "I *will have been*"	future perfect

use of present tense in describing past events	**historical present**
the mood of commands, e. g., "Do this"	**imperative**
verb mood used when discussing an accepted fact	**indicative**
the speaker's view of the likelihood of the action expressed, in English, indicative, subjunctive, or imperative	**mood**
the voice of the verb when a subject is acted upon, e.g. "I *was seen*"	**passive**
the participle voice of "*having been baked*"	**passive participle**
the participle tense of "*baked* fish" or "*sung* song"	**past participle**
the tense of "I *was*"	**past or preterit**
the tense of "I *had been*"	**past perfect or pluperfect**
the tense of "I *have been*"	**perfect**
the participle tense of "*having baked*"	**perfect participle**
the tense of "I *am*"	**present**
the participle tense of "*smoking* gun"	**present participle**
verb mood used in expressing a hypothetical or contingent action	**subjunctive**
a form of a verb showing time, e.g., past or future	**tense**
the subject-verb relation, i.e., active or passive	**voice**

Grammatical Cases

Among cases in grammar, which is for . . . ?

words indicating "away from," in Latin	**ablative**
a direct object, e.g., "I did *that*," in Latin	**accusative**
an indirect object or object of a preposition, as "to *him*," in Latin	**dative**
indicating place in some languages, e.g., Latin	**locative**
a subject or a predicate complement, in English and Latin	**nominative**

a word acting as object, e.g., "I hit *it*,"	**objective**
words showing possession, e.g., "of *it*"	**possessive (English) or genitive (Latin)**

Other Grammar Language

In the area of grammar and writing, what is or are . . . ?

a language that forms words mainly by combining little-changed word elements, as in "*Going-to-the-sun* Mountain"	**agglutinative language**
matching of number, case, gender, and person for related words, e.g., "He is," not "He are"	**agreement**
the letters of a language arranged in usual order	**alphabet**
an inconsistent grammatical shift in a sentence	**anacoluthon**
classification of verbs as to duration of action	**aspect**
bad handwriting or spelling	**cacography**
the relation of a noun, pronoun, or adjective to the rest of the sentence, shown by position or endings, e.g., "I" for a subject or "me" for an object	**case**
joining 2 independent clauses with a comma, rather than a conjunction or semicolon	**comma splice**
regular changes in the form of a verb, esp. in its ending, to show case, number, and gender in a sentence, e.g., "I *am*" and "You *are*"	**conjugation**
loss of vowel when 2 words join	**crasis**
a participle not clearly linked with the word it modifies, e.g., "*Sitting alone*, the bell rang"	**dangling participle**
a sentence that makes a statement	**declarative**

regular changes in form, esp. endings, of nouns, adjectives, and pronouns, showing case, number, and gender in a sentence, e.g., "I, you, he"	**declension**
a sudden exclamation, e.g., "Oh!"	**ejaculation** or **interjection**
omitting an unstressed vowel or syllable	**elision**
the "I" or "we" forms in a sentence, the speaker	**first person**
an incomplete sentence, e.g., a free-standing subordinate clause	**fragment**
masculine, feminine, or neuter, for purposes of grammatical agreement	**gender**
finding rules governing a language's structure, by transforming equivalent sentences	**generative transformational grammar**
the system of rules by which a language operates	**grammar**
a language with regular changes in word form, e.g., conjugations and declensions, to show use in a sentence	**inflected language**
a question, also a form of word used in asking one	**interrogative**
a verb that takes no direct object, e.g. "I *think*"	**intransitive**
an amusing misuse of a word	**malapropism**
singular or plural, often shown by an ending	**number**
having pairs or series of words, phrases, or clauses of similar pattern, e.g., "I came, I saw, I went"	**parallelism**
to break down a sentence, explaining the form and function of each part	**parse**
a long sentence, with the main clause complete only at the end	**periodic sentence**
joining 2 independent clauses with no punctuation or conjunction, "I saw him he went inside"	**run-on** or **fused sentence**
the "you" form in a sentence, the person spoken to	**second person**

a violation of standard grammatical or usage rules	**solecism**
a word inserted in an infinitive, e.g., "to *really* see"	**split infinitive**
dropping a mid-part of a word, as in "cap'n"	**syncope**
agreeing in meaning, though not in number, as in "If *anyone* hears it, *they* should whistle"	**synesis**
the pattern of word arrangement in sentences	**syntax**
the smallest unit of grammatical analysis	**tagmeme**
the "he, she, it, they" forms in a sentence, neither the speaker nor the person spoken to	**third person**

Types of Speech Sounds

Relating to types of speech sounds, what is or are . . . ?

a sound stopped and released sharply at articulation, as in "hut*ch*" or "*j*am"	**affricative**
a sound formed by the tip of the tongue at upper teeth, e.g., "t" or "d"	**alveolar** or **dental**
a sound formed with the tip of the tongue, e.g., "t"	**apical**
a sound from a puff of breath, as in "h"	**aspiration**
a sound formed with both lips, e.g., "b" or "m"	**bilabial**
a sound formed with the tongue tip turned back and at the roof of the mouth	**cacuminal** or **retroflex**
a sound formed by drawing in air and clicking the tongue, as in some African languages	**click** or **suction stop**
a sound formed by fully or partly obstructing the air flow past the speech organs	**consonant**
a consonant that can be drawn out, e.g., "s" or "f"	**continuant**
relating to the back, as in speech	**dorsal**
a sound made by closing the glottis, then sharply releasing air	**glottal stop**

a sound produced in the throat	**guttural** or **velar**
a sound formed mostly with the lips, e.g., "m"	**labial**
formed using the lips and teeth	**labiodental**
formed using the lips and soft palate	**labiovelar**
a sound made using the blade of the tongue	**laminal**
a sound produced by air along the side(s) of the tongue	**lateral**
a sound made with the tongue and other parts, e.g., "t"	**lingual**
a sound formed by air through the nose, e.g., "m"	**nasal**
formed by closing air passages, esp. nasal	**occlusive**
relating to the roof of the mouth	**palatal**
a speech sound made by closing the air passage, e.g., "di*p*"	**plosive** or **explosive**
a sound made with the tongue turned back to the roof of the mouth	**retroflex**
a "hissing" speech sound, e.g., "s" or "z"	**sibilation**
a voice spoken sound	**sonant**
a consonant formed by fully blocking air, e.g., "t"	**stopped**
a sound formed by organs above the glottis	**supraglottal**
a voiceless sound	**surd**
whispering or murmuring	**susurration**
a wordless, rhythmical wail	**ululation**
relating to the soft palate; in forming sound often with the back of the tongue as well, e.g., "g"	**velar**
a sound made by air passing rather freely through the mouth, usually the key sound of a syllable	**vowel**

Other Words About the Spoken Language

(See also The Brain and Nervous System: Speech Problems in *In Sickness and in Health*)

Relating to the spoken language, what is or are . . . ?

pretending to be at loss for words	**apophasis**

a dramatic breaking off in mid-sentence	**aposiopesis**
moving to produce speech sound, esp. consonants	**articulation**
a strong Irish accent	**brogue**
a rough whirring of the "r," as in Scotland	**burr**
a vowel in a stopped or closed syllable	**checked**
2 sounds pronounced with no intervening break	**close juncture**
a regional pattern of speech, differing from the standard	**dialect**
pronunciation of adjoining vowels separately	**diaeresis**
moving from one vowel sound to another within a syllable, as in "*toy*"; also the joined letters "æ" and "œ" now pronounced as 1 vowel	**diphthong**
replacing one sound with another, e. g., "purpure" became "purp*le*"	**dissimilation**
lengthening a vowel or making it a diphthong, when it usually is not	**drawl**
an old-fashioned public speaking style, with gestures and forced voice	**elocution**
making clear speech sounds	**enunciation**
speech without preparation or without notes	**extemporaneous**
mispronunciation of "g" or "k" sounds	**gammacism**
relating to the tongue	**glossal**
an individual's speech	**ideolect**
use of pitch in speaking	**intonation**
replacing "r" with "l" in a lulling way	**lallation**
misuse of the "l" sound, esp. to replace "r"	**lambdacism**
soft, vowel-like consonants, "l" and "r"	**liquid**
replacing sibilants with easier-to-produce sounds, e.g., "th" for "s"	**lisp**
a change in pitch or loudness	**modulation**
a single vowel sound, even if written as 2, e.g., in "*oat*"	**monophthong**

a silent letter, e.g., "one"; a sound made by stopping the breath, e.g., "b"; also one who cannot or does not speak, i.e., is dumb	**mute**
problems in making or using the "m" sound	**mytacism**
a break between 2 sounds	**open juncture**
the art of public speaking	**oratory** or **rhetoric**
problems using "l" with other sounds	**paralambdacism**
denying the statement you are making or about to	**paraleipsis**
problems using "r" near other sounds	**pararhotacism**
a comment delivered after a feigned retreat; in effect, "the last word"	**Parthian shot**
to make speech sounds	**phonate** or **vocalize**
acoustic frequency, heard as "higher" or "lower"	**pitch**
the act or style of making speech sounds	**pronunciation**
misuse of the "r" sound, or its replacement by another sound	**rhotacism**
an intermediate sound made while moving from pronouncing 1 sound to another	**semi-vowel** or **glide**
sound quality that makes a voice distinctive, apart from pitch or volume	**timbre** or **tone**
heavy nasality in a voice	**twang**
making speech sounds appear to come from another source, e.g., a dummy	**ventriloquism**

Language of Linguistics

Relating to linguistics, what is or are . . . ?

a morpheme's various forms, e.g., "hats" and "ices"	**allomorph**
a phoneme's various forms, e.g. "*pa*" and "*spa*"	**allophone**
loss of the vowel from a word's beginning, e.g., "esquire" to "squire"	**aphesis**

dropping the last part of a word, e.g., "doin' "	**apocope**
modification of a sound by its neighbor	**assimilation**
not accented	**atonic**
a word formed by changing or dropping another word's supposed affix, e.g., *kudo*, mistakenly treated as the singular for *kudos*	**back-formation**
mispronunciation of words	**cacoepy**
inserting a sound in mid-word, esp. to make it easier to pronounce	**epenthetis** or **svarabhakti**
emission of incoherent sounds, or "speaking in tongues"	**glossolalia**
a pattern of changes from Indo-European consonants to Germanic, e.g., "p" to "f"	**Grimm's Law**
words that sound the same but differ in spelling, meaning, or origin	**homophones**
private speech, e.g., between 2 children	**idioglossia**
the special language of a profession or group	**jargon**
excessive talkativeness	**logorrhea**
the smallest meaningful linguistic unit	**morpheme**
the varying sound pattern of morphemes, which distinguish morphemically related words	**morphophonemics**
a word with its last syllable stressed, as with an acute accent, e.g., "café"	**oxytone**
having an acute accent on the next-to-last syllable	**paroxytone**
the smallest distinct units of sound recognized in a language, e.g., "cat" and "*p*at"	**phonemes**
speaking multiple languages; also a book with text in 2 or more languages	**polyglot**
following a stressed syllable	**posttonic**
a consonant directly following a vowel	**postvocalic**
preceding a stressed syllable	**pretonic**
adding a phoneme at the start of a word, making it easier to pronounce	**prothesis**

the hypothetical or reconstructed language before a later, known language	**protolanguage**
the shift of a morpheme's sound in different contexts	**sandhi**
analysis of language as a formal system, esp. of phonemes, morphemes, and syntax	**structural linguistics**
a unit of spoken sound, and the letters to show it	**syllable**
pronouncing 2 normally separate vowels as 1	**syneresis** or **synizesis**
a change in pitch indicating the end of a statement or clause	**terminal juncture**
a language that uses pitch and tone to distinguish between otherwise similar words	**tone language**
stress shown by rising pitch, not more loudness	**tone** or **pitch accent**
representing a word from one language in the letters of another language	**transliteration**
3 vowel sounds pronounced in a row, e.g., "wow"	**triphthong**
a modification of Grimm's Law	**Verner's Law**
a word seen as a set of sounds, not a unit of meaning	**vocable**

Types of Books

Among the various types of books, what is or are . . . ?

a shortened work, cut or rewritten	**abridgment** or **condensation**
a collection reflecting a person or place's character	**ana**
selections from literary work	**analect**
a collection of short works in a larger one	**anthology**
a book of maps and other illustrative matter	**atlas**
a catalogue of information about books; also the profession of preparing such catalogues	**bibliography**
a textbook of cases, esp. in the law	**casebook**
an organized, descriptive catalogue	**catalogue raisonné**

literary passages used in language study	**chrestomathy**
a handwritten manuscript bound as a book	**codex**
an alphabetical index to every word in a work	**concordance**
printed materials on unusual topics, often erotic	**curiosa**
a limited edition, specially printed and bound, mostly for collectors and libraries	**de luxe edition**
a collection of defined words or phrases	**dictionary, lexicon,** or **glossary**
a book of names, addresses, and related data	**directory**
a first edition, in France	**editio princeps**
a substantial, ready-access reference book, often multi-volume and alphabetically arranged	**encyclopedia**
printed matter of short-lived interest	**ephemera**
works about or thought to stimulate sexuality	**erotica**
works of interest only to a very few	**esoterica**
an exact copy of something	**facsimile**
a book of articles in tribute, esp. of a scholar	**Festschrift**
a copy from those printed from the original plates, even if in several printings	**first edition**
a copy from a work's first press run	**first printing, issue,** or **impression**
a dictionary of geographical names and data	**gazetteer**
a practical book with articles and often step-by-step instruction	**handbook, manual,** or **enchiridion**
an early children's reader	**hornbook**
works printed in movable type before 1501	**incunabula**
a work on 1 subject, esp. scholarly	**monograph**
works with sexual content thought to tend toward the obscene	**pornography**
an elementary text in a subject	**primer**
a book of synonyms and antonyms	**thesaurus**

a formal systematic account of a subject	**treatise**
an edition with varying versions of a work and scholarly notes	**variorum**

Parts of a Book

Among the parts of a book, what is or are . . . ?

the publisher's identifying mark	**colophon**
the printed inscription at the start of a book	**dedication**
the specially made lining inside the cover of a book	**doublure**
the heavy leaves of paper connecting a book's cover to its contents	**end papers** or **flyleaves**
errors to be corrected in a reprint	**errata** or **corrigenda**
introductory comments, esp. by an expert	**foreword**
a finding device, esp. alphabetical	**index**
explanatory comments, usually by the author	**introduction**
matter printed in margins, e. g., notes	**marginalia**
introductory comments, often personal views	**preface** (Fr. **avant-propos**)
words, e.g., titles or key words, printed at the top of each page	**running heads**

Language About Printing

In the world of printing, what is or are . . . ?

a typeface heavier and darker than the rest in a book	**boldface**
a photographic negative plate	**cliche** or **stereotype**
the full set of type in a size or style	**font**
a feathery, uncut paper edge	**deckle** or **feather edge**
using personal computers to set type and design for works to be published	**desktop publishing**

a page number; a numbered leaf; or a group of book sizes	**folio**
the first proofs of a book's text, usually in long single-columned sheets	**galleys** or **galley proofs**
Gothic characters, as in German printing	**Fraktur**
type set at a slant, e.g., *this*?	**italic**
a printed sheet, with each side a page	**leaf**
a symbol that stands for a word, e.g., $ for dollar	**logogram**
one piece of type with two or more elements, e.g., a company's name and trademark	**logotype**
a piece of written work, esp. ready for printing	**manuscript**
a sheet folded to create 8 leaves, for a book	**octavo** or **8vo**
the second proofs, with galleys made into pages	**page proofs**
pages glued to the book's spine, not sewing	**perfect binding**
a unit of type measurement	**point**
a sheet folded twice to give 4 leaves for a book	**quarto** or **4to**
a book's right-hand pages, with odd numbers	**recto**
a standard straight, not slanted, modern type	**roman**
a type without knobs or strokes on the ends of letters	**sans serif**
strokes or knobs at the ends of letters in type	**serifs**
a single sheet, printed, folded, and trimmed in a book	**signature**
a page folded into 16 leaves for use in a book	**sextodecimo** or **16mo**
a proofreader's mark to leave material as was	**stet**
the range of type of a certain design or family	**typeface**
the left-hand pages of a book, with even numbers	**verso** or **reverso**

Other Language About Books and Printing

In the world of books and printing, what is or are . . . ?

the making of books	**bibliogenesis** or **-gony**
a book-stealer	**biblioklept**
extreme involvement with books, esp. with literal interpretations of the Bible	**bibliolatry**
an excessively avid book collector	**bibliomaniac** or **-taph**
a bookbinder	**bibliopegist**
the insect whose larva eat bookbinding paste	**bibliophage** or **bookworm**
a book lover, esp. a collector	**bibliophile** or **philobiblist**
a dealer in rare books	**bibliopole**
a book collection, esp. a library	**bibliotheca** or **-theque**
one who prepares copy for publication	**copy editor**
legal ownership of literary and artistic property	**copyright**
a newspaper's light literary section, in France	**feuilleton**
brownish stains on the pages of old books	**foxing**
one who writes books published under another's name, e.g., a celebrity	**ghost writer**
a document written in the signer's own hand	**holograph**
a license to publish	**imprimatur**
animal skin used for writing, esp. before paper	**parchment**
a work not, or no longer, protected by copyright	**public domain**
payment to authors of books borrowed from libraries, e.g., in Britain	**public lending right (PLR)**
payment to authors by a work's publisher	**royalties**
a note to indicate that an apparent error appeared in the original	**sic**
fine parchment made of young animals' skins	**vellum**

Accents, Punctuation, and Other Manuscript Marks

Among accents, punctuation, and other manuscript marks, what is or are . . . ?

the ´ accent, indicating a rise in the voice	**acute**
the & symbol for "and"	**ampersand**
the ' mark, as in don't	**apostrophe**
the * mark	**asterisk**
3 asterisks arranged in a triangle	**asterism**
the { } marks, to enclose matter, as in brackets	**braces**
the [] marks, to enclose matter, as in parentheses	**brackets**
the ˘ mark over a vowel to indicate a short sound	**breve**
the • used for emphasis	**bullet or centered dot**
the ^ mark, to show where to insert matter in text	**caret**
the mark under a c as in ç	**cedilla**
the ^ accent, as in être	**circumflex**
the : mark, as in "Now hear this:"	**colon**
the , sign between words	**comma**
the † symbol, used as a reference mark	**dagger or obelisk**
marks indicating sounds, e.g. ´ and ¨	**diacritical marks**
the 2 dots over the 2nd of 2 vowels, e.g., oö	**diaeresis or trema**
the ‡ symbol, used as a reference mark	**double dagger or diesis**
the " mark, indicating a repetition	**ditto**
the periods at a sentence break, as here . . .	**ellipsis**
the horizontal line used in "yes—or no"	**em dash**
1/2 an em dash, used in "1900–01"	**en dash**
the ! at the end of a word or sentence	**exclamation point**
the ` accent, indicating a fall in the voice	**grave**
the ˇ mark, used in Czech	**haček or wedge**
the - mark, as in "put-down"	**hyphen**
the ☞ symbol, with a pointing finger	**index, fist, or hand**

the ¯ mark over a vowel, to indicate a long sound	**macron**
the ¶ mark at a break point	**paragraph mark** or **blind P**
the () marks to enclose matter	**parentheses**
the . dot at the end of a sentence	**period** or **full stop**
marks used within text	**punctuation** or **reference marks**
the ? at the end of a word or sentence	**question** or **interrogation mark**
the ' ' or " " marks around words	**quotation marks (single** or **double)**
the § mark to begin a new section	**section mark**
the ; mark, as in "I am; so are you"	**semicolon**
the ˜ mark over an "n," making it a "ny" sound	**tilde**
the double dots ¨ (in Germany) or the small circle ° (in Scandinavia) over a vowel	**umlaut** or **zweipunkt**
the / mark, used for various purposes	**virgule, solidus, slash,** or **diagonal**

Reference Words and Phrases

Among reference words and phrases from the Latin, what is or are . . .?

above, as referring to an earlier mention	**supra (sup.)**
according to	**secundum (sec.)**
according to their value, as in taxation	**ad valorem**
among other things	**inter alia**
and elsewhere	**et alibi (et al.)**
and everything of this sort	**et hoc genus omne**
and other things	**et cetera (etc.)**
and others	**et alii** or **aliae (et al.)**
and the following	**et sequens (et seq.)**
around or about, as in reference to a date	**circa (c.** or **ca.)**
as	**qua**
for example	**exempli gratia (e.g.)**
in and of itself, lit. by itself	**per se**
in the matter of or concerning	**re**
in the place already cited	**loco citato (loc. cit.)**

in the same book or place	**ibidem (ibid.)**
in the work already cited	**opere citato (op. cit.)**
namely or that is, introducing a list	**viz. (videlicet)**
note well	**nota bene (n.b.)**
of its own nature	**qua se**
refer to or see	**confer (cf.)**
same	**idem (id.)**
same as	**idem quod (i. q.)**
see above	**vide supra**
see the following	**vide post**
so (it is) everywhere	**sic passim**
that is	**id est (i.e.)**
under the word (title)	**sub verbo (voco) (s.v.)**
what is needed but not yet in hand	**desideratum (pl.-ta)**
which (you should) note	**quod nota**
which (you should) see, as in a cross-reference	**quod vide (q.v.)**
which is	**quod est (q.e.)**
which was to be demonstrated, as in geometry	**quod erat demonstrandum (Q.E.D.)**
which was to be done	**quod erat faciendum (Q.E.F.)**

Language of Higher Learning

In the world of higher learning, what is the word or phrase for . . . ?

the basic 4-year university arts degree	**Bachelor of Arts (B.A.) or Artium Bacalaureus (A.B.)**
the basic 4-year university science degree	**Bachelor of Science (B.S.) or Scientiae Baccalaureus (Sc.B.)**
someone from Cambridge University	**Cantabrigian**
with praise, referring to college graduates	**cum laude**
a long, formal treatise, as for a doctoral degree	**dissertation or thesis**
a licensed teacher	**docent**
the degree following a master's	**Doctor of Philosophy or Philosophiae Doctor (Ph.D.)**
a school or university, in France	**école**
Paris's famous school of fine arts	**École des beaux-arts**

an honorary title kept after retirement	**emeritus**
a person of low general IQ but extraordinary ability in special areas, e.g., mathematics or music	**idiot savant**
with great praise, referring to college graduates	**magna cum laude**
the arts degree following a bachelor's	**Master of arts (M.A.) or Artium Magister (A.M.)**
a trusted teacher and advisor	**mentor**
someone from Oxford University	**Oxonian**
the art or profession of teaching	**pedagogy**
an overly rule-bound teacher or scholar	**pedant**
someone "brought along" by an influential person	**protégé**
the 4 mathematical disciplines of the medieval 7 liberal arts: arithmetic, astronomy, music, and geometry	**quadrivium**
the person who keeps a school's records	**registrar**
the person who gives the welcoming address at a graduation, usually the 2nd highest in a class	**salutatorian**
with highest praise, referring to college graduates	**summa cum laude**
the 3 nonmathematical disciplines of the medieval 7 liberal arts: grammar, rhetoric, and logic	**trivium**
the person who gives the closing address at a graduation, usually the highest in a class	**valedictorian**

World of the Arts

Actors from the Past

Among actors from the past, who . . . ?

was the 19th-c. head of the Barrymore family	**Maurice Barrymore**
was a prime 19th-c. Shakespearean actor, brother of Lincoln's assassin	**Edwin Booth**
was the London-born head of the Booth family	**Junius Brutus Booth**
originated the roles of Hamlet, Lear, and MacBeth	**Richard Burbage**
was the actor whose family joined the Barrymores	**John Drew**
was 18th-c. actor-manager at Drury Lane	**David Garrick**
was famed for his turn-of-the-century Holmes	**William Gillette**
was the 19th-c. British actor who played with Ellen Terry	**Henry Irving**
was famed for *Rip Van Winkle*	**Joseph Jefferson**
was a great, early-19th-c., British tragic actor	**Edmund Kean**
is the 1st actor known by name, a Greek	**Thespis**

Actresses from the Past

Among actresses from the past, who . . . ?

was John Drew's late-19th-c. leading lady	**Maude Adams**
continued to play after losing a leg	**Sarah Bernhardt**
was acclaimed as "La Duse"	**Eleanora Duse**
became Charles II's mistress	**Nell Gwyn**

was starring at the theater where Lincoln was shot	**Laura Keene**
was a London-born, 19th-c., Shakespearean, US actress	**Fanny Kemble**
was a British, late-18th to early-19th-c. tragic actress	**Sarah Siddons (née Kemble)**
was Henry Irving's leading lady	**Ellen Terry**
became empress of Byzantium in the 6th c.	**Theodora**

Classic Movie Duos

Astaire-Rogers Movies

Among Fred Astaire-Ginger Rogers movies, which had . . . ?

them as a team that split and made up	*The Barkleys of Broadway*
him as a psychiatrist and her as a patient	*Carefree*
them doing the Carioca, their 1st pairing	*Flying Down to Rio*
them as a sailor and his would-be girl	*Follow the Fleet*
them in a divorce-case mix-up	*The Gay Divorcée*
them singing, in support, "I Won't Dance"	*Roberta*
them as dancers pretending they're married	*Shall We Dance?*
them playing a legendary real dance team	*The Story of Vernon and Irene Castle*
them as a dance team, him with a fiancée	*Swing Time*
them in a mistaken-identity mix-up	*Top Hat*

Bogart-Bacall Movies

Among Humphrey Bogart-Lauren Bacall movies, which had . . . ?

him as Marlowe and her as a spoiled divorcée	*The Big Sleep*
him as an ex-con, with her aiding him	*Dark Passage*
them trapped in a hotel in a hurricane	*Key Largo*

them on a French Caribbean island in WWII — *To Have and Have Not*

Tracy-Hepburn Movies

Among Spencer Tracy-Katharine Hepburn movies, which had . . . ?

them as lawyers on opposite sides of a case	*Adam's Rib*
him as a computer engineer and her as a network researcher	*Desk Set*
them as parents whose daughter wanted to marry a black man	*Guess Who's Coming to Dinner*
him as a reporter and her as a widow	*Keeper of the Flame*
her as an athlete and him as a manager	*Pat and Mike*
them in a SW farmer vs. rancher drama	*The Sea of Grass*
them as a presidential candidate and his wife	*State of the Union*
them in a marriage of convenience	*Without Love*
them as reporters, he on sports, she on politics	*Woman of the Year*

Other Movie, Stage, and TV Duos

Among other movie, stage, or TV duos, who were paired in or as . . . ?

Adams Chronicles	**George Grizzard** and **Kathryn Walker**
Addams Family as Gomez and Morticia	**John Astin** and **Carolyn Jones**
Alice Doesn't Live Here Any More	**Ellen Burstyn** and **Kris Kristofferson**
All Creatures Great and Small, on TV, as Siegfried and Tristan	**Robert Hardy** and **Peter Davison**
All Creatures Great and Small, on TV, as James and Helen	**Christopher Timothy** and **Carol Drinkwater,** later **Linda Bellingham**
All in the Family as the Bunkers	**Carroll O'Connor** and **Jean Stapleton**
American in Paris	**Gene Kelly** and **Leslie Caron**

Avengers as John Steed and Mrs. Emma Peel	**Patrick MacNee** and **Diana Rigg**
Beauty and the Beast on TV	**Linda Hamilton** and **Ron Perlman**
Ben-Hur as enemies	**Charlton Heston** and **Stephen Boyd**
Bikini Beach	**Frankie Avalon** and **Annette Funicello**
Bob and Ray	**Bob Elliott** and **Ray Goulding**
Born Free	**Virginia McKenna** and **Bill Travers**
Brideshead Revisited	**Jeremy Irons** and **Anthony Andrews**
Brief Encounter	**Celia Johnson** and **Trevor Howard**
Burns and Allen	**George Burns** and **Gracie Allen**
Butch Cassidy and the Sun-Dance Kid	**Paul Newman** and **Robert Redford**
Cabaret, the movie	**Liza Minnelli** and **Michael York**
Cagney and Lacey	**Sharon Gless** and **Tyne Daly**
Camille	**Greta Garbo** and **Robert Taylor**
Captain Horatio Hornblower, the movie	**Gregory Peck** and **Virginia Mayo**
Caruso and his love in the movie	**Mario Lanza** and **Kathryn Grayson**
Casablanca as Elsa and her husband	**Ingrid Bergman** and **Paul Henreid**
Charly as patient and doctor	**Cliff Robertson** and **Claire Bloom**
Cheers, early in the TV series	**Ted Danson** and **Shelley Long**
Chicago, on Broadway	**Gwen Verdon** and **Jerry Ohrbach**
Chico and the Man	**Freddie Prinz** and **Jack Albertson**
Children of a Lesser God, the movie	**Marlee Matlin** and **William Hurt**
Crocodile Dundee	**Paul Hogan** and **Linda Kozlowski**
Dallas as Bobby and Pam	**Patrick Duffy** and **Victoria Principal**
Dallas as J.R. and Sue Ellen	**Larry Hagman** and **Linda Gray**
Deep Throat	**Linda Lovelace** and **Harry Reems**
Defenders on early TV	**E. G. Marshall** and **Robert Reed**
Dick Van Dyke Show as Buddy and Sally	**Morey Amsterdam** and **Rose Marie**

Doctor Zhivago and Lara	Omar Sharif and Julie Christie
Double Indemnity	Fred MacMurray and Barbara Stanwyck
Dragnet on early TV	Jack Webb and Henry Morgan
Drs. Kildare and Gillespie	Richard Chamberlain and Raymond Massey
Dynasty as competitive ex's	John Forsythe and Joan Collins
Eddie and Debbie before Liz came along	Eddie Fisher and Debbie Reynolds
Eleanor and Franklin on TV	Jane Alexander and Edward Herrmann
48 Hours	Eddie Murphy and Nick Nolte
42nd Street, the movie	Dick Powell and Ruby Keeler
Father Knows Best	Robert Young and Jane Wyatt
Foul Play	Goldie Hawn and Chevy Chase
Fountainhead	Gary Cooper and Patricia Neal
F Troop	Forrest Tucker and Larry Storch
Gentlemen Prefer Blondes	Marilyn Monroe and Jane Russell
Get Smart as agents	Don Adams and Barbara Feldon
Ghostbusters	Dan Aykroyd and Bill Murray
Gin Game	Hume Cronyn and Jessica Tandy
Gone With the Wind as Ashley and Melanie	Leslie Howard and Olivia de Havilland
Gone With the Wind as Scarlet and Rhett	Vivien Leigh and Clark Gable
Goodbye Girl	Richard Dreyfuss and Marsha Mason
Good Neighbors on TV	Richard Briers and Felicity Kendall
Graduate	Dustin Hoffman and Katharine Ross
Green Acres	Eddie Albert and Eva Gabor
Guardsman	Alfred Lunt and Lynn Fontanne
Guess Who's Coming to Dinner as lovers	Sidney Poitier and Katharine Houghton
Gunsmoke as Matt Dillon and Kitty	James Arness and Amanda Blake
Hanky Panky and real life	Gene Wilder and Gilda Radner
Happy Days	Henry Winkler and Ron Howard
Hardcastle and McCormick	Brian Keith and Daniel Hugh Kelly
Harold and Maude	Bud Cort and Ruth Gordon
Hill Street Blues as captain and lawyer	Daniel J. Travanti and Veronica Hamel

Holmes and Watson in the 1940s movies	Basil Rathbone and Nigel Bruce
Honeymooners as the Kramdens	Jackie Gleason and Audrey Meadows
I Love Lucy as Fred and Ethel	William Frawley and Vivian Vance
I Love Lucy as the Ricardos	Lucille Ball and Desi Arnaz
I Married Joan	Joan Davie and Jim Backus
I Spy	Bill Cosby and Robert Culp
Jane Eyre and Mr. Rochester in Hollywood	Joan Fontaine and Orson Welles
Jeffersons on TV	Sherman Hemsley and Isabel Sanford
Kate and Allie	Jane Curtin and Susan St. James
Klute	Jane Fonda and Donald Sutherland
La Cage aux Folles	Ugo Tognazzi and Michel Sarraut
Lady Vanishes as sparring lovers	Michael Redgrave and Margaret Lockwood
L.A. Law and in real life	Jill Eikenberry and Michael Tucker
Laugh-In as hosts	Dan Rowan and Dick Martin
Laura	Gene Tierney and Dana Andrews
Laurel and Hardy	Stan Laurel and Oliver Hardy
Laverne and Shirley	Penny Marshall and Cindy Williams
Life and Death of Colonel Blimp	Roger Livesey and Deborah Kerr
Les Liaisons Dangereuses, the movie	Glenn Close and John Malkovich
Lone Ranger and Tonto	Clayton Moore and Jay Silverheels
Love Story	Ryan O'Neal and Ali MacGraw
M*A*S*H early in the TV series	Alan Alda and Wayne Rogers
Magnum, P.I.	Tom Selleck and John Hillerman
Man and a Woman	Jean-Louis Trintignant and Anouk Aimée
Man from U.N.C.L.E	Robert Vaughn and David McCallum
Marriage Italian Style	Marcello Mastroianni and Sophia Loren
Martin and Lewis	Dean Martin and Jerry Lewis
Mayberry's sheriff and deputy	Andy Griffith and Don Knotts
Miami Vice	Don Johnson and Philip Michael Thomas
Min and Bill	Wallace Beery and Marie Dressler

Minivers, Mr. and Mrs.	**Greer Garson** and **Walter Pidgeon**
Miracle Worker, the movie	**Patty Duke** and **Anne Bancroft**
Mr. Smith Goes to Washington	**James Stewart** and **Jean Arthur**
Moon for the Misbegotten on Broadway in the 1970s	**Colleen Dewhurst** and **Jason Robards, Jr.**
Moonlighting on TV	**Cybill Shepherd** and **Bruce Willis**
Munsters as Hermann and Lily	**Fred Gwynne** and **Yvonne De Carlo**
Music Man	**Robert Preston** and **Shirley Jones**
My Dinner with André	**Wallace Shawn** and **André Gregory**
My Fair Lady, the originals	**Rex Harrison** and **Julie Andrews**
My Favorite Martian	**Bill Bixby** and **Ray Walston**
Never On Sunday	**Melina Mercouri** and **Jules Dassin**
Nichols and May, doing comic improvisations	**Mike Nichols** and **Elaine May**
Norma Rae as union organizers	**Sally Field** and **Ron Leibman**
Odd Couple on TV	**Tony Randall** and **Jack Klugman**
Officer and a Gentleman	**Richard Gere** and **Debra Winger**
On a Clear Day . . . on Broadway	**John Cullum** and **Barbara Harris**
Orphans of the Storm	**Dorothy** and **Lillian Gish**
Pallisers	**Susan Hampshire** and **Philip Latham**
Perry Mason and Della Street	**Raymond Burr** and **Barbara Hale**
Petries on early TV	**Dick Van Dyke** and **Mary Tyler Moore**
Pillow Talk	**Rock Hudson** and **Doris Day**
Police Woman on TV	**Angie Dickinson** and **Earl Holliman**
Popeye and Olive Oyl	**Robin Williams** and **Shelley Duvall**
Postman Always Rings Twice, the 1946 movie	**Lana Turner** and **John Garfield**
Private Lives, the originals	**Noel Coward** and **Gertrude Lawrence**
Psycho	**Anthony Perkins** and **Janet Leigh**
Quiet Man	**John Wayne** and **Maureen O'Hara**
Reds as John Reed and Louise Bryant	**Warren Beatty** and **Diane Keaton**

Rich and Famous	Jacqueline Bisset and Candice Bergen
Road pictures	Bing Crosby and Bob Hope
Rose Marie	Nelson Eddy and Jeannette MacDonald
Route 66	George Maharis and Martin Milner
Scenes from a Marriage	Liv Ullman and Erland Josephson
Servant as master and servant	James Fox and Dirk Bogarde
silents' reigning stars	Mary Pickford and Douglas Fairbanks
Some Like It Hot as female musicians	Tony Curtis and Jack Lemmon
South Pacific on Broadway	Mary Martin and Ezio Pinza
South Pacific, the movie	Mitzi Gaynor and Rossano Brazzi
Starsky and Hutch	Paul Michael Glaser and David Soul
Star Trek as Capt. Kirk and Mr. Spock	William Shatner and Leonard Nimoy
Streets of San Francisco	Karl Malden and Michael Douglas
Summer Place as young lovers	Troy Donahue and Sandra Dee
Sunset Boulevard as sponger and silent stars	William Holden and Gloria Swanson
Superman and Lois Lane	Christopher Reeve and Margot Kidder
Tarzan and His Mate	Johnny Weissmuller and Maureen O'Sullivan
Thin Man as Nick and Nora Charles	William Powell and Myrna Loy
To Catch a Thief	Cary Grant and Grace Kelly
Tom and Dick on a censored, cancelled 1960's TV show	Smothers Brothers
Tom Jones as parted lovers	Albert Finney and Susannah York
Top Gun	Tom Cruise and Kelly McGillis
To the Manor Born	Penelope Keith and Peter Bowles
Touch of Class	Glenda Jackson and George Segal
Trapper John, M.D.	Pernell Roberts and Gregory Harrison
Unmarried Woman	Jill Clayburgh and Michael Murphy
Waltons as the parents	Michael Learned and Ralph Waite
Who's Afraid of Virginia Woolf?	Elizabeth Taylor and Richard Burton

"Who's on first?" routine	**Bud Abbott** and **Lou Costello**
Witness for the Prosecution as lawyer and nurse	**Charles Laughton** and **Elsa Lanchester**
Witness for the Prosecution as killer and wife	**Tyrone Power** and **Marlene Dietrich**
Wuthering Heights	**Laurence Olivier** and **Merle Oberon**
Your Show of Shows	**Sid Caesar** and **Imogene Coca**
Zelig as doctor and patient	**Mia Farrow** and **Woody Allen**
Zorba the Greek	**Alan Bates** and **Anthony Quinn**

Other Modern Actors

Among other modern actors, who was (in) . . . ?

Addams Family as Uncle Fester	**Jackie Coogan**
Aguirre Wrath of God	**Klaus Kinski**
Alfie	**Michael Caine**
All About Eve as the cynical critic	**George Sanders**
All That Jazz	**Roy Scheider**
Andy Hardy	**Mickey Rooney**
Arch of Triumph as the illegal alien doctor	**Charles Boyer**
Around the World in 80 Days as Phineas Fogg	**David Niven**
Arthur, as the butler	**John Gielgud**
Banacek and *The A-Team*	**George Peppard**
Bang the Drum Slowly as the pitcher	**Michael Moriarty**
Baretta	**Robert Blake**
Barfly as Charles Bukowski	**Mickey Rourke**
Barnaby Jones	**Buddy Ebsen**
Barney Miller	**Hal Linden**
Bat Masterson on TV	**Gene Barry**
Batman in the 1989 movie	**Michael Keaton**
Batman on early TV	**Adam West**
Ben Casey on TV	**Vincent Edwards**
Best Years of Our Lives as the banker	**Frederic March**
Beyond the Fringe	**Dudley Moore, Peter Cook, Jonathan Miller,** and **Alan Bennett**
Big	**Tom Hanks**
Big Chill as the host	**Kevin Kline**
Birdman of Alcatraz	**Burt Lancaster**
Bluebeard, in 1944, a Shakespearean	**John Carradine**
Bonanza as Hoss	**Dan Blocker**

Bonanza as the father	**Lorne Greene**
Bowery Boys, the sad-faced one	**Huntz Hall**
Breaking Away as the father	**Paul Dooley**
Breaking Away as the bicyclist	**Dennis Christopher**
Buddy Holly Story	**Gary Busey**
Bugs Bunny's voice	**Mel Blanc**
Button Down Mind	**Bob Newhart**
Buzz Corey on early TV	**Ed Kemmer**
Cabaret as the host	**Joel Grey**
Camelot as Lancelot in Broadway's original	**Robert Goulet**
Camelot, the movie, as King Arthur	**Richard Harris**
Cannon on early TV	**William Conrad**
Captain Blood	**Errol Flynn**
Captain Kangaroo	**Bob Keeshan**
Cat Ballou in a double role	**Lee Marvin**
Catch-22 as Capt. Yossarian	**Alan Arkin**
Champ as the child	**Ricky Schroder**
Charade as Dyle	**Walter Matthau**
Chariots of Fire as Harold Abraham	**Ben Cross**
Chariots of Fire as Eric Liddell	**Ian Charleson**
Chariots of Fire as Lord Linley	**Nigel Havers**
Chariots of Fire as the trainer	**Ian Holm**
Charley Weaver in the 1950's	**Cliff Arquette**
Children of a Lesser God on Broadway	**John Rubenstein**
Chinatown as the father	**John Huston**
Chips on TV	**Erik Estrada**
Citizen Kane	**Orson Welles**
Clem Kaddiddlehopper on 1950's TV	**Red Skelton**
Clockwork Orange	**Malcolm McDowell**
Coal Miner's Daughter	**Tommy Lee Jones**
Cocoon, winning a supporting Oscar	**Don Ameche**
Columbo on TV	**Peter Falk**
the comic rope-twirler with folksy humor	**Will Rogers**
the comic of the 1960's played by Hoffman	**Lenny Bruce**
the comic, on radio, in the 1940's and 50's known for his baggy eyes	**Fred Allen**
the comic skinflint on 1950's TV	**Jack Benny**
the comic who "gets no respect"	**Rodney Dangerfield**
the comic who got pies in his face on early TV	**Soupy Sales**
Coming Home as the troubled husband	**Bruce Dern**

Conan the Barbarian	**Arnold Schwarzenegger**
Damned Yankees, the movie	**Tab Hunter**
Davy Crockett and Daniel Boone on early TV	**Fess Parker**
Day of the Jackal as the assassin	**Edward Fox**
Death of a Salesman, the original on Broadway	**Lee J. Cobb**
Death Wish	**Charles Bronson**
Deer Hunter playing Russian roulette	**Christopher Walken**
Deer Hunter as the man who lost his legs	**John Savage**
Desk Set, losing Hepburn to Tracy	**Gig Young**
Dial M for Murder as the detective	**John Williams**
Dial M for Murder as the other man	**Robert Cummings**
Diary of a Mad Housewife as the husband	**Richard Benjamin**
Diff'rent Strokes	**Gary Coleman**
"dirty bird" on 1950's TV	**George Gobel**
Dirty Harry	**Clint Eastwood**
Dodsworth	**Walter Huston**
double-talker featured on TV commercials	**John Moschitta**
Dracula in the 1931 movie	**Bela Lugosi**
Dracula in the 1979 movie	**Frank Langella**
Dresser in the title role	**Tom Courtenay**
Dukes of Hazzard	**John Schneider**
Easy Rider as star and director	**Dennis Hopper**
Eight Is Enough	**Dick Van Patten**
Elephant Man in the title role on Broadway	**Philip Anglim**
Emperor Jones, the original	**Paul Robeson**
Equalizer	**Edward Woodward**
Equus as the psychiatrist, on Broadway in 1974	**Anthony Hopkins**
Equus as the boy, on Broadway in 1974	**Peter Firth**
Evita as Juan Péron on Broadway	**Bob Gunton**
Fallen Idol as the butler	**Ralph Richardson**
Family Ties	**Michael J. Fox**
Fantasy Island	**Ricardo Montalban**
Fatty's Flirtation and other silents	**Roscoe Arbuckle**
Fawlty Towers, from Monty Python	**John Cleese**
FBI on early TV	**Efrem Zimbalist, Jr.**
Ferris Bueller's Day Off	**Matthew Broderick**

Fiddler on the Roof as the father in the movie	**Topol**
Fiddler on the Roof as the father on Broadway	**Zero Mostel**
Flash Gordon on early TV	**Steve Holland**
Flesh and the Devil	**John Gilbert**
Frankenstein	**Boris Karloff**
French Connection as Popeye Doyle	**Gene Hackman**
Freshman, a silent film	**Harold Lloyd**
Fugitive	**David Janssen**
Gandhi	**Ben Kingsley**
Gigi, who married	**Louis Jourdan**
Gilligan's Island in the title role	**Bob Denver**
Glass Key	**George Raft**
Glittering Prizes on British TV	**Tom Conti**
Godfather as Sonny	**James Caan**
Godfather as the adopted lawyer	**Robert Duvall**
Godfather as the ultimate heir	**Al Pacino**
God's Little Acre	**Robert Ryan**
Gomer Pyle, USMC	**Jim Nabors**
Grandmaw Frickett	**Jonathan Winters**
Grapes of Wrath	**Henry Fonda**
Great Expectations as Pip in Lean's movie	**John Mills**
Great White Hope	**James Earl Jones**
Greystoke as Tarzan	**Christopher Lambert**
Gunsmoke as Arness's original deputy	**Dennis Weaver**
Have Gun, Will Travel as Paladin	**Richard Boone**
Hawaii Five-O on early TV	**Jack Lord**
Heart Like a Wheel as the husband	**Beau Bridges**
Here Comes Mr. Jordan	**Robert Montgomery**
Hill Street Blues as Henry	**Joe Spano**
Hogan's Heroes as Commandant Klink	**Werner Klemperer**
Hogan's Heroes as Hogan	**Bob Crane**
Hollywood's highest-paid actor in early days	**Francis X. Bushman**
Honeymooners as Gleason's sidekick	**Art Carney**
Hopalong Cassidy	**William Boyd**
Hunter on TV	**Fred Dryer**
I, Claudius, in the title role on British TV	**Derek Jacobi**
imitator of public figures, esp. politicians	**Frank Gorshin; Rich Little**
In the Heat of the Night as the local police chief	**Rod Steiger**
Incredible Hulk in the title role	**Lou Ferrigno**

Indiana Jones	Harrison Ford
Invisible Man	Claude Rains
It Takes a Thief	Robert J. Wagner
James Bond and the Saint	Roger Moore
James Bond in the late 1980's	Timothy Dalton
James Bond, the movies' original	Sean Connery
Jazz Singer	Al Jolson
Jewel in the Crown as the historian	Charles Dance
Jewel in the Crown as Hari Kumar	Art Malik
Jewel in the Crown as the twisted cop	Tim Pigott-Smith
José Jiminez	Bill Dana
Judgment at Nuremberg as the defense lawyer	Maximilian Schell
Just Tell Me What You Want	Alan King
Kennedy as TV's president	Martin Sheen
Key Largo as the father	Lionel Barrymore
King and I	Yul Brynner
Kojak	Telly Savalas
Kung Fu on TV	David Carradine
L.A. Law as the divorce lawyer	Corbin Bernsen
La grande illusion	Jean Gabin
La guerre est fini	Yves Montand
La Strada as the slack rope walker	Richard Basehart
Last of the Red Hot Lovers	James Coco
Last Picture Show	Timothy Bottoms
Laugh-In and in *Nashville*	Henry Gibson
Laugh-In, who ran for president	Pat Paulsen
Laura as the murderer	Clifton Webb
Lawrence of Arabia in the title role	Peter O'Toole
Liar's Moon	Matt Dillon
Life of Riley	William Bendix
Lili as the crippled puppeteer	Mel Ferrer
Lili as the dashing rake	Jean-Pierre Aumont
Little House on the Prairie and *Bonanza*	Michael Landon
Little Rascals, the best known of "Our Gang"	Jackie Cooper
Longest Day as a deafened parachuter, a comic	Red Buttons
Lost Horizon	Ronald Colman
Lost Weekend	Ray Milland
Lou Grant	Edward Asner
Love at First Bite	George Hamilton
Luv, on Broadway	Eli Wallach and Anne Jackson
Macbeth in Hallmark's early TV version	Maurice Evans

Madigan in the title role	**Richard Widmark**
Mad Max	**Mel Gibson**
Make Room for Daddy	**Danny Thomas**
Maltese Falcon as Joel Cairo	**Peter Lorre**
Maltese Falcon as the Fat Man	**Sydney Greenstreet**
Man for All Seasons as Thomas More	**Paul Scofield**
Man in Grey	**James Mason**
"man of a thousand faces"	**Lon Chaney**
Man of La Mancha on Broadway	**Richard Kiley**
Mannix	**Mike Connors**
Many Loves of Dobie Gillis	**Dwayne Hickman**
Mark Twain in a one-man show	**Hal Holbrook**
Marty in the movie	**Ernest Borgnine**
Me and My Girl on Broadway	**Robert Lindsay**
Midnight Cowboy with Dustin Hoffman	**Jon Voight**
Mike Hammer on TV	**Stacy Keach**
Mission Impossible	**Peter Graves**
Mister Ed, co-starred with a horse	**Alan Young**
Mr. Peepers on early TV	**Wally Cox**
"Mr. Television" in the 1950's	**Milton Berle**
My Left Foot	**Daniel Day-Lewis**
My Little Chickadee	**W. C. Fields**
Naked Civil Servant on British TV	**John Hurt**
Nashville, singing "I'm Easy"	**Keith Carradine**
Network, as the TV anchor who went mad	**Peter Finch**
9 to 5, the boss tied up	**Dabney Coleman**
Officer and a Gentleman as the drill sergeant	**Lou Gossett, Jr.**
Oliver! as Bill Sykes	**Oliver Reed**
One Flew over the Cuckoo's Nest	**Jack Nicholson**
Paler Shade of White: A History of White People	**Martin Mull**
Paper Chase as Professor Kingsfield	**John Houseman**
Patton	**George C. Scott**
Percy Dovetonsils on 1950's TV	**Ernie Kovacs**
Peter Gunn	**Craig Stevens**
Peter Pan as Captain Hook on early TV	**Cyril Ritchard**
Phantom of the Opera on Broadway	**Michael Crawford**
Pink Flamingos as a female impersonator	**Divine**
Pink Panther movies as Inspector Clouseau	**Peter Sellers**

Poldark on British TV	Robin Ellis
Porgy and Bess, the movie, as Sportin' Life	Sammy Davis, Jr.
"Profile"	John Barrymore
Public Enemy	James Cagney
Real McCoys as Grampa	Walter Brennan
Real McCoys as Luke	Richard Crenna
Rebel Without a Cause	James Dean
Reilly, Ace of Spies	Sam Neill
Remington Steele	Pierce Brosnan
Return of Martin Guerre	Gerard Depardieu
Riders of the Purple Sage, the silent film	Tom Mix
Rifleman on early TV	Chuck Connors
River Niger	Douglas Turner Ward
Riverboat on early TV	Darren McGavin
Rockford Files	James Garner
Rocky and *Rambo*	Sylvester Stallone
Room at the Top	Laurence Harvey
Room Service	Marx Brothers (Chico, Groucho, Gummo, Harpo and Zeppo)
Roots as Kunta Kinte	Le Var Burton
Roots with Le Var Burton	Ben Vereen
Running on Empty as the son	River Phoenix
St. Elsewhere, winning an Emmy	Ed Flanders
Sanford and Son	Redd Foxx
Saturday Night Fever	John Travolta
Saturday Night Live as Father Guido Sarducci	Don Novello
Saturday Night Live, who later OD'd	John Belushi
Save the Tiger	Jack Lemmon
Scaramouche	Stewart Granger
"Schnozz," who said "Goodnight, Mrs. Calabash"	Jimmy Durante
Sea Hunt on TV	Lloyd Bridges
Secret Agent and *The Prisoner*	Patrick McGoohan
Secret Life of Walter Mitty	Danny Kaye
Sergeant Bilko	Phil Silvers
Seven Beauties	Giancarlo Giannini
Seven Days in May, uncovering the plot	Kirk Douglas
77 Sunset Street, combing his hair	Edd "Kookie" Byrnes
Shaft	Richard Roundtree
Shane as the boy	Brandon de Wilde
Shane as the main villain	Jack Palance
Shane in the title role	Alan Ladd
Sheik in silent films	Rudolph Valentino
Sherlock Holmes on 1980s British TV	Jeremy Brett

"Singing Cowboy" in the movies and TV	Gene Autry
Six-Million-Dollar Man	Lee Majors
Smokey and the Bandit	Burt Reynolds
S.O.B. as the director	Richard Mulligan
Some Like It Hot, saying, "Nobody's perfect!	Joe E. Brown
Sounder as the father	Paul Winfield
Sound of Music as Captain von Trapp	Christopher Plummer
Spenser: For Hire in the title role	Robert Urich
Star Trek as McCoy	De Forest Kelley
Star Wars as Luke Skywalker	Mark Hamill
Sting as the stung	Robert Shaw
Stop the World, I Want to Get Off	Anthony Newley
Stranger as the Nazi-hunter	Edward G. Robinson
Streetcar Named Desire as Stanley	Marlon Brando
Summer Wishes, Winter Dreams	Martin Balsam
Sunset Boulevard as the silents director	Erich von Stroheim
Superman on early TV	George Reeves
Sweeney Todd, the original on Broadway	Len Cariou
Swimming to Cambodia	Spalding Gray
Taxi as Alex	Judd Hirsch
Taxi as Louie	Danny De Vito
Taxi Driver as Travis Bickle	Robert De Niro
That Nigger's Crazy	Richard Pryor
Thin Man series on TV	Peter Lawford
Third Man's novel-writing innocent	Joseph Cotton
Thirty-Nine Steps	Robert Donat
Three's Company as Jack	John Ritter
Three Stooges	Joe De Rita, Moe Howard, and Larry Fine
Tinker, Tailor, Soldier, Spy as Bill Haydon	Ian Richardson
Tinker, Tailor, Soldier, Spy as George Smiley	Alec Guinness
Tommy in the title role	Roger Daltrey
To Kill a Mocking Bird	Gregory Peck
Too Close for Comfort	Ted Knight
Topkapi, winning an Oscar	Peter Ustinov
Tramp in silent films	Charlie Chaplin
Treasure Island as Long John Silver	Robert Newton
Tucker	Jeff Bridges
Twenty-three Paces to Baker Street	Van Johnson
2001: A Space Odyssey	Keir Dullea

Untouchables on TV as Elliot Ness	**Robert Stack**
Upstairs, Downstairs as Hudson	**Gordon Jackson**
Wagon Train on early TV	**Ward Bond**
Walking Tall	**Joe Don Baker**
Waltons as the son	**Richard Thomas**
Wanted—Dead or Alive as the bounty hunter	**Steve McQueen**
Welcome Back, Kotter	**Gabriel Kaplan**
Wells Fargo on early TV	**Dale Robertson**
Who Is Killing the Great Chefs of Europe as the dieter	**Robert Morley**
Wild, Wild West on early TV	**Robert Conrad**
Winds of War as Brian (Briney)	**Jan-Michael Vincent**
Winds of War as Pug Henry	**Robert Mitchum**
Wise Guys with De Vito	**Joe Piscopo**
Wizard of Oz as the Cowardly Lion	**Bert Lahr**
Wizard of Oz as the Scarecrow	**Ray Bolger**
Wizard of Oz as the Tin Man	**Jack Haley**

Other Modern Actresses

Among other modern actresses, who was (in) . . . ?

Ain't Misbehavin' on Broadway	**Nell Carter**
Alice on TV	**Linda Lavin**
All About Eve as Davis's best friend	**Celeste Holm**
All About Eve in the title role	**Anne Baxter**
All About Eve, saying "Fasten your seat belts"	**Bette Davis**
All in the Family as the daughter	**Sally Struthers**
All That Jazz	**Ann Reinking**
Anastasia as the grandmother	**Helen Hayes**
And God Created Woman	**Brigitte Bardot**
Annie in the title role on Broadway	**Andrea McArdle**
Atlantic City	**Susan Sarandon**
Auntie Mame in the original movie	**Rosalind Russell**
Autobiography of Miss Jane Pittman	**Cicely Tyson**
Baby Doll	**Carroll Baker**
Baby Snooks and starred in the Ziegfeld *Follies*	**Fannie Brice**
Barretts of Wimpole Street on Broadway	**Katherine Cornell**

Belle de Jour	Catherine Deneuve
Best Years of Our Lives, paired with Dana Andrews	Teresa Wright
Bewitched as Endora	Agnes Moorehead
Bewitched as Samantha	Elizabeth Montgomery
"Big Mouth," 1950's TV comic	Martha Raye
Big Show, radio's gravel-voiced host	Tallulah Bankhead
Bionic Woman	Lindsay Wagner
Blithe Spirit as the medium in the movie	Margaret Rutherford
Blume in Love	Susan Anspach
Body Heat	Kathleen Turner
Call Me Madam	Ethel Merman
Carnal Knowledge with Nicholson	Ann-Margret
Charlie's Angels, the original 3	Farrah Fawcett (Majors), Kate Jackson and Jaclyn Smith
Chorus Line	Donna McKechnie
Civic Repertory Theatre star and founder	Eva Le Gallienne
Close Encounters of the Third Kind	Teri Garr
Coal Miner's Daughter	Sissy Spacek
Color Purple	Whoopi Goldberg
Corn Is Green on Broadway in the 1940's	Ethel Barrymore
Country	Jessica Lange
Cousin, Cousine	Marie-Christine Barrault
Cross Creek	Mary Steenburgen
Dallas as the original elder Mrs. Ewing	Barbara Bel Geddes
Days of Wine and Roses	Lee Remick
Dead End	Sylvia Sidney
Diabolique	Simone Signoret
Divorcee	Norma Shearer
Dynasty as Krystle	Linda Evans
Emmanuele, the orginal	Sylvia Kristel
Evita on Broadway	Patti LuPone
Exorcist as the possessed girl	Linda Blair
Falcon Crest as matriarch	Jane Wyman
Fame on TV	Debbie Allen
Family as the daughter	Kristy McNichol
Fatal Attraction, going wild	Glenn Close
Five Easy Pieces, paired with Nicholson	Karen Black
Funny Girl	Barbra Streisand
Georgy Girl and TV's House Calls	Lynn Redgrave
Gertrude Stein	Pat Carroll
Getting of Wisdom	Sigrid Thornton
Gigi as the grandmother	Hermione Gingold

Gloria	**Gena Rowlands**
Godfather as the daughter	**Talia Shire**
Golden Girls as Rose	**Betty White**
Good Earth	**Luise Rainier**
Grapes of Wrath as Ma Joad	**Jane Darwell**
Great Expectations as Lean's young Estella	**Jean Simmons**
Gypsy, the show-inspiring burlesque artist	**Gypsy Rose Lee**
Halloween, the 1978 original	**Jamie Lee Curtis**
Hamlet in 1971 and Hallmark's Lady Macbeth	**Judith Anderson**
Harry and Tonto as the old girlfriend	**Geraldine Fitzgerald**
Hazel on early TV	**Shirley Booth**
Hello, Dolly on Broadway	**Carol Channing**
Hester Street	**Carol Kane**
High Sierra	**Ida Lupino**
Homecoming	**Vivien Merchant**
Honeysuckle Rose as the wife	**Dyan Cannon**
I Dream of Jeannie as the genie	**Barbara Eden**
I, Claudius as Livia on British TV	**Sian Phillips**
I'm No Angel	**Mae West**
Inside Daisy Clover	**Natalie Wood**
"It" girl, Hollywood's original	**Clara Bow**
It Happened One Night with Gable	**Claudette Colbert**
It's a Wonderful Life	**Donna Reed**
Jewel in the Crown as Daphne Manners	**Susan Wooldridge**
Jewel in the Crown as Sarah Layton	**Geraldine James**
Julia with Fonda	**Vanessa Redgrave**
L.A. Law as Van Owen	**Susan Dey**
La Strada as the waif	**Giulietta Masina**
Laugh-in as Ernestine the telephone operator	**Lily Tomlin**
Les enfants du paradis	**Arletty**
Lili, paired with Aumont	**Zsa Zsa Gabor**
Limelight	**Claire Bloom**
Little Miss Marker, Hollywood's original	**Shirley Temple**
Little Night Music on Broadway	**Glynis Johns**
Lolita as the mother	**Shelley Winters**
Lou Grant as Mrs. Pynchon	**Nancy Marchand**
M*A*S*H as Hollywood's Hotlips	**Sally Kellerman**
M*A*S*H as Hotlips on TV	**Loretta Swit**
Maltese Falcon	**Mary Astor**
Marriage of Maria Braun	**Hanna Schygulla**
Mary Hartman, Mary Hartman	**Louise Lasser**
Maude on TV	**Beatrice Arthur**

Member of the Wedding as the young girl	**Julie Harris**
Mildred Pierce, subject of *Mommie Dearest*	**Joan Crawford**
Million Dollar Mermaid, a swimming champion	**Esther Williams**
Modern Times with Chaplin	**Paulette Goddard**
Mogambo paired with Gable	**Ava Gardner**
Moonstruck, winning a starring Oscar	**Cher**
Moonstruck, winning a supporting Oscar	**Olympia Dukakis**
Murder, My Sweet as the villain	**Claire Trevor**
Murder, She Wrote	**Angela Lansbury**
My Brilliant Career	**Judy Davis**
My Fair Lady as Hollywood's Eliza Doolittle	**Audrey Hepburn**
My Man Godfrey as the ditsy blonde	**Carole Lombard**
Nashville as the singer who was shot	**Ronee Blakley**
Network	**Faye Dunaway**
One Day at a Time	**Bonnie Franklin**
One Flew over the Cuckoo's Nest, for an Oscar	**Louise Fletcher**
On the Waterfront	**Eva Marie Saint**
Our Miss Brooks on early TV	**Eve Arden**
Out of Africa	**Meryl Streep**
Paper Moon with her father	**Tatum O'Neal**
Pennies from Heaven	**Bernadette Peters**
Pete 'n Tillie and her own TV show	**Carol Burnett**
Peter Pan on Broadway and TV	**Mary Martin**
Phyllis	**Cloris Leachman**
Playboy of the Western World, the movie	**Siobhan McKenna**
Pretty Baby	**Brooke Shields**
Prime of Miss Jean Brodie	**Maggie Smith**
Private Benjamin paired with Hawn	**Eileen Brennan**
Private Secretary as TV's Susie McNamara	**Ann Sothern**
Prizzi's Honor as the granddaughter	**Anjelica Huston**
Pygmalion as Eliza Doolittle in the 1930's movie	**Wendy Hiller**
Raisin in the Sun	**Ruby Dee**
Red Dust as the sexy lead in the 1931 movie	**Jean Harlow**
Red Shoes	**Moira Shearer**
Rhoda	**Valerie Harper**

Road pictures with Hope and Crosby	**Dorothy Lamour**
Rose as the singer	**Bette Midler**
Royal Wedding	**Jane Powell**
Search for Fire	**Rae Dawn Chong**
Seventh Heaven for her 1st Oscar	**Janet Gaynor**
Sixteen Candles	**Molly Ringwald**
Sound of Music as the Baroness	**Eleanor Parker**
Splash as the mermaid	**Daryl Hannah**
Star Trek as Lt. Uhura	**Nichelle Nichols**
Star Wars as Princess Leia	**Carrie Fisher**
Story of Adele H.	**Isabelle Adjani**
Stranger as the young wife	**Loretta Young**
Sugar Babies, making a comeback on Broadway	**Ann Miller**
Summer of '42	**Jennifer O'Neill**
Sweet Charity, Broadway's original	**Gwen Verdon**
Swept Away . . .	**Mariangela Melato**
Taxi Driver	**Jodie Foster**
10 as Dudley Moore's obsession	**Bo Derek**
Terms of Endearment as the mother	**Shirley MacLaine**
Three Faces of Eve	**Joanne Woodward**
Three-Penny Opera's original Pirate Jenny	**Lotte Lenya**
Three's Company as Chrissy	**Suzanne Somers**
Trip to Bountiful	**Geraldine Page**
Upstairs, Downstairs as the maid Rose	**Jean Marsh**
"vamp," Hollywood's original	**Theda Bara**
Who's Afraid of Virginia Woolf as the young wife	**Sandy Dennis**
Wiz on Broadway	**Stephanie Mills**
Wizard of Oz as Dorothy	**Judy Garland**
Wizard of Oz as the bad witch who melted	**Margaret Hamilton**
Wizard of Oz as the Good Witch	**Billie Burke**
WKRP in Cincinnati as a sexy secretary	**Loni Anderson**
Wonder Woman on TV	**Lynda Carter**
Year of Living Dangerously for an Oscar as a man	**Linda Hunt**
Year of Living Dangerously with Gibson and Hunt	**Sigourney Weaver**
Zorba the Greek	**Irene Papas**

Variety Players

Among variety players, e.g., puppeteers, ventriloquists, clowns, and magicians, who . . . ?

was the human playing with Kukla and Ollie	**Fran Allison**
talked with and for his dummy Charlie McCarthy	**Edgar Bergen**
starred in Broadway's 1974 *The Magic Show*	**Doug Henning**
created the Muppets	**Jim Henson**
excelled in escape acts	**Harry Houdini**
was Weary Willie with the Ringling/Barnum circus	**Emmett Kelly**
played with TV's Lamb Chop and Charlie Horse	**Shari Lewis**
turned his skill to indicting faith-healers for fraud	**James "The Amazing" Randi**
created Rootie Kazootie	**Todd Russell**
was the ventriloquist-host on *Howdy Doody*	**Buffalo Bob Smith**
created the Kuklapolitans	**Burr Tillstrom**
had a head in a box saying, "It's all right!"	**Señor Wencez**
worked with dummy Jerry Mahoney	**Paul Winchell**

TV Families

Among families on TV series, which was or were the central family on . . . ?

All in the Family	**Bunker**
Andy Griffith Show	**Taylor**
The Beverly Hillbillies	**Clampett**
Bewitched	**Stephens**
Bonanza	**Cartwright**
The Cosby Show	**Huxtable**
Dallas	**Ewing**
Day by Day	**Harper**
The Dick Van Dyke Show	**Petrie**
The Donna Reed Show	**Stone**
Dynasty	**Carrington**
Eight Is Enough	**Bradford**
Falcon Crest	**Channing**
Family	**Lawrence**

Family Ties	**Keaton**
Father Knows Best	**Anderson**
Good Neighbors	**Good**
The Honeymooners	**Kramden** and **Norton**
I Love Lucy	**Ricardo** and **Mertz**
I Married Joan	**Stevens**
Leave It to Beaver	**Cleaver**
Life with Father	**Day**
Little House on the Prairie	**Ingalls**
Lost in Space	**Robinson**
Make Room for Daddy (The Danny Thomas Show)	**Williams**
My Three Sons	**Douglas**
Ozzie and Harriet	**Nelson**
Upstairs, Downstairs	**Bellamy**

Broadcasters

In the world of radio and television broadcasters, who was or were . . . ?

the early "Voice of the Yankees"	**Mel Allen**
the mid-1950's *Tonight* host, later on game shows	**Steve Allen**
the premier early radio and TV baseball sportscaster	**Red Barber**
host of the 1970's *Gong Show*	**Chuck Barris**
host of early TV's *Bell Science Series*	**Dr. Frank Baxter**
longtime news editor on the early *Today*	**Frank Blair**
the 1st host of the *Original Amateur Hour*	**Major Bowes**
news correspondent from 1981 on TV's *60 Minutes*	**Ed Bradley**
a movie reviewer and Movie Channel host	**Joe Bob Briggs**
longtime NBC news anchor, later with ABC	**David Brinkley**
NBC nightly news anchor	**Tom Brokaw**
host of TV's *The Ascent of Man*	**Jacob Bronowski**
host of NBC's *Tonight* from 1962	**Johnny Carson**
host of a PBS interview show from 1977	**Dick Cavett**
Garroway's successor on *Today*, later on NBC's evening news	**John Chancellor**

longtime host of *American Bandstand*	**Dick Clark**
host of TV's *Civilization*	**Kenneth Clark**
longtime TV tennis commentator	**Bud Collins**
host of Masterpiece Theater	**Alistair Cooke**
the grating and controversial longtime sportscaster	**Howard Cosell**
longtime anchor of CBS's evening news	**Walter Cronkite**
host of *The $25,000 Pyramid* from 1974	**Bill Cullen**
a Chicago, later NYC, daytime talk-show host	**Phil Donahue**
ABC's 1980's White House correspondent	**Sam Donaldson**
singing host of a longtime afternoon show	**Mike Douglas**
host of *20/20* with Walters, once from *Today*	**Hugh Downs**
CBS news anchor before Cronkite	**Douglas Edwards**
host of TV's *This Is Your Life*	**Ralph Edwards**
linked with "And so it goes . . ." on late-night TV	**Linda Ellerbee**
longtime *What's My Line* panelists	**Arlene Francis** and **Dorothy Kilgallen**
longtime producer for Murrow and others	**Fred Friendly**
star of Britain's *That Was The Week That Was*	**David Frost**
longtime host of *Candid Camera*	**Allen Funt**
the original host of the *Today* show	**Dave Garroway**
host of early TV's *Talent Scouts*	**Arthur Godfrey**
longtime host of an early-evening TV talk show	**Merv Griffin**
co-host on NBC's *Today* show	**Bryant Gumbel**
host of the old *Let's Make a Deal* show	**Monte Hall**
longtime host of *Good Morning America*	**David Hartman**
the computer-generated TV host	**Max Headroom**
early TV's "Mr. Wizard"	**Don Herbert**
host of early TV's *Ding Dong School*	**Dr. "Miss Frances" Horwich**
a reporter on PBS's evening news, one of the first blacks to attend the U. of Georgia	**Charlayne Hunter-Gault**
Brinkleys' co-anchor on early NBC's evening news	**Chet Huntley**

anchor of ABC's evening news	**Peter Jennings**
host of *Lake Wobegon Days*	**Garrison Keillor**
host of CNN's evening call-in show	**Larry King**
interviewer-host on ABC's *Nightline*	**Ted Koppel**
host of CBS's folksy "On the Road"	**Charles Kuralt**
sports editor on the early *Today* show	**Jack Lescoulie**
NBC's off-the-wall late-night host	**David Letterman**
longtime host of *People Are Funny*	**Art Linkletter**
early host of TV's *G. E. College Bowl*	**Allen Ludden**
host of the *Original Amateur Hour* after Bowes	**Ted Mack**
Carson's longtime sidekick on *Tonight*	**Ed McMahon**
co-anchors of PBS's evening news	**Robert MacNeil** and **Jim Lehrer**
longtime NBC sportscaster, as at the Seoul Olympics	**Jim McKay**
longtime host of *I've Got a Secret*	**Garry Moore**
the PBS, earlier CBS, interviewer	**Bill Moyers**
network anchor, then PBS commentator	**Roger Mudd**
early TV's conscience and *See It Now* host	**Edward R. Murrow**
NBC commentator and language maven	**Edwin Newman**
the CBS-TV anchor who favors bow-ties and rhymes	**Charles Osgood**
late '50's to early '60's late-night talk-show host	**Jack Paar**
the architect of early CBS	**William S. Paley**
longtime MC of the Miss America pageant	**Bert Parks**
co-host of NBC's *Today* show	**Jane Pauley**
Host of early TV's *Zoo Parade*	**Marlin Perkins**
Cronkite's successor at *CBS Evening News*	**Dan Rather**
onetime ABC anchor, a *60 Minutes* regular	**Harry Reasoner**
Carson's sometime replacement and later rival	**Joan Rivers**
NPR, then ABC, commentator	**Cokie Roberts**
the 1st black network anchor, on ABC	**Max Robinson**
60 Minutes's resident humorist	**Andy Rooney**
the radio operator who founded NBC	**David Sarnoff**

NBC anchorwoman drowned in an auto accident	**Jessica Savitch**
the lone female in 1980's on CBS's *60 Minutes*, later with ABC	**Diane Sawyer**
NBC's *Today* show meteorologist	**Willard S**
longtime commentator on CBS's news	**Eric Sevareid**
CNN's nightly news anchor	**Bernard Shaw**
a longtime key member of *Meet the Press's* panel	**Lawrence E. Spivak**
host of *The Toast of the Town*	**Ed Sullivan**
anchor of early TV's *Camel News Caravan*	**John Cameron Swayze**
host of an early TV travel series	**Lowell Thomas**
first among equals on *60 Minutes*	**Mike Wallace**
a surprising star on early *Today* with Downs	**Barbara Walters**
the retired judge on *People's Court*	**Joseph A. Wapner**
radio and TV's dispenser of sexual advice	**Dr. Ruth Westheimer**
the letter-turner on *Wheel of Fortune*	**Vanna White**
ABC News's conservative commentator	**George Will**
the daytime host and sometime movie actress	**Oprah Winfrey**
back-up reporter, with Hunter-Gault, on PBS news	**Judy Woodruff**

Directors and Producers

(See also Dancers and Choreographers)

Among stage and screen directors and producers, who produced and/or directed . . . ?

Actors' Studio students in The Method	**Lee Strasberg**
Alice's Restaurant	**Arthur Penn**
All That Jazz	**Bob Fosse**
Annie Hall	**Woody Allen**
Around the World in 80 Days	**Mike Todd**
Atlantic City	**Louis Malle**
Badlands	**Terence Malick**
Barbarella	**Roger Vadim**
Battleship Potemkin	**Sergei Eisenstein**

Beauty and the Beast	**Jean Cocteau**
Being There	**Hal Ashby**
Best Years of Our Lives	**William Wyler**
Birth of a Nation	**D. W. Griffith**
Blazing Saddles	**Mel Brooks**
Blow-Up	**Michaelangelo Antonioni**
Breathless	**Jean-Luc Godard**
Broadcast News	**James L. Brooks**
Carnal Knowledge	**Mike Nichols**
Carrie	**Brian De Palma**
Cats	**Trevor Nunn**
Chariots of Fire	**Hugh Hudson**
Chinatown	**Roman Polanski**
Citizen Kane	**Orson Welles**
Close Encounters of the Third Kind	**Steven Spielberg**
Closely Watched Trains	**Jiri Menzel**
Darling	**John Schlesinger**
Death in Venice	**Luchino Visconti**
Decameron	**Pier Paolo Pasolini**
Deer Hunter	**Michael Cimino**
Discreet Charm of the Bourgeoisie	**Luis Buñuel**
Doctor Zhivago and *Lawrence of Arabia*	**David Lean**
Elvis Presley's career	**"Col." Tom Parker**
Everyman	**Max Reinhardt**
Five Easy Pieces	**Bob Rafelson**
Follies on Broadway	**Florenz Ziegfeld**
42nd Street, the 1980's revival	**David Merrick**
Four Feathers, the 1939 movie, as film producer, director, and set designer, 3 brothers	**Alexander, Zoltan,** and **Vincent Korda**
Fountainhead	**King Vidor**
400 Blows	**François Truffaut**
French Connection	**William Friedkin**
Gandhi	**Richard Attenborough**
Garden of the Finzi-Continis	**Vittorio de Sica**
Gigi	**Vincente Minnelli**
Gimme Shelter	**David** and **Albert Maysles** and **Charlotte Zwerin**
Go-Between	**Joseph Losey**
Godfather	**Francis Ford Coppola**
Golden Boy	**Rouben Mamoulian**
Gone With the Wind	**David O. Selznick**
Grapes of Wrath and *The Quiet Man*	**John Ford**
Greed	**Erich von Stroheim**
Gregory's Girl and *Local Hero*	**Bill Forsyth**
Guess Who's Coming to Dinner	**Stanley Kramer**
Hester Street	**Joan Micklin Silver**

Hiroshima, Mon Amour	**Alain Resnais**
Home and the World	**Satyajit Ray**
Hospital	**Arthur Hiller**
Husbands	**John Cassavetes**
In Harm's Way	**Otto Preminger**
It's a Wonderful Life	**Frank Capra**
Keystone Kops comedies and Chaplin's Tramp	**Mack Sennett**
Klute	**Alan J. Pakula**
Kramer vs. Kramer	**Robert Benton**
La Cage aux Folles	**Edouard Molinaro**
La Grande Illusion	**Jean Renoir**
La Strada and *La Dolce Vita*	**Federico Fellini**
Last Emperor	**Bernardo Bertolucci**
Last Leaf	**Elaine May**
Last Picture Show	**Peter Bogdanovich**
Little Night Music	**Harold Prince**
Maltese Falcon and *African Queen*	**John Huston**
Man and a Woman	**Claude Lelouch**
Man for All Seasons	**Fred Zinnemann**
Man of Iron	**Andrzej Wajda**
Man Who Fell to Earth	**Nicolas Roeg**
Manon of the Spring	**Claude Berri**
Marat/Sade	**Peter Brook**
Marriage of Maria Braun	**Rainer Werner Fassbinder**
Metropolis	**Fritz Lang**
Midnight Express	**Alan Parker**
Minneapolis repertory company, its founder	**Tyrone Guthrie**
Morgan!	**Karel Reisz**
Moscow Arts Theatre, e.g., Chekhov plays	**Constantin Stanislavsky**
Mr. Hulot's Holiday	**Jacques Tati**
My Night at Maud's	**Eric Rohmer**
Napoleon, silent film	**Abel Gance**
Nashville	**Robert Altman**
Network	**Sidney Lumet**
Ninotchka	**Ernst Lubitsch**
Norma Rae	**Martin Ritt**
Nosferatu	**Friedrich Murnau**
Oh, God	**Carl Reiner**
Olympia, on the 1936 Berlin Olympics	**Leni Riefenstahl**
On Golden Pond	**Mark Rydell**
On the Waterfront	**Elia Kazan**
On Your Toes	**George Abbott**
One Flew Over the Cuckoo's Nest	**Milos Forman**
Open City	**Roberto Rossellini**
Outlaw	**Howard Hughes**

Paper Chase	**James Bridges**
Pink Panther movies	**Blake Edwards**
Platoon	**Oliver Stone**
Polish Laboratory Theater	**Jerzy Grotowski**
Psycho and *Rear Window*	**Alfred Hitchcock**
Public Theater in NYC	**Joseph Papp**
Rain Man	**Barry Levinson**
Red Shoes	**Michael Powell** and **Emeric Pressburger**
Reds	**Warren Beatty**
Romeo and Juliet, the 1968 movie	**Franco Zeffirelli**
Room with a View	**James Ivory**
Roots	**David Wolper**
Royal Shakespeare Company, then National Theatre	**Peter Hall**
Saturday Night Fever	**John Badham**
Seven Beauties	**Lina Wertmuller**
Sunset Boulevard	**Billy Wilder**
Seven Days in May	**John Frankenheimer**
7 Up and *28 Up*	**Michael Apted**
Sorrow and the Pity	**Marcel Ophuls**
Star Trek series	**Gene Roddenberry**
Star Trek—The Motion Picture	**Robert Wise**
Star Wars	**George Lucas**
Sting	**George Roy Hill**
Sullivan's Travels	**Preston Sturges**
Taxi Driver	**Martin Scorsese**
Ten Commandments	**Cecil B. de Mille**
Third Man	**Carol Reed**
This Is Spinal Tap	**Rob Reiner**
Thomas Crown Affair	**Norman Jewison**
Titicut Follies	**Frederick Wiseman**
To Have and Have Not	**Howard Hawks**
Tom Jones	**Tony Richardson**
Tommy and *Women in Love*	**Ken Russell**
Tootsie	**Sydney Pollack**
Turning Point	**Herbert Ross**
2001: A Space Odyssey	**Stanley Kubrick**
Unmarried Woman	**Paul Mazursky**
Upstairs, Downstairs	**John Hawkesworth**
Wild Bunch	**Sam Peckinpah**
Wild Strawberries	**Ingmar Bergman**
Woodstock	**Michael Wadleigh**
Z	**Constantin Costa-Gavras**

Dancers and Choreographers

(See also Directors and Producers)

In the world of dancers and choreographers, who . . . ?

choreographed *Blues Suite*	**Alvin Alley**
choreographed *Enigma Variations*	**Frederick Ashton**
debuted in the Paris Revue Nègre in 1925	**Josephine Baker**
choreographed *Slaughter on Tenth Avenue*	**George Balanchine**
defected from the Kirov Ballet in 1974	**Mikhail Baryshnikov**
choreographed *Sacre du Printemps*	**Maurice Béjart**
created *A Chorus Line*	**Michael Bennett**
staged the 1930's movie dance extravaganzas	**Busby Berkeley**
choreographed *La Sylphide*	**August Bournonville**
were ballroom dancers portrayed by Astaire and Rogers	**Vernon** and **Irene Castle**
danced together on their own 1950's TV show	**Marge** and **Gower Champion**
won a Tony for *My One and Only*	**Charles "Honi" Coles**
built the modern Stuttgart Ballet	**John Cranko**
choreographed *Images* and *Rainforest*	**Merce Cunningham**
was a male star in the 1970's NYC Ballet	**Jacques d'Amboise**
choreographed *Oklahoma*	**Agnes de Mille**
directed the early Sadler's Wells Ballet	**Ninette de Valois**
led the Ballets Russe in Paris	**Sergey Diaghilev**
was the early 20th-c. spark of modern dance	**Isadora Duncan**
was Nureyev's partner at the Royal Ballet	**Margot Fonteyn**
defected from the Bolshoi to the US in 1979	**Alexander Godunov** and **Leonid** and **Valentina Koslov**
choreographed *Appalachian Spring*	**Martha Graham**
was a female star in the 1970's ABT	**Cynthia Gregory**
was a female star in the 1970's NYC Ballet	**Melissa Hayden**
choreographed *Water Study*	**Doris Humphrey**

was premier dancer with the Alvin Ailey troupe	**Judith Jamison**
formed a company linked with City Center	**Robert Joffrey**
was ABT's premier dancer on coming to the West	**Natalia Makarova**
starred at the Royal Danish and NYC ballets	**Peter Martins**
created and danced *L'après-midi d'un faune*	**Vaslav Nijinsky**
partnered Margot Fonteyn on coming to the West	**Rudolf Nureyev**
was known for her dying Swan	**Anna Pavlova**
choreographed *The Sleeping Beauty*	**Marius Petipa**
choreographed *African Ceremonial*	**Pearl Primus**
was famous for her fan dance	**Sally Rand**
choreographed and directed *West Side Story*	**Jerome Robbins**
was the 1930's tap dancer called "Bojangles"	**Bill Robinson**
founded a key US dance school in 1915	**Ruth St. Denis** and **Ted Shawn**
created the modern ballet style in the early 19th c.	**Marie Taglioni**
danced with the NYC Ballet, an Amerindian	**Maria Tallchief**
choreographed *The Book of Beasts*	**Paul Taylor**
choreographed *Push Comes to Shove*	**Twyla Tharp**
choreographed *Pillar of Fire*	**Anthony Tudor**
co-choreographed, co-directed, and starred in *My One and Only*	**Tommy Tune**
was a NYC Ballet Star and early TV celebrity	**Edward Villella**

Prehistoric or Anonymous Works of Art

Among prehistoric or early anonymous works of art, what is or are . . . ?

the striking Greek statue found at Pergamum	**Dying Gaul**
the Parthenon statues in the British Museum	**Elgin Marbles**

the Roman silver cache unearthed in Britain in 1942	**Mildenhall Treasure**
the now-headless sculpture of a Greek goddess, in the Louvre	**Nike of Samothrace**
the 20,000-year-old limestone carving in Vienna's Museum of Natural History	**Venus of Willendorf**

Painters, Sculptors, and Architects

Among known painters, sculptors, and architects, who created . . . ?

Through Renaissance Times

Abduction of the Sabine Women	**Giovanni Bologna**
Birth of Venus (on the Half Shell)	**Sandro Botticelli**
Christ Before Pilate	**Tintoretto**
David and *St. George*	**Donatello**
Dead Christ	**Andrea Mantegna**
Delivery of the Keys to St. Peter	**Pietro Perugino**
Descent from the Cross	**Roger van der Weyden**
Discovery and Proving of the True Cross	**Piero della Francesca**
Erasmus, Henry VIII, and Thomas More portraits	**Hans Holbein the Younger**
Flight Into Egypt	**Caravaggio**; also **Adam Elsheimer**
Florentine sculptures and an Autobiography	**Benvenuto Cellini**
Four Horsemen of the Apocalypse	**Albrecht Dürer**
Garden of Delights	**Hieronymus Bosch**
Gates of Paradise, the Florentine Baptistery's doors	**Lorenzo Ghiberti** **Hubert** and **Jan van Eyck**
Giovanni Arnolfini and His Bride	**Jan van Eyck**
Hermes	**Praxiteles**
Isenheim Altarpiece, with Crucifixion	**Matthias Grünewald**
Jupiter and Io	**Correggio**
Last Supper and *Mona Lisa* (*La Joconde*)	**Leonardo da Vinci**
Life of Saint Francis frescoes	**Giotto**
Madonna and Angels, at Florence	**Luca Della Robbia**
Madonna of the Harpies	**Andrea del Sarto**
Madonna with the Long Neck	**Parmigianino**
Man with the Glove	**Titian**
Marriage at Cana	**Paolo Veronese**
Old Man and His Grandson	**Domenico Ghirlandaio**

Piazzetta, Venice	**Canaletto (né Antonio Canal)**
Providence Fountain in Vienna	**Georg Raphael Donner**
Return of the Hunters	**Pieter Breughel the Elder**
San Lorenzo Church in Florence	**Filippo Brunelleschi**
Sistine Chapel frescoes and the *Pietà*	**Michelangelo Buonarroti**
Sistine Madonna	**Raphael (Raffaello Sanzio)**
St. Francis in Ecstasy	**Giovanni Bellini**
Very Rich Book of Hours of the Duke of Berry illustrations	**Limbourg brothers**
Villa Rotonda, in Italy, inspiring 18th-c. British architects	**Andrea Palladio**
Village Fair	**Pieter Breughel the Younger**
Virgin Adoring the Christ Child	**Fra Filippo Lippi**
Vision of St. Bernard, Fra Filippo's son	**Filippino Lippi**

In the 17th–19th Centuries

Alice's Adventures in Wonderland illustrations	**John Tenniel**
Andes of Ecuador	**Frederick Church**
Annakirche, in Vienna	**Daniel Gran**
Arrangement in Black and Gray: The Artist's Mother	**James Abbot MacNeill Whistler**
At the Moulin Rouge	**Henri de Toulouse-Lautrec**
Balzac illustrations, in France	**(Paul) Gustave Doré**
Bath's Georgian layout, in England	**John Wood**
Bathers	**Jean-Honoré Fragonard**
Bathers	**Pierre-Auguste Renoir**
bird illustrations rivaling Audubon's	**Alexander Wilson**
birds of America in watercolors	**John James Audubon**
black-and-white illustrations in the 1890's	**Aubrey Beardsley**
Blenheim Palace's and Petworth's landscaping	**Lancelot "Capability" Brown**
Blenheim Palace, at the start	**John Vanbrugh**
Blenheim Palace, after replacing Vanbrugh	**Nicholas Hawksmoor**
Blue Boy	**Thomas Gainsborough**
Breakers, at Newport, Rhode Island	**Richard Morris Hunt**
Bronco Buster	**Frederick Remington**
Café Concert: at Les Ambassadeurs	**Edgar Dégas**
Capitol in Washington, D.C.	**William Thornton**
Central Park in NYC	**Frederick Law Olmsted** and **Calvin Vaux**
Covent Garden and Whitehall, "English Palladio"	**Inigo Jones**

David, in Rome's Borghese Gallery	**Gianlorenzo Bernini**
Death of Marat	**Jacques-Louis David**
Dejeuner sur l'Herbe (Luncheon on the Grass)	**Édouard Manet**
Downton's Gothic castle, in Britain	**Richard Payne Knight**
Emigrants Crossing the Plains, Sunset	**Albert Bierstadt**
Englischer Garten in Munich, a British-American	**Benjamin Thompson (Count Romford)**
Frogner Park sculptures in Oslo	**Gustav Vigeland**
Fur Traders on the Missouri	**George Caleb Bingham**
Gallery of Indians	**George Catlin**
Garden of Love	**Peter Paul Rubens**
Gibson girl drawings in the 1890s	**Charles Dana Gibson**
Greece Expiring on the Ruins of Missolonghi	**Eugène Delacroix**
Gross Clinic	**Thomas Eakins**
Haywain	**John Constable**
Hina Maruru	**Paul Gauguin**
Holkham Hall and other Palladian buildings	**William Kent**
Intrigue	**James Ensor**
Iron Forge	**Joseph Wright of Derby**
James Stuart, Duke of Lennox	**Anthony Van Dyck**
Japanese wood-block prints of Mt. Fuji	**Katsushika Hokusai**
Japanese wood-block prints that attracted Whistler	**Ando Hiroshige**
Jewish Graveyard	**Jacob van Ruysdael**
Jolly Toper	**Frans Hals**
Joseph the Carpenter	**Georges de la Tour**
Karlskirche, in Vienna, after his father died	**Joseph Emmanuel Fisher von Erlach**
Kitchen Still Life	**Jean-Baptiste Chardin**
Landscape with the Burial of Phocion	**Poussin**
Lincoln Memorial's statue of Lincoln	**Daniel Chester French**
Maids of Honor	**Diego Velásquez**
Man with a Hoe	**Jean Millet**
Massacre at Chios	**Eugène Delacroix**
medieval crafts revival in Britain	**William Morris**
Morning Bell	**Winslow Homer**
Mounted Officer of the Imperial Guard	**Théodore Géricault**
Mrs. Henry Adams (Grief)	**Augustus Saint-Gaudens**

Mrs. Siddons as the Tragic Muse	Joshua Reynolds
Night Watch	Rembrandt van Rijn
nursery rhyme illustrations in watercolor	Kate Greenaway
Odalisque	Jean Auguste Dominique Ingres
Pagoda at London's Kew Gardens	William Chambers
Palm House at London's Kew Gardens	Decimus Burton
Peace and Plenty	George Inness
Peterhof, Peter the Great's Leningrad palace	Alexandre Le Blond
Peterskirche in Vienna	Johann Lukas von Hildebrandt
Petworth Park's carvings	Grinling Gibbons
Pickwick Papers illustrations	Phiz (H. W. Browne)
Pilgrimage to Cythera	Antoine Watteau
Portrait of Madam X	John Singer Sargent
portraits of cowboys	Charles M. Russell
portraits of early Americans, e.g., Washington	Gilbert Stuart
portraits of Washington and other patriots	Charles Wilson Peale
Postsparkasse in Vienna	Otto Wagner
Rake's Progress	William Hogarth
River	Claude Monet
Royal Pavilion at Brighton, England	John Nash
Snow Storm: Steamboat Off a Harbor's Mouth	J. M. W. Turner
Songs of Innocence	William Blake
St. Martin-in-the-Fields Church	James Gibbs
St. Paul's Cathedral in London	Christopher Wren
Statue of Liberty	Frederic Auguste Bartholdi
Stourhead's landscaped park, in Britain	Henry Hoare
Sunday Afternoon on the Island of Grande Jatte	Georges Seurat
Sunflowers	Vincent van Gogh
Syon House, 18th-c. British architect-brothers	Robert and James Adam
Third-Class Carriage	Honoré Daumier
Third of May, 1808	Francisco de Goya (y Lucientes)
Vaux-le-Vicomte gardens	André Le Nôtre
View of Delft	Jan Vermeer
View of Toledo	El Greco (né Domenico Theotocopoulos)
Ville d'Avray	Jean-Baptiste Camille Corot
Washington Crossing the Delaware	Emanuel Leutze

Washington, D.C.'s, layout | **Pierre-Charles L'Enfant**
Washington Square Arch in New York City | **Stanford White**
Watson and the Shark | **John Singleton Copley**
wax figures in a London exhibition | **Madame Tussaud**
White House, in Washington, D.C. | **James Hoban**
Winterpalace in Vienna | **Johann Bernhard Fischer von Erlach**
Winterpalace's sculptures, in Vienna | **Giovanni Giuliani**
Woman Bathing | **Mary Cassatt**
Wurzburg Palace's ceiling frescoes | **Giovanni Tiepolo**

In the 20th Century

Allies Day, May, 1917 | **Childe Hassam**
American Gothic | **Grant Wood**
Animobiles and *Universe* in Chicago's Sears Tower | **Alexander Calder**
Ballets Russes designs for Diaghilev | **Léon Bakst**
Beanery | **Edward Kienholz**
Biotite | **Barbara Hepworth**
Bird in Space | **Constantin Brancusi**
Blue Guitar | **David Hockney**
Blue Poles | **Jackson Pollock**
Bottle and Glass | **Juan Gris**
Broadway Boogie-Woogie | **Piet Mondrian**
Brooklyn Bridge | **Frank Stella**
Burlington Square, renewal in Vermont | **Ludwig Miës van der Rohe**
Campbell's soup cans paintings | **Andy Warhol**
Capacious Forms | **Wassily Kandinsky**
cats, often in repose | **Théophile-Alexandre Steinlen**
Chairman of the Board | **Helen Frankenthaler**
Christina's World and paintings of Helga | **Andrew Wyeth**
City | **Fernand Léger**
Dawn | **Lyonel Feininger**
Dinner Party | **Judy Chicago**
Double Isometric Self-Portrait | **Jim Dine**
Double White Map | **Jasper Johns**
Dream | **Henri Rousseau**
Early Sunday Morning | **Edward Hopper**
East Wing of Washington's National Gallery | **I(eoh) M(ing) Pei**
Ecce Homo | **Jacob Epstein**
fabric rapped around huge areas | **Christo**

Fallingwater and NYC's Guggenheim Museum	**Frank Lloyd Wright**
Fiddler on the Roof Broadway set	**Boris Aronson**
flowers and skulls in the American Southwest	**Georgia O'Keeffe**
F-111, an 86-foot-long sculpture	**James Rosenquist**
Friedrichstrasse 12, a Vienna Secession building	**Joseph Olbrich**
Friedrichstrasse 12's doors for Vienna	**Gustav Klimt**
Germany, a Winter's Tale	**George Grosz**
Giant Trowel, a pop artist pair	**Claes Oldenburg** and **Oosje Van Bruggen**
Girl at Piano	**Roy Lichtenstein**
Girl Seated by the Sea	**Robert Henri**
Glass House, in New Canaan, Connecticut	**Philip Johnson**
glass window wall, an innovation at the Bauhaus	**Walter Gropius**
Golconda, or The Rape	**René Magritte**
Guernica	**Pablo Picasso**
Harmony in Red (Red Room)	**Henri Matisse**
Harpist	**Jacques Lipchitz**
Homage to the Square series	**Josef Albers**
I and the Village	**Marc Chagall**
illustrations for gothic fables and PBS's *Mystery*	**Edward Gorey**
illustrations for many juvenile classics	**N. C. Wyeth**
illustrations for many special editions of books	**Rockwell Kent**
impressionist works with erotic charge	**Egon Schiele**
Justice Center portal in Cleveland, Ohio	**Isamu Noguchi**
Kennedy Center, Washington, D.C.	**Edward Durell Stone**
Le Courrier	**Georges Braque**
Lever House in New York City	**Gordon Bunshaft**
Lindisfarne Castle, Edwardian-style, in Britain	**Edward Lutyens**
McDonald Pickup	**Ralph Goings**
Man Pointing	**Alberto Giacometti**
March of Humanity murals	**David Alfaro Siqueiros**
Mick Jagger's face, et al., in distorted pictures	**Francis Bacon**
Mont Sainte-Victoire Seen from Bibemus Quarry	**Paul Cézanne**
Morning Sunlight	**Pisarro**

Mount Rushmore sculptures of presidents	Gutzon Borglum
Mr. and Mrs. Rembrandt	Red Grooms
murals at Mexico's U. of Guadalajara	José Clemente Orozco
murals in Houston's interdenominational chapel	Mark Rothko
Mystery and Melancholy of a Street	Giorgio de Chirico
Nude Descending a Staircase	Marcel Duchamp
Observing Time	Man Ray
Old Clown	Georges Rouault
Out for the Christmas Trees	Grandma (Anna Mary Robertson) Moses
Parades and many graphics	Saul Steinberg
Paris Metro entrance design	Hector Guimard
Peasant War	Kathe Köllwitz
Persistence of Memory	Salvador Dali
Picton Castle art works	Graham Sutherland
posters of European ocean liners	A. M. Cassandre
psychedelic posters emblematic of the 1960's	Peter Max
Radiant City in Marseilles	Le Corbusier
Reclining Figure at NYC's Lincoln Center	Henry Moore
Rouen cathedral and water lilies studies	Claude Monet
Russian Revolution in a 76-panel work	Larry Rivers
Sacco and Vanzetti works	Ben Shahn
Sagrada Familia (Holy Family) cathedral, in Barcelona	Antoni Gaudi
San Simeon Castle, Hearst's California palace	Julia Morgan
Saturday Evening Post covers	Norman Rockwell
Scream	Edvard Munch
sculptures and paintings of elongated forms	Amedeo Modigliani
sculptures of massive female nudes	Aristide Maillol
sculptures of welded steel, as in the Seagram building	Louise Nevelson
Sex Pistols' graphic art	Jamie Reid
Stag at Sharkey's	George Bellows
stained-glass art works	Louis Tiffany
Standing Woman	Gaston Lachaise
Summer Lost at Night	Jennifer Bartlett
Summer Rental III	Robert Rauschenberg
Sunday in the Alameda in Mexico's Hotel Del Prado	Diego Rivera
Thinker	Rodin

"Three Servicemen," near the Vietnam Memorial	Frederick Hart
Threshing Wheat	Thomas Hart Benton
Totem and Taboo	Max Ernst
Truck and other life-size tableaux	George Segal
TWA terminal at NYC's Kennedy Airport	Eero Saarinen
Twittering Machine	Paul Klee
Umbrellas in the Rain	Maurice Prendergast
Vietnam Veterans Memorial	Maya Lin
View of Prague	Oskar Kokoschka
Wake of the Ferry	John Sloan
Western US in paintings	Charles M. Russell
Whitney Museum in New York City	Marcel Breuer
Woman I	Willem de Kooning
World Trade Center in New York City	Minoru Yamasaki
Yale University Center for British Art	Louis Kahn
Zig	David Smith

Cartoonists

Among modern cartoonists, who created . . . ?

ghoulish cartoons, as in the *New Yorker*	Charles Addams
the noted *Washington Post* editorial cartoons	Herbert "Herblock" Block
the *New Yorker* cartoons with scads of cats	George Booth
Bloom County	Berke Breathed
Terry and the Pirates and *Steve Canyon*	Milton Caniff
Li'l Abner and the people of Dogpatch	Al Capp
the X-rated comic and film star Fritz the Cat	R. (Robert) Crumb
the food-loving tiger cat, Garfield	Jim Davis
the Katzenjammer Kids	Rudolph Dirks
Mickey Mouse and *Fantasia*	Walt Disney
ultra-NYC cartoons, as in the *Village Voice*	Jules Feiffer
Mutt and Jeff	Harry "Bud" Fisher
the WWI "Uncle Sam Wants You" poster	James Montgomery Flagg

Sylvester and the always-elusive Tweety Bird	I. ("Fritz") Freland
the anti-hero cat Heathcliff	George Gately
Dick Tracy	Chester Gould
Little Orphan Annie	Harold Gray
the Flintstones and Yogi Bear	Bill Hanna and Joe Barbera
BC and the *Wizard of Id*	Johnny Hart
Krazy Kat	George Herriman
Pogo	Walt Kelly
Dennis the Menace	Hank Ketcham
Gasoline Alley	Frank King
the assorted cats who "love to eat mousies"	B. (Bernard) Kliban
the Far Side	Gary Larsen
Spiderman	Stan Lee
the cartoon soldiers Willie and Joe	William Mauldin
the Rep. elephant and the Dem. donkey	Thomas Nast
the Oscar-winning Tom and Jerry	Fred Quimby, William Hanna, and Joseph Barbera
Snoopy, Charlie Brown, Lucy, and Linus	Charles Schultz
Popeye and Olive Oyl	Elzie Segar
Superman	Jerry Siegel and Joe Shuster
the original Felix the Cat, later a Disney Star	Pat Sullivan
Doonesbury	Gary Trudeau
Calvin and Hobbes	Bill Watterson
ghoulish cartoons, as in the *New Yorker*	Gahan Wilson
Blondie and Dagwood Bumstead	Murat "Chic" Young

Photographers

Among photographers, who is or was famous for . . . ?

her photos of a changing NYC	Berenice Abbott
his Sierra Club nature photos	Ansel Adams
her photos of odd or disturbing people	Diane Arbus
his photos of turn-of-the-c. Paris and its people	Eugène Atget
his *Vogue* and celebrity portraits	Richard Avedon
his photos of royal and cultural celebrities	Cecil Beaton
her Time-Life war photos and Depression studies	Margaret Bourke-White

his Civil war photography	**Mathew Brady**
his war photos, as of the Spanish Civil War	**Robert Capa**
his "decisive moment" photos	**Henri Cartier-Bresson**
early photography	**Louis Daguerre**
his war photos in *Life*, as of Korea	**David Douglas Duncan**
his candid photos in *Life*	**Alfred Eisenstaedt**
doing *Let Us Now Praise Famous Men*	**Walker Evans**
his *Life* photos, esp. of architecture	**Andreas Feininger**
his stunt photos for *Life*	**Philippe Halsman**
his photos of immigrants and child laborers	**Lewis Hine**
photos of the 19th-c. American West	**William Henry Jackson**
her 1930's Farm Security Administration photos	**Dorothea Lange**
his documentary photos for *Life*, esp. of blacks	**Gordon Parks**
the unusual effects in his portraits	**Man Ray**
his 1930's Farm Security Administration photos	**Arthur Rothstein**
his royal, society, and fashion photos	**Lord Snowden, Anthony Armstrong-Jones**
organizing the *Family of Man* exhibition	**Edward Steichen**
his photos of O'Keeffe and his Gallery 291	**Alfred Stieglitz**
his photos on international social issues	**Paul Strand**
heading the Farm Security Administration photo effort	**Roy Stryker**
calotypes, which allowed prints to be made	**William Fox Talbot**
his secret photos of Jews in 1930's Europe	**Roman Vishniac**
his focus on shapes and forms, not messages	**Edward Weston**
his mystical, abstract photos	**Minor White**
his photos of New York society folk	**Jerome Zerbe**

Early Classical Musicians

Among classical composers before the 20th century, who wrote or created . . . ?

Academic Festival Overture	Johannes Brahms
Aida and La Traviata	Giuseppe Verdi
Au Matin and Berceuse from Joselyn	Benjamin Godard
Barber of Seville and the William Tell Overture	Gioacchino Rossini
Brandenburg Concértos	Johann Sebastian Bach
Caprices for Unaccompanied Violin	Nicolo Paganini
Carmen and L'Arlesienne Suite	Georges Bizet
Choros	Heitor Villa-Lobos
Clock Symphony and Toy Symphony	Franz Josef Haydn
Coppelia	Clement Philibert Leo Delibes
Dido and Aeneas	Henry Purcell
Die Fledermaus and the Blue Danube waltz	Johann Strauss, Jr.
D Minor Symphony	César Franck
"do, re, mi . . ." and musical notation	Guido d'Arezzo
Eine Kleine Nachtmusik and the theme used in Elvira Madigan	Wolfgang Amadeus Mozart
Faust	Charles Gounod
Four Seasons	Antonio Vivaldi
Giselle	Adolphe Adam
Grand Polonaise	Frédéric Chopin
"Harp that Once Through Tara's Halls"	Thomas Moore
harpsichord sonatas, over 500 of them	Domenico Scarlatti
Invitation to the Dance	Carl Maria von Weber
Iphigenie en Tauride	Christoph Gluck
I Promessi Sposi	Amilcare Ponchielli
Kamennoi-Ostrow	Anton Rubinstein
Kreisleriana	Robert Schumann
Le Bourgeois Gentilhomme	Jean-Baptiste Lully
Le Prophète	Giacomo Meyerbeer
Les Préludes and Hungarian Rhapsodies	Franz (Ferenc) Liszt
Lucia di Lammermoor	Gaetano Donizetti
Ma Vlast (My Country)	Bedrich Smetana
"Marseillaise"	Roger de Lisle
Martha	Friedrich von Flotow
Messiah and Royal Fireworks Music	George Frederick Handel

Moonlight Sonata and the *Ode to Joy*	**Ludwig von Beethovern**
Mozart catalog	**Ludwig von Köchel**
Murmuring Zephyrs	**Adolf Jensen**
Namouna	**Edouard Lalo**
Norma	**Vincenzo Bellini**
Nuit des Tropiques	**Louis Gottschalk**
Nutcracker Suite and the *1812 Overture*	**Peter Ilyich Tchaikovsky**
On the Steppes of Central Asia	**Alexander Borodin**
Orfeo and many madrigals	**Claudio Monteverdi**
Parzival	**Wolfram von Eschenbach**
Peer Gynt Suite	**Edvard Grieg**
Pictures at an Exhibition	**Modest Mussorgsky**
Pirates of Penzance	**William Gilbert** and **Arthur Sullivan**
Poet and Peasant Overture	**Franz von Suppé**
Ring Cycle	**Richard Wagner**
Ruslan and Ludmilla	**Mikhail Glinka**
Rustle of Spring	**Christian Sinding**
Scotch Poem	**Edward MacDowell**
"Silent Night, Holy Night"	**Franz Gruber**
Suite Española	**Isaac Albéniz**
Symphonie Fantastique	**Hector Berlioz**
Tales of Hoffman	**Jacques Offenbach**
violins of superb quality in 17th–18th-c. Cremona	**Antonio Stradivari**
violins of superb quality in 18th-c. Cremona	**Giuseppe Anatonio Guarneri (del Gesù)**
Wanderer and the *Unfinished Symphony*	**Franz Schubert**
"Wedding March" and *Spring Song*	**Felix Mendelssohn**

Modern Classical Musicians

Among classical composers working in the 20th century, who wrote . . . ?

Adagio for Strings	**Samuel Barber**
Air Music	**Ned Rorem**
Amahl and the Night Visitors	**Gian Carlo Menotti**
American Festival Overture	**William Schuman**
Andrea Chenier	**Umberto Giordano**
Appalachian Spring	**Aaron Copland**
avant-garde operas of great length	**Robert Wilson**

Beatrix Cenci	**Alberto Ginastera**
Bohemian Folk Dances	**Leos Janacek**
Bolero	**Maurice Ravel**
Brigg Fair	**Frederick Delius**
Carmina Burana	**Carl Orff**
Carnival of Animals	**Camille Saint-Saëns**
Caucasian Sketches	**Michael Ipolitoff-Ivanoff**
Cavalleria Rusticana	**Pietro Mascagni**
Cave of the Winds	**Lukas Foss**
Crétion de Monde	**Darius Milhaud**
Crown Imperial coronation march	**William Walton**
De Profundis	**Arnold Schönberg**
Einstein on the Beach	**Philip Glass**
Enigma Variations	**Edward Elgar**
Etudes Australes	**John Cage**
Finlandia	**Jean Sibelius**
Fountains of Rome	**Ottorino Respighi**
Grand Canyon Suite	**Ferde Grofé**
Gymnopédies	**Erik Satie**
Hansel and Gretel	**Englebert Humperdinck**
Hungarian Folk Songs	**Béla Bartók**
Ice Break	**Michael Tippett**
Kleine Kammermusik	**Paul Hindemith**
Kol Nidrei	**Max Bruch**
Lady Macbeth of Mzensk	**Dmitri Shostakovich**
Lark Ascending	**Ralph Vaughan Williams'**
Le Sacre du Printemps (Rite of Spring)	**Igor Stravinsky**
Les Biches	**Francis Poulenc**
Madame Butterfly and *Tosca*	**Giacomo Puccini**
Manon	**Jules Massenet**
Mary, Queen of Scots	**Thea Musgrave**
Merry Mount Suite	**Howard Hanson**
Merry Widow	**Franz Lehár**
Mother of Us All	**Virgil Thomson**
Much Ado About Nothing	**Erich Wolfgang Korngold**
New England Holidays	**Charles Ives**
New World Symphony	**Antonin Dvorák**
Nights in the Gardens of Spain	**Manuel de Falla**
Nixon in China	**John Adams**
Peter and the Wolf and *Love of Three Oranges*	**Sergei Prokofiev**
Peter Grimes	**Benjamin Britten**
Pélleas and Mélisande	**Gabriel Fauré**
Planets	**Gustav Holst**
Plow That Broke the Plains	**Virgil Thomson**
Prelude in C Sharp Minor	**Sergei Rachmaninoff**
Prélude à l'àprès-midi d'un faune	**Claude Debussy**
Prometheus	**Alexander Scriabin**
Psalmus Hungaricus	**Zoltán Kodály**

Pulsations	Iao Schifrin
Rhapsody in Blue and *Porgy and Bess*	George Gershwin
Romantic Symphony	Anton Bruckner
Sabre Dance	Aram Khachaturian
Scheherazade and the *Russian Easter Overture*	Nikolai Rimsky-Korsakoff
Schelomo (Hebrew Rhapsody)	Ernest Bloch
Skaters	Emil Waldteufel
Song of the Earth and *Symphony of a Thousand*	Gustav Mahler
Sorcerer's Apprentice	Paul Dukas
Syringa	Elliott Carter
Through the Looking Glass	Deems Taylor
Thursday for Light	Karlheinz Stockhausen
Thus Spake Zarathustra	Richard Strauss
Wozzeck	Alban Berg

Modern Conductors

Among conductors of the 20th century, who . . . ?

led the Utah Orchestra for over 30 years	Maurice Abravanel
led Manchester's (UK) Hallé and in Houston	John Barbirolli
founded Britain's Royal Philharmonic Orchestra	Thomas Beecham
is a popular conductor who wrote *West Side Story*	Leonard Bernstein
managed the Metropolitan Opera for 22 years	Rudolf Bing
conducts, often for his wife, Joan Sutherland	Richard Bonynge
was the 1st woman conductor at London's Royal Philharmonic and the Boston Symphony	Nadia Boulanger
was NY Philharmonic conductor 1971–77	Pierre Boulez
conducted at the Metropolitan from 1976	Sarah Caldwell
led at the Met and the NY Symphony for decades	Walter Damrosch
led the Boston Pops Orchestra for almost 50 years	Arthur Fiedler
was the premier mid-20th-c. German conductor	Wilhelm Furtwängler

conducted the Los Angeles Philharmonic from 1978	**Carlo Maria Giulini**
led Amsterdam's Concertgebouw Orchestra	**Bernard Haitink**
was Carson's early musical director on *Tonight*	**Skitch Henderson**
was the key mid-20th-c. music and dance impresario	**Sol Hurok**
was a German conductor in Los Angeles in WWII	**Otto Klemperer**
was the Boston Symphony's Russian-born leader	**Serge Koussevitzky**
was a German conductor in NY, Rochester, and Boston	**Erich Leinsdorf**
was the Metropolitan's musical director from 1975	**James Levine**
led the Cleveland Orchestra for a decade	**Lorin Maazel**
recorded much with London's St.-Martin-in-the-Fields	**Neville Marriner**
conducted the NY Philharmonic from 1978	**Zubin Mehta**
led the Philadelphia Orchestra for over 40 years	**Eugene Ormandy**
is the longtime Boston Symphony conductor	**Seiji Ozawa**
led at Cincinnati, Pittsburgh, Chicago, and NY's Met	**Fritz Reiner**
is a Russian-born cellist, conductor in Washington	**Mstislav Rostropovich**
was linked with the NYC Opera from 1943	**Julius Rudel**
led the Chicago Symphony from 1969	**Georg Solti**
conducted the music for *Fantasia*	**Leopold Stokowski**
led the Cleveland Symphony for 24 years	**George Széll**
founded and led the NBC Symphony	**Arturo Toscanini**
was longtime conductor of the Berlin Philharmonic	**Herbert von Karajan**
was a German-Jewish conductor in the US in WWII	**Bruno Walter (Schlesinger)**
succeeded Fiedler at the Boston Pops	**John Williams**

Modern Classical Singers

Among classical singers working in the 20th century, who . . . ?

was the black contralto once barred by the DAR	Marian Anderson
recorded Mahler's *Kindertoten-lieder* in 1975	Janet Baker
was the acclaimed Swedish tenor at the Met	Jussi Bjoerling
made her Met debut in a notable 1965 *Faust*	Montserrat Caballé
was the popular mid-20th-c. dramatic soprano	Maria Callas
was the popular early-20th-c. Italian tenor	Enrico Caruso
was the great early-20th-c. Russian bass	Feodor Challapin
was the famed British counter-tenor	Alfred Deller
is the premier late-20th-c. Spanish tenor	Placido Domingo
recorded acclaimed Brunhilde selections in 1961	Eileen Farrell
is a key late-20th-c. baritone and lieder singer	Dietrich Fischer-Dieskau
was a Norwegian Wagnerian soprano at the Met	Kirsten Flagstad
was an early-20th-c. Italian coloratura soprano	Amelita Galli-Curci
sang notably in Houston's *Falstaff*	Donald Gramm
is a late-20th-c. US-born mezzo-soprano	Marilyn Horne
was a mid-20th-c. German soprano and lieder singer	Lotte Lehmann
was the 19th-c. "Swedish Nightingale"	Jenny Lind
was a premier Irish tenor, who sang with Kreisler	John McCormack
was an early-20th-c. Australian coloratura soprano	Nellie Melba
was a mid-20th-c. Danish Wagnerian tenor	Lauritz Melchior
was a leading US-born Met baritone 1945–73	Robert Merrill
sang notably in the Metropoli-tan's *Thaïs*	Sherrill Milnes
starred in the Metropolitan's 1970's Ring cycle	Birgit Nilsson

is a wide-ranging late-20th-c. soprano	**Jessye Norman**
is the Italian tenor often singing with Sutherland	**Luciano Pavarotti**
sang notably in *Death in Venice*	**Peter Pears**
was the US-born longtime Met tenor and radio star	**Jan Peerce**
was a French-born coloratura soprano at the Met	**Lily Pons**
is a US-born lyric soprano at the Met for 24 years	**Leontyne Price**
was the early-20th-c. Austrian contralto in the US	**Ernestine Schumann-Heink**
was a German-born, mid-20th-c. lyric soprano	**Elisabeth Schwarzkopf**
led the NYC Opera, earlier their star soprano	**Beverly Sills**
is the Australian bel canto soprano of the late 20th c.	**Joan Sutherland**
was the early-20th-c. Austrian linked with Lehar	**Richard Tauber**
was the Italian soprano who reopened La Scala in 1946	**Renata Tebaldi**
sang at Charles and Diana's wedding	**Kiri Te Kanawa**
was the Met's main baritone 1925–50	**Lawrence Tibbett**
was the US-born tenor, friend, and rival of Peerce	**Richard Tucker**
sang notably in the Metropolitan's *Peter Grimes*	**Jon Vickers**
emigré soprano, married to Rostropovich	**Galina Vishnevskaya**

Modern Classical Instrumentalists

(See also Modern Conductors)

Among classical intrumentalists working in the 20th century, who . . . ?

made the harmonica also a classical instrument	**Larry Adler**
is the Chilean-born piano virtuoso	**Claudio Arrau**
is the Russian-born pianist, often with Perlman	**Vladimir Ashkenazy**

is the pianist-conductor married to Du Pré	Daniel Barenboim
played the organ Sunday mornings on CBS radio	E. Power Biggs
is the popular British classical guitarist	Julian Bream
was a Spanish cellist, refugee from Franco	Pablo Casals
won the 1958 Moscow Tchaikovsky Piano Competition	Van Cliburn
is the cellist who died of multiple sclerosis	Jacqueline de Pré
was the Russian-born violinist in the US 1911–67	Mischa Elman
is the late-20th-c. most popular flautist	James Galway
was the USSR's premier mid-20th-c. pianist	Emil Gilels
was the reclusive pianist who died untimely	Glenn Gould
is the Russian-born violinist in the US from 1917	Jascha Heifetz
gave popular WWII piano concerts in London	Myra Hess
was the Russian-born pianist who played into his 80's	Vladimir Horowitz
is the pianist who often plays with Stern and Rose	Eugène Istomin
was a premier violinist, often with McCormack	Fritz Kreisler
is the key cellist who debuted in 1967	Kyung-Wha Chung
was the premier mid-20th-c. harpsichordist	Wanda Landowska
is a well-known Spanish pianist	Alicia de Larrocha
were Russian-born pianists who taught at Juiliard	Rosina and Josef Lhevinne
is the Chinese-French-American premier cellist	Yo-Yo Ma
played violin on *West Meets East,* with Shankar	Yehudi Menuhin
is the Russian-born violinist linked with Horowitz	Nathan Milstein
invented a synthesizer to make music electronically	Robert Moog
was the Soviet violinist who debuted in the US in 1955	David Oistrakh
was the early-20th-c. Polish pianist and patriot	Ignace Paderewski
won the 1972 Leeds piano competition	Murray Perahia

is the premier Israeli-born violinist who overcame polio	**Itzhak Perlman**
was the Russian-born cellist in the US from WWII	**Gregor Piatigorsky**
is the French-born flute virtuoso	**Jean-Pierre Rampal**
is the cellist who often plays with Stern and Istomin	**Leonard Rose**
was the Polish-born pianist who played into his 90's	**Arthur Rubinstein**
was the premier 20th-c. classical guitarist	**Andrés Segovia**
is the key pianist linked with the Curtis Institute	**Rudolf Serkin**
played sitar on *West Meets East*, with Menuhin	**Ravi Shankar**
sparked the Carnegie Hall restoration, a violinist	**Isaac Stern**
is the black pianist linked with Gershwin and Liszt	**Andre Watts**
is the violinist who headed the Curtis Institute	**Efrem Zimbalist**
is the Israeli-born violinist-violist	**Pinchas Zukerman**

Pop and Rock Musicians

(See also Jazz and Blues Musicians; also Country and Folk Musicians)

Among modern popular, rock, and country singers, instrumentalists, and composers, who did . . . ?

Alive!	**Kiss**
"Allison"	**Elvis Costello**
American Pie	**Don McLean**
Annie as composers	**Charles Strouse** and **Martin Charnin**
anti-gay campaign, a pop singer	**Anita Bryant**
Anything Goes as composer	**Cole Porter**
Aquarius/Let the Sun Shine In	**Fifth Dimension**
Are You Experienced	**Jimi Hendrix**
"As Nasty as You Wanna Be"	**Live Crew**
Arthur Godfrey's TV show	**McGuire Sisters**
"At Seventeen"	**Janis Ian**
"At the Hop"	**Danny and the Juniors**
Atlantic Crossing	**Rod Stewart**
Babes in Toyland as composer	**Victor Herbert**
Back in the High Life	**Steve Winwood**
Band-Aid concert for African relief	**Bob Geldof**

"Beat It"	Michael Jackson
Blow by Blow	Jeff Beck
"Blueberry Hill"	Fats Domino
Born in the USA	Bruce Springsteen
"Born to Be Wild"	Steppenwolf
Breakin' Away	Al Jarreau
"Breaking Up Is Hard to Do"	Neil Sedaka
"Bridge over Troubled Waters"	Paul Simon and Art Garfunkel
"California Dreamin' "	The Mamas and the Papas
"Candy Man"	Sammy Davis, Jr.
"Can't Take My Eyes Off You"	Frankie Valli
"Catch a Falling Star," the Singing Barber	Perry Como
"Champagne Music" on early TV	Lawrence Welk
"Chantilly Lace"	The Big Bopper
Chariots of Fire theme	Vangelis (Papathanassious)
Cheap Thrills with Big Brother and the Holding Company	Janis Joplin
"Chelsea Morning" as composer-singer	Joni Mitchell
"Cherish"	The Association
"Chestnuts Roasting on an Open Fire"	Nat "King" Cole
children's songs, from Canada	Raffi
"Close to You"	Carpenters
clowning with music on early TV	Spike Jones
Colgate Comedy Hour as singer-host	Gordon MacRae
Colour by Numbers with the Culture Club	Boy George
comic piano routines, as on TV	Victor Borge
"Control"	Janet Jackson
"Da Doo Ron Ron"	The Crystals
"Dancin' in the Streets"	Martha and the Vandellas
Dancing on the Ceiling	Lionel Ritchie
Different Drum	Linda Ronstadt
Divine Miss M	Bette Midler
"Do You Believe in Magic"	Lovin' Spoonful
"Doctor My Eyes"	Jackson Browne
"Dominique," the Singing Nun	Soeur Sourire
Double Fantasy with Lennon	Yoko Ono
"Downtown"	Petula Clark
"Everybody Loves Somebody"	Dean Martin
"Every Breath You Take"	The Police, incl. Sting
Everyday People	Sly and the Family Stone
Exodus and other two-piano movie themes	Ferrante and Teicher
"Ferry Cross the Mersey"	Gerry and the Pacemakers
52nd Street	Billy Joel
Fillmore East, NYC's 1960's rock promoter	Bill Graham

"For What It's Worth"	**Buffalo Springfield**
"For Your Love"	**The Yardbirds**
Funny Girl	**Jules Styne**
"Games People Play"	**Blood, Sweat, and Tears**
"Georgia on My Mind" as composer	**Hoagy Carmichael**
"Georgy Girl"	**The Seekers**
Gift from a Flower	**Donovan (Leitch)**
Gigi's score	**André Previn**
Girl from Ipanema	**Astrud Gilberto**
"Girls Just Want to Have Fun"	**Cyndi Lauper**
"Give My Regards to Broadway" as writer	**George M. Cohan**
"God Bless America" and "White Christmas" as writer	**Irving Berlin**
"God Bless America," making it a hit	**Kate Smith**
"Goldfinger"	**Shirley Bassey**
"Good Vibrations"	**Beach Boys**
Graceland with Paul Simon	**Miriam Makeba**
Gratitude	**Earth, Wind and Fire**
"Great Balls of Fire"	**Jerry Lee Lewis**
"Great Pretender"	**Platters**
Guys and Dolls as writer	**Frank Loesser**
"Heart of Glass"	**Deborah "Blondie" Harry**
Heart of Saturday Night	**Tom Waits**
"Heartbreak Hotel"	**Elvis Presley**
Heartlight	**Neil Diamond**
Heavy Weather	**Weather Report**
Hello, Dolly as composer	**Jerry Herman**
"Higher Plane"	**Al Green**
Hillbilly Jazz	**Rick Ulman**
Honey in the Horn	**Al Hirt**
"House of the Rising Sun," led by Eric Burdon	**The Animals**
"Hungry Like the Wolf"	**Duran Duran**
"Hurt So Good"	**John Cougar**
Hysteria	**Def Leppard**
"I Am Woman"	**Helen Reddy**
"I Can't Get Next to You"	**Temptations**
"(I Can't Get No) Satisfaction" with Mick Jagger	**Rolling Stones**
"I'd Like to Teach the World to Sing"	**The New Seekers**
"I Feel for You"	**Chaka Khan**
"If You Knew Susie"	**Eddie Cantor**
"I Got You Babe"	**Sonny and Cher**
"I Heard It Through the Grapevine"	**Marvin Gaye**
"I Just Want to Be Your Everything"	**Andy Gibb**

"I Left My Heart in San Franciso"	Tony Bennett
"I'll Be Seeing You" as composer	Sammy Fain
"I'll See You Again" as writer	Noel Coward
"I Love You Truly"	Carrie Jacobs Bond
I'm Leaving It All Up to You	Marie and Donny Osmond
"I'm So Excited"	Pointer Sisters
In the Dark	Grateful Dead
"In the Still of the Night"	The Five Satins
"I Want to Dance with Somebody"	Whitney Houston
"Jamming" with the Wailers	Bob Marley
"Joy to the World"	Three Dog Night
Just Like Old Times	Ink Spots
"Killing Me Softly with His Song"	Roberta Flack
La Bamba, making it a hit	Richie Valens
"La Vie en Rose"	Edith Piaf
Latin music on early TV	Xavier Cugat
Lawrence Welk TV show	Lennon Sisters
"Let Me Be There"	Olivia Newton-John
"Let's Dance"	David Bowie
"Light My Fire" with Jim Morrison	The Doors
"Light My Fire"	Jose Feliciano
Like a Virgin	Madonna
"Little Bit Me, a Little Bit You"	Monkees
Little Night Music, as composer	Stephen Sondheim
"Little Old Lady from Pasadena"	Jan & Dean
"Lollipops and Roses"	Jack Jones
"Lookin' Out My Back Door"	Creedence Clearwater Revival
"Love Letters in the Sand"	Pat Boone
Love's Only Love	Engelbert Humperdinck
Love Will Keep Us Together	Captain and Tennille
Masquerade	George Benson
Me Myself and I	Joan Armatrading
"Memories" in Broadway's *Cats*	Betty Buckley
"Midnight Train to Georgia" with the Pips	Gladys Knight
"Moon River"	Andy Williams
"Moon River" as composer	Henry Mancini
Motown hits with the Supremes	Diana Ross
"Mrs. Brown You've Got a Lovely Daughter"	Herman's Hermits
Music Man	Meredith Willson
"My Evening Star"	Lillian Russell
My Fair Lady with Lerner	Frederick Loewe
"My Mammy"	Al Jolson
"My Old Kentucky Home" as 19th-c. writer	Stephen Foster
Nel Blu Dipinto Di Blu (Volare)	Domenico Modugno
New Year's Eve on early TV	Guy Lombardo
"Nick of Time"	Bonnie Raitt

No Jacket Required	**Phil Collins**
No, No, Nanette	**Vincent Youmans**
"Old Cape Cod"	**Patti Page**
"Old Man River" in *Show Boat*	**Paul Robeson**
Oliver! as composer-writer	**Lionel Bart**
On a Clear Day . . . with Lerner	**Burton Lane**
"One Fine Day" as composer	**Carole King**
"On the Banks of the Wabash Far Away" as composer	**Paul Dresser**
"Ooh, Baby, Baby" with the Miracles	**Smokey Robinson**
"Our Love"	**Natalie Cole**
Pal Joey as lyricist with Rodgers	**Lorenz Hart**
"Papa's Got a Brand New Bag"	**James Brown**
"Paper Doll"	**Mills Brothers**
Phantom of the Opera as composer	**Andrew Lloyd-Webber**
pianist fond of sequins and candelabras	**Liberace**
Picture This with the News	**Huey Lewis**
Pins and Needles as writer	**Harold Rome**
Pirates	**Rickie Lee Jones**
"Proud Mary" with Tina	**Ike Turner**
Purple Rain	**Prince**
"Raindrops Keep Falling on My Head"	**B. J. Thomas**
Raising Hell	**Run-D. M. C.**
Rapture	**Anita Baker**
"Reach Out and I'll Be There"	**The Four Tops**
Red Octopus	**Jefferson Starship**
"Respect"	**Aretha Franklin**
"Right Stuff"	**New Kids on the Block**
"Rock Around the Clock" with the Comets	**Bill Haley**
Rose Marie as composer	**Rudolf Friml**
"Rum and Coca Cola" in WWII	**Andrews Sisters**
Rumours	**Fleetwood Mac**
"Runaway"	**Del Shannon**
"Sad Songs"	**Elton John**
satirical songs in the 1950's and 60's	**Tom Lehrer**
Saturday Night Fever's music	**Bee Gees**
"Save the Last Dance for Me"	**The Drifters**
"School's Out"	**Alice Cooper**
Second Helping	**Lynyrd Skynyrd**
"Sentimental Journey" with his "band of renown"	**Les Brown**
Sergeant Pepper's Lonelyhearts Club Band	**Beatles (Paul McCartney, John Lennon, George Harrison, and Ringo Starr)**
"Shadows of the Night"	**Pat Benatar**

"Shake, Rattle and Roll"	Big Joe Turner
"She Works Hard for the Money"	Donna Summer
Sheik Yerbouli with the Mothers of Invention	Frank Zappa
"Sherry"	The Four Seasons
Show Boat as a torch singer	Helen Morgan
Show Boat, with Hammerstein	Jerome Kern
Silkroad	Kitaro
"Sing Along" shows on early TV	Mitch Miller
"Singing Lady" on early radio and TV	Irene Wicker
"Ski Trails"	Jo Stafford
"Snowbird"	Anne Murray
So	Peter Gabriel
"Soldier Boy"	The Shirelles
"Soul Man"	Sam and Dave
South Pacific as composer, with Hammerstein	Richard Rodgers
South Pacific as lyricist with Rodgers	Oscar Hammerstein II
Splish Splash	Bobby Darin
"Stagger Lee"	Lloyd Price
"Stairway to Heaven"	Led Zeppelin
Star Wars theme	John Williams
Stars and Stripes Forever as composer	John Philip Sousa
"Stop! In the Name of Love"	The Supremes
Stormy Weather	Lena Horne
"Strangers in the Night"	Frank Sinatra
Student Prince as composer	Sigmund Romberg
"Suite: Judy Blue Eyes"	Crosby, Stills, Nash, and Young
Summer Place theme	Percy Faith
"Sweet Dreams (Are Made of This)" with the Eurhythmics	Annie Lennox
Taste of Honey with the Tijuana Brass	Herb Alpert
Tea for the Tillerman	Cat Stevens (Yusif Islam)
"Tears on my Pillow" with the Imperials	Little Anthony
Teenage Idol	Ricky Nelson
"Teenager in Love" with the Belmonts	Dion (Di Mucci)
"Thank Heaven for Little Girls"	Maurice Chevalier
"That'll Be the Day" with the Crickets	Buddy Holly
"That's What Friends Are For"	Dionne Warwick
"There's No Business Like Show Business"	Ethel Merman
"These Boots Are Made for Walkin' "	Nancy Sinatra

Third Man's zither theme	**Anton Karas**
This One's for You	**Barry Manilow**
Three-Penny Opera with Brecht	**Kurt Weill**
"Time in a Bottle"	**Jim Croce**
Time of My Life	**Bill Medley** and **Jennifer Warnes**
Toast to Those Who Are Gone	**Phil Ochs**
"Turn! Turn! Turn!"	**The Byrds**
"Tutti Frutti"	**Little Richard (Penniman)**
"Twelfth of Never"	**Johnny Mathis**
"Twist"	**Chubby Checker**
Unforgettable Fire	**U2**
Up a Lazy River	**Si Zentner**
"Up Where We Belong"	**Joe Cocker** and **Jennifer Warnes**
"Vagabond Lover"	**Rudy Vallee**
Victory at Sea music for TV, as composer	**Robert Russell Bennett**
Vox Humana	**Kenny Loggins**
"Wake Up Little Susie"	**Everly Brothers**
"Walk On By" as composer	**Burt Bacharach**
"Waltzing Matilda" as writer	**A. B. (Banjo) Paterson**
War Babies	**Daryl Hall** and **John Oates**
"Way We Were"	**Barbra Streisand**
We Are the World video, as producer	**Quincy Jones**
"Wear Some Flowers in Your Hair"	**Scott McKenzie**
We Got Us	**Steve Lawrence** and **Eydie Gormé**
"What a Feeling"	**Irene Cara**
"What a Fool Believes"	**Doobie Brothers**
"What's Love Got to Do with It"	**Tina Turner**
"What's New, Pussycat"	**Tom Jones**
"When a Man Loves a Woman"	**Percy Sledge**
"White Christmas" in the movie	**Bing Crosby**
Whiter Shade of Pale	**Procol Harum**
"Who Do You Love"	**Bo Diddley**
"Who's Sorry Now" as writer	**Harry Ruby**
"Why Do Fools Fall in Love"	**Frankie Lymon**
"Will the Circle Be Unbroken"	**Nitty Gritty Dirt Band**
"Winchester Cathedral"	**New Vaudeville Band**
"Wooly Bully" with the Pharaohs	**Sam the Sham**
"You Are the Sunshine of My Life"	**Stevie Wonder**
"You Can't Kill Rock 'n Roll"	**Ozzy Osbourne**
"You Light Up My Life"	**Debby Boone**
"(You're) Having my Baby"	**Paul Anka**
"You're So Vain"	**Carly Simon**
"You Send Me"	**Sam Cooke**

"You've Got a Friend"   **James Taylor**
"You've Lost That Lovin'   **Righteous Brothers**
    Feeling"

Country and Folk Musicians

(See also Pop and Rock Musicians; also Jazz and Blues Musicians)

Among modern country singers, instrumentalists, and
composers, who did . . . ?

"Ain't No More Cane on the   **Odetta**
    Brazos"
"Alabama Jubilee"   **Roy Clark**
"Alice's Restaurant"   **Arlo Guthrie**
Always on My Mind   **Willie Nelson**
"Amanda"   **Waylon Jennings**
"Are the Good Times Really   **Merle Haggard**
    Over"
"Baby Don't Get Hooked on Me"   **Mac Davis**
"Back in the Saddle Again"   **Gene Autry**
"Battle of New Orleans"   **Johnny Horton**
"Big Bad John"   **Jimmy Dean**
"Blue Suede Shoes"   **Carl Perkins**
Bluegrass Boys, as leader   **Bill Monroe**
bluegrass banjo songs   **Lester Flatt** and **Earl Scruggs**
blues and yodeling combined   **Jimmie Rodgers**
Bobbie Sue   **Oak Ridge Boys**
"Break It to Me Gently"   **Juice Newton**
"By the Time I Get to Phoenix"   **Glen Campbell**
Carry Me Back   **Statler Brothers**
"Cat's in the Cradle"   **Harry Chapin**
"Coal Miner's Daughter"   **Loretta Lynn**
"Day-O"   **Harry Belafonte**
"Elite Hotel"   **Emmy Lou Harris**
Everytime I Feel the Spirit   **Mahalia Jackson**
"Every Which Way But Loose"   **Eddie Rabbitt**
"Feel Like I'm Fixin' to Die" with   **Country Joe (McDonald)**
    the Fish
"First Time Ever I Saw Your   **Ewan MacColl**
    Face" as writer
folk music field recordings   **Alan Lomax**
"Forever and Ever, Amen"   **Randy Travis**
"Free and Equal Blues"   **Josh White**
Funny Way of Laughin'   **Burl Ives**
"Gambler"   **Kenny Rogers**
Grand Ole Opry with a price tag   **Minnie Pearl**
    on her hat

Had a Dream (For the Heart)	**Naomi** and **Wynnona Judd**
Happy Trails to You with the Sons of the Pioneers	**Roy Rogers** and **Dale Evans**
"Harper Valley P. T. A."	**Jeannie C. Riley**
Hello Darlin'	**Conway Twitty**
"Help Me Make It Through the Night" as writer	**Kris Kristofferson**
"Help Me Make It Through the Night"	**Sammi Smith**
"If I Were a Carpenter" with Cash	**June Carter**
"I Walk the Line"	**Johnny Cash**
"I'm Moving On"	**Hank Snow**
"I'm Walking the Floor Over You"	**Ernest Tubb**
"Is It Really Over"	**Jim Reeves**
"I've Been Loving You Too Long"	**Otis Redding**
"Johnny B. Goode"	**Chuck Berry**
"King of the Road"	**Roger Miller**
"Little Green Apples"	**O. C. Smith**
"Lost in the Fifties Tonight"	**Ronnie Milsap**
"Make the World Go Away"	**Eddy Arnold**
Midnight Special together	**Brownie McGhee** and **Sonny Terry**
Mountain Music	**Alabama**
"9 to 5"	**Dolly Parton**
"Now That the Buffalo's Gone"	**Buffy Sainte-Marie**
"Ode to Billie Joe"	**Bobbie Gentry**
"Oh, Pretty Woman"	**Roy Orbison**
On a Night Like This	**Buckwheat Zydeco**
"Puff, the Magic Dragon"	**Peter, Paul and Mary**
"Send in the Clowns"	**Judy Collins**
"Silver Dagger"	**Joan Baez**
Sixteen Tons	**Tennessee Ernie Ford**
"Sleeping Single in a Double Bed"	**Barbara Mandrell**
Smoky Mountain Boys as founder	**Roy Acuff**
"Stand By Your Man"	**Tammy Wynette**
Sure Feels Like Love	**Gatlin Brothers**
"Sweet Dreams"	**Patsy Cline**
"Take This Job and Shove It"	**Johnny Paycheck**
"Thank God I'm a Country Boy"	**John Denver**
"That Was the Last Thing on My Mind" as writer	**Tom Paxton**
"There Goes My Everything"	**Jack Greene**
"This Land Is Your Land" with Pete Seeger	**Weavers**
"This Land Is Your Land" as writer-singer	**Woody Guthrie**

Times They Are A'Changin' as singer-writer	**Bob Dylan**
We Must Believe in Magic	**Crystal Gayle**
"We'll Sing in the Sunshine"	**Gale Garnett**
"What Am I Gonna Do About You"	**Reba McEntire**
"Wonder Could I Live There Anymore"	**Charlie Pride**
"World Is Waiting for the Sunrise"	**Les Paul** and **Mary Ford**
"You Are My Sunshine"	**Tex Ritter**
"Your Cheatin' Heart"	**Hank Williams**

Jazz and Blues Musicians

(See also Pop and Rock Musicians; also Country and Folk Musicians)

Among jazz and blues singers, instrumentalists, and composers, who did . . . ?

"A-Tisket-a-Tasket"	**Ella Fitzgerald**
At the Golden Circle	**Ornette Coleman**
bandleader who hired Frank Sinatra in 1939	**Harry James**
Birds of Fire	**Mahavishnu Orchestra**
blues singer rediscovered in her 70's	**Alberta Hunter**
Blue Train	**John Coltrane**
"Body and Soul" as a jazz classic	**Coleman Hawkins**
Boogie Chillun	**John Lee Hooker**
Conversations with Myself	**Bill Evans**
Davenport Blues with his Rhythm Jugglers	**Leon Bismarck "Bix" Beiderbecke**
Desafinado	**Stan Getz**
Dixie Stompers, as leader in classic jazz	**Fletcher Henderson**
"Don't Worry, Be Happy"	**Bobby McFerrin**
"Downhearted Blues," The Empress	**Bessie Smith**
early jazz band including Armstrong	**Joe "King" Oliver**
Ebony Concerto, Stravinsky's work	**Woodrow "Woody" Herman**
"Every Day I Have the Blues"	**B. B. King**
"Georgia on my Mind" as singer	**Ray Charles (Robinson)**
"Goodnight Irene"	**Leadbelly**
Guitar from Ipanema	**Laurindo Almeida**

"Hello, Dolly" singing and trumpeting	**Louis "Satchmo" Armstrong**
"Honeysuckle Rose" as writer	**Thomas "Fats" Waller**
Hora Decubitis	**Charles Mingus**
"I'm Just Wild About Harry" as writer	**Euble Blake**
In a Silent Way	**Miles Davis**
Innovations in Modern Music Orchestra	**Stan Kenton**
Is That All There Is	**Peggy Lee**
Jazz Messengers, as leader	**Art Blakey**
jazz from the 1930's, two brothers	**Tommy** and **Jimmy Dorsey**
jazz quintet in 1949	**George Shearing**
"Jelly Roll," claiming to have invented jazz in 1902	**Ferdinand "Jelly Roll" Morton**
Let's Dance series on 1930's radio	**Benny Goodman**
Light as a Feather	**Chick Corea**
Looking Ahead	**Cecil Taylor**
Manhattan Wildlife Refuge	**Bill Watrous**
Mercy, Mercy together	**Julian "Cannonball"** and **Nat Adderly**
M. F. Horn	**Maynard Ferguson**
Minnie the Moocher	**Cab Calloway**
Modern Jazz Quartet, as leader	**Dave Brubeck**
"Mood Indigo"	**Duke Ellington**
"Natural Man"	**Lou Rawls**
Now's The Time Chucklebuck	**Charlie "Bird" Parker**
One O'Clock Jump, theme song	**William "Count" Basie**
Opus de Funk	**Horace Silver**
piano-less West-Coast jazz group	**Gerry Mulligan**
Piano Starts Here	**Art Tatum**
ragtime music used in *The Sting*	**Scott Joplin**
recordings of many blues greats	**John Hammond**
"Roll 'Em," the "first lady of Jazz"	**Mary Lou Williams**
"Rollin' Stone"	**Muddy Waters**
" 'Round Midnight" in 1944	**Thelonius Monk**
'Round Midnight, music for the movie	**Herbie Hancock**
'Round Midnight, portraying the saxophonist	**Dexter Gordon**
St. Louis Blues as writer	**W(illiam) C. Handy**
Strange Fruit, "Lady Day"	**Billie Holliday**
String of Pearls	**Glenn Miller**
That's All	**Mel Tormé**
Think of One	**Wynton Marsalis**
Toccata for Trumpet and Orchestra in 1947	**John Birks "Dizzy" Gillespie**

Trident	**(Alfred) McCoy Tyner (Sulaimon Saud)**
Valse Hot	**Theodore "Sonny" Rollins**
"Weather Bird" with Armstrong	**Earl "Fatha" Hines**
What Are You Doing the Rest of Your Life	**Sarah Vaughan**

Muses

Among the muses, daughters of the Greek gods Zeus and Mnemosyne, who was the muse of . . . ?

epic poetry and eloquence in general	**Calliope**
history	**Clio**
love poetry	**Erato**
lyric poetry	**Euterpe**
tragedy	**Melpomene**
sacred poetry	**Polyhymnia**
dancing and choral song	**Terpsichore**
comedy and idyllic poetry	**Thalia**
astronomy	**Urania**

Stage and Work Names

What are the real names of these people from show business and the visual arts . . . ?

Anouk Aimée	**Françoise Sorya**
Woody Allen	**Allen Stewart Konigsberg**
Julie Andrews	**Julia Elizabeth Wells**
Eve Arden	**Eunice Quedens**
Arletty	**Léonie Bathiat**
Fred Astaire	**Frederick Austerlitz**
Mary Astor	**Lucile Langhanke**
Lauren Bacall	**Betty Joan Perske**
Anne Bancroft	**Anna Maria Italiano**
Ann-Margret	**Ann-Margret Olsson**
Theda Bara	**Theodosia Goodman**
John Barbirolli	**Giovanni Battista Barbirolli**
Brigitte Bardot	**Camille Javal**
Léon Bakst	**Lev Samoilovich Rosenberg**
Pat Benatar	**Patricia Andrejewski**
Tony Bennett	**Anthony Benedetto**
Jack Benny	**Benjamin Kubelsky**
Irving Berlin	**Israel Baline**

Sarah Bernhardt	**Rosine Bernard**
Dirk Bogarde	**Derek Bentron Gaspart Ulric van den Bogaerde**
Pat Boone	**Charles Eugene Boone**
David Bowie	**David Robert Jones**
Boy George	**George Alan O'Dowd**
Joe Bob Briggs	**John Bloom**
Mel Brooks	**Melvin Kaminsky**
George Burns	**Nathan Birnbaum**
Richard Burton	**Richard Walter Jenkins**
Michael Caine	**Maurice Joseph Micklewhite**
Maria Callas	**Maria Kalogeropoulos**
Eddie Cantor	**Edward Israel Iskowitz**
Robert Capa	**André Friedmann**
Cher	**Cherilyn Sarkisian**
Van Cliburn	**Harvey Lavan Cliburn, Jr.**
Patsy Cline	**Virginia Patterson Hensley**
Lee J. Cobb	**Lee Jacoby**
Claudette Colbert	**Lily Claudette Chauchoin**
Alice Cooper	**Vincent Furnier**
Gary Cooper	**Frank Cooper**
Lou Costello	**Louis Cristillo**
Joan Crawford	**Lucille Le Sueur**
Tony Curtis	**Bernard Schwartz**
Bobby Darin	**Walden Robert Cassotto**
Doris Day	**Doris Kappelhoff**
Sandra Dee	**Alexandra Zuck**
John Denver	**Henry John Deutschendorf, Jr.**
Bo Derek	**Cathleen Collins**
Marlene Dietrich	**Marie Magdalene Dietrich von Losch**
Isak Dinesen	**Baroness Karen Dinesen Bilxen**
Kirk Douglas	**Issur Danielovitch,** later **Izzy Demsky**
Patty Duke	**Anna Marie Duke**
Bob Dylan	**Robert Zimmerman**
Douglas Fairbanks	**Douglas Ulman**
José Ferrer	**José Vincente Ferrer Otero y Cintrón**
W. C. Fields	**William Claude Dukinfield**
Ford Madox Ford	**Ford Madox Hueffer**
Joan Fontaine	**Joan de Havilland**
John Ford	**Sean Aloysius O'Fearna**
Redd Foxx	**John Sanford**
Connie Francis	**Concetta Franconero**
Greta Garbo	**Greta Gustafsson**
John Garfield	**Julius Garfinkle**
Judy Garland	**Frances Gumm**
James Garner	**James Baumgardner**
John Gilbert	**John Pringle**

Samuel Goldwyn	Samuel Goldfish
Robert Goulet	Stanley Appelbaum
Stewart Granger	James Stewart
Cary Grant	Alexander Archibald Leach
Jean Harlow	Harlean Carpenter
Rex Harrison	Reginald Carey
Laurence Harvey	Larushka Mischa Skikne
Rita Hayworth	Margarita Cansino
Audrey Hepburn	Edda Hepburn van Heemstra
Pee-Wee Herman	Paul Rubenfield
William Holden	William Franklin Beedle
Judy Holliday	Judith Tuvim
Harry Houdini	Ehrich Weiss
Leslie Howard	Leslie Stainer
Rock Hudson	Roy Harold Fitzgerald
Engelbert Humperdinck	Arnold Dorsey
Burl Ives	Burl Icle Ivanhoe
Robert Joffrey	Abdulla Jaffa Anver Bey Khan
Elton John	Reginald Kenneth Dwight
Al Jolson	Asa Yoelson
Tom Jones	Thomas Woodward
Boris Karloff	William Henry Pratt
Danny Kaye	David Daniel Kaminsky
Elia Kazan	Elia Kazanjoglou
Buster Keaton	Joseph Francis Keaton
Chaka Khan	Yvette Stevens
Cheryl Ladd	Cheryl Stoppelmoor
Veronica Lake	Constance Ockleman
Hedy Lamarr	Hedwig Kiesler
Dorothy Lamour	Dorothy Kaumeyer
Mario Lanza	Alfredo Arnold Cocozza
Stan Laurel	Arthur Jefferson
Leadbelly	Huddie Ledbetter
Le Corbusier	Charles Édouard Jeanneret
Gypsy Rose Lee	Rose Louise Hovick
Peggy Lee	Norma Dolores Egstrom
Vivien Leigh	Vivian Mary Hartley
Jerry Lewis	Joseph Levitch
Liberace	Wladziu Valentino Liberace
Herbert Lom	Herbert Charles Angelo Kuchacevich ze Schluderpacheru
Carole Lombard	Jane Peters
Sophia Loren	Sofie Scicolone
Bela Lugosi	Bela Ferenc Blasko
Shirley MacLaine	Shirley Maclean Beaty
Madonna	Madonna Louise Ciccone
Barry Manilow	Barry Alan Pincus
Dean Martin	Dino Crocetti
Chico Marx	Leonard Marx
Groucho Marx	Julius Marx

Gummo Marx	**Milton Marx**
Harpo Marx	**Adolph Marx**
Zeppo Marx	**Herbert Marx**
Viriginia Mayo	**Virginia May Jones**
Nellie Melba	**Helen Porter Mitchell**
Ethel Merman	**Ethel Zimmerman**
Ray Milland	**Reginald Truscott-Jones**
Carmen Miranda	**Maria de Carmo Mirando de Cunha**
Joni Mitchell	**Roberta Joan Anderson**
Marilyn Monroe	**Norma Jean Baker**
Yves Montand	**Ivo Levi**
Paul Muni	**Muni Weisengreund**
Mike Nichols	**Michael Peschowsky**
Kim Novak	**Marilyn Novak**
Annie Oakley	**Phoebe Anne Oakley Mozee**
Merle Oberon	**Estelle Merle O'Brien Thompson**
Molly O'Day	**LaVerne Williamson**
Maureen O'Hara	**Maureen Fitzsimmons**
Jack Palance	**Walter Palanuk**
Joseph Papp	**Joseph Papirofsky**
"Col." Tom Parker	**Andreas van Kuijk**
Minnie Pearl	**Sarah Ophelia Cannon**
Jan Peerce	**Jacob Pincus Perelmuth**
Edith Piaf	**Edith Giovanna Gassion**
Mary Pickford	**Gladys Mary Smith**
Lily Pons	**Alice Joséphine Pons**
Jane Powell	**Suzanne Burce**
Stephanie Powers	**Stefania Federklewicz**
Prince	**Prince Rogers Nelson**
Tony Randall	**Leonard Rosenberg**
Debbie Reynolds	**Mary Francis Reynolds**
Tex Ritter	**Woodward Maurice Ritter**
Larry Rivers	**Yitzroch Loiza Grossberg**
Edward G. Robinson	**Emanuel Goldenberg**
Ginger Rogers	**Virginia Katharine McMath**
Roy Rogers	**Leonard Slye**
Mickey Rooney	**Joe Yule, Jr.**
Susan St. James	**Susan Miller**
Randolph Scott	**Randolph Crane**
Mack Sennett	**Michael Sinott**
Omar Sharif	**Michael Shalhoub**
Martin Sheen	**Ramon Estevez**
Beverly Sills	**Belle Silverman**
Barbara Stanwyck	**Ruby Stevens**
Ringo Starr	**Richard Starkey**
Connie Stevens	**Concetta Ann Ingolia**
Sting	**George Sumner**
Donna Summer	**La Donna Gaines**
Richard Tauber	**Ernst Seiffert**
Robert Taylor	**Spangler Arlington Brough**

Danny Thomas	**Amos Jacobs**
Terry-Thomas	**Thomas Terry Hoar-Stevens**
Michael Todd	**Avrom Hirsch Goldbogen**
Sophie Tucker	**Sophia Abuzza**
Tina Turner	**Annie Mae Bullock**
Twiggy	**Lesley Hornby**
Richie Valens	**Ricardo Valenzuela**
Rudolph Valentino	**Rudolpho D'Antonguolla**
Rudy Vallee	**Hubert Prior Vallee**
Erich von Stroheim	**Hans Erich Maria Stroheim von Nordenwall**
Muddy Waters	**McKinley Morganfield**
John Wayne	**Marion Morrison**
Clifton Webb	**Webb Parmalee Hollenbeck**
Rebecca West	**Cicely Fairfield Andrews**
Mary Lou Williams	**Mary Elfrieda Scruggs**
Shelley Winters	**Shirley Schrift**
Stevie Wonder	**Stevland Morris**
Natalie Wood	**Natasha Gurdin**
Jane Wyman	**Sarah Jane Fulks**

Language of Dance

In the world of dance, what is the word or phrase for . . . ?

slow movements emphasizing grace and line, as in a classic pas de deux	**adagio**
a fast dance, with leaps, jumps, and turns	**allegro**
a German dance, from the French	**allemand**
a stance on one leg, with the other out straight	**arabesque**
a female ballet dancer	**ballerina** or **danseuse**
a ballet that tells a story in pantomime	**ballet d'action**
a masked ball	**bal masqué**
a Spanish dance in ¾ time	**bolero**
beating one leg against the other in a ballet leap	**cabriole**
the dance painted by Toulouse-Lautrec	**can-can**
a rhythmic Latin American ballroom dance	**cha-cha**
a fast-paced 1920's dance	**Charleston**
a type of quick, gliding step	**chassé**

a heavy, stamping folk dance, as in wooden shoes	**clog dance**
a ballet company's ensemble of dancers	**corps de ballet**
a intricate dance, as at an 18th-c. formal ball	**cotillion** or **quadrille**
a greeting or salutation in a dance	**coupé**
a dance often portrayed in medieval art, in which death as a skeleton plays a part	**danse macabre** or **dance of death**
a male ballet dancer, from the French	**danseur**
a square-dance instruction to pass your partner, back to back, from the French dos à dos	**do-se-do**
a ballet leap with seeming suspension in air	**élévation**
touching or crossing the feet during a ballet leap	**entrechat**
a triple-time Spanish folk dance	**fandango**
a lively group dance in Provence	**farandole**
a folk dance from Spain's Andalusia	**flamenco**
a lively 16th–17th-c. French dance	**galliard**
a double-time dance, orig. by French peasants	**gavotte** or **bourrée**
a slow Cuban dance	**habañera**
an Israeli round dance	**hora**
an undulating Hawaiian dance	**hula**
a popular dance from *Me and My Girl*	**Lambeth Walk**
a 17th-c. French, pattern dance for couples	**minuet**
an English folk dance, often done in costume	**morris dance**
a ballet step	**pas de ballet**
an even walking step, in ballet	**pas de bourrée**
a ballet telling a story	**pas d'action** or **ballet d'action**
a dance performed by 2 people	**pas de deux**
a dance performed by 3 people	**pas de trois**
a dance performed by 1 person	**pas seul**
bullfight march, a Latin-American 2-step	**paso doble**
a twirling movement	**pirouette**
a lively round dance for couples, orig. Bohemian	**polka**

a promenading, stately Polish dance for couples	**polonaise**
partners joining hands and swinging in a circle	**pousette**
a corp's leading male dancer	**premier danseur**
a corp's leading female dancer	**premiere danseuse**
a French square dance	**quadrille**
a fast dance from Scotland, later Virginia	**reel**
a black Cuban dance, and its ballroom version	**rumba**
a Brazilian ballroom dance, with African origins	**samba**
a slow 17th- and 18th-c. European court dance	**saraband**
a folk dance from Spain's Catalonia	**sardana**
a solo ballet dancer	**soliste**
a Latin American 2/4 or 4/4 ballroom dance	**tango**
a quick-paced, whirling Italian dance	**tarantella**
a female dancer's short skirt	**tutu**
a 3/4 dance, with the 1st beat strongly accented	**waltz**
rhythmic heel stamping, as in a flamenco	**zapateado**

Language of Music

Types of Music

Among the various types of music, what is or are . . . . ?

the part of a church service sung or spoken by the priest and altar assistants	**accentus**
responsive singing, as in a church service	**antiphony**
an operatic song sung by a single voice	**aria**
music to be played at dawn	**aubade**
a song that tells a story, often passed by word of mouth from singer to singer	**ballad**
a Venetian gondolier's song	**barcarole**
a lullaby, in France	**berceuse**

banjo and guitar, folk improvisational music in the US South	**bluegrass**
a jazz style with lowered thirds and sevenths	**blues**
Brazilian music linked with the Gilbertos	**Bossa Nova**
comic or humorous music	**bouffe**
a Trinidad music style, often improvised	**calypso**
a work in which different voices sing a melody in the same or related key, starting at different times	**canon** *or* **round**
a elaborate instrumental and choral composition, with many solo parts	**cantata**
a nonmetrical song with its text from the Bible	**canticle**
a fixed melody in medieval Gregorian music	**cantus firmus**
a plain song, as in a medieval Gregorian chant	**cantus planus**
a song or lyric poem, from the Italian	**canzone**
a brief, often sentimental aria	**cavatina**
a song or ballad	**chanson**
a dirge or funeral song	**chant funèbre**
a concerto with two or more alternating solo parts	**concertante**
an orchestral work featuring one or more soloists	**concerto**
a pleasant, light, diverting composition	**divertissement**
a song beginning "Praise God from whom all blessings flow"	**doxology**
opera, in France	**drame lyrique**
a work for 2 voices or instruments	**duet** or **duo**
a piece of music written primarily for practice	**étude**
a spring song, in Germany	**Frühlingslied**
a work with melodic lines introduced in sequence and worked out contrapuntally	**fugue** (lt. **fuga**)
the medieval Catholic song sung in unison	**Gregorian chant** or **plainsong**
massively amplified rock music	**heavy metal**
a playful musical work	**humoresque**
a hymn sung at the beginning of a church service	**introit**

rhythmic, improvisational, indigenous US music	**jazz**
love songs, in German	**Liebeslieder**
a song or lyric	**lied**
music used in Christian church worship	**liturgical music**
a work for several voices, as in the 16th–17th c.	**madrigal**
several melodies combined for a unified performance	**medley**
a sacred musical work for unaccompanied voice	**motet**
a musical work for the evening	**nocturne** or **notturno**
a work for 8 voices or instruments	**octet**
music accompanying the offering of communion	**offertory**
a comic opera, in Italy	**opera buffa**
a serious opera, in Italy	**opera seria**
a work, in music often numbered	**opus**
a sacred musical work for voices and orchestra	**oratorio**
a song of thanksgiving or joy, from the Greek	**paean**
an introductory piece, esp. of a suite	**prelude**
a march played while people file in or out	**processional** or **recessional**
a work built around a known story	**program music**
a hymn or sacred song	**psalm**
a work for 4 voices or instruments	**quartet**
a work for 5 voices or instruments	**quintet**
an improvisational Hindu form of music	**raga**
an early form of jazz, with heavy syncopation	**ragtime**
Jamaican popular jazz	**reggae**
a musical work for a mass for the dead	**requiem mass**
a free-form composition, often based on folk themes	**rhapsody**
a work that repeats the main theme after each subordinate one	**rondo**
Latin American popular jazz	**salsa**
a light, humorous work, often in 3/4 time	**scherzo**

a lover's musical gift, also a half-suite, half-sonata	**serenade**
a work for 7 voices or instruments	**septet** or **septuor**
a work for 6 voices or instruments	**sextet** or **sestet**
a work with 3 varying parts, exposition, development, and recapitulation	**sonata**
a black American relgious folk song	**spiritual**
a work with several dances in related keys	**suite**
orchestral program music based on a theme	**symphonic** or **tone poem**
a long, sonatalike orchestral work	**symphony**
a popular song lamenting unrequited love	**torch song**
a work for 3 voices or instruments	**trio** or **terzet**
solo organ music before, after, or during a service	**voluntary**
a cradle song, in Germany	**Wiegenlied**

Musical Nuts and Bolts

Among the nuts and bolts of music, what is or are . . . ?

notes linked to others, played without a break	**appoggiato**
a grace note or note of embellishment	**appoggiatura**
tones in a chord played in succession, not at once	**arpeggio**
a bass accompaniament on the keyboard	**basso continuo** or **figured bass**
a progression of chords moving to a harmonic conclusion	**cadence**
a virtuosic section added as ornament	**cadenza**
a movable bar on a guitar neck to regulate pitch	**capotasto**
the standard scale including half-tones	**chromatic**
the symbol on a staff indicating the pitch	**clef**
a formal ending, often after a repeat	**coda**
the A above middle C, to which orchestra musicians tune their instruments	**concert pitch**

tones regarded as pleasantly harmonious and not requiring resolution	**consonant**
independent melodic lines that yet make harmony	**counterpoint** or **contrapunto**
a 32nd note	**demisemiquaver**
a melodic line sung higher than the main melody	**descant**
standard pitch, to the French	**diapason normal**
the standard 8-tone major or minor scale	**diatonic**
tones considered discordant and requiring resolution	**dissonant**
a single sustained tone, as in a bagpipe	**drone**
sounding the same, but written differently	**enharmonic**
a secondary tone produced by a main one	**harmonic** or **overtone**
physical analysis of musical sound	**harmonics**
a 64th note	**hemidemisemiquaver**
the main tone around which a work is built	**key**
a work's basic rhythmic unit, marked off by bars	**measure**
a device to mark time when practicing music	**metronome**
moving from one tonality to another with a regular chord progression	**modulation**
a work with one part, sung by 1 or more	**monody, homophony,** or **unison**
an essential passage, also an accompaniment	**obbligato**
arranging how the music will actually be played	**orchestration**
the actual frequency at which a tone is sounded	**pitch**
combining 2 or more melodic lines in counterpoint	**polyphony**
an 8th note	**quaver**
a verse or phrase repeated in a song or poem	**refrain**
the completion of a progression from dissonant to consonant— that is, traditional—tones or chords	**harmonic close**
a brief, repeated phrase, as in jazz	**riff**
the written parts for a musical work	**score**

the sign that indicates a repeat	**segno**
a whole note	**semibreve**
a 16th note	**semiquaver**
a shift of accent in a musical work, as in ragtime	**syncopation**
a sign to say hold a note to its full value	**tenuto**
musical shorthand using numbers for chords	**thorough bass**
shifting a work into a different key	**transposition**

Singing or Playing Styles

Among the various styles of singing, or playing what is or are . . . ?

a woman's low singing voice	**alto** or **contralto**
a male singing range between bass and tenor	**baritone**
the lowest male singing range	**bass**
a deep bass for comic opera passages	**basso buffo**
a very deep bass singing voice or singer	**basso profundo**
a vocal style of purity and finish, lit. beautiful song	**bel canto**
a showy performance, often technically difficult	**bravura**
a female singer, as in a French cabaret	**chanteuse**
a singer specializing in music with runs and trills	**coloratura**
an orchestra's leading string player	**concertmaster**
an adult male with a voice higher than tenor, comparable to the alto range in a woman's voice	**counter tenor**
singing in an unnaturally high pitch	**falsetto**
technical skill or dexterity in music, in Germany	**Fertigkeit**
making up music on the spot, though within certain general bounds	**improvisation**
choirmaster, in Italy	**maestro di cappella**
a woman's voice in range between soprano and alto	**mezzo-soprano**
a medieval musician; also a 19th-c. US variety show, often with "blacked" performers	**minstrel**

an opera's leading female singer	**prima donna** or **diva**
half-singing, half-speaking lines, as in an opera	**recitative**
jazz singing using nonsense syllables	**scat singing**
singing the scale, as with sol-fa syllables	**solfeggio, solfège,** or **vocalization**
the musical syllables do, re, mi, et al.	**solmisation syllables**
a woman's (and young boy's) highest singing range	**soprano**
the male singing range above baritone	**tenor**
a repeated, rapid alternation between 2 tones, also an extreme vibrato	**tremolo** or **-ulo**
pulsing minute variations in a sung or played tone	**vibrato**
rapid variations between normal voice and falsetto	**yodel**

Musical Directions

In the world of music, what word or phrase means to play or sing . . . ?

unaccompanied by instruments	**a cappella**
interpreting at the performer's discretion	**a capriccio**
slowly and carefully	**adagio**
with 2 instruments at once	**a due**
in an agitated manner	**agitato**
in quick common time, 2 beats for 4	**alla breve**
at a brisk, lively tempo (moderately briskly)	**allegro (allegretto)**
an octave higher than written	**all' ottava**
at a moderate speed	**andante**
with passion	**appassionato**
gaily and melodiously	**arioso**
in the original time, after a change in tempo	**a tempo**
with emphasis, lit. well marked	**ben marcato** or **marcato**
stirringly and animatedly	**bewegt**
with an encore or repetition	**bis**
with gradually decreasing tempo and volume	**calando**
in a flowing, melodic style	**cantabile**
with the wood of the bow, not the string	**collegno**
quietly and easily	**commodo**

with passionate abandon	con abbandono
with tenderness and love	con amore or amoroso
with soulful involvement	con anima
with zest and spirit	con brio
with warmth and passion	con calore
with sweetness	con dolcezza
sadly and mournfully	con dolore
with expression	con espressione
with force	con forza
with fire and verve	con fuoco
with grace	con grazia
tastefully	con gusto
impetuously	con impeto
with great passion	con molto passione
with animation and movement	con moto
with simplicity	con semplicità
with the piano's mute pedal down	con sordino
with spirit	con spirito
in a continuous or sustained way	continuato
with growing loudness and force	crescendo
in dance style	da ballo
in church style	da cappello or chiesa
again from the beginning	da capo (d.c.)
repeating from the sign, earlier in the music	dal segno (d.s.)
with decreasing volume	decrescendo or diminuendo
in a lively and sprightly way	desto
so the music dies away	diluendo
dolefully or pathetically	doloroso
gently or softly	doucement
harshly	duramente
more, a call from an audience	encore
emphatically	enfaticamente
stopping here, marking the end	fine
loudly, lit. forceful (very loud)	forte (f.) (fortissimo)
loud, but then soft	forte-piano
in a slow, stately manner, lit. large	largo
smoothly	legato
slowly	lentamente
slowing the tempo	lentando
slowly (extremely slowly)	lento (lentissimo)
majestically	maestoso
with moderation	non troppo
softly (very softly)	piano (p.) (pianissimo)
more	più
by plucking	pizzicato
gliding from one note to the next	portamento
rapidly (very rapidly)	presto or con prestezza (prestissimo)

at a slowly decreasing tempo	**rallentando** or **ritardando**
suddenly and dramatically stressing one note	**rinforzando** or **sforzando**
alternating faster and slower tempos	**rubato**
humorously or playfully	**scherzando**
simply and unaffectedly	**semplice**
in a forcing manner	**sforzando** or **forzando**
sustaining the notes	**sostenuto**
short quick notes by bouncing the bow on the strings	**spiccato**
in a lively, spirited way	**spiritoso**
with brief short notes	**staccato**
at an accelerating tempo	**stringendo**
peacefully or in a tranquil manner	**tranquillo**
tremulously or in an emotional manner	**tremolando**
all together	**tutti**
with vigor	**vigoroso**
swiftly	**vite**
in a gay and lively way	**vivace**
turning the page at this point	**volti**

Visual Arts Language

In the visual arts, what is the word or phrase for . . . ?

not representing natural objects	**abstract, nonrepresentational** or **nonobjective**
post-WWII nonrepresentational movement	**abstract expressionism**
painting by dribbling or splashing, à la Pollock	**action painting**
a pigmented liquid polymer used in painting	**acrylic**
a narrow-necked Greek vase with 2 handles	**amphora**
a low relief carving on an ornament	**anaglyph**
the decorative placing of one fabric or material on another, as in needlework	**appliqué**
a small area off the central aisle of a church	**apse**
etching done in stages, to produce varying tones	**aquatint**

decorative art, from 1920s	**art deco**
decorative art following natural forms	**Art Nouveau**
an artist's or artisan's studio, in France	**atelier**
colored tiles, as in Portugal	**azulejos**
an ornate artistic style, esp. from 1550 to 1700	**baroque**
sculpture only slightly raised from its flat background, lit. low relief	**bas-relief** (Fr.) or **basso-rilievo** (It.)
dyeing material in designs, with undyed parts protected by removable wax, from Java	**batik**
the 20th-c. German school of functional architecture	**Bauhaus**
a print made from a carved or engraved block	**block print**
a raw, stark architectural style	**brutalism (art brut)**
a support to counteract a building's outward thrust	**buttress**
artistic styles from the Eastern Roman Empire	**Byzantine**
a polished and rounded, rather than cut, gem	**cabochon**
artistic handwriting or fine penmanship	**calligraphy**
a gem or stone with an engraved relief	**cameo**
the light-tight, image-creating chamber that was the precursor of today's camera	**camera obscura**
a projecting structure with one end unsupported	**cantilever**
the top of a column	**capital**
artistic representations of maternal love	**carità**
a drawn or carved scroll-like design	**cartouche**
reproducing an object, e.g., with metal or plaster	**casting**
a descriptive catalogue of an artist's work	**catalogue raisonné**
a hollow relief, as opposed to bas-relief	**cavo-rellevo**
the art of making works of fired clay or porcelain	**ceramics**
symmetrical decorations of bone or ivory inlaid with wood, especially in Italy	**certosina**

pouring pulverized enamel into prepared spots on an object, then fusing and polishing it	**champlevé**
powerful contrast between light and dark	**chiaroscuro**
making motion pictures	**cinematography**
a design of 5 symmetrical parts, after the pattern of the flower	**cinquefoil**
the lost-wax process of hollow casting, in sculpture	**cire perdue**
designing public buildings	**civil architecture**
soldering enamel into metal patterns on an object, e.g., a vase, then fusing and polishing it	**cloissoné**
a work of art formed from pasted-up materials	**collage**
a work's balance, as between form, color, and line	**composition**
a crackled pottery glaze, in France	**craquelé**
an early-20th-c. style focusing on the geometric essentials of natural forms	**cubism**
a series of images circling the wall of a room, as if to place the viewer in the center of a scene	**cyclorama**
a doubly curved molding, concave above and convex below	**cyma recta**
a doubly curved molding, convex above and concave below	**cyma reversa**
a 20th-c. style focusing on distorted and comic effects to break down traditional responses	**Dadaism**
inlaying steel with gold and silver, as in Moorish Spain	**damascening**
a small-scale scene presented in 3 dimensions	**diorama**
a pair of painted panels, hinged together	**diptych**
intaglio engraving with a steel needle on a plate	**drypoint**
an artist's stand, for show or work	**easel**
a rough start on a projected work, in French	**ébauche**
carving a design in relief	**embossing** or **chasing**

color mixed with wax and painted while it's hot	**encaustic**
cutting a design in reverse on a plate, which is then printed	**engraving** or **chasing**
a quick sketch of a projected work, in French	**esquisse**
drawing a design in reverse on a wax-coated plate, which is then bathed in acid and used in printing	**etching**
glazed or painted pottery, as from Faenza, Italy	**faïence**
an artist's model, lit. made to be painted	**fait à preindre**
early-20th-c. artistic rebels, lit. "the beasts"	**Fauvists (les Fauves)**
"he made it," referring to an art work's creator	**fecit**
drawing an object as if it recedes into space	**foreshortening**
a chance object or material made into art	**found object (objet trouvé)**
melting a material and pouring it into a mold	**founding** or **casting**
nonrepresentational images and patterns in art	**free form** or **formes libres**
a painting done on a freshly plastered wall	**fresco**
a horizontal part of a structure, with decorations, sculptures, or paintings	**frieze**
specially prepared charcoal used in drawing	**fusain**
an early-20th-c. style focusing on the energy of modern industrial life	**futurism**
an engraved inscription on a gem or stone	**glyptograph**
a 12th–15th-c. architectural style with pointed arches and flying buttresses	**Gothic**
an opaque, watercolorlike paint	**gouache**
arts involving lines on 2-dimensional surfaces	**graphic arts**
ornamental painting using shades of gray	**grisaille**
a relief partway raised, between high and low	**half relief, demirelief,** or **mezzo-relievo**
a much-raised, as opposed to low, relief	**high relief** or **alto-rilievo**

a negative that produces a three-dimensional image	**hologram**
a 19th-c. school of landscape painting, esp. in NY	**Hudson River School**
manuscript paintings, esp. from medieval works	**illuminations**
painting with thickly built-up layers of paint	**impasto**
a late-19th-c. style using small strokes and primary colors to simulate light as perceived	**impressionism**
a design cut into a surface, e.g., metal or stone	**intaglio**
a mosaic inlaid in wood	**intarsia**
a 17th-c. British style after James I's Latin name	**Jacobean**
a Japanese scroll painting mounted on brocade	**kakemono**
an oven for baking or hardening pottery	**kiln**
art works that include moving parts	**kinetic art**
work in vulgar or crude bad taste	**kitsch**
a system for showing full forms in 2 dimensions, using a single viewpoint	**linear perspective**
a print from a stone (or plate) treated so that the image to be printed will attract ink	**lithograph**
a 16th-c. style involving distortion, as of scale	**mannerism**
works depicting the sea	**marine**
a drawing to scale with measurements	**mechanical drawing**
a large medal or coin with a decorative design	**medallion**
a print made from a plate scraped or burnished to simulate light and shadow	**mezzotint**
folk pottery, in Japan	**mingei**
a sculpture that moves with air flow	**mobile**
using color and shadow to make a form in 2 dimensions appear to have 3; also shaping soft matter	**modeling**
using shades of just 1 color	**monochromatic**
an art work made from other pictures or designs	**montage**
making designs with pieces of colored stone or glass, as embedded in cement	**mosaic**

a Moorish/Christian style of Spanish craftworkers	**mudéjar**
a large work painted directly onto a wall or ceiling	**mural**
the 17th–18th-c. style based on Greek aesthetics	**neoclassicism**
small, carved ivory objects, in Japan	**netsuke**
any object considered to be art, often small	**objet d'art**
a work done in paint of pigment mixed with oil	**oil painting**
an abstract art form stressing the creation of optical illusion	**op art**
a work with an open style, distinguishing forms through color, not through outlining	**painterly**
a board on which to mix colors, with a thumbhold	**palette**
the 18th-c. style inspired by Andrea Palladio	**Palladian**
a series of scenes covering time or space, sometimes actually unrolled for the viewer	**panorama**
the aggressive photographers of the rich and famous	**paparazzi**
a paper-pulp-and-paste mixture, shaped while wet	**papier-mâché**
a thick mat used to frame pictures	**passe-partout**
powdered pigment in a molded stick, used for drawing	**pastel**
the re-emergence of previously painted-over images	**pentimento**
an art experience involving both visual and performing elements	**performance art**
a 17th–18th-c. English Gothic architectural style, stressing vertical lines	**Perpendicular**
a technique for representing a 3-dimensional scene in 2 dimensions	**perspective**
a print from a plate to which a photographic image has been mechanically transferred	**photoengraving**
a work showing Mary holding the crucified Christ	**Pietà**
material that gives color, as in pastels or paints	**pigment**

a gypsum-and-water paste used in casts and molds	**plaster of Paris**
painting, or at least sketching, in the open air	**plein-air**
a post-impressionist style using dots, à la Seurat	**pointillism**
art using commercial styles and everyday subjects	**pop art**
a fine, hard, white ceramic	**porcelain**
a 19th-c. revival of the style of Italian painting before Raphael, linked with Rossetti	**pre-Raphaelite**
an unsophisticated artistic style, e.g., without perspective	**primitivism**
a trial sheet for checking a print's quality	**proof**
using heated tools or a small flame to make images, as on wood or leather	**pyrography**
art aiming to represent objects accurately	**realism**
sculptured forms raised from an attached back	**relief**
metal with a design hammered in relief	**repoussé**
works portraying recognizable objects	**representative art**
a transitional 9th–12th-c. architectural style	**Romanesque**
art using colored sand on a neutral sand ground	**sand painting**
elaborately carved pieces of bones or ivory	**scrimshaw**
painted with a hazy effect	**sfumato**
scratching pottery to make a design from the color beneath the surface	**sgraffito**
a cut-out or outline filled in with black, as of a profile	**silhouette**
printing a design on fabric by coating areas not to be printed with a blocking substance	**silk screen printing** or **serigraphy**
a piece of enamel or glass inset in a mosaic	**smalto**
a sculpture with no moving parts	**stabile**
a print from ink forced through a design cut into a cover sheet	**stencil**
a work portraying nonliving objects	**still life**

applying paint in dots or short strokes, à la Seurat	**stippling**
an art form stressing the use of chance effects and the products of the unconscious	**surrealism**
inlaid wood pieces in mosaic patterns	**tarsia**
paint of pigment, egg, and water or oil	**tempera**
hard-baked earthenware, also a brown-orange	**terra-cotta**
working metal to produce images in relief	**toreutics**
3 painted panels connected by hinges	**triptych**
painting that "fools the eye"	**trompe l'oeil**
a 16th-c. English building style with exposed beams	**Tudor**
Japanese woodblock prints	**ukiyoe**
the lightness or darkness of a color	**value**
in perspective, the point where the parallel lines converge	**vanishing point**
a small drawing, esp. in a book	**vignette**
a thin layer of watercolor on a painting	**wash**
paint of pigments mixed with water	**watercolor**
engraving on wood	**xylography**

Centuries in Italian

About the recent centuries, as often used in art history, what is the Italian word for the . . . ?

14th century (the 1300's)	**trecento**
15th century (the 1400's)	**quattrocento**
16th century (the 1500's)	**cinquecento**
17th century (the 1600's)	**seicento**
18th century (the 1700's)	**settecento**
19th century (the 1800's)	**ottocento**

Language of the Theatre and Show Business

(See also words of Literary Criticism in *Worlds of Letters*)

In the world of the theatre and show business, what is or are . . . ?

the ending of a Roman play, meaning the play is over, also Augustus's last words	**acta est fabula**
an actor's improvisation of dialogue to cover a hitch in the production	**ad lib** (Lat. **ad libitum**)
the main opponent of a play's protagonist	**antagonist**
a stage surrounded by seats on at least three sides	**arena state** or **theatre in the round**
the New Wave view of the director as author	**auteur**
a Japanese puppet theatre	**bunraku**
the play's climax, to the Greeks	**catastasis**
a paid cheering and applauding section	**claque**
the high point or turning point of a play	**climax**
comedy, or theatre, in France	**comédie**
a play focusing on the wit and sparkle of people in sophisticated society	**comedy of manners**
the improvised comedy form long used by road troupes in Europe	**commedia dell'arte**
a dramatic stunt or trick	**coup de théâtre**
a forced device to move the plot along, from the Greeks' lowering of a god in a stage machine	**deus ex machina**
conversation between characters in a play	**dialogue**
when the audience foresees disaster that a play's characters do not	**dramatic irony**
the list of a play's cast of characters	**dramatis personae**
they exit, a stage direction	**exeunt**
everyone leaves, a stage direction	**exeunt omnes**
filling in the characters' background	**exposition**

Italian puppets, often worked by mechanical aids	**fantoccini**
a writer of or performer in farces	**farceur**
a play focusing on wildly improbable plot twists and requiring superb timing	**farce**
a stall in the theatre, also an armchair, in France	**fauteuil**
dark, seamy films, esp. of the 1940's	**film noir**
scenes of events before the story opened	**flashbacks**
a deliberately macabre or gory work	**grand guignol**
the room off-stage where actors relax	**green room**
an extension of a Kabuki stage into the audience	**hanimachi**
an actor's making up dialogue and action on the spot, not from a prepared script	**improvisation**
an actress who plays juvenile roles	**ingénue**
an actor who banters with the end men in a minstrel show	**interlocutor**
a short play or musical piece between the acts of a serious work	**interlude, entr'acte, intermezzo,** or **divertissement**
the period between two acts of a play	**intermission** or **entr'acte**
a traditional all-male Japanese dance-theatre	**kabuki**
Korean court entertainers, like Japan's geishas	**kisaeng**
medieval plays on the lives of saints and martyrs	**miracle plays**
the background of stage events, lit. a stage set	**mise en scène**
medieval plays based on Christ's life	**mystery plays**
a French directors' movement from the late 1950's	**New Wave**
Japanese dramas with masked players	**Noh**
female roles played by male kabuki actors	**onagata**
the area below the stage in a proscenium theatre	**pit** or **orchestra**
all or mostly wordless theatrical performances	**pantomime** or **panto**

an arch separating audience and stage in a traditional theatre	**proscenium**
to give cues to actors	**prompt**
the chief character or hero in a work	**protagonist**
witty, unfettered comedies written after 1660, when Charles II reclaimed the English throne	**Restoration comedies**
19th-c. Japanese drama forms rivaling kabuki	**shimpa** and **shingeki**
broad comedy involving falls, pies, et al.	**slapstick**
a character speaking his thoughts aloud	**soliloquy** or **monologue**
a pert, flirtatious young girl, esp. a servant	**soubrette**
characters and situations that follow hoary conventions, as with the stage Irishman	**stock**
a still scene arranged for dramatic effect	**tableau vivant**
hangings that block the wings from the audience	**tormentors**
to take the audience's attention from another actor	**upstage**
early-20th-c. variety theatre	**vaudeville**
the passages leading out of an arena theatre	**vomitories (voms)**
the areas out of sight on either side of the stage	**wings**

In Sickness and in Health

Fears and Phobias

Among people's fears and phobias, what is an abnormal fear of . . . ?

animals	**zoophobia**
bees	**apiphobia**
being alone	**autophobia** or **monophobia**
being buried alive	**taphephobia (also taphi-** or **tapho-)**
blood	**hemophobia** or **hematophobia**
blushing	**erythrophobia**
books	**bibilophobia**
cats	**ailurophobia** or **felinophobia**
children	**pedophobia**
closed or narrow spaces	**claustrophobia**
completion or perfection	**teleophobia**
crossing a bridge	**gephyrophobia**
crossing a street	**agyrophobia**
crowds or mobs	**demophobia** or **ochlophobia**
death or corpses	**necrophobia** or **thanatophobia**
depths	**bathophobia**
dirt	**mysophobia**
disease	**nosophobia**
dogs	**cynophobia**
drafts or fresh air	**aerophobia**
drugs	**pharmacophobia**
dust	**koniophobia** or **amathophobia**
everything	**panphobia**
fear	**phobophobia**
fire	**pyrophobia**
flowers	**anthophobia**
food or eating	**cibophobia**
foreign or strange things	**xenophobia**
frogs or toads	**batrachophobia**
fur	**doraphobia**
God's wrath	**theophobia**

hair	**chaetophobia**
heart disease	**cardiophobia**
heights	**acrophobia** or **hypsophobia**
imperfection	**atelophobia**
light or the sun	**photophobia** or **heliophobia**
men	**androphobia**
mirrors	**eisoptrophobia**
motion or wandering	**dromophobia**
night	**nyctophobia**
novelty or newness	**neophobia**
open spaces	**agoraphobia**
pain	**algophobia**
poisons	**toxicophobia**
priests	**hierophobia**
saints	**hagiophobia**
sea	**thalassophobia**
sex	**erotophobia** or **genophobia**
sleep	**hypnophobia**
snakes or reptiles	**herpetophobia** or **ophiclophobia**
sounds or speaking	**phonophobia**
speed	**tachophobia**
spiders	**arachnephobia**
standing still	**stasophobia**
strong or rapid breathing	**pantophobia**
13	**triskaidekaphobia** or **tredecaphobia**
thunder	**brontophobia** or **tonitrophobia**
travel	**hodophobia**
water	**hydrophobia**
women	**gynephobia** or **feminophobia**
words	**logophobia**
work	**ergophobia**

Manias and Obsessions

Among people's manias and obsessions, what is an obsession or mania regarding . . . ?

alcoholic drinks	**dipsomania** or **potomania**
animals	**zoomania**
becoming larger	**macromania**
becoming smaller	**micromania**
being active	**ergasiomania**
being alone	**automania**
being at rest	**eremiomania**
being in automobiles	**amaxomania**
being naked	**gymnomania** or **nudomania**
being possessed by a demon	**cacodemonomania**

being very rich	**plutomania**
birds	**ornithomania**
blushing	**erythromania**
books	**bibliomania**
buying anything	**oniomania**
cats	**ailuromania**
Christ's second coming	**parousiamania**
crossing bridges	**gephyromania**
crowds	**demomania** or **ochlomania**
death or corpses	**necromania** or **thanatomania**
dirty talk	**coprolalomania**
dogs	**cynomania**
feeling melancholy	**tristimania**
feeling that one is God	**theomania**
fires	**pyromania**
fish	**ichthyomania**
flowers	**anthomania**
food or eating	**phagomania** or **sitomania**
foreigners or strangers	**xenomania**
fur	**doramania**
going home	**nostomania**
hair	**trichomania**
heights	**acromania**
homesickness	**philpatridomania**
horses	**hippomania**
hypnosis	**mesmeromania**
imagined diseases	**nosomania**
insects	**entomomania**
lies and exaggerations	**mythomania** or **pseudomania**
light	**photomania**
lust for men by women	**nymphomania, hysteromania, oestromania,** or **uteromania**
lust for women by men	**satyromania**
medicines	**pharmacomania**
men	**andromania**
mice	**musomania**
moving	**kinesomania**
murder	**homicidomania**
music	**melomania** or **musicomania**
narcotics	**letheomania**
new things	**kainomania**
night	**noctomania (**or **nocti-)**
noise	**phonomania**
one's own importance	**megalomania**
one's own sagacity	**sophomania**
one's self	**egomania**
open spaces	**agoramania**
penis	**mentulomania**
picking at growths	**phaneromania**
pinching off one's own hair	**trichorrhexomania**
plants	**florimania**

pleasure	**hedonomania**
priests	**hieromania**
pulling out one's own hair	**trichotillomania**
religion	**entheomania**
reptiles	**ophidiomania**
sea	**thalassomania**
several things	**oligomania**
sexual desire	**erotomania**
sexual literature	**pornographomania**
sexual organs	**edeomania**
sexual pleasure	**aphrodisiomania**
sin	**hamartomania**
single subject	**monomania**
sitting	**kathisomania**
sleep	**hypnomania**
speech	**lalomania**
stealing	**kleptomania**
sun or sunlight	**heliomania**
surgery	**tomomania**
talking	**logomania**
testicles	**orchidomania**
thinking	**phronemomania**
traveling	**dromomania**
wandering	**poriomania**
water	**hydromania**
werewolves	**lycomania**
wine	**enomania** or **oenomania**
women	**gynecomania**
words	**logomania** or **verbomania**
work	**ergomania**
writing	**graphomania** or **scribomania**

The Mind and Personality

(See also Fears and Phobias, and Manias and Obsessions, and also Anthropology, Archaeology, and Sociology Language in *World of the Sciences*)

Relating to the mind and personality, in the fields of psychology, psychiatry, and parapsychology, what is or are . . . ?

Aspects of the Healthy Mind

another self, meaning a close friend	**alter ego**
the female part of the male unconscious	**anima**
the male part of the female unconscious	**animus**

inherited psychic experience, for Jung	**collective unconscious**
known through perception or reasoning	**cognitive**
growth of intelligence and problem-solving ability	**cognitive development**
the conscious self, the "I"	**ego**
a response reinforced by a stimulus	**conditioned response** or **reflex**
one whose attention is much focused on others	**extrovert**
the instinctive, primal part of the psyche	**id**
a restraint, esp. the superego over the id	**inhibition**
one whose attention is much focused on the self	**introvert**
sensual satisfaction, also sexual desire	**libido**
the self-conscious role a person displays	**persona**
the mind, both conscious and unconscious	**psyche**
not fully conscious, but able to be made so	**subconscious**
showing an instinct in a socially acceptable form	**sublimation**
the psyche's repository of moral standards	**superego**
the unobservable but inferred part of the psyche	**unconscious**

Diseases or Problem Conditions

full or partial loss of memory	**amnesia**
personal disorientation following strong alienation	**anomie**
unjustified apprehension or fear	**anxiety**
a severe withdrawal in a child	**autism**
an unusual fear of emasculation	**castration complex**
a condition of rigid muscles and unresponsiveness	**catalepsy**
a condition of immobility, stupor, and mutism	**catatonia**
making repressions conscious, relieving tension	**catharsis**
emotional concentration on a single idea	**cathexis**
an untrue belief, firmly held against evidence	**delusion**

an unresponsive, despondent condition	**depression**
the generation of multiple personalities	**dissociation**
unthinking repetition of others' words	**echolalia**
flaunting one's self for attention	**exhibitionist**
switching thoughts based on the sound and rhyme of words	**clanging**
a delusionary vision, unsupported by reality	**hallucination**
a neurosis of uncontrolled anxiety or excitability	**hysteria**
a persistent feeling of inadequacy	**inferiority complex**
excitement exaggerated to pathology	**mania**
a psychosis in which strong excitability alternates with deep despondency	**manic-depression** or **cyclothymia**
delight in one's own pain or mistreatment	**masochism**
excessive attention to oneself, esp. one's body	**narcissism**
hypersensitivity and nervousness leading to restlessness and fatigue	**neurasthenia**
a general mental or emotional disorder without an identifiable organic cause	**neurosis**
perfectionism and inhibition carried to pathology, as in constant hand-washing	**obsessive-compulsive disease (OCD)**
a persistent unreasonable suspicion of others	**paranoia**
a desire to eat unusual substances, e.g., ashes	**parorexia**
hostility expressed through nonviolent inaction	**passive-aggressive behavior**
an excessive, unreasonable, persistent fear	**phobia**
a recent mother's depression, sometimes lightly called the "baby blues"	**postpartum depression**
a condition suffered by many Vietnam veterans	**post-traumatic stress disorder (PTSD)**
the inability to recognize faces	**prosopagnosia**
the continuous concoction of a fictitious personal history	**pseudologia fantastica**
someone with a personality disorder, esp. aggressively antisocial behavior	**psychopath**

someone with a mental disorder involving loss of mental function and withdrawal from reality	**psychotic**
acting in a less mature way	**regression**
pleasure from others' pain	**sadism**
pleasure from one's own and other's pain	**sado-masochism**
disorganized thought patterns, often with hallucinations and delusions	**schizophrenia** or **dementia praecox**
someone pathologically antisocial, with no conscience or social responsibility	**sociopath**
a persistent feeling of being better than others	**superiority complex**
a major emotional shock, often causing neurosis	**trauma**

Treatments and Tests

changing behavior through conditioning or biofeedback, not exploring causes	**behavior modification**
the use of electric current to treat depression	**electroshock therapy**
a technique calling for spontaneous linking of ideas	**free association**
a technique for artificially inducing a sleeplike, suggestible condition	**hypnotism** or **mesmerism**
using narcotics to reach a patient's suppressed memories	**narcosynthesis**
a personality test in which people respond to ink blots	**Rorschach test**
therapeutic reliving of traumas, often with screaming	**primal therapy**
recall of past events to reveal the unconscious	**psychoanalysis**
psychotherapy focusing on psychological games and interactions	**transactional analysis (TA)**
shifting feelings from one person to another, esp. to one's psychoanalyst	**transference**

Other Related Terms

a theory that conditioning is the key to behavior	**behaviorism**
a power to perceive things beyond the normal range of perception	**clairvoyance**

a "Catch 22" situation in which all alternatives have negative consequences	**double bind**
perception by inexplicable means, beyond the normal range of the senses	**extrasensory perception (ESP)**
a strong, often immature, attraction to someone or something	**fixation** or **idée fixe**
a verbal error indicating repressed thoughts	**Freudian slip**
a theory stressing that the whole has special properties not in the parts	**Gestalt**
characterized by disease, e.g., a compulsive liar	**pathological**
something like or reminiscent of a penis	**phallic symbol**
knowing something before it occurs	**precognition**
someone supposed to be responsive to extrasensory forces	**psychic** or **medium**
maniacally uncontrolled movement; also moving objects using mental, not physical, powers	**psychokinesis**
the movement of objects by inexplicable means	**telekinesis**
communication by inexplicable means	**telepathy**

The Brain and Nervous System

Relating to the brain and nervous system, what is or are . . . ?

Anatomy and Physiology—General

the brain and spinal cord together	**central nervous system (CNS)**
the rest of the nervous system	**peripheral nervous system (PNS)**
the part of the PNS controlling the vital organs	**autonomic nervous system (ANS)**
the cells in nerve tissue that conduct impulses	**neurons**
the nerve cell's long, thin "transmitters"	**axons**

the nerve cell's short, thin "receivers"	**dendrites**
the neurotransmitter disrupted by Alzheimer's disease	**acetylcholine**
cells that support and nourish the neurons	**glial cells**
the connection between two neurons	**synapse**
the insulating sheath covering nerve fibers	**myelin**
glial cells that form the myelin sheath	**Schwann cells**
groups of neurons outside the CNS	**ganglia**
ANS nerve fibers that prepare for a crisis	**sympathetic**
ANS nerve fibers that return to normal	**parasympathetic**
the membranes covering the brain and spine	**meninges**
the outer, fibrous meninges	**dura mater (hard mother)**
the middle, weblike meninges	**arachnoid membrane**
the inner, delicate meninges	**pia mater (gentle mother)**

Anatomy and Physiology—The Brain

the part of the brain joining the spinal cord, controlling heart-beat and breathing	**medulla oblongata**
the oval bridge of tissue above the medulla oblongata	**pons varolii**
the large two-lobed part of the brain	**cerebellum**
the deep folds on the cerebellum's surface	**sulci**
the main nerves that serve the brain	**cranial**
the 10th and longest of the cranial nerves	**vagus**
the nerve from the lower spine to each leg	**sciatic**
the network of nerves in the abdomen	**solar plexus**
the brain part that regulates body temperature and other activities of the ANS	**hypothalamus**
the brain part that holds the hypothalamus	**diencephalon**
the section of the brain outside the cerebellum	**brain stem**
the cerebellum part that controls hearing	**temporal lobe**

the cerebellum part that controls seeing	**occipital lobe**
the cerebellum's "sensory center"	**the rear part of the frontal lobe**
the cerebellum's association or "thinking" center	**the front part of the frontal lobe**
the "activity center" in the mid-part of each half of the brain	**parietal lobe**
controlling the left side of the body, linked with spatial and artistic abilities	**right brain**
controlling the right side of the body, linked with speech and calculating ability	**left brain**
the mechanism that allows selective filtering of sensory data	**reticular activating system (RAS)**
the standard brain wave patterns of a resting person	**alpha rhythms**
the standard brain wave patterns of an alert, wakeful person	**beta rhythms**
brain spaces filled with cerebro-spinal fluid	**ventricles**

Seizures, Spasms, and Paralysis

the condition resulting from electrical overload or irregularity of the brain	**epilepsy**
partial or complete loss of consciousness, and muscle spasms, as in epileptic patients	**seizures, convulsions,** or **psychomotor attacks**
brief losses of consciousness in epileptics	**petit mal** or **absence seizures**
sudden convulsions, involving stiffening and jerking of the body	**grand mal, haute mal,** or **tonic-clonic seizures**
a warning sensation before a seizure	**aura**
inability to feel or to move	**paralysis**
partial or slight paralysis	**paresis**
paralysis on one side of the body	**hemiplegia**
partial paralysis of one side of the body	**hemiparesis**
paralysis of the lower half of the body	**paraplegia**
partial paralysis of the lower half of the body	**paraparesis**
paralysis of the body from the neck down, i.e., both arms and legs	**quadriplegia** or **tetraplegia**

having continual spasms or convulsions	**spastic**
motor damage, as from an injury in infancy	**cerebral palsy**
cerebral palsy with involuntary movements	**dyskinetic** or **ataxic cerebral palsy**
temporary or permanent facial paralysis	**Bell's palsy**
a disease with muscle rigidity and tremor	**Parkinson's disease** or **shaking palsy**

Speech Problems

full or partial loss of speech from brain damage	**aphasia**
full or partial loss of speech from damage to speech organs	**aphonia**
articulation problems, e.g., stuttering	**dysarthria**
speech problems due to physical malfunctioning	**dyslalia**
speech difficulty due to mental impairment	**dyslogia** or **dysphasia**
any speech impairment, e.g., a stutter or stammer	**dysphemia**
a problem in speaking, esp. hoarseness	**dysphonia**
a speech defect involving repetition of sounds, as in stuttering	**palilalia**
aphasia involving inaccurate naming of objects	**paranomia**
aphasia involving use of wrong or nonsense words	**paraphasia**

(See also Other Words About the Spoken Language in *World of Letters*)

Other Diseases and Problem Conditions

an abnormally enlarged brain	**macrencephaly**
an enlarged brain from excess water	**hydrocephalus**
missing all or most of a brain, a soon-fatal birth defect	**anencephaly** or **-lia**
an inherited disease of the autonomic nervous system, as among Ashkenazi Jews	**dysautonomia**
a brain inflammation, as from a viral infection	**encephalitis** or **sleeping sickness**
inflammation of the brain and spinal membranes	**meningitis**
inflammation of a spinal nerve, esp. the root	**radiculitis**

pain along the course of a nerve	**neuralgia**
pain and spasms of the 5th cranial nerve	**trigeminal neuralgia** or **tic douloureux**
a viral infection along a nerve path	**herpes zoster (shingles)**
mildly impaired coordination or learning ability	**attention deficit hyperactivity disorder, minimal brain dysfunction,** or **learning disability**
substantial brain damage from infancy	**mental retardation**
a disease that destroys the nerves' myelin covering, leading to impaired motion	**multiple sclerosis (MS)**
abnormal skin sensations, e.g., the "pins-and-needles" feeling of multiple sclerosis patients	**paresthesia**
progressive degeneration of nerve cells, a disease linked with Lou Gehrig	**amyotrophic lateral sclerosis (ALS)**
damage to the peripheral nervous system	**peripheral neuropathy**
a paralysis and weakening following a virus	**Guillain-Barré syndrome**
excessive, uncontrollable daytime sleepiness	**narcolepsy**
deep sleep with rapid eye movements	**REM sleep**
walking during sleep	**somnambulism**
talking during sleep	**somniloquy**
a head injury with no long-term effects	**concussion**
memory loss, temporary or permanent	**amnesia**

Treatments, Tests, and Tools

the taking of some cerebrospinal fluid from the base of the brain	**cisternal puncture** or **tap**
an X-ray scan of the cerebrospinal fluid	**intrathecal scan** or **cisternography**
the taking of some cerebrospinal fluid from the base of the spine	**spinal tap** or **lumbar puncture**
an X-ray view of the space between the spinal cord and the arachnoid membrane	**myelography**
a record of the electrical impulses of the brain	**electroencephalography (EEG)**
surgery to de-activate the brain's frontal lobe	**lobotomy**

Sex and the Reproductive System

(See also Personal Relationships in *Everyday Life*)

Relating to sex and the reproductive system, what is or are . . . ?

Anatomy and Physiology—Male

the male sex cell with the full 46 chromosomes	**spermatocyte**
the result of meiosis (division) in a male sex cell	**spermatid**
spermatids after developing a head and tail	**spermatozoa** or **sperm**
the development of spermatozoa	**spermatogenesis**
the male organs that produce sperm and male sex hormones, e.g., testosterone	**testes**
the protective pouch covering the testes	**scrotum**
an abdominal slit through which testes descend before birth	**inguinal canal**
the inguinal area, where trunk and legs join	**groin**
the small organ that stores sperm	**epididymis**
the fluid in which the sperm travel	**semen**
the glands that produce most of the fluid in semen	**prostate gland** and **seminal vesicles**
the tubes that pass from the testes to the urethra, carrying semen	**vas (ductus) deferens**
the glands secreting a clear, sticky fluid	**bulbourethral** or **Cowper's glands**
the tubes passing sperm to the urethra	**ejaculatory ducts**
the external organ through which urine and semen pass to the outside	**penis or phallus**
the head of the penis	**glans penis**
the folded-back covering of the glans penis	**prepuce or foreskin**
removal of the foreskin, as at birth	**circumcision**
the penis's "caverns" that fill with blood	**sinuses**
the penis tissue once it has filled with blood	**erection**
the male discharge of semen at the climax	**ejaculation**

a sexual dream leading to a climax	**wet dream or nocturnal emission**
the muscle that causes ejaculation	**bulbocavernous**
the fleshy area over a man's pubic bone	**mons pubis**
a sac of fluid in the testes membrane	**hydrocele**
male sexual prowess	**virility**
sexually able, holding an erection to climax	**potency**

Anatomy and Physiology—Female

the female sex cell, with the full 46 chromosomes	**oöcyte**
the female sex cell, or egg, after meiosis (division)	**ovum (pl. ova)**
the glands that produce ova and secrete female sex hormones	**ovaries**
the sites in ovaries where ova mature	**follicles (Graafian)**
the degeneration of unused ova in the ovaries	**atresia**
the organ commonly called the womb	**uterus**
the thin outer layer of the uterus wall	**peritoneum**
the thicker middle layer of the uterus wall	**myometrium**
the inner, variable layer of the uterus wall	**endometrium**
the tube carrying ova from ovary to uterus	**Fallopian tubes or oviducts**
the narrow necklike lower part of the uterus	**cervix**
the cavity between the cervix and the external genitals	**vagina**
the glands that keep the vagina entrance moist	**Bartholin's glands**
the fatty tissue over a woman's pubic bone	**mons veneris**
the area from the mons veneris to the anus	**vulva**
the folds of tissue covering the vagina and urethra	**labia majora and minora (large and small lips)**
the sensual organ where the labia meet the mons veneris	**clitoris or glans clitoris**
the secretion around the clitoris (the foreskin, in a man)	**smegma**
the periodic rupture of a follicle, releasing an ova	**ovulation**

the temporarily transformed ruptured follicle	**corpus luteum**
the female sex hormone normally produced by the corpus luteum	**progesterone**
the female sex hormone produced by the corpus luteum if pregnancy occurs	**estrogen**
the monthly shedding of the uterus's lining in a nonpregnant woman	**menstruation**
the rebuilding of the lining after menstruation	**estrogenic** or **proliferative phase**
the resupply of nourishment in the uterus in preparation for a possible pregnancy	**progesteronal** or **secretory phase**
the onset of menstruation in a young girl	**menarche**
the end of menstruation in an older woman	**menopause** or **climacteric**
the breasts a woman develops at puberty	**mammary glands**
the part of the breast through which a child can suck milk	**nipple**
the brownish area around the nipple	**areola**
the membrane over a female virgin's vagina	**hymen**
periods of ovulation and excitement in female mammals other than human	**estrus, oestrus,** or **heat**

Anatomy and Physiology—General

the release culminating sexual activity, in males resulting in ejaculation	**orgasm** or **climax**
sexual organs, taken together, male or female	**genitals** or **pudenda**
sex glands in general, testes or ovaries	**gonads**
sexual changes that mark the beginning of adolescence, e.g., growth of breasts	**secondary sex characteristics**
the age when sex organs become functional and secondary sex characteristics appear	**puberty**
the age between puberty and full maturity	**adolescence**
sexual intercourse, in formal discussion	**copulation, coitus, fornication,** or **carnal knowledge**

someone who has not had sexual intercourse	**virgin**
something that stimulates sexual desire	**aphrodisiac**
licking or sucking a woman's clitoris or vulva	**cunnilingus**
licking or sucking a man's penis	**fellatio**
self-stimulation to orgasm	**masturbation** or **onanism**
having both male and female characteristics	**androgynous**

Anatomy and Physiology—Conception and Birth

the joining of a sperm and ovum	**fertilization** or **conception**
2 babies formed from 1 fertilized egg	**identical twins**
2 babies formed from 2 fertilized eggs	**fraternal twins**
the ability to bear children	**fertility**
the sex chromosome found in pairs in women	**X chromosome**
the sex chromosome paired with an X chromosome in men	**Y chromosome**
a characteristic both parents must carry to pass on to their child	**recessive trait**
a characteristic that can be passed on to a child through just one parent	**dominant trait**
a trait expressed differently depending on the individual's sex	**sex-influenced trait**
a trait expressed only in one sex	**sex-limited trait**
a gene located on a sex chromosome	**sex-linked trait**
a trait carried on a woman's gene	**X-linked trait**
the early stages of a being in the uterus, before fully recognizable forms appear	**embryo**
a being in the uterus, usu. from 8 weeks after conception to birth	**fetus**
the time when the baby is in the womb	**gestation** or **pregnancy**
the stage when the fetus can first be felt moving in the womb	**quickening**
the birth sac, which holds the fetus	**amniotic sac**
the muscle contractions that move the child out of the womb to be born	**labor** or **parturition**

the uterine tissue that nourishes the fetus, and is later expelled as the afterbirth	**placenta**
the hormone produced by the placenta, used in pregnancy tests	**human chorionic gonadotropin**
a woman who bears a child for another	**surrogate mother**
the fluid surrounding the fetus	**amniotic fluid**
the cord that connects mother and fetus	**umbilical cord**
the place where the umbilical cord is tied off	**umbilicus** or **navel**
the widening of the cervix during labor	**dilation**
a baby in a normal head-down uterine position	**vertex presentation**
a baby with feet or buttocks, not head, first	**breech presentation**
secretion of milk from the breasts	**lactation**
the first milk produced after a birth	**colostrum**
the period of time just after a birth	**postpartum**

Diseases and Problem Conditions

testes remaining in the abdomen, usually corrected surgically	**undescended testicles** or **cryptorchidism**
an enlarged prostate gland, as in older men	**prostatic hypertrophy**
inability to maintain an erection	**impotence** or **erectile dysfunction**
release of semen too early in a sex act	**premature ejaculation**
someone who has both male and female parts	**hermaphrodite**
a sterile form of hermaphroditism from having 2 X (female) and 1 Y (male) chromosomes	**Klinefelter's syndrome**
abnormally large male breasts	**gynecomastia**
a woman who has some male external parts	**gynandroid**
inability to have an orgasm, esp. of a woman	**anorgasmia**
having no sexual desire, especially of women	**frigidity**
genital pain during intercourse	**dyspareunia**
involuntary contraction of the vagina	**vaginismus**

a pattern of symptoms before a menstrual period	**premenstrual syndrome (PMS)**
the absence of menstruation	**amenorrhea**
painful or abnormal menstruation	**dysmenorrhea**
widely separated or very light menstruation	**oligomenorrhea**
abnormally heavy menstrual flow	**menorrhagia**
uterine bleeding between normal periods	**mertorrhagia**
waves of heat associated with menopause	**hot flashes**
the inability to bear children	**infertility** or **barrenness**
vomiting during pregnancy, or morning sickness	**hyperemesis gravidarum**
the inability to produce milk after a birth	**agalactia**
a fertilized egg outside the uterus, e.g., in a tube	**ectopic pregnancy**
the involuntary inability to continue a pregnancy	**spontaneous abortion** or **miscarriage**
uterine contractions without dilation of the cervix	**false labor**
a baby born dead	**stillborn**
the spontaneous abortion of a dead fetus	**inevitable abortion**
a disease with high blood pressure, blurred sight, and edema in pregnant women	**preeclampsia, eclampsia,** or **toxemia of pregnancy**
the placenta partly blocking the cervix	**placenta previa**
the placenta tearing away from the uterus	**placenta abruptia**
a severe bacterial infection following childbirth	**puerperal** or **childbed fever**
a benign fibrous growth in the uterus	**myoma** or **fibroid**
uterine tissue growing outside the uterus	**endometriosis**
sexual disease, in general	**venereal disease (VD)** or **sexually transmitted disease (STD)**
a highly contagious bacterial form of VD	**gonorrhea**
an increasingly common bacterial form of VD	**chlamydia**
a complication of gonorrhea and chlamydia	**pelvic inflammatory disease (PID)**
a bacterial form of VD, fatal if untreated	**syphilis**
an infected ulcer linked with early syphilis	**chancre**

a fibrous tumor of the vital organs in syphilis	**gumma**
a contagious form of VD, with genital ulcers	**granuloma inguinale**

Treatments, Tests, and Tools

a device to open the vagina for examination	**speculum**
a look at the vagina and cervix through a tube	**colposcopy**
a look at the uterus, Fallopian tubes, and ovaries, through a small abdominal incision	**laparoscopy**
the removal of tissue from the uterus lining	**D & C (dilation and curettage)**
removal of a fibroid tumor from the uterus	**myomectomy**
taking some fluid from the womb to test for birth defects	**amniocentesis**
an analysis of semen for fertility, also in rape cases	**semen analysis** or **sperm count**
a test of the progress of sperm in a woman's body	**Huhner test**
the fertilization of an ovum in a test-tube and implantation in a woman's uterus	**in vitro fertilization**
a device placed on a woman's abdomen to show the progress of labor	**external fetal monitor**
a look at the fetus using a tube inserted through an incision	**fetoscopy**
curved "tongs" to help pull the baby out	**forceps**
a suction cup to help pull the baby out	**vacuum extractor**
an incision at the vagina to aid childbirth	**episiotomy**
a birthing operation in which the baby is taken out through an abdominal incision	**Caesarean section** or **C-section**
local anesthesia used during a C-section	**epidural anesthesia**
a cross-wise Caesarean incision	**Pfannenstiel** or **bikini**
a vertical Caesarean incision	**midline**
removal of an embryo outside the uterus	**embryectomy**
the X-ray examination of breasts	**mammography**
breast cancer with an ulcerated nipple	**Paget's disease**
the removal of a breast	**mastectomy** or **mammectomy**

the removal of a breast and the lymph nodes	**modified radical mastectomy**
the removal of breast tissue, leaving skin and nipple intact	**subcutaneous mastectomy**
test for cancer that involves testing cells scraped from the cervix	**Pap** or **Papanicolaou smear** or **test**
an X-ray of the uterus and Fallopian tubes	**hysterosalpingography**
excision of the testes (or ovaries)	**castration**
a castrated man, as employed in harems	**eunuch**

Contraception and Abortion

the termination of a pregnancy before the fetus can sustain independent life	**abortion**
an abortion using suction for extraction	**vacuum abortion**
an abortion using a syringe for extraction	**menstrual abortion**
an abortion by injecting a drug into the fetal fluid, causing death and expulsion	**intraamniotic injection of hypertonic saline**
the birth control pills of synthetic hormones	**oral contraceptives**
a loop or coil inserted in the uterus to prevent conception	**intrauterine device (IUD)**
a rubber cup that fits loosely over the cervix to block sperm from entering the uterus	**diaphragm** or **pessary**
sperm-killing substances for birth control	**spermicides**
birth control based on the ovulation cycle	**rhythm method** or **Billings method**
a stream of water, often medicated, e.g., in the vagina for cleansing or for contraception	**douche**
a sheath that fits over the penis	**condom** or **rubber**
removal of the penis from the vagina before ejaculation, as a birth control method	**coitus interruptus, withdrawal,** or **onanism**
the cutting and tying off of the vas deferens, as a means of birth control	**vasectomy**
the cutting and tying off of the Fallopian tubes, as a means of birth control	**tubal ligation** or **salpingectomy**

burning the Fallopian tubes to close them	**coagulation** or **cauterization**
a device to support or reorient the uterus, also a vaginal suppository	**pessary**

The Eyes and Seeing

Relating to the eyes and seeing, what is or are . . . ?

Anatomy and Physiology

the "white of the eye," its outer coating	**sclera**
the clear, bulging, centered outer coating	**cornea**
the eye's middle layer, supplying blood	**choroid**
the eye's inner layer	**retina**
the sight receptors for light and color	**cones**
the many sight receptors for light alone	**rods**
the eye part that has cones, but not rods	**fovea**
the eye part that has neither rods nor cones	**blind spot**
the nerve stimulated by rods and cones	**optic nerve**
the place where the optic nerves meet and divide	**optic chiasma**
the dark center of the eye	**pupil**
the colored membrane that acts as a shutter	**iris**
the part that focuses light rays on the retina	**lens**
the mucous membrane of eyelid and eye	**conjunctiva**
the place where tears are collected	**lacrimal sac**
the corner of the eye, where the lids meet	**canthus**
the upper-eyelid fold common in people of East Asian lineage	**epicanthus (-ic) fold**
the clear, watery fluid in the cornea	**aqueous humor**
the gelatinous fluid in the back of the eye	**vitreous humor**

bits of vitreous humor, "spots before the eye"	**floaters**
normal vision, with signals from both eyes	**binocular vision**
ability to see objects off to both sides	**peripheral vision**
day vision	**photopia**

Diseases and Problem Conditions

double vision, with imperfect focus	**diplopia**
nearsightedness or shortsightedness	**myopia**
farsightedness or longsightedness	**hyperopia**
difficulty in focusing as the lens hardens with age	**presbyopia**
lack of symmetry in the shape of the cornea	**astigmatism**
lack of perfect focus because eye muscles are of unequal strength	**strabismus** or **heterotropia**
a form of strabismus where eyes diverge	**wall-eye** or **exotropia**
a form of strabismus where eyes turn inward	**cross-eye** or **esotropia**
upward strabismus	**anoöpsia**
lack of peripheral vision	**tunnel vision**
unaligned eyes, leading to "lazy eye"	**amblyopia**
loss of vision in one eye because of severe injury to the other	**sympathetic ophthalmia**
progressive loss of sharp central vision	**macular degeneration**
night blindness	**nyctalopia**
day blindness	**hemeralopia**
an inherited inability to distinguish some colors	**color blindness**
clouding of the lens, tending to blindness	**cataract**
vision loss with pressure on the optic nerve	**papilledema**
hardening of the eye and loss of vision due to blockage of the aqueous humor	**glaucoma**
total blindness	**amaurosis** or **gutta serena**
winking or blinking	**nication** or **nictitation**
involuntary spasmodic moving of the eyeball	**nystagmus**
bulging eyeballs	**exophthalmos**
an abnormally dilated or widened pupil	**mydriasis**

an inflammation at the back of the eye	**uveitis** or **iritis**
an inflammation of the eye's blood vessels	**choroiditis**
patchy degeneration of the retina	**retinitis pigmentosa**
loosening of the retina	**retinal detachment**
a cancer of the retina found in children	**retinoblastoma**
retinal damage due to diabetes	**diabetic retinopathy**
inflammation of the eye's mucous membrane	**conjunctivitis** or **pink eye**
abnormal dryness of the conjunctiva	**xerophthalmia**
a contagious viral disease of the conjunctiva, tending to blindness	**trachoma**
an inflammation or pimple on the eyelid	**sty** or **hordeolum**
an infection of the eyelid	**blepharitis**
an infection of the tear ducts	**dacrocystitis** or **dacryoadenitis**
a lump in the eyelid from a blocked gland	**chalazion**
yellowish growths on the eyelid, associated with high cholesterol	**xanthelasmae**
yellowish patches on the eyeball	**pinguecula**
a fleshy growth from the corner of the eye	**pterygium**
the turning inward of the eyelid	**entropion**
the abnormal looseness of the lower eyelid	**ectropion**
drooping eyelids, often in old age	**ptosis**
softening of the cornea, as from lack of vitamin A	**keratomalacia**

Treatments, Tests, and Tools

the type of lenses used to correct myopia	**concave**
the type of lenses used to correct hyperopia	**convex**
glasses for both myopia and presbyopia	**bifocals**
glasses for near, middle, and far sight	**trifocals**
lenses placed directly over the cornea	**contact lenses**
the masklike device used in a vision test	**phoropter**
the chart used in a vision test	**Snellen Chart**
a device used to look into the eye	**opthalmoscope**

surgery sometimes used to correct myopia	**radial keratotomy**
an X-ray view of the eye's blood circulation	**fluorescein retinal angiography**
a physician who diagnoses and treats eye diseases	**opthalmologist** or **oculist**
a person who tests vision and prescribes lenses to correct vision problems	**optometrist**
a person who fills prescriptions for lenses	**optician**

The Ears and Hearing

Relating to the ears and hearing, what is or are . . . ?

Anatomy and Physiology

the outer ear that gathers sound waves	**auricle** or **pinna**
the cavity beyond the auricle	**middle ear**
the ear drum that vibrates with sound waves	**tympanic membrane**
the tube connecting the middle ear and the throat, equalizing pressure on both sides of the ear drum	**Eustachian** or **auditory tube**
the small bones that vibrate, passing sound waves to the ear drum	**ossicles (malleus, incus** or **anvil, and stapes)**
the opening between the middle and inner ear	**oval window**
the inner ear's shell-like hearing receptors	**cochlea**
the organ with hair cells that pass on sound impulses	**organ of Corti**
the inner ear's organs of balance	**labyrinth (semicircular canals and maculae)**
"ear stones" in maculae, signaling head position	**otoliths**
the nerve transmitting sound impulses to the brain	**auditory** or **vestibulo-cochlear**
a honeycombed piece of bone behind the ear	**mastoid process**

Diseases and Problem Conditions

hearing loss due to mechanical problems	**conductive hearing loss**
hearing loss due to nerve damage	**sensorineural** or **perceptive hearing loss**

severe sensorineural hearing loss with aging	**presbycusis**
hearing loss from accident or excessive noise, or "rock-and-roll deafness"	**acoustic trauma**
supersensitivity to sound	**hyperacusia**
ringing or buzzing in the ears	**tinnitus**
dizziness and feeling that the room is moving	**vertigo**
a disease with tinnitus, vertigo, and loss of hearing, the "watchmaker's disease"	**Ménière's disease**
loss of balance caused by a virus	**vestibular neuronitis**
infection in the ear canal or "swimmer's ear"	**external otitis**
infection in the middle ear	**otitis media**
infection of the middle ear and mastoid bone	**acute mastoiditis**
infection of the whole inner ear	**labyrinthitis**
water blisters on the eardrum	**bullous myringitis**
a cyst in the mastoid and middle ear	**cholesteatoma**
a retracted eardrum with a blocked Eustachian tube and a change in pressure, as when flying with a cold	**barotitis media, barometric otitis,** or **bauro trauma**
benign tumors in the ear canal	**exostoses**
a benign tumor on a nerve in the ear	**acoustic neurinoma**
a buildup of bone around the stapes	**otosclerosis**

Treatments, Tests, and Tools

measurement of a patient's hearing	**audiometry**
removal of all or part of the mastoid bone	**mastoidectomy**
replacement of the stapes after otosclerosis	**stapedectomy**
a slit in the eardrum to equalize pressure	**myringotomy**
tiny tools to remove objects from the ear	**alligator forceps**

The Teeth

Relating to the teeth, what is or are . . . ?

Anatomy and Physiology

the cutting teeth at the front	**incisors** or **foreteeth**
the pointed teeth beside the incisors	**canines, eyeteeth,** or **cuspids**
the 2-pointed teeth beyond the canines	**bicuspids** or **premolars**
the flat-topped teeth beyond the bicuspids	**molars**
the late-arriving final molars in adults	**wisdom teeth**
the 20 teeth that are lost in childhood	**baby, milk, primary,** or **deciduous teeth**
the loss of deciduous teeth	**exfoliation**
the 32 adult teeth, replacing baby teeth	**permanent** or **secondary teeth**
the tissue that surrounds teeth at the roots	**gums, periodontal tissue,** or **gingiva**
the part of the tooth below the gum	**root**
the part of the tooth above the the gum	**crown**
the hard outer covering of the crown	**enamel**
the less hard substance under the enamel	**dentin**
the soft core of the tooth, containing nerves and blood vessels	**pulp** or **root canal(s)**
the bonelike material covering the root	**cementum**
the points or elevations on teeth	**cusps**
the flat top of teeth used for chewing	**occlusal surface**
meeting of the teeth	**occlusion**
the tooth socket in the jawbone	**alveolus**
teeth all the same size	**isodont**
secretions in the mouth	**saliva** or **mucus**
the digestive enzyme in saliva	**amylase**
chewing	**mastication**
the taste receptors on the tongue	**taste buds**
the four basic tastes the buds respond to	**sweet, sour, salt,** and **bitter**

Diseases and Problem Conditions

tooth decay	**caries**
a hole in the tooth left by decay	**cavity**

hard deposits on teeth	**tartar, plaque,** or **calculus**
inflammation of tissue surrounding teeth	**gingivitis, periodontitis, ulitis,** or **pyorrhea**
a sac or gap in the gum	**gingival** or **periodontal pocket**
craterlike sores in the mouth	**apthous ulcers** or **canker sores**
a tooth unable to break the gum surface	**impacted tooth**
exposure of bone after extraction	**dry socket**
abnormally decreased saliva flow, or "dry mouth"	**xerostomia**
describing toothlessness	**edentulous**
adjoining teeth spaced too widely apart	**diastema** or **gap teeth**
projecting top front teeth	**buckteeth** or **prognathism**
involuntary grinding of teeth	**bruxism**
improper meeting of the teeth	**malocclusion, cross-bite,** or **overbite**
malfunctioning jaw joints and muscles	**temporomandibular joint syndrome (TMJ)**

Treatments, Tests, and Tools

the material used to replace decayed dental matter	**filling, amalgam,** or **alloy**
a cast filling, usually gold	**inlay**
an artificial covering for a tooth	**crown** or **cap**
a replacement for a lost tooth	**false tooth**
a false tooth with metal roots lodged in the gum or jawbone	**implant**
false teeth anchored to natural teeth	**bridge**
a bridge affixed to the back of other teeth	**Maryland bridge**
false teeth anchored in the gums	**dental plate** or **denture**
thorough cleaning of teeth	**prophylaxis**
removal of tartar or calculus	**scaling**
painting discolored teeth with chemicals	**bleaching**
painting discolored or damaged teeth with plastic	**bonding**
the plastic used in bonding	**laminate veneer**
a plastic coating to prevent tooth decay	**sealant**
cutting away infected dental tissue	**gingivectomy, curettage** or **gingival surgery**
smoothing root surfaces to restore gums	**root planing**
cleaning out and replacing the pulp in the root cavity	**pulpectomy, root canal work,** or **endodontic therapy**
removal of teeth	**extraction** or **exodontia**

temporary devices to correct tooth position	**braces, splints,** or **plates**
a device to avoid bruxism and help keep teeth in proper position	**night guard**
correction of malocclusion	**occlusal reconstruction** or **stomatognathics**
decay-retarding chemicals added to water	**fluorides** or **fluorine**

The Digestive System

Relating to the digestive system, what is or are . . . ?

Anatomy and Physiology

the throat's passage for food	**esophagus** or **gullet**
the food or liquid passing into the stomach	**bolus**
the muscular contractions that move the bolus	**peristalsis**
the body's rejection of food	**regurgitation** or **vomiting**
the valve between esophagus and stomach to help prevent backward flow	**esophagus sphincter**
the muscular organ that digests the food	**stomach**
the upper, wide part of the stomach	**fundus**
the lower, tapering part of the stomach	**pyloric canal**
the acid produced by the stomach wall	**hydrochloric (gastric) acid (HCl)**
a digestive enzyme that breaks down protein	**pepsin**
the upper part of the small intestine	**duodenum**
the valve between stomach and duodenum	**pyloric valve**
the middle part of the small intestine	**jejunum**
the lower part of the small intestine	**ileum**
the organ that pours digestive juices into the duodenum	**pancreas**
the organ that produces bile, a digestive juice	**liver**
the organ that stores bile and pours it into the duodenum	**gallbladder**

the tiny "fingers" through which digested food moves into the capillaries	**villi** or **microvilli**
the organ that receives leftover undigested food	**large intestine** or **colon**
the upper part of the large intestine	**cecum**
the troublesome projection off the cecum	**veriform appendix**
the lower part of the large intestine	**sigmoid colon**
the organs of the abdomen, together	**viscera**
the membrane lining the abdominal cavity	**peritoneum**
the two bean-shaped organs that filter unwanted substances from the blood	**kidneys**
the waste fluid excreted from the kidneys	**urine**
the expandable organ that collects urine	**bladder**
the tubes leading from the kidneys to the bladder	**ureters**
the place where urine exits the body	**urethra**
releasing urine from the bladder	**urinating** or **micturating**
the waste matter in the colon	**feces** or **stool**
indigestible matter in feces, such as fiber	**roughage**
the place where the feces exit the body	**anus**
the passage leading to the anus	**rectum**
releasing feces from the body	**defecating**
gas released through the anus	**flatus** or **rectal gas**
the intestinal system	**bowels**
the whole digestive system	**gastrointestinal (GI) system**

Diseases and Problem Conditions

the backward flow of acids from the stomach into the esophagus	**gastroesophageal reflux**
an excess of gas in the body	**flatulence**
a bulge of the stomach into the chest cavity	**hiatal** or **esophageal hernia**
a sore in the mucous lining that protects the stomach from its acids	**gastrointestinal** or **peptic ulcer**
inflammation of the stomach	**gastritis**
an esophagus ending in a pouch, not in the stomach, requiring surgery after birth	**esophageal atresia**

pouches, often food-filled, in the GI system	**diverticula**
infected and inflamed diverticula	**diverticulitis**
inflammation of the abdominal membrane	**peritonitis**
an inflammation of the kidneys	**nephritis**
a protein whose presence in urine may indicate kidney disease	**albumin**
a disease of the kidneys' filtering system	**nephrosis** or **Bright's disease**
an inflammation of the liver, often viral	**hepatitis**
a liver inflammation from blood contact	**hepatitis B** or **serum hepatitis**
a liver ailment producing yellowish skin	**jaundice** or **ictus**
progressive liver destruction and scarring	**cirrhosis**
a liver enzyme deficiency leading to mental retardation	**phenylketonuria (PKU)**
a malformed urethra	**hypospadias**
poisoning resulting from urine not flushing unwanted substances out of the body	**uremia**
inflammation of the gall bladder	**cholecystitis**
inflammation of the urinary bladder	**cystitis**
irregular, cramplike colon contractions	**spastic** or **irritable colon**
inflammation of the colon	**colitis**
chronic inflammation in the intestines	**regional ileitis** or **Crohn's disease**
a paralysis of the intestines	**adynamic** or **paralytic ileus**
abnormally enlarged veins in the anus	**hemorrhoids** or **piles**
a narrow ulcer within the anus	**anal fissure**
an abnormal skin opening from the colon	**anal fistula**
heartburn	**purosis**
that "sick to the stomach" feeling	**nausea**
an inability to digest certain kinds of foods	**food intolerance**
an inability to digest milk, for lack of lactase	**lactose intolerance**
an intolerance to gluten, in wheat and rye	**celiac disease** or **sprue**
a tropical disorder involving inability to absorb nutrients from food	**tropical sprue**

a mostly male inability to absorb nutrients	**Whipple's disease**
abnormal digestion or upset stomach	**dyspepsia** or **indigestion**
difficulty in swallowing	**dysphagia**
difficulty in passing stool	**constipation**
excessive liquid content in stool	**diarrhea**
an infection—amebic, viral, or bacillary—of the lower intestines, with diarrhea	**dysentery**
a food bacteria often causing diarrhea and vomiting	**Salmonella**
the type of bacteria causing most travelers' intestinal infections, or "la turista"	**Eschericheria (E.) coli**
pale, fat-filled feces	**steatorrhea**
a strenuous desire to relieve the bowels and bladder, but inability to do so	**tenesmus**
urination during the night	**nocturia**
urinating involuntarily, as in bed-wetting	**enuresis**
painful or difficult urination	**dysuria**
an inability to control bladder or bowels	**incontinence**
stones formed in various parts of the body	**calculi (sing. calculus)**
the process of stone formation	**lithiasis**
a stone in the stomach	**gastrolith**
stones from cholesterol in the gall bladder	**cholelithiasis**
abnormal excretion of the amino acid cystine causing kidney stone formation	**cystinuria**
stones in the kidneys	**nephroliths**
a GI infection caught from puppies and kittens	**campylobacter infection**
a dysentery spread through infected food and water, involving ulcers in the colon	**amebiasis, amebic dysentery, or colitis**
an infection of the small intestine	**giardiasis**
infections of the bladder, ureters, and urethra	**urinary tract infections (UTI's)**
parasites that live in the lower intestines	**pinworms**
intestinal parasites that cause anemia, often picked up by walking barefoot	**hookworms**
parasites common in the tropics, causing abdominal pain	**threadworms or strongyloidiasis**

Treatments, Tests, and Tools

a device for viewing the stomach	**gastroscope**
removing all or part of the stomach	**gastrectomy**
surgically creating a passage between the stomach and small intestines	**gastroenterostomy**
a pair of X-ray views of the kidneys	**renal scan** and **renogram**
artificial filtering for a malfunctioning kidney	**dialysis** or **hemodialysis**
an X-ray of the pancreas and gallbladder ducts	**endocopic retrograde cholangiopancreatography**
an X-ray view of the kidneys, ureters, and bladder	**intravenous pyelography (IVP)** or **excretory urography**
a test of the bladder's nerve and muscle function	**cystometry**
a look at the urethra and bladder, using flexible tubes	**cystourethroscopy**
X-rays of the duodenum and pancreas	**duodenography**
a common test for rectal bleeding	**Hemocult** or **stool gualac test**
a look at the large intestine through a tube	**colonoscopy**
a look at the rectum and lower large intestine through a flexible tube	**proctosigmoidoscopy** or **proctoscopy**
a surgically created opening for the colon	**colostomy**
surgical formation of an opening between the stomach and small intestine	**gastroenterostomy**
removal of all or part of the stomach	**gastrectomy**
an X-ray examination of both the large and small intestine, using barium	**gastrointestinal (GI) series**
an X-ray examination of the large intestine	**lower GI series** or **barium enema**
an X-ray used to show the esophagus, stomach, and small intestine	**upper GI** and **small bowel series,** or **barium milkshake**
a drug to stimulate and ease defecation	**laxative**
a laxative meant to melt in the colon	**suppository**
flushing of the rectum with liquid, for cleansing or as a laxative	**enema**

X-rays to spot gallstones or related problems	**cholangiography** or **cholecystrography**
crushing and removing stones in the bladder, using a catheter	**litholapaxy**
the machine that uses sound waves to break up gall-stones and kidney stones	**lithotripter**

The Respiratory System

Relating to the respiratory system, what is or are . . . ?

Anatomy and Physiology

breathing in air	**inspiration** or **inhalation**
breathing out air, as when speaking	**aspiration**
the air holes in the nose	**nares** or **nostrils**
the division between the two nostrils	**septum**
a septum that is off to one side	**deviated septum**
mucous membranes that warm and dry air	**turbinates**
hairlike projections in the nose that clean air	**cilia**
the smell receptors in the upper nasal cavity	**olfactory receptors**
air-filled cavities in bones near the nose	**sinuses**
the 4 pairs of sinuses	**sphenoid, maxillary, frontal, and ethmoid**
the salivary glands	**parotid glands**
the roof of the mouth, hard or soft	**palate**
the soft part of the palate	**velum**
the soft tissue hanging down behind the palate	**uvula**
the throat	**pharynx**
the opening of the pharynx	**fauces**
the "wind pipe," the throat's passage for air	**trachea**
the voice box, between the mouth and trachea	**larynx**
the two flaps of tissue in the larynx	**vocal cords**
the space between the vocal cords in the larynx	**glottis**
cartilage projecting from the front of the larynx	**Adam's apple**

the "lid" covering the larynx	**epiglottis**
the disease-filtering structures in the throat	**tonsils** and **adenoids**
the main passages for air into the lungs	**bronchi**
the smaller air passages in the lungs	**bronchioles** and **alveoli**
the two main divisions of the lungs	**lobes**
the area between the lungs, holding the heart	**mediastinum**
the lining of the lungs and chest cavity	**pleura**

Breathing Problems

vibration of the soft palate, as during sleep	**snoring**
shortness of breath	**dyspnea**
lack of breathing	**apnea**
a condition in which breathing must be done sitting or standing up	**orthopnea**
chronic lack of breathing during sleep	**sleep apnea** or **hypersomnia-sleep apnea syndrome**
overbreathing	**hyperventilation**
suffocation from lack of oxygen	**asphyxiation**
involuntary diaphragm spasms	**hiccups** or **hiccoughs**
a sound some babies produce as they inhale	**stridor**

Special Infant and Child Problems

blockage of the nasal passages in infants	**choanal atresia**
a benign nose or pharynx tumor, often in boys	**juvenile angiofibroma**
warts on vocal cords, esp. of boys	**juvenile papillomas**
poorly developed or blocked lungs from which air cannot be expelled easily	**congenital lobar emphysema**
oxygen starvation during the birth process	**perinatal asphyxia**
collapsing of the alveoli, common in newborns	**respiratory distress syndrome (RDS)** or **hyaline membrane disease**
lung damage common in RDS babies	**bronchopulmonary dysplasia (BPD)**
undeveloped lungs leading to infant death	**pulmonary hypoplasia**

underdeveloped lungs in under-weight babies	**pulmonary immaturity** or **Wilson-Mikity syndrome**
unexpected and unexplained infant deaths	**sudden infant death syndrome (SIDS)**
a child's viral infection with noisy breathing and a severe cough, treated with humidifiers	**croup**

Infectious Respiratory Diseases

a head cold	**coryza**
a viral disease of the parotid glands	**mumps** or **parotitis**
the disease of the lungs once called consumption	**tuberculosis**
a common lower respiratory viral infection	**influenza** or **flu**
the kind of influenza that caused the terrible 1918 pandemic	**swine flu**
an infectious disease with heavy coughing spasms and gasps for breath	**whooping cough** or **pertussis**
tuberculosis of the lymph glands	**scrofula**

Occupational Lung Diseases

a disease of dust accumulation in the lung, as in miner's black lung disease	**pneumoconiosis** or **phthisis**
potter's lung, or silica dust in the lung	**silicosis**
fibrosis caused by asbestos dust	**asbestosis**
lung inflammation from iron particles	**siderosis**
farmer's lung, or organic dust in the lung	**allergic alveolitis**
brown lung, or hypersensitivity to cotton, flax, or hemp fibers	**byssinosis** or **Monday fever**

Other Diseases and Problem Conditions

a palate or lip not properly united	**cleft palate** or **harelip**
ulceration and infection of the mucous membranes of throat and mouth	**Vincent's infection** or **trench mouth**
lack of the sense of smell	**anosmia**
a runny nose and swollen nasal membranes	**chronic rhinitis**
an allergic catarrh with asthmatic symptoms	**allergic rhinitis, pollinosis,** or **hay fever**
oozing of excess mucus onto the pharynx	**postnasal drip**

a nosebleed	**epitaxis**
a thickening of the nose's outer surface	**rhinophyma**
inaction or thinning of mucous membrane	**atrophic rhinitis** or **ozena**
a blocked sinus and inflamed sinus lining	**sinusitis**
a sore or inflamed throat	**pharyngitis**
inflammation or irritation of the vocal cords	**laryngitis**
infected tonsils	**tonsilitis**
abscessed tonsils	**quinsy** or **amygdalitis**
an abscess near the tonsils	**peritonsillar abscess** or **quinsy**
inflammation of the bronchial passages	**bronchitis** or **bronchiolitis**
chronic expansion of the bronchial passages	**bronchiectasis**
inflammation of the pleura	**pleurisy**
a chronic disease involving muscle spasms and swelling in the bronchial tubes	**asthma**
pus in the pleural area	**empyema**
a disease of inflamed lungs filled with fluid	**pneumonia**
loss of elasticity of the lungs	**emphysema**
excess mucus, brought up in coughing	**sputum** or **phlegm**
filling of the alveoli with granules of fat or protein	**pulmonary alveolar proteinosis**
any of several diseases involving poor lung function, e.g., emphysema	**chronic obstructive pulmonary (lung, or respiratory) disease (COPD, COLD, or CORD)**
lung malfunction leading to death of the right side of the heart	**cor pulmonale (CP)**
leaking of air from the lungs into the chest, or a collapsed lung	**pneumothorax**
an airless, collapsed portion of a lung	**atelectasis**
bad breath	**halitosis**
a lung problem caused by worm infestation	**Loeffler's syndrome**
an autoimmune disease of lung hemorrhaging and kidney malfunction	**Goodpasture's syndrome**
a genetic disease involving excessive mucus and blockage of the air passages	**cystic fibrosis**
cancer of the lining of the chest or abdomen	**mesothelioma**

inflammation of nose and throat mucous membranes	**catarrh**

Treatments, Tests, and Tools

removal of tonsils	**tonsillectomy**
removal of adenoids	**adenoidectomy**
a surgical reshaping of the nose, or "nose job"	**rhinoplasty**
an X-ray of the trachea and bronchial tree	**bronchography**
a view of the trachea and bronchial tree using a flexible tube	**bronchoscopy**
a lung scan using an intravenous radioisotope	**perfusion scan**
a test of breathing effectiveness	**pulmonary function** or **lung capacity test**
a device used in a pulmonary function test	**spirometer**
a lung scan involving an inhaled radioisotope	**ventilation scan**
taking some fluid from between the lungs and chest wall	**thoracentesis** or **pleural tap**
an artificial breathing machine, for patients unable to breathe on their own	**respirator** or **iron lung**

The Heart and Circulatory System

Relating to the heart and circulatory system, what is or are . . . ?

Anatomy and Physiology—the Blood

the fluid part of the blood	**plasma**
the joining of platelets and proteins to seal a hole in the circulatory system	**blood clotting**
the fluid left after blood clots	**serum**
glucose in blood, serving as fuel	**blood sugar**
the red blood cells or corpuscles	**erythryocytes (RBC's)**
the iron-containing material in erythryocytes	**hemoglobin**
the white blood cells or corpuscles	**leukocytes**
specialized disease-fighting white blood cells	**granulocytes**
white cells controlling the immune reactions	**lymphocytes**
lymphocytes that produce antibodies	**B lymphocytes**, also **plasma cells**

lymphocytes that recognize foreign bodies	**T lymphocytes**
T cells that help produce other T cells	**T helper cells**
T cells that kill T helper cells, as in AIDS	**T suppressor cells**
blood-clotting elements in blood	**platelets** or **thrombocytes**
a clot-forming protein linked to heart disease	**fibrinogen**
the amount of blood cells in the blood	**hematocrit**
the amount of hemoglobin in the blood	**hemoglobin concentration (HGB)**
the forming of blood clots	**coagulation**

Anatomy and Physiology—the Circulatory System

tiny blood vessels that receive oxygen and take away carbon dioxide	**capillaries**
the vessels carrying blood from the heart	**arteries**
small arteries leading into capillaries	**arterioles**
the vessels carrying blood to the heart	**veins**
small veins leading away from capillaries	**venules**
the vessel bypassing the lungs in a fetus	**patent ductus arteriosis**
the inner layer of the heart's tissue	**endocardium**
the middle layer of the heart's tissue	**myocardium**
the outer layer of the heart's tissue	**epicardium**
the membrane surrounding the heart	**pericardium**
the walls dividing the heart's 4 chambers	**septa** (sing. **septum**)
the 2 receiving chambers of the heart	**atria** (sing. **atrium**)
the 2 pumping chambers of the heart	**ventricles**
the opening-and-shutting devices connecting the heart's chambers	**valves (pulmonary, aortic, mitral,** and **tricuspid)**
the large veins entering the right atrium	**superior** and **inferior vena cavae**
the artery taking blood to the lungs	**pulmonary artery**
the veins carrying blood from the lungs	**pulmonary veins**

the body's largest artery	**aorta**
the arteries circling the heart, like a crown	**coronary arteries**
the main blood vessel to the brain	**carotid artery**
the large veins in the front of the neck	**jugular veins**
the arteries and veins to and from the head and arms	**brachiocephalic**
the arteries and veins to and from the digestive system	**hepatic** or **celiac trunk**
the artery to the legs	**iliac artery**
the veins involved in varicose veins	**saphenous veins**
the veins that trouble hemorrhoid sufferers	**rectal veins**
the artery used to measure the pulse	**radial artery**
the artery used to measure blood pressure	**brachial artery**
the regulator of fluid balance in the body	**lymphatic system**
purifying filters within the lymphatic system	**lymph nodes**
the neck's lymph nodes, as in "swollen glands"	**cervical nodes**
the lymph nodes in the armpits	**axillary nodes**
the lymph nodes in the groin	**inguinal nodes**
the organ that destroys un-wanted blood cells	**spleen**
the filtering and destroying of unwanted cells	**phagocytosis**
the producer of specially immune lymph cells	**thymus**
a natural substance formed in the lungs for maintaining blood pressure	**angiotensin**
normal heartbeat rhythm	**sinus rhythm**

Heart Diseases and Problem Conditions

improper valve closing, with blood backflow	**valve prolapse**
the sound of a diseased valve	**heart murmur**
improper valve opening	**valvular stenosis**
disturbance in heart rhythm	**cardiac arrhythmia**
abnormally fast and violent heartbeat	**palpitations**
too fast a heart rhythm	**tachycardia**
too slow a heart rhythm	**bradycardia**
an irregular, too-fast beat of an atrium	**atrial fibrillation**

an irregular, too-fast beat of a ventricle	**ventricular tachycardia**
dangerously fast, uncoordinated heart rhythm	**ventricular fibrillation**
severe vasculitis of the aorta in young women	**Takayasu's disease**
blockage of a coronary artery with a clot	**coronary thrombosis**
heart tissue damage due to lack of blood	**myocardial infarction**
the inability of the heart to pump enough blood	**congestive heart failure**
an abnormally constricted aorta	**coarctation of the aorta**
intense chest pain, from blood-deprived heart muscle	**angina pectoris**
frequent, seemingly unprovoked chest pain	**unstable angina**
heart malformations causing blood from veins to be repumped through arteries, causing cyanosis, or "blue babies"	**cyanotic heart disease**
a disease of the heart valves or muscles	**cardiomyopathy**
abnormal enlargement of the heart	**hypertrophic cardiomyopathy**

Blood Diseases and Problem Conditions

lack of red blood cells for transporting oxygen	**anemia**
anemia caused by lack of iron	**iron-deficiency anemia**
anemia caused by lack of vitamin B_{12}	**pernicious** or **Addison's anemia**
anemia caused by destruction of more red blood cells than are produced	**hemolytic anemia**
a genetic disease causing hemolytic anemia	**spherocytosis**
a genetic anemia causing premature destruction of red blood cells	**glucose-6-phosphate dehydro-genase deficiency**
anemia caused by malfunction of the marrow	**aplastic anemia**
crescent-shaped red blood cells, esp. in black people	**sickle cell anemia**
a genetic anemia, esp. in Mediterranean people	**thalassemia** or **Cooley's anemia**
uncontrolled production of plasma cells	**multiple myeloma**
a blood factor that, if incompatible, can destroy red blood cells	**Rhesus (Rh) factor**

someone who has the Rhesus factor	**Rh-positive**
someone who lacks the Rhesus factor	**Rh-negative**
when mother and fetus have different Rh factors	**Rhesus incompatability**
the anemic disease resulting from RH incompatability	**erythroblastosis fetalis**
excessive blood cells, thickening blood	**polycythemia vera**
excessive production of white blood cells	**leukemia**
a marked decrease in granulocytes	**granulocytopenia** or **agranulocytosis**
a marked decrease in platelets	**thrombocytopenia**
an autoimmune breakdown of platelets	**idiopathic thrombocytopenia purpura**
pinpoint bleeding, as in thrombocytopenia	**petechiae**
an inherited coagulation or "bleeding" disorder	**hemophilia**
excessive coagulation and diffuse bleeding	**disseminated intravascular coagulation**
bacteria in the blood, or blood poisoning	**septicemia**

Other Diseases and Problem Conditions

high blood pressure	**hypertension**
low blood pressure	**hypotension**
inflammation of blood vessels	**vasculitis**
inflammation and thickening of blood vessels and nerves, often found in smokers	**Buerger's disease** or **thromboangiitis obliterans**
spasms in the blood vessels of fingers and toes, reducing blood flow	**Raynaud's phenomenon**
inflammation of a vein	**phlebitis**
weak or impaired bulging veins	**varicose veins**
vein inflammation caused by a blood clot	**thrombophlebitis** or **venous thrombosis**
fat and cholesterol that build up in arteries	**plaques** or **atheromas**
progressive narrowing of the arteries	**coronary athero-** or **arteriosclerosis**
obstruction of a vessel by a "plug" or embolus, such as a blood clot, fat, or air	**embolism**
a blood clot that obstructs flow in an artery	**thrombosis**
blockage of blood vessels in the lower limbs	**arteriosclerosis obliterans**

cramping or pain caused by artery blockage	**intermittent claudication**
lack of blood, as caused by arterial blockage	**ischemia**
blueness of lips and nails from lack of oxygen	**cyanosis**
reduction of the brain's blood flow, leading to tissue death, or bleeding in the brain	**stroke** or **cerebrovascular accident (CVA)**
a stroke with blockage in a brain blood vessel	**cerebrovascular hemorrhage occlusion**
a stroke with bleeding from a ruptured vessel	**cerebral hemorrhage**
mini-strokes	**transient ischemic attacks (TIA's)**
a weak bulge in a vessel that can rupture	**aneurysm**
bleeding from a ruptured blood vessel	**hemorrhage**
a "black-and-blue mark" from a hemorrhage	**hematoma** or **bruise**
a bruise without broken skin	**contusion**
a bruise with broken skin	**laceration** or **abrasion**
a hemorrhage under the brain's outer cover, as from a head injury	**subdural hematoma**
a cancer of the lymphatic system	**lymphoma**
a kind of lymphoma linked with the unique Reed-Sternberg cell	**Hodgkin's disease**
a viral disease often confused with leukemia	**infectious mononucleosis ("mono")** or **glandular fever**
progressive fibrosis of the bone marrow	**agnogenic myeloid metaplasia**
bacteria infection of the lymph nodes	**lymphadenitis**

Treatments, Tests, and Tools

an analysis of the components of the blood	**complete blood count (CBC)**
the number of red blood cells in blood	**red blood count (RBC)**
the number of white blood cells in blood	**white blood count (WBC)**
often used to analyze blood-clotting time	**Thrombin time** or **Prothrombin time**
the device used to measure blood pressure	**sphygmomanometer**
the blood pressure during heart contraction	**systolic** (e.g., 120)

the blood pressure during heart relaxation	**diastolic** (e.g., 80)
used to record the electrical impulses of the heart	**electrocardiogram (ECG or EKG)**
an ECG administered after exercise	**stress test**
an ECG taken over one or more days	**ambulatory ECG or Holter monitoring**
a scan that shows injured heart muscle through radioisotope imaging	**technetium pyrophosphate scan**
a scan that shows normal heart muscle through radioisotope imaging	**thallium scan**
a device that uses electric shock to restore normal heartbeat	**defibrillator**
an implanted device to regulate heart rhythm	**pacemaker or sinoatrial node**
the application of heavy jolts of electricity to restore normal heartbeat	**electrical cardioversion**
using sound waves to show blood flow in the arms, legs, and head	**Doppler ultrasonography**
showing blood actually pumping in the heart	**blood pool scanning**
an X-ray of blood vessels to spot abnormalities	**angiography**
an X-ray of arteries to spot abnormalities	**arteriography**
an X-ray of the veins to spot abnormalities	**venography**
an X-ray of the leg and foot veins	**phlebography**
a taking of blood from an artery to test the lung's ability to deliver oxygen	**arterial puncture or blood gas**
surgical removal of atherosclerotic deposits	**endartectomy**
implanting a healthy vessel for alternative blood flow, in severe atherosclerosis	**coronary bypass**
insertion of a tiny balloon to open blocked arteries	**angioplasty**
the artificial heart tried for permanent use in the 1980's	**Jarvik-7**
an alternative to a permanent, full, artificial heart	**left ventricular assist device (LVAD)**
the use of a dye to outline the lymphatic system	**lymphoangiography**
a test for Rh incompatability	**Rh titer**

extracting bone marrow to test for leukemia	**bone marrow aspiration** or **sternal tap**
a device used to stop blood flow in an artery	**tourniquet**

The Hormone System

Relating to the hormone system, what is or are . . . ?

Anatomy and Physiology

body organs that secrete special substances used in other parts of the body	**glands**
tubes to send secretions to certain locations	**ducts**
glands with ducts	**exocrine**
glands without ducts, secreting into the blood	**endocrine**
substances secreted by endocrine glands	**hormones**
the "master gland," near the base of the brain	**pituitary** or **hypophysis**
the front part of the pituitary	**adenohypophysis**
the rear part of the pituitary	**neurophypophysis**
the neck glands that regulate metabolic rates	**thyroid**
the 4 neck glands that control blood calcium	**parathyroid**
the 2 glands on top of the kidneys	**adrenal**
the outer part of each adrenal gland	**adrenal cortex**
the center of each adrenal gland	**adrenal medulla**
the gland below the stomach	**pancreas**
the groups of endocrine cells in the pancreas, producing insulin and glucagon	**islets of Langerhans**
a pituitary hormone affecting the thyroid	**thyroid-stimulating hormone (TSH)**
a pituitary hormone affecting the adrenal glands	**adrenocorticotropic hormone (ACTH)**
a pituitary hormone that causes eggs (ova) or sperm to mature	**follicle-stimulating hormone (FSH)**
a pituitary hormone affecting production of the female sex hormone, progesterone	**luteinizing hormone (LH)**

a pituitary hormone affecting production of the male sex hormone, testosterone	**interstitial cell stimulating hormone (ICSH)**
a pituitary hormone controlling body growth plus fat and sugar metabolism	**somatotropic hormone (STH)**
a pituitary hormone that stimulates milk production after a birth	**prolactin**
a pituitary hormone that stimulates uterine contractions and milk production at birth	**oxytocin**
a pituitary hormone that takes water from the urine for the blood	**antidiuretic hormone (ADH)**
the hormone produced by the thyroid	**thyroxin**
a paired X-ray view of the thyroid and its functioning	**thyroid scan** and **iodine uptake test**
hormones produced by the parathyroids to control calcium and phosphate use	**calcitonin** and **parathormone (PTH)**
the main hormones produced by the adrenal glands	**epinephrine (adrenaline), aldosterone,** and **cortisol**
the hormones by which the pancreas controls blood sugar levels	**insulin** and **glucagon**

Diseases and Problem Conditions

too much thyroxin in the blood, as from an overproductive thyroid gland, leading to excessive activity	**hyperthyroidism or Graves' disease**
too little thyroxin in the blood, leading to low metabolic rate or even retardation	**hypothyroidism** or **myxedema**
an enlarged thyroid gland	**goiter**
the disease resulting from too little secretion from the adrenal cortex	**Addison's disease**
the disease resulting from too much secretion from the adrenal cortex	**Cushing's disease**
any of several metabolic disorders with excessive thirst and urination	**diabetes**
a disease caused by lack of insulin	**diabetes mellitus**
cancerous tumors on the adrenal glands	**pheochromocytomas**

Muscle and Bone

Relating to the skeletal and muscular system, what is or are . . . ?

Anatomy and Physiology—The Skeletal System

cells that form bone, using calcium	**osteoblasts**
in bone cavities to help form blood	**marrow**
the place where two bones connect	**joint**
the set of bones that enclose the brain	**cranium**
the bone that forms the forehead	**frontal bone**
the bone that forms part of the eye socket	**ethmoid**
the small bones that form part of the eye socket	**lacrimal bones**
the bones in the nasal cavity	**palatine bones, nasals, inferior nasal conchae,** and **vomer**
the bone covering the top rear of the head	**parietal**
the bone covering the lower back of the head	**occipital**
the bone covering the area behind the ears	**temporal**
the small flat bone forward of the ears	**sphenoid**
the nonmovable joinings of the cranial bones	**sutures**
the membrane covering the not-yet-joined parts of an infant's skull	**fontanel**
the two bones forming the upper jaw	**maxillae**
the bone forming the lower jaw	**mandible**
the joint between the upper and lower jaw	**temporomandibular joint (TMJ)**
the bone that forms the curve of the cheek	**zygomatic arch**
the thyroid cartilage at the front of the neck	**Adam's apple**
the "great opening" in the rear of the skull, through which the spinal cord passes	**foramen magnum**
the lining of a joint	**synovial membrane**
the lubricating fluid in a joint	**synovial fluid**

Bones of the Trunk and Limbs

the bones that make up the spinal column	**vertebrae**
the cartilage-and-fiber "shock absorber" between vertebrae	**disk**
the outer fiber part of the disk	**anniulus fibrosis**
the inner jellylike part of the disk	**nucleus pulposus**
the vertebrae that make up the neck	**cervical vertebrae**
the vertebrae to which ribs are attached	**thoracic vertebrae**
the vertebrae in the "small of the back"	**lumbar vertebrae**
the triangular bone of 5 fused vertebrae joining the hips	**sacrum**
the "tailbone" at the base of the spine	**coccyx**
the normal curvature of the spine	**cervical lordosis**
the breastbone down the center chest	**sternum**
the upper part of the breastbone	**manubrium**
the bones of the shoulder region	**pectoral girdle**
the roughly triangular shoulder blade	**scapula**
the collar bone	**clavicle**
the upper arm bone	**humerus**
the two lower arm bones	**radius** and **ulna**
the "funny bone," part of the ulna	**olecranon process**
the bones of the wrist	**carpal bones**
the bones of the palm of the hand	**metacarpal bones**
the bones of the fingers and toes	**phalanges**
the bones that form the hips	**pelvic girdle**
the large part of the pelvic girdle	**illum**
the part of the hip joined to the sacrum	**os coxa**
the joint connecting pelvic girdle and sacrum	**sacroiliac joint**
the rear, inner part of the os coxa	**ischium**
the front, inner part of the os coxa	**pubis** or **pubic bone**
the wide opening in the os coxa	**obturator foramen**
the pelvic depression where the leg joint fits	**acetabulum**
the bone of the upper leg	**femur**
the rounded projections on the upper leg bone	**condyles**

the knee cap, which moves with the condyles	**patella**
the bones of the lower leg	**tibia** and **fibula**
the tibia extension that moves with the ankle	**medial malleolus**
the bones of the ankle	**tarsal bones**
the tarsal bone that forms the heel	**calcaneus**
the tarsal bone that moves with the lower leg bones, bearing the body's weight	**talus bone**
the bones of the flat of the foot	**metatarsals**
the big toe	**hallus**
fingers or toes	**digits**

Anatomy and Physiology—The Muscular System

a firm, somewhat rigid connective tissue, e.g., covering the ends of bones	**cartilage**
cells that give cartilage its firmness	**chondrocytes**
tough bands of tissue holding bones together	**ligaments**
voluntary muscles attached to bone	**skeletal muscle**
involuntary muscles in the heart	**cardiac muscle**
involuntary muscles of the other organs	**smooth muscle**
heavy tissue connecting muscle to bone	**tendons**
a muscle that decreases the angle between 2 bones	**flexor**
a muscle that increases the angle between 2 bones	**extensor**
a muscle that moves away from the body's midline	**abductor**
a muscle that moves toward the body's midline	**adductor**
rotating toward the body's midline	**medial rotation**
rotating away from the body's midline	**lateral rotation**
a muscle used to raise a body part	**levator**
a muscle used to lower a body part	**depressor**
the muscle surrounding the eye	**orbicularis oculi**
the muscles used in chewing	**temporalis** and **masseter**
the sheetlike muscle from mandible to shoulder that pulls down the mouth	**platysma**

the large, flat muscles that support and move the head and shoulders	**trapezius**
the muscle used in nodding the head	**sternocleidomastoid**
a major muscle at the back of the neck	**complexus**
the muscles around the ribs	**intercostals**
the dome-shaped muscle that moves as you breathe, separating chest and abdomen	**diaphragm**
the muscles that move the shoulders	**pectoralis major** and **minor**
a muscle that flexes the forearm	**biceps brachii**
a muscle that extends the forearm	**triceps brachii**
being able to use both hands equally well	**ambidextrous**
the muscles in the buttocks, used to move the leg	**gluteus maximus, gluteus medius,** and **gluteus minimus**
the muscle running from the buttocks to the back of the thigh	**hamstring**
the muscles used in moving the femur	**biceps femoris, triceps femoris,** and **quadriceps femoris**
the long muscle connecting the ilium and tibia	**sartorius**
the large muscle in the calf of the leg	**gastrocnemius**
the muscle in the calf, just above the heel	**soleus muscle**
the tendon near the soleus muscle at the heel	**Achilles tendon**
a muscle around an opening, e.g., the anus	**sphincter**
muscular perceptions, as of movement	**kinesthesia**

Special Muscle Problems

a small tear within a muscle	**strain**
an injury to the ligaments	**sprain**
a sudden, sharply painful muscle contraction	**spasms** or **Charley horse**
small spasms from overuse or too little blood	**cramps**
inflammation of muscles from overuse	**myofascitis**
a tear in the muscle wall, allowing internal organs to push through, or rupture	**hernia**
a disease of muscle weakness and wasting	**muscular dystrophy**

an inherited male-only muscular dystrophy	**Duchenne dystrophy**
lack of muscle tone	**atony**
the inability of muscles to relax after use	**myotonia**
short-term muscle-resistance exercise	**isotonic**
pain in the muscles	**myalgia**
weakness of the muscles	**myasthenia**
a progressive muscle-weakening disease	**myasthenia gravis**
sudden, short bouts of muscle weakness	**cataplexy**

Other Diseases and Problem Conditions

a break in a bone	**fracture**
a child's bone that cracks but does not break	**green-stick fracture**
a partial break in a bone	**hairline** or **stress fracture**
a broken bone with little damage to tissue	**simple fracture**
a broken bone with tissue damage	**compound fracture**
a bone partly crushed at a break	**comminuted fracture**
bones forced or jammed together	**compression** or **buckle fracture**
bones that cannot be returned to normal position	**irreducible**
the separation of bones from joints and ligaments	**dislocation**
tissue that knits broken bones together	**callus**
an irritation of the tendon on the outer elbow	**tennis elbow**
pressure on a nerve in the narrow passage between the wrist bones and a ligament	**carpal tunnel syndrome**
inflammation of rib cartilage	**costochondritis** or **Tietze's syndrome**
inflammation of the membrane on the tibia	**shin splints**
a fluid sac where bone meets skin or tendons	**bursa**
an inflamed bursa	**bursitis**
an inflamed bursa on a toe	**bunion** or **hallus valgus**
the bulging of a disk from between vertebrae	**herniated** or **slipped disk**
the breakdown of the disk material	**disk degeneration**
loss of spine flexion due to disk degeneration	**spondylosis**
stiffening of the spine as soft spinal tissues turn into bone	**ankylosing spondylitis**

weakening of bones through calcium loss	**osteoporosis**
weakening of bones through vitamin D deficit	**osteomalacia**
rounded shoulder and tucked-in chest	**kyphosis** or **hunchback**
swayback or excessive lumbar curve	**hyperlordosis**
a sideways curving of the lumbar spine	**scoliosis**
a malformed or twisted foot	**talipes** or **clubfoot**
lower back pain	**lumbago**
a bacterial infection of bone tissue	**osteomyelitis**
replacement of strong bone by diseased bone	**Paget's disease** or **osteitis deformans**
an inherited disease of the bones, causing dwarfism	**acromesomelic dysplasia**
possession of extra fingers or toes	**polydactyly**
an inherited malformation of hands and feet, with digits webbed together	**syndactyly** or **-tylism**
a birth defect with part of the spine exposed	**spina bifida**
inflammation of a joint	**arthritis**
a degenerative disease of the joints, esp. of the synovial area	**osteoarthritis** or **rheumatoid arthritis**
arthritis from crystal deposits in the joints	**gout, pseudogout,** or **calcium pyrophosphate dihydrate (CPPD)**
a fungal arthritis common in deserts	**coccidiomycosis, desert rheumatism,** or **valley fever**
a fungal arthritis common to gardeners	**sporotrichosis**
a fungal arthritis spread from skin or lungs	**blastomycosis**
arthritis with deformity of fingers and nails	**psoriatic arthritis**
inflammation of large joints and tissue areas	**Reiter's disease**
arthritis linked to inflamed bowels	**enteropathic arthritis**
a clawlike permanent bending of the toe	**hammertoes**

Treatments, Tests, and Tools

realignment of broken bones externally	**closed reduction**
realignment of broken bones using surgery	**open reduction**
implanting a bone from elsewhere	**bone graft**

an X-ray view of the skeletal structure	**bone scan**
an implanted device to hold bones together	**plate** or **pin**
an external device to hold bones rigid	**splint, cast,** or **traction**
an X-ray of a joint	**arthrography sampling**
a view of a joint through a small incision, also used in joint surgery	**arthroscopy**
used to record the electrical impulses of muscles	**electromyography (EMG)**

The Skin

Relating to the skin, what is or are . . . ?

Anatomy and Physiology

the type of tissue that covers the body and lines the internal organs	**epithelial tissue** or **epithelium**
the type of tissue that lies under the epithelium	**connective tissue**
the type of cells that form connective fibers	**fibroblasts**
"fat cells," filled with oil	**adipose cells**
the outer layer of the skin	**epidermis**
the middle layer of the skin	**dermis**
the fatty inner layer of the skin	**hypodermis**
the tissue binding skin and underlying tissue	**fascia**
the skin glands that cool the body	**sweat glands**
oil glands that lubricate hair and skin	**sebaceous glands**
the oil in a sebaceous gland	**sebum**
the skin parts that respond to deep pressure	**Pacinian corpuscles**
the skin parts that respond to light touches	**Meissner's corpuscles**
the skin parts that respond to heat and cold	**Krause end bulbs**
the tissue under the skin	**subcutaneous**
the subcutaneous part of a hair	**hair follicle**
the hair muscle that causes "goose bumps"	**arrector pili**
the hardened skin that makes up nails	**keratin**
the white crescent on a nail	**lunula**
the dead skin around a nail	**cuticle**

partly detached skin at the side of a nail	**hangnail**
the tissue from which the nail grows	**nail matrix** or **onych**

Diseases and Problem Conditions

inflammation of the nail matrix	**onychia**
inflammation of the skin around the nail	**paronychia**
the habit of nail-biting	**onychopagy**
hardening of the skin	**scleroderma**
abnormal thickening of the skin	**pachydermia**
fatty deposits under the skin	**xanthoma**
a lack of pigment in the skin	**albinism** or **alphosis**
variously pigmented benign areas in babies	**birthmarks** or **nevi**
benign pigmented growths appearing from early child-hood on	**moles**
birthmark from excess blood vessels	**hemangioma** or **port wine stain**
rough brownish growths on the upper body	**seborrheic keratoses**
pink, scaly spots, as on sun-exposed skin	**actinic** or **solar keratoses**
flat brown spots linked with age and sun	**liver spots** or **lentigines**
a spot of discolored skin	**macula**
scar tissue, as after surgery	**keloid**
a patch of diseased skin, also an injury	**lesion**
cancer of the skin's epithelial cells	**carcinoma**
a skin cancer linked with sun exposure	**basal cell carcinoma**
a skin cancer of the head, face, and hands	**squamous cell carcinoma**
the most serious form of skin cancer	**malignant melanoma**
the rare skin cancer associated with AIDS	**Kaposi's sarcoma**
recurrent or permanent flushing	**rosacea**
a raised sac of fluid under the skin's surface	**blister**
small wens that form around oily glands	**sebaceous cysts**
inflammation of oil glands, as in adolescence	**acne**
clogging of a hair follicle with oil	**blackhead** or **open comedo**
an infected, pus-filled hair follicle	**boil** or **furuncle**

an infection of the hair follicles, causing boils	**furunculosis**
bacterial abscesses larger than boils	**carbuncles**
severe itching	**pruritis**
reddening and inflammation of the skin	**dermatitis** or **eczema**
itchy skin inflammation from the cold	**chilblains**
scalp and skin scaling, common in mild form	**seborrheic dermatitis** or **dandruff**
a congenital disease of dry, scaly skin	**ichthyosis**
temporary loss of hair	**telogen effluvium**
loss of hair in patches, often temporary	**alopecia areata**
chronic production of scaly patches of skin	**psoriasis**
condition of pale, de-pigmented patches of skin	**vitiligo**
irritation of skin surfaces rubbing together	**intertrigo** or **chafing**
thickening of skin from frequent use	**corns** or **calluses**
a bedsore	**decubitus ulcer**
a heat rash or "prickly heat"	**miliaria**
an itchy swelling, as from a bite or allergy	**hives** or **urticaria**
a more serious form of hives	**angioedema**
an upper body rash, usually in adolescents	**pityriasis rosea**
skin tumors caused by viral growths	**warts**
white, pimply, viral growths	**mollusca**
a bacterial skin infection with blistering	**impetigo**
a bacterial infection in the deep levels of skin	**cellulitis**
a severe bacterial skin disease, often facial	**erysipelas** or **St. Anthony's fire**
death of tissue from a bacterial infection	**gas gangrene**
a contagious scalp disease that often barred immigrants from entering the US	**favus**
an infection causing pale patches on the skin	**tinea versicolor** or **sun fungus**
a fungal skin infection	**ringworm** or **tinea**
a form of ringworm common on the feet	**athlete's foot** or **tinea pedis**

a form of ringworm common in the crotch	**jock itch** or **tinea cruris**
a fungal infection of the feet, as in India	**mycetoma** or **Madura foot**
infestation with a mite, causing strong itching	**scabies** or "**the itch**"

Other Diseases and Symptoms

Among other diseases and symptoms, what is or are . . . ?

General Symptoms and Conditions

a pocket of pus in an inflamed area	**abscess**
disruption of the body's acid/alkaline balance	**acidosis**
abnormal enlargement of extremities	**acromegaly**
abnormal joining of tissues, as after an operation	**adhesions**
a hypersensitivity, as to pollens or penicillin	**allergy**
a severe allergic reaction, as to penicillin, that can lead to collapse of the circulatory system, shock, and death	**anaphylaxis** or **anaphylactic shock**
lack of oxygen	**anoxia**
suffocation from too little oxygen	**asphyxia**
loss of coordination or control of movements	**ataxia**
wasting away, as of unused muscle tissue	**atrophy**
a swollen, inflamed lymph gland, esp. in the groin or armpit, as in bubonic plague	**bubo**
wasting of the body from a chronic disease	**cachexia**
fibrous tissue, as builds up in arteries	**collagen**
a long, deep unconsciousness	**coma**
lessened ability to function	**debility**
delusions or visions, as with fever or drug use	**delirium**
the tremulous shaking and hallucinations linked with alcohol abuse	**delirium tremens (DT's)**
progressive loss of intellectual functioning	**dementia**

a widening, as of an air passage or cervix	**dilation**
abnormal development, as of organs or tissues	**dysplasia**
swelling from excess fluid in the body	**edema** or **dropsy**
thinness from illness or starvation	**emaciation**
collection of pus in a cavity, as in the lungs	**empyema**
reddening of the body, as with a rash	**erythema**
forming abnormal amounts of fibrous tissue	**fibrosis**
an abnormal opening between two body parts	**fistula**
an inability to break down milk sugar	**galactosomia**
death and decay of tissue, as from lack of blood	**gangrene**
the body's collapse as blood rushes to skin, and away from vital organs, to keep cool	**heat exhaustion**
life-threatening failure of the body's cooling mechanism	**heat stroke**
vomiting of blood	**hematemesis**
blood in the urine	**hematuria**
spitting up blood	**hemoptysis**
keeping a balance among the body's systems	**homeostasis**
excess activity or movement	**hyperactivity** or **hyperkinesis**
an imagined belief that one is ill or about to be	**hypochondria**
the death of tissue, due to lack of blood	**infarction**
the inability to sleep	**insomnia**
lack of immunity to infection	**maglobulinemia**
the softening of a body part	**malacia**
general listlessness and irritability	**malaise**
a fatal reaction to anesthetics, with extremely high body temperatures	**malignant hyperthermia**
a severe headache with throbbing and nausea	**migraine**
the death of living tissue	**necrosis**
small knots or lumps of tissue	**nodules** or **nodes**
being 20% or more above "ideal" weight	**obesity**
blockage, as of a blood vessel	**occlusion**
a puncture or other hole, as in an ear or ulcer	**perforation**
hypersensitivity to light	**photosensitivity**

getting better after taking a "dummy" drug	**placebo effect**
pus-filled	**purulent**
a thick fluid formed in bacterial infections	**pus**
pus in the blood	**pyemia**
pus in the urine	**pyuria**
pain felt in one place but coming from another	**referred pain**
an automatic, involuntary reaction to a stimulus	**reflex**
a severe body reaction including rapid pulse and low blood pressure, as after an accident	**shock**
the narrowing of a tube or opening	**stenosis**
a conscious, but impaired state	**stupor**
to form pus	**suppurate** or **fester**
a faint	**syncope**
an injury, esp. a sudden one	**trauma**
swelling or enlarging of a body part	**tumescence**
a lesion, often pus-filled, on skin, or on an internal mucous membrane, as in the stomach	**ulcer**
deep, dull aching in the abdomen	**visceral pain**
the body's readjustment after cut-off of a habit-forming substance	**withdrawal symptoms**

Infectious or Parasitical Diseases

the deadly sexually transmitted disease that destroys the immune system	**AIDS (acquired immune deficiency syndrome)**
a syndrome with swollen glands and fever, often preceding full-blown AIDS	**AIDS-related complex (ARC)**
a deadly infection often passed by cattle	**anthrax**
a fungal disease of people with weak immune systems	**aspergillosis**
deadly food poisoning, as from canned food	**botulism**
14th-c. Europe's "Black Death"	**bubonic plague**
a yeast infection from the fungus candida, as in AIDS patients	**candidiasis, moniliasis,** or **thrush**
an acute viral disease with skin eruptions	**chicken pox** or **varicella**
an epidemic disease with diarrhea and vomiting, spread by polluted water	**cholera**

an acute fungal infection in the SW US	**coccidioidomycosis** or **San Joaquin fever**
a worldwide fungal infection spread by pigeons	**cryptococcosis**
an acute infectious disease with clogging of air passages	**diphtheria**
enlarging and swelling of the body, due to a parasitical worm	**elephantiasis**
the virus linked with mononucleosis	**Epstein-Barr virus**
a disease linked with many birth defects	**German measles** or **rubella**
a liver disease associated with poor hygiene	**hepatitis A**
a serious blood-borne liver disease common among intravenous drug users	**hepatitis B**
the virus that causes cold sores	**herpes simplex Type 1**
the virus that causes genital sores	**herpes simplex Type 2**
the virus that cause AIDS	**HIV (human immuno-deficiency virus)** or **HTLV-III**
a fungal disease common in the central US	**histoplasmosis**
a sandfly-spread tropic and Asian infection	**kala azar**
a bacterial disease ulcerating skin and nerves, with victims isolated in colonies	**leprosy** or **Hansen's disease**
often linked with bacteria in cheese	**listeriosis**
a disease with arthritis, heart, or nerve damage, caused by infection from a tick bite	**Lyme disease**
a mosquito-spread parasitical infection, common in the tropics	**malaria**
an acute viral disease with red spots and fever	**measles** or **rubeola**
river blindness in West Africa	**onchocerciasis**
an infestation of lice in the pubic area	**pediculosis pubis** or **crabs**
a viral disease with sharp chest pain and mild fever	**pleurodynia** or **the devil's grip**
a viral disease causing paralysis and muscular atrophy	**polio, poliomyelitis,** or **infantile paralysis**
a bird-spread from of pneumonia	**psittacosis, ornithosis,** or **parrot fever**
a deadly nervous system disease spread by a bite from an infected animal	**rabies** or **hydrophobia**

an infectious disease with fever and joint inflammation, and often heart damage	**rheumatic fever**
a disease spread by mites or ticks	**rickettsialpox**
a serious tick-transmitted disease caused by rickettsiae parasites	**Rocky Mountain spotted fever**
an acute disease with reddish skin and high fever	**scarlet fever** or **scarlatina**
a tropical disease with worm infestation	**schistosomiasis, bilharziasis,** or **snail fever**
any bacterial disease	**schizomycosis**
a severe infectious disease recently eliminated from the world	**smallpox** or **variola**
bacteria causing much food poisoning	**staphylococci**
bacteria causing scarlet fever and strep throat	**streptococci**
a deadly infection involving muscle rigidity	**tetanus, lockjaw,** or **trismus**
bacterial blood poisoning linked with tampons	**toxic shock syndrome**
an infectious disease transmitted by rodents	**tularemia** or **rabbit fever**
a severe tropical fever spread by contaminated food or water, with intestinal hemorrhaging	**typhoid** or **enteric fever**
a rickettsiae-caused disease spread by lice	**typhus** or **prison fever**
a persistent bacterial fever causing weakness and aching joints	**undulant fever** or **brucellosis**
fungal infections in various parts of the body	**yeast infections**
a tropical and subtropical mosquito-borne disease, e.g., in Panama	**yellow fever**

Cancers and Other Abnormal Growths

not harmful or malignant, as of a tumor	**benign**
abnormal, often deadly growth of body cells	**cancer**
cancer-causing substances	**carcinogens**
harmful or dangerous, as of a tumor	**malign**
a cancer spreading to other sites	**metastasizing**
a general name for cancer genes	**oncogenes**

small mushroomlike growths on thin stalks	**polyps**
excess production of fibrous tissue in the body	**progressive systemic sclerosis (PSS)**
cancer of the connective tissues	**sarcoma**
a nonfunctional, noninflammatory growth in existing tissue	**tumor**

Diseases or Conditions from Deficiency or Excess

(See also The Hormone System: Diseases and Problem Conditions)

a thiamin-deficiency disease with paralysis, anemia, and wasting	**beriberi**
a disease resulting from malnutrition or poor absorption of nutrients	**deficiency disease**
not enough fluid in the body	**dehydration**
improper nutrition, and disorders caused by it	**dystrophy**
a disease from excess iron in the body	**hemochromatosis** or **bronzed diabetes**
excess blood sugar, as in diabetes	**hyperglycemia**
a high cholesterol condition	**hyperlipidemia**
unnaturally high body temperature	**hyperthermia** or **fever**
too little blood sugar, sometimes from an overdose of insulin	**hypoglycemia, insulin shock,** or **hyperinsulinism**
a potassium deficiency	**hypokalemia**
too little oxygen in the body's tissues	**hypoxia**
unnaturally low body temperature	**hypothermia**
a life-threatening buildup of acidic substances called ketones, as in diabetes	**ketosis**
a protein-deficiency disease, as in Africa	**kwashiokor**
a wasting away from too little or unassimilated food	**marasmus**
a niacin-deficiency disease	**pellagra**
excessive thirst, as in untreated diabetics	**polydipsia**
a vitamin D–deficiency disease of the spine	**rickets** or **rachitis**
caused by lack of Vitamin C	**scurvy** or **scorbutus**

Other Diseases and Conditions

an inherited form of dwarfism	**achondroplasia**
air bubbles in the blood from too rapid a change in atmospheric pressure, as among divers or tunnel workers, "the bends"	**aeroembolism, decompression sickness,** or **caisson disease**

a progressive disease with symptoms like senility	**Alzheimer's disease**
severe, life-threatening self-starvation	**anorexia nervosa**
a disease in which the body attacks itself	**autoimmune disease**
excessive secretion of mucus	**blenorhea**
abnormally heavy eating, often with vomiting	**bulimia**
an inherited degeneration of the nervous system, with spasmodic jerking	**chorea (Huntington's)** or **St. Vitus' dance**
a Caribbean disease from poisoned fish	**ciguatera**
replacement of muscles, skin, and other tissues with useless scar tissue	**dermatomyositis** or **polymyositis**
a genetic disease, with abnormal chromosome patterns causing retardation	**Down's syndrome, mongolism,** or **trisomy 21**
a disease from a cereal fungus, basis for LSD	**ergotism**
a genetic disease of the bones, blood, liver, and spleen, among Eastern European Jews	**Gaucher's disease**
an inherited juvenile cholesterol condition	**hypercholesterolemia**
an auto-immune disease that can affect any of the body's organs	**lupus** or **systemic erythematosus (SLE) lupus**
lead poisoning	**plumbism**
food poisoning caused by protein decay	**ptomaine poisoning**
any of several diseases of muscles, bones, nerves, and their connective tissue	**rheumatism**
a fatal brain disease found mostly among Eastern European Jews	**Tay-Sachs disease**
a tropical skin disease with red pimples	**yaws** or **frambesia**

Other Medical and Health Language

Relating to other language in the world of medicine and health, what is the word or phrase for . . . ?

The Body's Disease-Fighting Mechanisms

the parts of the body's immune system that fight foreign substances	**antibodies**
a foreign substance that stimulates antibodies	**antigens**
natural genes that protect against some cancers	**anti-oncogenes**
the body's defense network against disease	**immune system**
not susceptible to contracting a specific illness	**immune**
an infection that mainly strikes people with an impaired immune system, as by AIDS	**opportunistic infection**
the body's attack on a transplanted organ seen as foreign	**rejection**
immune system cells that stop a reaction	**suppressor T-cells**

Terms of Diagnosis and Prognosis

reaching a crisis quickly	**acute**
of unknown origin	**agnogenic**
someone harboring but not catching a disease	**asymptomatic carrier**
prolonged or lingering	**chronic**
a disease easily spread to others	**communicable** or **contagious**
existing from birth	**congenital**
a disease of deterioration	**degenerative disease**
determination of the nature of a disease	**diagnosis**
a congenital tendency toward a disease or weakness	**diathesis**
a disease that recurs in a particular community	**endemic**
a disease spreading rapidly in an area	**epidemic**
a disease induced inadvertently by a doctor	**iatrogenic**
of unknown origin, i.e., unique to an individual	**idiopathic**
the time after contact before symptoms of a contagious disease show	**incubation period**

able to be seen only with technical aid	**occult**
the minimum energy to sustain life at rest	**basal metabolism**
the 2 serpents twined around a staff, the symbol of medicine, from the Greeks	**caduceus**
gymnastic exercises, in general	**calisthenics**
able to destroy or burn tissue	**caustic**
in an epidemic, the line marking infected districts	**cordon sanitaire**
the outer area of an organ, e.g., the brain	**cortex**
an experiment where neither patients nor doctors know which drug is real and which a placebo	**double blind**
low cholesterol lipoprotein that carries fat away from body cells	**high-density lipoprotein (HDL)**
a digestive chemical that inflames tissue during allergic reactions	**histamine**
a place for the terminally ill, once a medieval monastic shelter	**hospice**
a medical student or graduate working under supervision	**intern**
a fatty substance	**lipid**
a fatty substance combined with a protein	**lipoprotein**
high cholesterol lipoprotein, that carries fat to body cells	**low-density lipoprotein (LDL)**
dark pigment in both hair and skin	**melanin**
relating to smell	**olfactory**
anything that causes a disease	**pathogen**
colored matter, e.g., in the eyes or hair	**pigment**
preventing the spread of a disease	**prophylaxis** or **-lactic**
an artificial replacement for a body part	**prosthesis**
amino acid–based compounds vital to the body	**protein**
relating to the lungs	**pulmonary**
isolation of people with contagious diseases	**quarantine**
a physician serving in a place while receiving specialized practical training	**resident**

| unease and nausea when traveling on water | **seasickness** or **mal de mer** |
| the presence of disease-causing microbes | **sepsis** |

Other Medical Tools, Tests, and Techniques

Among other medical tools, tests, and techniques, what is or are . . . ?

Treatments and Approaches

a Chinese medical treatment using long needles	**acupuncture**
treatment with drugs that produce effects unlike those of the disease	**allopathy**
inducing loss of feeling or sensation	**anesthesia**
removing fluids using suction, as from lungs	**aspiration**
listening to the body, as with a stethoscope	**auscultation**
a way to consciously regulate normally involuntary functions	**biofeedback**
the outdated practice of draining blood from the body through cuts or leeches	**bleeding, leeching,** or **venesection**
mouth-to-mouth breathing and external heart massage to revive heart attack victims	**cardiopulmonary resuscitation (CPR)**
burning away unwanted tissue with electricity or chemicals such as silver nitrate	**cautery** or **cauterization**
use of a needle to obtain body fluid samples	**centesis**
controversial treatment to remove deposits from arteries, by filtering heavy metals from the blood	**chelation therapy**
treating disease using chemicals	**chemotherapy**
destroying tissue with extreme cold, e.g., with liquid nitrogen	**cryosurgery**
outdated use of a heated cup to draw blood to the skin's surface	**cupping**
taking an ultrasound picture of a body part	**echography**

burning away growths with electrical current	**electrodesiccation (EST)**
injection of small pellets of material into a tumor to block off the blood supply	**embolization**
examining internal organs through a hollow tube	**endoscopy**
an upward thrust under the ribs of a choking person	**Heimlich "hug"** or **maneuver**
treatment with small doses of drugs that, in large doses, produce effects like those of the disease	**homeopathy**
treating diseases with hormones, natural or synthetic	**hormone therapy**
treatment by baths or wet compresses	**hydrotherapy**
introducing a substance using a needle	**injection**
introduction of a disease to the body to cause a mild case, and so immunity	**inoculation** or **vaccination**
introducing liquids through a vein	**intravenous (IV)**
tying off blood vessels during surgery	**ligature** or **ligation**
an attempt to promote longevity through diet	**macrobiotics**
therapeutic rubbing or kneading body parts	**massage**
a view of the area behind the sternum, through a small incision	**mediastinoscopy**
treatment with light	**phototherapy**
bombarding tumors with protons from an accelerator, or cyclotron	**proton therapy**
the use of radioactive materials or X-rays in treatment	**radiotherapy**
treatment given through the skin	**transdermal**
injecting blood, plasma, or other solutions directly into a vein	**transfusion**
surgical transfer of an organ or tissue from one body to another, or to elsewhere on a body	**transplant**
treating first those who will benefit most, when not all can be treated	**triage**
inserting a needle into a vein to draw blood	**venipuncture**

Tools and Tests

often used to provide contrast in X-rays	**barium**
a sample of body tissue	**biopsy**
a thin tube inserted into the body	**catheter**
the use of radioisotopes and successive cross-sections to picture body organs	**computerized axial tomography (CT or CAT)**
growing microorganisms, as for identification	**culture**
a scooplike knife used to cut away tissue	**curette** or **curet**
an AIDS test with a high margin of error	**Elisa method**
an X-ray showing moving images, used when inserting catheters	**fluoroscope**
a system for rating the development of preschool children	**Gesell's development scale**
a clamp to stop bleeding from a vessel	**hemostat**
a skin test for allergies	**intracutaneous test** or **patch test**
a surgical knife, sharp on both sides	**lancet**
the use of magnets and radiowaves to depict body organs and biochemistry	**nuclear magnetic resonance (NMR)** or **magnetic resonance imaging**
tapping or thumping on the body	**percussion**
the use of X-rays to produce a picture	**radiography**
picturing organs highlighted by radioactive material ingested by the patient	**radioisotope, nuclear scanning,** or **imaging**
instruments to hold back a cut's edges	**retractors**
a test for diptheria immunity	**Schick test**
an X-ray of the salivary glands	**sialography**
a device for listening to sounds in the body	**stethoscope**
sewing two edges together, as after surgery	**suture**
measuring varying heat of body tissues	**thermography**
the device that records the pattern of uterine contractions	**tocodynameter**
the use of sound waves to picture body organs	**ultrasound** or **sonogram**

a test to detect syphilis | **Wasserman test**
the AIDS test often used to check the Elisa test | **Western Blot method**

Medical Specialties

(See also Scientific and Technical Specialties in *World of the Sciences*)

In the area of medicine and health, what specialty focuses on . . . ?

anesthetics administration	**anesthesiology**
animals and their diseases	**veterinary medicine**
artificial dentures	**prosthodontics**
artificial replacements for body parts	**prosthetics**
blood	**hematology**
body as a whole, rather than as a collection of specialized parts	**holistic medicine**
cancer	**oncology**
childbirth	**obstetrics, midwifery,** or **tocology**
children and childhood diseases	**pediatrics**
children's teeth	**pedodontics** or **pediatric dentistry**
dental surgery to correct problems	**oral** and **maxillofacial surgery**
disease classification	**nosology**
disease identification	**diagnostics**
disease nature and consequences	**pathology**
disease origins and causes	**etiology**
disease treatment not with traditional medicine but with massage and bone manipulation	**osteopathy**
disease treatments in general	**therapeutics**
ears, nose, and throat	**otorhinolaryngology** or **otolaryngology**
ears	**otology**
elderly people's health and ills	**gerontology** or **geriatrics**
endocrine (ductless) glands and hormones	**endocrinology**
eye examinations and correcting vision with lenses	**optometry**
eyes and their diseases	**ophthalmology**
feet	**podiatry**
gum diseases	**periodontics**
hands and feet	**chiropody**

health and disease prevention	**hygiene**
hearing and sound	**audiology**
heart	**cardiology**
immunity and the immune system	**immunology**
link between biological and mental processes	**psychobiology**
measures of psychological factors, e.g., intelligence	**psychometrics**
medical evidence for legal proceedings	**forensic medicine**
medical use of physical means, e.g., manipulation or massage, to treat disease	**physical medicine**
medicine preparation and prescription	**materia medica**
medicines and their effects	**pharmacology**
mental illnesses, as a medical specialty	**psychiatry**
mind and behavior	**psychology**
mouth diseases	**oral pathology**
mouth	**stomatology**
nervous system surgery	**neurosurgery**
nervous system	**neurology**
newborn infants	**neonatology**
nonmedical manipulation of skeletal structures	**chiropractic** or **-praxis**
phenomena not explainable by current knowledge, e.g., telepathy or psychokinesis	**parapsychology**
poisons and treatment for poisoning	**toxicology**
radiation for diagnosis and therapy	**radiology**
rectum and anus	**proctology**
root canal therapy	**endodontics**
serum	**serology**
skeletal system and movement	**orthopedics**
skin	**dermatology**
stomach and intestines	**gastroenterology**
stomach and its diseases	**gastrology**
surgery that is highly delicate, using magnification	**microsurgery**
surgery to remodel or repair	**plastic surgery** or **chiroplasty**
surgery with extreme cold	**cryosurgery**
symptoms associated with disease	**symptomatology** or **semiology**
teeth cleaning	**dental hygienics**
teeth extractions	**exodontics**
teeth placement correction	**orthodontics**
teeth	**dentistry**

therapeutic use of physical means, e.g., heat or massage, to treat disease or injury	**physiotherapy,** or **physiatry**
treating illnesses with natural substances, esp. vitamins, not drugs	**orthomolecular medicine**
treatment using instruments	**surgery**
women's diseases, esp. of the reproduction system	**gynecology**

World of the Sciences

Scientific and Technical Specialties

(See also Medical Specialties in *In Sickness and In Health*)

In the world of science and technology, what is or was the special study of . . . ?

agriculture or farming	**geoponics**
air and gases	**pneumatics**
aircraft and aviation	**aeronautics**
algae	**algology**
algae and seaweed	**phycology**
ancient animals and their fossils	**paleozoology**
ancient plants and their fossils	**paleobotany**
ancient life forms and fossils	**paleontology**
ancient people's knowledge of the heavens	**paleoastronomy**
ancient written documents	**paleography**
animals	**zoology**
animal behavior	**ethology**
animal disease	**zoopathology**
animal comparative anatomy and physiology	**zootomy**
arithmetic generalized using symbols and numbers	**algebra**
artistic alteration and planting of grounds	**landscape architecture** or **gardening**
atmosphere, esp. weather	**meteorology**
atmospheric aspects of meteorology	**aerology**
bacteria	**bacteriology**
behavior of fluids	**hydraulics**
biological aspects of animal distribution	**zoogeography** or **zoography**
biological cycles and rhythms	**chronobiology**
biological principles as applied to engineering	**bionics**
birds	**ornithology**
butterflies and moths	**lepidopterology**
caves	**speleology**

228

cells	**cytology**
cell structure as it affects genetics	**cytogenetics**
character and intelligence from one's skull shape	**phrenology**
character as read from facial features	**physiognomy**
charting a course, esp. for a ship or airplane	**navigation**
chemical compounds that are not in or from living things	**inorganic chemistry**
chemical technology as applied to large-scale production	**chemical engineering**
chemistry as applied to medicine	**iatrochemistry**
chemistry of biological processes	**biochemistry**
chemistry of carbon compounds, as from living things	**organic chemistry**
children, their behavior and development	**pedology**
classifying plants and animals	**taxonomy**
climate	**climatology**
climate's effect on living organisms	**bioclimatology**
clouds	**nephology**
coins	**numismatics**
color	**chromatology**
continuously changing quantities, in mathematics	**calculus**
crime and criminal behavior	**criminology**
crystals	**crystallography**
deforming and flow of matter	**rheology**
descriptive study of the universe	**cosmography**
deserts	**eremology**
designing buildings, as both art and science	**architecture**
detailed description and representation of places	**topography**
development in beings' early stages, before birth or hatching	**embryology**
diagnosing and treating the body and mind	**medicine**
disciplines dealing with society, e.g., sociology, anthropology, economics, and political science	**social sciences**
diseased tissue	**pathology**
DNA's role in genetics	**molecular genetics**
Earth and its atmosphere, esp. geology and meteorology	**earth sciences**
Earth's changes in structure over the ages	**historical geology**

Earth's crust and the forces reshaping it	**geotectonics** or **structural geology**
Earth's features and distribution of life on it	**geography**
Earth's structure and development	**geology**
earthquakes and their origins	**seismology**
ecological relationships between plants	**phytosociology**
economic data using statisical techniques	**econometrics**
economics as affected by its political setting	**political economics**
economics as theory	**plutology**
economics at the general level, e.g., national	**macroeconomics**
economics at the local level, e.g., a small business	**microeconomics**
effects of breeding and mutation on living populations	**population genetics**
electricity and motion	**electrodynamics**
electron flows controlled in technical applications	**electronics**
electronics in aviation and astronautics	**avionics**
energy and nonliving matter, as in physics, astronomy, chemistry, and geology	**physical sciences**
engraving or carving on precious stones	**glyptography**
epidemics and the diseases that cause them	**epidemiology**
etching or engraving, or any writing with a stylus	**stylography**
evolution of the universe	**cosmogony**
evolving shape of land forms	**geomorphology**
extinct beings in the genus Homo	**paleoanthropology**
extremely low temperatures and their effects	**cryogenics**
feedback systems, as in biology and computers	**cybernetics**
fish	**ichthyology**
fluid behavior	**hydraulics**
food balance in the diet, for proper nutrition	**dietetics**
food use by animals and plants	**nutrition**
forces on objects or systems, and making machinery using such forces	**mechanics**

form and structure, as in biology and geology	**morphology**
form, characteristics, and reactions of matter, esp. as atomic or molecular systems	**chemistry**
fossil footprints	**ichnology**
fruit	**pomology**
fungi	**mycology** or **fungology**
gases and their interactions with moving objects	**aerodynamics**
gases in equilibrium, including balloon flight	**aerostatics**
genetic manipulation to change DNA	**genetic engineering**
geographical distribution of plants and animals	**biogeography**
geometric figures using algebraic techniques and coordinates	**analytic, coordinate,** or **algebraic geometry**
germ-free life, as in laboratory conditions	**gnotobiotics**
glaciers	**glaciology**
grapes, esp. for wines	**vinivulture** or **viticulture**
grasses	**agrostology**
growing citrus fruits	**citriculture**
growing fruit	**pomiculture**
growing ornamental plants, as in a garden	**horticulture**
growing plants in water	**hydroponics** or **aquiculture**
growing plants that flower	**floriculture**
growing trees	**arboriculture** or **silviculture**
growing vegetables	**olericulture**
growth and change in cultures, esp. "primitive" ones	**ethnology**
heavenly bodies so as to predict human affairs	**astrology**
hereditary degeneration	**cacogenics** or **dysgenics**
hereditary improvement through environmental adjustment	**euthenics**
hereditary improvement through genetic control	**eugenics**
heredity and evolution	**genetics**
history just before recorded records	**protohistory**
human beings, origin and behavior	**anthropology**
human cultures	**cultural anthropology**
human social behavior and societies	**sociology**
human social behavior, e.g., sociology or anthropology	**behavioral sciences**

human use of plants and animals, esp. in "primitive" societies	**ethnobiology**
inscriptions, e.g., writings on ancient statues	**epigraphy**
insects	**entomology**
language and related behavior or understanding	**psycholinguistics**
language as part of society's culture	**sociolinguistics**
life and life processes	**biology**
life processes of organisms	**physiology**
light and vision	**optics**
likelihood that given events will occur	**probability**
living tissue	**histology**
making gold from "baser" metals, a vain attempt	**alchemy**
mammals	**mammalogy**
mapmaking	**cartography**
mapping	**chorology**
material evidence of civilization's development	**archaeology**
material evidence of human evolution	**physical anthropology**
material evidence of industrial development	**industrial archaeology**
mathematics of groups of numerical data	**statistics**
mathematics of triangles' sides and angles	**trigonometry**
matter and energy and their interactions	**physics**
measuring bodies for anthropological classification	**anthropometry**
measuring deep bodies of water	**bathymetry**
measuring social behavior, esp. preferences	**sociometrics**
measuring time	**chronometry**
measuring time, and timepieces	**horology**
mechanics of stationary bodies in equilibrium	**statics**
metals, esp. obtaining them from ores	**metallurgy**
microscopic fossils	**micropaleontology**
microscopic organisms	**microbiology**
molecular, atomic, and nuclear systems	**microphysics**
mollusks	**malacology**
money and material goods, from production to consumption	**economics**

monsters	**teratology**
mosses and liverworts	**bryology**
motion, without considering mass and force	**kinematics**
motion and the forces involved in it	**dynamics** or **kinetics**
motion of heavenly bodies	**astrodynamics**
mountains	**orology**
natural substances of use to humans	**mineralogy**
natural things, in general; once much of science	**natural history**
number forms and relationships, using sharply defined symbols	**mathematics**
nutrition, diet, and food, as a general science	**sitology**
objectively quantifiable sciences, e.g., biology, chemistry, and physics	**natural sciences**
oceans and their characteristics	**oceanography** or **thalassography**
organisms as they relate to their environment	**ecology**
origins of the universe	**cosmology**
parasitism	**parasitology**
periodic biological events, e.g., bird migrations	**phenology**
physical analysis applied to chemical systems	**physical chemistry**
physics of biological processes	**biophysics**
physics of geological events	**geophysics**
physics of stars	**astrophysics**
places and surfaces, as in geography or mathematics	**topology**
plant and animal growth in varying soils	**agrobiology**
plant diseases	**phytopathology**
plant distribution	**phytogeography**
plant or animal structures	**anatomy**
plants, in general	**botany** or **phytology**
plates in the Earth's crust; also construction of large buildings	**tectonics**
points, lines, angles, plane surfaces, and solids	**geometry**
political principles, processes, and structures	**political science**
politics and geography as intertwined	**geopolitics** or **political geography**
population size, distribution, and composition	**demography**

primates, such as gorillas	**primatology**
printing material using movable type	**typography**
protozoans	**protozoology**
psychic phenomena	**parapsychology**
purpose in nature	**teleology**
purposelessness in nature	**dysteleology**
raising animals	**animal husbandry** or **zooculture**
raising bees	**apiculture**
raising fish	**pisciculture**
relationship between heat and other forms of energy	**thermodynamics**
reptiles and amphibians	**herpetology**
rocks	**petrology** or **lithology**
rock strata	**stratigraphy**
scientific agriculture and soil management	**agronomy**
scientific animal breeding or husbandry	**zootechnics** or **zootechny**
scientific breeding of animals and plants	**thremmatology**
scientific applications in industry or business	**technology**
scientific knowledge as applied to construction	**engineering**
sea life	**marine biology**
selective breeding of animals	**stirpiculture**
shells and mollusks	**conchology**
size and shape of the Earth	**geodesy** or **geodetics**
snakes	**ophiology**
soils, esp. for agricultural uses	**soil science** or **pedology**
soils, in relation to crops	**agrology**
space effects on living organisms and search for life in space	**exobiology, space, xeno-,** or **astrobiology**
space flight	**astronautics**
stamps	**philately**
statistical study of biological information	**biometrics**
storage, retrieval, and transmission of data	**information theory**
structure of cellular molecules, such as viruses	**molecular biology**
structure of the Earth and its constituents	**geognosy**
structures and life on the Earth's surface	**physical geography** or **physiography**
stuffing dead animals	**taxidermy**
societies with only "primitive" technologies	**ethnography**
topics that later became physics, an early study	**natural philosophy**

transmitting data by remote means	**telegraphy**
trees	**dendrology**
types, esp. trying to classify them	**typology**
universe outside Earth	**astronomy**
upper atmosphere, esp. ionized gas layers	**aeronomy**
viruses	**virology**
volcanoes	**vulcanology**
water underground	**hydrogeology**
water, bodies of, analyzing and mapping	**hydrography**
ways of life among the world's peoples	**enthnology** *or* **cultural anthropology**
whales	**cetology**
winds	**anemology**
worms, esp. parasites	**helminthology**

People of Science and Invention

Early Scientists and Inventors

Among early scientists and inventors, who . . . ?

invented the catapult and formulated laws about the lever and pulley	**Archimedes**
was the Greek (Roman) deified physician	**Asklepios (Aesculapius)**
1st said the Earth revolves around the Sun	**Aristarchus**
is called the "Chinese Hippocrates"	**Chang Chung-ching**
thought that all matter was made up of atoms	**Democritus**
is considered the father of algebra	**Diophantus**
developed the pharmacopeia *De Materia Medica*	**Dioscorides**
thought that all was earth, fire, water, and air	**Empedocles**
estimated the Earth's circumference and its distance from the Sun and Moon	**Eratosthenes**

formulated the fundamentals of geometry	**Euclid**
was the first experimental physiologist	**Galen**
1st used latitude and longitude	**Hipparchus**
developed the oath still taken by doctors	**Hippocrates of Cos**
designed Egypt's early step Pyramid	**Imhotep**
developed distillation techniques	**Mary the Jewess**
thought the Sun revolved around the Earth	**Ptolemy**
formulated a key theorem about right triangles	**Pythagoras**
used mathematics to predict the Sun's eclipse	**Thales**

Medieval and Renaissance Scientists and Inventors

Among medieval and Renaissance scientists and inventors, who . . . ?

wrote the classic *De Re Metallica*	**Georgius Agricola**
transmitted Hippocrates's teachings to Europe	**Avicenna**
developed the modern scientific method	**Roger Bacon**
initiated basic methods of chemical analysis	**Robert Boyle**
made the 1st measurements of parallax	**Tycho Brahe**
was burned at the stake for his Copernican views	**Giordano Bruno**
developed the centigrade temperature scale	**Anders Celsius**
showed that the Earth revolved around the Sun	**Nicolaus Copernicus**
developed analytical geometry based on coordinates	**René Descartes**
developed the mercury thermometer	**Gabriel Fahrenheit**
developed the telescope and warred with the church	**Galileo Galilei**
developed printing from movable type, in Europe	**Johann Gutenberg**
forecast the return of the comet named for him	**Edmund Halley**
outlined the human circulatory system	**William Harvey**
detected cells seen through a microscope	**Robert Hooke**

demonstrated the Earth's geological changes	**James Hutton**
developed light-wave theory and a pendulum-clock	**Christian Huygens**
formulated basic laws of planetary motion	**Johannes Kepler**
wrote the classic *Celestial Mechanics*	**Pierre Simon Laplace**
outlined the role of oxygen in combustion	**Antoine Lavoisier**
discovered bacteria using a microscope	**Anton van Leeuwenhoek**
developed calculus, independently of Newton	**Gottfried Wilhelm Leibniz**
developed the classificatory system of taxonomy	**Carl Linnaeus**
reintroduced anatomical dissection into medicine	**Mondino de'Luzzi**
invented logarithms	**John Napier**
formulated basic laws of gravity and motion	**Isaac Newton**
used chemistry to find new medicines	**Paracelsus**
pioneered in using artificial limbs	**Ambroise Paré**
founded the theory of probability	**Blaise Pascal**
developed the mercury barometer	**Evangelista Toricelli**
wrote the classic anatomy *De Humani Corporis Fabrica*	**Andreas Vesalius**
wrote the key work *De Architectura*	**Vitruvius**

Modern Anthropologists, Archaeologists, and Sociologists

(See also Modern Economists and Political Theorists, Modern Explorers, and Modern Chemists)

Among 19th- and 20th-century anthropologists, archaeologists, and sociologists, who . . . ?

wrote *Patterns of Culture*	**Ruth Benedict**
excavated Dilmun, on Bahrein	**Geoffrey Bibby**
developed the pattern-process theory of culture	**Franz Boas**
copied and analyzed cave paintings, as at Lascaux	**Abbé Edouard Breuil**
wrote *The Hero with a Thousand Faces*	**Joseph Campbell**
found King Tut's tomb	**George Carnarvon**
excavated King Tut's tomb	**Howard Carter**
wrote *The Dawn of European Civilization*	**V(ere) Gordon Childe**

wrote *Positive Philosophy*, introducing sociology	**Auguste Comte**
1st found Australopithecus remains	**Raymond Dart**
developed dendrochronology, tree-ring dating	**Andrew Ellicott Douglass**
started using statistics in sociological work	**Emile Durkheim**
led excavations of Mycenaean sites at Cnossus	**Arthur Evans**
wrote *The Golden Bough*	**James George Frazer**
discovered Neanderthal Man	**Johann Fuhlrott**
pioneered in statistical opinion polling	**George Gallup**
was a key post-WWII public opinion analyst	**Louis Harris**
found a new hominid species in Ethiopia	**Donald Johanson**
excavated Jericho	**Kathleen Kenyon**
wrote *The Structure of Scientific Revolutions*	**Thomas Samuel Kuhn**
1st identified Cro-Magnon humans	**Edouard Larter**
did key early anthropology work in Kenya	**Louis and Mary Leakey**
found a nearly 3-million-year-old complete human skull in Kenya	**Richard Leakey**
wrote *Structural Anthropology*	**Claude Lévi-Strauss**
wrote *Middletown*	**Robert Staughton Lynd and Helen Merrell Lynd**
developed the structural-functional theory of culture	**Bronislaw Malinowski**
wrote *Coming of Age in Samoa*	**Margaret Mead**
wrote *The Power Elite*	**C. Wright Mills**
focused on races, as with UNESCO	**Ashley Montagu**
opined that work expands to fill the time available	**C. Northcote Parkinson**
developed sociology's structural-functional theory	**Talcott Parsons**
thought that employees are promoted to their level of incompetence	**Laurence J. Peter**
developed ideas on pluralism and interest groups	**David Riesman**
was an early 20th-c. poller, as for *Fortune*	**Elmo Burns Roper, Jr.**
found the lost city of Troy	**Heinrich Schliemann**
applied Darwin's "survival of the fittest" theory to human society	**Herbert Spencer**

wrote *Folkways* and "The Forgotten Man"	**William Graham Sumner**
helped identify Peking Man	**Pierre Teilhard de Chardin**
wrote *The Theory of the Leisure Class*	**Thorstein Veblen**
deciphered the Mycenaean Linear B script	**Michael Ventris**
developed key ideas on class, status, and power	**Max Weber**
discovered Mohenjo-Daro and Harappa	**(Robert Eric) Mortimer Wheeler**
wrote *The Organization Man*	**William H. Whyte**
discovered Ur of the Chaldees	**Leonard Woolley**

Modern Astronomers

(See also Modern Physicists)

Among 19th- and 20th-century astronomers, who . . . ?

catalogued and classified thousands of stars	**Annie Jump Cannon**
posited the idea of a red shift	**Christian Doppler**
discovered stars' mass-luminosity relationship	**Arthur Eddington**
suggested that Stonehenge was an ancient observatory	**Gerald Stanley Hawkins**
discovered Uranus	**William Herschel**
hypothesized that the universe is expanding	**Edwin Powell Hubble**
discovered radio waves emissions in space	**Karl Jansky**
predicted the discovery of the planet later named Pluto	**Percival Lowell**
catalogued the stars of the northern sky	**Charles Messier**
wrote *Intelligent Life in the Universe*	**Carl Sagan**
1st described the Milky Way's shape	**Harlow Shapley**
predicted belts of radiation circling Earth	**James Alfred Van Allen**

Modern Aviators

(See also Modern Engineers and Inventors)

Among modern aviators, who . . . ?

were lost over the Pacific in 1937 on a round-the-world attempt	**Amelia Earhart and Frederick Noonan**

1st flew over the North Pole, in 1926	**Richard Byrd and Floyd Bennett**
developed glider designs that helped the Wrights	**Octave Chanute**
headed the WASPs (Women's Airforce Service Pilots) in WWII	**Jacqueline Cochran**
built the 1st practical seaplane	**Glenn Curtiss**
built the "Spruce Goose," the world's largest plane, in 1947	**Howard Hughes**
built many private jet aircraft	**William Lear**
flew *The Spirit of St. Louis* solo across the Atlantic in 1927	**Charles Lindbergh**
built the *Gossamer Albatross*, a human-powered craft that in 1979 crossed the English Channel	**Paul MacReady**
flew hydrogen balloons over 50,000 feet high in the 1930's, twin brothers	**Auguste Antoine and Jean Felix Piccard**
was a barnstormer killed in 1935 with Will Rogers	**Wiley Post**
developed the helicopter and the transoceanic "clippers"	**Igor Sikorsky**
built and flew the 1st motor-driven airplane, in 1903	**Wilbur and Orville Wright**
1st broke the sound barrier	**Charles "Chuck" Yeager**
1st flew non-stop around the world, in 1988 in the *Voyager*	**Jeana Yeager and Dick Rutan**
developed the rigid airship, the dirigible	**Graf Ferdinand von Zeppelin**

Modern Biologists

(See also Modern Chemists)

Among 19th- and 20th-century biologists, who . . . ?

was a key early 20th-c. Bronx Zoo researcher	**William Beebe**
helped create the mid-20th-c. "green revolution".	**Norman Borlaug**
developed hundreds of new crop strains	**Luther Burbank**
developed crops from products like the peanut	**George Washington Carver**
developed the theory of natural selection in his *The Origin of Species*	**Charles Darwin**

wrote *So Human an Animal* and discovered natural antibiotics	**René Dubos**
discovered penicillin	**Alexander Fleming**
worked with "gorillas in the mists" in Rwanda	**Dian Fossey**
discovered vitamins	**Casimir Frank**
coined the term "eugenics"	**Francis Galton**
studied chimpanzees in Uganda	**Jane Van Lawick-Goodall**
was a key Darwin defender, head of a scientific family	**Thomas Henry Huxley**
outlined the basic cycle of metabolic reactions	**Hans Adolf Krebs**
believed environment can cause inheritable biological changes	**Jean Baptiste Lamarck**
1st recognized basic blood types	**Karl Landsteiner**
wrote *On Aggression*	**Konrad Lorenz**
was Stalin's Lamarckian state biologist	**Trofim Lysenko**
believed population would out-grow food supply	**Thomas R. Malthus**
outlined the theory of immunity	**Peter Medawar**
was imprisoned for attacking Lysenko's ideas	**Zhores Medvedev**
advanced genetics with his sweet-pea studies	**Gregor Mendel**
wrote *Chance and Necessity*	**Jacques Monod**
identified genes as the basic units of heredity	**Thomas Hunt Morgan**
proposed establishment of a sperm bank	**Hermann Joseph Muller**
developed the technique of heating to kill microorganisms	**Louis Pasteur**
developed the 1st birth control pill	**Gregory Pincus**
discovered the structure of DNA	**James D. Watson and Francis C. H. Crick**
founded Yale's famed Florida primate laboratory	**Robert Yerkes**

Modern Chemists

(See also Modern Biologists)

Among 19th- and 20th-century chemists, who . . . ?

discovered that all gases had the same number of particles	**Amedeo Avogadro**
developed the 1st all-synthetic plastic	**Hendrik Baekeland**
developed basic chemical symbols and formulas	**Jöns Jakob Berzelius**

outlined the chemical reactions in photosynthesis	**Melvin Calvin**
introduced modern atomic theory	**John Dalton**
developed the spectroscope	**G. R. Kirchhoff**
developed the technique of radiocarbon dating	**Willard Frank Libby**
developed the periodic table of elements	**Dimitri Mendeleev**
developed DDT	**Paul Müller**
built molecule models and theorized that vitamin C prevents colds	**Linus Pauling**
discovered oxygen	**Joseph Priestley**
discovered several new elements and chaired the Atomic Energy Commission	**Glenn Seaborg**
discovered isotopes	**Frederick Soddy**
discovered heavy water	**Harold Urey**
led the early 20th-c. fight against food adulteration	**Harvey Washington Wiley**

Modern Economists and Political Theorists

(See also Modern Anthropologists, Archaeologists, and Sociologists)

Among 19th- and 20th-century economists and political theorists, who . . . ?

put forth the theory of utilitarianism	**Jeremy Bentham**
co-authored *The Communist Manifesto* with Marx	**Friedrich Engels**
is a key advocate of conservative monetarist theories	**Milton Friedman**
coined the term "The Affluent Society"	**John Kenneth Galbraith**
wrote *The Road to Serfdom*	**Freidrich August von Hayek**
wrote *General Theory of Employment, Interest and Money*	**John Maynard Keynes**
wrote *Capital*, basis of Communism	**Karl Marx**
wrote *On Liberty* and *The Subjection of Women*	**John Stuart Mill**
wrote *An American Dilemma* and coined the term "stagflation"	**Gunnar Myrdal**
wrote *The Wealth of Nations*	**Adam Smith**
wrote *The Theory of the Leisure Class* and coined the term "conspicuous consumption"	**Thorstein Veblen**

Modern Engineers and Inventors

(See also Modern Aviators, Modern Chemists, and Modern Physicists)

Among 19th- and 20th-century engineers and inventors, who . . . ?

developed the 1st fully electronic computer, the ABC (Atanasoff-Berry Computer) 1939-42	**John Vincent Atanasoff and Clifford E. Berry**
designed a mechanical computer in the 1830's	**Charles Babbage**
built the 1st practical television in 1926	**John Logie Baird**
invented the telephone	**Alexander Graham Bell**
developed the 1st gas-powered automobile	**Karl Benz**
developed the electroencephalograph (EEG)	**Hans Berger**
learned how to convert pig iron to steel	**Henry Bessemer**
invented the process for quick-freezing foods	**Clarence Birdseye**
used Boolean algebra in his 1930's computer	**Vannevar Bush**
invented xerography	**Chester Floyd Carlson**
built an "artificial heart" pumping machine in 1936	**Alexis Carrel and Charles Lindbergh**
designed the 1st practical hovercraft	**Christopher Cockerell**
developed the CAT (Computerized Axial Tomography) scanning device	**Allan MacLeod Cormack and Godfrey N. Hounsfield**
invented the Aqua-Lung (scuba gear) for underwater breathing	**Jacques-Yves Cousteau**
developed the electron tube (triode) and sound for movies	**Lee De Forest**
built the 1st industrial robot	**George Devol**
developed the phonograph, the electric light bulb, and the kinetoscope (motion picture)	**Thomas Alva Edison**
developed the electrocardiograph (ECG or EKG)	**Willem Einthoven**
developed the modern moving assembly line	**Henry Ford**
popularized the geodesic dome	**Buckminster Fuller**
developed the steamboat	**Robert Fulton**
developed the M-1 rifle	**John Cantius Garand**

was an early 20th-c. US rocket pioneer	**Robert Goddard**
supervised the building of the Panama Canal	**George Washington Goethals**
refined color television and invented the long-playing record	**Peter Carl Goldmark**
developed the 1st computer microchips	**Marcian "Ted" Hoff**
invented the Polaroid camera	**Edwin Herbert Land**
developed the 1st sonar	**Paul Langevin**
built the Suez Canal, but failed at Panama	**Ferdinand de Lesseps**
was a key USSR aeronautical engineer	**Sergei Korolev**
sent the 1st transatlantic wireless transmission	**Guglielmo Marconi**
built the 1946 ENIAC (Electronic Numerical Integrator and Computer)	**John William Mauchly and John Presper Eckert**
designed the Germans' basic WWII plane	**Willy Messerschmitt**
invented the telegraph	**Samuel F. B. Morse**
made the 1st photograph	**Joseph Niepce**
invented dynamite	**Alfred Nobel**
developed an elevator brake	**Elisha Otis**
developed the modern transistor	**William Shockley, John Bardeen, and Walter Brittain**
found how to transmit electricity for practical use	**Charles Steinmetz**
built the 1st practical railroad	**George Stephenson**
built the code-breaking computer *Colussus* in 1943	**Alan Turing**
led the rocket teams that developed the V-1 and V-2	**Wernher von Braun**
developed the idea of storing programs in computers	**John von Neumann**
developed a practical steam engine	**James Watt**
developed the 1st all-electronic television	**Vladimir Zworykin**

Modern Explorers

(See also Modern Aviators)

Among the world's modern explorers and adventurers, who . . . ?

1st traveled the Northwest Passage in 1903-6 and in 1911 1st reached the South Pole	**Roald Amundsen**

explored Asia on American Museum of Natural History expeditions	**Roy Chapman Andrews**
proved in 1728 that North America and Asia were divided	**Vitus Bering**
discovered Machu Picchu in 1911	**Hiram Bingham**
1st flew over both the North and South Poles	**Richard E. Byrd**
sailed around the world alone in his *Gipsy Moth*	**Francis Chichester**
claimed to have reached the North Pole in 1908	**Frederick A. Cook**
wrote *The Silent World* and *The Living Sea*	**Jacques-Yves Cousteau**
was an early 20th-c. Asian explorer, later a Nazi sympathizer	**Sven Hedin**
crossed the Pacific on a log raft and wrote *Kon-Tiki*	**Thor Heyerdahl**
1st scaled Mt. Everest	**Edmund Hillary and Tenzing Norgay**
explored and helped preserve Yosemite	**John Muir**
explored by sea nearly to the North Pole 1895-96	**Fridtjof Nansen**
opened Russia's Northeast Passage in 1878-9	**Baron Nils Nordenskiöld**
are credited with 1st reaching the North Pole, in 1909	**Robert Peary and Matthew Henson**
descended over 10,000 feet in his bathyscape in 1953	**Jacques Piccard**
founded Thule, Greenland, as an exploration base	**Knud Rasmussen**
reached the South Pole 2nd and died trying to return	**Robert Falcon Scott**
was a key 20th-c. Arctic explorer and US advisor	**Viklhjalmur Stefanson**
found the oldest printed book in desert China	**Marc Aurel Stein**
made 4 expeditions to the Antartic, dying at the start of the last	**Henry Shackleton**
British officer who explored Tibet 1903-4	**Francis Younghusband**

Modern Geologists and Earth Scientists

Among 19th- and 20th-century geologists and earth scientists, who . . . ?

theorized that ice ages had occurred on Earth	**Louis Agassiz**
theorized that a dust cloud from collision with an extraterrestrial object killed much life, e.g., dinosaurs	**Luis Wo and Walter Alvarez (father and son)**
wrote the 1st geographical encyclopedia, *Kosmos*	**Alexander von Humboldt**
wrote the groundbreaking *Principles of Geology*	**Charles Lyell**
outlined the wind, current, and weather patterns of the Atlantic	**Matthew Fontaine Maury**
developed cylindrical projection for world maps	**Gerardus Mercator**
discovered the "discontinuity" between Earth's crust and mantle	**Andrija Mohorovicic**
made the 1st US survey of the Grand Canyon	**John Wesley Powell**
developed a 9-point rating scale for earthquakes	**Charles F. Richter**
proposed the continental drift theory	**Alfred Wegener**

Modern Mathematicians

(See also Modern Engineers and Inventors and Modern Physicists)

Among 19th- and 20th-century mathematicians, who . . . ?

developed a symbolic logic system widely used in computer systems	**George Boole**
was a fictitious author, pseudonym for a French mathematical group	**Nicolas Bourbaki**
formulated the theory of sets	**Georg Cantor**
developed modern number theory, key to laws of electromagnetism	**Carl Friedrich Gauss**
showed that some axioms must be unprovable	**Kurt Gödel**
developed abstract or noncommutative algebra	**William Rowan Hamilton**
outlined 23 key unsolved problems in 1900	**David Hilbert**

founded modern probability theory	A. N. Kolmogorov
developed non-Euclidean geometry independently of each other	Nikolai Ivanovich Lobachevsky and Johann Bolyai
formulated the theory of fractals	Benoit Mandelbrot
developed the mathematics for the quantum theory	Erwin Schrödinger
wrote *Principia Mathematica*, with Bertrand Russell	Alfred North Whitehead
developed the theory of cybernetics	Nobert Wiener

Modern Physicians, Psychologists, and Other Medical Figures

(See also Modern Biologists, Modern Chemists, and Modern Engineers and Inventors)

Among 19th- and 20th-century physicians, psychologists, and other medical figures, who . . . ?

developed the idea of the inferiority complex	Alfred Adler
wrote *Pattern and Growth in Personality*	Gordon Allport
found that insulin was a treatment for diabetes	Frederick Banting and C.H. Best
did the 1st successful human heart transplant	Christiaan Barnard
founded the American Red Cross	Clara Barton
formulated the "double bind" theory	Gregory Bateson
wrote bestsellers about Transactional Analysis	Eric Berne
wrote *The Uses of Enchantment* on child psychology	Bruno Bettelheim
pioneered in using amniocentesis	Douglas Bevis
developed standard intelligence testing	Alfred Binet and Théodore Simon
was the 1st woman physician in the US	Elizabeth Blackwell
developed surgery to repair heart defects in "blue babies"	Albert Blalock and Helen Taussig
was the psychologist famed for appearing on *The $64,000 Question*	Joyce Brothers
1st isolated the Lyme disease bacteria	Willy Burgdorfer
studied twins, working from later-questioned data	Cyril Lodowic Burt
pioneered in studying the pituitary gland	Harvey Cushing

1st used surgery to repair damaged blood vessels	**Michael DeBakey**
implanted the 1st Jarvik-7 artificial heart	**William DeVries**
was active in MEDICO, for Third World health care, working especially in Laos	**Tom Dooley**
developed the idea of blood banks	**Charles Richard Drew**
developed the "magic bullet" cure for syphilis	**Paul Ehrlich**
wrote *Studies in the Psychology of Sex*	**Henry Havelock Ellis**
propounded an influential theory of the stages of psychosocial growth	**Erik Erikson**
did the 1st coronary bypass operation	**Rene Favalaro**
discovered penicillin	**Alexander Fleming**
developed the psychoanalytic approach	**Sigmund Freud**
developed the Type A behavior theory	**Meyer Friedman**
wrote *The Sane Society*	**Erich Fromm**
headed the international medical team to Chernobyl	**Robert Peter Gale**
developed developmental schedules for children	**Arnold Lucius Gesell**
supervised mosquito control at Panama 1904-14	**William Crawford Gorgas**
emphasized environmental causes of anxiety	**Karen Horney**
posited the idea of a stream of consciousness	**William James**
developed vaccinations to prevent smallpox	**Edward Jenner**
posited the Collective Unconscious	**Carl Jung**
wrote *Sexual Behavior in the Human Male*	**Alfred Charles Kinsey**
developed play therapy in child psychoanalysis	**Melanie Klein**
identified the organisms causing tuberculosis	**Robert Koch**
wrote *On Death and Dying*	**Elisabeth Kubler-Ross**
tried to explain schizophrenia in *The Divided Self*	**Ronald D. Laing**
developed popular natural childbirth techniques	**Fernand Lamaze**
developed antiseptic surgery	**Joseph Lister**
founded the Saranac Lake TB sanitorium in 1884	**Edward Livingston**

founded humanistic psychology, much used in management	**Abraham Maslow**
wrote *Against Therapy*, attacking Freud establishment	**Jeffrey Moussaieff Masson**
wrote *Human Sexual Response*	**William Masters and Virginia Johnson**
founded a famed Rochester, Minnesota, clinic	**William Mayo and sons**
founded a psychiatric clinic in Topeka, Kansas	**Charles Menninger and sons**
revolutionized nursing in the Crimean War	**Florence Nightingale**
developed chiropracty	**Daniel David Palmer**
developed the "Pap smear" test to detect cancer	**George Papanicolaou**
demonstrated conditioned reflexes	**Ivan Pavlov**
explored children's concepts of space and time	**Jean Piaget**
focused on the birth trauma	**Otto Rank**
first treated hypothyroidism with thyroid extract	**George Redmayne**
identified the causes of yellow fever	**Walter Reed**
focused on sexual energy, or "orgone"	**Wilhelm Reich**
pioneered in parapsychology and coined "ESP"	**Joseph Rhine**
laid the basis for sensitivity training	**Carl Rogers**
developed the oral live-virus polio vaccine	**Albert Sabin**
wrote *The Man Who Mistook His Wife for a Hat*	**Oliver Sacks**
developed the 1st polio vaccine	**Jonas Salk**
coined the term "birth control"	**Margaret Sanger**
spent his life treating patients in Gabon, Africa	**Albert Schweitzer**
developed theories of antiseptic childbirth, independently of Oliver Wendell Holmes	**Ignaz Semmelweiss**
developed a skin test for diphtheria	**Béla Shick**
developed modern theories of behaviorism	**B. F. Skinner**
wrote *The Common Sense Book of Baby and Child Care*	**Benjamin Spock**
recognized the illness called Lyme disease	**Allen Steere**
developed *in vitro* fertilization	**Patrick Steptoe**
founded Britain's 1st birth control clinic	**Marie Stopes**

wrote *The Interpersonal Theory of Psychiatry*	**Harry Stack Sullivan**
developed intelligence tests, including mazes and puzzle boxes	**Edward Lee Thorndike**
developed early theories of behaviorism	**John Watson**
pioneered in using the EKG to monitor the heart	**Paul Dudley White**

Modern Physicists

(See also Modern Mathematicians, Modern Chemists, Modern Aviators, and Modern Engineers and Inventors)

Among 19th- and 20th-century physicists, who . . . ?

pioneered in studying radioactivity	**Antoine Henri Becquerel**
explained solar and stellar energy production	**Hans Bethe**
described electrons orbiting around a nucleus	**Niels Bohr**
discovered radium together	**Marie Sklodowska Curie and Pierre Curie**
invented the electric arc and a miner's safety lamp	**Humphry Davy**
1st posited the wave nature of particles	**Louis De Broglie**
1st predicted the existence of antimatter	**Paul Dirac**
posited the theory of relativity and $E = mc^2$	**Albert Einstein**
pioneered work in magnetism and electricity	**Michael Faraday**
1st split the atom through nuclear fission	**Enrico Fermi**
worked on subatomic particles and demonstrated the *Challenger*'s O-ring failure on TV	**Richard Feynman**
used a pendulum to show the Earth's rotation	**Jean Foucault**
worked on the 1st A-bomb, a spy for Soviet Union	**Klaus Fuchs**
was a key exponent of the Big Bang theory	**George Gamow**
developed a device to count radiation particles	**Johannes Geiger**
predicted and classified sub-atomic particles	**Murray Gell-Mann**
wrote *A Brief History of Time*	**Stephen Hawking**
1st posited the uncertainty principle	**Werner Heisenberg**

described electromagnetic waves	Heinrich Hertz
used high-energy bombardment to produce isotopes	Frédéric Joliot and Irene Joliot-Curie
outlined the principle of conservation of energy	James Joule
invented the cyclotron	Ernest O. Lawrence
developed the theory of electromagnetism	James Clerk Maxwell
calculated the energy released by uranium fission	Lise Meitner
invented the interferometer	Albert Michelson
1st measured an electron's charge	Robert Millikan
led the Manhattan Project to build the atom bomb	J. Robert Oppenheimer
posited the exclusion principle	Wolfgang Pauli
developed the basis for quantum theory	Max Planck
pioneered in the US development of radar	Isidor Isaac Rabi
discovered X-rays	Wilhelm Roentgen
described the atom's structure and produced protons	Ernest Rutherford
was a key USSR hydrogen bomb expert and dissident	Andrei Sakharov
helped build the 1st nuclear reactor and drafted the physicists' letter to Roosevelt	Leo Szilard
is called the father of the US hydrogen bomb	Edward Teller
discovered electrons	Joseph Thomson
discovered heavy hydrogen (deuterium)	Harold Urey
developed an early electric battery	Alessandro Volta

Language of Science

General Scientific Language

(See also Philosophies, also Language of Logic and Reasoning, in *World of Philosophy and Belief*)

In the world of science in general, what is the word or phrase for . . . ?

metabolism of complex molecules from simple ones	anabolism
units of heat, watched by dieters	calories

change from complex to simple molecues	**catabolism**
substances that become ions in solution, and so conduct electricity	**electrolytes**
the full range of radiation of all types	**electromagnetic spectrum**
using observation and experiment	**empirical**
the gradual process by which modern life and matter have developed, as opposed to creationism	**evolution**
a test to try a hypothesis or show a truth	**experiment**
a theoretical conjecture to be proved	**hypothesis**
the theory that everything has material causes	**mechanism**
the biochemical reactions essential to life	**metabolism**
too small to see without a microscope	**microscopic**
carbon compounds found in living matter	**organic compounds**
development and testing of hypotheses, in building scientific knowledge	**scientific method**
a standard, simple periodic oscillation	**sine wave**
the range of a phenomenon, e.g., radiation	**spectrum**
too small to see with an optical microscope	**submicroscopic**
joint action greater than that of the individuals	**synergy**

Units of Everyday Measurement

In the world of everyday measurement, what is or are the units for measuring . . . ?

length	**meters;** or **inches, feet,** and **yards**
angles	**degrees, minutes,** and **seconds**
large areas	**ares, hectares,** and **square kilometers;** or **square yards, rods, acres,** and **miles**
small areas	**square millimeters, centimeters,** and **meters;** or **square inches, feet,** and **yards**

large weights	kilograms; or hundredweights and tons (short or long measure)
small weights	milligrams and centigrams; or grains, drams (or pennyweights), ounces, and pounds
fluid volume	liters; or pints, quarts, and gallons
dry volume	pints, quarts, pecks, and bushels
temperature, with freezing at 32° and boiling at 212°	Fahrenheit degree (°)

Units of Scientific Measurement

In the world of scientific measurements, what is or are the units for measuring . . . ?

the amount of a substance	mole (mol)
the amount of electricity	coulomb (C)
capacitance	farad (F)
conductance	siemens (S)
electric current	ampere (A)
electrical resistance	ohm (Ω)
energy	electronvolt (eV)
flux density	tesla (T)
force	newton (N)
frequency	hertz (Hz)
illuminance	lux (lx)
inductance	henry (H)
intensity of light	candela (cd)
length, in astronomy	astronomical unit (AU); also parsec (pc)
length	meter or metre (m)
luminous flux	lumin (lm)
magnetic flux	weber (Wb)
mass, in chemistry or nuclear physics	atomic mass unit (u)
mass	kilogram (kg)
a plane angle	radian (rad)
potential difference, relating to electricity	volt (V)
power	watt (W)
pressure	pascal (Pa)
a solid angle	steradian (sr)
temperature, with freezing at 0° and boiling at 100°	kelvin (K), Celsius, or centigrade
work or energy	joule (J)

Prefixes for Large and Small Numbers

Among standard prefixes for large and small numbers, what is the prefix for . . . ?

10^1 or ten times	**deka (da)**
10^2 or a hundred times	**hecto (h)**
10^3 or a thousand times	**kilo (k)**
10^6 or a million (US) times	**mega (M)**
10^9 or a billion (US) times	**giga (G)**
10^{12} or a trillion (US) times	**tera (T)**
10^{15} or a quadrillion (US) times	**peta (P)**
10^{18} or a quintillion (US) times	**exa (E)**
10^{-1} or a tenth	**deci (d)**
10^{-2} or a hundredth	**centi (c)**
10^{-3} or a thousandth	**milli (m)**
10^{-6} or a millionth (US)	**micro (μ)**
10^{-9} or a billionth (US)	**nano (n)**
10^{-12} or a trillionth (US)	**pico (p)**
10^{-15} or a quadrillionth (US)	**femto (f)**
10^{-18} or a quintillionth (US)	**atto (a)**

Names for Large Numbers

Relating to large numbers, what is the American (US) or European (EU) name for . . . ?

1,000,000	**million**
1,000,000,000	**billion (US)** or **milliard (EU)**
1,000,000 X 1,000,000, or 10^{12}	**trillion (US)** or **billion (EU)**
10^{15}	**quadrillion (US)**
10^{18}, or $1,000,000^3$	**quintillion (US)** or **trillion (EU)**
10^{33}	**decillion (US)**
10^{60}, or $1,000,000^{10}$	**decillion (EU)**
10^{100}	**googol (US)**
10^{303}	**centillion (US)**
10^{600}, or $1,000,000^{100}$	**centillion (EU)**

Anthropology, Archaeology, and Sociology
Language

(See also The Mind and Personality in *In Sickness and in Health*)

In the world of anthropology, archaeology, and sociology, what is the word or phrase for . . . ?

In Sociology and Cultural Anthropology

adjusting to fit into the culture of others	**acculturation**

being isolated or outside	**alienation**
seeing humans as central in the universe	**anthropocentrism**
attributing human feelings to the nonhuman	**anthropomorphism**
cannibals, i.e., eaters of human flesh	**anthropophagi**
inheritances that pass from and to both male and female lines	**bilineal**
formation of close, special personal ties	**bonding**
the middle class	**bourgeoisie**
any of 4 hereditary social classes in Hindu India	**caste**
an official count of population	**census**
exceptional leadership ability and personal charm	**charisma**
awareness of common interest within a class	**class consciousness**
actions following current norms	**conformity**
a family in which blood relatives are central	**consanguine**
a group whose cultural patterns deliberately differ from those of the dominant culture	**counter culture** or **contraculture**
a father imitating the childbirth experience	**couvade**
the theory that norms and values stem from their cultural context	**cultural relativity**
a family where males and females share power	**democratic**
differing from a norm	**deviant**
the spread of culture from one group to another	**diffusion**
leaving one country to settle in another	**emigration**
choosing mates from inside a group	**endogamous**
belief that one's race or ethnic group is superior	**ethnocentrism**
choosing mates from outside a group	**exogamous**
a family with three or more generations together	**extended family**
unquestioned, shared social behavior	**folkways**
organization into graded ranks	**hierarchy**
coming to settle in a country, having left another	**immigration**

all one's relatives	**kinship group**
where family power is concentrated in females	**matriarchy**
where inheritance follows the female line	**matrilineal**
a married couple living with the wife's parents	**matrilocal**
moral rules in a society, often strongly felt	**mores**
a married couple establishing their own home	**neolocal**
a family in which blood relations are not central	**nonconsanguine**
standard behavior in a group	**norms**
two generations, parents and children, together	**nuclear family**
independent development of culture by separate groups	**parallel development**
where family power is concentrated in males	**patriarchy**
where inheritance follows the male line	**patrilineal**
a married couple living with the husband's parents	**patrilocal**
a core of leaders exercising great power	**power elite**
the working class	**proletariat**
learning how to act in group life	**socialization**
the existence of discrete levels in society	**stratification**
a group whose cultural patterns differ somewhat from those of the dominant culture	**subculture**
opinions about what is or is not desirable	**value judgment**

In Archaeology and Physical Anthropology

walking on two feet	**bipedalism**
swinging by the arms; also branching in an evolutionary "tree"	**brachiation**
wide-headed, almost to roundness	**brachycephalic**
a technique using the half-life of a carbon-14 isotope to tell the age of old objects	**carbon 14 dating**
using growth rings in trees for dating	**dendrochronology**
long-headed	**dolicocephalic**
having a skull about 70–75% as wide as it is long	**orthocephalic**

limestone flakes with ink inscriptions, as in Egypt	**ostraca**
having a flat-topped head	**platycephalic**
the period before written records	**prehistory**
the period just before written records	**protohistory**

Prehistoric Cultures and Human Ancestors

a very early Paleolithic culture from France	**Abbevillian** or **Chellian**
an early Paleolithic culture from northern France	**Acheulian**
a late Paleolithic culture centered in France and linked with Cro-Magnon people	**Aurignacian**
extinct humanlike primates identified from Pleistocene remains in southern and eastern Africa	**Australopithecus**
an early form of human, named for finds in southern France	**Cro-Magnon**
an extinct early human found in West Germany	**Heidelberg man**
the primate from which modern man evolved	**Hominid**
an extinct human species found at Choukoutien, China	**Homo erectus, Pithecanthropus,** or **Peking Man**
an extinct human species found in East Africa	**Homo habilis**
the species of modern humans	**Homo sapiens**
a late Paleolithic culture, after the Aurignacian	**Magdalenian**
the cultural period marked by cutting tools and the bow, from about 15,000 years ago	**Mesolithic** or **Middle Stone Age**
a middle Paleolithic culture from SW France	**Mousterian**
an extinct line of humans, named for finds in West Germany	**Neanderthal**
the cultural period marked by refined stone tools and farming, from about 10,000 years ago, in the Near East	**Neolithic** or **New Stone Age**
the stone tools found in Africa's Olduvai Gorge	**Oldowan**
the cultural period marked by crude tools of chipped stone, from about 750,000 years ago	**Paleolithic,** or **Old Stone Age**

faked bones found in England in 1911   **Piltdown Man**

the Pleistocene skeleton found in Java in 1891   **Pithecanthropus erectus**

Astronomy Language

(See also Religious and Occult Language in *World of Philosophy and Belief*)

In the world of astronomy, what is the word or phrase for . . . ?

About Orbits and Eclipses

the sun covered by the moon, except for a bright ring   **annular eclipse**

a planet's orbit point farthest from the Sun   **aphelion**

a planet's orbit point farthest from the Earth   **apogee**

a thin, C-shaped moon, mostly in darkness   **crescent** or **new moon**

an orbit that is off center   **eccentric**

the blocking from sight of a celestial body   **eclipse**

the seeming path of the Sun among the stars   **ecliptic**

a small circle, whose center moves around a larger circle, as in Ptolemy's view   **epicycle**

the moon appearing as a fully lit disk   **full moon**

the moon between half and fully lit   **gibbous moon**

the moon when only a semicircle is lit   **half moon**

the full moon around the autumnal equinox   **harvest moon**

a natural body revolving around a planet   **moon**

movement between an observer and a body, as in an eclipse   **occultation**

a body's path as it revolves around another body   **orbit**

one body being partly obscured by another   **partial eclipse**

the moon or satellite's orbit point nearest to the Earth   **perigee**

a planet's orbit point nearest to the Sun	**perihelion**
the time it takes to complete an orbit.	**period of revolution**
the time it takes to complete a 360° turn on an axis	**period of rotation**
regular changes in the appearance of a planet or moon	**phases**
a body revolving around a star, without its own light	**planet**
the celestial shift of the equinoxes as the Earth's axis of rotation shifts	**precession of the equinoxes**
apparent backward motion of a planet	**retrograde motion**
moving in an orbit around a point	**revolution**
the position of a body on the celestial sphere	**right ascension**
moving in a circle around an internal axis	**rotation**
a natural or manmade orbiting body	**satellite**
the point where the orbits of 3 or more bodies are in line, e.g., the Sun, Earth, and Moon	**syzygy**
the passage of a small body across a larger one	**transit**
the dark part of a sunspot; also the shadow on the Earth during a total solar eclipse	**umbra**
the moon as it grows thinner	**waning moon**
the moon as it grows fatter	**waxing moon**
the highest point, as of a body's pass above the horizon	**zenith**

Other Astronomy Terms

dark lines on an electromagnetic spectrum, showing the radiation of a particular substance	**absorption spectrum**
the amount of radiation from a surface	**albedo**
small bodies, or "minor planets," revolving around the Sun	**asteroids**
a medieval device to find the altitude of the sun, lit. "star-taker"	**astrolabe**
bright, colored flashes in the polar night sky	**aurora**
aurora in the Southern Hemisphere, "southern lights"	**aurora australis**

aurora in the Northern Hemisphere, "northern lights"	**aurora borealis**
the theoretical explosion that began the universe	**big bang**
two stars orbiting around the same center	**binary stars**
an intense gravitational field in space, giving off no radiation	**black hole**
stars with regular variations in light emission	**cepheid variables**
the bright nebula around the head of a comet	**coma**
a body with a bright head and vapor tail, seen as its orbit nears the Sun	**comet**
two bodies being in the same celestial region	**conjunction**
a grouping or cluster of stars	**constellation** or **asterism**
a bright ring around a celestial body	**corona**
high-energy radiation from outer space	**cosmic ray**
occurring daily	**diurnal**
the apparent change in light or sound waves as two bodies move apart	**Doppler effect**
a star with low mass and brightness	**dwarf**
the radiation given off by a substance, as shown on the electromagnetic spectrum	**emission lines**
the times when day and night are equally long, in spring (vernal) and fall (autumnal)	**equinox**
stars that show in the west just after sunset	**evening stars**
millions of stars, gas, and dust bonded by gravity	**galaxy**
the view that the Earth was the universe's center	**geocentric theory**
a very large, very bright star	**giant**
the view that the planets revolve around the Sun	**heliocentric theory**
a graph comparing stars' brightness and heat	**Hertzsprung-Russel (H-R) diagram**
vast voids in the universe	**Hubble bubbles**
a ratio of a galaxy's speed away from to its distance from Earth	**Hubble constant**
the distance light covers in a year	**light year**

a body that glows as it enters Earth's atmosphere	**meteor** or **shooting star**
stars that show in the east just before sunrise	**morning stars**
a gas-and-dust mixture, remains of a supernova	**nebula**
a star that suddenly and temporarily becomes much brighter	**nova**
an apparent change in an object's position, due to the observer's movement	**parallax**
the shadowy fringe around a sunspot	**penumbra**
celestial sources of variable radio signals	**pulsar**
active cores of galaxies, erupting with energy as they draw in nearby mass	**quasars (quasi-stellar objects or QSO's)**
an increase in a body's radiation, toward the red end of the spectrum, due to the Doppler effect	**red shift**
the minimum distance from a body for formation of a moon	**Roche limit**
about or measured by the stars	**sidereal**
the Sun, its planets, and their orbiting bodies	**solar system**
blasts of electrically charged particles from the Sun	**solar wind**
the longest (summer) and shortest (winter) days in the year	**solstices**
the idea that the universe stays the same, creating new material as the old flies apart	**steady state theory**
a part of the sun brighter than its setting	**sun spot** or **facula**
a star that explodes	**supernova**
the time between conjunctions of a planet or moon with the Sun	**synodic month**
devices for viewing the stars, by sight or by measuring radiation	**telescopes**
everything that exists	**universe** or **cosmos**
bands of high radiation circling the Earth	**Van Allen belts**

The Solar System

Within the solar system, what is or are . . . ?

the small planet closest to the Sun	**Mercury**
the 2nd planet, between Mercury and Earth	**Venus**
the possibly habitable 4th planet, nearest Earth	**Mars**
Mars's 2 moons	**Phobos** and **Deimos**
the 5th and largest planet	**Jupiter**
Jupiter's 4 brightest moons, discovered by Galileo	**Io, Europa, Ganymede,** and **Callisto**
Jupiter's 3 largest moons	**Titan, Rhea,** and **Iapetus**
the 6th planet	**Saturn**
the 7th planet	**Uranus**
Uranus's largest moon	**Titania**
the 8th planet	**Neptune**
Neptune's largest moon	**Triton**
the 9th planet	**Pluto**

Stars and Constellations

Relating to stars and constellations, what is or was . . . ?

a double star in Centaurus, its brightest	**Alpha Centauri**
the constellation of the Chained Lady	**Andromeda**
the constellation of the Water Bearer	**Aquarius**
the constellation of the Ram	**Aries**
the constellation of the Charioteer	**Auriga**
the nearest star neighboring our Sun	**Barnard's Star**
the supergiant star in Orion	**Betelgeuse**
the constellation of the Herdsman	**Boötes**
the constellation of the Crab	**Cancer**
the constellation of the Hunting Dogs	**Canes Venatici**
the constellation including Sirius	**Canis Major (Larger Dog)**
the constellation east of Orion	**Canis Minor (Lesser Dog)**
the constellation of the Goat	**Capricornus**
the constellation of the Queen, or the Lady in the Chair	**Cassiopeia**
the constellation of the King (of Ethiopia), Andromeda's father	**Cepheus**
Pluto's moon	**Charon**
the constellation of the Southern Crown	**Corona Australis**

the constellation of the Northern Crown	**Corona Borealis**
the constellation of the Crow	**Corvus**
the remains of an 11th-c. A.D. supernova in Taurus	**Crab Nebula**
the constellation of the Swan, the Northern Cross	**Cygnus**
the constellation of the Dragon	**Draco**
the constellation of the Twins	**Gemini**
the 1st comet whose return astronomers predicted	**Halley's Comet**
a nebula in the constellation Orion	**Horsehead Nebula**
the constellation of the Sea-Serpent	**Hydra**
the comet discovered in 1973	**Kohoutek**
the constellation of the Lion	**Leo**
the constellation of the Hare	**Lepus**
the constellation of the Scales	**Libra**
the constellation of the Harp	**Lyra**
the Milky Way's neighboring 2 galaxies, seen in the Southern Hemisphere	**Magellanic Cloud**
the galaxy of which Earth is a part	**Milky Way**
the constellation of the Unicorn	**Monoceros**
the constellation of the Serpent-Bearer	**Ophiuchus**
the constellation of the Hunter	**Orion**
the constellation of the Winged Horse	**Pegasus**
the constellation of the Fish	**Pisces**
the stars named for Atlas's 7 daughters	**Pleiades**
the North Star, at the Little Dipper's handle end	**Polaris**
a smoke ring–shaped nebula in the Lyra	**Ring Nebula**
the constellation of the Archer	**Sagittarius**
the constellation of the Scorpion	**Scorpio**
the constellation of the Serpent	**Serpens**
the main star in Canis Major	**Sirius (the Dog Star)**
a cross-shaped constellation seen in the Southern Hemisphere	**Southern Cross** or **Crux**
the constellation of the Bull	**Taurus**
the constellation of the Great Bear, the Big Dipper	**Ursa Major**
the constellation of the Little Bear, the Little Dipper	**Ursa Minor**
a star in the constellation Lyra	**Vega**

| the constellation of the Virgin | **Virgo** |
| the constellation of the Fox | **Vulpecula** |

Astronauts and Spacecraft

Relating to astronauts and spacecraft, who or what was or were . . . ?

the developer of the V-2, Jupiter, and Saturn rockets	**Wernher von Braun**
the 1st craft to orbit the Earth, in 1957	**Sputnik**
the 1st human to orbit Earth, in 1961	**Yuri Gagarin**
the 1st line of Soviet manned spacecraft	**Vostok**
the US space agency	**National Aeronautic and Space Administration (NASA)**
the 1st American in space, in 1961	**Alan Shepard, Jr.**
the 1st line of US manned spacecraft	**Mercury**
the 2nd American in space, rescued from the sea in 1961	**Virgil Grissom**
the line of unmanned US craft exploring Venus and Mars from 1962	**Mariner**
the 1st American to orbit the Earth, in 1962, later an Ohio senator	**John Glenn, Jr.**
the 1st woman in space, in 1963	**Valentina Tereshkova**
the 1st American to walk in space, in 1965	**Edward White**
the 2nd line of US manned spacecraft	**Gemini**
the rocket that boosted Gemini into orbit	**Titan**
the US astronauts killed on the launch pad in 1967	**Virgil Grissom, Edward White, and Roger Chaffee**
the USSR astronaut killed in a 1967 re-entry crash	**Vladimir Komarov**
the 3rd line of US manned spacecraft	**Apollo**
the rocket that boosted Apollo into orbit	**Saturn**
the astronauts on the 1st manned Apollo flight, in 1968	**Walter Schirra, Jr., Donn Eisele**, and **R. Walter Cunningham**
the astronauts on the 1st flight to the moon, in 1968	**Frank Borran, James Lovell, and William Anders**

the 3rd line of USSR spacecraft, docking since 1969	**Soyuz**
the astronauts who landed the lunar module on the moon in July 1969	**Neil Armstrong** and **Edwin Aldrin, Jr.**
the astronauts who 1st used the lunar rover	**Alan Shepard, Jr.**, and **Edgar Mitchell**
the unmanned spacecraft launched in 1972 to explore Mars, Jupiter, Pluto, and Neptune	**Pioneer 10**
the 1st US manned space station in orbit, in 1973–74	**Skylab**
the pair of unmanned US spacecraft that landed on Mars in 1975	**Viking 1 and 2**
the spacecraft that linked on a 1975 US-USSR mission	**Apollo 18** and **Soyuz 19**
the pair of unmanned US spacecraft sent to Jupiter, Saturn, and Uranus in 1977	**Voyager 1** and **2**
the 1st US space shuttle craft, flying from 1981	**Columbia**
the 2nd US space shuttle craft, flying from 1983	**Challenger**
the 3rd US space shuttle craft, flying from 1984	**Discovery**
the 4th US space shuttle craft, flying from 1985	**Atlantis**
the astronauts killed when the *Challenger* exploded on takeoff in Jan. 1986, due to an O-ring failure	**Francis Scobee, Michael Smith, Gregory Jarvis, Christa McAuliffe, Robert McNair, Ellison Onizuka**, and **Judith Resnik**
the company that designed the *Challenger's* O-ring seals	**Morton Thiokol, Inc.**
the unmanned rocket planned to explore Jupiter in 1989 or later	**Galileo**
the Soviet astronaut who spent a record-breaking 326 days in space in 1987	**Yuri Romanenko**

Biology and Ecology Language

In the world of biology, what is or are . . . ?

General Terms

adjustment to a changing situation	**adaptation**
common microorganisms, often causing disease	**bacteria**
decomposable by natural biological processes	**biodegradable**
a built-in mechanism for periodicity of behavior	**biological clock**
all the living matter in an area, taken together	**biomass**
an interrelated community of plants and animals	**biome**
natural periodicity of life processes, e.g., sleeping	**biorhythms**
the part of the Earth occupied by living matter	**biosphere**
a region's animal and plant life	**biota**
an organism's chance of survival in a setting	**biotic potential**
the husk or outer coating of a plant seed	**bran**
starchy fuel-providing foods, organic compounds of carbon, hydrogen, and oxygen	**carbohydrates**
a flesh-eating animal	**carnivore**
the theory that massive sudden events caused evolution	**catastrophism**
indigestible plant carbohydrates, or roughage	**cellulose**
a moth or butterfly's hard shell during the pupa stage of development	**chrysalis**
having roughly a 24-hour periodicity	**circadian**
recurring about once a year	**circannual**
the final stage; in ecology, a mature community	**climax**
the spun covering of an insect in the pupa stage	**cocoon**
a system using feedback for self-control	**cybernetic system**
occurring during the day or daily	**diurnal**
the changing of ecosystems over time	**ecological succession**

a system of living beings and their necessities	**ecosystem**
the nutrient part of a plant seed	**endosperm**
substances that act as catalysts in living beings	**enzymes**
increased nutrients in an aging aquatic ecosystem	**eutrophication**
animals, in general	**fauna**
a self-controlling mechanism that tends to center activity around a set point	**feedback**
plants, in general	**flora**
feeding relationships, or who eats whom	**food chain**
a series of connected food chains	**food web**
geologically transformed organic matter, used for energy, e.g., coal and oil	**fossil fuels**
the place where a species normally lives	**habitat**
animals that eat plants	**herbivores**
the body's natural chemical balance	**homeostasis**
a being that provides nourishment for a parasite	**host**
the wingless, wormlike 1st stage of a moth or butterfly	**larva**
regions with similar plants and animals	**life zones**
the chemical reactions of a being, in general	**metabolism**
transformation during stages of normal growth, as a caterpillar becoming a butterfly	**metamorphosis**
tiny life forms, esp. disease-causing ones	**microbes**
plants or animals of microscopic size	**microorganisms**
1-crop agricultural ecosystems	**monocultures**
the idea that organisms best suited to their environment are most likely to survive, over time	**natural selection**
a setting that fills a being's survival requirements	**niche**
occurring during the night or nightly	**nocturnal**
lack of organic fertilization in monoculture	**nutrient stress**
animals that eat both plants and other animals	**omnivores**

an individual organism's course of development	**ontogeny**
diffusion of liquid through a semipermeable membrane, equaling pressure on both sides	**osmosis**
a type of being that nourishes itself on another	**parasite**
killing bacteria by heating, as in milk	**pasteurization**
a membrane that liquid can pass through	**permeable**
the flat-bottomed, circular dish used for cultivating microorganisms	**Petri dish**
the behavioral chemicals re-leased by insects	**pheromones**
plant movement in response to light	**phototaxis**
growth in response to light	**phototropism**
a species's course of evolution-ary development	**phylogeny** or **phylogenesis**
a being that attacks and kills another	**predator**
the object of a predator's attack	**prey**
breeding or reproducing plants or animals	**propagation**
a moth or butterfly's inactive stage of development, between larval and adult forms, when it is encased in a hard-shelled chrysalis	**pupa**
chemical reactions that fuel the metabolism	**respiration**
the interrelationships between living organisms	**symbiosis**
the giving off of water vapor by a plant	**transpiration**
a position in the food chain	**trophic level**
a submicroscopic, disease-causing nucleic acid in a protein coat, replicating only in living cells	**virus**
a water-saturated area, esp. as a wildlife habitat	**wetland**

About DNA and Cells

the 4 bases that bind the double helix	**adenine, thymine, guanine,** and **cytosine**
key organic compounds found in proteins	**amino acids**

the compound that carries energy in living creatures	**ATP (adenosine triphosphate)**
the "container" for a cell's cytoplasm	cell or **plasma membrane**
a being's smallest, independent structural unit	**cells**
the substance around the nucleus of a cell	**cytoplasm**
the life-perpetuating double helix	**DNA (deoxyribonucleic acid)**
the double twisting chain of life, formed of DNA	**double helix**
where protein is stored in cells	**Golgi body** or **apparatus**
within a cell digesting waste products	**lysosomes**
a type of cell that "eats" foreign or dead matter	**macrophage**
energy-providers for a cell	**mitochondria**
the "activity director" of a cell, controlling heredity and growth	**nucleus**
important living substances with amino acids	**proteins**
the jellylike substance that performs the basic life functions of living matter	**protoplasm**
the cell parts that produce protein	**ribosomes**
carriers of the information for making proteins	**RNA (ribonucleic acid)**
to RNA as thymine is to DNA	**uracil**

About Botany and Plant Propagation

a plant with no seed leaves, e.g., a moss or fern	**acotyledon**
the plant part that produces pollen	**anther**
succulents that need very little water, like the century plant	**agave**
plants that normally grow above the timberline	**alpines**
plants having their full life span in one season	**annuals**
plants that complete a life cycle in 2 years	**biennials**
small bulbs formed when a "mother bulb" splits	**bulbils**
an underground, scale-covered, food-storing stem	**bulb**
succulent plants that store water	**cacti**
the outer part of a flower, made up of sepals	**calyx**

green pigment used in photosynthesis	**chlorophyll**
two or more leaflets on one leaf stalk	**compound leaf**
trees that have needles	**conifers**
bulblike structures, as in the gladiolus	**corms**
small corms formed from an old, large corm	**cormels**
the outer part of a flower, made up of petals	**corolla**
the 1st leaf from a sprouting seed	**cotyledon**
plants with stems that grow along the surface	**creepers**
the part of a plant cut off and planted so as to take root	**cutting**
shedding in season, not permanent, e.g., maple tree	**deciduous**
the outer layer of a plant and its leaves	**epidermis**
persistent green foliage, not shedding annually	**evergreens**
the slim stalks that hold the anthers	**filaments**
plants, in general	**flora**
the leaves of plants, taken together	**foliage**
sprouting from a seed	**germination**
to join a shoot or bud to a living plant	**grafting**
the soft tissue of a leaf	**mesophyll**
a bulb grown to its fullest size before splitting	**mother bulb**
runnerlike, short-stemmed shoots	**offsets**
the plant part that produces the seed (ovule) to be fertilized	**ovary**
a leaf like a hand with spread fingers	**palmate**
plants that have a life span of 2 or more years	**perennials**
a leaf's stalk	**petiole**
plant tissue that conducts food	**phloem**
creating chemical energy and organic compounds in the presence of light	**photosynthesis**
a plant's seed-bearing, "female" part, including stigma, style, and ovary	**pistil**
a soft, spongy tissue of plant stems	**pith**

the "male" part of plant reproduction, produced by the anthers	**pollen**
to move pollen from an anther to a stigma, and so to fertilize	**pollination**
a fleshy, stoneless fruit, e.g., an apple	**pome**
the plant part that becomes the main root	**radicle**
underground or partly underground stems	**rhizome**
slim shoots on the ground, rooting at intervals	**runners**
thick-walled supportive plant tissue	**sclerenchyma**
a young plant after germination from the seed	**seedling, shoot,** or **sprout**
one of the green pieces that form around a flower	**sepal**
a leaf with notched, toothlike edges	**serrate**
leaves attached without a stalk	**sessile**
reproductive organs in nonflowering plants	**spores**
the reproduction part that includes the anther and filament	**stamen**
the tip of the pistil, where pollination occurs	**stigma**
branches formed above the soil that bend down and take root	**stolons**
the pores of a leaf	**stoma**
the thin part that holds the stigma	**style**
plants that need little water, such as cacti	**succulents**
branches formed below the soil, as in a lilac	**suckers**
a plant's main root	**tap root**
a large underground stem with buds, e.g., a potato	**tuber**
having vessels to transport sap	**vascular**
supporting or woody tissue in plants	**xylem**

About Gardens and Gardening

a tree-lined avenue in a French-style garden	**allée**
a water-filled tank or bowl for plants and animals	**aquarium**
plants that live and grow in water	**aquatics**

a shaded shelter in a garden	**arbor** or **bower**
a place for study and display of trees	**arboretum**
a Persian pleasure garden, often with a house	**bagh**
placing growing plants in the ground as a group	**bedding**
a vine-covered, arched trellis over a walk	**berceau** or **berso**
the creation of dwarf trees or shrubs	**bonsai**
a grove of trees in a park or garden	**bosquet** or **bosco**
evergreens often cut into hedges and mazes	**box** or **boxwood**
plants cut in designs to look like embroidery	**broderie** or **ricami**
an outdoor throne or platform in a Persian garden	**chabutra**
a Japanese tea garden	**chaniwa**
a hole, like a window, made in a hedge or wall	**clairvoyée**
a glass-covered frame to protect plants from the cold	**cold frame**
decayed organic matter to be used as fertilizer	**compost**
a trellis used to force plants to grow in defined patterns	**espalier**
artificially speeding up the growth process	**forcing**
destroying pests with smoke or fumes	**fumigation**
a long, narrow trench for planting seeds	**furrows** or **drills**
a pruned bower in a Spanish garden	**glorieta**
leveling or smoothing ground	**grading**
a glass-enclosed structure for raising and displaying plants	**greenhouse** or **conservatory**
low-growing plants	**ground cover**
semiformal style in a Japenese garden	**gyo**
an often-walled ditch to keep out animals in an English park or garden	**ha-ha**
solid, untilled ground or bedrock	**hardpan**
shrubs or trees used as a fence or boundary	**hedge**
a level Japanese garden	**hira-niwa**
a heated shelter for germination or protection	**hotbed** or **hothouse**

decayed vegetable matter used for its nutrients	**humus**
the art of arranging flowers, in Japan	**ikebana**
a dry landscape in a Japanese garden	**kare-sansui**
dwarf shrubs clipped in an interlaced design, as in Elizabethan times	**knot garden**
an open framework, as used for vines	**lattice**
covering a shoot with earth, so it will take root	**layering**
dissolving substances from a plant by soaking	**leaching**
animal waste matter used as fertilizer	**manure**
matter, often organic, placed around plants for protection	**mulch**
converting nitrogen into usable compounds	**nitrogen fixation**
a water-filled Roman pleasure pavilion	**nymphaeum**
plant food made from living matter, not chemicals	**organic fertilizers**
a patterned garden, in the 18th-c. French style	**parterre**
3 avenues leading from one spot, like a goose foot	**patte d'ole**
a vine-covered, open, arched walk in an English garden	**pergola**
an area where pines are planted and studied	**pinetum**
a fish pool in a Roman garden	**piscina**
decorative containers for house plants	**planters**
a walkway formed by interlaced tree branches in an English garden	**pleached alley**
to trim, promoting growth or better shape	**pruning**
rock-and-stucco formations in a French garden	**rocaille**
a pool found in a Roman garden	**savina**
a Japanese water garden	**sen-tei**
a device for watering an Egyptian garden or farm	**shaduf**
formal style in a Japanese garden	**shin**
informal style in a Japanese garden	**so**

an Italian conservatory for citrus trees in winter	**stanzone**
the layer of earth just beneath the surface	**subsoil**
an enclosed container for small plants and animals	**terrarium** or **wardian case**
an alcove for art objects or flowers in a Japanese garden	**tokonoma**
cutting shrubs or trees into decorative shapes	**topiary**
a Japanese gateway in the Shinto style	**torii**
a latticework frame for training vines	**trellis**
a Japanese garden using artificial elevations	**tsuki-yama**
grass-covered, matted surface soil	**turf** or **sod**
a pond or reservoir in an Italian park or garden	**vasca**

Taxonomy Categories

In the world of taxonomy, what is or are . . . ?

Types of Categories

the animal kingdom's main subcategory	**phylum**
the plant kingdom's main subcategory	**division**
animals and plants' next main category	**class**
animals and plants' next main category	**order**
animals and plants' next main category	**family**
animals and plants' next main category	**genus**
animals and plants' next main category, members of which can breed with each other	**species**
animals' last main category	**subspecies**
plants' last main category	**variety**

Classes of Animals

bats	**Chiroptera**
birds	**Aves**
bony fishes	**Osteichthyes**
fishes, in general (superclass)	**Pisces**
frogs	**Amphibia**
horses	**Equus**

human	**Mammalia**
kangaroos	**Marsupialia**
lobsters and crabs	**Crustacea**
octopuses and squids	**Cephalopoda**
sea urchins	**Echinoidea**
segmented worms	**Annelida**
sharks	**Chondrichthyes**
snails	**Gastropoda**
spiders	**Arachnida**
starfishes	**Asteroidea**

Other Animal Categories

animals with spines (subphylum)	**Vertebrata**
butterflies (order)	**Lepidoptera**
cats (family)	**Felidae**
dogs (genus)	**Canis**
human (phylum)	**Chordata**
humans and apes (order)	**Primates**
whales (order)	**Cetacea**

Divisions of Plants

algae and fungi	**Thallophyta**
mosses	**Bryophyta**
vascular (sap-carrying) plants	**Tracheophyta**

Classes of Plants

angiosperms with one seed leaf at germination	**Monocotyledonae**
angiosperms with two seed leaves at germination	**Dicotyledonae**
ferns	**Filicinae** or **Pteridophyta**
flowering plants	**Angiosperms**
mushrooms	**Basidiomycetes**
naked-seeded plants, e.g., firs	**Gymnosperms**

Extinct Prehistoric Animals

Among extinct prehistoric animals, which was or were . . . ?

a half-bird, half-reptile	**archaeoopteryx**
the ancestor of cows	**aurochs** or **urus**
a large, herbivorous dinosaur	**brontosaurus**; also **diplodocus**
the ancestor of the horse	**eohippus**
a dinosaur with short front limbs and a wide jaw for eating plants	**hadrosaur** or **duck-billed dinosaur**
fishlike sea-living reptiles	**ichthyosaurus**
a huge, ancient form of elephant	**mammoth**
an elephantlike mammal	**mastodon**
a flying reptile	**pterodactyl** or **pterosaur**
a large cat with long canine teeth	**saber-toothed tiger**

a herbivorous dinosaur with 2 rows of plates along its back	**stegosaurus**
a herbivorous dinosaur with horns and a bony neck-covering	**triceratops** ·
a large carnivorous dinosaur with short front limbs	**tyrannosaurus**

Chemistry Language

(See also Physics Language)

In the world of chemistry, what is or are . . . ?

a substance that frees hydrogen ions in solution, often turning litmus red	**acid**
chemical attraction	**affinity**
a substance that neutralizes acids and turns litmus blue	**alkali**
negatively charged ions	**anions**
nitric acid, Latin for "strong water"	**aqua fortis**
an aromatic cordial once popular in pharmacies, literally wonderful water	**aqua mirabilis**
distilled water	**aqua puris**
a mixture of nitric and hydrochloric acids	**aqua regia (royal water)**
the smallest part of an element that can be part of a chemical reaction	**atom**
the number of protons (or electrons) in an atom	**atomic number**
a substance that reacts with an acid to form a salt and water	**base**
chemical forces holding atoms together in molecules	**bonds**
a common laboratory burner	**Bunsen burner**
a marked glass tube for measuring liquids	**burette**
the worthless remains after chemical analysis, literally dead head	**caput mortuum**
a substance that starts or increases a chemical reaction, while itself remaining unchanged	**catalyst**
positively charged ions	**cations**

the amount of a substance, in grams, that would replace a standard; a combining weight	**chemical equivalent**
2 or more elements combined in definite proportions in a substance	**compounds**
a container used by high-temperature reactions	**crucible**
converting a liquid to a vapor and then collecting the condensed vapor	**distillation**
breaking apart a substance with electric current	**electrolysis**
a negatively charged particle orbiting a nucleus	**electron**
matter composed of just one type of atom	**element**
a simple chemical formula showing the proportion of elements present	**empirical formula**
a flat-bottomed, narrow-necked laboratory flask	**Erlenmayer flask**
the changing of liquid into vapor	**evaporation**
the principle that energy can be transformed, but not created or destroyed	**First Law of Thermodynamics**
the acid found in the stomach	**hydrochloric acid**
breaking apart a substance by adding water	**hydrolysis**
compounds with the same molecular formulas, but different arrangements and properties	**isomers**
atoms with the same atomic number but a different mass number	**isotopes**
paper used in a pH test	**litmus**
the number of nucleons in an atom's nucleus	**mass number**
a substance in which the constituents are not chemically bonded to each other	**mixture**
the smallest part of a substance to show its chemcial properties and exist independently	**molecule**
the total of all the atomic weights in a molecule	**molecular weight**
gases that resist forming chemical bonds, e.g., helium, neon, argon, and xenon	**noble gases**

the positively charged central core of an atom	**nucleus**
the parts of a nucleus, i.e., protons or neutrons	**nucleons**
the uncharged part of an atom's nucleus	**neutron**
massless, subatomic particles	**neutrinos**
the combination of oxygen with, or the removal of hydrogen from, a substance	**oxidation**
the degree of acidity or alkalinity of a solution	**pH**
a glass tube for transferring a precise volume of a liquid	**pipette**
substances of high molecular weight, formed from chains of linked molecules of a compound	**polymer**
the positively charged part of an atom's nucleus	**proton**
identifying the substances present in a mixture	**qualitative chemical analysis**
determining the amount of substances present	**quantitative chemical analysis**
a substance used to produce a chemical reaction	**reagent**
the subtraction of oxygen from, or the addition of hydrogen to, a substance	**reduction**
a large-based, narrow-necked glass vessel for a chemical reaction, e.g., distillation	**retort**
formed when an acid's hydrogen is replaced by a metal	**salt**
the principle that energy becomes less concentrated each time it is transformed	**Second Law of Thermodynamics**
to heat powders without melting them	**sinter**
examining a spectrum to determine a substance's chemical nature	**spectrographic analysis**
the apparatus used in distillation	**still**
finding the amount of a substance in a solution by adding to it precise amounts of a reagent	**titration**
the number of hydrogen atoms an atom will combine with or replace	**valence** or **combining power**

Computer Language

(See also Physics Language)

In the world of computers, what is the word or phrase for . . . ?

a computer showing data as measurements, not numbers	**analog computer**
attempted replication of human mental processes by computers	**artificial intelligence**
the rate of data transmission over a modem	**baud rate**
the 2-state (on-off) number system in computers	**binary**
the minimal unit of computer data, 0 or 1	**bit (binary digit)**
to start up a computer, making it ready to operate	**boot**
an error in a program or in the computer itself	**bug**
an 8-bit sequence representing 1 character	**byte**
the TV-like screen in a computer	**CRT (cathode ray tube or terminal)**
a computer-coded disk read by laser	**CD (compact disk)**
where the computer's main work is done	**central processing unit (CPU)**
copies of brand-name computers	**clones**
the mark on a screen at the present work point	**cursor**
a wheel with letters and symbols used in impact printing	**daisy wheel**
a computer designed for one purpose alone	**dedicated**
a computer program to identify errors	**diagnostics**
a computer showing data as numbers, not measurements	**digital computer**
forming letters from dots, not type	**dot matrix**
an early vacuum tube computer	**first generation**
a thin, plastic, somewhat flexible disk common in microcomputers	**floppy disk**
10^9 or a billion (US) bytes	**gigabyte**
garbage in, garbage out	**gigo**
a rigid computer disk, often built-in	**hard disk**

the physical parts of the computer	**hardware**
the 16-number system used by some machines	**hexadecimal**
printers that hit the page, like typewriters	**impact printers**
the connections allowing systems to communicate	**interface**
spraying ink to print letters	**jet** or **ink-jet printing**
roughly 1000 bytes, in practice 1024	**kilobyte**
an electro-static printer using lasers to form dot-matrix letters	**laser printers**
a large central computer unit, often in a network	**main frame**
2^{20} or roughly a million (US) bytes	**megabyte**
a piece of semiconducting material containing a transistor or an integrated circuit	**microchip**
small, inexpensive computers, as in homes and small business	**microcomputer or personal computer (PC)**
an integrated chip that functions as a CPU	**microprocessor**
an intermediate-size computer, between a micro- and a main frame	**minicomputer**
a device for transmitting data over lines	**modem**
a small, hand-operated device to move the cursor or to draw	**mouse** or **joystick**
linking of microcomputers or terminals with each other or with a main frame	**networks**
MS-DOS and its kin	**operating systems**
tiny dots that make up images on a CRT	**pixels**
rules for handling material, e.g., in what order	**protocol**
material that can be reached directly, not after reading serially	**RAM (random access memory)**
material that can only be read, not worked with	**ROM (read-only memory)**
computers using solid-state devices	**second generation**
the programs or applications used in the computer	**software**
a sequential series of instructions to the computer	**string commands**
computers using integrated circuits and microprocessors	**third generation**

Geography Language

In the world of geography, what is or are . . . ?

the boundary of the Southern Frigid Zone	**Antarctic Circle**
places on opposite sides of the Earth	**antipodes**
a group or chain of islands	**archipelago**
the boundary of the Northern Frigid Zone	**Arctic Circle**
land built up at the mouth of a river	**delta**
the falling tide, between a high and the next low	**ebb tide**
the circle dividing the Earth's Northern and Southern hemispheres	**equator**
the lower river as it meets the sea's tides	**estuary**
a finger-shaped inlet from the sea	**firth** or **fjord**
the rising tide, between a low and the next high	**flood tide**
the areas between each pole and the Arctic and Antarctic circles	**Frigid Zones**
the time at the meridian that passes through Greenwich, England	**Greenwich Mean Time**
half of a circle, on Earth divided north-south by the equator, or east-west by a meridian	**hemisphere**
an imaginary line in the Pacific, with the date one day earlier to its east	**International Date Line**
a neck of land connecting 2 larger land masses	**isthmus**
a measurement north or south of the equator, where an imaginary line meets a meridian	**latitude**
a shore or coast	**littoral**
a measurement east or west of the prime meridian	**longitude**
a circle around the Earth, passing through both poles	**meridian**
a raised, flat piece of land with cliffs for sides	**mesa**
tides lower than normal	**neap tide**

a deep bend in a river, later often cut off	**oxbow**
a wide, grassy plain, esp. in South America	**pampas**
in the open ocean, rather than near land	**pelagic**
land projecting into water	**peninsula**
at the foot of a mountain	**piedmont**
a raised, level piece of land	**plateau** or **tableland**
a wide grassy plain, esp. in North America	**prairie**
the 0° meridian through Greenwich, England, from which east-west position, or longitude, is measured	**prime meridian**
relating to the bank of a river, pond, or lake	**riparian**
a subsurface current running against the tide	**rip tide** or **undertow**
a treeless, grassy tropical or subtropical plain	**savannah**
tides higher than normal	**spring tide**
a wide, grassy plain, esp. in Eurasia	**steppe**
evergreen forests below the Arctic	**taiga**
a high wave at flood tide in a narrow passage	**tidal bore**
the middle latitudes of the Northern and Southern hemispheres	**Temperate Zones**
the Earth's surface features	**topography**
the region around the equator, between the Tropics of Cancer and of Capricorn	**Torrid Zone**
a stream that pour its waters into a larger one	**tributary**
the most northern line where the sun reaches 90°, the north boundary of the "Torrid Zone"	**Tropic of Cancer**
the most southern line where the sun reaches 90°, the south boundary of the "Torrid Zone"	**Tropic of Capricorn**
treeless, permanently frozen northern regions	**tundra**
grassy plains in southern Africa	**veldt**
the region that provides water for a certain spot	**watershed**
open, rolling, once-forested land, in England	**weald**

Geology Language

In the world of geology, what is or are . . . ?

soil deposited by a river	**alluvial**
a dense, dark, often glassy volcanic rock	**basalt**
the rock underlying surface soil	**bedrock**
basins from collapsed, central volcanic craters	**caldera**
the movement of huge land masses over time	**continental drift**
the Earth's molten heart	**core**
the surface point nearest an earthquake's origin	**epicenter**
the wearing away of the Earth's surface by wind and water	**erosion**
a flowing river of ice	**glacier**
a layered metamorphic rock	**gneiss**
the ancient supercontinent that included Africa, South America, India, and Australia	**Gondwana**
a light-colored igneous rock often used in building	**granite**
rock formed from a molten state, or partly so	**igneous** or **pyrogenic**
metal that may indicate collision with an object from space 65 million years ago	**iridium**
molten rock, as from a volcano	**lava**
sedimentary rock mostly of calcium carbonate from remains of ancient sea creatures	**limestone**
becoming like a liquid, e.g., some types of earth in an earthquake	**liquefaction**
the solid part of Earth, in general	**lithosphere**
molten rock under the Earth's crust, from which igneous rock is made	**magma**
the layer between the Earth's crust and its core	**mantle**
rocks transformed by pressure or heat	**metamorphic**
nonliving, natural substances of use to humans	**minerals**
the place where the Earth's crust and mantle join	**Mohorovicic discontinuity** or **Moho**

the top of a glacier, where snow changes to ice	**névé**
the mountain-building process	**orogeny**
the supercontinent that existed 200,000,000 years ago	**Pangaea**
radioactive gas that seeps from rocks	**radon**
a logarithmic scale for indicating the strength of an earthquake	**Richter scale**
sedimentary rock mostly of quartz grains	**sandstone**
grainy metamorphic rock, with much mica	**schist**
rocks from deposits of soil as sediment	**sedimentary**
a device to measure the size of earthquakes	**seismometer**
a fine-grained, layered sedimentary rock	**shale**
sections of crust that move around the Earth's surface	**tectonic plates**
a hole in the Earth's crust, pouring out lava	**volcano**

Geological Time Periods

Relating to geological time periods, what . . . ?

era saw rocks formed by cooling, pressure, and sedimentation, and 1st life begin, over 570 million years ago	**Precambrian**
era saw proliferation of life, about 230–570 million years ago	**Paleozoic (Old Life)**
Paleozoic period is marked by trilobites and shellfish, about 500–570 million years ago	**Cambrian**
Paleozoic period is marked by primitive fish and fungi, about 425–500 million years ago	**Ordovician**
Paleozoic period saw the 1st land plants, about 405–425 million years ago	**Silurian**
Paleozoic period saw the 1st amphibians, the age of fishes, about 345–405 million years ago	**Devonian**
Paleozoic period was warm and moist, and had many amphibians, insects, and plants that later formed coal, about 280–345 million ago	**Carboniferous (Missisippian and Pennsylvanian)**

Paleozoic period saw reptiles living on land, about 230–280 million years ago	**Permian**
era was dominated by reptiles, about 65–230 million years ago	**Mesozoic (Middle Life)**
Mesozoic period saw the rise of dinosaurs, about 190–230 million years ago	**Triassic**
Mesozoic period saw the 1st birds, about 140–190 million years ago	**Jurassic**
Mesozoic period saw the 1st flowering plants and the extinction of the dinosaurs, about 65–140 million years ago	**Cretaceous**
era began with heavy glaciation and is marked by evolution of living beings and geology into our times, from about 65 million years ago	**Cenozoic (Recent Life)**
Cenozoic period saw the rise of modern flowers and large mammals, about 2–65 million years ago	**Tertiary**
Tertiary epoch saw the rise of mountains, the splitting of continents, and the rise of mammals, about 55–65 million years ago	**Paleocene**
Tertiary epoch saw the decline of reptiles and the rise of modern birds and mammals, about 40–55 million years ago	**Eocene**
Tertiary epoch was marked by volcanic eruptions, rising mountains, flourishing grasses, and saber-toothed tigers, about 25–40 million years ago	**Oligocene**
Tertiary epoch was marked by very large, grass-eating mammals and whales, about 10–25 million years ago	**Miocene**
Tertiary epoch was cold and dry, when some forms of mammals became extinct, about 2–10 million years ago	**Pliocene**

Cenozoic period saw the 1st humans, about 2 million years ago to present	**Quaternary**
Quarternary epoch was the great Ice Age, about 2 million to 10,000 years ago	**Pleistocene**
Quarternary epoch covers the last 10,000 years	**Holocene**

Mathematics Language

In the world of mathematics, what is or are . . . ?

General Terms

a hand computing device with rods and counters	**abacus**
the distance of a point from the y-axis, in a coordinate system	**abscissa**
the number a logarithm stands for	**antilogarithm**
a line that infinitely curves toward a right angle	**asymptote**
a number that is typical of a group of numbers	**average**
basic, seemingly self-evident assertions	**axioms**
a reference or orientation line, as in a system of coordinates	**axis**
a number that has an exponent or power	**base**
algebra based on symbolic logic	**Boolean algebra**
a number showing quantity only, e.g., 1 or 289	**cardinal number**
2 or more points that give a location in space	**Cartesian coordinates**
fixed, measured perpendicular lines used to locate points in a plane or in space	**Cartesian coordinate system**
constants in an equation	**coefficient**
computations that are not affected by order	**commutative**
a digit's position to the right or left of a decimal point	**decimal place**
a number system based on 10	**decimal system**
x in $y = f(x)$	**dependent variable**
the quotient of 2 limits, in calculus	**derivative**

the limit of a variable, in calculus	**differentials**
limits of the mathematical quotient $\triangle y / \triangle x$, as $\triangle x$ nears zero	**differential calculus**
a superscript, placed above and to the right, indicating how many times a number should be multiplied by itself, e.g., the ^{2} in $3^2 = 3 \times 3$	**exponent** or **power**
a structure so irregularly shaped as to behave like a larger structure	**fractal**
a number shown as the quotient of 2 other numbers	**fraction**
f in $y = f(x)$	**function**
growth by a standard ratio, as in 1, 2, 4, 8, 16	**geometric growth**
a curved line between two asymptotes, formed by a conic section	**hyperbola**
y in $y = f(x)$	**independent variable**
a number so small as to be practically zero	**infinitesimal**
a whole number	**integer** or **integral**
calculus focusing on whole numbers and their properties	**integral calculus**
an equation with 2 variables	**linear equation**
statistical analysis of the relationship between independent and dependent variables	**linear regression**
the exponent of a number that will make it equal another, given number, as in trigonometry	**logarithm**
an average in which a group of numbers are added and divided by how many there are	**mean (arithmetic)**
the middle number of a ranked group, a type of average	**median**
the number that appears most often in a group of numbers	**mode**
computations affected by the order in which they are performed	**noncommutative**
a number showing rank in order, e.g., 1st or 98th	**ordinal number**
the distance of a point from the x-axis, in a coordinate system	**ordinate**
a flat surface, one with 2 dimensions	**plane**

an equation with 2 or more terms, esp, of the form $ax^2 + bx + c$	**polynomial equation**
assumptions made by mathematicians	**postulates**
the result of division	**quotient**
the relation between 2 numbers, e.g., 1 to 2 or ½	**ratio**
one of an equation's unknowns	**root**
the rate at which a curve or line rises or falls in a coordinate system	**slope**
in 3 dimensions	**solid**
a provable proposition, given certain assumptions	**theorem**
a quantity represented by a symbol, whose value is to be discovered	**unknown**
a value expressed as a magnitude and a direction	**vector**
the bar over two or more algebraic terms, so they will be treated as one	**vinculum**
a fixed horizontal line in a coordinate system	**x-axis**
a fixed vertical line in a coordinate system	**y-axis**

Geometry Language

In geometry, what is or are . . . ?

a plane figure with every point equally far from the center	**circle**
a straight line from circle's center to its edge	**radius (r)**
a straight line through the circle at the center	**diameter (d = 2r)**
the distance around the outside of a circle, or $2\pi r$	**circumference (c)**
the ratio between the circumference and the diameter of a circle, a constant 3.14 . . .	**π (pi)**
the amount of surface a figure covers, e.g., for a circle a $= \pi r^2$	**area (a)**
a line joining any 2 points on a curve or circle	**chord**
a line intersecting a curve at any 2 points	**secant**

a line that touches another line, curve, or surface at just one point, not intersecting it	**tangent**
the area or curve marked off by a chord	**segment**
¼ of the circle's arc, i.e., 90°	**quadrant**
an elongated, symmetrical oval	**ellipse**
elongated in one dimension, as in a rectangle or ellipse	**oblong**
2 lines equally distant from one another	**parallel lines**
the meeting of 2 nonparallel lines	**angle**
the point where 2 lines meet	**vertex (pl. vertices)**
a line joining 2 nonadjoining vertices	**diagonal**
a line that cuts through 2 or more other lines	**transversal**
an angle of less than 90°	**acute angle**
an angle of more than 90° and under 180°	**obtuse angle**
an angle of exactly 90°	**right angle** or **perpendicular**
any angle that is not 90°, i.e., acute or obtuse	**oblique**
corresponding exactly	**congruent**
a plane figure with 3 or more sides	**polygon**
a polygon with 3 sides	**triangle** or **trilateral**
a triangle with 1 right angle	**right triangle**
the side of a right triangle opposite the 90° angle	**hypotenuse**
a triangle with no right angle	**oblique triangle**
a triangle with all angles less than 90°	**acute triangle**
a triangle with one angle more than 90°	**obtuse triangle**
a triangle with 2 sides equal	**isosceles triangle**
a triangle with the 3 sides unequal	**scalene triangle**
a triangle with sides and angles equal	**equilateral triangle**
a 4-sided polygon	**quadrilateral, quadrangle,** or **tetragon**
a quadrilateral with no parallel sides	**trapezium**
a quadrilateral with 2 parallel sides	**trapezoid**
a quadrilateral with opposite sides parallel	**parallelogram**
a parallelogram with all 4 sides equal	**rhombus**

a parallelogram with unequal adjoining sides	**rhomboid**
a quadrilateral with opposite sides parallel and with right angles	**rectangle**
a quadrilateral with all sides equal and parallel	**square**
a 5-sided polygon	**pentagon**
a 6-sided polygon	**hexagon**
a 7-sided polygon	**heptagon**
an 8-sided polygon	**octagon**
a 9-sided polygon	**nonagon**
a 10-sided polygon	**decagon**
a 12-sided polygon	**dodecagon**
a solid figure with 4 or more faces	**polyhedron**
a polyhedron with a polygon as a base and each face a triangle, all meeting at a point	**pyramid**
a pyramid with the pointed top cut off and replaced by a face parallel to the base	**truncated pyramid**
a polyhedron with 2 congruent, parallel polygons as bases, and the sides parallelograms	**prism**
a 4-faced polyhedron	**tetrahedron**
a 5-faced polyhedron	**pentahedron**
a 6-sided polyhedron	**hexahedron**
a 6-faced prism with each face a rhombus	**rhombohedron**
a 6-faced prism with each face a parallelogram	**parallelepiped**
a polyhedron with each face a trapezium	**trapezohedron** or **trisoctahedron**
a 6-faced polyhedron, with all faces square and equal	**cube**
a 7-faced polyhedron	**heptahedron**
an 8-faced polyhedron	**octahedron**
a 10-faced polyhedron	**decahedron**
a 12-faced polyhedron	**dodecahedron**
a 20-faced polyhedron	**icosahedron**

Meteorology Language

In the world of meteorology, what is or are . . . ?

General Terms

the Earth's gaseous envelope	**atmosphere**
a device for measuring atmospheric pressure	**barometer**

the flow of heat through atmospheric motion	**convection**
parts of the ocean with only light winds	**doldrums**
a warm, variable current often appearing off South America around Christmas time	**El Niño**
a sea mirage of cliffs and castles	**Fata Morgana**
the borderline between two air masses differing in temperature	**front**
the Earth's absorption, rather than reflection, of solar rays, leading to a rise in temperature	**greenhouse effect** or **global warming**
ocean regions, about 30–35° above and below the equator, with high pressure and calm winds	**horse latitudes**
the water on the Earth's surface	**hydrosphere**
the condition of warm air trapping cold air, and its pollutants, near the Earth	**inversion**
the electrically active atmospheric layer 30 miles up	**ionosphere**
a line between points of the same pressure	**isobar** or **isopiestic line**
the side protected from the wind	**lee**
the atmospheric region about 20–50 miles up, with sharply decreasing temperature	**mesosphere**
a warm front blocked by a cold front	**occluded front**
the atmospheric layer 10–20 miles up that absorbs ultraviolet solar rays	**ozonosphere** or **ozone layer**
water falling to Earth, in any form	**precipitation**
the windy, rough ocean regions between 40° and 50° latitude, north and south	**roaring 40's**
the borderline between two roughly equal air masses	**stationary front**
the atmosphere layer above the troposphere	**stratosphere**
the part of the atmosphere nearest the surface	**troposphere**
on the side open to the wind	**windward**

Winds, Storms, and Clouds

winds swirling around a high-pressure center, in the Northern Hemisphere moving clockwise	**anticyclone** or **high**

the strong north wind in Europe's Alps	**bise**
a snowstorm, esp. with winds over 35 MPH and temperature below 20°F	**blizzard**
a warm, wet wind in the Pacific NW; a warm, dry wind in the eastern Rockies	**chinook**
high, thin, streaky bands of clouds	**cirrus**
fluffy, white, flat-bottomed clouds linked with storms	**cumulus**
dense, very high clouds usually producing heavy storms and often hail	**cumulonimbus**
winds swirling around a low-pressure center, in the Northern Hemisphere moving counterclockwise; also a violent, whirling storm	**cyclone** or **low**
from the east	**easterly**
a strong south wind in Europe's Alps	**foehn** or **föhn**
a wind with speeds of 32–63 miles per hour	**gale**
a wet fog off the North Sea, in Britain	**haar**
a dry wind out of Africa's Sahara	**harmattan**
a cyclone with winds over 75 miles per hour	**hurricane**
a hot wind out of the Sahara toward Egypt	**khamsin**
an easterly wind, in the Mediterranean	**levanter**
a cold, dry, northerly wind in southern France	**mistral**
a low, dark cloud linked with precipitation	**nimbostratus** or **nimbus**
a storm from the northeast	**northeaster** or **nor'easter**
from the north	**northerly**
a small, local whirling wind, carrying dust and debris high into the air	**sand spout** or **dust devil**
a hot, dusty wind in southern California	**Santa Ana**
a heavy, hot, sand-laden wind out of the Sahara and Arabian deserts	**simoom, samiel,** or **shaitan**
a hot, wet southerly wind, esp. from the Sahara across the Mediterranean toward Europe	**sirocco**

a storm from the southeast	**southeaster** or **sou'easter**
from the south	**southerly**
a foglike, low altitude cloud	**stratus**
a violently rotating, destructive column of air below a cumulonimbus cloud	**tornado, whirlwind,** or **twister**
steady winds, esp. over ocean tropics	**trade winds** or **trades**
a cold north wind, in Italy	**tramontane**
a huge wave, as from an underground earthquake	**tsunami** or **tidal wave**
a powerful tropical hurricane, esp. in the Pacific	**typhoon**
a whirlwind over water, raising a column of spray	**waterspout**
from the west	**westerly**
a gentle west wind	**zephyr**

Physics Language

(See also Chemistry Language and Computer Language)

In the world of physics, what is or are . . . ?

matter composed of mirror-image, or antiparticles, such as antineutrons and antiprotons	**antimatter**
the force that pushes whirling bodies away from the center of motion	**centrifugal force**
a whirling device to separate matter of varying density	**centrifuge**
X-ray images recorded on film or videotape	**cineradiography**
sunken inward	**concave**
material that readily transmits, esp. electricity	**conductor**
bulging outward	**convex**
the mass per volume, compared to a standard	**density**
a ringlike pattern of radio emissions from a far galaxy	**Einstein ring**
fluids that thicken in an electric field	**electro-rheological fluids**
increasing disorder in a system	**entropy**
the number of cycles in a given time	**frequency**
electromagnetic rays from radioactive decay	**gamma rays**

a desired theory to cover all the theories of subatomic particles and forces	**GUT (grand unified theory)**
the time for one-half of a radioactive sample's nuclei to decay	**half-life**
electromagnetic radiation beyond the visible red rays in the spectrum	**infrared**
material that does not readily transmit, esp. electricity	**insulator**
an intense beam of light, as used in space and medicine	**laser (Light Amplification by Stimulated Emission of Radiation)**
a substance that attracts iron with its field	**magnet**
radio frequency used in radio work	**megaherz**
the radio waves between infrared and short-wave	**microwaves**
splitting an atom's nucleus	**nuclear fission**
joining nuclei, while releasing energy	**nuclear fusion**
a machine to speed up and "smash" atoms, e.g., a cyclotron	**particle accelerator**
the time interval between two events	**period** or **cycle**
the theoretical operation of a device or system with no energy input	**perpetual motion**
a particle of energy with no mass or charge	**photon**
the constant proportion between radiation and its frequency	**Planck's constant**
having two opposite attributes, as in a magnet	**polarity**
the basic unit of subatomic energy	**quantum**
best known of the various supposed subatomic particles	**quarks** and **charm**
a device using radiowaves for detection of distant objects	**radar**
an image thrown back from a surface	**reflection**
the bending of light, e.g., on passing through water	**refraction**
the theory that motion, space, and time are not absolute, but exist in a frame of reference	**relativity**

friction and loss of electrical current in a medium	**resistance**
partly conductive materials used in electronic circuits	**semiconductors**
current-controlling devices used in transistors	**solid state**
an object's mass compared to the mass of an equal volume of water	**specific gravity**
the amount of heat needed to raise an object's temperature 1°, as compared to a standard	**specific heat**
electrical flow with no resistance, in certain matter	**superconductivity**
the tendency to keep turning about an axis	**torque**
twisting or turning an object	**torsion**
semiconductors used in a radio for detecting and amplifying signals	**transistors**
electromagnetic radiation beyond the visible violet rays in the spectrum	**ultraviolet rays**
a theory extending Einstein's general theory of relativity	**unified field theory**
the distance between the same point in 2 cycles	**wavelength**
streams of high-energy photons	**X-rays**

World of Philosophy and Belief

Specialties in Philosophy and Religion

In the world of philosophy and religion, what is or was the special study of . . . ?

the art and theory of happiness	**eudemonics**
the art of preaching	**homiletics**
being, in general	**ontology**
human conduct	**praxiology** or **praxeo-**
identifying right and wrong from ethical principles	**casuistry**
interpretation, esp. of the Bible	**hermeneutics**
the limits of knowledge	**gnoseology**
morals and moral choices	**ethics** or **moral philosophy**
the nature of knowledge	**epistemology**
the nature of religious truth	**theology**
philosophic first principles and primal reality	**metaphysics**
purpose in nature	**teleology**
reasoning as a formal discipline	**logic**
signs and symbols	**semantics** or **semiotics**
the theory of beauty and the fine arts	**aesthetics**
values and value judgments	**axiology**

Philosophies

Among the various philosophies, what is the view that . . . ?

denies the possibility of knowing if God exists	**agnosticism**
all creatures are harmless, to Hindus	**ahimsa**

296

the soul is the heart of life	**animism**
focuses on Rudolf Steiner's theory of spiritual experience	**anthroposophism**
faith alone leads to salvation	**antinomianism**
no God exists	**atheism**
life and matter were created by God as they exist, and did not evolve	**creationism**
involves belief in God	**deism**
combined Hegel's dialectic with Marxian theory	**dialectical materialism**
reality has two aspects, esp. mind and matter	**dualism**
knowledge is gained through experience, esp. the senses	**empiricism**
focuses on human isolation and choice	**existentialism**
pleasure equals good	**hedonism**
differs from accepted church belief	**heresy**
focuses on human beings, rather than abstractions or theology	**humanism**
material things are only examples of the ideas about them, a higher reality	**idealism**
statements of fact must pass the test of observation	**logical positivism**
the universe is ruled by 2 opposing powers, light-good and dark-evil	**manichaeism**
only matter and physical laws are real, and explain ideas or feelings	**materialism**
all is explainable using physical and mechanical principles, i.e., the world is like a machine	**mechanism**
reality is a unified whole	**monism**
involves belief in a single God	**monotheism**
seeks union with the divine through experiences or intuitions	**mysticism**
natural laws can explain reality, without resorting to the supernatural	**naturalism**
nothing exists or is knowable, hence a rejection of morality and social institutions	**nihilism**
abstract concepts have no reality, but are only names	**nominalism**

reality exists independent of the mind; also Ayn Rand's capitalist philosophy	**objectivism**
things generally tend to the good	**optimism**
society is like a living being	**organicism**
sees God or many gods in the forces of nature	**pantheism**
things generally tend to the bad	**pessimism**
ideas are the only reality, and that external objects are unknowable	**phenomenalism**
everything can be described in scientific terms, and is hence verifiable	**physicalism**
reality has many aspects, and no one view can account for them all	**pluralism**
belief in more that one god	**polytheism**
sense perceptions form the base for all human knowledge	**positivism**
practical actions and their results carry more weight than theory and tradition	**pragmatism**
reason is the true basis for belief or action, not observation, tradition, or revelation	**rationalism**
to be born again in a new body	**reincarnation**
socio-political motives, not religious ones, should have priority, e.g., in schools	**secularism**
sure knowledge is impossible, but doubting can help one approach certainty	**skepticism**
reality consists only of the self	**solipsism**
matter is real; or that material realities underlie all else	**substantialism**
focuses on reconciling divergent beliefs	**syncretism**
sees a human or humans as godlike	**theomorphism**
knowledge is intuitive, not stemming from objective experience	**transcendentalism**
a soul passes from one body to another at death	**transmigration** or **metempsychosis**
the Eucharist bread and wine become Christ, though appearing unchanged	**transubstantiation**
life cannot be explained wholly by biochemical descriptions	**vitalism**

Language of Logic and Reasoning

Relating to logic and reasoning, what is the word or phrase for . . . ?

a conclusion made stronger by logical force	**a fortiori**
the opposite in Hegel's dialectic	**antithesis**
reaching a conclusion after experiment and observation, rather than reasoning	**a posteriori**
reaching a conclusion by reasoning from general principles, not experiment or observation	**a priori**
the proposition made inevitable if a syllogism's major and minor premises are properly made	**conclusion**
reasoning in which a conclusion is drawn from premises	**deduction**
the meeting of thesis and antithesis and their transformation to synthesis, for Hegel	**dialectic**
a situation with 2 or more solutions, none favorable	**dilemma**
something actual, not potential, to Aristotle	**entelechy**
a syllogism in which one premise is implicit	**enthymeme**
reasoning from the particular to the general	**induction**
a deduction from facts	**inference**
intrinsic and inseparable from the thing itself	**inherent**
the premise that will form the predicate of a syllogism's conclusion	**major premise** .
the term in a syllogism's major premise that forms the predicate of the conclusion	**major term**
the premise that will form the subject of a syllogism's conclusion	**minor premise**
the term in a syllogism's minor premise, forming the conclusion's subject	**minor term**
a logical fault unknown to the reasoner	**paralogism**
a proposition from which a conclusion will be drawn	**premise**

a logical statement, with the subject affirmed or denied by the predicate	**proposition**
plausible but faulty reasoning	**sophistry**
a pattern of formal reasoning with a major premise (e.g., All dogs are sad), a minor premise (e.g., Spot is a dog), and a conclusion (e.g., Therefore, Spot is sad)	**syllogism**
the "higher truth" resulting from the clash of thesis and antithesis, in Hegel's dialectic	**synthesis**
the starting idea, in Hegel's dialectic	**thesis**
whether a proposition is true or false	**truth value**
a syllogism's middle term, when it does not cover the entire class in either premise	**undistributed middle**

Divination and Fortune-telling

Relating to divining the future, what type of fortune-telling focuses on . . . ?

animal droppings	**scatomancy**
animal entrails, as in ancient Rome	**haruspicy**
ashes	**spodomancy**
communing with the spirits of the dead	**necromancy** or **sciomancy**
crystal-gazing	**crystallomancy**
divining by lots, in general	**sortilege**
dreams	**oneiromancy**
finding a favorable time for an action, e.g., a wedding	**chronomancy**
flight pattern of birds	**ornithomancy**
horoscopy or palmistry, in general	**astrodiagnosis**
interpreting omens and portents, in general	**augury**
letters in a name	**onomancy** or **nomancy**
lines and geometric figures	**geomancy**
movements of an ax on a post	**axinomancy**
numbers	**arithmomancy** or **numerology**
number of lines in written work	**stichomancy**

oracles supposedly possessed of divine inspiration	**theomancy**
order in which a bird eats grains of corn placed on letters in a circle around it	**alectryomancy**
pebbles	**psephomancy**
position of the stars at someone's birth	**genethlialogy** or **genethliacs**
positions of heavenly bodies, as related to human affairs	**astrology, -mancy,** or **horoscopy**
reading fortunes from a person's palm	**chiromancy, -gnomy,** or **palmistry**
selecting arrows at random from a holder	**belomancy**
selecting random passages in a book, esp. the Bible	**bibliomancy**
shapes formed by melted wax in water	**ceromancy**
shoulder blades of animals	**scapulimancy, spatulamancy,** or **omoplatoscopy**
throwing dice	**cubomancy**
throwing lots	**cleromancy**
using a forked stick or rod to help find water	**dowsing**
using rods and wands	**rhabdomancy**
visions seen in liquids, e.g., in tides	**hydromancy**
where one falls from dizziness after much circling	**gyromancy**

Religious Works

Among the world's religious works, what is or was . . . ?

the main book of the Confucians	**Analects**
the 14 books of the Septuagint not accepted by Protestants	**Apocrypha**
the *Song of the Blessed One* from the Vedas	**Bhagavad-Gita**
the book of Christian scripture, containing the Old and New Testaments, sometimes more	**Bible**
the service and prayer book used by Anglicans	**Book of Common Prayer**
the book of Joseph Smith's key new revelations	**Book of Mormon**

books of the Bible once, but no longer, accepted by various church authorities	**deuterocanonical books**
Roman Catholic bible that includes 11 of the books of the Apocrypha, translated from the Vulgate	**Douay Bible**
first chapter or book of the Koran, also a prayer for the dying	**Fatihah**
1st 4 books of the New Testament, telling of Jesus's life	**Gospels**
text read aloud at a Passover Seder	**Hagadah**
Chinese *Book of Changes* hexagrams for divination	**I Ching**
17th-c. Anglican translation of the Bible from the Hebrew and Greek into English	**King James** or **Authorized Version**
scripture of the Moslems	**Koran (Quran)**
books of the Bible that form the basis of Christianity alone, not shared with the Jews	**New Testament**
books of the Bible accepted as scripture by both Jews and Christians	**Old Testament**
1st five books of the Bible, from the Greek	**Pentateuch**
modern US version of the Bible, based on the King James Version	**Revised Standard Version**
modern British and American version of the Bible, based on the King James Version	**Revised Version**
3rd-c. B.C. Jewish translation of the Old Testament into Greek	**Septuagint**
the 1st 5 books of the Old Testament, to Jews	**Torah**
the *Secret Doctrines* of the Vedas	**Upanishads**
the main scripture of the Hindus	**Vedas**
St. Jerome's 4th-c. translation of the Bible into Latin	**Vulgate**

Religious and Occult Langauge

In the language of religions and the occult, what is or are . . . ?

In Christianity

priestly forgiveness of sins following confesssion, as part of the sacrament of penance	**absolution**
a priest's attendant, esp. at a Mass	**acolyte**
a celebration of Christian love linked with the Eucharist among early Christians	**agape**
a formal curse of excommunication	**anathema**
against withdrawal from an established church, esp. the 19th-c. Church of England	**antidisestablishmentarianism**
Jesus's originial 12 disciples; also other missionaries	**apostles**
baptism by sprinkling	**aspersion**
the ceremony in which heretics were sentenced for execution in the Spanish Inquisition	**auto-da-fé (act of faith)**
a Roman Catholic prayer, "Hail Mary"	**Ave Maria**
a Christian sacrament involving water, for sprinkling or immersion, and the giving of a name, to symbolize cleansing from original sin	**baptism** or **christening**
a building where columns set off two aisles from the central nave, as in early Christian churches	**basilica**
a clerical book with hymns, offices, and prayers	**breviary**
prayers prescribed by canon law for 7 set times of the day	**canonical hours**
a question-and-answer book about a religion's basic doctrines	**catechism**
the Lord's Supper, in Latin	**Cena Domini**
a church vessel holding incense	**censer** or **thurible**
an early symbol of Christ	**chi-ro**
canonical hours set for just before going to bed	**complin**

declaring sins, esp. to receive absolution	**confession**
formal admission of a baptized person into the church	**confirmation**
the body of Christ, in Latin	**Corpus Christi**
a parish priest, in France	**curé**
day of wrath, in Latin, from a hymn in a Catholic mass for the dead	**dies irae**
a religious organization closely linked with political institutions	**ecclesia**
a movement toward a single Christian church	**ecumenism**
hell, in French	**enfer**
the Christian sacrament imitating the Last Supper	**Eucharist** or **Communion**
being forbidden to partake in the Eucharist	**excommunication**
the sacrament of anointing and prayer for one on the point of death	**extreme unction**
a sacred image, esp. in Eastern Christianity	**icon**
an investigation, esp. against heretics	**inquisition**
a day when meat may be eaten, lit. fat day in French	**jour gras**
a day of no meat or of fasting, lit. a meager day in French	**jour maigre**
Jesus's final meal with his disciples before crucifixion	**Last Supper**
hymns of praise accompanying matins	**lauds**
a prayer with alternating speech from a leader and the congregation	**litany**
the Christian rite of worship, esp. as in the Book of Common Prayer; also the Eucharist	**liturgy**
the common Christian prayer drawn from Jesus's teachings in the Book of Matthew	**Lord's Prayer**
morning prayer, esp. canonical hours set for the early morning	**matins**
the expected king of and deliverer of the Jews; for Christians, Jesus Christ	**Messiah**
the holy 1000-year period during which Christ is supposed to rule	**millennium**

a book containing prayers for a full year's Roman Catholic masses	**missal**
the 5th canonical hour, usually the 9th hour after sunrise	**nones**
a 9-day set of specific prayers, to Catholics	**novena**
ecclesiastical rites; also canonical hours or prayers	**offices**
a person's formal admission to a church's ministry	**ordination**
the belief that humans are inherently evil	**original sin**
the schedule of holidays and festivals, to Catholics	**ordo**
the Lord's Prayer, from "our father" in Latin	**paternoster**
Christian sacrament involving contrition, confession, punishment, and absolution	**penance**
the day's 2nd canonical hours set for around 6 A.M.	**prime**
a hymn sung as the clergy enter the church	**processional**
sacred hymns, esp. from the Old Testament	**psalms**
a book of psalms	**psalter**
a parish priest, in England	**rector** or **vicar**
the 16th-c. attempts to revitalize Catholicism, leading to the formation of Protestant churches	**Reformation**
beads used in counting prayers, esp. by Catholics	**rosary beads**
a service for the dead; also the music for it	**Requiem Mass**
one of the basic Christian rites	**sacrament**
an X-shaped cross from early Christian art	**St. Andrew's cross**
a red vertical cross on a white background	**St. George's cross**
a red X-shaped cross on a white background	**St. Patrick's cross**
the expected return of Christ to judge the world	**Second Coming** or **Second Advent**
the 4th of the canonical hours, set for about noon	**sext**
the T-shaped cross common in medieval times	**tau** or **St. Anthony's cross**
the 3rd of the canonical hours, usually the 3rd hour after sunrise	**tierce**

the belief that the Father, Son, and Holy Ghost are one god	**Trinity**
anointing as part of a ceremonial ritual	**unction**
canonical hours set for late afternoon	**vespers**
Eucharist given to one on the point of death	**viaticum**

Religious Invocations from Latin

bless you	**benedicite**
by God's grace	**Dei gratia**
Glory be to God the Highest	**Gloria in Excelsis Deo**
Glory to the Father	**Gloria Patri**
God be merciful	**Deus misereatur**
God (the Lord) be with you	**Deus (Dominus) vobiscum**
God is the chief good	**Deus est summum bonum**
God willing	**Deo volente**
God (the Lord) will provide	**Deus (Dominus) providebit**
God with us, who can stand against us	**Deus nobiscum, quis contra**
God's will be done	**fiat Dei voluntas**
God wills it, a Crusaders' slogan	**Deus vult**
go in peace	**vade in pace**
Lord be with you, in Latin, ending a mass	**Dominus vobiscum**
Lord direct us, London's motto	**Domine, dirige nos**
Lord is my light, Oxford's motto	**Dominus illuminatio mea**
peace be with you	**pax vobiscum**
rest in peace	**requiescat in pace**
thanks to God	**Deo gratias**
thee God, we praise, a Christian hymn	**te Deum laudamus**
to God, the best, the greatest, a motto of the Benedictine order	**Deo, Optimo, Maximo (D.O.M.)**
with God's help	**Deo juvante**

In Hinduism and Buddhism

a nectar, food of the gods, for Hindus	**amrita**
the state of bliss	**ananda**
a spiritually perfect sage, to Lamaist Buddhists	**arhat**
the posture assumed for meditation in yoga	**asana**
a Hindu monastery or place of retreat	**ashram**
the divine, eternal part of the self, to Hindus	**atman**

the incarnation of a god on earth, to Hindus	**avatar**
ignorance of one's true self, to Hindus	**avidya**
a plane human souls pass through after death, to Tibetan Lamaist Buddhists	**bardo**
devotion to duty and God, to Hindus	**bhakti**
a Buddhist monk who lives by daily begging	**bhikku**
a Buddhist who forgoes nirvana to save others	**bodhisattva**
a Buddhist priest, in Japan	**bosan**
the hereditary social classes of the Hindus	**castes**
energy centers in the body, like "glowing wheels" to some	**chakras**
a guru's disciple, in India	**chela**
a Hindu temple	**devalaya**
concentrating on a single idea or image during meditation	**dharana**
a person's individual duty, calling, or fate, the law of all things	**dharma**
thoughtless concentration during meditation	**dhyana**
a religious teacher, to Hindus	**guru**
a huge, wheeled statue of Vishnu, hence an unstoppable force	**Juggernath**
one's fate or destiny, to Hindus	**karma**
latent energy force at the base of the spine, in Sanskrit mythology	**kundalini**
a monastery among Lama Buddhists	**lamasery**
a word repeated as an aid to meditation, to Hindus	**mantra**
release from the necessity of transmigration, to Hindus	**mokshu**
freedom from all earthly constraints, to Buddhists	**nirvana**
a supposedly powerful word used in Hindu prayer	**Om**
a soul consigned to suffering, to Buddhists	**pretas**
an ascetic holy person, among the Hindus	**sadhu**
the continuing cycle of life and death, in India	**samsarma**

the passive or creative force of the cosmos, seen as a goddess, to Hindus	**Shakti**
the drink of the gods, to Hindus	**soma**
a Buddhist shrine with a bell-shaped domed top	**stupa** or **tope**
a Hindu collection of wise sayings or proverbs	**sutra**
philosophy and spiritual exercises, to Hindus	**yoga**

In Islam

Shi'ite religious leader, e.g., Khomeini	**ayatollah**
the call to prayer, 5 times a day	**azan**
the pilgrimage to Mecca required of all Moslems	**haj, hajj,** or **hadj**
the prophet Mohammed's flight from Mecca to Medina in 622 A.D.	**Hejira** or **Hegira**
a female guide in paradise	**houri**
the robe a pilgrim wears at Mecca	**ihram**
the prayer leader, in Islam	**imam**
holy war, in Islam	**jihad**
the tower from which Moslems are called to prayer	**minaret**
places of worship	**mosques**
a person who calls Moslems to prayer	**muezzin**
a teacher, esp. of Islamic basics	**mullah**
the direction facing Mecca, to	**qibla**
Moslems learned in the Koran and Islamic law	**ulema**
the giving of alms	**zakat**

In Judaism

reading the Torah at a synagogue service; also a visit to Jerusalem	**aliyah**
the ceremony marking a Jewish boy's move into adulthood, usually at 13	**bar mitzvah**
the ceremony marking a Jewish girl's move into adulthood, usually at 13	**bas** or **bat mitzvah**
a ceremony at circumcision	**bris**
an occult mystical view of Jewish scriptures	**cabala** or **kabbala**

the scattering (dispersion) of Jews from the Middle East, esp. after the 1st c. A.D.	**Diaspora**
a Gentile, to the Jews	**goy (pl. goyim)**
Hebrew school	**heder**
the 6-pointed star, symbol of Judaism	**hexagram, Magen (Mogen) David,** or **Star of David**
attempt to exterminate Jews, by Nazi Germany in WW II	**Holocaust**
a prayer for the dead	**Kaddish**
a prayer for Yom Kippur eve	**Kol Nidre**
food prepared according to Jewish dietary laws	**kosher**
a book with prayers for the Jewish holidays	**mahzor**
the candelabrum lit on Hanukkah	**menorah**
a box of verses affixed to the doorway of an Orthodox Jew's home	**mezuze** or **mezuzah**
an Orthodox Jewish ritual bath	**mikvah**
the 10 male Jews needed for a religious service	**minyon**
a professional Jewish circumciser	**moyl** or **mohel**
violence and massacre against Jews	**pogroms**
a Jewish congregational leader	**rabbi** or **rebbe**
the feast Jews celebrate during Passover	**Seder**
a ram's horn sounded in synagogues at special times	**shofar**
a Jewish book with prayers for the year	**siddur**
a prayer shawl	**tallith**
unclean, not kosher, food	**tref**
the anniversary of a person's death	**yahrzeit**
rabbinical school; also a Hebrew high school	**yeshiva**

In Other Religions and Occult Beliefs

the food of the Greek and Roman gods	**ambrosia**
an ancient Egyptian T-shaped cross with a loop on top, symbolizing the life force	**crux ansata** or **ankh**
the Brazilian "positive" form of voodoo	**candomblé**
a means of reaching the spirit world	**channeling**

the 36 stars, one for each 10° in the zodiac, whose risings are charted by astrologers — **decan stars**

a voodoo priest, on Haiti — **hougan**

any of the 12 parts of the zodiac — **house**

a local voodoo temple, on Haiti — **hounfor**

the belief that one has or can become a werewolf — **lycanthropy**

a voodoo priestess, on Haiti — **mambo**

someone thought able to communicate with the dead — **medium**

the drink of the Greek and Roman gods — **nectar**

a board supposedly for receiving spiritual messages — **Ouija board**

the catalyst alchemists sought in vain, to turn ordinary metals into gold — **philosopher's stone**

a ghost that makes noise, as with rappings — **poltergeist**

someone believed to have extrasensory powers — **psychic**

occult letters or characters, in general — **runes**

a symbol of resurrection or talisman in early Egypt — **scarab**

the home of the gods, in Japan — **shintai**

the 12 divisions of the zodiac, each linked with a major constellation — **signs**

a Chinese program for mental and bodily harmony — **T'ai Chi Ch'uan**

a 22-card deck used in fortune-telling — **tarot**

a popular, African-linked Haitian religion — **voodoo**

the 360° circle representing the heavens — **zodiac**

General Terms

a cabalistic word thought to have mystical power — **abracadabra**

a sign of the future, in general — **auspice, omen,** or **portent**

the ability to see things beyond the normal range of the senses — **clairvoyance** or **second sight**

a special contract with God—or the Devil — **covenant**

a group strongly devoted to a charismatic leader — **cult**

a church quite separate from the state, as in the US	**denomination**
a ceremony to drive out the devil or evil spirits	**exorcism**
perception by means beyond the normal senses	**extrasensory perception (ESP)**
ceremonial purification	**lustration**
an idea of foreboding	**premonition**
the day of rest and worship in a religion	**sabbath**
relating to priests or the priesthood	**sacerdotal**
the profaning of something sacred	**sacrilege**
a small, often zealous, religious group	**sect**
worldly, as opposed to spiritual	**secular**
the supposed power of mind over matter	**telekinesis** or **psycho-kinesis**
communication through inexplicable means	**telepathy**
a recital of the gods' origin and genealogy, as in early epic poetry	**theogony**
a god's appearance before a human	**theophany**
a relaxation method based on Hindu techniques	**transcendental meditation**

Religious Groups and Orders

Among religious groups and orders, which . . . ?

In the Judeo-Christian Tradition

focus on the nearness of the Second Coming and the end of the world	**Adventists** or **Seventh-Day Adventists**
was a 13th-c. anti-priest sect in southern France	**Albigensians**
are followers of 17th-c. Mennonite Jacob Amman	**Amish**
were 16th-c. Protestants stressing adult baptism, pacifism, and church-state separation	**Anabaptists**
belong to the Church of England or its affiliates	**Anglicans**

were followers of St. Augustine, often hermits	**Augustinian**
are saintly Jews, chosen by God for special work	**Baal Shem**
baptize after age 12 with total immersion	**Baptists**
are "Black Monks" noted for their learning	**Benedictines**
was an order formed by ex-Franciscans in 1525	**Capuchins**
were a 12th-c. order of White Friars, later nuns	**Carmelites**
are followers of Jesus Christ	**Christians**
are faith healers, inspired by Mary Baker Eddy	**Christian Scientists**
belong to an 11th-c. order founded by St. Robert	**Cistercians** or **Bernardines**
are evangelicals emphasizing fellowship	**congregationalists**
follow a modified type of Judaism, between Orthodox and Reform	**Conservative Jews**
were Jews converted to Christianity in 15th-c. Spain	**Conversos**
are Black Friars known for their teaching	**Dominicans** or **Jacobins (France)**
do not accept the Church of England, esp. other English Protestant sects	**Dissenters** or **Nonconformists**
stresses simplicity of religious life and total immersion baptism	**Dunkers**
split with the Roman Catholics in 1054	**Eastern Orthodox**
are American cousins to Britain's Anglicans	**Episcopalians**
1st-c. B.C. Jewish sect of the Dead Sea Scrolls	**Essenes**
believe in ethical behavior based on humanist ideals	**Ethical Culturalists**
are Protestants stressing the Gospels, faith, and grace over sacraments and good works	**Evangelicals**
are associated with poverty and love of nature	**Franciscans**
believe in literal interpretation of the Bible	**fundamentalists**
tried early to reconcile Greek philosophy with Christianity	**Gnostics (Knowers)**
are a sect of ultra-pious Jews from Poland	**Hasidim**

is the Anglican branch with services similar to those in Catholicism	**High Church**
were French followers of John Calvin	**Huguenots**
are US evangelicals stressing the nearness of the millennium and opposition to war	**Jehovah's Witnesses**
belong to St. Ignatius of Loyola's Society of Jesus	**Jesuits**
have as their scripture the Old Testament	**Jews** or **Hebrews**
is the Anglican branch that eschews Catholic-like rituals	**Low Church**
follow the reforms of Martin Luther	**Lutherans**
follow the 16th-c. Anabaptist Simons Menno	**Mennonites**
split off from the Anglicans, following John Wesley	**Methodists**
follow Joseph Smith's revelations	**Mormons** or **Latter-Day Saints**
hold to the old Jewish religious ways	**Orthodox Jews**
are evangelical US Protestants, once called "holy rollers"	**Pentecostals**
follow John Knox's form of Calvinist reform	**Presbyterians**
broke away from the Roman Catholics in the 16th c.	**Protestants**
the Society of Friends	**Quakers**
are people following a modern version of Judaism, esp. strong in the US	**Reform Jews**
follow John Calvin's Protestant reforms	**Reformed Protestants or Calvinists**
accept the authority of the Pope in Rome	**Roman Catholics**
were a secret religious society from the 15th–17th c.	**Rosicrucianists**
are Adventists stressing celibate communal living	**Shakers**
was founded by St. Ignatius Loyola	**Society of Jesus (Jesuits)**
were early Christian hermits who lived on pillars	**stylites**
are Cistercian monks who keep absolute silence	**Trappists**
reject the Trinity and stress religious freedom	**Unitarians**

In Other Religions

stress the spiritual unity of humanity	**Baha'ists**
are Moslem Iranian "volunteers for martyrdom"	**Basiji**
belong to the US Nation of Islam, proposing racial segregation and a black nation	**Black Muslims**
is the highest, priestly caste of the Hindus	**Brahmins**
are followers of Siddhartha Gautama's religion	**Buddhists**
are followers of the precepts of China's Confucius	**Confucians**
are Moslem ascetics, famed for their whirling dances	**dervishes**
were early Celtic priests and sorcerors	**Druids**
are Moslem ascetics and beggars	**fakirs**
were Hindu ascetics from Classical times	**gymnosophists**
is the group that chants the name of Krishna	**Hare Krishna**
are members of India's ancient caste religion	**Hindus**
were Indian ascetics stressing the soul's immortality and transmigration	**Jains**
is the Hindu caste of soldiers and rulers	**Kshatriya (Shatriya)**
follow Buddhist Tibet's Dalai Lama	**Lamaists**
are followers of Islam	**Moslems (Muslims) or Mohammedans (Muhammadans)**
are Hindus with no caste	**Outcastes**
are non-Christians, in the eyes of some Christians	**pagans**
are the main dissident Moslems, as in Iran	**Shiites**
follow the old Japanese "way of the gods"	**Shintoists**
follow a religion centered in India's Punjab	**Sikhs**
are the Hindu caste of farm and craft workers	**Sudra**
belong to a Moslem mystic sect	**Sufis**
are the main "orthodox" body of Moslems	**Sunnis**

follow early China's Lao-tzu	**Taoists**
follow a mystical or occult sect, with some links to Eastern religions	**Theosophists**
are the Hindu caste of herders and traders, and in modern times merchants and entrepreneurs	**Vaisya**
are Hindus who stress unity with the single principle, Brahman	**Vedantists**
are males practicing sorcery or wizardry	**warlocks**
are women practicing sorcery or wizardry	**witches**
are Hindus stressing spiritual insight and inner peace	**Yogists** or **Yogi**
are Buddhists stressing direct religious experience	**Zen Buddhists**
are followers of Zoroaster	**Zoroastrians** or **Zarathustrians**

Key Figures in Religion and Philosophy

(See also Christian Saints and also Key Figures in World History and Key Figures in American History in *People from the Past*)

Among the world's key figures in religion and philosophy, who . . . ?

in the Ancient World

founded the Jewish priesthood, brother of Moses	**Aaron**
is regarded as the founder of Judaism	**Abraham**
wrote *Politics* and *Poetics* and tutored Alexander the Great	**Aristotle**
founded Buddhism in 6th-c. B.C. India	**Buddha (Siddhartha Gautama)**
laid out basic guides to behavior in his *Analects* in 6th–5th-c. B.C. China	**Confucius**
led 1500 Jews back from Babylon to Jerusalem	**Ezra**
was a leading 1st-c. B.C. Talmudic scholar	**Hillel**
betrayed Jesus for 30 pieces of silver	**Judas Iscariot**
founded Christianity, as told in the New Testament	**Jesus Christ**

was deliberately tested by adversity	**Job**
was the prophet swallowed by a whale	**Jonah**
founded Taoism in 6th-c. B.C. China	**Lao Tzu**
received the 10 Commandments and led his people to the Promised Land	**Moses**
was told by Jesus he must be "born again"	**Nicodemus**
wrote *The Republic*, a student of Socrates	**Plato**
danced for Herod and demanded the head of John the Baptist on a plate	**Salome**
was a 5th-c. B.C. Greek philosopher and teacher of Aristotle, condemned to death by Athens	**Socrates**
founded a new Persian religion in the 6th-c. B.C.	**Zoroaster (Zarathustra)**

In the Medieval World

founded the Abbasid Caliphate, uncle of Mohammed and of Ali, the fourth caliph	**Abbas**
was the monk who loved Heloise	**Peter Abélard**
wrote *The Confessions* and *The City of God*	**St. Augustine**
was the pope France charged with heresy, leading to the great schism and the 2nd "Babylonian Captivity"	**Boniface VIII**
was the French pope installed during the schism	**Clement V**
founded the Franciscan order in the 13th c.	**St. Francis of Assisi**
founded the Jesuit order in the 16th c.	**St. Ignatius Loyola**
translated the Bible into Latin	**St. Jerome**
was the prophet who founded Islam in the 7th c.	**Mohammed (Muhammad)**
wrote *Moreh Nevukhim (Guide for the Perplexed)*	**Moses ben Maimon (Maimonides)**
led a heretical, refugee, 5th-c. Asian Christian sect	**Nestorius**
was a 16th-c. French astrologer given to prophecy	**Michel Nostradamus**

was the 12th-c. archbishop murdered in Canterbury Cathedral by Henry II's men — **St. Thomas à Becket**

wrote *Imitation of Christ (Imitatio Christi)* — **St. Thomas à Kempis**

wrote *Summa Theologiae* — **St. Thomas Aquinas**

preached reform in 14th-c. England — **John Wycliffe**

was a key 16th-c. Swiss Protestant reformer — **Huldreich Zwingli**

In the Renaissance and Early Colonial World

wrote *Religio Medici* — **Thomas Browne**

was executed in Rome in 1600 — **Giordano Bruno**

was a 16th-c. Protestant, whose views led to the Presbyterian and Reformed churches — **John Calvin (Jean Cauvin)**

founded the Hasidic movement in the 18th c. — **Israel ben Eliezer (Besht)**

was an early fire-and-brimstone New England preacher — **Jonathan Edwards**

wrote *In Praise of Folly*, a key Renaissance scholar — **Desiderius Erasmus**

founded the Quakers' Society of Friends — **George Fox**

wrote *Leviathan* — **Thomas Hobbes**

stressed skepticism in his *An Enquiry Concerning Human Understanding* — **David Hume**

was the 15th-c. Czech religious reformer and martyr — **Jan Hus (John Huss)**

founded Scottish Presbyterianism, following Calvin — **John Knox**

wrote *An Essay Concerning Human Understanding* — **John Locke**

created the "mythical and magical" Golem — **Rabbi Löw**

sparked the Reformation with his "95 Theses" — **Martin Luther**

wrote *Il Principe (The Prince)* — **Nicolló Machiavelli**

founded Sikhism in 16th-c. India's Punjab — **Guru Nanak**

whipped 15th-c. Florence into a pious frenzy — **Girolamo Savonarola**

was a 17th-c. Dutch-Jewish rationalist-pantheist — **Baruch (Benedict) Spinoza**

In the 18th and 19th centuries

founded the Bahai religion in the 19th c.	Baha'ullah (né Mirza Husayn Ali)
suggested that things exist only when perceived	Bishop George Berkeley
wrote *Karma*, a theosophist and Fabian socialist	Annie Besant
was a key 19th-c. Unitarian	William Ellery Channing
founded positivism	Auguste Comte
founded the Christian Science movement	Mary Baker Eddy
was the main New England exponent of transcendentalism	Ralph Waldo Emerson
wrote *An Enquiry Concerning Political Justice*	William Godwin
wrote *The Phenomenology of the Spirit*	Georg Friedrich Wilhelm Hegel
was the rabbi "seer of Lublin," a key figure in Hasidism	Jacob Hurwitz
wrote *The Varieties of Religious Experience*	William James
wrote *A Critique of Pure Reason*	Immanuel Kant
wrote *Either-Or*, the father of existentialism	Søren Kierkegaard
suggested that this was "the best of all possible worlds"	Gottfried von Leibnitz
was an 18th-c. German-Jewish reformer, grandfather of Felix	Moses Mendelssohn
wrote *The Spirit of Laws*	Charles de Montesquieu
wrote of supermen in *Thus Spake Zarathustra*	Friedrich Nietzsche
propounded the theory of pragmatism	Charles Peirce
wrote *The Social Contract*	Jean Jacques Rousseau
wrote *The World as Will and Representation*	Arthur Schopenhauer
was the 1st American-born saint	Elizabeth Ann Seton
founded the Mormon church	Joseph Smith
wrote *First Principles*	Herbert Spencer
calculated that the world began in 4004 B.C.	Archbishop James Ussher
founded the Methodist church	John Wesley
wrote *Vindication of the Rights of Women*	Mary Wollstonecraft
led the Mormons west in America	Brigham Young

In the Modern World

founded the Ethical Culture Society	**Felix Adler**
lost the PTL (Praise the Lord) operation	**Jim** and **Tammy Bakker**
was the German Lutheran pastor killed for being anti-Hitler	**Dietrich Bonhoeffer**
wrote *I and Thou*	**Martin Buber**
wrote *Resistance, Rebellion, and Death*	**Albert Camus**
wrote *The Tao of Physics*	**Fritjof Capra**
wrote *The Teachings of Don Juan: A Yaqui Way of Knowledge*	**Carlos Castaneda**
was an American faith healer and clairvoyant	**Edgar Cayce**
was the 1930's anti-Semitic Catholic priest on radio	**Charles Coughlin**
was the Catholic U. priest-professor suspended by the Vatican for his writings on sexual ethics	**Rev. Charles E. Curran**
was a popular astrologist of the 1960's	**Jeanne Dixon**
headed the Moral Majority	**Jerry Falwell**
was the Black Muslim leader linked with Jesse Jackson	**Louis Farrakhan**
founded Boys' Town in 1917	**Father Edward Joseph Flanagan**
wrote *The Prophet*	**Kahlil Gibran**
wrote *Sun Signs*	**Linda Goodman**
started his TV evangelism in 1953	**Billy Graham**
taught "The Fourth Way," a Russian mystic	**G(eorgi) I. Gurdjieff**
focused on being and becoming, an existentialist	**Martin Heidegger**
is called the father of modern Zionism	**Theodor Herzl**
wrote *The True Believer*, a longshoreman-philosopher	**Eric Hoffer**
founded Scientology and wrote *Dianetics*	**L. Ron Hubbard**
wrote *Man and the Modern World*	**Karl Jaspers**
channeled sayings from Ramtha	**J. Z. Knight**
was the Indian ascetic and philosopher of freedom, popular in the 1960's	**Khrishnamurti (Jiddu)**
wrote *Transcendental Meditation: Science of Being and Art of Living*	**Yogi**

was the Black Muslim leader assassinated in NYC on Feb. 21, 1965	Malcolm X
was an American Catholic priest, Trappist monk, and civil rights activist	Thomas Merton
wrote *A Gift of Prophecy*	Ruth Montgomery
founded the Unification Church, from Korea	Rev. Sun Myung Moon
led the Black Muslims to 1975	Elijah Muhammad
led the 19th-c. Oxford Movement for Anglican reform, later converting to Catholicism	John Henry Newman
was a key American Christian theologian	Helmut R. Niebuhr
is NYC's controversial cardinal	John Cardinal O'Connor
wrote *The Power of Positive Thinking*	Norman Vincent Peale
wrote *The Revolt of the Masses*	José Ortega y Gasset
said God would "take him home" if he didn't raise $8 million	Oral Roberts
was the televangelist and 1988 presidential hopeful	Pat Robertson
wrote *Principia Mathematica* (with Alfred North White-head) and *A History of Western Philosophy*	Bertrand Russell
founded the Jehovah's Witnesses	Charles Russell
wrote *Skepticism and Animal Faith*	George Santayana
broadcasts TV's *Hour of Power* from his Crystal Cathedral	Robert Schuller
hosted early TV's *Life Is Worth Living*	Bishop Fulton J. Sheen
was an early-20th-c. revivalist	Billy Sunday
was the televangelist who weepily confessed his sexual indiscretions on TV	Jimmy Swaggart
wrote *The Phenomenon of Man*	Pierre Teilhard de Chardin
was a German-American religious existentialist	Paul Tillich
wrote "A proposition is a model of reality as we think it to be"	Ludwig Wittgenstein

Gods and Devils

Among the world's gods and devils, who was or were . . . ?

In Ancient Egypt and the Near East

Egyptian king of the gods	**Ammon** or **Amon-Ra**
Egyptian jackal-god who took souls to judgment	**Anubis**
Phoenician goddess of love and fertility	**Astarte**
single god promoted by Amenhotep IV in Egypt	**Aton**
Egyptian cat goddess	**Bastet**
Egyptian avenging god, shown as a hawk	**Horus (Harpocrates)**
sister and wife of the Egyptian god Osiris	**Isis**
Egyptian judge of the dead, guard of the tombs	**Osiris**
Egyptian sun god, later joined with Ammon	**Ra** or **Re**
Egyptian (Greek) god of evil	**Set (Typhon)**
a half-lion, half-man representation of the sun god Ra in Egypt; also a lion-bird-woman monster in Greece, who posed a riddle to Oedipus	**Sphinx**
Egyptian god of wisdom and truth	**Thoth**

In Classical Greece and Rome

Greek god of the winds	**Aeolus**
queen of the sea and wife of Poseidon	**Amphitrite**
son of Ge and Poseidon, invincible as long as he touched earth	**Antaeus**
Roman (Greek) god of the sun	**Apollo (Phoebus)**
Greek (Roman) goddess of wisdom	**Athena (Minerva)**
Greek (Latin) god of wine, associated with orgies	**Bacchus (Dionysus)**
Roman (Greek) goddess of farming	**Ceres (Demeter)**
oldest Greek god, of mixed earth, air, and sea	**Chaos**
Roman (Greek) god of love	**Cupid (Eros)**
wife of Roman god Saturn	**Cybele**

Roman (Greek) goddess of hunting and the moon	**Diana (Artemis)**
12 most important Roman gods	**Dii Majores**
lesser Roman gods	**Dii Minores**
Greek god of the cavernous pathway to Hades	**Erebus**
Greek (Roman) goddess of Earth, mother and wife of Uranus	**Ge or Gaea (Tellus)**
Roman (Greek) queen of the gods	**Juno (Hera)**
Roman household gods	**Lares and Penates**
Roman (Greek) god of war	**Mars (Ares)**
Roman (Greek) messenger god	**Mercury (Hermes)**
Roman (Greek) god of the oceans	**Neptune (Poseidon)**
Greek god of night	**Nyx**
god of the waters beyond the Greek world	**Oceanus**
Roman (Greek) god of the underworld	**Pluto (Pluton)**
Roman (Greek) wife of Pluto (Pluton)	**Proserpine (Persephone)**
Greek god who assumed any shape at will	**Proteus**
wife of the Greek god Kronus	**Rhea**
Roman (Greek) god of time	**Saturn (Kronus)**
wife of Oceanus and daughter of Uranus and Ge	**Tethys**
mother of Achilles	**Thetis**
mother of the Greek god Poseidon	**Triton**
Greek god of heaven	**Uranus**
Roman (Greek) goddess of love and beauty	**Venus (Aphrodite)**
Roman (Greek) goddess of house and home	**Vesta (Hestia)**
Roman (Greek) blacksmith god	**Vulcan (Hephaistus)**
Greek (Roman) king of the gods	**Zeus (Jupiter)**

In the Germanic and Scandinavian Tradition

celestial gods	**Aesir**
home of celestial gods	**Asgard**
god of the sun	**Balder**
god of poetry	**Bragi**
goddess of love	**Freya**
messenger god	**Hermoder**
god of mischief	**Loki**
home of nature gods	**Noatun**
"home of darkness" of the Nibelungs	**Nibelheim**

dwarfs with a great hoard of gold	**Nibelungs**
water god	**Niörd**
chief of the gods	**Odin (Wotan)**
god of thunder, son of Odin	**Thor**
god of wisdom	**Tiu**
god of justice	**Vali**
Valhalla's 12 nymphs, who chose who should die	**Valkyries**
gods of nature and the earth	**Vanir**
god of silence	**Vidar**
heavenly home of dead heroes	**Valhalla**

In the Hindu and Buddhist Tradition

god of fire, sun, and lightning	**Agni**
Creator	**Brahma**
god of wisdom	**Ganesh**
monkey-god	**Hanuman**
god of heaven and thunderous storms	**Indra**
goddess of death, sickness, and chaos, the wife of Siva	**Kali (Durga)**
godly winged white horse, who will destroy the earth	**Kalki**
god of youthful love	**Kama**
god of fire and storms, the "black one"	**Krishna**
god of riches and evil powers	**Kubera**
Destroyer, but also a creator, a dancing figure with 2 extra arms	**Siva**
god of the sun	**Surya**
top three Hindu gods, together	**Trimurti**
Preserver	**Vishnu**
god of death	**Yama**

In the Islamic Tradition

Moslem (also Jewish) angel of death	**Azrael**
demons of good or evil in Arab myth	**djinn** (sing. **djinnee**)
a god or deity, to the Hindus	**deva**

In the Judeo-Christian Tradition

substitutes for the name of God, to Jews	**Adonai, Adoshem, Bore Olam, Elohim, Ha-Shem, Jehovah, Ribon,** or **Yahweh**
popular medieval phrase for Jesus Christ	**Agnus Dei (Lamb of God)**

Jewish (and Moslem) angel of death	Azrael
a spirit that possesses and controls a human, to Eastern European Jews	dybbuk
God, to Christians	Jehovah

In Other Religions

Japanese sun goddess	Amaterasu
female wraith bringing tidings of evil and death, in Ireland and Scotland	banshee
Aztec goddess of the earth and death	Chicomecoatl
Aztec goddess of the earth	Itzpapalotl
gods who supposedly formed the Japanese islands	Izanagi and Izanami
great spirit, good or evil, of Amerindians	manitou
Aztec god-king whose return was expected	Quetzalcoatl

Christian Saints

(See also Key Figures in Religion and Philosophy)

Among Christian saints, who was associated with . . . ?

brewers, esp. in Flanders	Adrian
artists and nurses, who had her breasts cut off	Agatha
young girls, esp. virgins, honored on Jan. 20	Agnes
scientists	Albert
pilgrims, beggars, hermits, and nurses	Alexius
confessors	Alphonsus Liguori
innkeepers and hoteliers	Amand
beehives, from 4th-c. Milan	Ambrose
fishers, Scotland, and Greece, 1 of the 12 disciples, Peter's brother, honored on Nov. 30	Andrew
Canada, cabinetmakers, house-wives, and women in child-birth, the mother of the Virgin Mary	Anne
Denmark	Ansgar
butchers	Anthony of Egypt

barren women, searchers, travelers, and the poor	**Anthony of Padua**
gravediggers	**Anthony the abbott**
swineherds	**Anthony the Great**
dentists and toothache sufferers	**Apollonia**
millers	**Arnold**
Canterbury, as its 1st archbishop	**Augustine of England**
printers and brewers	**Augustine of Hippo**
guns, mining, lightning, prisoners, and the dying	**Barbara**
laboring alongside the Apostle Paul	**Barnabas**
plasterers and knives, 1 of the 12 disciples	**Bartholomew**
poison victims	**Benedict**
visions of the Virgin Mary at Lourdes	**Bernadette**
founding the Cistercian monastery at Clairvaux	**Bernard of Clairvaux**
mountain climbers and skiers, founding Alpine hospices	**Bernard of Menthon**
advertisers	**Bernardine of Siena**
woolcombers and sore throats	**Blaise**
Germany, an 8th-c. apostle	**Boniface**
Dante's *Paradiso*, the "Seraphic Doctor"	**Bonaventura**
sailors, who traveled in the Atlantic in the 6th c.	**Brendan**
Sweden	**Bridget**
Ireland, scholars, and dairies	**Brigid**
the possessed	**Bruno**
emigrants	**Frances Xavier Cabrini**
nurses and the sick	**Camillus de Lellis**
Denmark	**Canute**
Poland	**Casimir**
scholars, and was killed on a wheel	**Catharine**
students, teachers, jurists, and philosophers	**Catherine of Alexandria**
Italy	**Catherine of Siena**
the blind, poets, musicians, and singers	**Cecilia**
travelers, esp. sailors and automobile drivers, and protection against earthquakes, fires, floods, and bad dreams	**Christopher**
sculptors	**Claude**
tanners, shown with an anchor	**Clement**
Ireland and Scotland	**Columba**

physicians, surgeons, pharmacists, and barbers, 2 brothers	**Cosmas** and **Damian**
shoemakers, 2 brothers	**Crispin** and **Crispian**
sailors and rosary beads	**Cuthbert**
being the 1st martyred Christian bishop	**Cyprian**
Wales, poets, and leeks	**David**
France and the possessed, apostle to the Gauls	**Denis**
undertakers, prisoners, and robbers, himself a repentant thief	**Dismas**
astronomers, also a sparrow and a dog with a torch, called Inquisitor-General	**Dominic**
choir singers	**Dominic Savio**
florists, gardeners, roses, and apples	**Dorothy**
goldsmiths, blacksmiths, and musicians	**Dunstan**
the insane	**Dymphna**
being the English St. Sebastian	**Edmund**
queens and bakers	**Elizabeth of Hungary**
artists, jewelers, smiths, and metalworkers	**Eligius, Eloi, or Eloy**
sailors	**Erasmus**
Sweden	**Eric**
sailors and Barcelona	**Eulalia**
hunters	**Eustachius**
barren women	**Felicitas**
engineers	**Ferdinand III**
gardeners and taxi drivers	**Fiacre**
being rediscovered in Rome's 19th-c. Catacombs	**Filumena**
Poland, firefighters, and mercers	**Florian**
automobile drivers	**Frances of Rome**
Italy, nature, and merchants, founder of the Franciscan order	**Francis of Assisi**
writers and the deaf	**Francis of (Francois de) Sales**
Ethiopia	**Frumentius**
messengers, broadcasters, and postal workers	**Gabriel**
actors, printers, secretaries, and attorneys	**Genesius**
Paris	**Genevieve**
England, farmers, soldiers, and boy scouts, a dragon-slayer	**George**
pregnant women	**Gerard Majella**
children	**Germayne**

travelers, protecting against rats and mice	**Gertrude**
the retarded, supposed to restore their wits	**Gildas**
crippled people and beggars	**Giles**
tailors	**Goodman**
potters	**Gore**
musicians, singers, and teachers	**Gregory the Great**
Brussels	**Gudule or Gudila**
butchers and soldiers	**Hadrian**
being mother of Constantine the Great	**Helena**
Whitby, England, as its wise abbess	**Hilda or Hild**
tailors	**Homobonus**
hunters	**Hubert**
soldiers, supposedly the little child Jesus used as an example for his disciples	**Ignatius**
farmers and laborers	**Isidore**
attorneys	**Ivo**
Spain, pharmacists, pilgrims, rheumatism victims, and laborers, 1 of the 12 disciples and brother of St. John	**James the Great (also Santiago or San Diego)**
being killed by a club, 1 of the 12 disciples	**James the Less (Shorter)**
Naples	**Januarius**
priests	**Jean-Baptiste Vianney**
librarians and healing a lion	**Jerome**
orphans	**Jerome Aemilian**
being father of the Virgin Mary	**Joachim**
France and soldiers	**Joan of Arc**
teachers	**John Baptist de la Salle**
altar boys	**John Berchmans**
editors and laborers	**John Bosco**
jurists	**John Capistrano**
public speakers	**John Chrysostom**
confessors	**John Nepomucene**
booksellers, printers, nurses, and the sick, esp. heart patients	**John of God**
founding the Carmelite order, a mystical poet	**John of the Cross (San Juan de la Cruz)**
missionaries, baptized by Jesus in a river and later beheaded for Salome	**John the Baptist**
being "the beloved disciple," 1 of the 12, brother of St. James	**John the Evangelist or the Divine**
booksellers	**John Port Latin**

carpenters, China, and the dying, the Virgin Mary's husband and Jesus's earthly father	**Joseph**
prisoners	**Joseph Cafasso**
undertakers, supposedly kept alive by the Holy Grail	**Joseph of Arimethea**
aviators	**Joseph of Cupertino**
being 1 of the 12 disciples, a carpenter	**Jude** or **Thaddeus**
travelers and hospitality	**Julian**
philosophers	**Justin**
Wessex, England, as its 9th-c. prince	**Kenelm**
Glasgow, "the Dearest"	**Kentigern** or **Mungo**
Ireland, a 6th-c. hermit	**Kevin**
Celtic Cornwall, a 5th-c. saint	**Keyne**
cooks, curriers, and the poor	**Lawrence**
protection from leprosy, a beggar	**Lazarus**
prisoners, from France	**Leonard**
skaters	**Lidwina**
barbers, a 13th-c. French king	**Louis (IX)**
social workers	**Louise de Marillac**
being a virgin martyred in 4th-c. Syracuse	**Lucia**
the blind and sight-impaired	**Lucy**
physicians, painters, glassworkers, butchers, and brewers, 1 of the 12 disciples and a gospel author	**Luke**
infertile women and pregnant women, a model of feminine innocence and submission	**Margaret**
Venice since the 14th c., who wrote the 2nd gospel	**Mark**
proper housewives, servants, and cooks, sister of Lazarus and Mary	**Martha**
innkeepers and drinkers	**Martin**
soldiers	**Martin of Tours**
being mother of Jesus and husband of Joseph	**Mary,** also **the Virgin Mary, Mater Dolorosa, Our Lady of Mercy,** and **the Madonna**
the repentant, esp. prostitutes	**Mary Magdelene**
fools	**Mathurin**
bankers, bookkeepers, accountants, and tax collectors, 1 of the 12 disciples and a gospel author	**Matthew (Levi)**
being the disciple who replaced Judas Iscariot	**Matthias**
infantry soldiers	**Maurice**

Germany, grocers, police officers, paratroopers, and the sick, the prince of the angels, linked with Mercury	**Michael**
mothers	**Monica**
attorneys	**Thomas More**
Russia, Greece, scholars, clerks, pawnbrokers, brides, bakers, and little boys, inspiration of Santa Claus	**Nicholas**
travelers, merchants, brewers, and children	**Nicholas of Myra**
the blind	**Odilia**
musicians, Norway's first Christian king	**Olaf**
France and India	**Our Lady of Assumption**
Poland	**Our Lady of Czestochowa**
motorcyclists	**Our Lady of Grace**
Mexico	**Our Lady of Guadalupe**
aviators	**Our Lady of Loreto**
children, and with a sword and a palm branch	**Pancras**
physicians	**Pantaleon**
Ireland, associated with serpents and shamrocks	**Patrick**
ministers and tentmakers, an apostle and missionary	**Paul (Saul of Tarsus)**
Egypt, as its 1st hermit-saint, in the 4th-c.	**Paul the Hermit**
cancer victims	**Peregrine**
being supposed to ward off ague	**Pernel** and **Petronella**
blacksmiths, the fisherman who denied Jesus 3 times, 1 of the 12 disciples, an apostle, missionary, and founder of the Papacy	**Peter (Simon,** also **the Rock,** *petra***)**
sailors	**Peter Gonzales**
being 1 of the 12 disciples and a missionary	**Philip**
gardeners	**Phocas**
travelers, physicians, nurses, and the blind	**Raphael**
pregnant women and people accused falsely	**Raymund Nonnatus**
France, as a 5th-6th-c. bishop	**Remigius** or **Remy**
anesthetists	**René Goupil**
being 1 of 12 disciples and a missionary	**Philip**
invalids and plague victims	**Roch** or **Roque**
Palermo, as its 12th-c. patron saint	**Rosalia** or **Rosalie**

archers, athletes, and soldiers	**Sebastian**
Ireland, a hermit-saint on Scattery Island	**Senanus**
fullers	**Severus**
being shown carrying Jesus as a baby	**Simeon**
being 1 of the 12 disciples, a fishseller	**Simon (Zelotes)**
Poland	**Stanislaus of Cracow**
being the 1st Christian martyr	**Stephen**
Hungary, its 1st Christian king, in the 11th c.	**Stephen**
protection of chastity	**Susan**
being "master of the rain," from 6th-c. France	**Swithins (St. Martin of Bullions); (in France, Médard or Gervais)**
Wales, a strongly anti-heretical saint	**Teilo**
being the 1st woman martyr	**Thecla**
being Venice's patron saint before Mark	**Theodore**
selling his soul to the Devil in 6th-c. Cilicia	**Theophilus**
being a Spanish nun who helped found the Carmelites	**Theresa**
Spain and headaches, who helped found the Carmelite order	**Theresa of Avila**
aviators, florists, and France	**Thérèse of Lisieux**
architects, the 1 of the 12 disciples who doubted	**Thomas**
students	**Thomas Aquinas**
bishops and other high church officials	**Timothy** and **Titus**
gardeners	**Trypon**
winemakers	**Urban**
being the Cornish princess supposedly killed with 11,000 virgins	**Ursula**
lovers, a 3rd-c. Roman martyr	**Valentine**
portraitists, who supposedly gave Jesus her handkerchief on his way to the cross	**Veronica**
drinkers	**Vincent**
builders	**Vincent Ferrer**
comedians and chorea, a Sicilian martyr	**Vitus**
replacing Celtic rituals with Roman ones, as a Northumbrian bishop	**Wilfrid**
hatters	**William**

sheperds	**Windelines**
virgins and bakers	**Winifred**
servants	**Zita**

Religious Holidays

Among religious holidays, which . . . ?

On Specific Dates

on Jan 6. marks the visit of the Magi to Jesus	**Epiphany, Three Kings' Day, or Twelfth Night**
on Feb. 2 honors the purification of Mary	**Candlemas Day**
on Feb. 14 is celebrated by the sending of cards	**Valentine's Day**
on Mar. 1 honors Wales patron saint with leeks	**St. David's Day**
on Mar. 17 honors the Irish patron saint with shamrocks	**St. Patrick's Day**
on Mar. 25 honors the angel Gabriel's telling Mary she would bear the Messiah	**Annunciation** or **Lady Day**
on Apr. 23 honors the English patron saint	**St. George's Day**
on June 15 was linked with manic dancing, supposedly for luck	**St. Vitus's Day**
is July 15, on which rain signals 40 more days of rain	**St. Swithin's (St. Martin of Bullions Day)**
is Aug. 1, from a "loaf mass" for the bread from the 1st corn harvest	**Lammas Day**
on Aug. 15 marks the death of Mary	**Assumption Day**
falls on Aug. 16, an old harvest festival	**St. Roch's (Roque) Day**
falls on Sept. 29	**Michaelmas** or **St. Michael's Day**
is on Oct. 25, also the date of the British victory at Agincourt in 1415	**St. Crispin's Day**
is on Oct. 31, the eve of Hallowmass	**Halloween**
falls on Nov. 1	**Hallowmass** or **All Hallow's (All Saints) Day**
falls on Nov. 2	**All Soul's Day**

is on Nov. 11	**Martinmas** or **St. Martin's Day** (in Rome, the **Feast of Bacchus**)
is on Nov. 30, marking the start of Advent	**St. Andrew's Day**
is on Dec. 13	**St. Lucia's Day**
falls on Dec. 24	**Christmas Eve**
on Dec. 25 honors Jesus's birth	**Christmas Day**
is Dec. 26, with boxes of money given to servants and shopkeepers	**Boxing Day**
falls on Dec. 26	**Feast of Stephen**
is celebrated on Dec. 31	**New Year's Eve**

Other Holidays

are the 4 weeks before Christmas	**Advent**
is on the Sun. nearest Nov. 30	**Advent Sunday**
is the Thurs. 40 days after Easter, marking Jesus's rising to heaven	**Ascension Day** or **Holy Thursday**
is the 1st day of Lent	**Ash Wednesday**
is 1 of 2 festivals following Ramadan	**Bairam**
is the 1st Mon. after Easter	**Black Monday**
is the Mon. before Lent	**Blue Monday**
is on the Thurs. after Trinity Sun.	**Corpus Christi (Body of Christ) Day**
marks Jesus's rising from the dead	**Easter Sunday**
is the last day of the haj, with a feast of sacrifice	**Eid-al-Azha**
is the holiday after the fasting month of Ramadan	**Eid-al-Fitr**
are the Christian fasting days set in 1095	**Ember Days**
is the day of Jesus's death, the Friday before Easter	**Good, Holy,** or **Long Friday**
is the 8-day Jewish Feast of Lights, often around December	**Hanukkah** or **Feast of the Dedication**
is the 10-day celebration of the Jewish New Year, including Rosh Hashonah and Yom Kippur	**High Holy Days**
is the last week of Lent	**Holy** or **Passion Week**
is the Sat. before Easter	**Holy Saturday** or **the Great Sabbath**
is the season around Lammas Day	**Lammastide**

is the 40-day fasting-and-penitence period between Ash Wednesday and Easter	**Lent**
is the day before Ash Wednesday, the beginning of Lent	**Mardi Gras (Fat Tuesday), Shrove Tuesday,** or **Pancake Day**
is the Thurs. before Easter	**Maundy** or **Holy Thursday**
is the festival in the 1st 10 days of the 1st month of the Moslem year, also the month's name	**Muharram**
is the Sun. before Easter	**Palm Sunday**
is an 8-day festival honoring the Jews' deliverance from Egypt	**Passover** or **Pesach**
honors the rescue of the Jews from Persia	**Purim** or **Feast of Lots**
is the 9th month of the Moslem year, with all-day fasting	**Ramadan (Holy Month)**
is the Jewish New Year's Day	**Rosh Hashonah**
is the 3rd Sun. before Lent	**Septuagesima**
honors the sheltering of the Jews in the wilderness, a harvest festival	**Sukkoth** or the **Feast of Tabernacles**
is the 8th Sun. after Easter	**Trinity Sunday**
is the 7th Sun. after Easter	**Whitsunday (White Sunday)** or **Pentecost (50th Day)**
is the week, esp. the 1st 3 days, beginning with Whitsunday (Pentecost)	**Whitsuntide**
is the holiest Jewish holiday	**Yom Kippur** or **Day of Atonement**
is the festive period beginning with Christmas	**Yule**

Everyday Life

Life and Death

Personal Relationships

(See also Sex and the Reproductive System in *In Sickness and in Health* and *In other words*: Words from the French: Life and Loving)

About personal relationships, sexual and otherwise, what is the word for . . . ?

anal intercourse	**sodomy** or **buggery**
born of unmarried parents	**illegitimate**
brothers and sisters, in general	**siblings**
concubine confined to a harem	**odalisque**
courtesan or kept woman in French	**fille de joie**
deriving pleasure from giving pain	**sadism**
deriving pleasure from pain	**masochism**
deriving sexual pleasure from giving or receiving pain	**sadomasochism** or **algolagnia**
desire for unusual forms of sex	**paraphilia**
dissolving of a marriage	**divorce**
fascination by sexual matters	**prurience**
fatherhood	**paternity**
female having more than one husband at a time	**polyandry**
hated of mankind, or men	**misanthropy**
hatred of women	**misogyny**
having more than one spouse at a time	**polygamy**
having more than one wife at a time	**polygyny**
having one spouse at a time	**monogamy**
having sex with a female under legal age	**statutory rape**
having sex with animals	**zooerastia** or **bestiality**
house of prostitution, in Italy	**bordello**
lover, esp, adulterous, an old-fashioned term	**paramour**

man's heavy, uncontrollable sexual desire	**satyriasis**
marital joining of several men and women	**group marriage**
marriage after an earlier spouse's death or divorce	**digamy**
marriage legally considered never to have occurred	**annulment**
marriage for material, not personal, reasons	**marriage of convenience**
marriage in which a spouse and any offspring have no claim on titles or estates	**morganatic**
marriage of people from different races	**miscegenation**
marriage while still married to another	**bigamy**
money or property a bride brings to a marriage	**dowry**
noisy serenade once given to newlyweds	**charivari**
one attracted to people of both sexes	**bisexual**
one attracted to people of the opposite sex	**heterosexual**
one attracted to people of the same sex (esp. male)	**homosexual, homophile,** or **gay**
one who converts to the opposite sex, esp. a male	**transsexual**
one who dresses like the other sex	**transvestite**
one who likes to watch sex acts, often secretly	**voyeur**
one who obtains sexual partners for others	**panderer, procurer,** or **pimp**
one's ancestral line	**pedigree**
people sharing one parent, not two	**half-brothers** or **-sisters**
prostitute or woman of the "half-world," in French	**demimondaine**
relating to marriage	**conjugal, marital, matrimonial,** or **nuptial**
relation between a parent and child	**filiation**
relationship by blood	**consanguinity**
"right of first night," the feudal lord's right to take the virginity of his vassals' brides	**droit du seigneur,** or **jus primae noctis**
sexual attraction to corpses	**necrophilia**
sexual attraction to animals	**zoophilia**
sexual attraction to children	**pedophilia**

sexual attraction to feces	**coprophilia**
sexual feeling excited by a thing or body part	**fetishism**
sexual intercourse between close blood relatives, e.g. siblings or parent and child	**incest**
sexual relations between a man and a boy	**pederasty**
third party named in a divorce case charging adultery	**corespondent**
virgin, from the Latin	**virgo intacta**
woman homosexual, attracted to other women	**lesbian, sapphist,** or **tribadist**
woman's heavy, uncontrollable sexual desire	**nymphomania**
world of the streets, lit. half-world	**demimonde**

Kinds of Killing

Among the various kinds of killing, what is the word or phrase for killing . . . ?

animals for use	**butchering** or **slaughtering**
another human being	**homicide**
as a sacrifice	**immolation**
brother	**fratricide**
by a suicidal plane attack, as by the Japanese in WWII	**kamikaze**
by cutting off the flow of air	**strangulation, suffocation, throttling, smothering,** or **asphyxiation**
by fire, as of a sacrifice, a term applied to some cases of genocide	**holocaust**
by stoning to death	**lapidation**
by strangling, esp, with a metal collar or wire	**garotting**
father	**patricide**
fetus	**feticide, aborticide,** or **abortion**
fungi	**fungicide**
germs	**germicide** or **microbicide**
heretics by burning, as in the Inquisition	**auto-da-fé**
infant	**infanticide**
insects	**insecticide**
king	**regicide**
living things, in general	**biocide**
mother	**matricide**
on a cross	**crucifixion**
1 in every 10; more loosely, a large part	**decimation**

oneself by ritual suicide, by disembowelment, in Japan	**hara-kiri** or **seppuku**
oneself by ritual suicide, on a dead husband's pyre, in India	**suttee**
parent	**parenticide**
pests	**pesticide**
plants	**herbicide**
prophet	**vaticide**
public or celebrated person	**assassination**
race	**genocide**
relative	**parricide**
self	**suicide** or **felo-de-se**
sister	**sororicide**
spouse, normally referring to a husband	**mariticide**
to provide a blessed release for someone	**euthanasia** or **mercy killing**
tyrant	**tyrannicide**
wife	**uxoricide**
without due process of law, esp. hanging	**lynching**
without premeditation	**manslaughter**

Death and Funeral Rites

Regarding death and funeral rites, what is the word or phrase for . . . ?

ancient monument of a single, large stone	**menhir**
ancient mound grave	**barrow** or **tumulus**
bell tolled announcing a death	**passing of death bell**
box in which corpse is buried	**coffin** or **casket**
bugle call at military funerals, also at night	**taps**
burial in the ground	**inhumation** or **interment**
burial or entombment within a wall	**immurement**
burial or storage of ashes of the dead in an urn	**inurnment**
burial site for the penniless and unknown	**potter's field**
burning of a corpse	**cremation** or **incineration**
Catholic mass for the dead	**requiem mass**
Central Asian "towers of silence" where corpses are left to be picked clean by vultures	**dokhmas**
ceremonial procession, esp. at a funeral	**cortege**

church's caretaker, earlier a gravedigger	**sexton**
dead body	**corpse, cadaver,** or **carcass**
death notice, often a brief printed biography	**obituary**
embalming and drying a corpse	**mummification**
Eucharist given to someone dying	**viaticum**
funeral director or embalmer	**undertaker** or **mortician**
funeral rites	**obsequies** or **exequies**
heap of burnable matter in which a corpse is placed for incineration	**pyre** or **funeral pile**
large cemetery, lit. city of the dead	**necropolis**
large stones covering an ancient mound	**cromlech** or **dolmen**
man who ferried the dead across the River Styx to Hades	**Charon**
monument to someone buried elsewhere	**cenotaph**
people who carry the coffin at a funeral	**pallbearers**
place for storing dead bodies, as before burial	**morgue, mortuary,** or **charnel house**
place for storing the bones of the dead	**ossuary**
place for storing urns of ashes of the dead	**cinerarium** or **columbarium**
place to house the dead	**tomb, vault,** or **sepulchre**
public speech of praise, esp. of the recently dead	**eulogy**
river of forgetfulness in Hades	**Lethe**
riverside platform where corpses are burned in India	**ghat**
sacrament given at point of death	**extreme unction** or **last rites**
stand on which a coffin sits in a state funeral	**catafalque**
stately tomb or tomb building	**mausoleum**
stone coffin	**sarcophagus**
3-headed dog at the door to Hades	**Cerberus**
tomb inscription, or a brief text honoring the dead	**epitaph**
tomb with rectangular base and sloping sides, meeting at a point, as in ancient Egypt	**pyramid**
treating a corpse to slow or prevent decay	**embalming**
underground burial vault, esp. under a church	**crypt**

underground tunnels with graves, as in Rome	**catacombs**
vase to hold the ashes from cremation	**urn**
vehicle for transporting the dead	**hearse**
vigil over a corpse, esp. to look for signs of life	**wake** or **deathwatch**

The Times of Our Lives

Time, Calendars, and Anniversaries

About time in daily life, what is . . . ?

before noon	**A.M. (ante meridian)**
after noon	**P.M. (post meridian)**
referring to a year before Christ's birth	**B.C. (before Christ)**
before the year 0 to non-Christians	**B.C.E. (before the common era)**
after the year 0 to non-Christians	**C.E. (common era)**
referring to a year after Christ's birth	**A.D. (anno Domini)**
in the year of the king	**A.R. (anno regni)**
before the current year	**B.P. (before present)**
before the war, as in the US Civil War	**antebellum**
before the Biblical flood, or very long ago	**antediluvian**
the calendar in widest use today	**Gregorian**
the calendar introduced in Roman times	**Julian calendar**
the day of the new moon, the 1st day of the month, to the Romans	**calends**
the day of the full moon, to the Romans	**ides**
the 9th day before the full moon, to the Romans	**nones**
twice a week	**semiweekly (less often biweekly)**
every 2 weeks	**biweekly** or **fortnightly**
twice a month	**semimonthly (less often bimonthly)**
every 30 days, effectively every month	**tricennial**
every 2 months	**bimonthly**
every 3 months	**quarterly**
twice a year	**semiannual** or **biannual**

every year	**annual**
every 2 years	**biennial**
every 3 years	**triennial**
every 4 years	**quadrennial**
every 5 years	**quinquennial**
every 6 years	**sexennial**
every 7 years	**septennial**
every 8 years	**octennial**
every 10 years	**decennial**
every 12 years	**duodecennial**
every 15 years	**quindecennial**
a person in his or her fifties	**quinquagenarian**
a person in his or her sixties	**sexagenarian**
a person in his or her seventies	**septuagenarian**
a person in his or her eighties	**octogenarian**
a person in his or her nineties	**nonagenarian**
a person aged over 100	**centenarian**
a special anniversary, as of a certain no. of years	**jubilee**
a 25-year anniversary, as of a reign or wedding	**silver**
a 50-year anniversary	**gold**
a 75-year anniversary	**diamond**
a 100-year anniversary	**centennial** or **-enary**
a 150-year anniversary	**sesquicentennial** or **-enary**
a 200-year anniversary	**bicentennial** or **-enary**
a 300-year anniversary	**tercentennial, tricentennial** or **-enary**
a 400-year anniversary	**quadricentennial** or **quartercentenary**
a 500-year anniversary	**quincentennial** or **-enary**
a 600-year anniversary	**sexcentennial** or **-enary**
a 1000-year anniversary	**millennium** or **-ennary**

International Foods and Dining

Places for Dining, Drinking, and Preparing Food

Among places for dining, drinking, and preparing food, what is or are . . . ?

In France

a slaughterhouse	**abbatoir**
an inn (country inn)	**auberge (ferme auberge)**
a small tavern or alehouse	**bistro** or **brasserie**
a shop selling meat, esp. beef	**boucherie**
a shop selling horse meat	**boucherie chevaline**
a bakery or bread shop	**boulangerie**
a coffeehouse or small restaurant	**café** or **estaminet**

a shop for cooked meats, esp. pork	**charcuterie**
an ice cream and candy shop	**confiserie**
shops for dairy products	**crèmeries**
restaurants specializing in crêpes	**crêperies**
a grocery store	**épicerie**
an outdoor market	**marché**
a restaurant specializing in omelettes	**omeletterie**
a pastry and candy shop	**pâtisserie**
a tea shop	**salon du thé**
a supermarket	**supermarché**

In Italy

an inn	**albergo**
a grocery store	**alimentari** or **salumeria**
an ice cream bar	**gelateria**
a relatively inexpensive restaurant	**osteria**
a pastry shop	**pasticceria**
delicatessens	**pizzicherie**
a fine restaurant	**ristorante**
a grill for light meals	**rosticceria**
a cheap eating place, lit. hot table	**tavola calda**
a small restaurant	**trattoria**
a Roman table with couches for diners on 3 sides	**triclinium**

Elsewhere (Outside France and Italy)

a store or department featuring Jewish delicacies	**appetizing store**
a bakery, in Austria	**Bäckerei**
a small tavern or eating place in Spain or SW US	**cantina**
a Japanese garden teahouse, and the tea ceremony	**chanoyu**
a roadside inn or hotel, in Spain	**fonda**
a dairy shop, in Greece	**galaktoboúreko**
cheese dairies, in Germany	**Käskuchä**
pastry shops, in Austria	**Konditorei**
a bar or drinking place, in Japan	**nomiya**
an alehouse or tavern, in Germany	**Ratskeller** or **Bierhaus**
a tap-room, in Germany	**Bierstube**
a Korean teahouse	**tabang, tadang,** or **tashil**
Spanish restaurants serving tapas	**tascas**
fast-food stalls in Taiwan	**yam cha**

Language of Dining and Nutrition

In the language of dining and nutrition around the world, what is the word or phrase for . . . ?

In France

the check or bill	addition
a menu with dishes each priced separately	à la carte
good appetite	bon appétit
drinks included, on a prix fixe menu	boisson compris
the day's menu or bill of fare	carte du jour
wine list	carte du vins
master chef or head cook	chef de cuisine or chef (or gros) bonnet
masterpiece in cookery	chef d'oeuvre
lunch	déjeuner
dinner	dîner
appetizer	entrée
side dish or sweets	entremets
celebratory feast or banquet	fête
someone who loves hearty, good eating	gourmand
a connoisseur of fine food and wine	gourmet or epicure
master chef's "big hat"	gros bonnet
head waiter or steward	maître d' (hôtel)
a meal at a fixed price	menu à prix fixe
breakfast	petit déjeuner
the main dish in a meal	pièce de résistance
prepared meals, as sold in charcuteries	plats cuisine
main course	plat principal or plat
restaurant owner	restaurateur
late-night snack	réveillon
service not included, on a restaurant bill	service non compris (S.N.C.)
a wine steward	sommelier
a meal for guests at a fixed hour and price	table d'hôte

In Italy

dining in the open air	al fresco
breakfast or lunch	colazione
the check	conto
a cover charge on a check	coperto
a holiday or feast	festa
dinner's 1st course, pasta or soup	primo piatto

the receipt given by law in Italy's restaurants	**Ricevuta Fisecale (R.F.)**
dinner's second or main course	**secondo** or **entree**
service included, meaning no tipping	**servizio compreso**
service not included, meaning tipping is expected	**servizio non compreso**

Elsewhere in Europe, the Americas, and the Commonwealth

breakfast or the day's 1st main meal, in Spain	**almuerzo**
the 2nd breakfast, c. 9–10 A.M., in Germany	**Brotzeit** or **z'Nuni**
supper, in Spain	**cena**
dinner, or meal in general, in Spain	**comida**
the special feast on German carnival day	**Faschingsfest**
a holiday or feast, in Spain	**fiesta**
breakfast, in Denmark	**Frokost**
breakfast, in Germany	**Frühstuck**
a vegetarian who eats only fruits or nuts harvested without killing the plant	**fruitarian**
the art or science of good eating	**gastronomy, -logy,** or **aristology**
a no-meat Austrian feast, on fast day	**Heringschmaus**
a light lunch, in The Netherlands	**koffietafel**
a vegetarian who eats eggs and dairy products	**lacto-ovo-vegetarian**
a vegetarian who eats dairy products	**lactovegetarian**
fats that are soft or liquid at room temperature	**polyunsaturated**
fats that are solid at room temperature	**saturated**
a cook of quickly prepared, often frozen items	**short-order cook**
a large afternoon-evening meal in Britain, esp. in the north	**tea** or **high tea**
someone who eats no animal products in any form	**vegan**
someone who eats no animal flesh, and sometimes no animal products at all, e.g., eggs or cheese	**vegetarian**

In Asia, Africa, and the Pacific

snacks, in Korea	**anju**
a large breakfast, in India	**bari haziri**
a large banquet, lit. a big dinner, in India	**bara khana**

a small light breakfast, in India	**chhoti haziri**
food in general, in Cantonese Chinese	**chow**
prepared in accordance with Jewish dietary laws	**kosher**
between-meals snack, to Jews	**nosh**
chopsticks, in Japan	**o hashi**
food that is not kosher, to Jews	**treyf**

Cooking Styles and Sauces

Among cooking and serving styles and sauces, what is . . . ?

In France—Cooking and Serving Styles

American style	**à l'Américaine**
English style	**à l'Anglaise**
with paprika and cream	**à l'archiduc**
garnished with potatoes, mushrooms, and ham	**à la Basquaise**
Brittany-style, with white kidney beans	**à la Bretagne** or **Bretonne**
on a skewer or spit	**à la broche** or **en brochette**
with carrots, Crécy-style	**à la Crécy**
with capers and lemon slices, Grenoble-style	**à la Grenobloise**
with paprika and cream, Hungary-style	**à la Hongroise**
Kiev-style, esp. stuffed, coated, and sautéed, as of chicken breasts	**à la Kiev**
with juniper berries, Liège-style	**à la Liègoise**
in the style of the house	**à la maison**
made plainly, with parsley, butter sauce, and lemon juice	**à la maître d'hôtel**
with a scoop of ice cream	**à la mode**
Périgord-style, with truffles	**à la Périgourdine**
Polish-style, e.g., topped with browned bread crumbs and eggs	**à la Polonaise**
with garlic and onions, Provençale	**à la Provencale**
with a cream sauce with mushrooms and truffles, esp. chicken, "in the queen's style"	**à la reine**
Russian-style, generally with sour cream or caviar	**à la Russe**
Vichy-style, with carrots	**à la Vichy**
with tarragon	**à l'estragon**
with sausage, ham, sauerkraut, and boiled potatoes	**Alsacienne**
with almonds	**amandine**

with asparagus	**Argenteuil**
in a sauce of melted butter	**au beurre fondu**
in a sauce of browned butter	**au beurre roux**
poached with vinegar, turning fish skin blue	**au bleu**
in a white wine sauce	**au chablis**
with cabbage	**au choux**
with preserved fruits	**au confitures**
with cheese	**au gratin**
with natural juices as gravy	**au jus**
with milk	**au lait**
with pepper	**au poivre**
with aromatic herbs and vegetables	**aux aromates**
with watercress	**aux cressons**
with morel mushrooms	**aux morilles**
with onions	**aux oignons**
with green peas	**aux petits pois**
well-cooked	**bien cuit**
unattractive fare designed to shoo away unwanted guests, lit. to chase cousins	**chasse-cousins**
the art or style of cooking	**cuisine**
good quality, home-style cooking	**cuisine bourgeoise**
in the cooking style of the provinces or country	**cuisine des provinces** or **compagnarde**
done just right, lit. cooked to a point	**cuit à point**
with mustard, Dijon-style	**dijonnaise**
in a mayonnaise aspic, as of lobster	**en bellevue**
braised	**en daube**
with oil, tomatoes, onions, and peppers, Spanish style	**Espagnole**
set aflame	**flambé** (fem. **-bée**)
glazed, as carrots or a cake with icing	**glacé**
heavy, rich, traditional cooking	**haute cuisine**
made with fresh vegetables	**jardinière**
with thin strips of vegetables	**julienne**
a cold plate	**l'assiette froid**
with onions, Lyon-style	**Lyonnaise**
dusted with flour and sautéed in butter	**meunière**
Nice-style, with seafood and vegetables	**Niçoise**
lean-style, rather than rich, cooking	**nouvelle cuisine** or **cuisine malgreure**
fried in fat and browned	**rissolé**
with white grapes	**Véronique**

In France—Sauces

a mayonnaise-like oil-and-garlic sauce	**aïoli**
a rich egg-and-butter sauce with shallots	**béarnaise**
a rich cream sauce	**béchamel**

a sauce of shallots, white wine, butter, and broth	**bercy**
butter and shallots with vinegar or white wine	**beurre blanc**
browned butter with vinegar or lemon	**beurre noir**
a bitter orange sauce, as for duck	**bigarade**
a sauce with red Bordeaux wine	**bordelaise**
a well-spiced Burgundy-based sauce	**Bourguignonne**
a butter and white-wine seafood sauce	**duglère**
a "Dutch" sauce of egg yolks and lemon juice	**hollandaise**
a cream sauce thickened with egg yolks	**maintenon**
a butter-and-flour paste for thickening	**roux**
an onion sauce	**soubise**
a "velvet" sauce of flour, butter, and broth	**velouté**

In Italy—Cooking Styles and Sauces

with sea food	**ai frutti di mare**
prepared with oregano	**arreganata**
with a hearty meat-and-tomato sauce	**alla bolognese**
hunter-style, esp. sautéed with onions and mushrooms	**alla cacciatore**
with a bacon-and-egg sauce	**alla carbonara**
Florence-style, generally with spinach	**alla Florentina**
Genoa-style, with herbs, esp. basil	**alla Genoese**
"sailor-style," in a tomato sauce	**alla marinara**
as in Milan, esp. a cutlet battered and sautéed	**alla Milanese**
with tomato sauce, eggplant, and cheese	**alla norma**
with Parmesan cheese	**alla parmigiana**
with a Neapolitan-style tomato sauce	**alla pizzaiola**
Sicilian-style, with eggplant	**alla Siciliana**
with a sweet wine and broth sauce	**al Marsala**
with a meatless tomato sauce	**al pomodoro**
a white wine and hot chili pepper sauce	**arrabbiata**
with cream sauce, in northern Italy	**con panna**

dipped in batter and sautéed; French-style	**Francese**
boiled	**in bianco**
a light white-wine sauce	**luciana**
French-Italian white wine, tomato, and cognac sauce, esp. for veal or chicken	**marengo**
a sauce of whole fruits in sweet mustard, served with boiled meats, from Cremona	**mostarda di Cremona**
a sauce of ground basil, garlic, olive oil, and parmesan cheese, a Genoese specialty	**pesto**
sautéed with butter and lemon	**piccata**
homemade	**produzione propria**
a basic tomato-and-meat sauce	**ragù**

In Europe (Outside France and Italy)—Cooking Styles and Sauces

fish pickled, fried, and served in jelly, in Belgium	à l'escavèche
a Greek lemon, egg, and chicken broth sauce	**avgolemono**
boiled or poached, in Germany	**blau**
a spicy, red currant and port, British game sauce	**cumberland**
a very hot, spicy sauce, filling, or spread	**diablo (deviled)**
breaded and fried, in Germany	**gebacken**
roasted, in Holland	**gebraden**
smoked, in Holland	**gerookt**
a parsley sauce, as served with eel pie in Britain	**green liquor**
baked in almonds, as fish, in Germany	**Müllerin**
Dutch-Indonesian "rice-table" of many dishes	**rijsttafel**
a green sauce of olive oil, lemon, capers, and garlic	**salsa verde**
a varied array of hors d'oeuvres, in Scandinavia	**smörgåsbord (Finn. vollelpäpöytä)**

Outside Europe—Cooking Styles and Sauces

mild stir-fried cooking from southern China	**Cantonese**
a spicy French-style tomato sauce, in New Orleans	**créole**
a spicy Indian sauce	**curry**
an onion curry, in India	**doopiaza**
a super-hot Indian curry	**frithath**
pure clarified butter, in India	**ghee**

a Tunisian red pepper, salt, oil, and garlic sauce	**harissa**
a spicy, sweet, soybean-based Chinese sauce	**Hoisin**
a very hot, spicy cooking style from south China	**Hunan**
a Japanese sauce of sweetened sake	**mirin**
a food additive common in Chinese cooking	**monosodium glutamate (MSG)**
a Mexican chili sauce, sometimes with chocolate	**mole**
a Chinese-Malaysian style of cooking	**Nonya**
a Haitian hot sauce	**piment oiseau**
an Indonesian peanut sauce	**pinda**
an Indian curd-and-spices sauce	**raita**
a hot and spicy Indonesian sauce	**sambal**
a Malaysian coconut cream	**santan**
soy sauce, in Japan	**shoyu**
"angel's brazier" with a wide range of ingredients, in Korea	**sinsullo**
stirring small pieces of food over high heat, in Chinese cooking	**stir fry**
a spicy Chinese cuisine, featuring hot chili peppers	**Szechuan**
a Haitian onion-and-herb sauce	**ti malice**
a spicy, green, horseradishlike japanese sauce	**wasabi**

Delicacies and Garnishes

Among delicacies and garnishes from around the world, what is or are . . . ?

In France

a garnish of artichokes with mushrooms, horseradish, and creamed potatoes	**ambassadeur**
a patty or tasty mouthful	**bouchée**
brains, such as calves' brains	**cervelles**
pieces of toasted bread in soup or salad	**croutons**
cut-up, raw vegetables	**crudités**
a delicacy, in general	**délicatesse**
delicacies, e.g., cheese or fish on toast or crackers, served before a main meal	**hors d'oeuvres, appetizers,** or **canapés**

a chopped vegetable mixture	**macédoine**
minced pork paste, served cold	**rillettes**
loaves of spicy ground meat	**pâté**
pâté served hot in a pastry crust	**pâté chaud**
country-style pâté	**pâté de campagne**
pâté made from the livers of force-fed geese	**pâté de foie gras**
blackbird paté, in Corsica	**pâté de merle**
calves' sweetbreads	**ris de veau**
a prized fungus	**truffles**

Elsewhere in Europe (Outside France)

oysters and bacon on toast, in Britain	**angels on horseback**
sweetbreads, in Italy	**animelle**
a 1st course or appetizer, often with meats and raw vegetables, in Italy	**antipasto**
jellied broth, often molded	**aspic**
tiny, tasty tidbits, in Italy	**bocconcini**
Greek red caviar	**brik**
Sicilian eggplant sauce or appetizer	**caponata di melanzana**
sweetish Portuguese paprika	**colorão**
dried seaweed, in Ireland	**dulsea**
goose fat, in Germany	**Gänseschmalz**
Rhineland rabbit paté made with port	**Hase im Topf**
jellied broth of boiled animal parts, esp. the head	**headcheese**
Greek meatballs	**keftédes**
Greek appetizers	**mezés**
Rhineland meat paste with buckwheat meal	**Panhas**
a spice central to Hungarian cooking	**paprika**
a Polish type of pâté	**pasztety**
tastily prepared thymus gland of an animal	**sweetbreads**
small dishes, as of fish, ham, or eggs, in Spain	**tapas**
Greek fish roe spread	**taramasaláta**

Outside Europe

a Filipino papaya-and-carrot relish	**achara**
a mashed, baked eggplant and sesame paste, in the Middle East	**baba-ghanoug**
a Filipino fermented shrimp and salt mixture	**bagoong**

an egg with a half-formed duck chick, a Filipino aphrodisiac	**balut**
Egyptian caviar	**batarikh**
Turkish pistachio-stuffed pastries	**bülbül yuvasi**
fried pork rinds, in the Dominican Republic	**chicharrón**
the Indian relish of fruit or vegetables, vinegar, and a Worcester-like sauce	**chutney**
the rich, Mexican avocado sauce or dip	**guacamole**
the Middle Eastern paste of mashed chick peas and tahini	**humus**
cactus fruit preserve, in Mexico	**melcocha**
areca nut and spice mixture in a leaf, in India	**pan**
African pepper used in Portugal	**piripiri**
acorn mash, esp. for the sick, in North Africa	**racahout**
Chinese-Malaysian mixture of ground spices	**rempah**
oily sesame seed paste, in the Middle East	**tahini**
spicy, pickled, mixed vegetables, in Egypt	**turshi** or **bickley**

Breads and Rolls

Among breads and rolls from around the world, what is or are . . . ?

In France

the traditional long, crisp bread	**baguette**
small pastrylike round breads, often meat-filled	**brioches**
a light pastry	**chou**
the crescent-shaped light pastry	**croissant**
a thin pretzel-shaped bread with ham, from Provence	**fougasse**
a pastry made with cheese and pâté à choux	**gougère**
bread, in general	**pain**
the round, soft, whole-wheat bread	**pain de campagne**
Parisian sourdough bread baked in wood ovens	**pain Poilâne**
toast	**pain grillé**

In Italy

hard biscuits with anise and nuts	**biscoti**
a kind of garlic bread	**bruschetta**
the flat pastry from bologna	**crostata**
fried bread, served with sausages	**gnocco**
Genoese flat bread	**focaccia**
Genoese sweet bread	**pandolce**
Perugian cheese bread	**pane al formaggio**
northern Italian rolls made with yogurt	**panini allo yogurt**
Milanese raisin-and-citron sweet bread	**pannettone**
the chewy cornbread popular around Venice	**polenta**

Elsewhere in Europe (Outside France and Italy)

a Polish-Jewish roll with baked onion	**bialy**
a roll, in Holland	**broodje**
Polish rye bread	**czarny chleb**
wheat bread, in Scandinavia	**franskbrød**
a puffy breakfast roll, often with poppy seeds	**kaiser**
hard, unleavened Scandinavian rye bread	**Knekkebrød**
a popular Belgian bread	**pain à la grecque**
dark, slightly sour Eastern European rye bread	**pumpernickel**
rye bread, in Scandinavia	**rugbrød**
sweet rolls coiled like a snail, in Germany	**schnecken**
doughy Scotch pastry, orig. an oatmeal cake	**scone**
toasted biscuit, in Germany	**Zwelback**

In the Americas

flat, biscuitlike crackers in the Dominican Republic	**calletas**
Argentinian manioc (potato), egg, and cheese bread	**chipa**
corn bread sans milk or eggs, in the US South	**corn pone**
deep-fried corn-dough balls, in the US South	**hush puppies**
French-style Bolivian bread	**marraqueta**
coarse country bread, in Puerto Rico	**pan de agua**
Chilean country bread, baked in an earthen oven	**pan de horno**

In Asia, Africa, and the Pacific

a puffy Japanese rice cracker	**arare**
a doughnut-shaped boiled roll, favored by Jews	**bagel**
the braided loaf, favored by Jews on the Sabbath	**challah**
flat, unleavened disks of bread, in India	**chappati**
crepelike south Indian rice bread	**dosa**
steamed Indian rice cake	**idlis**
unleavened Jewish crackers linked with Passover	**matzoh**
Indian flat bread baked in a clay oven	**nan**
small Filipino buns	**pan de sal**
Indian bread with pepper and aniseed	**pappar**
rich Indian pastry often stuffed with vegetables	**paratha**
Middle Eastern, unleavened "pocket" bread	**pita** or **pitta**
deep-friend Indian dough balls	**poories** or **loochi**
Filipino rice cakes	**puto**
Turkish bread rings with sesame seeds	**simit**

Noodles, Dumplings, and Other Light Dishes

Among noodles, dumplings, and other light dishes from around the world, what is or are . . . ?

In France

boat-shaped pastry shells for fillings	**barquette**
a pancake	**crêpe**
pancakes cooked in brandy	**crêpes suzette**
a grilled ham-and-cheese sandwich with an egg	**croque-madame**
a grilled ham-and-cheese sandwich	**croque-monsieur**
a salty crepe, from northern France	**galette**
scrambled eggs	**ouefs brouillés**
a hard-boiled egg	**oeuf dur**
poached eggs	**oeufs pochés**
a dumpling-like ball of veal, chicken, or fish	**quenelles**
a custard pie, with meat or vegetables	**quiche**
a cheese pastry, baked in a mold	**ramequin**
an oblong roll filled with meat or fish	**rissole**

pastry-encrusted baked sausage	**saucisson en croûte**
meat-stuffed puff pastry	**vol-au-vent**

In Italy

ravioli stuffed with meat and cabbage	**agnolotti**
meat- or rice-filled, fried dough balls, from Sicily	**arancine**
a dish of song birds fed on figs and grapes	**beccafico**
Genoese torte stuffed with greens and meat	**cima**
wide "ribbon" spaghetti, as favored by Alfredo	**fettuccine** or **tagliatelle**
dumplings	**gnocchi**
pasta shaped like an earthworm	**lombriche**
fried, chick pea–flour dumplings, from Sicily	**panelle**
Genoese spinach-stuffed ravioli in a nut sauce	**pansotti**
Genoese torte stuffed with greens and eggs	**pasqualina**
pasta with sardines and fennel, as in Sicily	**pasta con sarde**
pasta pockets, a Genoese specialty	**ravioli**
rice with meat sauce and cheese	**risotto**
pasta folded around cheese or meat	**tortellini**
very thin spaghetti, lit. little worms	**vermicelli**

Elsewhere in Europe (Outside France and Italy)

stuffed pancakes, in Russia (Germany)	**blinis (blintzes)**
Dutch sandwiches on a roll	**brodjes**
Hungarian dumplings, as for goulash	**csipetke** or **galuska**
rice- and meat-stuffed grape leaves, in Greece	**dolmádes** or **dolma**
bacon and eggs, in Holland	**erten met spek**
a crepe with ham, cheese, and mushrooms	**ficelle picard**
melted cheese, as for dipping bread into	**fondue**
a Greek meat sandwich, usually on pita bread	**gyro**
Czechoslovakian dumplings for soup or with cheese	**halusky**
a hard-boiled egg with tomato, lettuce, and pickle, in Holland	**huzarensla**

Bavarian cheese noodles	**Kässpatzen**
German dumplings	**Knödel**
Polish beef or lamb turnovers, in bouillon	**kolduny**
Eastern European Jewish raviolilike treats	**kreplach**
Polish pastry of mushrooms and cabbage	**kuleblak**
noodles, in Poland	**lazanki**
Hungarian noodles	**metélt** or **nudli**
crescent-shaped, handheld pie from Cornwall	**pasty**
hot meat or cabbage pasties with soup, in Poland	**paszteciki** or **kapúsniaczki**
poached potato or cheese dumplings, in Poland	**pierogi**
Russian pasties	**pirozhki**
cheese, crusty bread, and pickles, in Britain	**ploughman's lunch**
a hot beefsteak sandwich, in Portugal	**prego**
dumplings, in Poland	**pyzy** or **kopytka**
Polish sour-milk pancakes	**racuszki**
scrambled eggs, in Holland	**roerel**
meat-stuffed cabbage leaves, in the Balkans	**sarmi** or **sarmale**
a hard-boiled egg inside a sausage, baked and served cold, in Britain	**Scotch eggs**
ground meat topped with mashed potatoes, in Britain	**shepherd's pie**
Scandinavian open-faced sandwiches	**Smørbrød, smørre-brød, smörbröd, smögås,** or **vollelpä**
Greek meat-and-rice balls, in a tomato or avgolemono sauce	**souzoukákia**
German, string-style, pan-fried dumplings	**Spätzle** or **Spaetzle**
fried eggs, in Holland	**spiegeleieren**
a British deep-dish pie of beef, kidneys, and onions	**steak and kidney pie**
a Greek cheese pie, sometimes with egg	**tyrópitta**
an open-faced sandwich of fried eggs and meat or cheese, in Holland	**uitsmijter**
a baked pancake-style mixture served with roast beef, in Britain	**Yorkshire pudding**
a Southern German onion tart	**Zwelbelkichen**

In the Americas

dumplings with bean mash, in northern Brazil	**acaraje**
Mexican tacos with fillings, e.g., ground beef	**burritos**
poached eggs and ham on English muffins with hollandaise sauce	**eggs Benedict**
a Chilean pastry with meat, egg, olive, and raisins	**empanada**
a hearty Argentinian meat-and-potato pie	**empanadas Jujeuñas**
a meat or cheese-stuffed tortilla with a chili sauce	**enchilada**
a corn tamale cooked in leaves, in Argentina or Chile	**humita (en chala)**
a Chilean corn pie	**pastel del choclo**
a Mexican fried tortilla with a cheese-based filling	**quesadilla**
a beef, olive, egg, potato, and pea mixture in dough, in Bolivia	**saltena**
Chilean fried pumpkin patties	**sopaipillas**
an Argentinian corn, cheese, and egg pie	**sopa Paraguayan**
fried, filled corn-dough cups, in Mexico	**sopes**
a crisp-fried tortilla, with a filling, in Mexico	**taco**
spicy meat with a cornbread crust, in Mexico	**tamale**
an unleavened pancake, in Mexico	**tortilla**

In Asia, Africa, and the Pacific

eggs, potatoes, and vegetable in puff pastry, in Tunisia	**brik à l'oeuf**
Filipino rice with thick chocolate and beef	**champurrado**
thin, vermicelli-like Japanese noodles	**chasoba**
small Chinese dumpling delicacies	**dim sum**
an Indian pancake with coconut chutney	**dosal**
Japanese soy noodles	**harusame**
a meatless fish-and-vegetable meal served with a Japanese tea ceremony	**kaiseki**
Anglo-Indian dish of rice, smoked fish, and eggs, also a lentil-and-rice side dish, in India	**kedgeree** or **khichri**

small, made-at-the-table meat- or vegetable-filled pancakes, in Korea	**kujoipan**
bean sprouts and vegetables in a fried thin pastry, in Indonesia	**loempia**
boiled noodles, in Malaysia	**mee jawa**
fried noodles, in Malaysia	**mee goreng**
fried rice or noodles with bits of meat or shellfish, in Indonesia	**nasi** or **bami goreng**
eggs with tomato sauce and sausage, in Tunisia	**odja**
fritterlike treats, in India	**pakoras**
fried noodles, in Thailand	**phad Thai**
small Korean pancakes with vegetables	**pindaedok**
Thai or Malaysian stuffed pancakes (spring rolls)	**poh piah**
fried rice with meat, currants, and nuts, in Egypt	**roz bel khalta**
a Turkish pastry stuffed with spiced meats	**sambouse**
a stuffed pastry in India	**samosa**
Japanese buckwheat flour noodles	**soba**
Japanese deep-fried vegetables or seafood	**tempura**
Japanese wheat-flour noodles	**udon**
Egyptian dolma	**waraq anab**
a Thai salad with sweet Chinese sausages	**yam koon-chiang**

Soups, Stews, and One-Dish Meals

Among soups, stews, and one-dish meals from around the world, what is or are . . . ?

In France

the mussel-and-shallot soup from Maxim's in Paris	**billi bi**
a creamy soup, often made with seafood or game	**bisque**
an aromatic broth stew, as of veal or lamb	**blanquette**
beef stew	**boeuf Bourguignon**
black pudding	**boudin noir** or **ordinaire**
a Marseilles soup of fish and mixed vegetables	**bouillabaisse**
clear broth, as of beef	**bouillon**
a dish of white beans and meat or poultry	**cassoulet**

goose stew, in Champagne	**civet d'oie**
a casserole	**cocotte**
clear broth, as of chicken or beef	**consommé**
wine broth used when boiling fish or meat	**court-bouillon**
a mutton and spring vegetable stew	**navarin**
a light basil-flavored vegetable soup	**pistou**
the soup of the day	**potage du jour**
split pea soup	**potage purée de pois cassés**
meat broth with vegetables, lit. a pot in fire	**pot-au-feu**
thick vegetable stew from Lorraine	**potée Lorraine**
spicy vegetable soup with tomato sauce	**soupe au pistou**
meatless vegetable soup	**soupe maigre**
potato soup	**vichyssoise**

In Italy

Genoese fish stew	**burrida**
wide Italian noodles layered with ricotta cheese and tomato or meat sauce	**lasagna**
Neapolitan pork-and-cabbage soup	**maritata**
Italian white-bean-and-pasta soup	**pasta e fagioli**
soft pizza with green vegetables, from Abruzzi	**pizza e fojje**
beef stew, in Austrian-speaking NE Italy	**Rindsgulasch**
a Neapolitan dish of rice, liver, mozzarella, eggs, and ground beef	**sartù**
Italian egg drop soup	**stracciatella**
Florentine bean soup	**zuppa de fagioli**
Italian chestnut soup	**zuppa di mosciarelle**

In Spain and Portugal

Portuguese sailors' stew, with fish, onions, tomatoes, and potatoes	**caldeiradas**
a Portuguese soup of cabbage and sausages in a potato broth	**caldo verde**
a Portuguese broth-and-rice-soup	**canja**
a Portuguese boiled dinner, with meat, poultry, rice, and chick peas, the broth making a soup	**cozido**

the cold, spicy Spanish vegetable soup	**gazpacho**
Spanish saffron rice with mixed vegetables, meats, poultry, and fish	**paella**
Portuguese vegetable soup	**sopa alentejana**

Elsewhere in Western Europe (Outside France, Italy, Spain, and Portugal)

Bremen summer eel soup	**Aalsuppe grün**
a Dutch dish of kale, potatoes, and smoked sausage	**Boerenkool met Rookworst**
sweet goulash, Flanders style	**carbonades flamandes**
Scottish fish soup	**cullen skink**
Berlin yellow bean soup	**Erbsensuppe**
thick, winter-hearty Dutch pea soup	**Erwtensoep**
pork, kidney, onion, and sage, served with peas, in the British Isles	**faggots and peas**
German consommé with shredded pancakes	**Flädlesupp**
leftovers made into a hash	**gallimaufry**
vegetable consommé with vermicelli and meatballs, in The Netherlands	**Groentensoep**
Austrian paprika-and-onion soup	**Gulyassuppe**
a Dutch dish of potatoes, carrots, and onions	**hutspot**
a Dutch dish of marrowfat peas, with stewed beef, bacon, potatoes, and various garnishes	**Kapucijners**
meat broth with liver dumplings, in Austria	**Leberknödlsuppe**
German ravioli, served in a broth with chives	**Maultaschen**
a Belgian soup of fresh fish and herbs	**waterzooi**

In Greece and the Balkans

Greek egg, lemon, rice, and chicken broth soup	**avgolemono**
fish soup from Danubian Romania	**bors pescaresc**
a sour Romanian soup with fish or meatballs	**chorba**
Romanian sour-cream-and-chicken soup	**ciorba de perisoare**
Romanian sour-cream-and-meatball soup	**ciorba de pui**
Bulgarian spicy hotpot	**Gyuvech**

the Greek ground-meat-and-eggplant-layered casserole	**moussaká**
Greek fish soup	**psarósoupa**
a Bulgarian soup of beef innards in spicy milk	**Shkembe Churba**
Greek veal, tongue, or hare stew	**styphádo**
cold yogurt soup, in Bulgaria	**tarator**

Elsewhere in Eastern Europe (Outside Greece and the Balkans)

Polish sour rye or oat soup	**alzur**
Hungarian ham and bean soup	**bableves**
Polish beet-root soup	**barszcz**
Russian beet soup, often with cabbage	**borscht**
Czech potato and vegetable soup	**bramboracka**
Polish cold sour-cream and crayfish soup	**chlodnik**
Polish "black" soup of blood, bones, and innards with prunes or cherries	**czarinina**
Polish pea soup with croutons	**grochówka**
Polish mushroom soup	**grzybowa**
Hungarian spicy beef and vegetable soup	**gulyás (goulash)**
Hungarian rich fish soup, like a bouillabaisse	**halászlé**
Hungarian bouillon, often with a raw egg	**húsleves**
Polish vegetable soup	**jaryznowa**
Hungarian cabbage soup	**káposztaleves**
Polish barley soup	**krupnik**
the thick, brown Hungarian soup, with croutons	**rántott leves**
Polish beef bouillon	**rosól**
hearty Russian cabbage soup	**shchi**
Polish sorrel soup, with hard-boiled eggs	**szczawiowa**
Polish onion soup	**zalewajka**
Polish beer soup	**zupa piwna**

In the Americas

thick potato soup, in Columbia	**ajiaco**
thick northern Mexican tripe soup	**birria, menudo,** or **café de hueso**
a Jamaican pepper pot soup	**callalou**
a Chilean soup with chicken, rice, pumpkin, and vegetables	**cazuela de ave**
a Bolivian soup of beef, potatoes, and fava beans	**chairo**

northern Mexican spicy beef soup	**chili con queso**
an American meat and vegetable dish, inspired by the Chinese for "odds and ends"	**chop suey**
California seafood stew of Italian descent	**cioppino**
a Brazilian stew of pork, sausage, and vegetables	**feijoadas**
a Creole soup/stew featuring okra	**gumbo**
spicy Creole stew	**jambalaya**
an Argentinian soup of corn, sausages, potatoes, pumpkin, and bacon	**locro**
various corn soups, in Mexico	**pozole**
Bolivian highland potato soup	**sopa de papa lisa**
Bolivian soup with quinoa grain	**sopa de quinoa**

In Africa

Algerian chicken with vegetables and vermicelli	**chorba beïda**
Algerian bean soup	**chorbe loubia**
a hearty North African soup of chicken, mutton, rice, vegetables, spices, and bread yeast	**harira**
a West African rice and vegetable dish with meat, poultry, or fish	**jollof rice** or **benachin**
Zambian corn flour and meat or fish dish	**mealie-mealie**
Zambian corn meal and meat stew	**nshima**
West African fish, escargot, rice, and vegetable stew	**thie Bou Diene** or **che bu gen**
Kenyan maize and spicy meat porridge	**ugali**

In Asia and the Pacific

the Filipino version of paella	**arroz valenciana**
a thick Filipino soup of pork meat and innards	**batsoy**
a sumptuous Indian dish of chicken and lamb, rice, and whole spices, topped with fruits	**biriani**
a one-pot Jewish Sabbath dish prepared ahead	**cholent** or **hamin**
a Chinese dish of vegetables, meat, and noodles	**chow mein**

the Indian lentil and split pea soup	**dhal**
Turkish meat broth, egg yolk, and lemon soup	**dügün çorbasi**
a simple meal of soup and side dishes, in Korea	**hanjong-shik**
Burmese sweet-and-sour vegetable soup	**hinga**
Turkish lamb and eggplant stew	**hünker begend**
Korean clam soup	**joge tang**
Thai rice noodle soup	**kuay tiaw**
Singapore soup with noodle, coconut, and herbs	**laksa**
Tunisian chick-pea soup	**lebabli**
Bengali vegetable and fish curry soup	**machher jhol**
Korean fish soup	**maeun-tang**
Bengali prawn and coconut curry	**malai curry**
Korean soup with dough-wrapped meatballs	**mandu-kuk**
a soybean-based Japanese soup	**miso**
a Japanese sukiyaki-type dish with chicken or pork	**mitzutaki**
a Cantonese chicken-and-vegetable dish	**moo goo gai pan**
a spicy Anglo-Indian vegetable soup	**mulligatawny**
a Korean cold dish of noodles, vegetables, eggs, and meat	**naeng-myon**
a Middle Eastern spiced dish of meat, rice, and raisins	**pilau**
a simpler version of India's biriani	**pulao**
soup, in general, in Indonesia	**sajor**
a Burmese fish or meat stew	**sibyan**
the Filipino version of bouillabaisse	**sinigang na hipon**
a Filipino sourish pork stew	**sinigang no baboy**
a clear Japanese soup	**suimono**
Japanese dish of beef, vegetables, bean curd, and sake	**sukiyaki**
the turkish vegetable, yogurt, and flour soup	**tarhana**
the Filipino chicken and green-papaya soup	**tinolang manok**
a fruit or vegetable stew, to Jews	**tsimmes**
a vinegary Indian curry	**vindaloo**
a Turkish yogurt soup	**yayla çorbasi**

Fruits, Grains, Nuts, and Vegetables

Among fruits, grains, nuts, and vegetables, and dishes centered on them, from around the world, what is or are . . . . ?

In France

almond	amande
pineapple	ananas
artichoke	artichaut
asparagus with a butter-and-egg sauce	asperges à la flamande
eggplant	aubergine
beet, or beetroot	betterave
soft "butter" pear	beurré
cherry	cerise
mushrooms	champignons or cèpes
cucumber	concombre
cabbage	chou
sauerkraut	choucroute
cauliflower	choufleur
Brussels sprouts	choux de Bruxelles
pumpkin or gourd	courge
watercress	cresson
squash	courge à la moelle
shallots	échalotes
fennel	fenouil
bean (broad)	fève (de marasi)
kitchen herbs such as parsley, sage, or tarragon	fines herbes
strawberry	fraise
raspberry	framboise
dried fruit	fruit sec
hot potato cake	galette de pommes de terre
vegetables and potatoes in a cream-and-cheese sauce	gratin dauphinois
vegetables cut in thin strips	julienne
grapefruit	pamplemousse
potato	pomme de terre

In Italy

orange	arancio
nutty-flavored aromatic salad green	arrugula or arugula
vegetables dipped in a heated sauce at the table, lit. a hot bath	bagna cauda or calda
flour or cereal	farina
eggplant	melanzane
stuffed zucchini and peppers, as in Genoa	ripieni
rice and peas, as in Venice	risi e bisi

| rice with saffron, as in Lombardy | **riso giallo** |
| mixed fruits | **tutti-frutti** |

In Spain and Portugal

almond, in Spain	**almendra**
custard apples, in Portugal	**anonas**
cherry, in Spain	**cereza**
passionfruit, in Portugal	**maracujá**
Portuguese fruit of the "strawberry tree"	**medronha**
Portuguese nectarines	**péssegos carecas**

Elsewhere in Europe (Outside France, Italy, Spain, and Portugal)

potatoes, in Holland	**aardappelen**
nutritious Swiss cereal exported around the world	**Birchermüesli**
cauliflower, in Holland	**bloemkool**
fried potatoes in batter, in Czechoslovakia	**bramborák**
German bean-carrot-and-apple dish	**Bunte oder Gepflückte Finten**
lemon, in Holland	**citroen**
peas, in Holland	**doperwten**
grapes, in Holland	**druiven**
potatoes, in Austria	**Erdäpfel**
green beans, in Austria	**Fisolen**
plate of varied, cooked and raw vegetables, in Austria	**Gemischter Salat**
mushrooms, in Poland	**grzyby**
sauerkraut, in Poland	**kapu'sniak**
cauliflower, in Austria	**Karfiol**
potato, in Poland	**kartoflanka**
buckwheat groats, in Poland and Russia	**kasha** or **kasza**
cherries, in Holland	**kersen**
German turnip cabbage	**kohlrabi**
cucumber, in Holland	**komkommer**
cabbage, in Holland	**kool**
Romanian corn mush	**mamaliga**
tomatoes, in Austria	**Paradeiser**
potato pancakes, in Poland	**placki kartoflane**
roasted sliced potatoes, in Austria	**Röstkartoffeln**
red cabbage, in Germany	**Rotkohl**
red cabbage, in Austria	**Rotkraut**
orange, in Holland	**sinaasappel**
lettuce or salad, in Holland	**sla**
cabbage salad with vinegar dressing, in Austria	**Slaw**
tomato stuffed with shrimps and mayonnaise, in Belgium	**tomatoes aux crevettes (cold)** or **croquette aux crevettes (hot)**

onions, in Holland	**ulen**
squash, to the British	**vegetable marrow**
fruit salad, in Holland	**vruch tensla**
carrots, in Holland	**worteljes**
pear fritters, in Switzerland	**Ziegerkrapfen**
sauerkraut, in Holland	**zuurkool**

In the Americas

rice and beans, in Puerto Rico	**arroz y habichuelas**
persimmon, in Mexico	**chapote**
rice and black mushrooms, in Haiti	**diri et djondjon**
black bean of Hispanic America	**frijole**
Jamaican salad of oranges and star apples	**matrimony**
rice and kidney beans, in Haiti	**riz et pois**
deep-fried bananas (plantains), in Puerto Rico	**tostones**

In Africa, Asia, Australia, and the Pacific

West African dish of the potatolike manioc	**attieke**
a type of Filipino mango	**carabao**
tiny pear-shaped "roseapples," from SE Asia	**chompoo**
fried rice, in China	**chow fan**
steamed semolina wheat, often topped with meat	**couscous**
white radish, in Japan	**daikon**
Indian lentil served with rice	**dal**
a foul-smelling Filipino fruit	**durian**
deep-fried, spicy, mashed fava-bean patties, as in Egypt	**falafel** or **taameyya**
guava, in Thailand	**farang**
fava beans and tomatoes in a spicy sauce, in Egypt	**fool mudhammas**
West African starchy, gooey staple	**foufou**
cold vegetables in peanut sauce, in Indonesia	**gado gado**
a root used for long life and potency in China	**ginseng**
burdock root, in Japan	**gobo**
boiled white rice, in Japan	**gohan**
Turkish eggplant stuffed with tomato and garlic, lit. the imam (a Moslem cleric) fainted	**imàm baylldi**
persimmons, in Japan	**kaki**
pickled cabbage, radish, or cucumbers, in Korea	**kimchee**

a fuzzy-rinded Asian fruit, a "Chinese gooseberry"	**kiwi**
finger-sized bananas, in Thailand	**klue khai**
pale brown Thai berries	**langsat** or **langsard**
rich, oily nuts, orig. from Australia	**macadamia**
rich with lentils and onions, in the Middle East	**majadra**
a tropical Asian fruit, with orangy flesh	**mango (ma-muang)**
a SE Asian hybrid fruit with purple rind and white fruit	**mangosteen** or **mangokhud**
a crisp, South Indian pancake with cashews, peas, potatoes, and raisins, with coconut chutney	**masala dosa**
Tunisian tomato, cucumber, and onion salad	**mechoula**
mandarin oranges, in Japan	**mikan**
spinachy, mintlike Egyptian vegetable	**moulukhiya**
a Japanese apple or pearlike fruit	**nashi**
rice, in Indonesia and Malaysia	**nasi**
Thai "custard" apples, eaten with a spoon	**noina**
the thin seaweed used to wrap sushi, in Japan	**nori**
rape flowers, in Japan	**na-no-hana**
watermelon, in the Philippines	**pakwan**
mainstay fruit in the Philippines	**papaya**
a type of Filipino mango	**pico**
a grapefruitlike Filipino fruit	**pomelo**
plum-sized Thai crabapples	**pood-sa**
a SE Asian hairy-rinded fruit with translucent flesh	**rambutan** or **ngo**
stewed vegetables in general, in Indonesia	**sambalans**
popular South Indian vegetarian dishes	**sambar** and **pachadi**
pineapples, in Thailand	**saparot**
a mangolike fruit from SE Asia	**sapodilla** or **lamood**
Indonesian, fried coconut meat and peanuts	**seroendeng** or **apenhaar**
mushrooms, in Japan	**shiitake**
fresh bamboo shoots, in Japan	**takenoko**

Other Fruits, Grains, Nuts, Vegetables, and Vegetarian Dishes

an alligator pear, used in guacamole	**avocado (Fr. avocat)**
the outer husk of cereal grains, once byproducts	**bran**

cracked wheat, in western Asia	**bulgur** or **burghul**
a salad of romaine, egg, lemon, anchovies, croutons, and Parmesan cheese	**Caesar salad**
a dish of fruit cooked in sugar	**compote**
fried chunks of potatoes	**French fries, frites,** or **chips**
tropical fruit used in jellies	**guava** or **jambu batu**
thin-sliced potatoes in a buttery casserole	**potatoes Anna**
an eggplant-zucchini-and-tomato dish	**ratatouille**
cold salad of bulgar and vegetables	**tabouli**
bean curd	**tofu**
the nutritious embryo of a wheat kernel	**wheat germ**

Meat, Poultry, and Fish Dishes

Among meat, poultry, and fish, and dishes centered on them, what is or are . . . ?

In France

lamb	**agneau**
anchovies	**anchois**
a Lyonnais dish of sausage and entrails	**andouillette grillée**
a marinated meat-and-potato casserole, in the Alsace	**baeckaoffe**
sea bass	**bar** or **bar rayé**
beefsteak	**bifteck**
chicken in a champagne sauce	**blanc de volaille au champagne**
beef or ox	**boeuf**
spicy French sausage	**boudin**
boiled or stewed meat	**bouilli**
puréed fish with oil and spices, in Provence	**brandade de morue**
cod	**cabillaud**
quail	**caille**
duck or duckling	**canard** or **caneton**
the loin cut of meat or fillet	**carré**
a rooster castrated for better eating	**chapon**
broiled beef fillet with potatoes and mushrooms	**châteaubriant** or **-land**
venison, or deer meat	**chevreuil**
varied meats with Madeira and mushrooms	**choesel au Madère**
an Alsatian mixed grill with sauerkraut in a white wine sauce	**choucroute garnie**

a ragout of game with wine, onions, and spices	**clvet**
varied French pork dishes, served hot or cold	**cochonailles chaud ou froid**
pigeon ragout	**compote**
chicken in a white sauce, as in Alsace	**coq au Riesling**
chicken cooked in wine	**coq au vin**
shellfish	**coquillage**
scallops	**coquilles St. Jacques**
veal rolled around cheese and ham, dipped in a batter and fried, as in Austria	**Cordon Bleu**
a chop or cutlet	**côtelette**
ribs or beef	**côtes de bœuf**
the thigh or rump of meat or leg of poultry	**cuisse, cuissot, or culotte**
a slice of fish	**darne**
tenderloin steak carved from the ribs	**entrecôte**
ragout or small cutlet	**épigramme**
snails	**escargots**
stewed meat	**étuvée**
mock turtle	**fausse tortue**
a piece of meat or fish with bones removed	**filet or fillet**
prawns, in Corsica	**gambas**
cooked leg of meat	**gigot**
lobster	**homard**
ham	**jambon**
ham and parsley pâté, in Dijon	**jambon persillé**
mussels in a white-wine broth	**moules marinières**
seafood	**poisson de mer**
fresh-water fish	**poisson de rivière**
a young hen, spayed for better eating	**poulard**
young chicken	**poulet**
chicken roasted in red wine, in central France	**poulet en barbouille**
fish balls in a creamy sauce, as in Lyon	**quenelles sauce Nantua**
a spicy stew of meat and vegetables	**ragoût**
wild boar, in Corsica	**sanglier**
dry salami	**saucisson**
smoked salmon	**saumon fumé**
a meat pie, with a mushroomy cream sauce	**tourte Bourguignon**
mutton wrapped in intestines, in central France	**tripaux d'Aurillac**
trout	**truite**

sea urchins, in Corsica	**ursens**
veal	**veau**
meat, in general	**viande**

In Italy

duck	**anatra** or **anitra**
herring	**aringa** or **aringhe**
roast pork	**arista**
crayfish	**aragosta**
a roast of meat	**arrosto** or **arrostito**
beefsteak	**bistecca**
steamed or boiled meats plain or in a parsley sauce	**bollito misto (bolliti misti)**
stuffed meat rolls	**brasciole**
squid	**calamari** or **totani**
meat-filled pasta tubes in sauce	**cannelloni**
a pork-and-cabbage mixture from Lombardy	**cazzoeula**
a sausage popular in Modena	**ciccioli**
rabbit	**coniglio**
a kind of prosciutto, like ham	**cotto**
mussels	**cozze**
smoked raw pork, a kind of prosciutto	**crudo**
NW Italian mussels, lit. dates of the sea	**datteri di mare**
a mixed fry	**fritto misto**
grilled and roasted meats	**grigliate ed arrosti**
plain grilled veal	**lombatta di vitello**
a sausage popular in Modena	**lòppa**
edible snails	**lumache**
bologna	**mortadella**
a NW Italian dish of baby squid with basil and tomato	**moscardini affogati**
braised veal shanks, as made in Milan	**osso buco (ossi buchi)**
raw bacon	**pancetta**
spicy, hard, Italian sausage	**pepperoni**
fish baked with herbs and garlic	**pesce al cartoccio**
octopus	**polipi**
raw, cured ham	**prosciutto**
frog	**rana**
rice and fish, in Venice	**risotto al pesce**
slices of ham and veal cooked together	**saltimbocca**
tripe	**trippa**
clams prepared with oregano	**vongole arreganata**
pig's feet	**zampóne**

In Spain and Portugal

a porridgy Portuguese dish of white fish, wheat bread, and boiled eggs	**açorda**
tiny Portuguese shellfish	**ameijoas**
chicken in rice in many Latin regions	**arroz con pollo**
dried cod, in a sauce or grilled, in Portugal	**bacalhau**
beefsteak in a sweet-paprika-and-red-wine sauce, in Portugal	**bifes a portugesa**
shrimp or crawfish, in Spain	**camarón**
beef, in Iberia	**carne de vaca**
sheep or mutton, in Spanish	**carnero**
cockles with chicken or sausages, in Algarve	**cataplana**
sun-dried or smoked meat strips, in Spanish	**charqui (jerky)**
spicy Spanish sausages	**chorizos**
a Portuguese dish of chicken, sausages, tripe, beans, carrots, and tomatoes	**dobrada a moda do Porto**
a Madeira kebab roasted on bay tree twigs	**espetadas**
steamed Portuguese crayfish	**lagosta suada**
mussels, in Portugal	**mexilhões**
dried cod in rissoles, in Portugal	**pasteis de bacalhau**
Portuguese oysters	**percebes**
dried ham, in Portugal	**presuntos**

Elsewhere in Western Europe (Outside France, Italy, Spain, and Portugal)

baby eels in an herb sauce, in NW Europe	**anguilles au vert**
breaded, deep-fried chicken, in Austria	**Backhuhn** or **-hendl**
a stuffed meat roll, braised or poached	**ballotine** or **ballottine**
sausages, in Britain	**bangers**
an Austrian boiled dinner, with ham, pork, sausage, sauerkraut, and dumpling	**Bauernschmaus**
a Berlin-style hamburger	**Berliner Bouletten**
a plump German frankfurter sausage	**Bockwurst**
German sour pickled herring	**Brathering**
whitish German pork sausage	**Bratwurst**
a North German dish of sweetbreads, chicken, veal meatballs, clams, peas, and asparagus	**Breme Küken ragout**

air-dried beef, in Switzerland	**Bündnerfleisch**
game such as hare, with prunes, as in Flanders	**civet de lièvre à la flamande**
an Irish Halloween dish of potatoes, onions, cabbage, and heavy cream	**colcannon**
pickled pigs' feet, in Ireland	**cruibins**
duck, in Holland	**eend**
spicy pork shank with sauerkraut, in Germany	**Eisbein mit Sauerkraut**
minced meat, in Austria	**Faschiertes**
smoked haddock, in Scotland	**finnan haddie**
fried sole, in The Netherlands	**gebakken zeetong**
pork chops stuffed with apples, raisins, and toast, topped with rum, in North Germany	**Gefüllte Schweinerippchen**
thin-sliced veal in a cream sauce, in Switzerland	**Geschnetzeltes**
lightly salted pig's feet, in Switzerland	**Gnagi**
spiced, minced innards, cooked in the animal's stomach, in Scotland	**haggis**
roast lamb, in North Germany	**Heidschnückenbraten**
Wiener Schnitzel with fried egg and anchovies	**Holsteiner Schnitzel**
a Dutch-Indonesian dish of rice, eggs, steak, potatoes, and vegetables in a curry sauce	**Java honden povtle (a hound's portion)**
veal shank, in Germany	**Kalbshax'n**
German salt pork, butter-fried, then slow-cooked	**Kasseler Rippenspeer**
cheese stuffed with meat or fish and baked, to the Dutch	**Keshi Yena**
salted and smoked herring	**kippers**
a German meatball with herring and capers	**Königsberger Klopse**
a North German stew of meat, herring, potatoes, and beetroot	**Labskaus**
Bavarian pork roast loaf	**Leberkäs**
fried whiting, in The Netherlands	**lekkerbekjes**
ham with juniper, smoked over oak, in Ireland	**Limerick ham**
Swiss pork sausages with caraway and anise	**longeoles**
smoked salmon	**lox**
steak filet, in Austria	**Lungenbraten**
Scandinavian cod marinated in potash lye	**lutefisk**
young wild boar, in Belgium	**marcassin**

herring and unpeeled boiled potatoes, in Germany	**Matjeshering**
Swiss beef marinated in cider, then air-dried	**Moschtbröckli**
a Dutch-Indonesian spicy meatball	**nasibal**
Belgian goose boiled with vegetables, then fried	**oie à l'instar de Visé**
crab with rice and cream, in Scotland	**partan bree**
an herb-flavored German sausage	**Pfälzer**
peppery German goulash	**Pfefferpothast**
spring chicken, in Holland	**piepkuiken**
North German sausage of fatty pork	**Pinkelwurst**
Scandinavian aged fish	**rakørret**
north German smoked eel	**Räucheraal**
jugged venison, in Switzerland	**Rehpfeffer**
venison, in Austria and Switzerland	**Rehrücken**
roast beef, in Germany	**Riderbraten**
Belgian roast kidneys with juniper and gin	**rognons de ceau à la Liègeoise**
pickled herring with onion and pickle on a toothpick, in Germany	**Rollmops**
Dutch beef and tripe, pickled, minced, and sautéed in butter, served with apple and red cabbage	**Rolpens met Rodekool**
German pickled beef	**Sauerbraten**
ham, in Germany	**Schinken**
roast goose or pork with potato dumplings and fried fruit	**Schlesisches Himmelreich**
bacon smoked over Black Forest fir cones	**Schwarzwaldgeräuchertes**
roast pork belly, in Germany	**Schweinebauch**
roast pork, in Germany	**Schweinebraten**
Sunday roast, in Germany	**Sonntagsbraten**
a flavorful smoked bacon, in Germany	**Speck**
highly seasoned, double-ground raw beef	**steak tartare**
spit-roasted chicken, in Austria	**Steirisches Brathuhn** or **Poulard**
dried whitefish cooked in milk, with potatoes, rice, and other garnishes, in The Netherlands	**Stokvis**
pigs' ears and feet with sauerkraut and peas, in Germany	**Sulperknocken**

chopped meat in aspic, in Germany	**Sulze**
a sour herring dish, in Scandinavia	**surströmming**
boiled beef, in Austria	**Tafelspitz**
pork chops, in Holland	**varkenskotelet**
a molded pork-and-bread mix, in Germany	**Weckewerk**
a white German sausage of veal with calves' brains and spleen	**Weisswurst**
batter-covered fried veal steak, in Austria	**Wiener Schnitzel**

In Eastern Europe

grilled innards, in Bulgaria	**agneshki drebuliiki**
strips of beef in a sour cream sauce	**beef Stroganoff**
a Hungarian type of Wiener Schnitzel	**bécsi szelet**
sauerkraut, cabbage, onions, and leftover meat, in Poland	**bigos**
a Hungarian mixed grill	**fatányéros**
tripe with ginger and cheese, in Poland	**flaki**
Greek roast lamb and pasta	**giuvetsi**
Polish cabbage leaves stuffed with meat and rice	**golabki**
charcoal-grilled Baltic herring, in Finland	**hiiliillä paistettue silakkaa**
"poor man's caviar" with herring roe, in Romania	**irka**
baked pork and fish in a rye crust, in Finland	**kalakukko**
marinated, charcoal-grilled, skewered meat chunks	**kebab** or **shashlik**
Bulgarian spicy, grilled minced-meat rolls	**Kebapcheta**
Polish sausage	**kielbasa**
a layered Hungarian dish of sour cabbage, smoked sausage, pork, eggs, and rice	**kolozsvári rakottkáposzta**
flavorful Finnish meatballs	**lihapulilla**
a Bulgarian mixed grill	**Meshana skara**
skinless Romanian cocktail sausages	**mititei**
pork stuffed with ham and cheese, in Romania	**muschi clobanesc**
beef stuffed with mushrooms, bacon, and peppers, in Romania	**muschi polana**

pig's knuckles, in Poland	**nózki**
Hungarian paprika chicken	**paprikás csirke**
beef or chicken in aspic, in Romania	**piftie**
Bulgarian chicken with tomatoes and peppers	**Pile paprikash**
chicken stuffed with bacon, sausage, and vegetables, in Romania	**piu cimpulungean**
Hungarian paprika stew, in the US called goulash	**pörkölt** or **tokány**
reindeer casserole, in Finland	**poronkäristys**
Finnish reindeer tongue with lemon sauce	**poronkieltä**
Hungarian fried chicken	**rántott csirke**
meat or poultry with a sour cream and horseradish sauce, in Moldavia	**rasol Moldovenesc cu hrean**
Hungarian steak, onion, and potato dish	**serpenyós rostélyos**
spit-roasted Greek kebabs	**souvláki**
a Transylvanian form of goulash	**székelygulyús**
a Romanian pork stew	**tocana**
Hungarian meat-filled cabbage	**töltött káposzta**
Hungarian meat-filled peppers	**töltött paprika**
Polish beef rolls, with mushroom, sour cream, and rice or kasha	**zrazy zawijane**

In the Americas

open-fire roasted meat, in Argentina	**asado**
the Puerto Rican almost-soup of chicken or seafood	**asopao**
mutton wrapped in thin leaves, in Mexico	**barbacoa**
Mexican beef fillet with peppers and guacamole	**carne asada**
northern Brazil shrimp creole	**caruru,** or **camarones a baiano**
baby shark, in the Yucatan	**cazón**
meat with spicy sauce and often beans, in the US	**chile con carne**
thinly sliced, dried smoked beef	**chipped beef**
meat broiled over charcoal, in Latin regions	**churrasco**
a spicy Bolivian chicken dish	**ckocko**
spicy suckling pig baked in banana leaf, in the Yucatan	**cochinita pibil**
a Chilean pork, seafood, potato, and vegetable dish, cooked in sacks over hot stones in the ground	**curanto**

a turkey hen (cock), in the Caribbean	**dinde (dindon)**
a Brazilian beef-tongue-and-shrimp stew	**efo**
bits of grilled meat or poultry served with tortillas, in Mexico	**fajitas**
Brazilian rice, black bean, and smoked pork dish	**feijoada completa**
meat and vegetables in a flour-thickened broth	**fricasée**
a Bolivian dish of pork with mint and hot peppers	**fritanga**
pickled raw salmon, in Iceland	**gravlax**
fried Haitian pork and bananas	**grillot et banane pese**
cured shark meat, in Iceland	**hákarl**
smoked lamb, a festive Icelandic dish	**hangikjöt**
dried fish, in Iceland	**hardfiskur**
baby crawfish, in Chile	**langostinos**
flaming Haitian lobster	**langouste flambé**
spit-roasted suckling pig, in Puerto Rico	**lechón asado**
Mexican jerky	**machacado**
northern Brazil fish creole	**muqueca de peixe**
smoked salmon, less salty than lox	**Nova Scotia salmon**
Argentinian, Chilean, or Uruguayan mixed grill	**parrillada**
minced meat and corn flour in banana leaf, in the Spanish West Indies	**pastelles**
dried buffalo meat, for frontier Americans	**pemmican**
dried spicy meat and onions, fried, in Argentina	**reviro**
a Brazilian stew of pig innards in pig's blood	**sarapatel**
raw fish in a spicy marinade, in Peru	**seviche**
sherry-marinated herring, in Iceland	**sherry síld**
dried turkey, in Haiti	**tassot de dinde**
a spicy fish-and-shrimp dish in Brazil	**vatapa**
chicken with peanuts and coconut, in northern Brazil	**ximxim de galinha**

In Asia, Africa, Australia, and the Pacific

Filipino chicken or pork stewed in soy sauce	**adobo**
chicken, in Indonesia	**ajam**

Filipino grilled crab in vinegar sauce	**allmango**
Malaysian fish curry with a tamarind sauce	**assam pedas**
Indonesian roast young pork in a mildly spicy sauce	**babi pangang**
meat steamed in coconut milk, in Indonesia	**bebottok**
a sea slug, a delicacy to the Chinese	**bêche-de-mer**
North African ground meat, plus pasty	**bourak**
meat boiled with vegetables, sliced, then fried, in India	**buffaths**
stewed meat, in Indonesian cooking	**daging**
pig's entrails stewed with blood and chili, in the Philippines	**dinuguan**
slightly cooked shrimp, in Japan	**ebi**
a mushy, Indonesian meatball	**fricadel**
a Jewish fish mixture, lit. stuffed fish	**gefiltefish**
a Thai fish pudding with banana leaves	**hoh mok pla**
red caviar, in Japan	**ikura**
Nonya (Malaysian) spicy deep-fried chicken	**inche kabin**
grilled meat or fish with a chili-garlic sauce, in the Philippines	**inihaw**
Thai chicken curry with bamboo shoots	**kaeng kai noh mai**
oxtail in a thick Filipino peanut sauce	**kare kare**
chicken pieces cooked in coconut milk, in Malaysia	**kari kapitan**
spit-roasted Turkish swordfish	**kilic sis**
spiced meat baked in intestines, a Jewish dish	**kishke**
ground meat broiled on a skewer, in Egypt	**kufta**
chicken in peanut sauce, in Senegal	**mafe**
tender, lean, raw tuna, in Japan	**maguro**
grilled, meat-stuffed sheep's stomach, in North Africa	**melfouf**
highly spiced North African lamb sausage	**merguez**
Malaysian grilled fish pâté	**otak otak**
leeks and clams fried in a batter, in Korea	**pachon**

deep-fried pig's thigh with chili and vinegar sauce, in the Philippines	**pata**
Thai sweet-and-sour fish	**phad priew wan pla**
marinated strips of beef, in Korea	**pulgogi** or **pulgoki**
Koran shortribs	**pulkalbi**
a spicy Indian meat or fish crêpe in Trinidad	**roti**
mackerel, in Japan	**sanma**
Malaysian meat kebabs marinated in spicy coconut milk	**satay**
Indonesian skewered bits of pork in a peanut sauce	**saté babi**
spit-roasted lamb, in the Middle East	**schawarma**
seafood served raw, in Japan	**sushi** or **sashimi**
octopus, in Japan	**tako**
Moghul-style chicken, in India	**Tandoori chicken**
seafood, beef, and vegetables cooked at a table grill, in Japan	**teppanyaki**
Japanese breaded pork cutlet and cabbage	**tonkatsu**
eel, in Japan	**unagi**
Japanese grilled chicken and vegetable on a skewer	**yakitori**
grilled seafood, in Japan	**yakizakana**
West African chicken in a spicy lemon sauce	**yassa au poulet**

Cheeses and Other Dairy Dishes

Among cheese and other dairy dishes from around the world, what is or are . . . ?

In France

butter	**beurre**
Normandy triple-crème cheeses	**Boursault** and **Boursin**
a cheese from sheep's milk, in Corsica	**brebis**
a rich white-rinded cheese in a disk	**Brie**
a creamy white cheese, from Corsica	**brucciu**
a soft, creamy, pungent cheese from Normandy	**Camembert**
a rich goat cheese	**chabichou**
a cheese from around Bourges	**chavignot**
a fresh goat's-milk cheese	**fromage de chèvre**
a doubly thick heavy cream	**crème fraîche**
cheeses with 60–74% butterfat	**double crème**
cheese, in general	**fromage**

Alsatian cow's-milk cheese	**Münster**
white-rinded Normandy cow's-milk cheese	**Neufchâtel**
a semi-soft cheese made by Trappists	**Port Salut**
a tangy, fermented cheese from Languedoc	**Roquefort**
an Alpine cheese of half goat's milk	**St-Marcellin**
a tangy cheese from Languedoc and the Auvergne	**Saint-Nectaire**
a cheese with 75 + % butterfat	**triple crème**

In Italy

a soft, mild cheese, lit. beautiful land	**Bel Paese**
cheeses from the Valle D'Aosta region	**Fontina** and **Oma Valdostana**
a mild blue cheese	**Gorgonzola**
an Italian Swiss cheese	**groviera**
a dessert cheese	**Mascarpone**
a fresh white cheese flavored for pizzas	**mozzarella**
grating cheese originating in Parma	**Parmesan** or **Parmigiano**
a relatively strong cheese	**pecorino**
cheeses from the Bergamo region of Lombardy	**provolone** and **taleggio**
a creamy cottage cheese used in lasagna	**ricotta**

Elsewhere in Europe (Outside France and Italy)

a Swiss yellow cheese with a brownish rind	**Appenzell**
an Austrian farmhouse cheese	**Bergkäse**
a German "beer cheese"	**Bierkäse**
a sharp cheese with moldy blue veins	**bleu cheese**
an Eastern Europe cream cheese from ewes' milk	**bryndza**
a mild Swiss cheese	**caciotta**
a Welsh white cheese soaked in brine	**Caerphilly**
a pressed cheese from Chester, England	**Cheshire**
a Dutch red- or yellow-rinded, part-skim cheese	**Edam**
a light yellow, holey cheese from Bern, Switzerland	**Emmenthal**
a fresh, brine-pickled Greek cheese	**féta**

melted cheese and white wine with bread for dipping, in Switzerland	**fondue Neuchâteloise** or **Savoyard**
a Scandinavian goat cheese	**geitost**
a yellow-rinded whole-milk cheese from Holland	**Gouda**
a light yellow cheese with small holes, from Switzerland and Gruyere	**Gruyere**
a smelly cheese from Mainz, Germany	**Handkäs**
a sharp cheese with caraway, from mid-Germany	**Harzer**
a Danish semi-soft cow's milk cheese	**Havarti (Harvarti)**
alternating slabs of Stilton and Double Gloucester	**Huntsman**
a swiss cheese–like Norwegian cheese	**Jarlsberg**
yogurt, in Bulgaria	**kisselo mleko**
a spicy, salty, strong North-German cheese	**Limburger**
a salted cottage cheese, in Portugal	**queijinhos de Tomar**
cheese eaten fresh, in Portugal	**queijinho fresco**
a hearty Portuguese ewes'-milk cheese	**queijo d'Azeitão**
an ewes'-milk cheese that "sheds tears," in Portugal	**queijo da Serra**
strong cheese melted over boiled potatoes and perhaps dried beef, as in the Alps	**raclette**
a dry Portuguese cheese	**Serpa**
a Bulgarian baked cheese dish	**Sirene po shopski**
Britain's premier cheese, from the Vale of Belvoir	**Stilton**
a Limburger-type cheese from the Saarland	**Stinkes**
a German, medium-firm, yellow cheese	**Tilsit**
a Swiss soft-ripened cheese	**Vacherin Mont d'Or**
a seasoned, melted cheese with beer over toast, in Britain	**Welsh Rarebit** or **Rabbit**
a pale, delicate Yorkshire cheese	**Wensleydale**
yogurt, in Greece	**yaoúrti**

In the Americas, Asia, Africa, and the Pacific

fétalike Egyptian cheese	**gibna beida**
thick, creamy Egyptian yogurt	**leban zabadi**
a US cheese, originally akin to Limburger	**Liederkranz**

an Egyptian paste of dried cheese and spices	**mish**
a cheddarlike California cheese	**Monterey Jack**
a soft cheese with sugar cane honey, in Argentina	**quesillo con miel de caña**

Desserts and Sweets

Among desserts and sweets from around the world, what is or are. . . ?

In France

a sweet cake soaked in rum and syrup, supposedly named after Ali Baba	**Baba au rhum**
a light, fruit-flavored, often molded custard	**Bavaroise**
fritters or doughnut balls	**beignets**
a dessert, frozen in a rounded mold and filled	**bombe**
chocolate candy, often with cream or nut filling	**bonbon**
a popular Provence biscuit	**caladon**
a molded custard dessert with ladyfingers	**Charlotte Russe**
a country-style cherry tart	**clafouti**
jam or preserves	**confiture**
ice cream	**crème à la glace** or **glacée**
a molded pudding topped with burnt caramel	**crème caramel** or **flan**
whipped cream	**crème fouettée**
a dry almond cookie from Provence	**croquant villaret**
a kind of rich cream-cake	**dariole**
a sugar-coated almond (or pill)	**dragée**
a cream-filled, chocolate-covered pastry	**éclair**
a pastry like a pudding, from Brittany	**far Breton**
a frozen, sherbetlike dessert	**frappé**
sweets, also a sweet tooth	**friandise**
a cake filled with goat cheese, from Angoulême	**fromagier**
sweet waffles, as in France or Belgium	**gaufres**
soft ice cream	**glace italienne**
flaky, butter-rich Breton pastry	**kouign amann**
chewy cookies of almond paste and egg whites	**macaroons**
chestnuts in a heavy, sweet syrup	**marrons glacés**

a molded dessert of chestnut purée and custard	**Nesselrode**
frozen custard in a tall glass, with toppings and cream	**parfait**
tiny, delicate cakes	**petits fours**
the pastries that sparked Proust's memories	**petits madeleines**
cream-filled puff pastries with chocolate sauce	**profiteroles**
liqueur-filled chocolates, from the French Alps	**roseaux d' Annecy**
sherbet	**sorbet**

In Italy

macaroons of sugared egg whites and almonds	**amaretti**
northern Italian cream-puffs	**bignole**
strudel-like central Italian pastry	**bricciata umbria**
fried sweets, as at northern Italian carnivals	**bugie**
a cream-filled pastry roll	**cannoli**
a Genoese rice cake	**farinata**
ice cream	**gelato**
prized chocolates from Turin	**gianduiotti**
Perugian apple pie	**mele a Cartoccio**
fruit-and-nut ice cream	**spumone**
egg, honey, and almond candy from Cremona	**torrone**
the northern Italian hazelnut cake	**torta di nocciole**
rich ice cream with almond or macaroon topping	**tortoni**
a dessert of egg yolks, sugar, and wine	**zabaglione**

Elsewhere in Western Europe

festive rice pudding, in Portugal	**arroz doce**
a Dutch pastry formed like an initial and filled with almond paste	**bankeletter**
Irish spicy fruit-bread, baked with a gold ring	**barm brack**
a fried batter-ball with a fruit center, in Holland	**bollen**
an Irish potato cake with bacon fat and caraway	**boxty**
Belgian gingerbread	**couques de Dinant**
toasted, buttered, round tea breads, in England	**crumpets**
a custard tart with red currant jelly and cream, in England	**dariole**

crystallized fruits in Portugal	**dragée**
a rich Scottish fruit cake	**Dundee cake**
custard, in Spain	**flan**
Dutch dessert pancakes	**flensjes** or **pannekoeken**
a light sponge cake in the French Alps	**gâteau de Savole**
an Austrian sponge cake	**Guglhupf**
an Austrian dessert pancake with stewed fruit	**Kalserschmarren**
a crispy, jam-filled Austrian doughnut	**Krapfen**
a coffee cake or sweet roll, in Austria	**Kuchen**
pitted apricots filled with sugar and boiled in dough, in Austria	**Marillenkknödel**
a molded ground-almond confection	**marzipan**
egg yolks in baked sugar, in Portugal	**ovos moles**
Austro-Hungarian dessert pancakes	**Palatschinken**
a Spanish, boiled-bread and sweet-wine dish	**panada**
custard-and-cinnamon tarts, in Portugal	**Pastels de Nata**
filled pancakes, in Germany	**Pfannkuchen**
fried, sugar-dusted dough balls, in Holland	**poffertjes**
Austrian plum jam–filled dough triangles	**Powidltatschkerl**
cheese tarts, in Portugal	**queijadas**
an Austrian dessert soufflé	**Salzburger Nockerl**
whipped cream, in Austria	**Schlagobers**
German Black Forest cherry cake	**Schwarzwälderkirschtorte**
Dutch spiced ginger-cookies	**speculaas**
spiced, Dutch, butter sponge-cake	**spekkoek**
a British dessert of milk, wine or liquor, and gelatin	**syllabub (Edinburgh fog)**
pastry sheets alternating with fruit, in Germany	**Strudel**
a spiced Dutch Christmas cake	**taal-taal**
a Belgian cake of beet leaves and cheese	**tarte al djote**
a Belgian sugar tart	**tarte au sucre**
a rich Austrian pastry	**Torte**
a British layered sweet dessert	**trifle**
baked egg yolks in a heavy syrup, in Portugal	**trouxas d'ovos**
Irish brittle toffee	**yellow man**

stewed plums used in Austrian desserts	**Zwetschkenröster**

In Eastern Europe

a Polish Easter cake with raisins	**babka wielkanocna**
a Greek (and Middle Eastern) pastry of thin slices of pastry, honey, and nuts	**baklava**
a Bulgarian cheese pastry	**bánitsa**
a Hungarian pasta and jam dessert	**barátfüle (friar's ears)**
fried, sugar-sprinkled twists of dough, in Poland	**chrusty** or **hrusta**
a Hungarian cake with a burnt-sugar top	**dobostorta**
a Greek pastry treat of honey, nuts, and custard,	**galaktoboúreko**
a Romanian doughnut	**gogosi**
plum- or apple-stuffed Polish dumplings	**knedle**
a Polish poppy-seed pastry	**makowiec**
flaky Polish finger biscuits	**mazurki**
a Romanian doughnut, with cheese and cream	**papanasi**
dumplings with blueberries, cherries, or prunes, in Poland	**piero'zki**
a sweet, cream-stuffed cake, in Russia	**pirog**
Romanian cheese pie	**placinta cu brinza**
Hungarian poppy-seed strudel	**rétes**
a dessert cheese roll, in Romania	**rulada rarau**
Polish cheese cake	**sernik**
Hungarian dessert of pasta with curds, sour cream, and pork crackling	**túrós csusza**

In the Americas

slabs of ice cream and sponge cake in liqueur and meringue, baked	**baked Alaska**
Mexican caramel candy	**cajeta**
the Brazilian coconut dessert	**cocada**
the Argentinian dessert of long-boiled, sweet milk	**dulce de leche**
dessert pancakes, in Iceland	**islenzkar pönnukökur**
the Haitian sweet potato pudding	**pain patate**
the Chilean Christmas fruit cake	**pan de pascua**
cactus fruit cakes, from Mexico	**queso de tuna**

the Brazilian egg and coconut dessert	quindins
the Amish molasses and brown sugar pie	shoofly pie

In Asia, Africa, and the Pacific

the Egyptian dessert of custard topped with cake	aish el saraya
the special Egyptian dessert for Ramadan	ata'if
Filipino deep-fried, sugar-coated bananas	banana-cue
Egyptian milk ice or sherbet	dondurma
the Indian rice pudding with fruits and nuts	firnee
bananas served in coconut milk, in Thailand	gluay
the Middle Eastern honey-and-sesame-seed candy	halva
the sweet pastry with prune jam or poppy seeds, eaten by Jews at Purim	hamantasch or homentash
Indian dessert pancakes in syrup	jalebi
syrup-flavored shreds of wheat and chopped nuts in the Middle East	kanafa
the Indian desserts based on boiled-down milk	khoa
sticky rice baked in bamboo, in Thailand	kow laam
Thai egg custard	maw geng
the Bengali dessert of yogurt sweetened with milk	mishti dhoi
a cream of rice and pistachio dessert, in Egypt	muhalabiya
a lime paste, betel nut, aniseed, and cardamom dessert, in India	pan
a South Indian milk pudding	paysaam
fried bananas, in Indonesia	pisang goreng
an Egyptian bread pudding with pine nuts	umm ali
a Turkish rice pudding with saffron	zerde

Wines and Spirits

About wines and spirits around the world, what is . . . ?

In France

the licorice-flavored aperitif	anise
a light drink before a meal, to increase appetite	aperitif
brandy, often of fruits, lit, water of life	aqua vitae or eau de vie
dry, also crude	brut
an open-topped bottle for serving water or wine	carafe
brought to room temperature	chambré
an after-coffee liqueur	chasse
hard cider, from Brittany	cidre bouché
sweet, nonalcoholic cider, from Brittany	cidre doux
dry, dark-red table wine, esp. from Bordeaux	claret
the fine brandy from western France	Cognac
the black-currant brandy	crème de Cassis
a mint-flavored liqueur	crème de menthe
vintage wine	cru
wine contained in a vat	cuvée
raspberry brandy	framboise
liqueur over shaved ice	frappé
fine wines from the Côte d'Or region	grands crus
an anise-and-water drink, as with pernod	pastis
a milky, anisette-flavored apertif	pernod
a glass of beer	une pression or demie
a very good wine, aged 4 years	quadrimum
dry	sec
barrels for storing wine	tonneau
a wine smooth or velvety on the palate	velouté
the grape harvest	vendange
white wine with herbs and spices, as in cocktails	vermouth
white wine	vin blanc
mulled wine	vin chaud
mixed wines	vin coupé
sweet wine	vin doux
wine of the locality or region	vin du pays
light wine	vin léger
ordinary table wine	vin ordinaire or vin de table
pure, unadulterated wine	vin pur

| light-red wine | **vin rosé** |
| red wine | **vin rouge** |

In Italy

sweet	**abboccatto**
chianti simmered with beans and herbs	**chianti fagioli al fiasco**
an after-dinner liqueur	**digestivo**
anise liqueur	**Sambuca**
dry	**secco**
sweet or mild	**soave**
very old	**stravecchio**
old	**vecchio**
wine	**vino**

In Spain and Portugal

medium sweet wine, in Portugal	**adamado**
brandy, in Portugal	**aguardente**
white wine, in Portugal	**branco**
extra dry, as of sparkling wine, in Portugal	**bruto**
beer, in Spain	**cerveza**
sweet wine, in Portugal	**doce**
sparkling wine, in Portugal	**espumante**
fully aged fine wine, in Portugal	**garrafeira** or **reserva**
medium-dry wine, in Portugal	**meio seco**
the rich Portuguese wine from Oporto	**port**
rosé, in Portugal	**rosado**
the chilled, sweetened, wine punch, in Spain	**sangría**
strong wine from Jerez, Spain	**sherry**
red wine, in Portugal	**tinto**
old wine, in Portugal	**velho**
young or "green" wine, in Portugal	**vinho verde**

Elsewhere in Europe (Outside France, Italy, Spain and Portugal)

heavy Dutch eggnog	**advocat**
Scandinavian grain or potato alcohol liquor	**aquavit, akvavit,** or **snaps**
wine made from selected, late-gathered grapes	**Auslese**
dessert wines made from late grapes exposed to the fungus called "noble rot"	**Beerenuaslese**
standard draught beer in Britain	**bitter**
a tart herbal addition to drinks	**bitters**

a tot of jenever (Dutch gin), in Holland	**borrel**
a small, large-handled cup for alcohol, in Russia	**charka**
the sweet, citrusy Greek apertif	**citro**
a narrow-necked bottle encased in wicker	**demijohn**
wine from frozen grapes, in Austria	**Eiswein**
before-lunch German beer, esp, with a hangover	**Frühschoppen**
gin, in Holland	**jenever**
a very large wine bottle	**jeroboam**
dry wine, with no sugar added, in Germany	**Kabinett**
Danish cherry wine	**kijafa**
a drink of white wine and crème de Cassis	**kir**
cherry brandy from Germany's Black Forest	**Kirschwasser**
the juniper-scented North German brandy	**Korn**
vodka with honey and spices, in Poland	**krupnik**
a bitter beer of rye or barley, in Russia	**kvas**
German-style aged beer	**lager**
German export wine	**Liebfraumilch**
made with grains that have been let sprout	**malt**
a sweet, scented Greek aperitif	**mastika**
a milky, anisette-flavored aperitif, in Greece	**oúzo**
a homemade, vodkalike, Irish potato brew	**poteen**
a Greek white wine and resin drink	**retsina**
a powerful liquor, in Germany	**schnapps**
pure unblended whisky, in Scotland	**single malt**
a rich, Austrian wine from late-gathered grapes	**Spätlese**
a wine-and-soda combination, usually served cold	**spritzer**
strong dark beer, as in Britain	**stout**
a Hungarian dessert wine	**tokay**
Beerenuaslese wine made from almost-dry grapes	**Trockenbeerenauslese**
Russian whiskey, often of potato and grain mash	**vodka** or **wódka**

the liquor distilled from grain, e.g., corn or rye	**whiskey (whisky)**

In the Americas

powerful "fire water," in Chile	**aguardiente**
a Brazilian drink of fruit juices and rum	**batidas**
local Brazilian rum	**cachaça**
a South American liquor of maize and cane sugar; a grape-based drink akin to hard cider, in Chile	**chicha**
a Mexican drink of tequila and lime juice with salt	**margarita**
a distilled grape drink, in Chile	**pisco**
a drink of rums and fruit juice, in Martinique	**un planteur**
a distilled grape drink, in Bolivia	**singani**
a powerful Mexican liquor distilled from the century plant	**tequila**
a powerful punch, in Martinique	**ti-punch**

In Asia, Africa, and the Pacific

the Tunisian liqueur distilled from figs	**bookha**
Turkish brandy	**konyak**
fermented mare's milk, in Central Asia	**kummis**
a powerful Filipino drink	**lambanog**
milky-white rice liquor from Korea	**makkolli**
Egyptian bock beer	**marzen**
a Turkish orange liqueur	**mersin**
a milky, anisette-flavored aperitif	**raki (Turkey), arak (Lebanon),** or **zibib**
a Turkish grape and aniseed drink	**raki**
a powerful rice drink, in Japan	**sake**
a powerful rice or millet drink, in China	**samshu**
Korean "burned liquor"	**soju**
the Tunisian liqueur distilled from dates	**thibarine**
fermented palm juice, in India	**toddy**
plum wine, in Japan	**umeshu**

Coffees and Other Non-Alcoholic Drinks

Among coffees and other drinks from around the world, what is or are . . . ?

In Europe

coffee with a little milk, in Austria	**Brauner**
coffee, in France	**café**
coffee with milk, in France	**café au lait**
coffee with hot milk, in Italy	**caffèlatte**
decaffeinated coffee, in Italy	**caffè Hag**
coffee with a drop of milk, in Italy	**caffè macchiato**
espresso with steamed, foaming milk, in Italy	**cappuccino**
hot chocolate with whipped cream, in Italy	**cioccolata con panna**
lemonade	**citronade**
strong, black coffee served in a small cup	**demitasse**
whipped cream, with some coffee, in Austria	**Doppelschlag**
hot, black coffee in a glass, in Austria	**Einspänner**
cold coffee with ice cream, whipped cream and rum, in Austria	**Eiskaffee**
rich, black coffee, in Italy	**espresso**
frozen or iced drink, as made with fruit and milk	**frappé**
coffee and whipped cream, in Austria	**Kaffee mit Schlag**
black coffee with ice and rum, in Austria	**Mazagran**
half-coffee, half-milk, in Austria	**Melange**
sweet, black, after-dinner coffee, in Australia	**Mokka**

In the Americas

a thick Mexican drink of water from boiled tortilla dough	**atole**
syrup, soda, and milk drink, esp. in NYC	**egg cream**
a drink of milk, eggs, and rum, brandy, or wine	**egg nog**

In Asia, Africa, and the Pacific

a Filipino drink from young coconuts	**buko**
tea, in China and Central Asia	**cha**

a Filipino sugar-cane juice and fruit drink	**halo halo**
sugar-cane water, in Singapore	**kam chia chui**
a cooling raspberry-colored Egyptian drink	**karkade**
buttermilk, in India	**lassi**
medium-sweet thick coffee, in Egypt	**mazboota**
lemonade, in India	**nimboo pani**
coffee, in Arabia	**qahwah**
bitter thick coffee, in Egypt	**saada**
sugar-and-mint tea from Tunisia	**thé vert**
coconut water, in Singapore	**ya chui**
sweet thick coffee, in Egypt	**ziyada**

In Other Words

(See also sections on topics of special interest, e.g., International Foods and Dining in *Everyday Life*)

Words from the French

From the French language, what is the word or phrase for . . .?

Hail and Farewell

come in or enter	**entrez**
come on or let's go	**allons**
do you speak French	**parlez-vous français**
excuse me	**pardonnez-moi**
fair to middling or so-so, answering how are you	**Comme çi, comme ça**
forget it, or say no more about it	**brisons-là**
go away or be gone	**allez-vous-en**
goodbye or so long	**adieu**
good day, as a greeting	**bon jour**
good night or evening	**bon soir**
good trip, said in farewell	**bon voyage**
how are you, to a close friend	**ça va**
how are you, to a relative stranger	**comment allez-vous**
look here!	**tiens**
march forward	**en avant**
OK or that's good enough	**assez bien**
respond (if you) please, as to an invitation	**répondez s'il vous plaît (R. S. V. P.)**
see here	**voyez**
shut up or close your mouth	**fermez la bouche**
stop	**arrêtez**

thank you	**merci**
there (it is)	**voilà**
till we meet again or goodbye	**au revoir**
to your health, as in a toast	**à votre santé**
very well or very good	**très bien**
welcome, as a greeting	**bienvenue**

Time, Months, and Seasons

January	**Janvier**
February	**Février**
March	**Mars**
April	**Avril**
May	**Mai**
June	**Juin**
July	**Juillet**
August	**Août**
September	**Septembre**
October	**Octobre**
November	**Novembre**
December	**Décembre**
spring	**printemps**
summer	**été**
autumn	**automne**
winter	**hiver**
dawn	**aube**
morning	**matin**
afternoon	**après-midi**
twilight, lit. half-day	**demi-jour**
evening	**soir**
night	**nuit**
a week from today	**d'aujourd'hui en huit**
a fortnight from today	**d'aujourd'hui en quinze**
day	**jour**
week	**semaine**
month	**mois**
year	**année**
century or a cultural age	**siècle**
end of the century, esp. the 19th	**fin de siècle**
era or long period of time	**époque**

Numbers

one	**un**
two	**deux**
three	**trois**
four	**quatre**
five	**cinq**
six	**six**
seven	**sept**
eight	**huit**
nine	**neuf**
ten	**dix**

eleven	onze
twelve	douze
thirteen	treize
fourteen	quatorze
fifteen	quinze
sixteen	seize
seventeen	dix-sept
eighteen	dix-huit
nineteen	dix-neuf
twenty	vingt
fifty	cinquante
hundred	cent

Buildings and Habitations

administrative district, as in a city	arrondissement
bathroom	salle de bain
building with public toilets	chalet de nécessité
church	église
customs or customhouse	douane
defined section within a larger area	enclave
dining room	salle à manger
library	bibliothèque
living room, esp. where celebrities gather	salon
medieval dungeon entered by a trap door	oubliette
open-sided roofed carriage entrance	porte-cochère
round or oval window, lit. a bull's eye	oeil-de-boeuf
salt-water bath	bain d'eau de mer
school	école
shore or seacoast	côte
small second home, lit. a foot on the earth	pied-à-terre
steam bath	bain de vapeur
street	rue
suburb, quarter, or area around a city	faubourg
town house or city mansion	hôtel particulier
train's sleeping-car, as on the Orient Express	wagon-lit

In Fashion

according to strict rules of etiquette	de rigueur
beyond normal bounds or bizarre	outré
cap with no brim	beret
characteristic, orig. a stamp seal	cachet

clothing that is styled to be split or cut open	**fendu**
curtain across a door or arch	**portière**
decorative ball or tuft, esp. on a hat	**pompon**
dress designer or dressmaker	**couturier** (fem. **-rière**)
dressed in one's "Sunday best" clothes	**endimanché**
an expert, with taste and judgment	**connoisseur**
eyeglasses that perch on the end of the nose	**pince-nez**
fabric including metal threads, esp. gold or silver	**lamé**
fashionable, chic, stylish	**à la mode**
flower or small bouquet worn in a buttonhole	**boutonnière**
full, puffed-out hair style	**bouffant**
giving a shimmering effect	**moiré**
good style, also fashionable society	**bon ton**
grand or elegant	**de luxe**
hair stylist	**coiffeur** (fem. **-euse**) or **friseur** (**-euse**)
hat	**chapeau**
having a lining, applied to clothes	**doublé**
hood or cowl	**capuce** or **capuchon**
in bad taste	**de mauvaise goût**
in the American style or fashion	**à l'américaine**
in the Chinese style or fashion	**à la chinoise**
in the Dutch style or fashion	**à la hollandaise**
in the English style or fashion	**à l'anglaise**
in the French style or fashion	**à la française**
in the German style or fashion	**à l'allemand**
in the Greek style or fashion	**à la grecque**
in the Irish style or fashion	**à l'irlandaise**
in the Italian style or fashion	**à l'italienne**
in the Parisian style or fashion	**à la parisienne**
in the Provençe style or fashion	**à la provençale**
in the Russian style or fashion	**à la russe**
in the Spanish style or fashion	**à l'espagnole**
in the usual or ordinary style or fashion	**à l'ordinaire**
knot or hair behind or atop the head	**chignon**
latest fashion, lit. the latest cry	**dernier cri**
low-cut neckline, as on a gown	**décolletage**
model of perfection	**beau idéal**
odds and ends, miscellaneous knickknacks	**bric-à-brac**

old-fashioned, from the old times or out of vogue	du vieux temps, démodé, or déclassé
rustle of fabrics, as of silk, or fussy clothes	froufrou
sedan chair	porte-chaise
sheer, loose gown, esp. worn in private	négligé
square scarf, in France	foulard
stylish or smart	chic or chi chi
suitcase that opens into 2 halves	portmanteau
undressed or very casually dressed	déshabillé
the vanguard, esp. in art	avant-garde
with spirit or verve, lit. a plume of feathers	panache
woman's bathrobe	peignoir
woman's dressing room, lit. a pouting place	boudoir
world of fashion, lit. the beautiful world	beau monde

Life and Loving

(See also Personal Relationships in *Everyday Life*)

abstracted or absentminded	distrait
affair of honor, especially a duel	affaire d'honneur
always in love	toujours amoureux
American-born people of French or Spanish parents	créole
at the home or place of . . .	chez . . .
between us or between four eyes	entre nous or entre quatre yeux
body of work	oeuvre
boredom	ennui
born, referring to a person's name given at birth	né (m.) or née (f.)
brother	frère
buttocks or rear end	derrière
called or known as	dit
chambermaid, or generally a female servant	fille de chambre
charming, captivating woman	charmante
chubby or plump, a euphemism for fat	enbonpoint
composure under pressure, lit. cold blood	sang-froid
crib, nursery, or manger	crèche
custodian of a building	concierge
dean, the eldest, most senior person	doyen
dear or darling	chéri

distinguished, elegant, or aristocratic	**distingué**
dregs of society, a "pack of dogs"	**canaille**
elderly man, lit. old beard	**vieille barbe**
emigrant or expatriate	**émigré**
encounter, esp. an antagonistic one	**rencontre**
evening party or celebration	**soirée**
fair	**foire**
fantasized illness of a hypochondriac	**malade imaginaire**
feeling of having seen or experienced something before, contrary to fact	**déjà vu**
fellow member or comrade in an organization	**confrère**
first public appearance, such as a "coming out"	**début**
for two, as in an intimate relationship	**à deux**
forced labor without pay, originally feudal	**corvée**
foreign worker, usually a young woman, hired to care for children	**au pair**
former, the late, or ex-	**ci-devant**
free, easy, unrestrained, even flip	**dégagé**
friendly, easygoing disposition of person	**bonhomie**
gentleman or gallant knight	**chevalier**
German, esp. in WWI	**boche**
good friend, often also said of one's love	**bon ami ((f.) bonne amie)**
good will and warmth among good friends	**camaraderie**
grave digger or ditchdigger	**fossoyeur**
happiness	**bonheur**
headache	**mal de tête**
heartbreaking sorrow	**crêve-coeur**
here lies . . . , as in an epitaph	**ci-gît**
holiday, celebration, or festival	**fête**
homesickness	**mal du pays**
in love or infatuated	**épris**
in the privacy and informality of the family	**en famille**
joy of life	**joie de vivre**
juvenile or immature	**jejune**
knowing proper behavior, lit. to know how to do	**savoir-faire**
ladies' man, also a fair-haired man	**blondin**

last blow, to relieve the suffering of the dying	**coup de grâce**
long line of followers, as at a funeral	**cortège**
love affair or romance	**affaire d'amour** or **de coeur**
love at first sight, like thunder and lightning	**coup de foudre**
love letter, lit. a sweet note	**billet-doux**
love or self-respect, also vanity	**amour-propre**
loving looks, lit. sweet eyes	**yeux doux**
marriage to someone of a lower class	**mésalliance**
melancholy or sadness	**souci**
middle-ages, lit. between two ages	**entre deux âges**
middle-class people, in business or trade	**bourgeoisie**
midwife	**sage-femme**
misbehaving child	**enfant terrible**
newly rich	**nouveau riche**
noble gesture, often impressive but empty	**beau geste**
off color	**risqué**
one making a first public appearance	**débutant (f. -e)**
one taught or forwarded by another	**protégé**
one with recently achieved status or success	**arrivé** or **parvenu**
one with unfulfilled ambitions, often in the arts	**manqué**
outline of biographical data, esp. employment	**résumé**
person devoted to sensuous pleasures	**bon vivant**
person who enjoys life	**bon viveur**
person's specialty or profession	**métier**
polite courtesy or service	**devoir**
pregnant, also a fortress's defensive wall	**enceinte**
private meeting, esp. of 2, lit. head to head	**tête-à-tête**
quick reply, originally from fencing	**riposte**
rascally rake	**roué**
recountal of one's love life	**vie amoureuse**
revelation of a previously hidden scandal	**exposé**
rumor or gossip, a "noise"	**bruit**
rumor	**on-dit** or **ouï-dire**
seasickness	**mal de mer**

sore throat	**mal à la gorge**
self-possession, lit. perpendicularity	**aplomb**
self-styled, or pretended, lit. calling one's self	**soi disant**
siren or accomplished seductress	**femme fatale**
sister or nun	**soeur**
social blunder, lit. a false step	**faux pas**
social climber	**arriviste**
social ease, lit. to know how to live	**savoir-vivre**
something indefinable, lit. I do not know what	**je ne sais quoi**
son, or junior, as comparing father and son	**fils**
sophisticated and elegant	**soigné**
sour pout	**moue**
story-teller	**raconteur**
stranger or alien	**étranger**
student or pupil	**élève**
super-patriot or jingoist	**chauvinist**
sunstroke, also a blush or flushed face	**coup de soleil**
taunt or gibe	**coup de bec**
teasing, flirting woman	**coquette**
too much, often of an undesired person	**de trop**
toothache	**mal de dents**
to the final end, as in a duel to the death	**à outrance**
traveler, as in early North America	**voyageur**
traveling salesman	**commis-voyageur**
unacceptable in former social circles	**déclassé**
uproar or fuss	**brouhaha**
vile hoax or lie intended to deceive	**canard**
visiting or calling card	**carte de visite (c.d.v.)**
waiter or young boy	**garçon**
well-bred young lady	**demoiselle**
wise person	**savant**
well-known, often scandalous case	**cause célèbre**
well versed or knowledgeable	**au fair**
woman friend, commonly a mistress	**belle amie**
woman's confinement while giving birth	**accouchement**

Words from the German

From the German language, what is the word or phrase for . . . ?

Hail and Farewell

attention!	**Achtung**
certainly or yes	**ja wohl**
cheer up or look alive	**frisch auf**
do you speak German	**Sprechen sie Deutsch**
farewell or till we meet again	**auf Wiedersehen**
good health, said after a sneeze	**Gesundheit**
how are you	**wie geht's**
never mind	**das schadet nichts**
never mind or it doesn't matter	**das tut nichts**
please, also a response to thank you	**bitte**
thank you very much	**danke schön**
that's enough or that will do	**das tut's**

Time, Months, and Seasons

January	**Januar**
February	**Februar**
March	**März**
April	**April**
May	**Mai**
June	**Juni**
July	**Juli**
August	**August**
September	**September**
October	**Oktober**
November	**November**
December	**Dezember**
spring	**Frühling**
summer	**Sommer**
autumn	**Herbst**
winter	**Winter**
dawn	**Morgendämmerung**
morning	**Morgen**
afternoon	**Nachtmittage**
twilight	**Dämmerung**
evening	**Abend**
night	**Nacht**
day	**Tag**
week	**Woche**
month	**Monat**
year	**Jahr**
century	**Jahrhundert**

Numbers

one	**eins**

two	zwei
three	drei
four	vier
five	fünf
six	sechs
seven	sieben
eight	acht
nine	neun
ten	zehn
eleven	elf
twelve	zwölf
thirteen	dreizehn
fourteen	vierzehn
fifteen	fünfzehn
sixteen	sechzehn
seventeen	siebzehn
eighteen	achtzehn
nineteen	neunzehn
twenty	zwanzig
fifty	fünfzig
hundred	hundert

Words from the Italian

From the Italian language, what is the word or phrase for . . . ?

Hail and Farewell

by your leave, or with your permission	con permesso
good day, as a greeting	buon giorno
good evening, said in greeting	buona sera
good night, said in farewell	buona notte
good trip or bon voyage	buon viaggio
happy return	felice ritorno
hello or goodbye, hail or farewell	ciao
hello, a telephone greeting	pronto
how do you do or how are you	come sta or state
how goes it with you or how are things	come va
intimate meeting, esp. of 2, lit. to 4 eyes	a quatr'occhi
is Italian spoken	si parla italiano
stop, or enough	basta
till we meet again	arrivederci or arrivederla
to your health, as in a toast	alla vostra salute
welcome	ben venuto
wonderful or superb, as at a performance	bravo or bravissimo

Time, Months, and Seasons

January	gennaio
February	febbraio
March	marzo
April	aprile
May	màggio
June	giugno
July	lùllo
August	agosto
September	settèmbre
October	ottobre
November	novèmbre
December	dicèmbre
spring	primavera
summer	estate
autumn	autunno
winter	invèrno
dawn	alba
morning	mattina
afternoon	pomeriggio
twilight	crepùscolo
evening	sera
night	nòtte
day	giorno
week	settimana
month	mese
year	anno
century	sècolo

Numbers

one	uno
two	due
three	tre
four	quattro
five	cinque
six	sèi
seven	sètte
eight	otto
nine	nòve
ten	dièci
eleven	ùndici
twelve	dódici
thirteen	trédici
fourteen	quattòrdici
fifteen	quindici
sixteen	sédici
seventeen	diciassètte
eighteen	diciòtto
nineteen	diciannòve
twenty	vente

| fifty | cinquanta |
| hundred | cènto |

Words from the Latin

(See also specific topics, esp. Reference Words and Phrases in *World of Letters*, Times of Our Lives in *Everyday Life*, and Religious Invocations from Latin in *World of Philosophy and Belief*.)

From the Latin language, what is the word or phrase for . . . ?

Hail and Farewell

farewell	bene vale (b. v.)
farewell and be happy	vive, vale(que)
go with me, esp. of a guide carried with a person	vade mecum
hail and farewell	ave atque vale
hail, emperor, we who are about to die salute you	Ave Imperator! Morituri te salutamus
I am here, as in rollcall in some British schools	ad sum
let him go forth well, a good personal reference	bene exeat
long live the king (queen)	vivat rex (regina)

Time, Months, and Seasons

January	Ianuarius
February	Februarius
March	Martius
April	Aprilis
May	Maius
June	Iunius
July	Iulius or Quinctilis
August	Augustus or Sextilis
September	September
October	October
November	Novembris or November
December	December
spring	ver or tempus
summer	aestas
autumn	autumnus
winter	hiems or tempus hibernum (or hiemale)
dawn	aurora, prima lux, or diluculum
morning	mane, tempus matutinum, or matutino tempore
afternoon	post meridiem or postmeridianum tempus
twilight	crepusculum
evening	vesper or tempus vespertinum
night	nox or noct-

day	**dies**
week	**septem dies** or **septem dierum spatium**
month	**mensis**
year	**annus, annuum tempus,** or **anni spatium**
century	**centum anni** or **saeculum**

Numbers

one	**unus**
two	**duo**
three	**tres**
four	**quattuor**
five	**quinque**
six	**sex**
seven	**septem**
eight	**octo**
nine	**novem**
ten	**decem**
eleven	**undecim**
twelve	**duodecim**
thirteen	**tredecim**
fourteen	**quattuordecim**
fifteen	**quindecim**
sixteen	**sedecim**
seventeen	**septemdecim**
eighteen	**duodeviginti**
nineteen	**undeviginti**
twenty	**viginti**
fifty	**quinquaginta**
hundred	**centum**

Words from the Spanish or Hispanic Languages

From the Spanish or Hispanic languages, what is the word or phrase for . . . ?

Hail and Farewell

bravo	**olé**
exclamation, esp. of awe	**caramba**
go with God, said at parting	**vaya con Dios**
good afternoon	**buenas tardes**
good day or good morning	**buenos días**
good luck	**buena suerte**
good night or good evening	**buenas noches**
goodbye until we meet again	**hasta la vista**
goodbye	**adios**
how are you	**cómo está**
how goes it with you	**cómo le va**
I kiss your hands (or feet), said in greeting	**beso las manos (los pies)**

let us go	**vámonos**
Spanish is spoken	**se habla español**
to your health, as in a toast	**a vuestra salud**
watch out or be careful	**cuidado**
welcome	**bienvenido**
who kisses your hand, the formal ending of a letter to a woman	**que besa su mano (Q.B.S.M.)**
whose hands (feet) I kiss, a ritual phrase	**cuyas manos beso (c.m.b.)** or **cuyos pies beso (c.p.b.)**

Time, Months, and Seasons

January	**enero**
February	**febrero**
March	**marzo**
April	**abril**
May	**mayo**
June	**junio**
July	**julio**
August	**agosto**
September	**septiembre**
October	**octubre**
November	**noviembre**
December	**diciembre**
spring	**primavera**
summer	**verano**
autumn	**otoño**
winter	**invierno**
dawn	**alba** or **madrugada**
morning	**mañana**
afternoon	**tarde**
twilight	**crepúscolo**
evening	**noche** or **tarde**
night	**noche**
day	**día**
week	**semana**
month	**mes**
month we are now in	**corriente (cte.)**
year	**año**
century or a cultural age	**siglo**

Numbers

one	**uno**
two	**dos**
three	**tres**
four	**cuatro**
five	**cinco**
six	**seis**
seven	**siete**
eight	**ocho**

nine	nueve
ten	diez
eleven	once
twelve	doce
thirteen	trece
fourteen	catorce
fifteen	quince
sixteen	dieciseis
seventeen	diecisiete
eighteen	dieciocho
nineteen	diecinueve
twenty	veine
fifty	cincuenta
hundred	ciento

Buildings and Habitations

castle, palace, or fortress	alcázar
cattle ranch in Hispanic America	estancia
city or town	ciudad
deep, often-dry ravine, as in SW US	barranco or barranca
fountain or spring	fuente
house (little house)	casa (caseta)
military fort or prison	presidio
pier or wharf	embarcadero
post office	correro
royal road or highway	camino real
small canyon in SW US	cañoncito
state	estado
tree-lined public walk or avenue	alameda
ward or district	barrio
water course or dry gully	arroyo

Life and Loving

acquaintance	conocido
American-born people of Spanish parents	criollo
blanketlike cloak with a head opening	poncho or serape
brigand or highwayman	bandolero
bullfighter, in general	toreador or torero
cigar, a long, tapering one	panatela
companion or friend, originally a godfather	compadre
conqueror, especially in the New World	conquistador
cowboy, in Mexico	charro
cowboy's heavy jacket	chaqueta
exaggerated masculinity	machismo or macho
fan of a sport or activity	aficionado
fight or quarrel	camorra

fighter who actually kills the bull	**matador**
friend	**amigo**
herder or cowboy, in Hispanic lands	**vaquero**
judge or a justice of the peace, as in SW US	**alcalde**
knight, specifically a horseman	**caballero**
lacy scarf worn over a high comb	**mantilla**
lady	**doña**
the leather coverings for the front of the legs of horse riders in Mexico and the SW	**chaparajos** or **chaps**
married lady, often a chaperone	**dueña**
master or landlord of an estate or home	**dueño**
nap in the afternoon	**siesta**
one of mixed ethnic origin, esp. Indian-Spanish	**mestizo**
rider who irritates the bull, in bullfighting	**picador**
Spanish or a Spaniard	**español**
wide-brimmed hat, as in Mexico	**sombrero**
vestlike Spanish jacket, open at the front	**bolero**

Politics and People

Modern U.S. Presidents, Their Families and Advisors

The Bush Years (1989-)

Among George Herbert Walker Bush's family, friends, and advisors, who was or were his . . . ?

wife	**Barbara Pierce**
springer spaniel	**Millie**
Vice-President	**James Danforth Quayle, 3rd**
Sec. of State	**James Baker, 3rd**
Sec. of Defense	**Richard Cheney**
proposed Sec. of Defense, rejected by Senate	**John Tower**
National Security Advisor	**Lt. Gen. Brent Scowcroft**
delegate to the United Nations	**Thomas Pickering**
CIA head	**William Webster**
Chief of Staff	**John Sununu**
Sec. of Treasury	**Nicholas Brady**
Director of the FBI	**William Sessions**
Attorney General	**Richard Thornburgh**
Sec. of Commerce	**Robert Mosbacher**
Budget Director	**Richard Darman**
Sec. of Education	**Lauro Cavazos**
Sec. of Labor	**Elizabeth Hanford Dole**
Sec. of Interior	**Manuel Lujan**
Environmental Protection Agency head	**William Reilly**
Sec. of Agriculture	**Clayton Yeutter**
Sec. of Housing and Urban Development	**Jack Kemp**
Sec. of Health and Human Services	**Louis Sullivan**
Sec. of Energy	**Adm. James Watkins**
Sec. of Transportation	**Samuel Skinner**
Drug Czar	**William Bennett**
Trade Representative	**Carla Hills**
Press Secretary	**Marlin Fitzwater**

The Reagan Years (1981–1989)

Among Ronald Reagan's family, friends, and advisors, who was or were his . . . ?

wife while president	**Nancy (Anne Frances Robbins) Davis**
children with Nancy Davis	**Patricia** and **Ronald**
1st wife	**Jane Wyman**
children with Jane Wyman	**Maureen** and **Michael**
Vice-President and successor	**George Bush**
1st Sec. of State, former NATO rep.	**Gen. Alexander Haig, Jr.**
2nd Sec. of State	**George Shultz**
Ass't. Sec. of State for Latin America	**Elliott Abrams**
1st Sec. of Defense	**Caspar Weinberger**
National Security Advisors during Iran-Contra	**Robert MacFarlane,** then **Adm. John Poindexter**
successor to Poindexter, then Weinberger	**Frank Carlucci**
last National Security Advisor, Bush's head of Joint Chiefs	**Lt. Gen. Colin Powell**
civilian Sec. of the Navy, a novelist	**John Lehman**
1st CIA head	**William Casey**
2nd CIA head, formerly at the FBI	**William Webster**
1st Chief of Staff, then Treasury Sec.	**James Baker**
1st Sec. of Treasury, later Chief of Staff	**Donald Regan**
Chief of Staff after Iran-Contra hearings	**Howard Baker**
1st delegate to the United Nations	**Jeane Kirkpatrick**
Kirkpatrick's successor	**Vernon Walters**
Webster's successor at the FBI	**William Sessions**
1st Attorney General	**William French Smith**
controversial 2nd Attorney General and longtime advisor	**Edwin Meese, 3rd**
3rd Attorney General, ex-Pennsylvania gov.	**Richard Thornburgh**
Sec. of Commerce, killed in a rodeo accident	**C. Malcolm Baldridge**
1st Budget Director	**David Stockman**
Sec. of Education, who issued *A Nation at Risk* report	**Terrell Bell**
much-investigated 1st Sec. of Labor	**Raymond Donovan**

"silent" Sec. of HUD	**Samuel Pierce, Jr.**
embattled 1st Sec. of Interior	**James Watt**
2nd Sec. of Transportation	**Elizabeth Hanford Dole**
advisors convicted of influence-peddling	**Michael Deaver** and **Lyn Nofziger**
press sec. who said he made up quotes	**Larry Speakes**
press sec. shot in 1981 with Reagan	**James Brady**
Secret Service agent shot with Reagan	**Timothy ..... .hy**
Washington, D. C., police officer shot with Reagan	**Thomas Delahanty**

Other Iran-Contra Figures

Among figures in the Iran-Contra affair, who was or were . . . ?

Lt. Col. who ran the Iran-Contra operations from the White House	**Oliver North**
North's secretary	**Fawn Hall**
North's courier	**Robert Owen**
the ex-Air Force general who headed the Iran initiative	**Richard Secord**
Secord's Iranian-American partner	**Albert Hakim**
the Iran arms-dealer and Saudi Arabian financier involved in the Iran initiative	**Manucher Ghorbanifar** and **Adnan Khashoggi**
the potentate who donated $10 million to the Contras	**Sultan of Brunei**
Rep. heads of the Iran-Contra hearings	**Sen. Warren Rudman** and **Rep. Richard Cheney**
Dem. heads of the Iran-Contra hearings	**Sen. Daniel Inouye** and **Rep. Lee Hamilton**
Special Prosecutor (Independent Counsel)	**Lawrence Walsh**
Federal judge for North's Iran-Contra trial	**Gerhard Gesell**

The Carter Years (1977–1981)

Among Jimmy (James Earle) Carter's family, friends, and advisors, who was or were his . . . ?

wife	**Rosalynn Smith**
mother	**Miz' Lillian**
daughter who lived in the White House	**Amy**

brother linked with Libya	**Billy**
Vice-President, would-be successor	**Walter Mondale**
1st Sec. of State	**Cyrus Vance**
2nd Sec. of State	**Edmund Muskie**
Sec. of Defense	**Harold Brown**
1st Attorney General	**Griffin Bell**
1st HEW Sec.	**Joseph Califano, Jr.**
2nd HEW Sec., formerly with HUD	**Patricia Roberts Harris**
1st Sec. of Transportation	**Brock Adams**
1st Sec. of Energy	**James Schlesinger**
Sec. of Education	**Shirley Hufstedler**
embattled OMB director and old friend	**Bert Lance**
UN delegate, later Atlanta mayor, earlier Martin Luther King, Jr. advisor	**Andrew Young**

The Ford Years (1974–1977)

Among Gerald R. Ford's (born Leslie Lynch King) family, friends, and advisors, who was or were his . . . ?

wife	**Elizabeth "Betty" Warren Bloomer**
Vice-President, appointed by Congress	**Nelson Rockefeller**
Sec. of State	**Henry Kissinger**
1st Sec. of Defense (Nixon's 3rd)	**James Schlesinger**
Sec. of Treasury (Nixon's 4th)	**William Simon**
Chief of Staff	**Richard Cheney**
National Security Advisor	**Lt. Gen. Brent Scowcroft**
1st Sec. of Agriculture (Nixon's 2nd)	**Earl Butz**
1st HEW Sec. (Nixon's 3rd)	**Caspar Weinberger**
2nd Sec. of Transportation	**William Coleman, Jr.**

The Nixon Years (1969–1974)

Among Richard Milhous Nixon's family, friends and advisors, who was or were his . . . ?

wife	**(Thelma) Patricia Ryan**
daughter married from the White House	**Tricia**
daughter who married David Eisenhower	**Julie**
1st Vice President, forced to resign	**Spiro Agnew**

2nd Vice President	**Gerald Ford**
1st Sec. of State	**William Rogers**
2nd Sec. of State, previously National Security Advisor	**Henry Kissinger**
1st Sec. of Defense	**Melvin Laird**
2nd Sec. of Defense, then HEW Sec., later Attorney General who resigned rather than carry out the Sat. Night Massacre, Oct. 20, 1973	**Elliot Richardson**
1st Attorney General, then head of Committee to Re-elect the President (CREEP), later jailed re: Watergate	**John Mitchell**
Attorney General after Mitchell	**Richard Kleindienst**
Mitchell's talkative wife	**Martha**
2nd Sec. of Treasury, wounded with Kennedy	**John Connally**
1st Sec. of Commerce in Watergate	**Maurice Stans**
1st Sec. of Transportation	**John Volpe**
1st Sec. of Labor, then 2nd Sec. of Treasury	**George Shultz**
special counsel who pleaded guilty to obstructing justice over the break-in at Daniel Ellsberg's psychiatrist's, re: the Pentagon Papers	**Charles Colson**

Other Watergate Figures

Among other Watergate figures, who was or were (the) . . . ?

the people who actually broke into the Democratic Nat. HQ in Washington, D.C.'s Watergate building	**Bernard Barker, Virgilio Gonzalez, Eugenio Martinez, James McCord, and Frank Sturgis**
the novel-writing White House consultant and Watergate conspirator	**E. Howard Hunt**
a leading "plumber" in the Pentagon Papers affair	**G. Gordon Liddy**
head of Nixon's "dirty tricks" campaign	**Donald Segretti**
the White House counsel who wrote *Blind Ambition*	**John Dean**
the White House advisor who later wrote *Washington: Behind Closed Doors*	**John D. Ehrlichman**

the White House Chief of Staff convicted in the Watergate cover-up	**H. R. Haldeman**
The White House communications aide and deputy director of CREEP involved in the Watergate cover-up	**Jeb Stuart Magruder**
the acting FBI director who resigned over destruction of documents	**L. Patrick Gray**
Nixon's personal attorney, involved in CREEP disbursements	**Herbert Kalmbach**
the special Watergate prosecutor, fired in the Sat. Night Massacre	**Archibald Cox**
the Deputy Attorney General fired with Cox	**William Ruckelshaus**
the Justice Department official who did the Sat. Night Massacre firings, later a rejected Supreme Court nominee	**Robert Bork**
Cox's successor as Watergate special prosecutor	**Leon Jaworski**
the White House official who 1st testified about the existence of Nixon's office tapes	**Alexander Butterfield**
Nixon's secretary	**Rose Mary Woods**
House Watergate Committee leader	**Peter Rodino**
Senate Watergate Committee leader	**Sam Ervin**
Washington Post's investigative reporters	**Bob Woodward** and **Carl Bernstein**
Woodward and Bernstein's anonymous source	**Deep Throat**
Federal judge deciding on the Nixon tapes	**John Sirica**

The Johnson Years (1963–1969)

Among Lyndon Baines Johnson's family, friends, and advisors, who was or were his . . . ?

wife	**Claudia Alta "Lady Bird" Taylor**
daughters	**Lynda Bird** and **Luci Baines**
Vice-President	**Hubert Humphrey**
Sec. of State	**Dean Rusk**
2nd Sec of Defense	**Clark Clifford**

| 2nd Attorney General | **Nicholas Katzenbach** |
| 3rd Attorney General | **Ramsey Clark** |

The Kennedy Years (1961–1963)

Among John Fitzgerald Kennedy's family, friends, and advisors, who was or were his . . . ?

wife, later married to Greek shipping tycoon Aristotle Onassis	**Jacqueline Lee Bouvier**
daughter	**Caroline**
son who saluted his father's coffin	**John (John-John)**
son who died 2 days after birth	**Patrick**
father, FDR's SEC head and ambassador to Britain	**Joseph Kennedy**
mother	**Rose Fitzgerald Kennedy**
maternal grandfather, former mayor of Boston	**John "Honey Boy" Fitzgerald**
oldest brother, killed in WWII	**Joseph**
2nd brother, his attorney general, killed in 1968	**Robert Fitzgerald**
RFK's wife	**Ethel**
their youngest brother, a senator and presidential contender	**Edward (Ted) Kennedy**
Sec. of State	**Dean Rusk**
Sec. of Defense	**Robert McNamara**
Sec. of Treasury	**C. Douglas Dillon**
Sec. of Agriculture	**Orville Freeman**
Sec. of Interior	**Stewart Udall**
Sec. of Commerce	**Luther Hodges**
1st Sec. of Labor, later on the Supreme Court	**Arthur Goldberg**
1st HEW Sec	**Abraham Ribicoff**
head of the Peace Corps	**Sargent Shriver**
advisor and key speechwriter	**Theodore Sorenson**

The Eisenhower Years (1953–1961)

Among Dwight David Eisenhower's family, friends, and advisors, who was or were his . . . ?

wife	**Marie Geneva "Mamie" Doud**
brother, a college president	**Milton**
his WWII driver and lover	**Kay Summersby (Morgan)**
grandson and biographer, who married his V-P's daughter	**David Eisenhower**
Vice-President	**Richard M. Nixon**

Nixon's dog, part of a key speech	**Checkers**
1st Sec. of State	**John Foster Dulles**
1st Attorney General	**Herbert Brownell, Jr.**
2nd Attorney General	**William Rogers**
1st Sec. of Commerce	**Sinclair Weeks**
Sec. of Agriculture	**Ezra Taft Benson**
Sec. of Interior	**Douglas McKay**
1st Sec. of HEW	**Oveta Culp Hobby**
advisor forced to resign over a vicuna coat	**Sherman Adams**

The Truman Years (1945–1953)

Among Harry S Truman's family, friends, and advisors, who was or were his . . . ?

wife	**Elizabeth Virginia "Bess" Wallace**
daughter	**Margaret**
Vice-President	**Alben Barkley**
2nd Sec. of State	**James Byrnes**
3rd Sec. of State, later Sec. of Defense	**George Marshall**
4th Sec. of State	**Dean Acheson**
Sec. of the Navy, then Sec. of Defense	**James Forrestal**
1st Sec. of Commerce	**Henry Wallace**
2nd Sec. of Commerce	**W. Averill Harriman**

The Roosevelt Years (1933–1945)

Among Franklin Delano Roosevelt's family, friends, and advisors, who was or were his . . . ?

wife and distant cousin, later UN delegate	**Anna Eleanor Roosevelt**
lover, with him at his sudden death	**Lucy Rutherfurd**
powerful mother	**Sara Delano Roosevelt**
family dog	**Fala**
1st Vice-President	**John Nance Garner**
1st Sec. of Agriculture, later Sec. of Commerce and 2nd Vice-President	**Henry Wallace**
3rd Vice-President	**Harry S Truman**
longtime Sec. of State	**Cordell Hull**
2nd Sec. of State	**Edward Stettinius, Jr.**
wartime Sec. of War	**Henry Stimson**
longtime Sec. of Treasury	**Henry Morgenthau, Jr.**

4th Attorney General	**Francis Biddle**
1st Postmaster General	**James Farley**
2nd Sec. of Commerce	**Harry Hopkins**
Sec. of Labor	**Frances Perkins**
Sec. of the Interior	**Harold Ickes**
key political advisor, a journalist	**Louis Howe**
"unofficial whip" of the New Deal	**Thomas G. Corcoran**
lawyer on the "brains trust"	**Adolf Berle**

Modern Losing Presidential and V-P Contenders

Among the modern losing presidential and vice-presidential candidates, who were . . . ?

1988 Dem. presidential candidate	**Michael Dukakis**
1988 Dem. V-P candidate	**Lloyd Bentsen**
1984 Dem. presidential candidate	**Walter Mondale**
1984 Dem. V-P candidate	**Geraldine Ferraro**
1980 Dem. presidential candidate	**Jimmy Carter**
1980 Dem. V-P candidate	**Walter Mondale**
1980 Independent presidential candidate	**John Anderson**
1980 Citizens presidential candidate	**Barry Commoner**
1976 Rep. presidential candidate	**Gerald Ford**
1976 Rep. V-P candidate	**Robert Dole**
1976 Independent presidential candidate	**Eugene McCarthy**
1976 American Independent presidential candidate	**Lester Maddox**
1972 Dem. presidential candidate	**George McGovern**
1972 Dem. V-P candidate	**Sargent Shriver**
1972 originally nominated Dem. V-P candidate	**Thomas Eagleton**
1968 Dem. presidential candidate	**Hubert Humphrey**
1968 Dem. V-P candidate	**Edmund Muskie**
1964 Rep. presidential candidate	**Barry Goldwater**
1964 Rep. V-P candidate	**William Miller**
1960 Rep. presidential candidate	**Richard Nixon**
1960 Rep. V-P candidate	**Henry Cabot Lodge**
1956 and 1952 Dem. presidential candidate	**Adlai Stevenson**
1956 Dem. V-P candidate	**Estes Kefauver**
1952 Dem. V-P candidate	**John Sparkman**
1948 Rep. presidential candidate	**Thomas Dewey**
1948 Rep. V-P candidate	**Earl Warren**

1948 States' Rights presidential candidate	**Strom Thurmond**
1948 Progressive presidential candidate	**Henry Wallace**
1940 Rep. presidential candidate	**Wendell Willkie**
1936 Rep. presidential candidate	**Alfred Landon**

Other Key Modern US Political and Military Figures

Among other post-WWII US political and military figures, who was . . . ?

Westmoreland's successor in Vietnam in 1968	**Creighton Abrams**
the Speaker of the House 1970–76	**Carl Albert**
the former Arizona gov. and 1988 Dem. presidential hopeful	**Bruce Babbitt**
the NY Dem. representative convicted in Wedtech scandals	**Mario Biaggi**
the Delaware senator, and 1988 Dem. presidential hopeful	**Joseph R. Biden**
the racist Mississippi senator to the mid-1940's	**Theodore G. Bilbo**
the New Jersey Dem. senator, former basketball pro	**Bill Bradley**
the black mayor of Los Angeles	**Thomas Bradley**
the 1st black in the Senate since the 19th c.	**Edward Brooke**
the conservative columnist and Rep. speechwriter	**Patrick J. Buchanan**
the 1950's–1960's UN undersecretary, 1st black to win the Nobel Peace Price	**Ralph Bunche**
the West Virginia Senate Dem. Majority Leader to 1988	**Robert C. Byrd**
Chicago's mayor after Daley	**Jane M. Byrne**
a liberal Dem. senator from California	**Alan Cranston**
the 1st black woman in the House of Representatives	**Shirley Chisholm**
the head of the 1975–76 committee on the CIA, an Idaho senator	**Frank Church**

San Antonio's Hispanic-American mayor until 1989	Henry Cisnerno
the Maine senator and poet, on the Iran-Contra panel	William Cohen
the Birmingham, Alabama, official who used water hoses and dogs against civil rights activists	Eugene "Bull" Connor
NY State's 1980's Dem. gov. and presidential hope	Mario Cuomo
Chicago's long-time Dem. boss, as in 1968	Richard Daley, Sr.
key black Dem. representative from California	Ronald Dellums
California's Armenian-American Rep. gov.	George Deukmejian
NYC's first black mayor	David Dinkins
Iowa Senate Rep. leader and 1980's presidential hopeful	Robert Dole
San Francisco's woman mayor of the 1980's	Dianne Feinstein
Miami's 6-term Puerto Rican mayor	Maurice A. Ferre
Boston's nonpartisan mayor of the late 1980's	Raymond Flynn
the Washinton Dem., House Majority Leader after 1988	Thomas Foley
the sponsor of an educational exchange program	J. William Fulbright
Philadelphia's 1980's black Democratic mayor	W. Wilson Goode
the Tennessee Dem. senator and 1988 presidential hopeful	Albert Gore, Jr.
the 1st woman elected gov. in her own right, in Connecticut	Ella Grasso
the Colorado ex-senator nixed in the 1988 presidential race by links with Donna Rice	Gary Hart
a key conservative Rep. Utah senator	Orrin G. Hatch
the black mayor of Gary, Indiana	Richard Hatcher
the senior Rep. senator from Oregon	Mark Hatfield
the longtime Dem. senator from Alabama	Howell Heflin
the far-right senior senator, Rep. from North Carolina	Jesse Helms
the Dem. senator from South Carolina	Ernest Fritz Hollings

the much-feared head of the FBI, 1924–72	J. Edgar Hoover
a longtime liberal Rep. senator from NY	Jacob Javits
a former Texas representative and 1986 Dem. keynoter	Barbara Jordan
the junior Kansas senator, of Alf Landon's family	Nancy Kassebaum
the head of the 1950's Senate organized crime hearings, a Tennessee Dem.	Estes Kefauver
NYC's grating and controversial 1980's mayor	Ed Koch
NYC's mid-20th-c. mayor who read comics over the air during a newspaper strike	Fiorello La Guardia
Vermont's longtime Dem. senator	Patrick J. Leahy
the Louisiana gov. and presidential hopeful, the "Kingfish," assassinated in 1935	Huey Long
the senior Indiana senator, a Rep.	Richard Lugar
the head of the 1950's anti-Communist Senate hearings, a Wisconsin Rep.	Joseph McCarthy
the Speaker of the House 1962–70	John McCormack
the Arizona Rep. gov. who fought charges of misusing state money and obstructing justice	Evan Mecham
a liberal Dem. senator from Ohio	Howard Metzenbaum
the feisty Maryland representative, then senator	Barbara Mikulski
the Maine senator and Dem. leader from 1988	George Mitchell
the Wisconsin Rep., Ind., then Dem. senator, to 1968	Wayne Morse
NY's liberal Dem. senator, a sociologist	Daniel Patrick Moynihan
the Massachusetts Dem. Speaker of the House 1976–88	Thomas "Tip" O'Neill
the junior Rep. senator from Oregon	Bob Packwood
the Rhode Island Dem. head of the Senate Foreign Relations Committee	Claiborne Pell
the longtime Florida Dem. representative, who fought for senior citizens' rights	Claude Pepper

the black Harlem Dem. representative not at first seated in the House, in 1967	**Adam Clayton Powell, Jr.**
the Wisconsin Dem. senator who gave Golden Fleece awards	**William Proxmire**
the longtime Texas Dem. Speaker of the House	**Sam Rayburn**
the former Philadelphia Dem. mayor, later a Rep.	**Frank L. Rizzo**
the W.Va. Senator and Standard Oil heir	**John D. Rockefeller, 4th**
the Illinois Dem., head of the House Ways and Means Committee	**Dan Rostenkowski**
the New Hampshire Rep. senator, vice-chair of the Senate's Iran-Contra Committee	**Warren Rudman**
the California representative killed by Jim Jones's people in 1978	**Leo J. Ryan**
the senior Dem. senator from Maryland	**Paul Sarbanes**
the Colorado Dem. representative, who considered a 1988 run for the presidency	**Patricia Schroeder**
the Illinois senator and 1988 presidential hopeful	**Paul Simon**
the Wyoming Rep. senator, on Judiciary Committee	**Alan K. Simpson**
the Maine Rep. senator, author of *Declaration of Conscience*	**Margaret Chase Smith**
the conservative Georgia Dem. senator 1947–88	**John C. Stennis**
Miami's 1st Cuban-born mayor	**Xavier L. Suarez**
the Ohio senator and 1952 Republican presidential hopeful	**Robert A. Taft**
South Carolina's powerful far-right Rep. senator	**Strom Thurmond**
the Texas Rep. senator, head of Reagan's Iran-Contra commission	**John Tower**
the Arizona Dem. head of the House Interior Committee	**Morris K Udall**
the Virginia Rep. senator and one-time husband of Elizabeth Taylor	**John W. Warner**
Chicago's first black mayor	**Harold Washington**
the California Dem., chair of the House Subcommittee on Health and the Environment	**Henry A. Waxman**

Connecticut's liberal Rep. senator, to 1988	**Lowell P. Welcker, Jr.**
the US commander in Vietnam, then chief of staff	**William Westmoreland**
Houston's nonpartisan woman mayor	**Kathy Whitmire**
the Texas Dem., Speaker of the House from 1987	**Jim Wright**
the Vietnam officer who oversaw the use of Agent Orange, which apparently killed his own son	**Elmo Zumwalt**

Modern Supreme Court Judges

Among judges on the Supreme Court, who . . . ?

was appointed by Reagan in 1987	**Anthony Kennedy**
was appointed by Reagan in 1986	**Antonin Scalia**
moved from Associate to Chief Justice in 1986	**William Rehnquist**
was appointed by Reagan in 1981, the 1st woman	**Sandra Day O'Connor**
was appointed by Ford in 1975	**John Paul Stevens**
served 1971–87	**Lewis Powell, Jr.**
was appointed by Nixon in 1970	**Harry Blackmun**
was Chief Justice 1969–86, appointed by Nixon	**Warren Burger**
was appointed by Johnson in 1967, the 1st black	**Thurgood Marshall**
was appointed by Johnson in 1965, rejected by the Senate for Chief Justice in 1969	**Abe Fortas**
resigned to become UN Ambassador, after serving 1962–65	**Arthur Goldberg**
was football star "Whizzer" White, serving on the Court from 1962	**Byron White**
served 1958–81, later consultant for a PBS series	**Potter Stewart**
served from 1956	**William Brennan, Jr.**
was Chief Justice 1953–69, head of the commission on John F. Kennedy's assassination	**Earl Warren**

was Chief Justice 1946–53	**Frederick Vinson**
was chief US prosecutor at the Nuremberg Trials, and served on the Court 1941–44	**Robert Jackson**
was the Court's leading modern liberal, serving 1939–75	**William O. Douglas**
was the Court's leading liberal-turned-conservative, serving 1939–62	**Felix Frankfurter**
was a leading Court liberal, once a member of the Ku Klux Klan, serving 1937–71	**Hugo Black**
was one of the greatest lawyers of his time, serving on the Court 1932–38	**Benjamin Cardozo**
was Chief Justice 1930–41, Associate 1910–16	**Charles Evans Hughes**
served 1925–46, from 1941 as Chief Justice	**Harlan Fiske Stone**
was Chief Justice 1921–30	**William Howard Taft**
served 1916–39, the 1st Jew on the Supreme Court	**Louis Brandeis**
was the Court's "Great Dissenter," serving 1902–32	**Oliver Wendell Holmes**

Other Notable US Judges and Lawyers

Among other notable US judges or lawyers, who is or was . . . ?

the defense lawyer in Dr.Samuel Sheppard's murder trial	**F. Lee Bailey**
the lawyer who defended Jack Ruby after he killed Lee Harvey Oswald	**Melvin Belli**
Nixon's unsuccessful 1970 Supreme Court nominee	**G. Harrold Carswell**
senate counsel during the McCarthy hearings	**Roy Cohn**
the NY State judge who disappeared in 1930	**Joseph Crater**
the defense attorney in the Leopold and Loeb and the Scopes "Monkey" trials	**Clarence Darrow**
the Harvard Law School professor and commentator	**Alan M. Dershowitz**

Reagan's Supreme Court nominee forced to withdraw after tales of his smoking marijuana	Douglas H. Ginsburg
the Florida judge impeached by the House in 1988	Alcee Hastings
the judge in the Chicago 7 case	Julius Hoffman
the judge in the Rosenberg spy trial	Irving R. Kaufman
the lawyer for the Chicago 7	William Kunstler
the attorneys in the Howard Beach and Tawana Brawley cases	C. Vernon Mason and Alton H. Maddox
the attorney for Quentin Reynolds in his libel suit against columnist Westbrook Pegler	Louis Nizer
the Equal Opportunity Commission chairman and frequent PBS legal commentator	Eleanor Holmes Norton
the judge in the 1921 Sacco and Vanzetti trial	Webster Thayer
the U.S. Army attorney who said to McCarthy, "Have you no sense of decency, sir?"	Joseph Nye Welch
the defense attorney for unpopular people, e.g., Joseph McCarthy and Jimmy Hoffa	Edward Bennett Williams

Modern Activists and Social Critics

Among modern US activists and social critics, who . . . ?

led the SCLC (Southern Christian Leadership Conference) after King's assassination	Rev. Ralph Abernathy
wrote the critical *Inside the Company: CIA Diary*	Philip Agee
founded the Fund for Animals, an animal rights group	Cleveland Amory
led the draft-card burning at Catonsville in 1968	Fathers Daniel and Philip Berrigan
was at first refused his seat in the Georgia legislature in 1965	Julian Bond
succeeded Carmichael at SNCC in 1967	H. Rap Brown

was active in Physicians for Social Responsibility and founded Women's Action for Nuclear Disarmament	**Helen Caldicott**
led SNCC (Student Non-Violent Coordinating Committee) in 1966	**Stokely Carmichael**
were civil rights activists killed in 1967, as shown in *Mississippi Burning*	**James Chaney, Andrew Goodman, and Michael Schwerner**
was convicted for killing a New Jersey trooper, later escaping to live in Cuba	**Joanne Chesimard (Assata Shakur)**
wrote *Soul on Ice,* a Black Panther	**Eldridge Cleaver**
was a Yale chaplain active for civil rights and against the Vietnam War	**William Sloane Coffin**
was the black Communist professor indicted and acquitted of supplying guns in a 1970 prison shootout by Jonathan Jackson	**Angela Davis**
organized antiwar protests from 1965, 1 of the Chicago 7	**David Dellinger**
released the Pentagon Papers in 1969 to protest against the Vietnam War	**Daniel Ellsberg**
was the NAACP leader killed in Jackson, Mississippi, succeeded by brother Charles, June 12, 1963	**Medgar Evers**
founded CORE (Congress of Racial Equality) in 1942	**James Farmer**
was the black Mississippi delegate locked out of the 1964 Atlantic City Dem. convention	**Fannie Lou Hamer**
were the Black Panther leaders killed by Chicago police in 1970	**Fred Hampton and Mark Clark**
was a leading late-20th-c. Socialist, author of *The Other America*	**Michael Harrington**
was SDS (Students for a Democratic Society) president 1962–63, 1 of the Chicago 7, married to Fonda	**Thomas Hayden**
were Yippie leaders and anti-Vietnam War activists, 2 of the Chicago 7	**Abbie Hoffman and Jerry Rubin**

directed the NAACP from 1977	**Benjamin Hooks**
was a 1980's black presidential hopeful	**Jesse Jackson**
was the Nobel Peace Prize–winning leader of the nonviolent civil rights movement until his assassination in 1968	**Rev. Martin Luther King, Jr.**
wrote *Illiterate America*	**Jonathan Kozol**
wrote *Look Out, Whitey, Black Power's Gonna Get Your Momma*	**Julius Lester**
was the Detroit civil rights activist killed in Selma, Alabama, in 1965	**Viola Gregg Liuzzo**
was CORE leader from 1966	**Floyd McKissick**
founded the Organization of Afro-American Unity	**Malcolm X**
gained admission to the U. of Mississippi in 1962	**James Meredith**
founded the Black Panthers in 1966	**Huey Newton** and **Bobby Seale**
started the Montgomery, Alabama, bus boycott by refusing to give up her seat in 1955	**Rosa Parks**
organized the Brotherhood of Sleeping Car Porters	**A. Philip Randolph**
was the Boston Unitarian minister beaten to death in Selma, Alabama, in 1965	**James Reeb**
organized the 1963 March on Washington	**Bayard Rustin**
was a nonlegal advisor in the Howard Beach and Tawana Brawley cases	**Rev. Al Sharpton**
led the NAACP 1955–77, after White	**Roy Wilkins**
was the NAACP's exec. sec. 1931–55	**Walter Francis White**
headed the National Urban League from 1961	**Whitney Young, Jr.**

Modern Feminists

Among modern feminists, who . . . ?

wrote *The Second Sex*	**Simone de Beauvoir**
wrote *Against Our Will: Men, Women, and Rape*	**Susan Brownmiller**

wrote *Women and Madness*	**Phyllis Chesler**
wrote *The Feminine Mystique*	**Betty Friedan**
wrote *The Female Eunuch*	**Germaine Greer**
wrote *From Reverence to Rape*	**Molly Haskell**
wrote *Man's World, Woman's Place*	**Elizabeth Janeway**
wrote *Sexual Politics*	**Kate Millet**
drafted the Equal Rights Amendment	**Alice Paul**
wrote *Memoirs of an Ex-Prom Queen*	**Alix Kates Shulman**
founded and edited *Ms.* Magazine	**Gloria Steinem**

Modern Assassins and Terrorists

Among modern assassins and terrorists, who . . . ?

was the alleged architect of the *Achille Lauro* hijacking	**Mohammed Abul Abbas**
shot Pope John Paul II on May 13, 1981	**Hehmet Ali Agca**
paralyzed Alabama Gov. George Wallace on May 15, 1972	**Arthur H. Bremer**
murdered John Lennon in NYC, on Dec. 8, 1980	**John Chapman**
tried to assassinate Pres. Harry Truman on Nov. 1, 1963, Puerto Rican nationalists	**Oscar Collazo** and **Grissello Torresola**
shot Pres. William McKinley on Sept. 6, 1901	**Leon Czolgosz**
was disarmed in an attempt on Pres. Gerald Ford on Sept. 5, 1975, a Charles Manson follower	**Lynette (Squeaky) Fromme**
assassinated Mahatma Gandhi in New Delhi on Jan. 30, 1948	**Nathuran Vinayak Godse**
shot Pres. James A. Garfield on July 2, 1881	**Charles J. Guiteau**
shot Pres. Ronald Reagan, et al., on Mar. 30, 1981	**John W. Hinckley, Jr.**
killed Leon Trotsky on Aug. 20, 1940, probably on orders from Joseph Stalin	**Ramon Mercador del Rio**
missed Pres. Gerald R. Ford on Sept. 2, 1975	**Sara Jane Moore**
heads the radical terrorist wing of the Palestinian Al Fatah	**Abu Nidal**

killed Pres. John F. Kennedy on Nov. 22, 1963	**Lee Harvey Oswald**
killed Austro-Hungarian archduke Francis Ferdinand on June 28, 1914, sparking WWI	**Gavrilo Princep**
killed Rev. Martin Luther King, Jr. on Apr. 4, 1968	**James Earl Ray**
shot Lee Harvey Oswald, on live TV on Nov. 24, 1963	**Jack Ruby**
killed Robert F. Kennedy during the presidential primary campaign on June 5, 1968	**Sirhan Sirhan**
killed Louisiana senator Huey Long on Sept. 8, 1935, himself killed by Long's bodyguards	**Dr. Carl Austin Weiss**
killed Chicago Mayor Joseph Cermak in trying for Pres. Franklin Roosevelt on Feb. 15, 1933	**Joseph Zangara**

Recent Hostages and Other Terrorism Victims

Among recent hostages and other terrorism victims, who is (are) or was (were) . . . ?

the longest-held US hostage in Lebanon, since 1984	**Terry Anderson**
the CIA station chief tortured and killed in Lebanon	**William Buckley**
the US hostages taken in Lebanon in Sept. 1986	**Joseph James Cicippio** and **Frank Reed**
the heroine of the 1985 TWA hijacking to Lebanon	**Uli Dedrickson**
the ABC correspondent who escaped his captors	**Charles Glass**
the head of the UN Truce Supervision team in Lebanon, taken in 1988 and later killed	**Lt. Col. William R. Higgins**
the US man taken hostage in Lebanon in May 1985	**David Jacobsen**
the US hostage freed by terrorists in Lebanon in 1985	**Rev. Martin Jenco**
the US hostage taken in 1984 and killed by terrorists in Lebanon in 1986	**Peter Kilburn**

the US passenger murdered aboard the *Achille Lauro* in 1985 — **Leon Klinghoffer**

the journalist who escaped from captors in Lebanon — **Jeremy Levin**

the professors taken hostage in Lebanon in Jan. 1988, the last, an Indian-American, soon released — **Robert Polhill, Alan Steen, Jesse Turner, and Mithileshwar Singh**

the US sailor murdered by terrorists during the 1985 TWA hijacking to Lebanon — **Robert Steatham**

the US hostage taken in Lebanon in June 1985 — **Thomas Sutherland**

the US writer taken in Lebanon October 1986 — **Edward Austin Tracy**

the British hostage negotiator taken hostage himself — **Terry Waite**

the US hostage freed by terrorists in Lebanon in 1986 — **Rev. Benjamin Weir**

Figures in Modern Spy Cases

Among figures in spy cases, who was or were . . . ?

exchanged for Francis Gary Powers in 1962 — **Rudolf Abel**

the ex-CIA officer convicted as a Soviet spy in the 1980's — **David Barnett**

the "4th man," a British knighted art historian — **Antony Blunt**

the British spies who defected to Russia in 1951 — **Guy Burgess** and **Donald MacLean**

the CIA man convicted as a Chinese spy, a suicide — **Larry Wu-Tai Chin**

the *US News & World Report* reporter arrested by the USSR as a spy, exchanged for Zakharov in 1986 — **Nicholas Daniloff**

the Soviet spy who worked on the early A-bomb — **Klaus Fuchs**

the conduit for Fuchs's information for the USSR — **Harry Gold**

the witness against the Rosenbergs, Ethel's brother — **David Greenglass**

charged as a spy by Whittaker Chambers — **Alger Hiss**

the head of British counter-intelligence (MI5), accused by some as a Soviet spy	**Roger Hollis**
the British atomic physicist and WWII Soviet spy	**Alan Nunn May**
the FBI agent convicted as a Soviet spy	**Richard Miller**
the National Security Agency communications specialist and Soviet spy	**Ronald Pelton**
the master British spy who defected to Russia in 1963	**Kim (Harold) Philby**
the couple convicted of spying for Israel in the 1980's	**Jonathan Pollard** and **Anne Henderson-Pollard**
the US pilot shot down over the USSR in a U2 plane	**Francis Gary Powers**
the American couple executed in 1953 as Soviet spies	**Julius** and **Ethel Rosenberg**
the man convicted with the Rosenbergs, but not executed	**Morton Sobell**
the USSR spy exchanged for Daniloff in 1986	**Gennadi Zakharov**
the author of *Spycatcher*	**Peter Wright**

Villains and Victims

Among various criminals and victims (proven or alleged) in modern causes célèbres, who was or were . . . ?

the convicted killer of *Arizona Republic* reporter Don Bolles in 1976	**John Harvey Adamson**
the leaders of the 1930's Mafia assassination group, "Murder, Inc."	**Albert Anastasia** and **Louis "Lepke" Buchalter**
the Long Island male nurse who confessed to injecting patients with lethal doses of Pavulon	**Richard Angelo**
shot and killed, with 3 technicians, at the CBS-TV studios in New York in 1982	**Margaret Barbera**
convicted as the Mayflower Madam	**Sydney Biddle Barrow**
the Denver talk-show host killed by the neo-Nazi group The Order (Bruders Schweigen) in 1984	**Alan Berg**

NYC's 1976–77 "Son of Sam" murderer	**David Berkowitz**
the woman acquitted of the 1892 ax murders of her father and stepmother	**Lizzie Borden**
the NY State black girl who said she was kidnapped and raped by 6 white men, in 1988	**Tawana Brawley**
the serial murderer of the 1970's, a law student	**Ted Bundy**
convicted of the civilian murders at My Lai on Mar. 16, 1968	**Lt. William Calley, Jr.**
behind the 1929 St. Valentine's Day Massacre	**Al (Alphonse) Capone**
the admitted killer of Jennifer Levin in NYC's 1986 "Preppie Murder" case	**Robert E. Chambers, Jr.**
executed in California in 1960, after worldwide clemency campaigns, and many stays	**Caryl Chessman**
the hijacker who parachuted out of an airplane with $200,000 ransom over Washington State in 1971 and was never heard of again	**D. B. Cooper**
convicted of strangling her 4-year-old daughter Alice Marie in a 1965 cause célèbre	**Alice Crimmins**
the Boston Strangler, active 1962–64	**Albert De Salvo**
the FBI's "Public Enemy No. One" killed in 1934	**John Dillinger**
the black man accused of murder, lynched in South Carolina in 1947	**Willie Earle**
the Prohibition era criminal called Dutch Schultz	**Arthur Flegenheimer**
the 1930's Midwestern robber called "Pretty Boy"	**Charles Arthur Floyd**
NYC's boss of the Mafia bosses, killed in 1979	**Carmine Galante**
the Wisconsin man who inspired Hitchcock's *Psycho*	**Edward Gein**
the oil tycoon's grandson kidnapped in 1973 and released after $2.8 million was paid	**J. Paul Getty, 3rd**
the Chicago crime boss portrayed by his daughter, Antoinette	**Sam Giancana**

the Utah murderer executed in 1977, the 1st in the US after reinstatement of the death penalty	**Gary Gilmore**
NYC's "subway vigilante" who shot 4 black teenagers in 1984	**Bernhard Goetz**
the head of NYC's powerful Gambino family	**John Gotti**
the 6-year-old Kansas City boy kidnapped on Sept 28, 1953, by Bonnie Brown Heady and Carl A. Hall, later executed for his death	**Richard C. Greenlease**
the young black man chased to his death on a highway in Howard Beach, NY, in 1986	**Michael Griffith**
the woman found guilty of killing Scarsdale diet author Dr. Herman Tarnower in 1980	**Jean Harris**
the Symbionese Liberation Army members who kidnapped Patty Hearst in 1974	**William** and **Emily Harris**
the victim kidnapped Nov. 22, 1933, and killed by Thomas Thurmond and John Holmes, later lynched when the body was found floating in San Francisco Bay	**Brooke Hart**
the man convicted of kidnapping 20-month-old Charles A. Lindbergh, Jr. in Hopewell, NJ, on Mar. 1, 1932, later electrocuted for killing the baby, although $50,000 was paid	**Bruno Richard Hauptmann**
the newspaper heiress kidnapped on Feb. 4, 1974	**Patricia (Patty) Hearst**
the boy convicted of killing Westchester Yale student Bonnie Jean Garland in 1977	**Richard Herrin**
the young men who killed the Clutter family, in Holcomb, Kansas, in 1959, as described in Capote's *In Cold Blood*	**Richard Hickok** and **Perry Smith**
involved in murder and forgery of Mormon documents in Salt Lake City in the 1980s	**Mark Hofmann**
the author of *The Happy Hooker*	**Xaviera Hollander**

the convicted Massachusetts murderer who committed rape and assault while on furlough, a case used in the 1988 presidential campaign	**Willie Horton**
wrote a false Howard Hughes autobiography	**Clifford Irving**
the defendants in the 1986 Howard Beach case	**Scott Kern, Jason Ladone, Jon Lester** and **Michael Pirone**
the kidnappers and "thrill" killers of young Robert Franks on May 22, 1924, defended by Clarence Darrow in a sensational trial	**Nathan Leopold** and **Richard Loeb**
the British lord who disappeared in 1974 after apparently attacking his wife and killing their children's nanny	**Lucan (John Bingham)**
the creators of the Mafia's national syndicate in the US	**Charles "Lucky" Luciano** and **Meyer Lansky**
the Army doctor convicted of murdering his wife and 2 daughters in 1970, who later sued Joe McGinniss over his view of the case in *Fatal Vision*	**Jeffrey MacDonald**
the Atlanta woman kidnapped by Gary Steven Krist and Ruth Eisenmann-Schier on Dec. 17, 1968, found 3 days later, after a $500,000 ransom was paid, buried 18 inches underground in a wooden box	**Barbara Jane Mackle**
the mass murderer and cult leader convicted of Sharon Tate's 1969 murder	**Charles M. Manson**
the 1930's robber-killer called "Baby Face"	**George Nelson**
the battered common-law wife of Joel Steinberg	**Hedda Nussbaum**
the 1930's robbing couple cum folk heroes	**Bonnie Parker** and **Clyde Barrow**
the Exxon executive taken by guerrillas in Argentina, on Dec. 6, 1973, and released after a record $14.2 million was paid	**Victor E. Samuelson**
the black man beaten in the Howard Beach affair	**Cedric Sandiford**

the 9 young black men convicted, on tainted evidence, of raping 2 Alabama white women	Scottsboro "boys"
the Cleveland doctor convicted in 1954 of killing his wife, a decision later overturned, resulting in an acquittal on a retrial	Samuel Sheppard
the California rapist who cut off his victim's hands and left her for dead	Lawrence Singleton
the singer's son kidnapped on Dec. 8, 1963, later released after a $240,000 ransom was paid	Frank Sinatra, Jr.
the killer of 8 student nurses in Chicago in the 1960's	Richard Speck
the lawyer tried for battering to death his illegally adopted daughter, Lisa, in 1988	Joel Steinberg
the federal witness who wrote *My Life in the Mafia*	Vincent Teresa
the killer of architect Stanford White, former lover of his wife, Evelyn Nesbit, in 1906	Harry Kendall Thaw
the black youth lynched in Mississippi in 1955, for whistling at a white woman	Emmett Till
the Oklahoma City man kidnapped on July 22, 1933, by George (Machine Gun) Kelly and 5 others, released after $200,000 was paid	Charles F. Urschel
the Rhode Island man accused by his stepchildren of trying to murder his rich, socialite wife, Sonny	Claus von Bülow
convicted of 2 of Atlanta's 28 black child murders 1979–81	Wayne Williams
the killer of San Francisco officials George Moscone and Harvey Milk in 1978	Dan White

Key Political Figures Around the Modern World

For pre-WWII figures, see Politics and People)

In Africa

Among key political figures in post-WWII Africa, who is or was . . . ?

Algeria's leader after 1962 French eviction	Ahmed Ben Bella
Algeria's military leader from 1965–78	Col. Houari Boumedienne (né Mohamed Boukharouba)
Boumedienne's successor	Col. Chadli Benjedid
the leader of **Angola**'s Unita (National Union for the Total Independence of Angola) guerillas	Jonas Savimbi
Egypt's president after Sadat	Hosni Mubarak
Egypt's president after Nasser, assassinated 1981	Anwar el-Sadat
Egyptian leader 1954–70	Lt. Col. Gamal Abdel Nasser
the Egyptian king forced to abdicate in 1952	Farouk
the brutal **Equatorial Guinea** dictator 1972–79	Masie Ngueme Biyogo
Ethiopia's president after 1974, head of the Dergue Junta	Col. Mengistu Haile Mariam
Ethiopia's longtime emperor	Haile Selassie
Ghana's military leader from 1979	Flight Lt. Jerry Rawlings
Ghana's early key leader	Kwame Nkrumah
Guinea leader 1958–70	Sekou Toure
Liberia's president after a coup in 1980	Samuel K. Doe
the strongman of **Libya**, linked with terrorism	Col. Muammar al-Qaddafi
Kenya's leader from 1978	Daniel arap Moi
Morocco's leader from 1961	Hassan II (né Moulay)
Nigeria's military president after 1985	Maj. Gen. Ibrahim Babangida
Senegal's leader from 1981	Abdou Diouf
Sudan's president from 1986	Sadiq al Mahdi
Sudan's president and general 1958–64	Ibrahim Abboud
South Africa's president from 1978–89	P(ieter) W. Botha
South Africa's president from 1989	F(rederik) W. DeKlerk

foreign minister under P. W. Botha and DeKlerk	**Roelef "Pik" Botha**
the Anglican bishop and 1986 Nobel peace prize winner	**Rev. Desmond Tutu**
the Zulu chief, leader of the Inkatha organization	**Mangosuthu Buthelezi**
the long-jailed African National Congress leader, freed 1990	**Nelson Mandela**
Mandela's wife and often spokesperson	**Winnie Mandela**
the exiled African National Congress leader	**Oliver Tambo**
the black activist killed in South Africa in 1977	**Steve Biko**
Biko's journalist friend who escaped to England	**Donald Woods**
the leader who formalized South Africa's apartheid policy after his 1948 election	**Daniel Malan**
Tanzanian president 1962–85	**Julius Nyerere**
Tunisian prime minister from 1987	**Zine el-Abidine Ben Ali**
the longtime president of Tunisia	**Habib Bourguiba**
the Tunisian prime minister to 1986	**Samson Kisekka**
Uganda's bloody general-director 1971–79	**Idi Amin**
the Uganda prime minister ousted in 1971	**Milton Obote**
the president of **Zaire** from 1965	**Mobuto Sese Seko** (né Joseph Mobutu)
the premier overthrown by Mobutu in 1964	**Moïse Kapenda Tshombe**
the president who removed Lumumba	**Joseph Kasavubu**
the 1st premier of the Congo (now Zaire), killed in 1961, perhaps with CIA urging	**Patrice Lumumba** (né Kataka Kombe)
the **Zambia** president from 1964	**Kenneth Launda**
the **Zimbabwe** prime minister after 1980	**Robert Mugabe**
the head of the opposition Zimbabwe African People's Union and of the Ndebele	**Joshua Nkomo**
the leader who declared Rhodesia's independence from Britain in 1965	**Ian Smith**

In the Americas (Except the US)

Among key political figures in the post-WWII Americas (outside the United States) who is or was . . . ?

Argentina's president from 1989	**Carlos Saul Menem**
Argentina's president 1983–89	**Raul Alfonsin**
the Argentinian head during the Falklands war	**Leopoldo Galitieri**
the mid-20th-c. populist leader in Argentina	**Juan Péron**
Péron's 1st wife	**Eva (Evita) Duarte Péron**
Péron's 2nd wife and successor at his death	**Isabel Péron**
Brazil's president from 1990	**Fernando Collor de Mello**
Brazil's president 1986–90	**José Sarney**
the popular presidential choice who died in 1985	**Tancredo Neves**
the president 1979–85, ending military rule	**João Figueiredo**
the president 1975–79	**Gen. Ernesto Geisel**
the president 1969–75	**Gen. Emilio Garrastazu Médici**
the president from 1967, who closed congress	**Marshal Costa e Silva**
the leader who took over after a 1964 military coup	**Gen. Humberto de Alencar Castello Branco**
a protégé of Vargas, president 1961–64	**João "Jango" Goulart**
dictator from 1930 and president from 1951	**Getulio Vargas**
Canada's Conservative prime minister in the 1980's	**Brian Mulroney**
the Liberal party leader after Trudeau	**John Turner**
the Liberal prime minister 1968–79, 1980–84	**Pierre Elliot Trudeau**
the 1980's leader of the New Democratic Party	**Edward Broadbent**
the Liberal prime minister 1963–68	**Lester Pearson**
the Conservative prime minister 1957–63	**John G. Diefenbaker**
the longtime Québec leader to 1959	**Maurice Duplessis**
the longtime leader of the separatist Parti Québecois and Québec premier	**René Lévesque**
Chile's civilian president from 1990	**Patricio Aylwin**
Chile's military ruler 1973–90	**Gen. Augusto Pinochet Ugarte**
the Chilean ruler bloodily overthrown in 1970	**Salvador Allende Gossens**

Chile's ruler from 1964 who nationalized mines	**Eduardo Frei Montalva**
the president of **Colombia** in the late 1980's	**Virgilio Barco Vargas**
the Colombian attorney general killed by drug lords in 1988	**Carlos Mauro Hoyos**
Costa Rica's Nobel-winning president	**Oscar Arias Sanchez**
Cuba's leader since 1959	**Fidel Castro Ruz**
the Castro aide who took the revolution to Bolivia	**Che Guevara**
the Cuban dictator 1952–59	**Fulgencio Batista**
the **Dominican Republic**'s dictator 1930–61	**Gen. Rafael Leonidas Trujillo Molina**
the prime minister of **Grenada** 1984–89	**Herbert Blaize**
the prime minister executed in a 1983 coup	**Maurice Bishop**
elected president in **Haiti**'s army-controlled 1988 elections	**Lt. Gen. Henri Namphy**
his father's successor in 1971, "Baby Doc"	**Jean-Claude Duvalier**
dictator 1957–71, "Papa Doc"	**Dr. Francois Duvalier**
the dreaded secret police squad	**Tontons Macout**
the president of **Honduras** from 1986	**José Azcona Hoyo**
Jamaica's prime minister from 1980	**Edward Seaga**
the socialist prime minister 1972–80	**Michael Manley**
Mexico's president, from 1988	**Carlos Salinas de Cortari**
the president 1982–88	**Miguel de la Madrid Hurtado**
the president 1976–82, who nationalized the banks	**José Lopez Portillo**
the president 1970–76	**Luis Echeverria**
Nicaragua's coalition president from 1990	**Violetta Barrios de Chamorro**
Nicaragua's Sandinista president	**Daniel Ortega Saavedra**
Nicaragua's Sandinista defense minister	**Humberto Ortega Saavedra**
the Catholic mediator between Nicaragua's Sandinistas and Contras	**Miguel Cardinal Obando y Bravo**
the president of Nicaragua before 1979	**Anastosio Somoza Debayle**
Panama's president after Noriega	**Guillermo Endara**
the Panama general ousted by US	**Manual Antonio Noriega**
the elected president ousted by Noriega	**Eric Arturo Devalle**
Peru's president from 1990	**Alberto Fujimori**
Peru's president 1985–90	**Alan Garcia Perez**

the president before and after 1968–80	**Fernando Belaunde Terry**
the US-backed **Salvadoran** president from 1984	**José Napoléon Duarte**
the rightist head of Salvadoran "death squads"	**Roberto d'Aubuisson**
the Salvadoran Catholic archbishop assassinated by death squads in 1980	**Oscar Arnulfo Romero**
the exiled Democratic Revolutionary Front leader who returned to El Salvador in 1987	**Rubén Zamora**
Uruguay's president from 1985	**Julio Maria Sanguinetti**
the president ousted in 1976	**Juan Maria Bordaberry**
leftist guerilla group of recent decades	**Tupamaros**
Venezuela's president from 1984	**Jaime Lusinchi**

In Asia

Among key political figures in post-WWII Asia, who is or was . . . ?

the **Afghan** president from 1986	**Mohammad Najibullah**
soviet-backed president 1979–86	**Babrak Karmal**
the Afghani king exiled in the 1970's	**Mohammad Zahir Shah**
Saudi Arabia's king 1964–75	**Faisal (né Ibn-Abd-ad-Aziz al-Saud)**
the powerful Saudi oil minister 1962–86	**Sheikh Ahmed Zaki Yamani**
leader of **Burma** renamed Myanmar, from 1988	**Saw Maung**
Burma's leader 1962–88	**Ne Win**
the Burmese UN sec.-general in the 1960's	**U Thant**
Burma's leader after its 1948 independence	**U Nu**
Burma's WWII leader	**Aung San**
the head of **Cambodia**'s Khmer Rouge, which killed millions of people in the late 1970's	**Pol Pot**
the US-backed Cambodian premier from 1970	**Lon Nol**
the neutral Cambodian prince from WWII	**Norodom Sihanouk**
China's (People's Republic of) leader after the Tiananmen square protests	**Li Peng**
key leader 1987–89	**Zhao Ziyang (Chao Tzu-Yang)**

the party leader deposed in 1987, whose death sparked the Tiananmen square protests	**Hu Yaobang (Yao-pang)**
the senior leader after Chou	**Deng Xiaoping (Teng Hsiao-ping)**
Mao's successor in 1976	**Hua Guofeng (Kuo-feng)**
the toppled 1960's president, later rehabilitated	**Liu Shaoqi (Shao-ch'i)**
Mao's wife, leader of the "Gang of 4"	**Jiang Qing (Chiang Ch'ing, née Luan Shu-meng)**
the architect of Communist China, with Mao	**Zhou Enlai (Chou En-lai)**
the revered founder-leader of the Communists	**Mao Zedong (Mao Tse-Tung)**
the China (Nationalist) prime minister from 1984	**Yu Kuo-hwa**
the Taiwan government's leader to 1975	**Chiang Kai-shek**
the Nationalist Chinese Chiang Kai-Shek's wife	**Song Meiling (Soong Mei-ling)**
Sun Yat-sen's and Chiang Kai-shek's brother-in-law, a key financier	**T. V. (Tzu-wen) Soong**
India's leader after Rajiv Gandhi	**V. P. Singh**
India's ruler 1984–89, Indira's 2nd son	**Rajiv Gandhi**
Indira Gandhi's 1st son and heir before he died	**Sanjay Gandhi**
the assassinated prime minister, Nehru's daughter	**Indira Gandhi**
the 1st non-Congress Party prime minister, in the 1970's	**Moraji Desai**
India's leader 1947–64	**Jawaharlal Nehru**
the nonviolent leader of the Indian independence movement, called Mahatma (Great Soul)	**Mohandas K. Gandhi**
the Pathan Gandhi disciple, leader of nonviolent Servants of God (Red Shirts)	**Abdul Ghaffar Khan**
the Indonesian president from 1968	**Suharto**
Indonesia's president after its 1949 independence	**Sukarno**
Iran's 1980's parliament head, Khomeini's successor	**Hojatolislam Ali Akbar Hashemi Rafsanjani**
Iran's powerful ayatollah of the 1980's	**Ruhollah Khomeini**
Bakhtiar's successor as Iran's president	**Abolhassan Bani-Sadr**

the 1st leader of Iran's post-Shah government	**Shahpur Bakhtiar**
the Shah of Iran overthrown in 1979	**Mohammed Riza Pahlavi**
the Iran premier overthrown in 1953	**Mohammed Mosadegh**
Iraq's president in the 1980's	**Saddam Hussein At-Takriti**
the **Israeli** Likud leader of the 1980's	**Yitzhak Shamir**
the Israeli Labor leader of the 1980's	**Shimon Peres**
the leader of the early 1980's invasion of Lebanon	**Ariel Sharon**
the man who revealed details of Israel's A-bomb program	**Mordechai Vanunu**
the Israeli Likud prime minister 1977–83	**Menachem Begin**
Meir's successor, later defense minister	**Yitzhak Rabin**
the key 1960's Israeli general, with 1 eye	**Moshe Dayan**
Israel's premier during the Yom Kippur War	**Golda Meir**
the UN and US ambassador and foreign minister	**Abba Eban**
Israel's 1st premier	**David Ben-Gurion**
Israel's 1st prime minister	**Chaim Weizmann**
Japan's premier after Uno	**Toshiki Kaifu**
Takeshita's brief successor in 1989	**Sosuke Uno**
the elected head of Japan's Liberal Party in 1987	**Noboru Takeshita**
the head of Japan's Liberals to 1987	**Yasuhiro Nakasone**
the king of **Jordan** from 1952	**King Hussein**
the Jordanian king assassinated on July 20, 1951	**Abdullah ibn Hussein**
the president of North **Korea** from 1972	**Kim Il-Sung**
South **Korea**'s president from 1988	**Roh Tae Woo**
the South Korean president until 1988	**Chun Doo Hwan**
the South Korean opposition leader exiled in US	**Kim Dae Jung**
the South Korean opposition leader, along with Kim Dae Jung	**Kim Young Sam**
the head of a junta from 1961 until killed in 1979	**Park Chung Hee**

South Korea's 1st president, 1948–60	Syngman Rhee
Kuwait's longtime ruling dynasty	Al-Sabah
Laos's head of state since 1975	Prince Souphanouvong
the Laotian prime minister from 1975	Kaysone Phomvihan
Laos's premier for most years 1951–75	Prince Souvanna Phouma
the Lebanese premier assassinated in 1984	Rashid Karami
Gemayel's brother and successor	Amin Gemayel
the Lebanon Phalange president killed in 1982	Bashir Gemayel
the leader of Lebanon's Amal Shiite Moslem militia	Nabih Berri
Jumblat's son and successor	Walid Jumblat
the Lebanese Druze leader killed in 1977	Kamal Jumblat
the pro-Iranian Lebanese Shiite Moslem militia	Hezbollah (Party of God)
Oman's sultan from 1970	Qabus bin Said
Oman's sultan to 1970, overthrown by his son	Said bin Taimur
Pakistan's president from 1988, Ali Bhutto's daughter	Benazir Bhutto
the president killed in a 1988 plane crash	Mohammed Zia ul-Haq
the president overthrown and killed by Zia in 1977	Zulfikar Ali Bhutto
the general and leader after a 1958 coup	Mohammed Ayub Khan
the general and leader from 1969	Agha Mohammad Yahya Khan
the leader of Pakistan at its partition from India	Mohammed Ali Jinnah
the leader of the Al Fatah wing of the Palestinian Liberation Organization (PLO)	Yasir Arafat
the Philippines president from 1986	Corazon Aquino
the Philippines opposition leader assassinated in 1983	Benigno Aquino
the Philippines president 1965–86	Ferdinand Marcos
Marcos' shoe-loving wife, the "Iron Butterfly"	Imelda Marcos
the Philippines post-WWII president to 1957	Ramon Magsaysay
Saudi Arabia's ruler since 1982	King Fahd
King Faisal's successor as Saudi Arabia's king	Crown Prince Khalid

the Saudi Arabian ruler assassinated in 1975	**King Faisal**
the 1st **Singapore** prime minister, from 1959	**Lee Kuan Yew**
Sri Lanka's president from 1978	**Junius Jayawardene**
the prime minister from 1978	**Ranasinghe Premadasa**
the prime minister from 1959, Solomon W.R.D.'s widow	**Sirimavo Bandaranaike**
the prime minister assassinated in 1959	**Solomon W. R. D. Bandaranaike**
Syria's president from 1971	**Hafez al-Assad**
Thailand's prime minister from 1980	**Prem Tinsulanonda**
the prime minister to 1980	**Kriangsak Chomanan**
Thailand's post-WWII Massachusetts-born monarch	**Bhumibol Aduldej** or **Rama IX**
Turkey's president from 1980	**Kenan Evren**
the prime minister from 1983	**Turgut Ozal**
Vietnam's leader from 1986	**Nguyen Van Linh**
the North Vietnam negotiator with Kissinger in 1973	**Le Duc Tho**
the longtime North Vietnam leader, whose adopted name means "He Who Enlightens"	**Ho Chi Minh** (né **Nguyen That Tan**)
the South Vietnam leader from 1967	**Nguyen Van Thieu**
the South Vietnam prime minister from 1965	**Nguyen Cao**
the South Vietnam leader from 1955	**Ngo Dinh Dem**
the Annam emperor ousted in 1945, head of Vietnam from 1949	**Bao Dai**
the South **Yeman** leader from 1986	**Haidar Abu Bakr al-Atlas**
the South Yemen president assassinated in 1978	**Salem Robaye Ali**
the North Yemen president from 1978	**Ali Abdullah Saleh**
the North Yemen prime minister from 1983	**Abdul Aziz Abdel Ghani**
the Yemen leader from 1974, assassinated in 1977	**Col. Ibrahim al-Hamidi**
the revolutionary Yemen leader from 1962	**Abdullah al-Salal**
the Yemen heir forced to flee in 1962	**Imam Mohamad al-Badr**
the Yemen king assassinated in 1962	**Imam Ahmed**

In Australia and New Zealand

Among key political figures in post-WWII Australia and New Zealand, who was or is . . . ?

Australia's Labor prime minister from 1982	**Robert James Lee Hawke**
Australia's 1980's Liberal opposition leader	**Andrew Peacock**
the Liberal prime minister 1975–83	**John Malcom Fraser**
the Labor leader and prime minister 1972–75	**Edward Gough Whitlam**
the Liberal prime minister 1949–66 and earlier	**Robert Gordon Menzies**
New Zealand's prime minister from 1984, who barred nuclear ships from his country	**David Lange**

In Europe

Among key political figures in post-WWII Europe, who is or was . . . ?

Albania's leader after Hoxha	**Ramiz Alia**
Albania's leader 1944–85	**Enver Hoxha**
Austria's leader and UN General Sec., linked to Nazis	**Kurt Waldheim**
Austria's socialist chancellor 1970–1983	**Bruno Kreisky**
the president of **Cyprus** from 1977	**Spyros Kyprianou**
the Greek Cypriot president 1960–74	**Archbishop Makarios**
Czechoslovakia's reform-minded president from 1989, a playwright	**Vaclav Havel**
Czechoslovakia's president 1975–89	**Gustav Hasek**
Czechoslovakia's leader in the 1968 uprisings, parliament chairman from 1989	**Alexander Dubcek**
France's Socialist prime minister from 1981	**François Mitterand**
the neo-Gaullist leader of the 1980's	**Jacques Chirac**
the Republican leader before Mitterand	**Valéry Giscard d'Estaing**
the leader of France's far-right National Front	**Jean-Marie Le Pen**
the radical leader of the 1968 student protests	**Daniel Cohn-Bendit**

the premier from 1954–55, ending the Indochina War	Pierre Mendès-France
the Gaullist premier and president of the 1960–70's	Georges Pompidou
the key Free French and post-WWII leader	Charles de Gaulle
East Germany's president elected in 1990	Lothar de Maiziere
East Germany's leader, who opened the Berlin Wall in 1989	Egon Krenz
East Germany's leader from 1976–89	Erich Honecker
West Germany's chancellor from 1982	Helmut Kohl
the chancellor 1974–84	Helmut Schmidt
the chancellor 1969–74, who resigned over a spy case	Willy Brandt
the longtime right-wing Bavarian leader	Franz Josef Strauss
the terrorist leaders of the Red Army Faction	Andreas Baader and Ulrike Meinhof
the chancellor 1949–69	Konrad Adenauer
Great Britain's 1st woman prime minister, from 1979, the "Iron Lady"	Margaret Thatcher
the 1980's Labour Party head, whose speech Sen. Joseph Biden was accused of plagiarizing	Neal Kinnock
the left-wing Labour leader to 1983	Michael Foot
the left-wing Labour M. P. who renounced a title	Tony (Anthony Neil Wedgwood) Benn
the Labour leader defeated by Foot in 1980	Denis Healey
the Labour prime minister 1976–79	James Callaghan
the Conservative prime minister 1974–76	Edward Heath
the Labour prime minister 1964–70, 1974–76	Harold Wilson
the Conservative prime minister 1957–63	Harold Macmillan
the minister who resigned in 1960's sex scandal	John Profumo
the prime minister 1955–57, during the Suez Crisis	Anthony Eden
the prime minister in WWII and in the 1950's	Winston Churchill
the Labour leader after Clement Attlee	Hugh Gaitskell

the post-WWII Labour prime minister	**Clement Attlee**
the Welsh Labour designer of the National Health Service	**Aneurin "Nye" Bevan**
the Labour leader who founded the Transport and General Workers Union in 1921 (see also Modern British Royals, below)	**Ernest Bevin**
Greece's prime minister 1981–89	**Andreas Papandreou**
the founder of a military dictatorship in 1967	**George Papadopoulos**
the 1963–64 leader, forced to resign	**George Papandreou**
the post-WWII conservative leader	**Constantine Karamanlis**
Hungary's premier elected in 1990	**Jozsef Antall**
Hungary's leader from 1956	**János Kádár**
the Hungarian premier ousted in 1955, leading to open revolt and Soviet invasion	**Imre Nagy**
Hungary's 1st post-WWII president	**Zoltan Tildy**
the head of **Ireland**'s Fianna Fail (Soldiers of Destiny)	**Charles J. Haughey**
the head of Ireland's Fine Gael (Tribe of the Irish)	**Garret Fitzgerald**
the militant **Northern Ireland** M. P. 1969–74	**Bernadette Devlin**
the right-wing No. Ireland M. P. from 1970	**Ian Paisley**
Italy's 1st Socialist prime minister, from 1983	**Bettino Craxi**
the Italy-based US officer taken, then rescued, in 1981	**Brig. Gen. James Dozier**
the Christian Democrat leader and often premier	**Amintore Fanfani**
the prime minister in the mid-1960's, killed by terrorists in 1978	**Aldo Moro**
the terrorist group who killed Aldo Moro	**Red Brigade**
the liberal parliament member and chronicler of modern Italy	**Luigi Barzini**
the ruling scion of **Monaco**'s House of Grimaldi	**Prince Rainier III**
Monaco's late American princess, an actress	**Grace Kelly**

the queen of the **Netherlands** since 1980	**Beatrix**
the queen from 1948 to abdication in 1980	**Juliana**
Juliana's husband, involved in a scandal over the American Lockheed firm	**Prince Bernhard**
the post-WWII prime minister of the Netherlands	**Willem Drees**
Poland's 1st post-WWII non-communist premier from 1989	**Tadeusz Mazowiecki**
the leader who imposed martial law in 1981	**Gen. Wojciech Jaruzelski**
the prime minister of Poland in the 1980's	**Zbigniew Messner**
the founder of Solidarity in 1970's Poland	**Lech Walesa**
the leader after Gomulka in 1970	**Edward Gierek**
the leader of Poland 1956–70	**Wladislaw Gomulka**
Portugal's president from 1986	**Mario Soares**
the leader of the 1974 "Carnation Revolution"	**Gen. Antonio de Spinola**
Salazar's successor in 1968	**Marcello Caetano**
Portugal's 40-year dictator from the 1920's	**António de Oliveira Salazar**
Romania's president elected in 1990	**Ion Iliescu**
Romania's president from 1965–89	**Nicolae Ceausescu**
Romania's premier and general after WWII	**Ion Antonescu**
Spain's prime minister from 1982	**Felipe Gonzalez Marquez**
the king who took over after Franco died	**Juan Carlos**
Fascist dictator from the 1930's to 1975	**Gen. Francisco Franco**
Sweden's premier assassinated in 1986	**Olof Palme**
the **USSR** general sec. from 1985	**Mikhail Gorbachev**
Mikhail Gorbachev's wife	**Raisa Gorbachev**
Gorbachev's key foreign minister	**Edward Shevardnadze**
foreign ministry spokesman under Gorbachev	**Gennadi Gerasimov**
a dissident and physicist, long in internal exile in Gorky, who won 1975 Nobel Peace Prize	**Andrei Sakharov**
a prominent dissident, Sakharov's wife	**Yelena Bonner**
the mathematician-dissident released to Israel in 1986 in a spy swap	**Anatoly (Natan) Shcharansky**

the longtime foreign minister until 1985	Andrei Gromyko
Gorbachev no. 2 man, labeled obstructionist	Yegor Ligachev
the Moscow party chief ousted in 1987	Boris Yeltsin
Andropov's brief successor	Konstantin Chernenko
the KGB head who briefly succeeded Brezhnev	Yuri Andropov
the 1st sec. and main leader after Khrushchev	Leonid Brezhnev
Brezhnev's co-equal, then deputy	Alexei Kosygin
the USSR leader deposed in 1964	Nikita Khrushchev
key party ideologist 1950's–82	Mikhail Suslov
Stalin's supposed heir, in Khrushchev's shadow	Georgi Malenkov
the NKVD head and "liquidator" from 1938	Lavrenti Beria
Yugoslavia's communist leader 1946–80	Marshal Tito (Josip Broz)
the critic and author of *The New Class*	Milovan Djilas
the Yugoslavian partisan leader executed in 1946	Draja Mikhailovich

Modern British Royals

queen from 1952	Elizabeth II
Elizabeth II's consort	Prince Philip Mountbatten
Elizabeth II's sister	Princess Margaret
Margaret's artist-husband, later estranged	Lord Snowdon, Anthony Armstrong-Jones
Elizabeth II's heir, Prince of Wales	Charles
Prince Charles's wife from 1981	Lady Diana Spencer
Charles and Diana's eldest son and heir	Prince William
Charles's uncle and mentor, killed by the IRA in 1979, who oversaw India's independence	Lord Mountbatten
Charles's sister, an avid horsewoman	Princess Anne
Elizabeth II's 2nd-born son	Prince Andrew
Prince Andrew's wife	Sarah Ferguson
Andrew and Sarah's 1st-born, a daughter	Beatrice
Elizabeth II's 3rd-born son	Prince Edward

Language of Politics and Public Life

In the world of politics and public life, what is or are . . . ?

Types of Government and Social Rule

a lack of political authority	**anarchy**
the old regime, as before the French Revolution	**ancien régime**
rule by a privileged or "noble" class	**aristocracy**
a government requiring strict obedience to authority, suppressing individual freedom and dissent	**authoritarian**
benign autocracy	**benevolent** or **enlightened despotism**
an alliance among 2 or more parties	**coalition**
the people's ownership of the means of production	**collectivism**
a country's rule of foreign territories	**colonialism**
a voluntary association, e.g., the countries of the former British Empire	**commonwealth**
supposedly classless economic and political rule by a single group in the name of the people	**communism**
rule by the people or their representatives	**democracy**
government by 2 equal rulers	**diarchy, duarchy,** *or* **duumvirate**
absolute rule by one person, esp. oppressive	**dictatorship, autocracy,** or **autarchy**
a self-governing nation, esp. in the British Commonwealth	**dominion**
a nation, esp. a kingdom, and its territories	**empire**
an extreme right dictatorship, as in Nazi Germany	**fascism**
a union of states giving some, but not all, power to a central government	**federalism**
the medieval relationship of vassals and lords	**feudalism**
rule by elders	**gerontocracy**
the domestic self-government of a dependency	**home rule**
the spread of a nation's control or influence to other nations	**imperialism**

rule by a small group of military officers	**junta**
government by the most talented	**meritocracy**
rule by a king or emperor	**monarchy**
rule by the mob	**ochlocracy**
rule by a representative body	**parliamentary**
Coleridge's utopian community plan	**pantisocracy**
government by the wealthy	**plutocracy**
a country under rigid control, esp. with secret police	**police state**
rule by one person in place of another, e.g., when the legitimate ruler is a minor	**regency**
a government, esp. a democracy, relying on a constitution	**republic**
democratic combined with socialism	**social democracy**
a system in which the main economic features are controlled by the state, with or without democracy	**socialism**
self-government and full independence	**sovereignty**
ruling another nation in foreign affairs, but allowing it domestic self-government	**suzerainty**
a movement to have labor unions control business and the state	**syndicalism**
government by scientists and technicians	**technocracy**
rule by priests or the clergy	**theocracy** or **hiero-**
a government that achieves social unity by authoritarian means	**totalitarian**
government by 3 equal rulers	**triarchy** or **triumvirate**
government by a cruel, unjust single ruler	**tyranny**
a system in which the government agrees to care for its citizens	**welfare state**

Political Stances and Actions

a select, powerful group of unofficial advisors	**cabal**
excessive nationalist enthusiasm	**chauvinism** or **jingoism**
the refusal to obey laws seen as unjust	**civil disobedience**
the quick overthrow of an existing government	**coup d'état** or **putsch**

placing friends in key positions	**cronyism**
a leader appealing to people's emotions and prejudices	**demagogue**
deliberate spreading of false information	**disinformation**
the supposed basis for a medieval monarch's rule	**divine right**
the strong, sometimes extreme, support for freedom of action	**libertarianism**
freeing people from slavery or parental control	**emancipation** or **manumission**
a subversive group working for another country's or party's aims	**fifth column**
deriving unwarranted profit from political influence	**graft**
the trial of a public officer, e.g., a president	**impeachment**
the 19th-c. anti-immigrant, anti-Catholic party	**Know-nothings**
the 19th-c. belief that the US should expand from Atlantic to Pacific	**manifest destiny**
the temporary replacement of civil by military rule	**martial law**
the political theory giving rise to communism	**Marxism**
stressing domestic, rather than international, views	**nationalism**
the government takeover of private production or service organizations	**nationalization**
favoring family and friends, esp. in patronage	**nepotism**
not stemming from any single party	**nonpartisan**
an official to protect citizens from government abuse	**ombudsman**
the nonviolent refusal to comply with authority	**passive resistance**
distributing political offices on the basis of political friendship, not merit	**patronage**
politics focusing on fairer distribution of wealth and power, esp. among the general population	**populism**
politics associated with Robert La Follette	**progressivism**

to restore to favor a disgraced public official	**rehabilitate**
harming property or society for subversive aims	**sabotage**
fostering of resistance to the government	**sedition**
the people's right to determine how they shall be ruled	**self-determination**
the idea that government should be based on the consent of the governed	**social contract**
rights not conceded to the central government by the states, in federalism	**states' rights**
the replacement of 1 ruler by another	**succession**
the use of violence and induced fear for political ends	**terrorism**
the formal recognition of minority rights, esp. in religion	**sufferance**
seizing power that belongs to another	**usurpation**

Elections and Electioneering

voting for a single candidate when there is proportional representation	**bullet ballot**
a special election to fill a vacancy	**by-election**
soliciting votes or opinions	**canvass**
an outsider seeking political office in a region	**carpetbagger**
the voters or region served by an elected official	**constituency**
an outside shot in a political race	**dark horse**
the people who actually elect	**electors**
a right by law, e.g., the right to vote	**franchise**
moving district lines to benefit a political party	**gerrymandering**
a campaign from a widespread political base, not from a strong political center	**grass roots**
the electorate's views, as shown in an election	**mandate**
the declared principles of a party	**platform** or **plank**
the electorate's direct vote on a question	**plebiscite**

the largest number of votes in a contest, not necessarily a majority	**plurality**
voting by ranking choices	**preferential voting**
an election to select candidates for a later election	**primary**
voting to remove a public official from office	**recall**
putting a measure up to a popular vote	**referendum**
a small party split off from a large one	**splinter party**
voting for candidates of more than 1 party	**split ticket**
rewarding supporters after an election	**spoils system**
a supposed candidate preparing the way for another	**stalking horse**
voting for people of all 1 party	**straight ticket**
casting fake votes	**stuffing the ballot box**
the right to vote	**suffrage**
a district that might readily vote for either party	**swing district**
campaigning in many small towns, esp. by railroad	**whistle-stop campaign**

Legislatures and Lawmaking

a legislature with 2 houses	**bicameral**
supported by people from 2 parties	**bipartisan**
a party meeting to decide on candidates and issues	**caucus**
a bill full of special-interest group provisions	**Christmas tree bill**
ending a debate by taking an immediate vote on a question	**cloture**
a bill that puts an action into effect	**enabling**
delaying tactics, esp. long speeches in the Senate	**filibuster**
laws passed, and the process of passing them	**legislation**
the ability to veto parts, rather than all, of a bill	**line item veto**
to attempt to sway legislators	**lobby**
a formal call for a vote	**motion**
full or complete, as of a legislative session	**plenary**

a veto by failure to sign a bill within the specified time after Congress's adjournment	**pocket veto**
a project benefiting a legislator's constituency	**pork barrel**
a call for an immediate vote, ending debate, i.e., bringing on cloture	**previous question**
the subject under discussion	**question**
the number of members needed to vote or carry on business in a body	**quorum**
to control or restrict, but not bar, activities	**regulate**
to revoke a law	**repeal**
an expression of opinion, without the force of law	**resolution**
rules governing behavior in formal meetings	**Robert's Rules of Order**
calling of names for an oral vote	**roll call**
a small, weak remainder of a larger parliament	**rump**
sitting of the legislature, as of a court	**session**
a law passed by a legislature	**statute**
to delay consideration of a bill	**table** or **pigeonhole**
a legislature with 1 house	**unicameral**
a chief executive's rejection of a bill	**veto**
the person who tries to see that party members are present and vote as desired	**whip**

People From the Past

Key Figures in World History

(For post-WWII figures, see *Politics and People*; see also Key Figures in Religion and Philosophy and Christian Saints in *World of Philosophy and Belief*; People of Science and Invention in *World of the Sciences*, and appropriate sections of *World of Letters* and *World of the Arts*)

Among the key figures in history around the world, who . . . ?

In Africa

united Egypt by 3000 B.C.	**Menes**
built the Step Pyramid at Sakkara	**Zoser**
designed the Step Pyramid for his pharaoh	**Imhotep**
built the largest of Giza's 3 great pyramids	**Cheops (Khufu)**
invaded Syria in the time of Abraham	**Sesostris III**
ruled as regent, then as queen herself	**Hatshepsut**
was Hatshepsut's grandson, a monotheist	**Amenhotep IV**, later **Akhenaton**
was Akhenaton's wife	**Nefertiti**
was a 14th-c. B.C. pharaoh whose tomb was found untouched in the early 20th c.	**Tutankhamen**
was the 13th-c. B.C. Egyptian "king of kings"	**Ramses**
founded Carthage in 814 B.C., by legend	**Dido** or **Elissa**
was the great 5th-c. B.C. Carthaginian general	**Hamilcar**
explored the Atlantic coast of Africa, Hamilcar's son	**Hanno**
explored the Atlantic coast of Europe, Hamilcar's son	**Himilco**
crossed the Alps with elephants to attack Rome in the 3rd-c. B.C., Hamilcar's grandson	**Hannibal**

was the Greek ruler of Egypt after Alexander	Ptolemy
was the last of the Ptolemaic line, linked with Caesar and Antony	Cleopatra
founded a new dynasty during the Crusades	Saladin (Salah ed-Din)
led the 14th-c. Mali Empire	Mansa Kankan Musa
led the 16th-c. Songhai Empire	Askia Muhammad
explored the Niger and the Gambia in the 18th c.	Mungo Park
explored up the Nile, a Swiss	J. L. Burckhardt
separately reached Timbuktu in the early 19th c.	Alexander Laing and René Caillé
took control in Egypt in 1805	Muhammad Ali
crossed mid-Africa in the mid-19th c., a missionary	David Livingstone
explored the Nile and Lake Tanganyika	Richard Burton and John Speke
said, "Dr. Livingston, I presume" in 1871	Henry Stanley
led the Zulu campaigns called Mfecane, "The Crushing"	Shaka
killed a party of Boer immigrants in 1838	Dingaan
defeated Dingaan and helped settle Natal	Andreas Pretorius
was 1st president of the South African Republic in the Transvaal, from 1856	Marthinius Pretorius
had built, in 1869, and later sold the Suez Canal	Isma'il
led the Boer protest against annexation of the South African Republic by the Cape Colony	Paul Kruger
led the 1880's dervish rebellion in Sudan, called The Mahdi (The Expected One)	Mohammed Ahmed
was killed by the Mahdi at Khartoum in 1885	Charles "China" Gordon
was the Cape Colony's prime minister from 1890	Cecil Rhodes
established the 1920's Rif Republic in Morocco	Abd el-Krim
resisted the Italian invasion of Ethiopia in 1936	Haile Selassie

In the Americas (Outside the U.S.)

Among key historical figures in the Americas (outside the U.S.), who . . . ?

In Canada

1st reached the Pacific overland from the east, through Canada, in 1789	**Alexander Mackenzie**
was independent Canada's 1st prime minister	**John A. MacDonald**
led an 1860's prairie rebellion in Manitoba	**Louis Riel**
was prime minister 1896–1911	**Wilfrid Laurier**
was Canada's prime minister 1921–30, 1935–48	**William Lyon Mackenzie King**

In Latin America

discovered the Americas, looking for Asia, in 1492	**Christopher Columbus (né Cristoforo Colombo)**
explorer who gave his name to America	**Amerigo Vespucci**
discovered Brazil from the sea in 1500	**Pedro Alvares Cabral**
1st saw the Pacific Ocean from Panama in 1513	**Vasco Nuñuz de Balboa**
explored the Rio de la Plata in 1515	**Juan Diaz de Solis**
was the Aztec emperor who lost Mexico to Cortés	**Montezuma II**
explored Mexico in 1519	**Hernando Cortés**
invaded the Inca Empire in the 1530's	**Francisco Pizarro**
was the Inca ruler Pizarro held for ransom, then killed	**Atahualpa**
ransacked old Panama in the late 16th c.	**Francis Drake**
first rounded South America's Cape Horn, in 1616	**Willem van Schouten** and **Jacob Lemaire**
destroyed old Panama in the mid-17th c.	**Henry Morgan**
was a woman pirate captain of the early 18th c.	**Anne Bonney**
was a West Indies and Indian Ocean pirate captain in the late 18th c.	**William Kidd**
was an early-18th-c. pirate known as Blackbeard	**Edward Teach**
was the early-19th-c. Haitian independence leader	**Toussaint L'Ouverture**

took Lima, Peru, in 1821, Argentine's liberator	**José de San Martin**
successfully rebelled against the Spanish in Mexico in 1821	**Agustin Iturbide**
was the 19th-c. hero of Bolivian independence	**Simon Bolivár**
was Chile's 1st director after independence	**Bernardo O'Higgins**
was general of the 1830's Mexican army against Texas	**Antonio Lopez de Santa Anna**
was an American who made himself president of Nicaragua in 1856–57	**William Walker**
led Puerto Rico's fight for freedom from Spain in 1909	**Luis Muñoz Rivera**
was Mexico's Austrian ruler in the 1860's	**Maximilian**
led the successful Mexican revolution against Maximilian's rule	**Benito Juarez**
was the leading peasant revolutionary of the Mexican Revolution	**Emiliano Zapata**
was the ex-bandit who became a general in the Mexican Revolution	**Pancho Villa**
was the dictator overthrown by the Mexican Revolution of 1910	**Porfirio Diaz**
was the radical reformist president of Mexico 1934–40	**Lázaro Cardenas**

In Asia

In Central and East Asia (except Japan)

united China in the 1st B.C., the "Yellow Emperor"	**Shih Huang Ti**
was China's "Martial Emperor" of the 2nd–1st c. B.C.	**Wu Ti**
explored Central Asia for the Chinese in the 2nd c. B.C.	**Chang Ch'ien**
was the legendary founder of Korea	**Tan'gun**
founded China's T'ang Dynasty in the 7th c. A.D.	**Li Yüan**
was the expansionist 7th-c. A.D. Chinese emperor	**T'ai Tsung**
was the great 8th-c. Chinese ruler	**Hsüan Tsung (Ming Huang)**

ruled most of Asia and founded China's Yüan dynasty in the 13th c.	**Genghis Khan (Temujin)**
took China, founded Xanadu, and invaded Japan	**Kublai Khan**
was the 14th-c. conqueror called "the Lame"	**Timur (Tamerlane)**
sailed to East Africa for China in the 15th c.	**Cheng Ho**
was the turn-of-the-20th-c. dowager empress	**Ts'u Hsi**
founded the Chinese Republic in 1911	**Sun Yat-sen**
was Madame Sun Yat-sen	**Soong Qingling (Ch'ing-ling)**
was China's "Last Emperor"	**Henry P'u Yi (né Hsüan T'ung)**

In India

was the 4th-c. B.C. Indian emperor	**Chandragupta**
made India a Buddhist state in the 3rd c. B.C.	**Asoka**
was the 16th-c. Indian emperor, descended from Genghis Khan	**Babur**
was Babur's grandson and notable successor	**Akbar**
was the great 17th-c. Moghul emperor	**Aurengzeb**

In Japan

was the 7th-c. B.C. emperor, or Mikado	**Kamu-Yamato-Iware-Biko**
was the 6th–7th-c. A.D. Buddhist prince	**Shotoku**
was the 1st shogun, in 1185, from the Genji clan	**Yoritomo Minamoto**
tried to unite the country in the 16th c.	**Nobunaga Oda**
persecuted Christians in the late 16th c.	**Hideyoshi Toyotomo**
reorganized Japan in the 17th c.	**Ieyasu Tokugawa**
closed Japan's ports to outsiders in 1639	**Iemitsu**
opened Japan's ports in 1853, a US commodore	**Matthew Perry**
was prime minister 1929–30, killed by the right	**Hamaguchu Osachi**
was 1931 prime minister killed by the right	**Inukai Tsuyohi**

took Japan into WWII as prime minister	**Tojo Hideckl**
designed the attack on Pearl Harbor, an admiral	**Isoroku Yamamoto**
commanded the SE Asia invasion	**Tomoyuki Yamashita**
commanded the air fleet at Pearl Harbor and Midway	**Chuichi Nagumo**
developed kamikaze tactics	**Takijiro Onishi**
oversaw the Bataan death march in the Philippines	**Masaharu Homma**
broadcast for the Japanese as Tokyo Rose	**Iva Ikuko Toguri D'Aquino**
was emperor before, during, and after WWII	**Hirohito**

In the Near East

conquered northern Syria before 2350 B.C., king of Akkad and Naram-Sin	**Sargon**
established a code of laws in 18th-c. B.C. Babylon	**Hammurabi**
were early Jewish patriarchs from before 1500 B.C.	**Abraham, Isaac,** and **Jacob**
were key Jewish leaders from the age of judges, before 1000 B.C.	**Deborah, Gideon,** and **Samson**
was Israel's 1st king, killed fighting the Philistines	**Saul**
was Israel's 10th-c. B.C. king who took Jerusalem	**David**
built a temple in Jerusalem, David's wise successor	**Solomon**
sent out a Phoenician trading fleet with Solomon	**Hiram I of Tyre**
came to visit Solomon from southern Arabia	**Queen of Sheba**
was Israel's 9th-c. B.C. king, husband of Jezebel	**Ahab**
was the 9th-c. B.C. prophet who opposed idol-worship	**Elijah**
was the 9th-c. B.C. king of Judah	**Jehosophat**
invaded Judah from Syria in 701 B.C.	**Sennacherib**
was Judah's king against the Assyrians	**Hezekiah**
was a prophet of Hezekiah's period	**Isaiah**
was Judah's king, killed in 609 B.C.	**Josiah**
was a gloomy prophet of Josiah's period	**Jeremiah**
destroyed the Jews' temple in Jerusalem, a 6th-c. B.C. Babylonian king	**Nebuchadnezzar**

rebuilt Jerusalem's walls, in the 5th-c. B.C.	**Nehemiah**
Persia's king, defeated off Greece in 490 B.C.	**Darius**
Darius's son and heir, defeated by Alexander the Great	**Xerxes**
ruled in the Middle East after Alexander the Great	**Seleucid**
was the 3rd-c. B.C. queen of Palmyra	**Zenobia**
outlawed Jewish practices in 167 B.C.	**Antiochus IV**
reconsecrated the Jerusalem temple in 165 B.C.	**Judah the Maccabee**
made Israel a Roman province in 63 B.C.	**Pompey**
was the 1st-c. B.C. "king of Jews" named by Mark Antony	**Herod the Great**
ordered the crucifixion of Jesus Christ in 29 A.D.	**Pontius Pilate**
took and destroyed Jerusalem in 70 A.D.	**Titus**
built Jerusalem's Dome of the Rock in 691	**Caliph Abd el-Malik**
was the caliph in Baghdad from 786 to 809	**Harun al-Rashid**
was the Mongol who burned Baghdad in 1258	**Hulagu Khan**
was the 16th-c. ruler who did much building	**Suleiman the Magnificent**
was the British officer who helped organize the WWI Arab revolt against the Turks	**T. E. Lawrence (of Arabia)**
declared Arab independence from Turkey in 1916, the Grand Sherif of Mecca	**Hussein Ibn Ali**
took Jerusalem for the British in 1917	**Edmund Henry Allenby**
led Turkey to its post-WWI independence	**Mustafa Kemal Ataturk**
was the ruler installed in Jordan in 1921	**Abdullah**
headed the Arab Legion in the Transjordan	**John Glubb "Pasha"**
was king of Iraq from 1921, from *Lawrence of Arabia*	**Faisal**
formed the kingdom of Saudi Arabia in 1932	**Ibn-Saud (né Abd al-Aziz Ibn-Saud)**

In Southeast Asia

killed Magellan in the Philippines	**Lapu-Lapu**
was the 1st governor-general of the Philippines	**Miquel Lopez de Legazpi**
liberated Siam (now Thailand), in the 16th c.	**Naresuan**
founded Siam's Chakri dynasty in the 18th c.	**Chao Phya Chakri** or **Rama I**
founded Singapore in 1819, a Briton	**Thomas Stamford Raffles**
was the late-19th-c. Thai king, "The Beloved"	**Chulalongkorn** or **Rama V**
was the 19th-c. Thai ruler in *The King and I*	**Mongkut** or **Rama IV**
was the Philippine patriot executed in 1896	**Jose Rizal**
rebelled against Spanish rule, becoming the Philippines' 1st president in 1899	**Emile Aquinaldo**
became the Philippines' president in 1935	**Manuel Quezon**

In Australia and the Pacific

first circled Australia and discovered New Zealand	**Abel Janszoon Tasman**
sailed the strait between Australia and New Guinea	**Luis de Torres**
explored Australia, New Zealand, and the Pacific basin in the 19th c., a British captain	**James Cook**
was an early, powerful Australian sheepbreeder	**John MacArthur**
was the governor who sparked the Rum Rebellion in 1808	**William Bligh**
was Australia's 1st non-naval governor	**Col. Lachlan Macquarie**
oversaw Australian expansion in the 1820's	**Thomas Brisbane**
Brisbane's successor, who introduced trial by jury	**Ralph Darling**
2-time governor of New Zealand, from Australia	**George Grey**

In Europe

Before the Roman Empire

(See also Homer's Characters and Places in *World of Letters*)

was the king of Mycenae	**Agamemnon**
laid out Sparta's strict military life	**Lykourgos**
instituted harsh law in 7th-c B.C. Athens	**Draco**
reformed Athens in the 6th-c B.C.	**Solon**
led the Greeks at Marathon in 490 B.C.	**Miltiades**
led the Greeks at Thermopylae in 480 B.C.	**Leonidas**
rebuilt the Greek fleet after defeat by the Persians	**Themistocles**
led Athens during its 5th-c. B.C. Golden Age	**Pericles**
was a key Athenian general in the Peloponnesian War	**Alcibiades**
was Athens' great 5th-c. B.C. orator	**Demosthenes**
was the Macedonian king who conquered Greece	**Philip II**
was Philip's son, who conquered much of the Near East	**Alexander the Great**

In the Roman Empire

supposedly founded Rome, wolf-suckled twins	**Romulus** and **Remus**
urged in the Senate that Carthage be destroyed	**Cato**
crossed the Rubicon to spark civil war, later assassinated by Brutus and others	**Julius Caesar**
was defeated at Actium with Cleopatra in 31 B.C.	**Mark Antony**
succeeded Caesar, being Rome's 1st emperor and founder of the Pax Romana (Roman Peace)	**Caesar Augustus** (né **Octavian**)
was Caesar Augustus's wife	**Livia**
was Augustus's stepson and heir	**Tiberius**
led Rome's 1st-c. A.D. slave rebellion	**Spartacus**
was the mad emperor assassinated in 41 A.D.	**(Caius) Caligula**
conquered Britain for Rome	**Claudius**
was Claudius's nymphomaniacal wife	**Messalina**

was Claudius's 4th wife and niece	**Agrippina**
Agrippina's son, who supposedly fiddled while Rome burned	**Nero**
oversaw completion of the Colosseum in 80	**Titus**
firmed up Roman rule in the Balkans in the 2nd-c A.D.	**Trajan**
Trajan's road-building successor	**Hadrian**
died in 180 A.D., ending the Pax Romana	**Marcus Aurelius**
tried to revive the empire in the 3rd c. A.D.	**Diocletian**
made Christianity Rome's state religion in 313	**Constantine**
led the Visigoths to sack Rome in 410	**Alaric**
was the Ostrogoth king of Italy from 476	**Odoacer (Odovacar)**

From the Middle Ages to the Mid-20th Century

In the British Isles

was queen of the Iceni, who fought the Romans	**Boadicea**
reportedly ordered the sea to recede	**King Canute**
was king of the legendary Camelot	**King Arthur**
was King Arthur's wife	**Guinevere**
was Queen Guinevere's lover, in tradition	**Lancelot du Lac**
was the learned 9th-c. Saxon king	**Alfred the Great**
was the 10th-c. king nicknamed "the Unready"	**Ethelred**
built the central chapel in Westminster Abbey	**Edward the Confessor**
was the Irish king who held off the Norse in 1014	**Brian Boru**
successfully invaded Britain in 1066, a Norman	**William the Conqueror**
was defeated by William at Hastings in 1066	**Harold**
was the 12th-c. Norman king who founded the House of Plantagenet	**Henry II**
married Louis IX and later England's Henry II, mother of Richard Coeur-de-Lion	**Eleanor of Aquitaine**

was the archbishop killed at Canterbury in 1170	**Thomas à Becket**
succeeded Henry, nicknamed the Lionheart (Coeur-de-Lion)	**Richard I**
was Henry and Eleanor's 2nd son	**Geoffrey**
was Richard I's usurping brother, forced to sign the Magna Carta	**John**
was the legendary robber-hero of John's time	**Robin Hood**
ruled during England's first parliament	**Henry III**
was leader of the barons in the 13th-c. civil wars, creating the 1st parliament	**Simon de Montfort, Earl of Leicester**
won Scotland's independence in 1328	**Robert Bruce**
was the half-legendary 14th-c. London mayor	**Dick Whittington**
claimed the French throne, starting the Hundred Years' War; victor at Crécy	**Edward III**
was the 14th-c. king overthrown and then killed	**Richard II**
tried to drive the English from Wales in 1402	**Owen Glendower (Owain Glyndwr)**
defeated the French at Agincourt in 1415	**Henry V**
was deposed in 1460, starting the War of the Roses	**Henry VI**
was symbolized by the red rose	**House of Lancaster**
was symbolized by the white rose	**House of York**
was the hunchback king accused of killing his young nephews to gain the throne	**Richard III**
was the family who ended the War of the Roses	**House of Tudor**
was the first Tudor king	**Henry VII**
was the much-married Tudor king	**Henry VIII**
was Henry VIII's 1st wife, mother of Mary	**Catherine of Aragon**
was the cardinal who arranged for Henry VIII's divorce from Catherine	**Thomas Wolsey**
was Wolsey's successor	**Thomas Cranmer**
was Henry VIII's chancellor, later executed for refusing to approve of the divorce	**Thomas More**

was Henry VIII's 2nd wife, mother of Elizabeth, later executed	**Anne Boleyn**
was Henry VIII's 3rd wife, mother of Edward VI	**Jane Seymour**
was Henry VIII's 4th wife	**Anne of Cleves**
was Henry VIII's 5th wife, later executed	**Catherine Howard**
was Henry VIII's 6th wife, who outlived him	**Catherine Parr**
was Edward VI's brief successor	**Lady Jane Grey**
succeeded the sickly Edward VI and married Philip II of Spain	**Mary I**
succeeded Mary, ruling over England's great age	**Elizabeth I**
was Elizabeth I's general and great love	**Robert Dudley, Earl of Leicester**
was executed for rebellion, once a favorite	**Earl of Essex**
was the Scottish queen executed by Elizabeth	**Mary, Queen of Scots**
was husband of Mary, Queen of Scots	**Lord Darnley**
spread his cloak over a puddle for Elizabeth I	**Walter Raleigh**
fought the Spanish Armada out of Plymouth	**Francis Drake**
was both Mary and Elizabeth's sec. of state	**William Cecil, Lord Burleigh**
succeeded Elizabeth, first of the Stuart line, uniting England and Scotland	**James I (James VI of Scotland)**
tried to blow up Parliament in 1605	**Guy Fawkes**
succeeded James I, later beheaded	**Charles I**
supported Charles I in the 1640's Civil War	**Cavaliers**
were the Puritan supporters of Cromwell	**Roundheads**
led the Commonwealth founded in 1653	**Oliver Cromwell**
was Cromwell's successor as "Protector"	**Richard Cromwell**
replaced Cromwell at the Restoration	**Charles II**
succeeded Charles II, later deposed and exiled	**James II**
were the Protestant Dutch king and British queen brought in to replace Catholic James II in the "Glorious Revolution"	**William III and Mary II**

succeeded William and Mary	**Anne**
was the great 17th–18th-c. general in the wars against France	**John Churchill, Duke of Marlborough**
was Marlboroughs' wife, friend of Queen Anne	**Sarah Churchill**
was the ruling house after Anne's death	**House of Hanover**
was prime minister under George I and II	**Robert Walpole**
was the Stuart claimant defeated at Culloden in 1746	**Bonnie Prince Charlie**
hid and helped the Prince after Culloden	**Flora MacDonald**
was the king during the American Revolution	**George III**
was the key prime minister under George III	**William Pitt the Younger**
ruled as regent during George III's madness	**Prince George,** later **George IV**
won the 1805 fight against Napoleon at Trafalgar	**Horatio Nelson**
was Nelson's longtime mistress	**Emma Hamilton**
defeated the French at Waterloo in 1815, the "Iron Duke," later prime minister	**Duke of Wellington**
succeeded George IV in the 1830's	**William IV**
was a reform Whig prime minister of the 1830's	**Earl Grey**
was a mid-19th-c. liberal Conservative prime minister	**Robert Peel**
served alternately as prime minister in the 1840's–60's	**Lords Russell** and **Palmerston**
helped win Catholic emancipation in 1829, known in Ireland as "The Liberator"	**Daniel O'Connell**
became queen in 1837, giving her name to an age	**Victoria**
was Victoria's beloved German consort	**Prince Albert of Saxe-Coburg**
was Victoria's favorite prime minister, born a Jew	**Benjamin Disraeli**
was Disraeli's counterpart in the Liberal Party	**William Gladstone**
conquered the Sudan and put down the Boers	**Horatio Herbert Kitchener**
led the late-19th-c. Irish push for Home Rule until politically destroyed by a divorce suit	**Charles Stewart Parnell**

founded the Labour Party in 1888, a Scot	**Keir Hardie**
succeeded Victoria in 1901	**Edward VII**
helped found the socialist Fabian Society with Shaw	**Beatrice Potter Webb** and **Sidney Webb**
succeeded Edward VII in 1910	**George V**
was the central family of British feminists, who founded the Women's Social and Political Union in 1912	**Emmeline, Christabel,** and **Sylvia Pankhurst**
was liberal prime minister 1908–16	**Herbert Asquith**
said "the lamps are going out all over Europe"	**Edward Grey**
was Liberal prime minister 1916–22	**David Lloyd George**
was viceroy of India, Lloyd George's foreign sec.	**George Curzon**
was Winston Churchill's father, a British M.P.	**Randolph Churchill**
was Winston Churchill's mother, an American	**Jennie Jerome**
was an Irish revolutionary hanged for treason in 1916	**Roger Casement**
led the Irish Volunteers in the 1916 Rising	**Patrick Pearse**
led the Irish Citizen Army in the 1916 Rising	**James Connolly**
accepted partition for the Irish Republicans	**Michael Collins**
supported a Jewish homeland in Palestine	**Arthur Balfour**
was 1st Labour prime minister 1924, and 1929	**James Ramsey MacDonald**
was independent Ireland's 1st president in 1921 and prime minister 1930's–50's	**Eamon de Valera**
succeeded George V in 1936 and then abdicated	**Edward VIII**
was the American woman for whom Edward VII gave up his throne	**Bessie Wallis Warfield Simpson**
was prime minister 1923, 1924–29, 1936–37, during the General Strike and abdication crisis	**Stanley Baldwin**
was a leading 1930's British fascist	**Oswald Mosley**
ruled from 1936–52, during WWII	**George VI**
was George VI's wife, later the "Queen Mum"	**Elizabeth Bowes-Lyon**

was the prime minister who tried to appease Hitler	Neville Chamberlain
was the 1st woman M.P., an American heiress	Nancy Langhorne Astor
evacuated Dunkirk, later led in North Africa	Harold Alexander
was the victorious general at El Alamein in 1942	Bernard Montgomery
led the forces that liberated Burma in 1945	William Slim
was the British Nazi broadcaster in WWII as Lord Haw-Haw	William Joyce

In Eastern Europe

bedeviled Europe in the 5th c.	Attila the Hun
was Hungary's 1st Christian king, in the 11th c.	St. Stephen
was the Bohemian king celebrated in a carol	Wenceslas (Václav)
was a 19th-c. leader for Hungarian freedom	Lajos Kossuth
were key leaders of post-WWI Czechoslovakia	Thomas Masaryk and Eduard Benes
led Hungary's 1918 Liberal revolution	Mihály (Michael) Károlyi
was the Communist leader who followed Károlyi	Béla Kun
was independent Poland's 1st premier after WWI, a world-class pianist	Ignacy Paderewski
was the main Polish general in the 1920 Soviet-Polish War	Jósef Pilsudski
was the Ukrainian general allied with the Poles in 1920	Simon Petlyura
was the Yugoslavian dictator assassinated in 1934	Alexander I
was the 1930's Romanian king forced to abdicate	Carol II
was Carol II's puppet successor through WWII	Michael
was Romania's WWII pro-Nazi leader	Marshal Antonescu
was Hungary's WWII leader	István Bethlen

In France

| founded the Carolingian line in the 7th c. | Pepin |
| turned back the Moslems at Poitiers in 732 | Charles Martel |

was made Roman Emperor in 800	**Charlemagne**
made Paris the French capital in 987	**Hugh Capet**
was France's crusader-king, later sainted	**Louis IX**
had a schism with Rome in 1296	**Philip IV the Fair**
turned the Hundred Years' War toward France	**Joan of Arc**
was the Dauphin Joan of Arc made secure	**Charles VII**
was the 1st husband of Mary, Queen of Scots	**Francis II**
was Francis II's powerful mother	**Catherine de' Medici**
founded the Bourbon line and guaranteed religious tolera- tion in the Edict of Nantes	**Henry IV**
was Henry IV's wife, a powerful Catholic	**Marie de' Medici**
was the powerful cardinal allied with Marie	**Cardinal Richelieu**
was the Sun King, the extravagant 18th-c. ruler	**Louis XIV**
was the powerful cardinal of Louis XIV's reign	**Cardinal Mazarin**
were Louis XIV's 2 most notorious mistresses	**Marquise de Pompadour** and **Comtesse du Barry**
was king from 1774; guillotined in 1793	**Louis XVI**
was Louis XVI's queen, daughter of Maria Theresa, the Hapsburg empress	**Marie Antoinette**
was a moderate leader of the national assembly	**Comte de Honoré Mirabeau**
were the more moderate revolutionaries	**Girondins**
were the more radical revolutionaries	**Jacobins**
helped overthrow the Girondins, a revolutionary club	**Cordeliers**
was a Cordelier leader, later executed	**Georges Jacques Danton**
was the revolutionary assassi- nated in his bath by Charlotte Corday	**Jean Paul Marat**
led the guillotine-mad Reign of Terror	**Maximilian Robespierre**
ruled after Robespierre fell, a revolutionary group	**Directoire**

was the Corsican general who seized power in 1799, and started 15 years of war	**Napoleon Bonaparte**
married Bonaparte in 1796	**Josephine de Beauharnais**
was France's foreign minister under Napoleon and later, under the restored Bourbons	**Charles Maurice de Talleyrand-Périgord**
was the "citizen king" who took power in 1830	**Louis-Philippe**
was a nephew of Napoleon, elected president in 1848, later proclaimed emperor	**Louis Napoleon,** later **Napoleon III**
was Napoleon III's empress	**Eugénie**
was the 19th-c. French captain attacked by anti-Semites	**Alfred Dreyfus**
was premier 1906–9, 1917–20, helping shape the Treaty of Versailles	**Georges Clemenceau**
tried to appease Hitler over Czechoslovakia	**Édouard Daladier**
was designer of the fortified line on the French border	**André Maginot**
led France badly during the "Phony War"	**Maurice Gamelin**
was the WWI marshal, leader of the Vichy government	**Philippe Pétain**
was head of the Vichy government after 1942	**Pierre Laval**
was the North African leader appointed by Eisenhower	**François Darlan**
was the officer leading French North Africa after Darlan	**Henri Giraud**
was the general who took the German surrender in Paris	**Jacques Leclerc**

In the Germanies, Austria, and the Low Countries

defeated the Romans in 9 A.D.	**Hermann (Arminius)**
was crowned Holy Roman Emperor in 962	**Otto the Great**
was the 12th-c. Hohenstaufen emperor who battled with the pope	**Frederick Barbarossa**
were the supporters of Frederick Barbarossa	**Ghibellines**
were the supporters of the pope	**Guelphs**
was Austrian ruling dynasty from 13th–20th c.	**Hapsburgs**
was the 16th-c. emperor who retired to a monastery	**Charles V**

was Holland's Protestant leader against Spain	**William the Silent of Orange**
was Spain's anti-Protestant general in Holland	**Duke of Alva (Alba)**
came to the Hapsburg throne in 1740, sparking the Wars of the Austrian Succession	**Maria Theresa**
militarized Germany in the 18th c.	**Hohenzollerns**
was a key 18th-c. Prussian ruler	**Frederick the Great**
was president of the post-Napoleon Congress of Vienna, an Austrian prince	**Klemens Lothar Metternich**
was the Iron Chancellor, who unified Germany	**Bismarck**
was Wagner's patron, the "Dream King" of Bavaria	**Ludwig II**
was Hapsburg ruler from 1848 to WWI	**Franz Josef**
was the Hapsburg who died mysteriously at Mayerling in 1889	**Rudolf**
was Rudolf's mistress, also found dead at Mayerling	**Marie Vetsera**
was the archduke and Hapsburg heir killed in 1914	**Franz Ferdinand**
was Germany's kaiser in WWI, later abdicating	**William II**
led Germany's navy before and during WWI	**Alfred von Tirpitz**
was the German sec. of state who proposed an alliance with Mexico against the US in 1917	**Arthur Zimmerman**
was Germany's famed flying ace, the "Red Baron"	**Manfred von Richthofen**
was a WWI spy for the Germans, a Dutch dancer	**Mata Hari (né Margaretha Geertruida Zelle)**
led the 1919 Spartacist revolt and were assassinated by the right	**Rosa Luxemburg** and **Karl Liebknecht**
was 1st president of the Weimar Republic	**Friedrich Ebert**
was dictator of Austria 1932–34, killed by Nazis	**Engelbert Dollfuss**
was the German Communist leader killed in 1944	**Ernst Thaelmann**
was the Dutch queen from the 19th c. to 1948	**Wilhelmina**
led Nazi Germany to WWII and wrote *Mein Kampf*	**Adolf Hitler (né Schicklgruber)**

was Hitler's mistress and at the end his wife	**Eva Braun**
was leader of the Storm Troopers (SA or Brown-shirts), killed in the 1934 Nazi purge	**Ernst Roehm**
was Hitler's deputy, who flew to Scotland in 1941	**Rudolf Hess**
was creator of the SS (Blackshirts), including the Gestapo and the death camp system	**Heinrich Himmler**
was president during the Nazi Years	**Hermann Goering**
was chief propagandist during the Nazi years	**Joseph Goebbels**
was the key organizer of the Holocaust, "The Hangman"	**Reinhard Heydrich**
was the head of the Nazi high command from 1938	**Wilhelm Keitel**
was the general in North Africa, the "Desert Fox"	**Erwin Rommel**
was Hitler's personal assistant, long rumored to be alive	**Martin Bormann**
was the SS officer captured in 1960 and hanged in 1962	**Adolf Eichmann**
was the Austrian SS general and head of the Gestapo	**Ernst Kaltenbrunner**
was air force chief of staff from 1936	**Albert Kesselring**
was the chief racist theoretician during the Nazi years	**Alfred Rosenberg**
was the publisher who developed genocide proposals	**Julius Streicher**
was head of army intelligence and secret Hitler opponent	**Wilhelm Canaris**
was the colonel who tried to kill Hitler in 1944	**Klaus von Stauffenberg**
named Hitler Chancellor, the aging president	**Paul von Hindenburg**
was the chief "experimenting" doctor at Auschwitz	**Josef Mengele**
was the diplomat who made a 1939 nonaggression pact with the Russians	**Joachim von Ribbentrop**
was head of Nazi Germany's war production system	**Albert Speer**
was the main arms supplier to the Nazis	**Krupp family**
signed the German surrender in 1945	**Alfred Jodl**

was the American who broadcast for the Nazis as Axis Sally	**Mildred Gillars**
was Belgium's king imprisoned during WWII	**Leopold III**

In Greece

was Greece's leader in much of the early 20th c.	**Eleutherios Venizelos**
took the Greek throne in 1920	**King Constantine I**
took power in a 1934 coup	**Gen. John Metaxas**

In Italy

was the strong 15th-c. ruler of Florence	**Cosimo de' Medici**
was the late-15th-c. ruler of Florence, "the Magnificent"	**Lorenzo de' Medici**
led the 19th-c. nationalist "rebirth" movement, Risorgimento	**Giuseppe Mazzini, Giuseppe Garibaldi,** and **Camillo di Cavour**
was a 19th-c. Italian writer and patriot	**Gabriele d'Annunzio**
was the 1st king of united Italy, from 1861	**Victor Emmanuel**
was the king assassinated on Sept. 19, 1900	**Umberto I**
was Fascist leader from 1922	**Benito Mussolini**

- In Scandinavia

united the Vikings in 872 A.D.	**Harald the Fairhaired**
was the great 16-c. Swedish Protestant king	**Gustavus Adolphus**
was the Norwegian executed for collaborating with the Germans in WWII	**Vidkun Quisling**
was the Swedish diplomat who transmitted a German peace proposal to the Allies, later killed in Palestine	**Count Folke Bernadotte**
was the Swedish diplomat who saved tens of thousands of Jews from the Nazis during WWII	**Raoul Wallenberg**

In Spain and Portugal

made Castile an independent Christian state in the 10th c.	**Fernán González of Burgos**
united Castile and Navarre in the 11th c.	**Sancho the Great**
led the Christian reconquest in the 11th c.	**Alfonso VI of Castile**

was the popular leader of Alfonso's crusade	**Rodrigo Diaz de Bivar, El Cid (The Lord)**
organized expeditions along Africa's Atlantic coast	**Henry the Navigator**
rounded Africa's Cape of Good Hope in 1487	**Bartholomew Dias**
expelled the Moors from Granada, united Spain, and financed Columbus's voyages from 1492	**Ferdinand of Aragon** and **Isabella of Castile**
sailed around Africa to India in 1498	**Vasco Da Gama**
led the voyage that 1st circled the globe in 1520	**Ferdinand Magellan (Fernão de Magalhaes)**
married England's Queen Mary and sent Spain's Armada in 1588	**Philip II**
was Spain's dictator in the 1920's	**Primo de Rivera**
was forced to leave the Spanish throne in 1931	**King Alfonso XIII**
was Spain's 1936–37 socialist prime minister	**Francisco Largo Caballero**
was the Republican leader called "La Pasionara"	**Dolores Ibarruri**
was Spain's fascist dictator 1939–75	**Francisco Franco**

In Russia

was the 9th-c. Viking ruler of Novgorod, 1st of his dynasty	**Rurik**
adopted Byzantine Christianity in the 10th c.	**Vladimir**
defeated the Swedes in the 13 c.	**Alexander Nevsky**
was the 1st to be called czar, in the 16th c., also called "the Terrible"	**Ivan IV**
was regent, then czar, after Ivan	**Boris Godunov**
fostered Western ideas in early 18th c.	**Peter the Great**
discovered Bering Strait, between North America and Asia, in 1724, a Dane in Russian employ	**Vitus Bering**
expanded Russia in the late 18th c.	**Catherine the Great**
defeated Napoleon in Russia	**Mikhail Kutuzov**
was the late-19th-c. reforming czar, later killed	**Alexander II**
was the last Russian czar, killed with his family in 1917	**Nicholas II**

was the last czarina, grand-daughter of Victoria	**Alexandra** (née **Alix**)
was the monk who so influenced Alexandra and Nicholas	**Grigori Rasputin**
may have survived the Romanovs' murders	**Anastasia**
led the 1917 democratic government	**Alexander Kerensky**
led the 1917 Bolshevik revolution	**Vladimir Ilyich Lenin** (né **V. I. Ulyanov**)
was an early Bolshevik leader with Lenin, later expelled	**Leon Trotsky** (née **Lev Davidovich Bronstein**)
was a key Menshevik and early Lenin colleague	**Georgi Plekhanov**
was 1st chief of the USSR secret police, the Cheka	**Felix Dzerzhinsky**
were key generals in the 1920 Soviet-Polish War	**Mikhail Tukhachevsky** and **Semën Budënny**
was a Lenin associate later expelled with Trotsky	**Lev B. Kamenev** (né **L. B. Rosenfeld**)
was the all-powerful, purging leader after Lenin	**Joseph Stalin** (né **Iofij Dzhugashvili**)
was public prosecutor during the 1930's purges	**Andrei Vishinsky**
was a key Communist strategist, convicted as a Trotskyist in a 1937 show trial	**Karl Radek** (né **Sobelsohn**)
was a Lenin co-successor, later executed after a 1937 show trial	**Gregory Zinoviev**
was a Lenin associate and key Communist theorist executed after a 1938 show trial	**Nikolai Bukharin**
made a 1939 nonaggression pact with the Nazis, named himself "The Hammer"	**Vyacheslav Molotov** (né **V.M. Skriabin**)
was the Jewish diplomat dismissed after the Nazi-Soviet pact, later WWII ambassador to the US	**Maksim Litvinov**
was army chief of staff from 1941	**Georgi Zhukov**

Key Figures in Colonial American and US History

Colonial and Revolutionary War Figures

Among historical figures in colonial and revolutionary North America, who . . . ?

explored and settled for a time near and in North America in the 10th c.	**Leif Ericson**
came to the Canadian Maritimes in 1497	**John Cabot (Giovanni Caboto)**
entered the Hudson Strait in 1509, John's son	**Sebastian Cabot**
discovered Florida in 1513	**Ponce de Leon**
explored NY Bay for the French in 1524	**Giovanni da Verrazano**
explored the Gulf of St. Lawrence in 1534 and arrived at the site of Montréal in 1535	**Jacques Cartier**
explored Florida and the mid-Mississippi in 1539–41	**Hernando de Soto**
explored North America's Southwest in 1540	**Francisco de Coronado**
came to the Colorado's Grand Canyon in 1540	**Garcia Cardenas**
explored the California coast in 1542	**Juan Rodríguez Cabrillo**
founded St. Augustine, Florida, in 1565	**Pedro Menendez de Avilés**
discovered Frobisher's Bay in Canada in 1576	**Martin Frobisher**
claimed California for Britain in 1579	**Francis Drake**
sponsored a colony on Roanoke Island in 1585	**Walter Raleigh**
headed a 2nd Roanoke colony in 1587, later lost	**John White**
was the 1st child born in America of English parents, in Roanoke	**Virginia Dare**
explored Canada's fur routes 1603–9 and founded Québec in 1608	**Samuel de Champlain**
led the Jamestown settlers in 1607	**Captain John Smith**
sailed up the Hudson River in 1609–10	**Henry Hudson**
married John Rolfe, an Indian princess	**Pocahontas (Matoaka)**

was taken to England in 1615, but later returned	Squanto
led the Pilgrims to Plymouth from 1621	William Bradford
did Priscilla Mullins tell to speak for himself	John Alden
asked John Alden to speak for him, according to Longfellow	Miles Standish
bought Manhattan for the Dutch West India Co. in 1626	Peter Minuit
founded the Rhode Island colony in 1636	Roger Williams
sponsored the Maryland colony, founded in 1634	George Calvert, Lord Baltimore
was the 1630's head of the New Netherlands colony	Peter Stuyvesant
explored Lake Michigan in 1634	Jean Nicolet
explored the Mississippi to around Arkansas in the 1670's	Jacques Marquette and Louis Jolliet
founded the Pennsylvania colony in 1682	William Penn
reached the mouth of the Mississippi from the north in 1682	Sieur de La Salle
was a key Puritan leader, father of Cotton	Increase Mather
sparked the witchhunts in Salem, Massachusetts	Cotton Mather
founded the Georgia colony in 1733	James Oglethorpe
defeated the French at Québec in 1759	James Wolfe
lost to the British at Québec in 1759	Louis de Montcalm
founded California's late-18th-c. missions	Father Junípero Serra
said, "Give me liberty, or give me death!"	Patrick Henry
led the radical patriots at the 1st Continental Congress in 1774	Samuel Adams
was a black patriot killed in the 1770 Boston Massacre	Crispus Attucks
wrote *Common Sense*	Thomas Paine
established the freedom of the press	John Peter Zenger
dumped tea overboard in the Boston Tea Party	Sons of Liberty
wrote the Declaration of Independence	Thomas Jefferson

had the largest signature on the Declaration of Independence	**John Hancock**
warned that the British were coming	**Paul Revere**
were the soldiers who fought at Lexington and Concord	**Minutemen**
was Revolutionary commander and 1st president	**George Washington**
led the American troops at Ticonderoga in 1775	**Ethan Allen** and **Benedict Arnold**
was the American spy who had "but one life to lose"	**Nathan Hale**
was a patriot, printer, ambassador, and kite-flyer	**Benjamin Franklin**
was Washington's drillmaster at Valley Forge	**Friedrich von Steuben**
was a key French general in Washington's Continental Army	**Marquis de Lafayette**
was a German general in the Continental Army	**Baron de Kalb (Johann Kalb)**
commanded French forces allied with the American in the Revolutionary War	**Comte de Rochambeau (Jean-Baptiste-Donatien Vimeur)**
led Vermont's Green Mountain Boys	**Ethan Allen**
reportedly made the first American flag	**Betsy Ross**
commanded British forces early in the American Revolution	**Thomas Gage**
led the British to defeat at Saratoga in 1777	**"Gentleman Johnny" Burgoyne**
was the British general in New York	**Henry Clinton**
surrendered British forces at Yorktown	**Charles Cornwallis**
was the West Point commander and later traitor	**Benedict Arnold**
fortified West Point during the Revolution	**Thaddeus Kosciusko**
was the Polish cavalry general at Valley Forge	**Kazimierz Pulaski**
was Revolutionary general in the Carolina campaign	**Nathaniel Greene**
was a British ally, later moving to Canada, an Iroquois	**Joseph Brant**
led Virginians into the Old Northwest in 1779	**George Rogers Clark**

Early US Presidents

Among US presidents, their families, and advisors, before the Civil War, who was . . . ?

1789–97 president (no party)	George Washington
Washington's wife	Martha Dandridge Custis
Washington's 1st Sec. of State	Thomas Jefferson
Washington's 1st Sec. of War	Henry Knox
Washington's 1st Attorney General and 2nd Sec. of State	Edmund Randolph
Washington's 1st Sec. of Treasury	Alexander Hamilton
1797–1801 president (Federalist)	John Adams
Adams's wife	Abigail Smith
1801–9 president (Dem-Rep.)	Thomas Jefferson
Jefferson's wife	Martha Wayles Skelton
1809–17 president (Dem.-Rep.)	James Madison
Madison's wife	Dolley Payne Todd
1817–25 president (Dem.-Rep.)	James Monroe
1825–29 president, chosen from among the candidates by the House of Representatives	John Quincy Adams
Quincy Adams's and Jackson's 1st V-P and Tyler's 3rd Sec. of State	John Calhoun
1829–37 president (Dem.), "Old Hickory"	Andrew Jackson
1837–41 president (Dem.), Jackson's V-P	Martin Van Buren
1841 president (Whig) who died in a month	William Henry Harrison
1841-45 president (Whig)	John Tyler
1845–49 president (Dem.)	James Polk
1849–50 president (Whig), earlier fought in Mexico	Zachary Taylor
Fillmore's and Tyler's Sec. of State	Daniel Webster
1850–53 president (Whig)	Millard Fillmore
1853–57 president (Dem.)	Franklin Pierce
1857–61 president (Dem.)	James Buchanan
1861–65 Civil War president (Rep.)	Abraham Lincoln
Lincoln's wife	Mary Todd
Lincoln's Sec. of State	William Seward
Lincoln's 1st Sec. of War	Simon Cameron
Lincoln's 2nd Sec. of War	Edwin Stanton
Lincoln's Sec. of Navy	Gideon Welles
Lincoln's assassin on Aug. 14, 1865	John Wilkes Booth

Other Key Figures of Early US History

Among the other key figures of the United States before the Civil War, who . . . ?

lost the 1800 presidential race to Jefferson in the House of Representatives	**Aaron Burr**
wrote the Compromise of 1850, an 1832 and 1844 presidential candidate	**Henry Clay**
was 1812 Federalist presidential candidate	**DeWitt Clinton**
was 1860 Dem. presidential candidate	**Stephen Douglas**
was Chief Justice of the Supreme Court 1789–95	**John Jay**
said, "I have not yet begun to fight!"	**John Paul Jones**
was New Orleans pirate-hero of the War of 1812	**Jean Lafitte**
was Chief Justice of the Supreme Court 1801–35	**John Marshall**
took Mexico City in the 1846–48 war	**Winfield Scott**
was Chief Justice of the Supreme Court 1836–64	**Roger Brooke Taney**

Key Figures of the Civil War Era and After

Among the key figures in the Civil War era and after, who . . . ?

raided the Harper's Ferry arsenal in 1859	**John Brown**
succeeded McClellan after Antietam	**Ambrose Burnside**
was president of the Confederacy	**Jefferson Davis**
published the mid-19-c. abolitionist *Liberator*	**William Lloyd Garrison**
was the Union Army's commander-in-chief, later president	**Ulysses S. Grant**
wrote "Battle Hymn of the Republic"	**Julia Ward Howe**
was the Confederate general at Antietam and Bull Run	**Thomas "Stonewall" Jackson**
led the Confederate Army of Northern Virginia	**Robert E. Lee**
was Union commander at Antietam	**George B. McClellan**

was the Union general at Gettysburg	**George Meade**
led an ill-fated Confederate charge at Gettysburg	**George Pickett**
was the bloody Confederate guerrilla raider	**William Quantrill**
was the Union general who burned Atlanta	**William Tecumseh Sherman**
organized the 1st US women's rights convention in 1848	**Elizabeth Cady Stanton** and **Lucretia Mott**
was a key Confederate aide to Robert E. Lee	**J(ames). E. B. Stuart**
was a former slave and abolitionist born Isabella Van Wagener	**Sojourner Truth**
was an ex-slave, a key conductor on the Underground Railroad	**Harriet Tubman**
led an ill-fated slave rebellion in 1831	**Nat Turner**

US Presidents from the Civil War to WWII

Among US presidents, their families, and advisors between the Civil War and World War II, who was . . . ?

impeached (not convicted) 1865–69 president (Rep.)	**Andrew Johnson**
1869–77 president (Rep.)	**Ulysses S. Grant**
Grant's 2nd Sec. of State	**Hamilton Fish**
1877–81 president (Rep.)	**Rutherford B. Hayes**
1881 president (Rep.) killed in office	**James Garfield**
1881–85 president (Rep.) who succeeded Garfield	**Chester Arthur**
1885–89 and 1893–97 president, losing in 1889	**Grover Cleveland**
Cleveland's daughter, now a candy bar name	**Baby Ruth**
1889–93 president (Rep.)	**Benjamin Harrison**
1897–1901 president (Rep.) killed in office	**William McKinley**
1901–09 president (Rep.), who lost in 1912 as Progressive "Bull Moose" candidate	**Theodore Roosevelt**
Roosevelt's daughter, famed for her blue gown	**Alice Roosevelt Longworth**
Roosevelt's Sec. of War, then of State	**Elihu Root**
1909–13 president (Rep.)	**William Howard Taft**
1913–21 president (Dem.), during WWI	**Woodrow Wilson**

Attorney General who led the post-WWI anti-radical raids	**A. Mitchell Palmer**
1921–23 president (Rep.) who died in office	**Warren Gamaliel Harding**
Harding's Attorney General, charged with corruption in the Teapot Dome scandal	**Harry Daugherty**
Harding's Sec. of Interior, part of the Teapot Dome scandal	**Albert Fall**
Harding's and Coolidge's Sec. of State	**Charles Evans Hughes**
Harding's and Coolidge's Sec. of Treasury	**Andrew Mellon**
1923–29 president (Dem.), "Silent Cal"	**Calvin Coolidge**
Coolidge's wife	**Grace Anna Goodhue**
Coolidge's 2nd Sec. of State	**Frank Kellogg**
1929–33 president (Rep.) at the Crash	**Herbert Hoover**

Key 19th- and Early-20th-century Social Critics and Reformers

Among social critics and reformers before WWII, who . . . ?

founded Hull House, a peace activist	**Jane Addams**
was president of the National American Woman Suffrage Association in the late 19th c.	**Susan B. Anthony**
founded the Socialist Party in 1900	**Victor Berger**
was the Russian-American anarchist who tried to assassinate Henry Clay Frick in 1892	**Alexander Berkman**
led the American Communist Party before WWII	**Earl Browder**
founded the League of Women Voters	**Carrie Chapman Catt**
was co-founder of the pacifist *Catholic Worker*	**Dorothy Day**
was 1920, 1912, and 1908 Socialist presidential candidate	**Eugene Debs**
wrote *The Souls of Black Folk* and called for independent black colonies	**William E. B. Du Bois**
was an IWW member, Communist, and founder of the American Civil Liberties Union	**Elizabeth Gurley Flynn**

urged a Back to Africa movement	**Marcus Garvey**
was an anarchist associated with Berkman	**Emma Goldman**
wrote *Progress and Poverty*	**Henry George**
fought for the blind and handicapped, like herself	**Helen Keller**
founded the Girl Scouts	**Juliette Gordon Low**
was the early-20th-c. hatchet-wielding prohibitionist	**Carry Nation**
was the *Reds* American buried in the Kremlin	**John Reed**
wrote *How the Other Half Lives*	**Jacob Riis**
founded what became Planned Parenthood	**Margaret Sanger**
wrote *The Shame of the Cities*	**Lincoln Steffens**
was the early-20th-c. muckraker, as about Standard Oil	**Ida Tarbell**
was the pacifist and 6-time Socialist presidential candidate	**Norman Thomas**
founded Tuskegee Institute	**Booker T. Washington**
founded NYC's Henry St. Settlement House	**Lillian Wald**

Notables of the Frontier and the Old West

Among the notable people of the frontier of the Old West, who . . . ?

was the rough judge of Langtry, Texas	**Roy Bean**
was a Sauk leader in the Midwest in the 1830's	**Black Hawk**
opened up Kentucky through the Cumberland gap	**Daniel Boone**
was the smiling killer called "Billy the Kid"	**William Bonney**
invented a knife and died at the Alamo	**Jim Bowie**
founded a key fort on the old Oregon Trail	**Jim Bridger**
was a super-lumberjack in many tall tales	**Paul Bunyan**
was a frontier woman called Calamity Jane	**Martha Jane Burk**
was a trapper and a guide in early Taos	**Christopher "Kit" Carson**
were played on the screen by Newman and Redford	**Butch Cassidy** and the **Sundance Kid**
fought the Earp brothers at OK Corral	**the Clantons**

was the Apache leader of the 1860's and early '70's	Cochise
ran a Wild West show as "Buffalo Bill"	William Cody
wore a coonskin hat and died at the Alamo	Davy Crockett
led the Sioux and Cheyenne against Custer	Crazy Horse
fought with his brothers Virgil and Morgan at Tombstone, Arizona's, OK Corral in 1881	Wyatt Earp
mapped the West, 1856 Rep. presidential candidate	John C. Frémont
was the Apache leader in the 1870's	Geronimo
was the consumptive ally of the Earps at OK Corral	Doc Holliday
was killed in Deadwood and nicknamed "Wild Bill"	James Butler Hickok
led the 1830's Texas War of Independence	Sam Houston
were Missouri outlaw brothers after the Civil War	Jesse and Frank James
explored the Missouri and Pacific NW in 1804-6	Meriwether Lewis and William Clark
was Buffalo Bill's supreme markswoman	Annie Oakley
discovered a Rockies peak in 1806	Zebulon Pike
was a Comanche chief, last to surrender, in 1875	Quanah (Parker)
was Lewis and Clark's guide	Sacajawea
was an Oklahoma woman cattle thief	Belle Starr (Myra Belle Shirley)
owned the California mill where gold was found in 1848	John A. Sutter

Other Key US Figures from the Civil War to WWII

Among other key US figures between the Civil War and World War II, who . . . ?

was 1908, 1900, and 1896 Dem. presidential candidate, of the "Cross of Gold" speech	William Jennings Bryan
was 1920 Dem. presidential candidate	James Cox
died making a "last stand" in 1875	George Armstrong Custer
was 1924 Dem. presidential candidate	John Davis

headed the 1st House Committee to Investigate Un-American Activities (HUAC), in 1938	**Martin Dies**
was a slave and later minister to Haiti	**Frederick Douglass**
was 1924 Progressive presidential candidate	**Robert LaFollette**
was the last queen of the Hawaiian Islands	**Lydia Kamekeha Liliuokalani**
was 1872 Dem.-Liberal Rep. presidential candidate, and said, "Go West, young man"	**Horace Greeley**
was 1916 Rep. presidential candidate	**Charles Evans Hughes**
was the general who in the 1920's urged the US army to use air power	**William "Billy" Mitchell**
was the financier who personally halted the 1907 panic	**J(ohn) Pierpont Morgan**
led the US forces in WWI, called "Black Jack"	**John Pershing**
was the 1st woman to serve in Congress, in 1916, and the only person to vote against declaring WWII	**Jeannette Rankin**
was the 25-term Texas Representative, Speaker 17 years	**Samuel Rayburn**
was the US WWI air ace	**Edward "Eddie" Rickenbacker**
was 1928 Dem. presidential candidate	**Alfred Smith**
founded the *Woman's Journal* for suffrage in 1870	**Lucy Stone**
was the NY Senator who pioneered the National Labor Relations Act and Social Security	**Robert F. Wagner**
was the Congressional Medal of Honor–winner played by Gary Cooper	**Sgt. Alvin York**

Key US Figures in World War II

Among the key US figures in World War II and after, who was . . . ?

the army chief of staff, architect of postwar aid	**George C. Marshall**
the South Pacific commander from 1942	**William Halsey, Jr.**
the commander of the Pacific Fleet from Dec. 1941	**Chester Nimitz**

the admiral in charge at Pearl Harbor in 1941	**Husband Kimmel**
the general in charge at Pearl Harbor	**Walter Short**
the Atlantic commander, later chief of naval operations	**Ernest King**
the general leading the Flying Tigers in China	**Clare Chennault**
the lt. col. leading B-25 bombers to Tokyo in 1942	**James Doolittle**
the general nicknamed "Blood and Guts"	**George Patton**
the general who said "Nuts!" when asked to surrender	**Anthony McAuliffe**
the general of the 1st Army at Normandy and the 12th Army heading to Germany	**Omar Bradley**
the general commanding the 5th Army in Italy	**Mark Clark**
the American general advising the Chinese during WWII	**Joseph "Vinegar Joe" Stilwell**
the commanding general in occupied Japan and Korea, later fired by Truman	**Douglas MacArthur**
the head of the OSS (Office of Strategic Services)	**William "Wild Bill" Donovan**

Special Places

Bays and Gulfs

Among the world's bays and gulfs, which is or was . . . ?

In the Americas

where the St. Lawrence joins Lake Ontario	**Alexandria Bay**
south of Baton Rouge, Louisiana	**Atchafalaya Bay**
off Miami, Florida	**Biscayne Bay**
north of Alaska's Aleutian Islands	**Bristol Bay**
south of New Bedford, Massachusetts	**Buzzards Bay**
between Baja and mainland Mexico	**Gulf of California**
knifed between Maryland and Virginia	**Chesapeake Bay**
at the Panama Canal's Caribbean entrance	**Cristóbal Bay**
between Nova Scotia and New Brunswick, with the huge tidal bore	**Bay of Fundy**
on the Gulf Coast of Texas	**Galveston Bay**
off Lake Huron	**Georgian Bay**
site of Muir and other Alaskan glaciers	**Glacier Bay**
jutting off Lake Michigan, in Wisconsin	**Green Bay**
at Rio de Janeiro	**Guanamara Bay**
site of a US naval base, in Cuba	**Guantanamo Bay**
outlet for fur traders, in north Canada	**Hudson Bay**
off southern Hudson Bay	**James Bay**
off the Caribbean end of the Panama Canal	**Limón Bay**
between Long Island and Connecticut	**Long Island Sound**
off St. Augustine, Florida	**Matanzas Bay**
in the curve of Mexico and the SE US	**Gulf of Mexico**
south of Rhode Island	**Narragansett Bay**

south of Nome, Alaska	**Norton Sound**
in western Nova Scotia	**Passamaquoddy Bay**
off SE Maine	**Penobscot Bay**
site of an ill-fated 1961 invasion of Cuba	**Bay of Pigs (Bahiaide los Cochinos)**
site of the 1989 *Exxon Valdez* Alaska oil spill	**Prince William Sound**
off northern Alaska	**Prudhoe Bay**
curved deep into Washington State	**Puget Sound**
off SE Mexico	**Gulf of Tehuantepec**

In Europe

north of Iberia and west of France	**Bay of Biscay**
between Sweden and Finland	**Gulf of Bothnia**
just west of the Strait of Gibraltar	**Gulf of Cadiz**
off mid-Wales	**Cardigan Bay**
almost separates the Peloponnesus from Greece	**Gulf of Corinth**
on the coast of Kerry, Ireland	**Dingle Bay**
between Helsinki and Leningrad	**Gulf of Finland**
near Edinburgh, Scotland	**Firth of Forth**
on the Atlantic coast of central Ireland	**Galway Bay**
Istanbul's famous bay and harbor	**Golden Horn**
off Malta, site of 1989 summit	**Marsaxlokk Bay**
off Iverness, Scotland	**Moray Firth**
pushed into Scotland from the Irish Sea	**Solway Firth**
near England's Southampton	**Southampton Water**
off Thessalonica, Greece	**Gulf of Thermaikós**
long, thin inlet at the Vikings' old capital	**Trondheimsfjord**
draining eastern England's fen country	**The Wash**
now a fresh-water lake, in the Netherlands	**Zuider Zee (I Jsselmeer)**

In Asia, Africa, Australia, and the Pacific

where Nelson defeated the French in the 1798 Battle of the Nile	**Abukir (Abu Qir) Bay**
Moroccan site of a pre-WWI French-German crisis	**Agadir Bay**
between the Sinai and Saudi Arabia	**Gulf of Aqaba**
south of Bangladesh	**Bay of Bengal**
south of Biafra	**Bight of Biafra**
south of Sydney, explored by Cook in 1770	**Botany Bay**

scooped out of northern Australia	**Gulf of Carpentaria**
in the southern curve of Australia	**Great Australian Bight**
in the curve of West Africa	**Gulf of Guinea**
pointing like a finger into SE Turkey	**Gulf of Iskanderun**
site of WWII's largest Pacific battle	**Leyte Gulf**
Philippine site of 1945 American landings	**Lingayen Gulf**
off NW Antarctica	**McMurdo Sound**
curved into the south coast of New Guinea	**Gulf of Papua**
between Iran and Arabia	**Persian Gulf**
south of Thailand	**Gulf of Siam**
in the Philippines, with a US base	**Subic Bay**
between Egypt proper and the Sinai	**Gulf of Suez**
at Cape Town, South Africa	**Table Bay**
site of alleged attacks justifying US entrance into the Vietnam War	**Tonkin Gulf**

Capes and Points

Among the world's capes and points, which is or are . . . ?

In the Americas

in Alaska where the 3 whales were trapped in 1988	**Point Barrow**
near St. John's, in eastern Newfoundland	**Cape Bona Vista**
in NE Nova Scotia	**Cape Breton**
the Florida space center site called Cape Kennedy 1963–73	**Cape Canaveral**
in Massachusetts, where the pilgrims first landed	**Cape Cod**
on the western approach to Magellan Strait	**Cape Deseada (Desired)** or **Cape of Good Hope**
at old Québec, on the St. Lawrence River	**Cap Diamant (Diamond)**
on the Atlantic coast in North Carolina	**Capes Hatteras, Lookout,** and **Fear** (no. to so.)
on the Mississippi River in Missouri	**Cape Girardeau**
near Port-au-Prince, Haiti	**Cap Haitien, Cap-Français,** or **Le Cap**

in Virginia, where Jamestown settlers landed	**Cape Henry**
at the southern tip of South America	**Cape Horn, Cabo de Hornos,** or **Old Cape Stiff**
in southern Rhode Island	**Point Judith**
off San Diego, California	**Point Loma**
on the southern coast of New Jersey	**Cape May**
in northern California where Drake landed	**Point Reyes**
in SE Nova Scotia	**Cape Sable**
at the southern tip of Baja California	**Cabo San Lucas**
in New Jersey, with the US's oldest lighthouse	**Sandy Hook**
at the easternmost bulge of Brazil	**Cape São Roque**
at the eastern approach to Magellan Strait	**Cape Virgenes** or **Virgins**

In Europe

on the Riviera, favored in the 1920's	**Cap d'Antibes** and **Ferrat**
Britain's northernmost point, in Scotland	**John O' Groats**
at the far west point of Britain's Cornwall	**Land's End**
on the Ionian Sea, site of a WWII battle	**Cape Matapan** or **Tainaron**
at the nothernmost point of Scandinavia	**North Cape** or **Nordkapp**
in Greece near where Persian king Darius wrecked his fleet	**Cape Nymphaion** or **Nymphaeum**
where the British landed in Sicily in WWII	**Cape Passero** or **Passaro**
in Crete, that St. Paul mentions in Acts 27	**Cape Pláka** or **Salmone**
in SW Portugal, near Prince Henry the Navigator's navigation school	**Cape St. Vincent** or **Cabo São Vincente**

In Asia, Africa, Australia, and the Pacific

at the Horn of Africa, on the Arabian Sea, meeting place for the old spice trade	**Cape Aromata, Guardafi,** or **Cape of Spices**
on the coast of West Africa, important in early Portuguese explorations	**Capes Bojador, Blanca,** and **Verde** (no. to so.)

in NE Tunisia, pointing toward Sicily	**Cape Bon**
on the Mediterranean, near Haifa, Israel, where Napoleon was defeated	**Cape Carmel**
at the northernmost point in Asia	**Cape Chelyuskin**
at the southern tip of India	**Cape Comorin**
in NE Asia, on the Bering Strait	**East Cape** or **Cape Dezhnev**
at the southern tip of Africa	**Cape of Good Hope, Cabo da Boa Esperaça, or Cabo Tormentoso**
on the south coast of New Britain Island in Papua New Guinea	**Cape Merkus**
nearly dividing the Dead Sea in half	**Cape Molineux**
on the west coast of central and SW Africa	**Capes Palmas, St. Catherine, and St. Mary** (no. to so.)
beyond Russia's Ob River, in myth	**Cape Tabin**
NE tip of Australia	**Cape York**

Caves and Grottoes

Among the world's caves and grottoes, which is or are the . . . ?

In the Americas

in New Mexico	**Carlsbad Caverns**
Alabama caves discovered in 1540	**De Soto**
caves with pre-Columbian art on Aruba	**Fontein**
oil-bird cave in Venezuela	**Guácharo**
underground caverns in New York State	**Howe**
in South Dakota's Black Hills	**Jewel**
great system of caves in Kentucky	**Mammoth**
Alabama caves lived in 8000 years ago	**Russell**

In Europe

site of prehistoric paintings in Spain	**Altamira**
on the Isle of Capri, the "Blue Grotto"	**Grotta Azzura**
in France's Franche-Comté	**Baume-les-Messieurs**

"Ice Giants' World" near Salzburg, Austria — **Eisriesenwelt**

Ice Age caves in Germany's Franconia — **Gailenreuther Zoolithenhöhle**

chalk caves in England's Buckinghamshire — **Hell-Fire**

main 2 caves of dozens near Erpfingen, Germany — **Karlshöhle** and **Bärenhöhle**

sites of prehistoric cave paintings in France — **Lascaux** and **Les Eyzies-de-Tayac**

cave near Württemberg's Linchtenstein Castle — **Nebelhöhle**

fairytale caves in Thuringia, East Germany — **Saalfeld** and **Eisenach**

"Devil's cave" in Germany's Franconia — **Teufelshöhle**

In Asia, Africa, Australia, and the Pacific

site of 200 + year-old sculptures and paintings, near Bombay, India — **Ajanta caves**

Hindu pilgrimage site near Malaysia's Kuala Lumpur — **Batu caves**

in Thailand's Doi Indhanon Park — **Borijinda**

Zimbabwe caves with prehistoric remains — **Chinhoyi**

temple caves near Bombay, India — **Elephanta**

caves full of Hindu, Buddhist, and Jain Temples near Bombay, India — **Ellora (Elura)**

massive bat caves on Bali — **Goah Lawah**

Buddhist caves outside Luoyang, China — **Long Men**

caves with prehistoric paintings and edible birds' nests in Sarawak, on Borneo — **Niah**

caves near China's Dunhuang that yielded the world's oldest printed work — **Caves of the Thousand Buddhas** or **Magao**

New Zealand caves with a Glow-worm Grotto — **Waitomo**

Churches and Other Sacred Places

(See also Caves and Grottoes; Mountains and Peaks; and Statues, Tombs, and Other Special Sites)

Among the world's churches and other sacred places, which is or are . . . ?

In the Americas

basilica and pilgrimage site near Québec	Ste-Anne-de-Beaupré
old "home mission" in Carmel, California	San Carlos Borromeo del Rio Carmelo
Mexico's largest pre-Columbian pyramid	Cholula
one of the oldest pyramids near Mexico City	Culcuilco
"mother mission," oldest in California*	San Diego
San Francisco's old mission	Dolores
Martin Luther King, Jr.'s, Atlanta church	Ebenezer Baptist
wooden cathedral in George-town, Guyana	St. George's
1523 church in old San Juan, Puerto Rico	San José
California mission to which swallows annually return	San Juan Capistrano
Russian cathedral in Sitka, Alaska	St. Michael's
cathedral in the Caribbean's Santo Domingo	Santa Maria Le Menor
New World's oldest synagogue, on Curaçao	Mikve Israel
Santa Fe mission, oldest in use in the US	San Miguel
Boston church where Revere's signal was hung	Old North Church
NYC's striking 5th-Avenue cathedral	St. Patrick's
Santa Monica, California's, multi-religious shrine	Self-Realization Fellowship Lake
Aztec temple in Mexico City	Tenochtitlán
site of sacred Toltec pyramids near Mexico City	Teotihuacán
US's oldest synagogue, in Newport, RI	Touro
home of Mexico's god-king Quetzalcoátl	Tula

| Mayan site with the Pyramid of the Magician | **Uxmal** |
| 18th-c. white mission near Tucson, Arizona | **San Xavier del Bac** |

In Europe

the civic and religious center of Athens	**Acropolis**
13th-c. cathedral in Sofia, Bulgaria	**Alexander Nevsky**
Wiltshire stone circle larger than Stonehenge	**Avebury**
5th-c. abbey founded by St. Patrick in Ireland's County Mayo	**Ballintubber**
Ivan's cathedral in Moscow's Kremlin	**St. Basil's**
Prague church where John Huss preached	**Bethlehem Chapel**
church and old lighthouse in England's Boston	**St. Botolph's**
seat of the Church of England's primate	**Canterbury**
monastery site of a key WWII battle in Italy	**Monte Cassino**
13-c. French cathedral lauded by Henry Adams	**Chartres**
ruined Central France Benedictine and Cluniac abbey	**Cluny**
the site of Greece's main temple to Apollo, longtime home of the Oracle	**Delphi**
Paris basilica where French monarchs were buried	**St. Denis**
Vienna's church of the Teutonic Knights	**Deutschehordenskirche**
tall-towered medieval church in Utrecht	**Domkirk**
cathedral that is the symbol of Florence	**Duomo**
Paris's oldest church	**Eglise St-Germain-des-Près**
ancient sanctuary north of Athens's Parthenon	**Erechtheion**
Gothic cathedral in Sens, France	**St.-Etienne**
12-c. Gothic cathedral in Metz, France	**St-Etienne**
ruined abbey near Yorkshire's River Skell	**Fountains Abbey**
Prague church with 12-c. frescoes	**St. George's**

Palladian church facing Venice's Piazza San Marco	**San Giorgio Maggiore**
cathedral of the diocese of Rome, a pilgrimage site	**San Giovanni in Laterano**
minaret at Seville's grand mosque	**Giralda**
the ruined English abbey and old pilgrimage site linked with St. Joseph Arimathea and King Arthur	**Glastonbury**
6th-c. basilica, now a mosque, in Istanbul (then Constantinople)	**Hagia (Santa) Sofia** or **Ayasofya**
named after Welch martyr St. Winifred's well	**Holywell**
Polish shrine with the "Black Madonna" linked with St. Luke	**Jasna Góra (Hill of Light)**
Lisbon's Heronymites monastery	**Jerónimos**
rebuilt 14th-c. Warsaw cathedral	**St. John's**
Aachen's imperial cathedral	**Kaiserdom**
Vienna's church of the Capuchins	**Kapuzinerkirche**
18th-c. Vienna church, inspired by the plague	**Karlskirche**
Polish chapel carved out of the Wieliczka salt mine	**St. Kinga**
Nuremberg's 13th-c. Gothic church	**St. Lorenz**
Florence's basilica of the Medicis	**San Lorenzo**
French shrine where Bernadette had her vision	**Lourdes**
16th-c. church in Lisbon's old dock area	**Madre de Deus**
Vienna's church of the Knights of Malta	**Malteserkirche**
Venice's basilica with the 4 Constantinople horses	**San Marco (St. Mark's)**
Milan's convent with Leonardo's *The Last Supper*	**Santa Maria delle Grazie, Cenacolo Vinciano**
main church in Barcelona	**Santa Maria del Mar**
small church next to Westminster Abbey	**St. Margaret's**
church near London's National Gallery	**St. Martin-in-the-Fields**
London's Cockney church near St. Paul's	**St. Mary-le-Bow**
Budapest's rebuilt "Coronation Church"	**Matthias (Mátyás)**
many-columned mosque in Córdoba, Spain	**Mezquita**

Coventry, England, cathedral mostly destroyed in 1940 and rebuilt	**St. Michael's**
religious center on a rock off Cornwall	**St. Michael's Mount**
1th-c. monastery on a rock off Normandy	**Mont St.-Michel**
Roman temple in London's Bucklersbury House	**Mithras**
Kiev's striking 11th-c. church complex	**Monastery of the Caves**
12th-c. cathedral in Trondheim, Norway	**Nidaros**
Paris cathedral on the Ile de la Cité	**Notre Dame**
Gothic cathedral at Reims with Chagall windows	**Notre Dame**
temple on the Acropolis, symbol of Athens	**Parthenon**
Rome's greatest temple, later a Christian church	**Pantheon**
Dublin's cathedral for Ireland's patron saint	**St. Patrick's**
London's Wren-designed church where Charles and Diana were married	**St. Paul's Cathedral**
huge cathedral in Cologne	**St. Peter and St. Mary's**
church in the Vatican with the Sistine Chapel	**St. Peter's (San Pietro)**
modern, ark-shaped church in industrial Nowa Huta, near Cracow	**Church of the Queen of Poland**
fine abbey on Yorkshire's River Rye	**Rievaulx Abbey**
Vienna's church of St. Rupert, on a Roman site	**Ruprechtskirche**
pilgrimage site in Spain where St. James the Great was supposedly buried	**Santiago de Compostela**
120-foot-high steeple in Cork's St. Anne's Church	**Shandon Steeple**
11th-c. Kiev cathedral	**St. Sophia (Sofisky)**
old Vienna's main cathedral	**Stephansdom (St. Stephen's)**
Wiltshire stone circle, linked with Druids	**Stonehenge**
Istanbul's famous Blue Mosque	**Sultan Ahmet Cami**
Welsh abbey celebrated by Wordsworth	**Tintern Abbey**
Wren-designed bell tower at Oxford's Christ Church	**Tom Tower**
palaces that form a city-state within Rome	**Vatican City**

Cracow church from which a bugle often sounds	**Virgin Mary**
Germany's "Stonehenge," near Bremen	**Visbecker Bridegroom**
cathedral in Prague's old royal courtyard	**St. Vitus**
Cracow's cathedral, once Pope John Paul II's	**Wawel**
London site for crowning British monarchs	**Westminster Abbey**
Britain's Roman Catholic cathedral, in London	**Westminster**
British cathedral damaged in a 1984 fire	**York Minster**

In Asia, Africa, Australia, and the Pacific

Egyptian temple and statue rescued from Aswan High Dam Ramses	**Abu-Simbel**
10th-c. Jain temple in Palitana, India	**Adinath**
ruined Khmer temple in Cambodia	**Angkor Wat**
basilica built at Mary's Nazareth home	**Annunciation**
mosque built near Jerusalem's Dome of the Rock	**El Aqsa**
Haifa's Mt. Carmel shrine to a Bahai prophet	**Bab**
Bali's holiest Hindu temple	**Besakih Mother**
huge mosque in Samarkand	**Bibi Khanym**
Turkey's "Valley of 1001 Churches"	**Bin Bir Kilise Deresi**
India's 13th-c. Hindu temple to sungod Orissa	**Black Pagoda (Konarak)**
huge 9th-c. Buddhist monument on Java	**Borobudur**
in Varanasi, India, with Vishnu's footprints	**Charanpaduka pedestal**
Sinkh Golden Temple in Amristar, India	**Darbar Sahib**
Great Mosque in Algiers	**Djemaâ El Kebir**
Jerusalem's house of worship on Temple Mount, a site revered by Jews, Christians, and Moslems	**Dome of the Rock**
garden near Jerusalem where Jesus was arrested	**Gethsemane**
world's largest enclosed mosque, in Casablanca	**Great Hassan II**
site in Mecca all Moslems should visit	**Grand Mosque**

tallest wooden building in the world, in Nara, Japan	**Great Buddha Hall of Todaiji**
dominating temple of Bhubaneswar, Orissa, India	**Great Lingaraj**
church on the site of Jesus's tomb	**Holy Sepulcher**
largest and oldest of Japan's temples at Nara	**Horyuji**
Taoist temple in Taipei, Taiwan	**Hsing Tien**
1300-year-old temple in Lhasa, Tibet	**Jokhang** or **Dazhousi**
sacred stone in Mecca's mosque	**Ka'aba**
massive Egyptian temple to Amon, near Thebes and Luxor	**Karnak**
Penang's Buddhist temple with the Ban Hood Pagoda	**Kek Lok Si**
reconstructed 14th-c. Buddhist temple near Kyoto	**Kinkakuji**
7th- or 8th-c. Buddhist temple near Kyoto	**Kiyomizu-Dera**
Buddhist "Dragon Mountain" temple on Taiwan	**Lungsham**
the Shi'a Moslem shrine in Iran, tomb of Ali ar-Rida	**Mashhad (Meshed) Ali**
national mosque in Malaysia's Kuala Lumpur	**Masjid Jame**
1700-year-old Shinto shrine in Tokyo	**Meiji Shrine, Harajuku**
16th-c. Christian basilica in Cebu, Philippines	**Minore Del Santo Nino**
old Jewish synagogue near Cochin, India	**Mattancheri**
towering Cairo mosque	**Muhammad Ali**
6th-c. Bethlehem church built by Justinian	**Basilica of the Nativity**
shrine at the supposed grave of Moses	**Nebi Musa**
world's largest Christian church, in Yamassoukro, Ivory Coast	**Our Lady of Peace**
mid-Nile temple to Isis near Aswan, Egypt	**Philae**
Dalai Lama's palace in Lhasa, Tibet	**Potala**
Mohammed's mosque in Medina, Saudi Arabia	**Prophet**
Buddhist temple and pagodas in Kyongju, Korea	**Pulguk-sa**
12th-c. Moslem tower in Delhi	**Qutb Minar**

India's oldest mosque, in Delhi, with an iron pillar	**Quwwat-ul-Islam**
6th-c. B.C. Buddhist pagoda in Rangoon, Burma	**Shwedagon**
mosque named for the saint who brought Islam to North Africa	**Sidi Oqba**
Buddhist image in a shrine near Kyongju, Korea	**Sokkuram**
17th-c. shrine north of Tokyo, Japan	**Toshogu**
Great Mosque at Erzurum, Turkey	**Ulu Cami**
in Jerusalem where Jews mourn the loss of the 2nd Temple	**Wailing (Western) Wall**
Bangkok's "Temple of the Dawn"	**Wat Arun**
Bangkok's temple with Buddha's footprint	**What Phra Buddhabadh**
Bangkok's "Temple of the Emerald Buddha"	**Wat Phra Keo**

Deserts

Among the world's deserts and dry places, which is or are . . . ?

In the Americas or Europe

In Northern Chile	**Atacama**
rocky, arid region in South Dakota	**Badlands**
in eastern Poland, Europe's only desert	**Bledowska**
in Mexico and the US SW	**Chihuahua**
in the US SW, a Santa Fe Trail shortcut	**Cimarron**
lowest, dryest place in the US, in California	**Death Valley**
striking dunes of southern Colorado	**Great Sand Dunes**
where the space shuttle lands, in California	**Mojave**
on an Arizona plateau	**Painted**
in NW Mexico and southern Arizona and California	**Sonoran**
gypsum sand dunes in New Mexico	**White Sands**

In Asia, Africa, Australia, and the Pacific

between the Nile and the Red Sea	**Arabian (Eastern)**
in the heart of Australia	**Gibson, Great Sandy, Great Victoria,** and **Simpson**
in Mongolia and northern China	**Gobi**
in southern Africa	**Kalahari**
in Russian Turkmenistan	**Kara-Kum**
in the heart of Iran	**Kavir**
in Russian Kazakhstan and Uzbekistan	**Kyzyl Kum**
in North Africa west of the Nile	**Libyan (Western)**
in China's Xinjiang province, a salt waste	**Lop Nor**
in eastern Iran	**Lut (Dasht-e-Lut)**
in Saudi Arabia, crossed by Lawrence of Arabia	**Al Nafud (Red Desert)**
on Africa's SW coast	**Namib**
in southern Israel	**Negev**
part of the Sahara in NE Sudan	**Nubian**
north of Xian, China, in the Yellow River's loop	**Ordos**
in southern Arabia	**Rub al Khali** or the **Empty Quarter**
world's largest, in northern Africa	**Sahara**
on a peninsula between the gulfs of Suez and Aqaba	**Sinai**
from northern Saudi Arabia to Syria	**Syrian**
in China's Sinkiang province	**Taklamakan**
in southern Pakistan and northern India	**Thar**
China's "furnace" watered by underground canals	**Turpan (Turfan)**

Forts and Prisons

(See also Palaces, Castles, and Homes)

Among the world's forts and prisons, which is or was . . . ?

In the Americas

in San Antonio, where Texans died for independence	**Alamo**
on an island in San Francisco Bay	**Alcatraz**
Confederate military prison in Georgia	**Andersonville**

NY State prison with a bloody 1971 riot	**Attica**
infantry fort in Columbus, Georgia	**Fort Benning**
fur-trading post at the Missouri's head of navigation	**Fort Benton**
on a hilltop at Halifax, Nova Scotia	**The Citadel**
fortress in Haiti's Cap-Haïtien	**La Citadelle La Ferrière**
old Danish fort on St. Thomas, in the Caribbean	**Christian**
at the foot of NY's Manhattan Island	**Castle Clinton**
an east-facing fort in San Juan, Puerto Rico	**San Cristóbal**
fort in old Cartegena, Colombia	**San Felipe de Barajas**
in Ontario, a 17th-c. Jesuit mission-fort	**Huronia**
US fort and gold depository, in Kentucky	**Knox**
key Wyoming fort and fur-trading site	**Laramie**
in NE Nova Scotia, an old French fort	**Louisbourg**
restored Hudson's Bay Co. fort in Manitoba	**Lower Fort Garry**
fort where "The Star-Spangled Banner" was written	**McHenry**
in St. Augustine, Florida, an old Spanish fort	**Castillo de San Marcos**
Great Lakes fort, HQ for Astor's fur trade	**Michilimackinac**
in San Juan, Puerto Rico, an old Spanish fortress	**El Morro (orig. Castillo de San Felipe del Morro)**
in northern California, an old Russian fort	**Ross (Stawianski)**
Alabama fort of the US Army Aviation School	**Rucker**
huge Inca fortress in old Cuzco, Peru	**Sacsayhuaman**
"up the (Hudson) river" in old prison movies	**Sing Sing (Ossining)**
where the Civil War started, in Charleston, South Carolina	**Sumter**
fort just south off Lake Champlain	**Ticonderoga**
controversial NYC prison	**Tombs**
fort and military college on the Hudson River	**West Point**

In Europe

fortress guarding the Vatican in Rome	**Castel Sant'Angelo**
USSR prison where poet Irina Ratushinskaya was held	**Barashevo**
in Florence, a Renaissance fortress, now a museum	**Bargello**
in Paris, taken in the French Revolution	**Bastille**
Churchill's WWII London headquarters	**The Citadel**
where Marie Antionette awaited execution, in Paris	**Conciergerie**
fort on the chalk cliffs at the English Channel	**Dover Castle**
fortress on the Rhine at Koblenz	**Ehrenbreitstein**
Salzburg's 12th-c. fortress	**Festung Hohensalzburg**
where early British suffragettes were forcefed	**Holloway Prison**
pre-Roman earthen fort in Britain's Dorset	**Maiden Castle**
Rome prison that may have held St. Peter	**Mammertime**
in Moscow, favored by the KGB	**Lubyanka**
London's old prison in Holborn	**Newgate**
famed Leningrad fortress	**Peter-and-Paul**
Paris's prison for most people condemned to be guillotined	**Galerie des Prisonniers**
British hilltop fort linked with King Arthur	**South Cadbury**
in Nuremberg, where Rudolf Hess was held	**Spandau**
London's bloody Thameside prison, home of the Crown Jewels and the "Beefeater" guards	**Tower of London**

In Asia, Africa, Australia, and the Pacific

part of the old walled city of Manila, Philippines	**Intramuros**
15th-c. Alexandria fort on the site of Pharos, the old lighthouse	**Kait Bey**
citadel in old Algiers	**Kasbah**
South Africa's main prison in Cape Town	**Pollsmoor**
huge 17th-c. Moghul fort in Delhi, India	**Red Fort**

on Cebu, in the Philippines, a 16th-c. fort	**San Pedro**
the fort in old Manila, the Philippines	**Santiago**

Islands

Among the world's islands, which is or are . . . ?

In and Around the Americas and the Atlantic

off Alaska, called Fortress of the Bears	**Admiralty**
island city in San Francisco Bay	**Alameda**
chain between North America and Asia	**Aleutians**
in the West Indies, once linked with St. Kitts	**Anguilla**
at the mouth of the St. Lawrence	**Anticosti**
in the Caribbean east of St. Kitts	**Antigua**
the islands dividing the Caribbean and the Atlantic	**Antilles**
the Dutch Caribbean "ABC Islands" west of Curaçao	**Aruba, Bonaire,** and **Curaçao**
in the SE Atlantic used for satellite communications	**Ascension**
off Maryland, with wild ponies	**Assateague**
in the mid-North Atlantic, held by Portugal	**Azores (Açores)**
between Greenland and mainland Canada	**Baffin**
group in the Atlantic, off Florida and Cuba	**Bahamas**
British-style Caribbean luxury resort island	**Barbados**
home to Sitka, Alaska	**Baronof**
British-linked resort spot in the western Atlantic	**Bermuda**
off Rhode Island	**Block**
off New Brunswick, site of FDR's summer home	**Campobello**
Nova Scotia's large northern island	**Cape Breton (Île Royale)**
in the Caribbean famed for turtles and tax shelters	**Cayman**
off Virginia, with wild ponies	**Chincoteague**
off Mexico's Yucatan hit hard by a 1988 hurricane	**Cozumel**

90 miles off Florida, in Castro's hands	**Cuba**
off Puerto Rico famed for its underwater life	**Culebra**
resort island off Alabama in Mobile Bay	**Dauphin**
French Caribbean island off Guadeloupe	**Désirade**
penal island off South America's French Guiana	**Devil's Island**
northerly Windward Island, "Switzerland of the Caribbean	**Dominica**
off the Florida Keys	**Dry Tortugas**
off Manhattan, once the main US immigration inspection station	**Ellis**
fought over by Britain and Argentina, in the South Atlantic	**Falklands (Malvinas)**
popular sandy resort off NY's Long Island	**Fire Island**
where Vikings settled centuries before Columbus in north Atlantic	**Greenland (Kalaallit Nunaat)**
invaded by the US after a coup in 1983	**Grenada**
between Grenada and St. Vincent in the Caribbean	**Grenadines**
French Caribbean island favored by Club Med	**Guadeloupe**
resort island off South Carolina	**Hilton Head**
shared by Haiti and the Dominican Republic	**Hispaniola**
north Atlantic island with the world's oldest continuing democracy	**Iceland**
once the English base in the Caribbean	**Jamaica**
southernmost US chains of islands off Florida	**Keys**
Florida island, setting of a Bogart film	**Key Largo**
off southern Alaska, key wild-life breeding place threatened by the *Exxon Valdez* oil spill	**Kodiak**
chain from Puerto Rico SE marking off the Caribbean from the Atlantic	**Leeward Islands**
home to the Statue of Liberty	**Liberty (Bedloe's)**
east of Manhattan, jutting into the Atlantic	**Long**

resort island in the Michigan-Huron strait	**Mackinac**
Portuguese wine-making island in the Atlantic	**Madeira**
heart of New York City	**Manhattan**
most popular of Venezuela's resort islands	**Margarita**
French Caribbean island near Guadeloupe	**Marie-Galante**
old whaling islands off Massachusetts's Cape Cod	**Martha's Vineyard** and **Nantucket**
in the Carribbean, home of Mt. Pelée and Josephine	**Martinique**
south of Canada's Newfoundland	**Miquelon** and **St. Pierre**
at Bar Harbor, Maine	**Mt. Desert**
Leeward Island called "little Ireland"	**Montserrat**
Dutch-linked Leeward and Windward islands of the Caribbean	**Netherlands Antilles**
Canadian maritime province settled by Vikings	**Newfoundland**
off North Carolina, linked with Blackbeard	**Ocracoke**
in the St. Lawrence River off Québec	**Orleans**
barrier chain off North Carolina	**Outer Banks**
resort island off Corpus Christi, Texas	**Padre**
off Canada's New Brunswick and Nova Scotia	**Prince Edward (Isle St. Jean)**
Caribbean island that came to the US in 1898	**Puerto Rico**
chain off Canada's British Columbias	**Queen Charlotte**
off North Carolina, site of the lost colony	**Roanoke**
in the Dutch Caribbean, reached from St. Martin	**Saba**
in the Caribbean, reached from St. Martin	**St. Barthélemy (Barts)**
old slave-trading center in the Virgin Islands	**St. Croix**
politically united islands among the Caribbean's Leeward Islands	**St. Christopher (St. Kitts** or **Liamulga)** and **Nevi**
in the Caribbean and 1st recognized the US flag	**St. Eustatius (Statia)**
in the South Atlantic, where Napoleon died	**St. Helena**

in the US Virgin Islands, mostly a national park	**St. John**
independent Caribbean island south of Martinique	**St. Lucia**
part-Dutch, part-French Caribbean island	**St. Martin (Sint Maarten)**
in US Virgin Islands, linked with Captain Kidd	**St. Thomas**
in the Caribbean's Windward Islands, united	**St. Vincent** and **the Grenadines**
near Guadeloupe, favored by Cousteau	**Iles des Saintes**
off Panama's Caribbean coast	**San Blas**
off Florida, known for their shells	**Sanibel** and **Captiva**
between Washington State and Vancouver	**San Juan**
in the Bahamas where Columbus 1st landed	**San Salvador (Watling)**
chain off central and western California	**Santa Barbara**
large island SW of Los Angeles	**Santa Catalina**
west of Los Angeles	**Santa Cruz**
resort islands off Savannah, Georgia	**Sea Islands**
in the South Atlantic, near the Falklands	**South Georgia**
resort island off Brownsville, Texas	**South Padres**
just off Manhattan, generally reached by ferry	**Staten Island**
off Virginia, where Elizabethan accents are heard	**Tangier**
quarry islands in Long Island Sound	**Thimbles**
in Alexandria Bay in the St. Lawrence River	**Thousand Islands**
large island off the tip of South America	**Tierra del Fuego**
in the British Virgin Islands, a popular anchorage	**Tortola**
in the Caribbean linked with calypso	**Trinidad** and **Tobago**
in the South Atlantic, an old whaler's rest stop	**Tristan da Cunha**
British-linked islands south of the Bahamas	**Turks and Caicos**
seat of British Columbia's capital, Victoria	**Vancouver**
once-Danish Caribbean islands divided between the US and Britain	**Virgin Islands**

Caribbean islands, in general	**West Indies**
chain from Dominica south marking off the Caribbean from the Atlantic	**Windward Islands**

In and Around Europe and the Mediterranean

Finland's Baltic islands	**Åland**
off Holyhead, once called Mona or Mother of Wales	**Anglesey**
off western Ireland, that inspired Synge	**Aran**
off Scotland, SE of Strathclyde	**Arran**
in the Mediterranean off eastern Spain	**Balearics**
popular islands in the Bay of Naples	**Capri, Ischia,** and **Procida**
islands in the strait between England and France	**Channel (Guernsey, Jersey, Great** and **Little Sark** and **Herm)**
Paris's political and church center in the Seine	**Île de la Cité**
in Scotland's Western Isles, NW of Tyree	**Coll**
Greek island off Turkey, perhaps Homer's home	**Chios (Kíos)**
west of Greece, a popular tourist retreat	**Corfu (Kérkyra)**
south of France, Napoleon's birthplace	**Corsica**
in the Aegean linked with Hippocrates	**Cos (Kos)**
SE of Greece, home of the Minoans	**Crete**
center of Bronze Age Mediterranean culture	**Cyclades**
Greek-Turkish battleground in the Mediterranean	**Cyprus**
off Greece, linked with Aphrodite	**Cythera (K'ythira)**
island in the Cyclades, linked with Apollo	**Delos**
off Tunisia, home of the *Odyssey*'s lotus-eaters	**Djerba**
Greek islands around Rhodes	**Dodecanese (-kánissa)**
near-island in a Thames loop in east London	**Isle of Dogs**
Scottish island just south of Rum	**Eigg**
off Italy, once Napoleon's exiled home	**Elba**
in Scotland's Western Isles, where Bonnie Prince Charlie first landed	**Eriskay**

large island east of Greece	**Euboea (Évia)**
Danish islands in the North Atlantic	**Faeroes**
famed for its sweater designs, north of Scotland	**Fair Isle**
archipelago off northern Russia	**Franz Josef Land (Fridtjof Nansen)**
group in the North Sea, off Germany	**Frisian**
Sweden's Baltic island	**Gotland (Göteland)**
in the English Channel, famed for its cows	**Guernsey**
hundreds of islands off Scotland's west coast	**Hebrides (Outer** and **Inner)** or **Western Isles**
Stockholm's Island of the Holy Spirit	**Helgeandscholmen**
beyond the Frisians, in the North Sea	**Helgoland**
off northern Norway, "The Horseman"	**Hestmannen**
"golden isles" off the French Riviera near Toulon	**Iles d'Hyères**
site of St. Columba's shrine, in the Inner Hebrides	**Iona**
Scottish island south of Jura	**Islay**
off Greece, home to Odysseus	**Ithaca (Itháki)**
called *La Reine de la Manche* (Queen of the Channel)	**Jersey**
Scottish island north of Islay	**Jura**
hospital island on the Tiber in Rome	**Isola Tiberina**
large island in western Stockholm	**Kungsholmen**
in the Aegean where Hephaestos landed, lame	**Lemnos**
in the Aegean, linked with Sappho	**Lesbos**
main islands in Scotland's Outer Hebrides, famed for tweed	**Lewis** and **Harris**
"Holy Island" off NW Britain	**Lindisfarne**
off NE Sicily, home of Aeolus, Greek god of winds	**Lipari (Isole Eolie)**
largest of the Balearic Islands off Spain	**Majorca**
strategic island in the central Mediterranean, site of 1989 summit	**Malta**
in the Irish Sea, home of the Manx cats	**Isle of Man**
island just off Cornwall's Penzance, and its "twin" just off St.-Malo, France	**St. Michael's Mount (Mont St. Michel)**

2nd largest of the Balearic Islands off Spain	**Minorca**
Venetian island famed for its fine crafts	**Murano**
popular vacation island in the Cyclades	**Mykonos**
large island SW of Scotland's Fort William	**Mull**
"New Siberia" off northern Russia	**Novosibirskiye**
"New Land" off northern Russia	**Novya Zemlya**
off Kalmar, Sweden	**Öland**
NE of Scotland's John O'Groats	**Orkneys**
off the coast of Brittany, old Ushant	**Ile d'Ouessant**
off the Italian Riviera, home of the Blue Grotto	**Isola Palmaria**
largest of the Iles d'Hyères	**Porquerolles**
off Madeira, where Columbus sojourned	**Porto Santo**
off north Ireland, where Robert Bruce took refuge	**Rathlin**
off Turkey, once home to the Knights of St. John Hospitallers	**Rhodes (Ródos)**
Stockholm's Isle of Knights	**Riddarholmen**
Scottish island south of Skye	**Rum**
residential island east of Paris's Ile de la Cité	**Ile St.-Louis**
island off which the Greeks beat the Persians in 480 B.C.	**Sálamis (-mina)**
in the Aegean, homeland of Pythagoras	**Sámos**
in the Aegean, where *Winged Victory* was found	**Samothrace (-ráki)**
across the lagoon from Venice's Piazza San Marco	**San Giorgio Maggiore**
large island between Corsica and Sicily	**Sardinia (Sardegna)**
Channel Island where cars are banned	**Sark**
warm islands off Cornwall's Land's End	**Scilly Isles**
"North Land" off northern Russia	**Severnaya Zemlya**
NE of the Orkneys, famed for ponies	**Shetlands**
off the toe of Italy's "boot"	**Sicily**
"Garden of Skerries," an archipelago near Stockholm	**Skärgården**
main islands in Scotland's Inner Hebrides	**Skye, Mull,** and **Iona**

Norway's large Arctic archipelago	**Spitsbergen (Svalbard)**
"Scattered Isles" east of Greece	**Spórades**
active volcano among the Lipari Islands	**Stromboli**
off NE Greece, near an off-shore oil and gas field	**Thássos**
in the Cyclades, center of a 1450 B.C. volcanic eruption	**Thíra (Santorini)**
in Scotland's Western Isles, west of Mull	**Tyree**
large island off England's Southampton	**Isle of Wight**
Denmark's largest island, holding Copenhagen	**Zealand (Sjaelland)**

In and Around Asia, Africa, Australia, and the Pacific

chains of old pirate haunts off India	**Andaman** and **Nicobar**
off Arabia that was probably ancient Dilmun	**Bahrain**
lone Hindu island in Indonesia	**Bali**
Pacific site of a costly 1943 Marine assault	**Betio**
Pacific atoll used for hydrogen bomb tests	**Bikini**
volcanic group NE of New Guinea	**Bismarck Archipelago**
shared by Malaysia, Indonesia, and Brunei	**Borneo**
Spanish islands off NW Africa	**Canaries (Gran Canaria, Tenerife, and Fuerteventura)**
off South Korea's southern coast	**Cheju-do**
old pirate haunts in the Mozambique Channel	**Comoros**
near Tahiti, once linked with New Zealand	**Cooks**
in the Philippines, where MacArthur said, in 1942, "I shall return"	**Corregidor**
once-Portuguese island off Gujarat, India	**Diu**
in the Pacific, noted for its huge stone figures	**Easter (Rapa Nui)**
all the islands off SE Asia	**East Indies**
in the Nile at Aswan	**Elephantine**
Pacific atoll where Japanese fought to the death, later site of a hydrogen bomb blast	**Eniwetok**

largest of the Pacific's New Hebrides Islands	**Espiritu Santo**
off Africa's Guinea, was discovered in the 15th-c.	**Fernando Po (Bioko)**
So. Pacific islands near the Solomons and Tonga	**Fiji (Vanua Levu** and **Viti Levu)**
in the Pacific, are famed for turtles and Darwin	**Galapagos**
mid-Nile island near Cairo	**Gezira**
chain of coral islets off NW Australia	**Great Barrier Reef**
in the Solomons, was retaken by the Allies in 1943	**Guadalcanal**
in the Marianas, was retaken by the Allies in 1944	**Guam**
off Southern China	**Hainan**
mid-Pacific group in the US's westernmost state	**Hawaii**
largest of the Hawaiian Islands	**Hilo**
Japan's main northern island, home of the Ainu	**Hokkaido**
Japan's largest island	**Honshu**
site of a noted WWII flag-raising, later a statue	**Iwo Jima**
SE Asian island the Dutch called Batavia	**Java**
Hawaii's NW island	**Kauai**
in the Pacific, formerly the Gilberts	**Kiribati**
home to the huge dragon-lizard, in Indonesia	**Komodo**
strung out between Kamchatka and Japan	**Kurils**
atoll site of a 1944 assault, in the Marshalls	**Kwajalein**
Japan's main southern island	**Kyushu**
old pirate haunts west of SW India	**Laccadives**
large northern island of the Philippines	**Luzon**
where Magellan was killed in 1521	**Mactan**
in the Indian Ocean, once home of a pirate nation	**Madagascar**
chain of old pirate haunts SW of Sri Lanka	**Maldives**
chain in the western Pacific, once called the Ladrones	**Marianas**
islands to which Paul Gauguin retreated	**Marquesas**
US trust territories in the Pacific	**Marshalls**

2nd largest island in Hawaii	**Maui**
in the Indian Ocean, once called Ile de France	**Mauritius**
island group in the western Pacific Ocean	**Melanesian Archipelago**
large south island of the Philippines, home of the Tasaday	**Mindanao**
island just south of the Philippines' Luzon	**Mindoro**
SE Asian group once called the Spice Islands	**Moluccas**
French island in the Pacific	**New Caledonia (Nouvelle Calédonie)**
part of the Bismarck Archipelago, linked with Papua New Guinea	**New Britain** and **New Ireland**
shared by Papua New Guinea and Indonesia	**New Guinea**
island nation near Australia, home of the Maori	**New Zealand**
site of Hawaii's capital, Honolulu	**Oahu**
islands of the mid, western, and Southern Pacific	**Oceania**
so. of Japan, taken by the Allies in mid-1945	**Okinawa**
largest of the San Juan Islands	**Orcas**
island off the western Malay Peninsula	**Penang**
SE Asian islands taken by the US in 1898	**Philippines**
where the Bounty mutineers landed, in the Pacific	**Pitcairn**
group centered on Tahiti	**Polynesia**
between Taiwan and mainland China	**Quemoy, Matsu,** and **The Penghu (the Pescadores)**
France's island in the Indian Ocean	**Réunion (Bourbon)**
group south of Japan's Kyushu	**Ryukyu**
mid-1944 Pacific site where Japanese fought to the death	**Saipan**
off the USSR where the Korean jet was shot down in 1983	**Sakhalin**
Pacific islands, part of the US protectorates	**Samoas**
off Gabon, old slave trading centers	**São Tomé** and **Principe**
in the Indian Ocean NE of Madagascar	**Seychelles**

south of Japan's Honshu, a pilgrimage island	**Shikoku**
off the tip of the Malay Peninsula	**Singapore**
off the Horn of Africa, called Island of Spices	**Socotra**
in the Melanesian Archipelago, saw WWII battles	**Solomons**
off India's southern tip, once called Ceylon, Taprobane, and Serendip	**Sri Lanka**
Indonesian islands once called the Celebes	**Sulawesi**
Indonesia's largest island	**Sumatra**
large island off China, once called Formosa	**Taiwan**
large island politically linked with Australia	**Tasmania**
in the East Indies, once Portuguese, now Indonesian	**Timor**
in the SW Pacific, near Fiji	**Tonga**
in the SW Pacific, once the Ellice Islands	**Tuvalu**
SW Pacific island group once called New Hebrides	**Vanuatu**
part of Britain's Hong Kong colony	**Victoria Island**
central cluster in the Philippines	**Visayas**
French islands between Fiji and Samoa	**Wallis** and **Futuna**
old trading islands off Tanzania	**Zanzibar (Isle of Cloves)** and **Pemba**

Lakes

(See also Seas)

Among the world's lakes, which is or are . . . ?

In the Americas

west of Guatemala city	**Atitlán**
crater lake in Guatemala	**Coatepaque**
in the remains of a volcano, in Oregon	**Crater**
between Lakes Michigan and Ontario	**Erie**
swamp in south Florida, home of Seminoles	**Everglades**

in glacier-cut valleys of central NY State	**Finger Lakes**
in Canada's NW territories	**Great Bear** and **Great Slave**
at the US-Canada border	**Great Lakes**
in Utah's Mormon country	**Great Salt**
in NY State, north of the Hudson River	**George** and **Champlain**
2nd largest of the Great Lakes	**Huron**
the Mississippi's source, in Minnesota	**Itaska**
in NE Guatemala	**Izabal**
in Canada's Banff Nat. Park	**Louise**
in western Venezuela	**Maracaibo**
artificial lake formed by the Hoover Dam across the Colorado	**Mead**
3rd largest of the Great Lakes	**Michigan**
pollution-threatened lake in central Florida	**Okeechobee**
swamp in Georgia	**Okefenokee**
between Lake Erie and the St. Lawrence River	**Ontario**
near New Orleans, Louisiana	**Pontchartrain**
remnant of a prehistoric lake, near Reno	**Pyramid**
remains of a California sea	**Salton Sea**
largest and westernmost of the Great Lakes	**Superior**
California-Nevada vacation spot	**Tahoe**
highest in the world, between Peru and Bolivia	**Titicaca**
feeder for Wisconsin's Green Bay	**Winnebago**
in Canada's west-central plains	**Winnipeg**

In Europe

resort lake SW of Budapest	**Balaton**
Rome's reservoir	**Bracciano**
connected by wide rivers, in England's Norfolk	**The Broads**
France's largest, in the Alps	**(Lac du) Bourget**
on or near the Italian-Swiss border	**Como, d'Orta, Lugano,** and **Maggiore**
on the Swiss-Bavarian border	**Constance (Bodensee)**
in Cornwall, where King Arthur's sword, Excalibur, was supposedly thrown after his death	**Dozmary Pool**
west of Verona, Italy's most popular	**Garda**

in Ireland's Sligo, inspiration of Yeats's *The Lake Isle of Inisfree*	**Lough Gill**
NE of Leningrad, linked with the Vikings	**Lodoga**
Scottish loch celebrated in song	**Loch Lomond**
near Stockholm, Sweden	**Mälar**
supposed Scottish home of a monster	**Loch Ness**
salt-water lake in Austria and Hungary	**Neusiedler See**
NE of Russia's Lake Ladoga	**Onega**
largest of Munich's "Five Lakes"	**Starnbergersee**
in the heart of Germany's Black Forest	**Titisee**
where Hannibal defeated the Romans	**Trasimene**

In Asia, Africa, and Australia

northernmost of Africa's Rift Valley lakes	**Albert**
east of Irkutsk in south-central Russia	**Baikal**
in Russian Central Asia, north of Alma Ata	**Balkhash**
along the Suez Canal	**Bitter Lakes** and **Lake Timsah**
just south of Africa's Sahara	**Chad**
2 large Chinese lakes feeding the Yangtze	**Dongting (Tungting)** and **Poyang**
Russian Central Asia's "Warm Lake"	**Issyk Kul**
manmade resort lake in Zambia and Zimbabwe	**Kariba**
"wandering" lake in China's Sinkiang	**Lop Nor**
in Tanzania, famed for its flamingos	**Manyara**
along Tanzania, Mozambique, and Malawi	**Malawi (Nyasa)**
in Kenya, famed for its flamingos	**Nakuru**
in Cameroon where a 1986 cloud of carbon dioxide killed 1746 people	**Nyos**
6000 feet high in Soviet Armenia	**Sevan**
swampy source of the White Nile	**Sudd**
source of the Blue Nile	**Tana**
world's longest lake, in Africa's Rift Valley	**Tanganyika**
in a crater on Sumatra	**Toba**

in Africa near Richard Leakey's worksite	**Turkana (Rudolf)**
in ancient Armenia, now Turkey	**Van**
Africa's largest	**Victoria**

Mountains and Peaks

Among the world's mountains and peaks, which is or are . . . ?

In the Americas

highest peak in the Americas, in Argentina	**Aconcagua**
in northern New York State	**Adirondacks**
range running down South America's west coast	**Andes**
inland from North America's East Coast	**Appalachians**
range in western Massachusetts	**Berkshires**
beautiful range in Virginia	**Blue Ridge**
promontory on St. Kitts	**Brimstone Hill**
site of a key 1775 battle in Boston	**Bunker Hill**
in Maine's Acadia National Park	**Cadillac**
huge granite block at Yosemite	**El Capitan**
the range running through Oregon and Washington	**Cascades**
in southern New York State	**Catskills**
2nd highest peak in the Americas, in Ecuador	**Chimborazo**
Oregon Trail landmark in Nebraska	**Chimney Rock**
highest peak in the Great Smoky Mts.	**Clingmans Dome**
striking peak overlooking Quito, Ecuador	**Cotopaxi**
Wyoming's volcanic peak, a national site	**Devil's Tower**
fortified rock on Martinique	**Diamond Rock (Rocher du Diamant)**
jagged peaks in Wyoming	**Grand Tetons**
Appalachian range in Tennessee	**Great Smokies**
range running through Vermont	**Green**
granite peak facing El Capitan at Yosemite	**Half-Dome**
Aruba's "Haystack Mountain"	**Hooiberg**
21,000-foot-high peak at La Paz, Bolivia	**Illimani**

"Great Register" of the Oregon Trail, where pioneers carved their names	**Independence Rock**
El Salvador volcano, the "Lighthouse of the Pacific"	**Izalco**
in southern Alaska, erupted in 1912	**Katmai Volcano**
longtime Arizona astronomical observatory	**Kitt Peak**
tangle of mountains in Oregon and California	**Klamath Knot**
north of the St. Lawrence River	**Laurentians**
Canada's highest mountain, in the Yukon	**Logan**
range at the edge of the sea at California's Big Sur	**Lucia**
volcano that formed Crater lake 7000 years ago	**Mazama**
North America's highest mountain, in Alaska	**McKinley** or **Denali (The Big One)**
active volcano near León, Nicaragua	**Momotombo**
peak on Dominica, in the Caribbean	**Morne Diablotin**
range of Washington's Pacific coast	**Olympic**
in SW California, holds a famous observatory	**Palomar**
Martinique volcano that killed 40,000 people in 1902	**Pelée**
off the tip of Canada's Gaspé Peninsula	**Percé Rock**
Rockies peak that pioneers wanted to reach "or bust"	**Pike's Peak**
resort hills in SE Pennsylvania	**Poconos**
a dormant volcano SE of Mexico City	**Popocatepetl**
a landmark on the old Santa Fe Trail	**Rabbit Ears**
volcanic peak in the Cascades, once Mt. Tacoma	**Rainier**
Continental Divide for North America	**Rockies** ·
rock that old Santa Fe traders climbed for a view	**Round Mound**
site of the carved faces of Washington, Jefferson, Lincoln, and Theodore Roosevelt	**Rushmore**
volcano in Washington that killed 60 people in 1980	**St. Helens**

range running from Colorado into New Mexico	**Sangre de Cristo (Blood of Christ)**
Nebraska pioneer Oregon Trail landmark	**Scotts Bluff**
northern California peak, a tourist's favorite	**Shasta**
range running down Mexico's west coast	**Sierra Madre Occidental**
range running along Mexico's Gulf Coast	**Sierra Madre Oriental**
home of the largest sequoia, in California	**Sierra Nevada**
lookout point near St. John's, Newfoundland	**Signal Hill**
"drive-in" volcano on St. Lucia, in the Caribbean	**Soufrière**
Rushmore-like carving of Confederates, near Atlanta	**Stone Mountain**
peak overlooking Rio de Janeiro	**Sugar Loaf**
national landmark at Dickerson, Maryland	**Sugarloaf**
New Hampshire's highest, cold, windy peak	**Washington**
range in New Hampshire	**White**
spot with fine views of California's Death Valley	**Zabriskie Point**

In Europe

range with Europe's highest peaks	**Alps**
spine of Italy	**Appenines**
dead volcano overlooking Edinburgh	**Arthur's Seat**
Byzantine holy mountain on a Greek peninsula	**Athos**
sprawling range in SE Europe	**Balkans**
Britain's highest peak, in Scotland	**Ben Nevis**
range in southern Wales	**Brecon Beacons**
Europe's highest peak, a climbers' favorite	**Mont Blanc (Monte Blanco)**
hill near Worcester, with a Roman camp	**Bredon Hill**
in Wales, linked with the warrior-bard Idris	**Cader Idris**
civic center of Rome, one of the old 7 hills	**Capitoline Hill**
in a semicircle around Hungary's plain	**Carpathians**
range running from the Black Sea to the Caspian	**Caucasus**

on the England-Scotland border	**Cheviots**
west of Britain's Oxford	**Chilterns**
in the Pyrénées, in France's Gascony	**Cirque de Gavarnie**
rolling hills west of Britain's Thames	**Cotswolds**
striking limestone peaks in NE Italy	**Dolomites (Dolomiti)**
ranges of chalky hills in southern England	**Downs (South Downs)**
high point on Britain's Exmoor	**Dunkery Beacon**
2 most famous peaks in the Swiss Bernese Oberland	**Eiger** and **Jungfraujoch**
Europe's largest active volcano, on Sicily	**Etna**
on the European side of Gibraltar Strait, old Jabal al-Tariq	**Rock of Gibraltar**
between Scotland's Lowlands and Highlands	**Grampians**
squared-off mountain south of Dublin	**Great Sugar Loaf**
range in central West Germany	**Harz**
range between France and Switzerland	**Jura**
peaks overlooking Salzburg, Austria	**Kapuzinerberg** and **Mönchsberg**
Greek mountain linked with Pan	**Kitherón (Kitherónas)**
hills near Worcester that Elgar loved	**Malvern**
coastal mountains in NW Italy	**Maritime Alps**
plateau in southern France	**Massif Central**
climber's favorite on the Italian-Swiss border	**Matterhorn (Cervino)**
hills around England's Cheddar Gorge	**Mendip**
Parisian hill where St.-Denis was martyred and the Paris Commune started	**Montmartre**
home of the gods, highest in Greece	**Olympus (Olympos)**
most prominent of Rome's 7 hills	**Palatine**
peak in Attica, near Athens	**Parnis (Párnitha)**
site of England's first national park, in Derbyshire	**The Peaks**
spine of England	**Pennines**
between France and Spain	**Pyrénées**
home of Orpheus and Eurydice, in Bulgaria	**Rhodopean**
Provence peak linked with Cezanne	**Montagne de Ste-Victoire**

"snow-clad" mountains of southern Spain	**Sierra Nevada**
highest mountain in Wales	**Snowdon**
range on Czechoslovakia's north border	**Tatras**
home to San Marino, on the Italian Peninsula	**Titano**
pierced by a large hole, in northern Norway	**Torghatten**
range dividing European and Asian Russia	**Urals**
the volcano that erupted and buried Pompeii and Herculaneum in 79 A.D.	**Vesuvius**
resort peak near Sofia, Bulgaria	**Vitosha**
range in France's Alsace	**Vosges**
rolling uplands in England's Sussex	**The Weald**
chalky uplands of England's Lincolnshire	**Wolds**
Shropshire peak for viewing the Midlands	**The Wrekin**

In Asia and the Pacific

holy peak on Bali	**Agung**
range in Russian Central Asia, an early gold source	**Altai**
Philippines' tallest peak	**Apo**
where Noah's ark supposedly came to rest, in Turkey	**Ararat (Agri Dag)**
hill near Jerusalem, where Jesus was crucified	**Calvary** or **Golgotha**
overlooking Haifa, Israel	**Carmel**
promontory overlooking Honolulu's Waikiki Beach	**Diamond Head**
range south of the Caspian, in Iran	**Elburz**
highest peak in the world, in Nepal and Tibet	**Everest**
Japan's most famous mountain	**Fuji**
where Israel's Samaritans celebrate Passover	**Gezirim**
hill where Jesus was crucified	**Golgotha** or **Calvary**
range with the world's highest peaks	**Himalayas**
range in Afghanistan, once the Caucasus Indicus	**Hindu Kush**
range in Kashmir, the "Black Gravel Mts."	**Karakorum**

Hawaii volcano whose lava made the sea boil in 1986	**Kilauea**
sacred peak in the Sabah region of Borneo	**Kinabalu**
2nd highest peak in the world, in Kashmir	**K2 (Godwin Austen** or **Dapsang)**
Pacific volcano that exploded in 1883 creating the "year with no summer"	**Krakatoa**
Taiwan's "Goddess of Mercy" mountain	**Kuan Yin Shan**
Hawaii's highest volcano, with bubbling lava	**Mauna Loa**
active volcano near Manila, Philippines	**Mayon**
mountain near Mt. Zion in old Jerusalem	**Moriah**
mount for viewing old Jerusalem	**Olives**
tangle of mountains in west-central Asia, "the Roof of the World"	**Pamirs**
Java volcano that killed 3000 people in 1772	**Papandayan**
peak from which Moses saw the Promised Land	**Pisgah**
range south of China's Xi'an	**Qin Ling**
where Moses received the 10 Commandments	**Sinai**
peak on the island of Iwo Jima	**Suribachi**
Java volcano that killed 12,000 people in 1815	**Tamboro**
range in southern Turkey	**Taurus (Toros)**
Jerusalem mount that held the old Jewish temples	**Temple**
"Celestial Mountains" of Xinjiang	**Tien Shan (Tianshan)**
Japan volcano that killed 10,000 in 1792	**Unzen-Dake**
peak atop Hong Kong	**Victoria**
Taiwan's highest peak, the Jade Mountain	**Yu Shan**
Jerusalem mount where David is buried	**Zion**

In Africa, Australia, and Antarctica

ranges in Morocco	**Atlas**
hill in Australia's outback, sacred to Aborigines	**Ayers Rock**
on the African side of Gibraltar Strait	**Rock of Ceuta**

South Africa range the Boers trekked through	**Drakensbergs**
peak on Antarctica	**Erebus**
mountains in Algeria's Sahara, the Taureg's home	**Hoggar** or **Haggar**
Africa's 2nd highest peak, an extinct volcano	**Kenya**
Africa's highest peak, linked with Hemingway	**Kilimanjaro**
massif in the Sahara, linked with the Taureg	**Tibesti**

Museums, Galleries, and Libraries

(See also Palaces, Castles, and Homes)

Among the world's great museums, galleries, and libraries, which is or are . . . ?

In the Americas

famed museum in Chicago	**Art Institute of Chicago**
noted for its eccentric founder and Impressionist works, in Pennsylvania	**Barnes Foundation**
NYC's medieval museum and garden	**Cloisters**
Washington, D.C.'s, Shakespeare library	**Folger**
world's richest museum, near Los Angeles	**J. Paul Getty**
NYC's Frank Lloyd Wright–designed museum	**Guggenheim**
idiosyncratic art-filled palazzo in Boston	**Isabella Stewart Gardner**
Washington D.C.'s, main modern art museum	**Hirshhorn**
in San Marino, California	**Huntington**
Fort Worth's 2 major art museums	**Kimbell** and **Amon Carter**
US government library in Washington, D.C.	**Library of Congress**
NYC's museum of museums	**Metropolitan Museum of Art**
NYC library and gallery, gift of a financier	**Morgan**
NYC's largest collection of modern art	**Museum of Modern Art**
world-class museum in Boston	**Museum of Fine Arts**

in Washington, D.C., holds the Watergate tapes	**National Archives**
circus museum in Sarasota, Florida	**Ringling Museum**
national historical museum in Washington, D.C.	**Smithsonian**
NYC's Kahn-designed modern art museum	**Whitney**

In Europe, Asia, Africa, Australia, and the Pacific

center of Moslem learning in Cairo	**Al Azhar**
Vienna's premier graphic arts museum	**Albertina**
Ankara museum of Near East archaeology	**Anatolian Civilization**
Oxford's famed museum	**Ashmolean**
Tunis's museum of ancient art	**Bardo**
cultural center on the site of the old Les Halles marketplace	**Beaubourg** or **Centre Pompidou**
Oxford U.'s library	**Bodleian**
London home of Rosetta Stone and Elgin Marbles	**British Museum**
London's home for the Royal Academy of Arts	**Burlington House**
Manchester's museum of industry and cities	**Castlefield**
London's J.M.W. Turner museum	**Clore Gallery**
London galleries directed by Antony Blunt, now in Somerset House	**Courtauld Institute**
museum of Prussian art in West Berlin	**Dahlem**
main museum in England's Cambridge	**Fitzwilliam**
art museum in Cambridge, Massachusetts	**Fogg**
Leningrad's famed art museum	**Hermitage**
Museum of Fine Arts in Vienna	**Kunsthistorisches**
Paris's massive museum, once a palace	**Louvre**
London's popular wax-figure museum	**Madame Tussaud's**
The Hague's fine museum	**Mauritshuis**
smaller of Paris's Impressionist museums	**Musée de l'Orangerie**
Paris's now-closed museum of Impressionists	**Musée du Jeu de Paume**

Paris's Impressionist museum in former railroad station	**Musée d'Orsay**
Italy's oldest museum, on Rome's Piazza del Campidoglio	**Musei Capitolini**
Naples's museum with remains from Pompeii	**Museo Archeologico Nazionale**
Taiwan museum with Chinese mainland relics	**National Palace**
war museum in Overloon, Netherlands	**Oorlogsmuseum**
Peggy Guggenheim Venice art gallery	**Palazzo Venier dei Leoni**
East Berlin's museum with a 2nd-c B.C. altar	**Pergamon**
Milan's famed 17th-c. palazzo-gallery	**Pinacoteca de Brera**
Spanish national museum in Madrid	**Prado**
main hall of Vienna's National Library	**Prunksaal**
art gallery at Buckingham Palace	**Queen's Gallery**
Amsterdam's museum with *The Night Watch*	**Rijksmuseum**
art museum on London's Embankment	**Tate Gallery**
museum in an Istanbul palace	**Topkapi Saray**
Florence's famous Renaissance art gallery	**Uffizi**
London's museum of ornamental arts	**Victoria and Albert**
London's collection of French rococo art	**Wallace Collection**
Liverpool's main art collection	**Walker Art Gallery**
Israel's Holocaust archives	**Yad Vashem**

Palaces, Castles, and Homes

(See also Forts and Prisons; Museums, Galleries, and Libraries; and Parks, Gardens, and Forests)

Among the world's palaces, castles, and homes, which is or was . . . ?

In the Americas

Diego Columbus's 1503 palace in Santo Domingo	Alcazar
French château in Asheville, North Carolina	Biltmore House
Washington, D.C., presidential guest house	Blair House
Cornelius Vanderbilt's Newport mansion	Breakers
Ringling's Venetian palace in Sarasota, Florida	Ca' d' Zan
presidential retreat in Maryland, once called Shangri-La	Camp David
Ponce de Léon family home in Puerto Rico	Le Casa Blanca
Victorian villa at Newport, Rhode Island	Château-sur-Mer
John A. MacDonald's Ottawa home	Earnscliffe
house Frank Lloyd Wright built over a stream	Fallingwater
Ernest Hemingway's home in Cuba	Finca Vigía
official residence of Puerto Rico's governor	La Fortaleza
Elvis Presley's Memphis home, now a shrine	Graceland
residence of NYC's mayor	Gracie Mansion
Andrew Jackson's home in Nashville, Tennessee	Hermitage
where Reagan and Gorbachev met in Reykjavik	Hofdi House
Jane Addams's Chicago settlement house	Hull House
Franklin Delano Roosevelt's Hudson River home	Hyde Park (Springwood)
Gothic mansion in Tarrytown, New York	Lyndhurst
William Vanderbilt's Newport villa	Marble House
Thomas Jefferson's home, in Virginia	Monticello

George and Martha Washington's Virginia home	**Mount Vernon**
Frederick Church's Hudson River home	**Olana**
California home of Mary Pickford and Douglas Fairbanks	**Pickfair**
Ottawa home of Canada's governor-general	**Rideau Hall**
Teddy Roosevelt's Long Island home	**Sagamore Hill**
William Randolph Hearst's California castle	**San Simeon**
Lincoln's Kentucky birthplace	**Sinking Spring Farm**
Ottawa home of Canada's opposition leader	**Stornowaye**
Washington Irving's home near NYC	**Sunnyside**
Frank Lloyd Wright's Wisconsin and Arizona homes	**Taliesin**
Ottawa home of Canada's prime ministers	**24 Sussex Drive**
Victorian mansion in Wisconsin's Prairie du Chien	**Villa Louis**
Italianate palace near Miami, Florida	**Vizcaya**
U.S. president's home in Washington, D.C.	**White House**

In the British Isles

Sir Walter Scott's Scotland home	**Abbotsford House**
castle of the Percys, Dukes of Northumberland	**Alnwick**
Northamptonshire house of the Spencers, Princess Diana's family	**Althorp**
duke of Wellington's London house	**Apsley**
English castle of the dukes of Norfolk	**Arundel**
Leicestershire castle, setting of Scott's *Ivanhoe*	**Ashby**
Essex house created by Vanbrugh and Adam	**Audley End**
Northumberland castle linked with Lancelot du lac	**Bamburgh**
where Charles I was beheaded, part of Whitehall Palace	**Banqueting Hall**
early-19th-c. Gothic castle of the duke of Rutland	**Belvoir**
castle where England's Edward II was killed	**Berkeley**

Scottish home of the dukes of Atholl	**Blair Castle**
home of the Marlboroughs and Churchills	**Blenheim Palace**
Mountbatten Hampshire home where Charles and Diana honeymooned	**Broadlands**
reigning British monarch's London palace	**Buckingham**
restored castle near Shannon, Ireland	**Bunratty**
Northamptonshire house of the Cecil family	**Burghley**
Welsh castle of the princes of Wales	**Caernarfon**
castle, with a leaning tower, near Cardiff, Wales	**Caerphilly**
Roman-Norman Welsh castle rebuilt in the 19th-c. in a fantastic medieval style	**Cardiff**
Isle of Wight castle where Charles I was held	**Carisbrooke**
where *Brideshead* was filmed, in Yorkshire	**Castle Howard**
Ireland's largest private home, west of Dublin	**Castletown House**
Winston Churchill's home in southern England	**Chartwell**
Derbyshire home of the dukes of Devonshire	**Chatsworth**
country home of the British prime minister	**Chequers**
Queen Mother's house in London	**Clarence**
home of the Astors, earlier of George Villiers, duke of Buckingham	**Cliveden**
Wordsworth's home in Grasmere	**Dove Cottage**
Roman palace and garden in Britain's Sussex	**Fishbourne**
Cardinal Wolsey's palace, ceded to Henry VIII	**Hampton Court**
Derbyshire home of Bess, countess of Shrewsbury	**Hardwick Hall**
mid-Wales castle celebrated in patriotic song	**Harlech**
Hertfordshire home of the marquess of Salisbury, where Queen Elizabeth I once lived	**Hatfield House**
castle that houses Britain's Royal Observatory	**Herstmonceux**

castle of Anne Boleyn, later of the Astors	**Hever**
Thomas Hardy's earlier and later Dorset homes	**Higher Bockhampton** and **Max Gate**
Norfolk home of the earls of Leicester, the Coke family	**Holkham Hall**
royal palace in Edinburgh, Scotland	**Holyroodhouse**
Disraeli's home near High Wycomb, Buckinghamshire	**Hughenden Manor**
Warwickshire ruin romanticized by Scott	**Kenilworth**
favorite palace of Britain's Hanoverians	**Kew (the Dutch House)**
C. S. Lewis's house near Oxford	**The Kilns**
Tudor-built Kent home of the Sackville family	**Knole**
Henry James's Sussex house	**Lamb House**
archbishop of Canterbury's London palace	**Lambeth**
Buckinghamshire house turned bookstore	**Lilies**
marquess of Bath's Wiltshire home, with zoo	**Longleat**
British castle with an open-air summer theater	**Ludlow**
remains of an old British Roman villa	**Lullingstone**
Bedfordshire house designed by Adam	**Luton Hoo**
Berkshire house in *The Wind in the Willows*	**Mapledurham**
Tudor farmhouse, once a priory, in Sussex	**Michelham Priory**
Somerset house with topiary gardens	**Montacute House**
Lord Byron's home in Nottinghamshire	**Newstead Abbey**
Queen Victoria's retreat on the Isle of Wight	**Osborne House**
Welsh birthplace of England's Henry VII	**Pembroke Castle**
14th-c. Kent palace of Philip Sidney, now the de L'Isle family	**Penshurst**
Sussex home where Turner painted	**Petworth**
Brighton palace of the prince regent (later George IV)	**Royal Pavilion**
Wordsworth's Lake District home in Ambleside	**Rydal Mount**

British palace to which ambassadors are posted	**St. James's**
Norfolk home of England's monarch	**Sandringham House**
Bloom's Dublin home in Joyce's *Ulysses*	**7 Eccles Street**
castle on the Boyne, Ireland, used for rock concerts	**Slane**
Wiltshire house set in England's 1st landscaped garden, with classical temples	**Stourhead**
Hampshire house of the dukes of Wellington	**Stratfield Saye**
Catherine Parr's Gloucestershire castle	**Sudeley**
Robert Adam masterpiece outside London	**Syon House**
London residence of Britain's prime minister	**10 Downing Street**
Baron de Rothschild's Buckinghamshire château	**Waddesdon Manor**
castle on the Avon sold to Madame Tussaud's	**Warwick**
home of George Washington's ancestors, near Newcastle in NE England	**Washington Old Hall**
Wiltshire house where Eisenhower planned the Normandy invasion	**Wilton**
Thames Valley castle of England's monarchs	**Windsor**
Bedfordshire residence of the dukes of Bedford, with zoo	**Woburn Abbey**

In Continental Europe

Moorish palace and gardens of Granada, Spain	**Alhambra**
13th–16th-c. castle, now a museum, in Stuttgart	**Altes Schloss**
palace with Lisbon's Espirito Santo collection	**Azuara**
striking châteaux in the Loire Valley	**Azay-le-Rideau, Blois,** and **Chenonceau**
palace built in 60 days for Marie Antoinette, near Paris	**Bagatelle**
Prince Eugene's 18th-c. Viennese country palace	**Belvedere**
Hitler's "Eagle's Nest" retreat in the Bavarian Alps	**Berchtesgaden**
hilltop castle overlooking Lisbon	**Castelo de São Jorge**
Francois I's Loire château, the valley's largest	**Chambord**

château that holds the *Très Riches Heures du Duc de Berry,* near Paris	**Chantilly**
palace where Frederick the Great's treasures are kept, in West Berlin	**Charlottenburg**
restored château near Compiègne	**Château de Pierrefonds**
be-dungeoned Prague castle	**Daliborka**
Nero's palace in Rome, the "Golden House"	**Domus Aurea**
royal palace in Stockholm	**Drottningholm**
French château at Newport, Rhode Island	**Elms**
France's royal Renaissance palace near Paris	**Fontainebleau**
palace near Lisbon noted for its gardens	**Fronteira**
the pope's summer residence in Italy	**Castel Gandolfo**
13th-c. castle near the Danube, north of Augsburg	**Harburg**
Empress Elizabeth's home near Vienna	**Hermes Villa**
palace from which counsellors were thrown in the 17th-c. "defenestration of Prague"	**Hradcany**
home of the Dutch monarchs, near The Hague	**Huis ten Bosch**
ancient Minoan palace on Crete	**Knossós**
"Hamlet's Castle" in Helsingør, Denmark	**Kronborg**
rebuilt neo-classical palace in Warsaw	**Lazienki**
"Pleasure Castle" near Salzburg built by practical jokers	**Lustschloss Hellbrunn**
where Chekhov lived, south of Moscow	**Melikhovo**
Saxon royal castle near Meissen	**Moritzburg**
Bavarian royal palace near Munich	**Nymphenburg**
Cardinal Richelieu's Paris palace	**Palais Royal**
doges' palace in Venice near San Marco	**Palazzo Ducale**
Rome palace on the Piazza Venezia, from which Il Duce and popes hailed crowds	**Palazzo Venezio**
Peter the Great's seaside home at Leningrad	**Peterhof**
Portuguese royal palace	**Queluz**

Hohenzollern castle in Potsdam, imitated in Haiti	**Sans Souci**
Salzburg home built by a 17th-c. Medici bishop for his mistress	**Schloss Mirabell**
German birthplace of Britain's Prince Albert	**Schloss Rosenau**
Maria Theresa's Vienna palace, Marie Antoinette's home	**Schönbrunn**
palace cum hotel near Vienna's Belvedere	**Schwarzenberg**
Turgenev estate south of Moscow	**Spasskoye-Lutovinovo**
Paris palace built by Marie de' Medici	**Tuileries**
French château more opulent than Versailles, for which its owner was arrested	**Vaux-le-Vicomte**
Louis XIV's grand château outside Paris	**Versailles**
country palace of Portugal's dukes of Bragança	**Vila Viçosa**
Tuscany villa with spectacular gardens	**Villa Garzoni**
château near Tours with reconstructed parterre gardens	**Villandry**
papal summerhouse in the Vatican gardens	**Villa Pia**
German "Hall of Fame" castle near Regensburg	**Walhalla**
9-century-old castle in Eisenach, East Germany	**Wartburg**
rebuilt baroque palace outside Warsaw	**Wilanów**
Leningrad palace the Bolsheviks took in 1917	**Winter**
Tolstoy's home, south of Moscow	**Yasnaya Polyana**
old Saxon palace in Dresden	**Zwinger**

In Asia, Africa, Australia, and the Pacific

summer residence of the Thai monarchs	**Bang Pa-In**
palace where Tunisian independence was granted	**Bardo**
royal residence in Bangkok, Thailand	**Chakri Maha Prasad**
Korean "Palace of Illustrious Virtue" in Seoul	**Changdok**
shogun's castle in old Tokyo	**Edo** or **Chiyoda**

Peking palace compound of China's emperors	**Forbidden City (Zi Jin Cheng)**
Old Nawab's palace in Lucknow, India	**Great Imambara**
palace in India's Agra Fort	**Jahangir Mahal**
17th-c. imperial villa near Kyoto, Japan	**Katsura Rikyu**
Turkish palace in Algiers	**Khedaodj El Amia**
Sultan's palace on Java	**Kraton**
Seoul, Korea's "Shining Happiness Palace"	**Kyongbok**
Japanese medieval imperial palace	**Kyoto Gosho**
presidential palace in Manila, in the Philippines	**Malacanang**
2000-year-old royal castle near Seoul, Korea	**Namhansan**
17th-c. shogun's castle near Kyoto, Japan	**Nijo-Jo**
"Crescent Moon Castle" of Korea's Silla kings	**Panwol-song**
New Delhi's presidential (once viceroy's) palace	**Rashtrapati Bhavan**
imperial Summer Place outside Peking	**Yiheyuan**

Parks, Gardens, and Forests

(See also Palaces, Homes, and Castles)

Among the world's parks, gardens, and forests, what is or are . . .?

In the Americas

park and gardens at Bar Harbor, Maine	**Acadia**
Utah park of weather-hollowed sandstone	**Arches**
arboretum at Jamaica Plain, outside Boston	**Arnold**
Cincinnati's park of many gardens	**Ault**
Baffin I. park called "the Place That Does Not Melt"	**Auquittuq**
densely grown gardens in New Iberia, Louisiana	**Avery Island Jungle**
Spanish-Moorish-Mayan park in San Diego	**Balboa**

Canada's 1st nat. park, in Alberta	**Banf**
famed gardens at Theodore, Alabama	**Bellingrath**
huge botanical gardens in Hales Corners, Wisconsin	**Boerner**
the park in the heart of old Boston	**Boston Common**
research and public gardens in Montréal, Québec	**Jardin Botanique**
bridge-garden, in Shelburne Falls, Massachusetts	**The Bridge of Flowers**
botanical gardens at Wheaton, Maryland	**Brookside**
gardens near a Tampa, Florida, brewery	**Busch**
gardens in a resort in Pine Mountain, Georgia	**Callaway**
tropical gardens in Kingston, Jamaica	**Castleton**
mid-Manhattan park designed by Frederick Law Olmsted and Calvert Vaux	**Central**
park in the heart of Mexico City	**Chapultepec**
holly gardens on Pinehurst, North Carolina	**Clarendon**
gardens around Florida's Lake Eloise	**Cypress**
nat. park around Alaska's Mt. McKinley	**Denali**
gardens on California's Rancho San Raphael estate	**Descanso**
fossil-filled provincial park in Alberta, Canada	**Dinosaur**
nat. wildlife refuge in Virginia	**Dismal Swamp**
garden in the heart of Washington, D.C.	**Dumbarton Oaks**
vast watery park near Homestead, Florida	**Everglades**
fine tropical garden near Miami, Florida	**Fairchild**
Philadelphia's huge city park	**Fairmount**
New York City's garden-in-a-skyscraper	**Ford Foundation**
wild-flower garden in Framingham, Massachusetts	**Garden In the Woods**
world-class conservatory in Chicago, Illinois	**Garfield Park**
Montana park of glaciers and bighorn sheep	**Glacier**

magnolia gardens and arboretum in Mississippi	**Gloster**
extensive gardens near Many, Louisiana	**Hodges**
arboretum in Portland, Oregon	**Hoyt**
campus pinetum at Wellesley, Massachusetts	**Walter Hunnewell**
estate botanical gardens at San Marino, California	**Huntington**
huge park in São Paulo, Brazil	**Ibirapuera**
park on Lake Michigan's south shore	**Indiana Dunes**
multi-cultural garden in Salt Lake City, Utah	**International Peace**
multi-tiered glass St. Louis conservatory	**Jewel Box**
southern California forest of cactuslike trees	**Joshua Tree**
nat. park in the Aleutian region	**Katmai**
Canadian park around the Yukon's Mt. Logan	**Kluane**
El Salvador botanical gardens in an old crater	**La Laguna**
formal gardens at Kennett Square, Pennsylvania	**Longwood**
Spanish-style gardens in New Orleans	**Long-vue**
stand of huge sequoia in California's Yosemite	**Mariposa Grove**
US research gardens on Puerto Rico	**Mayagüez**
exotic estate garden in Grand Métis, Québec	**Parc de Métis**
nat. forest near Elkins, West Virginia	**Monongahela**
plantation gardens with butterfly lakes near Charleston, South Carolina	**Middleton Place**
boxwood gardens at Leesburg, Virginia	**Morven Park**
Oregon nat. forest and ski area	**Mt. Hood**
California nat. park famed for redwoods	**Muir Woods**
private, now public, garden at Jackson, Mississippi	**Mynelle**
nat. wildlife refuge in Georgia	**Okefenokee Swamp**
lush, wet forest in Washington State	**Olympic Rain**
forest where trees turned to rock, in Arizona	**Petrified**

New Jersey's low-lying, boggy, pine-filled area	**Pine Barrens**
gardens in Jefferson Island, Louisiana, once home of pirate Jean Lafitte	**Rip Van Winkle**
gardens at the White House	**Rose Garden**
famed rose gardens of Columbus, Ohio	**Park of Roses**
nat. forest of giant cactus, in Arizona	**Saguaro**
California park with the world's largest trees	**Sequoia**
tropical gardens at Ocho Rios, Jamaica	**Shaw Park**
park in Virginia's Blue Ridge country	**Shenandoah**
campus gardens at Northampton, Massachusetts	**Smith College**
San Francisco's famed park and arboretum	**Strybing Arboretum**
restored Colonial gardens of New Bern, North Carolina	**Tryon Palace**
Toscanini's estate, now a park, in the Bronx, NY	**Wave Hill**
gardens on an old du Pont estate in Delaware	**Winterthur**
Wyoming park graced by the Old Faithful geyser, the US's 1st nat. park	**Yellowstone**
California park with El Capitan and Half Dome	**Yosemite**
famed floating gardens near Mexico City	**Xochimilco**
gardens and park in Austin, Texas	**Zilker**

In the British Isles

100-acre Cambridgeshire gardens with Tudor manor	**Anglesey Abbey**
wild, common land in Sussex, A. A. Milne country	**Ashdown Forest**
riverside gardens behind Cambridge U.'s colleges	**The Backs**
Hampshire palace house and motor museum	**Beaulieu**
Buckinghamshire's stand of hugh old beeches, once pollarded	**Burnham Beeches**
park near Stratford-upon-Avon linked with Shakespeare	**Charlecote**
azalea and rhododendron gardens near Glasgow	**Crarae Lodge**

old English forest between the Severn and Wye	**Dean**
topiary garden of Fife, Scotland	**Earlshall**
island park in Ireland's Cork City	**Fota**
royal gardens at Britain's Windsor Castle	**Frogmore**
park between London's Piccadilly and Buckingham Palace	**Green**
medieval gardens at Britain's Henley-on-Thames	**Greys Court**
large park in NW London	**Hampstead Heath**
gardens near Britain's Chipping Camden	**Hidcote Manor**
London park with a free-speech corner	**Hyde**
Yorkshire site of a fine Alpine rock garden	**Ingleborough Hall**
gardens west of Hyde Park, in London	**Kensington**
Royal Botanic Gardens on London's outskirts	**Kew**
gardens, lakes, and fine views in Sussex	**Leonardslee**
fine topiary garden in Westmorland, Britain	**Levens Hall**
park in County Wicklow, south of Dublin	**Marley**
large park north of London's Buckingham Palace	**Regent's**
ancient royal park up the Thames from London	**Richmond**
forest near Salisbury, England	**Savernake**
forest in Nottinghamshire linked with Robin Hood	**Sherwood**
Kent gardens created by Vita Sackville-West and Harold Nicolson	**Sissinghurst**
nat. park in central Wales	**Snowdonia**
park that runs along The Mall, in London	**St. James's**
Bedfordshire bird zoo and sanctuary	**Stagsden Bird Gardens**
deer park near Yorkshire's Fountains Abbey	**Studley Royal**
popular 18th-c. gardens on London's South Bank	**Vauxhall Gardens**
Britain's Royal Horticultural Society gardens	**Wisley**

In Continental Europe

royal Spanish garden near Madrid	**Aranjuez**
park on the former Radziwill estates in Poland	**Arkadia**
old imperial park in Vienna	**Augarten**
striking international bird park in southern Holland	**Avifauna**
forest in East Bavaria, near Czechoslovakia	**Bayerischer Wald**
ancient forest on the Poland-USSR border	**Bialowieza**
Bohemian forest at the Austro-German-Czech border	**Böhmerwald**
Paris park that was once a slum	**Bois de Boulogne**
park designed by Pier Francesco Orsini near Viterbo, Italy	**Bomarzo (Sacro Bosco)**
forest in northern Poland with wild European bison	**Borecka**
park near Vienna's Albertina Museum	**Burggarten**
park near Paris's Eiffel Tower	**Champ de Mars**
Vienna park with the Donauturm (Danube Tower)	**Donaupark**
English-designed park in Munich	**Englischer Garten**
Spanish forest west of Madrid	**Extremadura**
parks with over 600 sculptures in Oslo	**Frogner** or **Vigeland**
parterre garden near Lisbon	**Fronteira**
classic Italian garden near Florence	**La Gamberaia**
safari park in lower Austria	**Gänserndorf**
restored Moorish gardens of Granada	**Generalife**
Moscow park in Martin Cruz Smith's book	**Gorky**
Berlin's largest park	**Grunewald**
park in the heart of Bucharest	**Herastrau**
nat. park in central Holland	**Hofe Veluwe**
Polish nat. forest near Warsaw	**Kampinos**
forest where thousands of Poles were killed in 1940	**Katyn**
famed bulb-flower garden near Amsterdam	**Keukenhof**
Stockholm's Royal Gardens	**Kungsträdgården**
wildlife preserve outside Vienna	**Lainzer Tiergarten**
north German heath filled with prehistoric ruins	**Lüneburger Heide**
popular park on Paris's Left Bank	**Jardin du Luxembourg**
wildlife preserve in lower Austria	**Marchauen**

Hampshire forest and heath, with wild ponies	**New Forest**
woods and gardens of old Prague	**Petrin**
botanical gardens east of Paris's Latin Quarter	**Jardin des Plantes**
Vienna amusement park where *The Third Man* climaxed	**Prater**
Portuguese royal gardens	**Queluz**
Saxon Woods east of Hamburg and the Elbe	**Sachsenwald**
famed Black Forest of Germany's upper Rhine	**Schwarzwald**
varied gardens at Mannheim, West Germany	**Schwetzingen**
Stockholm's amusement park	**Skansen**
Vienna park near the Karlskirche	**Stadtpark**
forest in Germany's Swabian Alps	**Schwäbischer Wald**
site of Munich's Oktoberfest	**Theresienwiese**
park in central Berlin	**Tiergarten**
famous water park outside Rome	**Tivoli**
amusement park in Copenhagen	**Tivoli Gardens**
Paris park built by Catherine de' Medici	**Jardin des Tuileries**
18th-c. garden with statuary, near Würzburg	**Veitshöchheim**
stand of twisted dwarf beeches in Champagne	**Forêt de Verzy**
Rome's largest park	**Villa Borghese**
wooded hills near Vienna	**Wienerwald**
"Great Poland" national park near Posnan, Poland	**Wielkopolski**
recreational woods outside Cracow, Poland	**Wolski**
park for Stuttgart vistas	**Zeppelin-Aussichtsplatte**

In Africa

wildlife park near Mt. Kilimanjaro, Kenya	**Amboseli**
main nat. park in Tanzania	**Arusha**
nat. park in SW Senegal	**Basse Casamance**
wildlife reserve in Botswana	**Chobe**
wildlife reserve in Namibia (Southwest Africa)	**Etosha**
botanical gardens in Harare, Zimbabwe	**Ewanrigg**
famed gardens of Cairo, Egypt	**Ezbeklya**
wildlife reserve in South Africa's Zululand	**Hluhluwe**

Zimbabwe's Connecticut-sized wildlife reserve	**Hwange**
huge wildlife reserve in Zambia	**Kafue**
nat. wildlife park in Togo, Africa	**Keran**
forest in SW Uganda, with many chimpanzees	**Kibale**
South Africa's main nat. park	**Kruger**
Kenya wildlife reserve, in the Serengeti Plains	**Masai Mara**
Kenya reserve where Elsa, the *Born Free* lioness, went wild	**Meru**
world's largest wildlife reserve, in Tanzania	**Selous**
African park with annual game migrations	**Serengeti Plains**
Zambia's wildlife reserve famed for its elephants	**South Luangwa**
Kenya's primate reserve	**Tana River**
Kenya's largest park, famed for hippo sightings	**Tsavo**

In Asia, Australia, and the Pacific

imperial park in Peking	**Bei Hai**
botanical gardens in Seoul, Korea	**Changgyong-won**
game reserve south of Kathmandu, Nepal	**Chitwan**
Honshu nat. park with Japan's highest peaks	**Chubu-Sangaku**
mountainous nat. park on Japan's Hokkaido	**Daisetsuzan**
nat. park in northern Thailand	**Doi Indhanon**
park on Kauai, Hawaii, featuring Silverswords	**Haleakola**
wildlife sanctuary in Assam, India	**Kaziranga**
famed landscape gardens in Tokyo	**Korakuen**
amusement park in Melbourne	**Luna**
Kyoto garden famed for its cherry trees	**Maruyama**
gardens near Poipu on Kauai, Hawaii	**Plantation (Moir's)**
sacred and royal park in Seoul, Korea	**Sajik**
Japanese Garden of Tranquillity in Singapore	**Seiwaen**
botanical gardens outside Calcutta	**Sibpur**
gardens on Honolulu, on Oahu, Hawaii	**Alice Cooke Spaulding**
landscaped gardens in Malaysia's Kuala Lumpur	**Titiwangsa**

Passes

Among the world's great passes, which . . . ?

is a key railroad tunnel in the Austrian Alps	**Arlberg**
leads into the Vale of Kashmir, in India	**Banihal**
links Verona, Italy, and Innsbruck, Austria	**Brenner**
feeds into the Garonne Valley from southern France	**Carcassone Gap**
was the main miners' pass in the Yukon gold rush	**Chilkoot**
is the old pass through Turkey's Taurus Mts.	**Cilician Gates**
took Daniel Boone through the Appalachians	**Cumberland Gap**
is the Appalachians notch through which the Delaware River passes	**Delaware Water Gap**
is where 1846 California pioneers died in a blizzard	**Donner Pass**
is a break in the mountains in Ireland's Killarney National Park	**Gap of Dunloe**
is the main pass between Mongolia and Russia	**Dzungarian Gap**
is popular with leafers, in New Hampshire	**Franconia Notch**
is famed for its dogs and hospice, between Italy and Switzerland	**Great St. Bernard**
is on the mountain route from Leh to Central Asia	**Karakorum Pass**
is where Americans lost in 1943, in Tunisia	**Kasserine**
guarded old India's Northwest Frontier	**Khyber**
is where the Scottish defeated the British in 1689	**Killiecrankie**
links SW France and NE Spain, in the Pyrénées	**Le Perthus**
was on the Santa Fe Trail	**Raton**
was where Roland made his last stand, in the Pyrénées	**Roncesvalles**
was the main Oregon Trail pass into the Rockies	**South**
is the main pass near Thailand's River Kwai	**Three Pagodas**

is the 10,000-foot-high pass in California's Sierra Nevada, near Yosemite	**Tioga**
was the main railroad pass in the Yukon gold rush	**White**

Rivers and Valleys

(See also Seaways, Straits, and Passages)

Among the world's rivers and valleys, which . . . ?

In the Americas

flows from the Peruvian Andes through Brazil	**Amazon**
is the highest falls in the world, in Venezuela	**Angel Falls**
are the best-known glaciers in Canada's Columbia Icefields	**Athabaska** and **Saskatchewan glaciers**
is the seasonally dry Yosemite falls, highest in North America	**Bridalveil Falls**
is a canyon of rainbow rock in southern Utah	**Bryce**
is used by the Panama Canal	**Chagres**
flows through Boston, Mass.	**Charles**
flows north into Hudson Bay	**Churchill**
cut the Grand Canyon	**Colorado**
winds from Canada into Washington State	**Columbia**
flows along Manhattan's east side	**East**
is the huge gorge cut by the Colorado River	**Grand Canyon**
forms the border between Mexico and Texas	**Rio Grande (Rio Bravo del Norte)**
flows in a circle in the Atlantic, a "river in the sea"	**Gulf Stream**
flows by New York City	**Hudson**
is California's main farming valley	**Imperial Valley**
includes over 275 falls, where Argentina, Brazil, and Paraguay join	**Iguaçu (Iguazú) Falls**
flows from Virginia into Hampton Roads	**James**
is the huge falls in Guyana	**Kaieteur**

flows from Canada's NW into the Arctic Ocean	**Mackenzie**
formed California's Yosemite Valley	**Merced**
drains mid-America through New Orleans	**Mississippi**
joins the Mississippi at St. Louis	**Missouri (Big Muddy)**
is the water-level route through the Appalachians	**Mohawk**
is the most famous "ice river" at Glacier Bay	**Muir Glacier**
in Canada's Northwest Territories has the huge Virginia Falls	**Nahanni**
forms the world-famous falls on the Canada–New York State border	**Niagara**
flows from NY and Pennsylvania to the Mississippi	**Ohio**
is the main river of Venezuela	**Orinoco**
forms the Iguaçu Falls, in Brazil-Argentina	**Paraná**
is Argentina's "River of Silver," where the *Graf Spee* fought in 1939	**Rio de la Plata (Plate)**
was followed by Oregon Trail travelers from the Mississippi west	**Platte**
flows through Washington, D.C.	**Potomac**
flows south into the St. Lawrence	**Saguenay**
connects the Great Lakes with the Atlantic	**St. Lawrence**
joins the Potomac at Harper's Ferry, West Virginia	**Shenandoah**
is tapped by the New Deal's TVA	**Tennessee**
in southern Alaska is filled with volcanic holes	**Valley of the 10,000 Smokes**
was the Mississippi-Alabama site of a controversial US dam project	**Tombigbee**
was sacred to Peru's Incas	**Urubamba**
is the glacier that feeds Canada's Lake Louise	**Victoria**
flows through Indiana	**Wabash**
drains NW Canada into the Bering Sea	**Yukon**

In the British Isles

is a beautiful ravine near Bristol, in Britain	**Avon Gorge**
is in Britain's Rutland Valley, famous for Stilton	**Vale of Belvoir**

is the fox-hunting valley in England's north Dorset	**Vale of Blackmoor**
was where William III defeated James II in Ireland in 1690	**Boyne**
flows through England's Cambridge	**Cam (Granta)**
is a limestone ravine with caverns, in Somerset	**Cheddar Gorge**
joins the Thames (Isis) at Oxford	**Cherwell**
flows through Glasgow	**Clyde**
flows by Aberdeen, Scotland	**Dee**
is the Worcestershire valley in the Cotswolds	**Vale of Evesham**
flows *under* the city of London	**Fleet**
flows through the port of Hull, in NE England	**Humber**
is the Thames's name as it flows through Oxford	**Isis**
flows through Dublin	**Liffey**
flows through Liverpool	**Mersey**
is where Virginia Woolf drowned, in Sussex	**Ouse**
near Britain's Gloucester has a striking tidal bore	**Severn**
flows through Limerick, Ireland	**Shannon**
is linked with John Constable in England's Suffolk	**Stour**
carved one of Yorkshire's wildest, finest dales	**Swale**
flows between Cornwall and Devon, Britain	**Tamar**
is Scotland's longest river, fine for fishing	**Tay**
runs from Cumberland, Britain, into the North Sea	**Tees**
flows through London and Oxford	**Thames**
flows through Newcastle, in NE England	**Tyne**
runs from Wales into Hereford and Gloucestershire	**Wye**

In Continental Europe

flows from Italy's Alps to the Adriatic	**Adige**
flows through Amsterdam	**Amstel** and **IJ**
runs through Tuscany, south of Florence, Italy	**Arno**
flows through Vienna and Budapest	**Danube (Donau)**
flows past Kiev and Chernobyl into the Black Sea	**Dnieper**

flows past Rostov into the Azov Sea	**Don**
is the narrow gorge of the Danube in Bavaria	**Donaudurchbruch**
in France has many prehistoric caves	**Dordogne**
is where much Portuguese wine is made	**Douro**
is the main Russian river flowing into the Baltic	**Dvina**
runs through NE Spain to the Mediterranean	**Ebro**
flows past Hamburg to the North Sea	**Elbe**
flows through SW France to the Atlantic	**Garonne**
runs past Córdoba and Seville to the Atlantic	**Guadalquivir**
flows from the Alps through Munich	**Inn**
is the spectacularly narrow part of the Danube in Romania	**Iron Gates**
is Balzac country, famous for its many chateaux	**Loire**
is near Germany's Frankfurt	**Main**
seemed like one long battlefield in WWI	**Marne**
flows through France, Belgium, and Holland	**Meuse (Maas)**
in Czechoslovakia inspired Smetana	**Moldau**
flows from France to the Rhine, a wine-making valley	**Moselle (Mosel)**
flows through Heidelberg	**Neckar**
flows from Czechoslovakia to the Baltic Sea	**Oder**
flows from Turin, Italy, to the Adriatic Sea	**Po**
flows through the heart of Germany and Holland	**Rhine (Rijn)**
flows into the Mediterranean near Marseilles	**Rhône**
is Bulgaria's central farming valley	**Valley of the Roses**
is a major industrial area in northern West Germany	**Rhur**
joins the Rhône at Lyon	**Saône**
flows by Antwerp	**Schelde** or **Scheldt**
flows through Paris to the Bay of Biscay	**Seine**
saw one of WWI's worst battles	**Somme**

flows through Lisbon, Portugal	**Tagus**
flows through the Old City of Rome	**Tiber**
flows through Warsaw	**Vistula**
flows through Prague	**Vltava**
is the main Russian river flowing into the Caspian	**Volga**

In Asia

drains west-central Asia, linked with Alexander the Great	**Amu** and **Syr**
is in SE Russia, on the Mongolian border	**Amur**
is where Syrians and Israelis fought, in Lebanon	**Bekaa** or **Bekka**
flows from the Himalayas into the Bay of Bengal	**Brahmaputra**
flows through Bangkok, Thailand	**Chao Praya**
is the more westerly of Mesopotamia's 2 main rivers	**Euphrates (Firat)**
flows through India to Calcutta	**Ganges (Ganga)**
flows through Seoul, Korea	**Han**
flows through Calcutta	**Hooghly**
is the oft-flooded "China's Sorrow"	**Huang (Yellow)**
was home to the Mohenjo-daro civilization	**Indus**
runs through Burma	**Irrawaddy**
flows into the Dead Sea	**Jordan**
is the Shangri-La–like valley in northern India	**Vale of Kashmir**
drains NE Siberia into the East Siberian Sea	**Kolyma**
is the Thai river that WWII POW's bridged	**Kwai**
drains mid-Siberia into the Laptev Sea	**Lena**
flows through Vietnam to the South China Sea	**Mekong**
drains the land east of the Urals into the Kara Sea	**Ob**
flows through Hong Kong	**Pearl**
is the joined Tigris and Euphrates rivers	**Shatt al-Arab**
runs along the north rim of the Taklamakan Desert	**Tarim**
is the more easterly of Mesopotamia's 2 main rivers	**Tigris (Dicle)**
is where MacArthur was stopped, in Korea	**Yalu**

is China's "River of Golden Sand;" so long it has 2 names	**Yangte (Yangzi)** and **Chang Jiang (Jinsha Jiang)**
drains western Siberia into the Kara Sea	**Yenesei**
flows through Tibet into the Brahmaputra	**Zangbo**

In Africa, Australia, and the Pacific

flows from Central Africa into the Atlantic	**Congo (Zaire)**
is in Australia's New South Wales	**Darling**
flows through mid-Morocco toward the Sahara	**Draa**
flows through Senegambia	**Gambia**
flows from northern South Africa to the Indian Ocean	**Limpopo (Crocodile)**
curves through West Africa	**Niger**
forms the lifeline of Egypt	**Nile**
is the site of key Leakey finds in East Africa	**Olduvai Gorge**
is where the African continent is tearing apart	**Rift Valley**
are the huge falls on Zambia's Zambezi River	**Victoria Falls**
runs through Melbourne, Australia	**Yarra**
forms the Victoria Falls, in Zambia	**Zambezi**

Seas

(See also Lakes)

Among the world's seas, which is . . . ?

between Italy and Yugoslavia	**Adriatic**
east of Greece and west of Turkey	**Aegean**
south of Burma and north of Sumatra	**Andaman**
east of the Caspian Sea in Russian Central Asia	**Aral**
atop the Black Sea	**Azov**
between Scandinavia, Germany, and the USSR	**Baltic (Ost See)**
north of Novaya Zemlya, served by Murmansk	**Barents**

linked to the Mediterranean, once Pontus Euxinus, "the Hospitable Sea"	**Black**
between the USSR, Turkey, and Iran	**Caspian**
between New Guinea and Australia	**Coral**
fed by the Jordan River, the world's lowest	**Dead**
where Jesus gathered his disciples	**Galilee**
between southern Italy and Greece	**Ionian**
between Eire and England	**Irish**
between China and Japan	**Japan**
south of Novaya Zemlya	**Kara**
between Siberia and the New Siberian Is.	**Laptev**
between Italy and Corsica	**Ligurian**
between the Mediterranean and Black seas	**Marmara**
between Europe and Africa	**Mediterranean**
between Britain and Norway	**North**
between Kamchatka and the Russian mainland	**Okhotsk**
between Egypt and Arabia	**Red**
the "inland sea" of Japan	**Seto Naikai**
south of China	**South China**
between Timor and Australia	**Timor**
between Italy and Sardinia	**Tyrrhenian**
between China and Korea	**Yellow**
in NW Russia, with the port of Archangel	**White**

Seaways, Straits, and Passages

Among the world's seaways, straits, or passages, which . . . ?

runs between the Virgin Islands and Anguilla	**Anegada Passage**
divides Arabia from North Africa, the "Strait of Tears"	**Bab al-Mandab or el Mandeb**
flows between Australia and Tasmania	**Bass Strait**
leads into the Gulf of St. Lawrence	**Strait of Belle Isle**
divides Asia and North America	**Bering Strait**

connects the Marmara and Black seas	**Bosporus (Bogaziçi)**
runs through Loch Ness	**Caledonian Canal**
is between New Zealand's 2 main islands	**Cook Strait**
connects the Mediterranean and the Sea of Marmara	**Dardanelles (Hellespont)**
is where the *Bismarck* sank the *Hood* in 1940	**Denmark Strait**
is the narrows of the English Channel	**Dover Strait**
lies between England and the Continent	**English Channel**
separates Cuba and the Florida Keys	**Straits of Florida**
runs between Vancouver I. and British Columbia	**Strait of Georgia**
connects the Mediterranean with the Atlantic, between Africa and Europe	**Gibraltar Strait (Pillars of Hercules)**
connects Stockholm and Götland	**Göte Canal**
is Venice's central water-highway	**Canal Grande**
runs south of Antigua and Montserrat	**Guadeloupe Passage**
lies between Arabia and Iran, troubled during the Iran-Iraq War	**Strait of Hormuz**
runs between Singapore and mainland Malaya	**Strait of Johore**
connects the Pacific and Puget Sound	**Juan de Fuca Strait**
runs between Sweden and Jutland	**Kattegat**
connects the Black Sea and the Sea of Azov	**Kerch Strait**
cuts across Schleswig Holstein between the North and Baltic seas	**Kiel Canal**
runs between Korea and Japan	**Korea Strait**
joins Lakes Michigan and Huron	**Mackinac**
lies between the South American mainland and Tierra del Fuego	**Magellan Strait**
runs between Sumatra and Malaysia	**Strait of Malacca**
runs between Italy and Sicily, home of Scylla and Charybdis	**Strait of Messina**
cuts across France between the Mediterranean and the Bay of Biscay	**Canal du Midi**

bisects the Netherlands	**Moerdijk**
passes between the Dominican Republic and Puerto Rico, where many emigrants were killed by sharks in a 1987 boat accident	**Mona Passage**
runs between Madagascar and Africa	**Mozambique Channel**
runs between Tunisia and Sicily	**The Narrows**
runs between the Caribbean's St. Kitts and Nevis	**The Narrows**
runs between Ireland and Scotland	**North Channel**
passes north of Eurasia	**Northeast Passage** or the **Northern Sea Route**
links Amsterdam and the North Sea	**North Sea Canal**
was the long-sought route north of America to Asia	**Northwest Passage**
connects the Atlantic and Pacific oceans across Central America	**Panama Canal**
lies between Ottawa and Lake Ontario	**Rideau Canal**
runs between Wales and Ireland	**St. George's Channel**
connects the Great Lakes and the Atlantic	**St. Lawrence Seaway**
runs through central Paris	**Canal St-Martin**
runs between the Caribbean's St. Lucia and St. Vincent	**St. Vincent Passage**
passes between mainland California and the Santa Cruz islands	**Santa Barbara Channel**
connects Lakes Huron and Superior, "the Soo"	**Sault Ste. Marie Canals**
lies between Denmark's Jutland and Norway	**Skaggerak**
is where Denmark collected dues from ships	**The Sound**
passes between the Red and Mediterranean seas in Egypt	**Suez Canal**
passes between Java and Sumatra	**Sunda Strait**
lies between China and Taiwan	**Taiwan (Formosa) Strait**
separates New Guinea from Australia	**Torres Strait**
divides Japan's Honshu and Hokkaido islands	**Tsugaru Straits**
passes between Mexico's Yucatan and Cuba	**Yucatan Channel**

Squares, Circles, and Plazas

Among the world's squares, circles or plazas, which is or was . . . ?

In the Americas

at the foot of Manhattan	**Bowling Green**
in Port-au-Prince, honoring Haiti's revolutionaries	**Champs de Mars (Place des Héros de l'Indépendence)**
at the heart of Puerto Rico's San Juan	**Plaza Colón**
in NYC, as in "remember me to"	**Herald Square**
in Phoenix, with restored Victorian homes	**Heritage Square**
museum-surrounded space in Washington, D.C.	**The Mall**
music square in Guadalajara, Mexico	**Plazuela de Mariachis**
where Argentinians protest, in Buenos Aires	**Plaza de Mayo (de Armas)**
in downtown Atlanta	**Margaret Mitchell Square**
main square in São Paulo, Brazil	**Praça de Patriarca**
where New Yorkers celebrate New Year's Eve	**Times Square**
main square in Mexico City	**Zocalo**

In the British Isles

in London, linked with the Russells	**Bedford Square**
in London, where the nightingale sang	**Berkeley Square**
site of a popular London junk/antique market	**Bermondsey Square**
in London, linked with Virginia Woolf et al	**Bloomsbury Square**
circle where le Carre's spy center was set	**Cambridge Circus**
in London's quiet Belgravia district	**Eaton Square**
in front of London's University College	**Gordon Square**
in London, where Dr. Johnson wrote his dictionary	**Gough Square**
in London, fronted by the American Embassy	**Grosvenor Square**
London's cinema theater center	**Leicester Square**
London square near Baker Street	**Manchester Square**
mall complex near London's St. Paul's Cathedral	**Paternoster Square**

London circle around which many theaters sit	**Piccadilly Circus**
near London's British Museum	**Russell Square**
near Buckingham Palace	**St. James's Square**
London square for rich young Britons	**Sloane Square**
a Bohemian, somewhat seedy London square	**Soho**
where Londoners celebrate New Year's Eve	**Trafalgar Square**
where London's old Courtauld Galleries were	**Woburn Square**

In Continental Europe

main square in East Berlin	**Alexanderplatz**
in Vienna, with columns to the plague, et al.	**Am Hof**
in Siena, where the Palio (a horserace) is run	**Campo**
main park in Lisbon	**Campo Grande**
where dancers celebrate Pamplona's bull-running	**Plaza del Castillo**
where thousands were guillotined in Paris, once Place de la Révolution	**Place de la Concorde**
in Salzburg, the Cathedral Square	**Dom Platz**
Leningrad's Palace Square	**Dvortsovaya Ploshchad**
Rome's trading and meeting center	**Forum**
at the heart of Nuremberg	**Hauptmarket**
Viennese square with old Roman ruins	**Hohe Markt**
Prague's Castle Square	**Hradcanské Námestí**
in Vienna near the National Library	**Josefplatz**
in the heart of Vienna's old ghetto district	**Judenplatz**
at the heart of Munich	**Karlsplatz or Stachus**
Prague's Square of the Knights of the Cross	**Krizovnické Námestí**
square at the heart of Kiev	**Lenkomsomol**
in Munich, has a noted clock tower	**Marienplatz**
Rome site known for its chariot races	**Circus Maximus**
Vienna square near the Hofburg	**Michaelerplatz**
Lvov square honoring a key Polish poet	**Adam Mickiewicz**
graced by Bernini's Triton Fountain, in Rome	**Piazza Barberini**

"Field of Miracles," home of Pisa's Leaning Tower	**Piazza del Duomo**, also **Campo dei Miracoli**
where coins are thrown in Rome's Trevi Fountain	**Piazza del Popolo**
where touring shoppers congregate in Rome	**Piazza di Spagna**
in Rome, sporting 3 Bernini fountains	**Piazza Navona**
in Rome's Old City, near the Pantheon	**Piazza Rotonda**
visitor's entryway to Venice	**Piazza San Marco**
in the Vatican, before Saint Peter's	**Piazza San Pietro**
near Capitoline Hill, usually traffic-clogged	**Piazza Venezia**
Berlin square near Hitler's bunker	**Potsdamer Platz**
in Moscow, holds Lenin's Tomb	**Red (Krasnaya) Square**
arcaded square in Barcelona	**Plaça Reial**
in front of Vienna's St. Stephen's Cathedral	**Stephansplatz**
in Paris, with a column honoring Napoleon	**Place Vendôme**
surrounded by arcades, in Paris	**Place de Vosges**
at the heart of Prague	**Wenceslas Square**
Warsaw's Castle Square	**Plac Zamkowy**

In Asia, Africa, Australia, and the Pacific

at the heart of Harare, Zimbabwe	**Cecil Square**
Bethlehem square at the Basilica of the Nativity	**Manger Square**
central Cairo's "Liberation Square"	**Midan al Tahrir**
facing Manila Cathedral, in the Philippines	**Plaza Roma**
"Heavenly Peace" square in Beijing, site of the 1989 student demonstrations and massacre	**Tiananmen Square**

Statues, Tombs, and Other Special Sites

(See also Churches and Other Sacred Places)

Among the world's statues, tombs, and other special sites, which is or are . . . ?

In the Americas

Indian mounds near Evansville, Indiana	**Angel Mounds**
national cemetery outside Washington, D.C.	**Arlington**
Indian burial mounds near Peoria, Illinois	**Dickson Mounds**
Indian mounds near Marquette, Iowa	**Effigy Mounds**
marker at 0°00′00″, near Quito, Ecuador	**Equatorial Monument**
Indian mound settlement in Georgia	**Etowah**
Washington site where Lincoln was killed	**Ford's Theatre**
in NYC where Washington bade his men farewell	**Fraunces Tavern**
Eero Saarinen's St. Louis arch	**Gateway Arch**
main set of locks on the Panama Canal	**Gatun Locks**
Washington dam across the Columbia	**Grand Coulee Dam**
across the Colorado, creating Lake Mead	**Hoover Dam**
Indian burial site on the Mississippi at Cahokia	**Hopewell Mounds**
New Mexico rock where people have left drawings and writings for centuries	**Inscription Rock** or **El Morro**
tower overlooking Mexico City	**Latin American Tower**
Philadelphia bell that stands for independence	**Liberty Bell**
where King made his "I have a dream" speech	**Lincoln Memorial**
mysterious lines in the Peruvian desert	**Nazca lines**
the Massachusetts site honoring Pilgrims' settlement	**Plymouth Rock**
most famous of Ohio's Indian Mounds	**Serpent Mounds**
statue greeting visitors to NY harbor	**Statue of Liberty**

crystal springs like 3 eyes, near Santo Domingo	**Los Tres Ojos**
name-covered V-shaped Washington, D.C., monument	**Vietnam Veterans Memorial**
New Orleans's French Quarter or "old quarter"	**Vieux Carré**
tall, simple spire dominating Washington, D.C.	**Washington Monument**
the idiosyncratic tower in Los Angeles	**Watts Tower**

In the British Isles

in London's Hyde Park, for Victoria's consort	**Albert Memorial**
Roman-built earthen wall in Scotland	**Antonine Wall**
stone that tourists kiss near Ireland's Cork City	**Blarney Stone**
main London memorial to the dead of WWI and WWII	**Cenotaph**
huge Dorset carving in the chalk hills	**Cerne Giant**
London's 15th-c. B.C. obelisk, a gift from Egypt	**Cleopatra's Needle**
wall the Romans built in northern England	**Hadrian's Wall**
London burial place of Marx and George Eliot	**Highgate Cemetery**
arch near London's old Tyburn Tree gallows	**Marble Arch**
chalk spires in the sea off the Isle of Wight	**The Needles**
in London's Trafalgar Square, to honor the 1805 victory over Napoleon	**Nelson's Column**
passage graves in Ireland's Boyne Valley	**Newgrange**
huge prehistoric mound near Avebury, England	**Silbury Hill**
prehistoric stone circle in Scotland	**Standing Stones of Callanish**
symbol of Scottish independence, embedded in Westminster Abbey's Coronation Chair	**Stone of Scone (Destiny)**
arch facing London's Hyde Park Corner	**Wellington Arch**
figure carved in the Oxfordshire chalk hills	**White Horse of Uffington**
giant figure cut into the Sussex chalk Downs	**Wilmington Long Man**

In Continental Europe

ancient Greek "upper town" of Athens	**Acropolis**
Viennese clock with statues parading time	**Anker Clock**
16th-c. Istanbul arch only a sultan could pass through on horseback	**Bab-I-Salem (Gate of Salutation)**
climbable statue in Munich's Theresienwiese	**Bavaria**
barrier dividing Berlin 1961-1989	**Berlin Wall**
Mouth of Truth, as in *Holiday in Rome*	**Bocca della Verità**
old city gate and triumphal arch, in East Berlin	**Brandenburger Tor**
site of thousands of prehistoric stone monuments in SW France	**Carnac**
Rome's underground tombs, where early Christians worshipped	**Catacombs**
main American crossing point between East and West Berlin, 1961-1989	**Checkpoint Charlie**
the site of ancient Rome's chariot races	**Circus Maximus**
place in Rome where gladiators once fought	**Colosseum**
triumphal arch near Rome's Colosseum	**Arch of Constantine**
Westphalian bas-relief of the Descent from the Cross	**Extern Stones**
14th-c. tower with a grand view of Istanbul	**Galata Tower**
old Jewish quarter in Venice	**Ghetto**
replica of the Liberty Bell in Berlin, a US gift	**Freiheitsglocke**
old Roman theater in Istanbul	**Hippodrome (At Meydani)**
Vienna's night-lit fountain near the Belvedere	**Hochstrahlbrunnen**
war veterans' home where Napoleon lies	**Hôtel des Invalides**
Hapsburgs' Imperial Vault in Vienna	**Kaisergruft**
2300-year-old tomb in Thrace	**Kazanluk**
old Roman defensive line along the Rhine	**Limes**
famed gate at Mycenae	**Lion Gate**
Virgin's Column in Vienna's Am Hof	**Mariensäule**

cemetery at the Vatican in Rome	**Necropolis**
Paris cemetery where Proust, Chopin, Gertrude Stein, and Jim Morrison lie	**Cimetière Père Lachaise**
Plague Column in Vienna's Graben	**Pestsäule**
old Roman aqueduct near Nîmes, France	**Pont du Gard**
massive Roman gateway to Trier, Germany	**Porta Nigra**
Odessa steps where Eisenstein filmed a massacre	**Potemkin Steps**
place in Rome where Keats and Shelley lie	**Protestant Cemetery**
22-ton bell in Vienna's Stephansdom	**Die Pummerin (Boomer)**
Berlin monument to its Franco-Prussian victory, once facing the Reichstag	**Siegessäule**
Vienna place where Lippizaner horses are taught their "dances"	**Spanish (Winter) Riding School**
popular gathering-place near where Keats died in Rome	**Spanish Steps**
Rome's arch just west of the Forum	**Arch of Tiberius**
Rome's arch just east of the Forum	**Arch of Titus**
in Rome's Piazza Venezia, with a spiral frieze	**Trajan's Column**
where coins are thrown, in Rome	**Fontana di Trevi**
Paris arch honoring Napoleon Bonaparte	**Arc de Triomphe de l'Etoile (Arch of Triumph)**
Fountain of the Virgin's Wedding in Vienna	**Vermählungsbrunnen**
ancient protected salt mine near Cracow	**Wieliczka mine**
NE Poland bunker where Hitler escaped assassination	**Wolf's Den**

In Asia, Africa, Australia, and the Pacific

great dam across the Egyptian Nile	**Aswan High Dam**
ancient cemetery outside Cairo, Egypt	**Beni Hassan**
4-arched "Arc de Triomphe" in Hyderabad, India	**Char Minar**
world's largest stone structure, in Giza, Egypt	**Great Pyramid**
China's old 2000-mile-long defensive line	**Great Wall**

remains of the sub-Sahara's oldest structures	**Great Zimbabwe Ruins**
Flora Fountain in the heart of Bombay, India	**Hutåtma Chowk**
18th-c. astronomical observatory in Delhi, India	**Jantar Mantar**
half-lion/half-fish guarding Singapore	**Merlion**
majestic tombs near Peking's Great Walls	**Ming Tombs**
Turkey's naturally formed "Cotton Fortress," once a spa called Hierapolis	**Pamukkale**
huge carved lion with a man's head at Giza	**Sphinx**
massive early Egyptian tomb at Saqqara	**Step Pyramid**
famed white marble mausoleum at Agra, India	**Taj Mahal**
Gate of Heavenly Peace in Peking's Forbidden City	**Tiananmen Gate**
royal tombs of Korea's Silla kings, near Kyongju	**Tumuli Park**

Towers and Skyscrapers

Among the world's towers and skyscrapers, which is . . . ?

observation tower in Munich's Peterskirche	**Alte Peter (Old Peter)**
14th–15th-c. tower over Vienna	**Alte Steffi (Old Steve)**
sailors' lookout tower in Lisbon	**Belém**
clock tower at Britain's Parliament Houses	**Big Ben**
elevator to upper Lisbon, built by Eiffel	**Campo**
7th-c. astronomical tower in Kyongju, Korea	**Chomsong-dae**
Vienna's tower with a rotating restaurant	**Donauturm**
Paris's striking iron tower built in 1889	**Eiffel Tower (Tour Eiffel)**
NYC's once-tallest building climbed by King Kong	**Empire State Building**
East Berlin's revolving observation tower	**Fernsehturm**
Bonn's 11th-c. watchtower	**Godesburg**
tower overlooking ruins in Rabat	**Hassan Tower**

tower at Marrakesh's mosque	**Koutoubia**
Pisa's off-perpendicular building	**Leaning Tower**
tower at Canada's Houses of Parliament	**Peace Tower**
Prague's version of the Eiffel Tower	**Petrin Tower**
site of Alexandria's lighthouse, a wonder of the world	**Pharos**
rose granite column in Alexandria	**Pompey's Pillar**
viewing tower in the west of London	**Post Office Tower (British Telecom Tower)**
tower from an old Prague fort	**Powder Tower**
Detroit's 7-tower complex	**Renaissance Center**
Chicago tower, built as the world's tallest	**Sears Tower**
tower from Seattle's 1962 World's Fair	**Space Needle**
tower whose flag flies when Britain's Parliament is sitting	**Victoria Tower**
twin towers with spectacular views, in NYC	**World Trade Center**

Cities and Regions

Africa

Egypt

Among the cities and regions of Egypt (Masr), what is or was . . . ?

archaeological site flooded by the Aswan Dam	**Abu-Simbel**
pilgrimage site linked with Osiris	**Abydos (Abdou)**
site of a key 1942 British victory	**El Alamein**
old port and intellectual center, site of Pharos lighthouse	**Alexandria**
region of the Nile flooded for a dam	**Aswan**
capital at the head of the Nile's delta	**Cairo**
largest oasis, west of Cairo	**Fayum**
site of 3 huge pyramids and the Sphinx	**Giza (Ghiza)**
early center of sun worship, now Cairo	**Heliopolis (On)**
on the Suez Canal, near Cairo	**Ismailia**
site near the Temple of Karnak	**Luxor**
1st capital, from about 3000 B.C.	**Memphis**
where the Suez Canal meets the Mediterranean	**Port Said**
site of Egypt's Step Pyramid, a city of the dead	**Sakkara (Saqqara)**
Egypt's canal region, in biblical times Goshen	**Suez**
capital from 2160 B.C., home of Amon	**Thebes**
region around Tutankhamen's tomb	**Valley of Kings**

North Africa

Among the cities and regions of North Africa (outside of Egypt), what is or was ... ?

Cities

capital of Ethiopia (Abyssinia)	**Addis Ababa**
Moroccan site of a 1960 earthquake that killed 20,000 people, also of a WWI incident	**Agadir**
capital of Algeria, home of the Kasbah	**Algiers (El Djazaïr)**
port of Libya	**Benghazi**
utterly destroyed by Rome in 146 B.C., now Tunis	**Carthage**
Moroccan port city of Bogart fame	**Casablanca**
historic Moslem centre of old Mali	**Djenne**
Morocco's 2nd largest city	**Fez**
Tunisia's gateway to the Sahara	**Gabes**
Tunisia's beachside town near Cape Bon	**Hammamet**
Africa's holiest Moslem city, in Tunisia	**Kairouan (Quairawan)**
Sudan's capital, where Gordon was killed	**Khartoum**
key city in central Morocco	**Marrakesh**
old coastal port in northern Eritrea, Ethiopia	**Massawa**
fortified old city within Tunis	**Medina**
Algier's port where the Allies attacked the French in 1940	**Mers el-Kebir** and **Oran**
birthplace of Tunisia's President Bourguiba	**Monastir**
capital of Chad	**N'Djamena**
capital of Mauritania	**Nouakchott**
Sudan's largest city	**Omdurman**
capital of Morocco	**Rabat**
where British took many Italian prisoners in 1940	**Sidi Barrani**
Libyan fortress besieged in 1941, taken in 1942	**Tobruk**
capital and port of Libya	**Tripoli**
Tunisia's capital and main port, once Carthage	**Tunis**

Regions

ancient kingdom in what is now Ethiopia	**Axum**
North African coast during the pirate era	**Barbary Coast**

land south of, and in sometime battle with, Libya	**Chad**
beaches of northern Tunisia	**Coral Coast**
small republic facing Arabia	**Djibouti**
Ethiopian coast province seeking independence	**Eritrea**
land southeast of Egypt on the Red Sea	**Ethiopia (Abyssinia)**
desert area south of coastal Libya	**Fezzan**
triangle pointing out from Ethiopia and Somalia	**Horn of Africa**
coastal strip of North Africa	**Maghreb**
nation of the upper Senegal and SW Sahara	**Mauritania**
kingdom of the NW coast of Africa	**Morocco**
ancient name of the mid-Nile region	**Nubia**
hilly strip along the Moroccan coast	**Rif**
peninsula between the gulfs of Suez and Aqaba	**Sinai**
land south of Egypt, once called Nubia	**Sudan**
city at the Moroccan entrance to Gibraltar Strait	**Tangier**
an Ethiopian province seeking independence	**Tigre**
region west of Mauritania	**Western Sahara**

South Africa

Among the cities and regions of South Africa, what is or are . . . ?

main judicial center	**Bloemfontein**
"Homelands" into which blacks have been herded	**Bophuthatswana, Ciskel, Transkel,** and **Venda**
old name for the state at Africa's southern tip	**Cape Colony**
main port and largest city	**Cape Town**
main east coast port, once Port Natal	**Durban**
key center in the north	**Johannesburg**
east coast region centered on Durban	**Natal**
South Africa's main southern port	**Port Elizabeth**
main administrative capital	**Pretoria**
site of a bloody 1960 protest	**Sharpeville**

site of a 1976 uprising of South Africa's blacks	**Soweto**
the region north of the Vaal River	**Transvaal**

Sub-Saharan Africa

Among the cities and regions of Sub-Saharan Africa (outside of South Africa), what is or was . . . ?

Cities

largest city of the Ivory Coast	**Abidjan**
Ghana's capital, a former trading post	**Accra (Akkra)**
capital of Malagasy Republic (Madagascar)	**Antananarivo**
Mali's capital	**Bamako**
capital of the Central African Republic	**Bangui**
capital of The Gambia	**Banjul**
Guinea-Bissau's capital	**Bissau**
capital of the Congo	**Brazzaville**
Burundi's capital	**Bujumbura**
Zimbabwe's 2nd largest city, "Place of Killings	**Bulawayo**
capital of Guinea	**Conraky**
Senegal's capital, the "Paris of Africa"	**Dakar**
capital and main port of Tanzania	**Dar-es-Salaam**
Ugandan site of a 1976 Jewish rescue of hostages	**Entebbe**
Sierra Leone's capital	**Freetown**
Botswana's capital	**Gaborone**
capital of Zimbabwe, once called Salisbury	**Harare**
Uganda's capital	**Kampala**
Rwanda's capital	**Kigali**
Zaire's capital	**Kinshasa**
Nigeria's capital	**Lagos**
Gabon's capital	**Libreville**
Malawi's capital	**Lilongwe**
Togo's capital	**Lomé**
Angola's capital	**Luanda**
Zambia's capital	**Lusaka**
Equatorial Guinea's capital	**Malabo**
old port on Kenya's north coast	**Malindi**
Mozambique's capital	**Maputo**
Tanzanian starting point for Kilimanjaro climbers	**Marangu**
Lesotho's capital	**Maseru**
Swaziland's capital	**Mbabene**

Somalia's capital	**Mogadishu**
Kenya's 2nd largest city and main port	**Mombasa**
Liberia's capital	**Monrovia**
Kenya's capital, "Place of Cool Waters"	**Nairobi**
main city in Kenya's Rift Valley region	**Nakuru**
Niger's capital	**Niamey**
Burkina Faso's capital	**Ouagadougou (Wagadugu)**
Mauritius's capital	**Port Louis**
Benin's capital	**Port Novo**
Cape Verde's capital	**Praia**
capital of Old French West Africa	**St-Louis**
fabled SW Sahara travel and trade center in Mali	**Timbuktu**
main city in Namibia (SW Africa)	**Windhoek**
capital of the Ivory Coast	**Yamoussoukro**
Cameroon's capital	**Youande**

Regions

large country south of the Congo and Zaire	**Angola**
nation once called Dahomey	**Benin**
famine-stricken, would-be independent region in eastern Nigeria	**Biafra**
region once called Bechuananaland	**Botswana**
region once called Upper Volta	**Burkina Faso**
state tucked between Zaire and Tanzania	**Burundi**
land east of Nigeria, where a carbon monoxide cloud killed 1746 in 1986	**Cameroon**
landlocked state north of Zaire, formerly part of French Equatorial Africa	**Central African Republic**
country between Gabon and Zaire	**Congo**
"African Riviera" near Abidjan, Ivory Coast	**Ebrie Lagoon**
tiny country on the Bight of Biafra, surrounded by Cameroon and Gabon	**Equatorial Guinea**
country where Albert Schweitzer worked, once part of French Equatorial Africa	**Gabon**
country surrounded by and linked with Senegal	**The Gambia**

West African state once called the Gold Coast	**Ghana (Wagadu)**
West African country between Senegal and Guinea	**Guinea-Bissau**
West African country between Liberia and Ghana	**Ivory Coast (Côte d'Ivoire)**
east African nation, home of the Mau Mau	**Kenya**
landlocked pocket country once called Basutoland	**Lesotho**
West African nation founded by US Blacks	**Liberia**
nation on the island of Madagascar	**Malagasy Republic**
Rift Valley republic once called Nyasaland	**Malawi**
landlocked republic on the upper Niger River	**Mali**
nation on Africa's SE coast	**Mozambique**
SW region freed from South Africa	**Namibia**
huge, landlocked country north of Nigeria	**Niger**
nation on the Gulf of Guinea, once a British colony	**Nigeria**
region claimed by both Somalia and Ethiopia	**Ogaden**
state near Uganda, where Fossey studied gorillas	**Rwanda**
formerly French West Africa	**Senegal**
1982 union of 2 West African countries for defense	**Senegambia (Senegal and Gambia)**
in West Africa, sits between Guinea and Liberia	**Sierre Leone**
occupies the east part of the Horn of Africa	**Somalia**
landlocked nation in SE Africa	**Swaziland**
nation formed by Tanganyika and Zanzibar	**Tanzania**
nation between Ghana and Benin	**Togo**
in high east-central Africa, home of Idi Amin	**Uganda**
nation along Congo, home of many pygmies	**Zaire**
nation that was once northern Rhodesia	**Zambia**
nation that was once southern Rhodesia	**Zimbabwe**

The Americas

Canada

Among the cities and regions of Canada, what is or are . . . ?

Cities

famed for highland games, in Nova Scotia	**Antigonish**
resort towns near Alberta's Lake Louise	**Banff and Jasper**
post-Revolution Iroquois home, in Ontario	**Brantford**
site of 1988's winter Olympics, in Alberta	**Calgary**
Prince Edward I. birthplace of federal Canada	**Charlottetown**
old Canadian fur trading port on Hudson Bay	**Churchill**
capital of Alberta, near the world's largest mall	**Edmonton**
capital of New Brunswick	**Fredericton**
Newfoundland airport where many soldiers were killed in a 1985 accident	**Gander**
Nova Scotia's capital, where a 1917 ship explosion killed 1600 people	**Halifax**
Nova Scotia home of Acadians exiled in 1713	**Grand Pré**
old English capital on Lake Ontario, Ft. Frontenac	**Kingston**
11th-c. Viking settlement in Newfoundland	**L'Anse Aux Meadows**
commercial capital on the St. Lawrence	**Montréal**
national capital, once called Bytown	**Ottawa**
popular Nova Scotia fishing village	**Peggy's Cove**
Québec site where Wolfe beat Montcalm	**Plains of Abraham**
1605 French settlement in Nova Scotia	**Port Royal** (now **Annapolis Royal**)
old French capital on the St. Lawrence	**Québec City**
capital of Saskatchewan	**Regina**
New Brunswick town founded by Loyalists	**St. John**
capital of Newfoundland	**St. John's**

Ontario city, old Fort William and Port Arthur	**Thunder Bay**
the thriving city on Lake Ontario's north side	**Toronto**
British Columbia's main city	**Vancouver**
capital of British Columbia, on Vancouver Island	**Victoria**
capital of Yukon Territory	**Whitehorse**
capital of Manitoba, once Fort Garry	**Winnipeg**
Nova Scotia port with ferries to Maine	**Yarmouth**
capital of the Northwest Territories	**Yellowknife**

Regions

Nova Scotia to the early French	**Acadia**
prairie province centered on Calgary	**Alberta**
province on the Pacific	**British Columbia**
peninsula at the mouth of the St. Lawrence	**Gaspé**
mainland region of Newfoundland province	**Labrador**
easternmost prairie province	**Manitoba**
province bordering Maine	**New Brunswick**
easternmost province	**Newfoundland**
huge region west of Hudson Bay	**Northwest Territories**
NE province, "New Scotland," once Acadia	**Nova Scotia**
huge province north of the Great Lakes	**Ontario**
huge province east of Ontario	**Québec**
the Wheat Province, between Alberta and Manitoba	**Saskatchewan**
region bordering Alaska	**Yukon Territory**

The Caribbean and Atlantic Islands

(See also Islands in *Special Places*)

Among the cities on Caribbean and Atlantic islands, what is or are . . . ?

capital of St. Christopher (St. Kitts) and Nevis	**Basseterre**
capital of Barbados	**Bridgetown**
Haiti's north coast town, once called Cap Francais	**Cap-Haïtien (Le Cap)**

capital of St. Lucia	**Castries**
capital of the US Virgin Is., on St. Thomas	**Charlotte Amalie**
resort city and old slave-trade center on St. Croix	**Christiansted**
capital of Martinique	**Fort-de-France**
capital of the Cayman Is.	**Georgetown**
huge American naval base in Cuba	**Guantánamo**
capital of Bermuda	**Hamilton**
capital of Cuba	**Havana**
capital of St. Helena	**Jamestown**
capital of Jamaica	**Kingston**
capital of St. Vincent and the Grenadines	**Kingstown**
main city on Bonaire	**Kralendijk**
Cuban take-off point of the 1980 refugee boat lift	**Mariel**
popular resort communities on Jamaica	**Montego Bay** and **Ocho Rios**
capital of the Bahamas	**Nassau**
main town of Aruba	**Oranjestad**
capital of Montserrat	**Plymouth**
capital of Haiti	**Port-au-Prince**
Falklands port where the Argentines surrendered	**Port Stanley**
capital of Trinidad	**Port of Spain**
capital of Dominica	**Roseau**
capital of Antigua and Barbuda, much restored	**St. John's**
capital of Grenada	**St. George's**
Martinique town buried by lava in 1902	**St. Pierre**
capital of Puerto Rico, with its old fortress	**San Juan**
old Spanish port and Cuba's 2nd city	**Santiago de Cuba**
capital of the Dominican Republic	**Santo Domingo**
capital of Trinidad and Tobago	**Port-of-Spain**
capital of the Netherlands Antilles, on Curaçao	**Willemstad**

Central America

Among the cities and regions of Central America, what is . . . ?

old capital of Guatemala	**Antigua**
capital of Belize	**Belmopan**
region once called British Honduras, and its capital	**Belize**

US-held strip along the Panama Canal	**Canal Zone**
Mayan village in Guatemala, famed for its market	**Chichicastenango**
city at the Caribbean entrance to the Panama canal	**Colón**
country between Panama and Nicaragua	**Costa Rica**
country where the Sandinistas and Contras fought	**El Salvador**
capital of Guatemala	**Guatemala City**
Nicaragua's oldest city	**Granada**
country bordering Guatemala, El Salvador, and Nicaragua	**Honduras**
Nicaragua town founded in 1524, moved after a 1610 volcanic eruption	**León Vieja (Old León)**
capital of Nicaragua	**Managua**
country between Honduras and Coast Rica	**Nicaragua**
country and city around the Canal Zone	**Panama**
Indian market town near San Salvador	**Panchimalco**
west highlands center in Guatemala	**Quezaltenango (Xela)**
capital of Costa Rica	**San José**
main industrial city of Honduras	**San Pedro Sula**
capital of El Salvador	**San Salvador**
capital of Honduras, in the highlands	**Tegucigalpa**
Honduras port founded in 1524	**Trujillo**

Mexico

Among the cities and regions of Mexico, what is . . . ?

Pacific port famed for diving and Manila galleons	**Acapulco**
peninsula named "Lower California"	**Baja California**
Yucatan resort hit hard by 1988's Hurricane Gilbert	**Cancun**
coastal center of Peru's pre-Inca Chimu culture	**Chan Chan**
region just south of Texas and New Mexico	**Chihuahua**
city across the river from El Paso, Texas	**Ciudad Juarez**
massive Mayan town on the Yucatan	**Dzibilchaltún**

home of mariachi music	**Guadalajara**
city across from El Paso, Texas	**Juárez (Ciudad or City)**
town across the Rio Grande from Brownsville	**Matamoros**
entryway to the Yucatan, with Mayan ruins	**Mérida**
capital of Baja California	**Mexicali**
national capital, once called Tenochtitlán	**Mexico City**
NE town hard-hit by 1988 Hurricane Gilbert	**Monterrey**
main town south of the Arizona border	**Nogales**
just south of the California border, in Baja	**Tijuana**
Caribbean port named "True Cross"	**Vera Cruz**
peninsula on the southern Gulf of Mexico	**Yucutan**

South America

Among the cities and regions of South America, what is or are . . . ?

Cities

Paraguay's capital	**Asunción**
Colombia's capital	**Bogotá**
Brazil's official capital	**Brasília**
Argentina's capital	**Buenos Aires**
old port of Lima, Peru	**Callao**
capital of Venezuela	**Caracas**
old Spanish port on the Colombian coast	**Cartagena**
capital of French Guiana	**Cayenne**
Bolivia's alpaca handcrafts center	**Cochabamba**
Chile's university town and mining center	**Concepcion**
popular beaches near Rio de Janeiro	**Copacabana, Ipanema, and Leblon**
old Inca capital in Peru's Andes	**Cuzco**
site of striking Jesuit ruins, in Paraguay	**Encarnación**
Mennonite community in Chaco, Paraguay	**Filadelfia**
capital of Guyana	**Georgetown**
Ecuador's main port	**Guayaquil**
Bolivia's main city	**La Paz**
Peru's capital	**Lima**

long-lost Inca stronghold in the Andean jungle	**Machu Picchu**
2nd largest city in Venezuela, on the Caribbean	**Maracaibo**
Colombian cities harboring the 2 main drug cartels	**Medellín** and **Cali**
capital and main port of Uruguay, where the *Graf Spee* was sunk in 1939	**Montevideo**
Suriname's capital	**Paramaribo**
silver-rich mining center in Bolivia	**Potosí**
southernmost city of South America and the world, on the Strait of Magellan	**Punta Arenas (Magallanes)**
popular beach resort south of Montevideo	**Punta del Este**
capital of Ecuador	**Quito**
Brazil's famed Atlantic port	**Rio de Janeiro**
Brazil's 1st capital	**Salvador (Bahia)**
Chile's capital	**Santiago**
Brazil's largest city	**São Paulo**
Bolivia's 2nd largest city	**Sucre**
striking Indian ruins in Bolivia	**Tihuanaco**
main port of Chile	**Valparaíso**
popular resort city in Chile	**Viña del Mar**

Regions

SE country claiming the Falklands	**Argentina**
landlocked Andes nation	**Bolivia**
huge nation centered on the Amazon	**Brazil**
region fought over by Bolivia and Paraguay in the early 1930s	**Chaco**
NW nation linked with drug cartels	**Colombia**
NW coast nation where a 1987 earthquake killed 4000 people	**Ecuador**
French territory on the NE coast	**French Guiana**
east of Venezuela, where Jim Jones lived and died	**Guyana**
large central state of Brazil	**Mato (Matto) Grosso**
landlocked country between Bolivia and Argentina	**Paraguay**
region of SE South America, in Argentina	**Patagonia**
nation at the heart of Inca country	**Peru**
once-Dutch republic neighboring French Guiana	**Suriname (-nam)**

region between Brazil and Argentina	**Uruguay**
oil-rich nation in NE South America	**Venezuela**

United States

Among the cities and regions of the United States, what is or are . . . ?

In the Northeast and Mid-Atlantic

capital of New York, on the old Mohawk Trail	**Albany**
Maryland's capital, home of the US Naval Academy	**Annapolis**
Maryland site of a bloody 1862 Civil War battle	**Antietam (Sharpsburg)**
NY State site of the 1957 Mafia meeting	**Apalachin**
New Jersey home of gambling and Miss America	**Atlantic City**
Maine's capital	**Augusta**
Maryland home of clippers and Johns Hopkins	**Baltimore**
Pennsylvania town linked with steel and Christmas	**Bethelehem**
"Cradle of Liberty," capital of Massachusetts	**Boston**
New Hampshire birthplace of the World Bank	**Bretton Woods**
NYC borough north of Manhattan	**Bronx**
NYC borough east of Manhattan	**Brooklyn**
Pennsylvania tourist and artist haven	**Bucks County**
home of Harvard U. and MIT, in Massachusetts	**Cambridge**
Maryland town where the Berrigans et al. burned draft cards in 1968	**Catonsville**
Massachusetts site where Mary Jo Kopechne died, with Edward Kennedy driving the car	**Chappaquiddick**
old NY State resort with world-famous programs	**Chatauqua**
New Hampshire's capital	**Concord**
home of the Baseball Hall of Fame, in NY	**Cooperstown**
famed glass center in western NY State	**Corning**

peninsula shared by Delaware, Maryland, and Virginia	**Delmarva**
region that includes the nation's capital	**District of Columbia**
Delaware's capital	**Dover**
Pennsylvania site of Lincoln's famed address	**Gettysburg**
home of the US Merchant Marine Academy in NY	**Great Neck**
home of Colgate U., in NY	**Hamilton**
resort towns on NY's eastern Long Island	**Hamptons**
home of Dartmouth U., in New Hampshire	**Hanover**
site of John Brown's 1859 raid, in West Virginia	**Harper's Ferry**
capital of Pennsylvania, where the Three Mile Island nuclear plant malfunctioned in 1979	**Harrisburg**
capital of Connecticut	**Hartford**
chocolate capital, in Pennsylvania	**Hershey**
reconstructed iron-town in Pennsylvania	**Hopewell Village**
Massachusetts town with the Kennedy Compound	**Hyannis**
site of FDR's home, in NY	**Hyde Park**
home of Cornell U., in NY	**Ithaca**
the Maine site of the Bushes' vacation home	**Kennebunkport**
center of Pennsylvania's Amish country	**Lancaster**
Massachusetts home of Tanglewood	**Lenox**
New England towns where the "shot heard round the world" was fired in 1775	**Lexington** and **Concord**
central borough of New York City	**Manhattan**
Vermont's capital	**Montpelier**
Continental Army winter base 1779–80, in New Jersey	**Morristown**
Connecticut town famed for its maritime museum	**Mystic**
famed for its whaling museum, in Massachusetts	**New Bedford**
home of Yale U., in Connecticut	**New Haven**
US Coast Guard Academy home in Connecticut	**New London**
Rhode Island summer resort and yachting center	**Newport**

art and financial center, born Nieuw Amsterdam	**New York City**
Maryland resort town near Assateague Island	**Ocean City**
home of the Liberty Bell and independence	**Philadelphia**
Pennsylvania steel town called "Smoke City"	**Pittsburgh**
Massachusetts town where the Pilgrims settled	**Plymouth**
main city in southern Maine	**Portland**
Rhode Island's capital	**Providence**
Cape Cod town where the Pilgrims first landed	**Provincetown**
home of Eastman Kodak, in NY	**Rochester**
Massachusetts town famous for witches and whales	**Salem**
New Hampshire site of an "American Stonehenge"	**Salem**
NY resort and site of a key British defeat in 1777	**Saratoga (Springs)**
Massachusetts home of the Basketball Hall of Fame	**Springfield**
recreated New England village in Massachusetts	**Sturbridge**
NY town linked with Irving and Sleepy Hollow	**Tarrytown**
New Jersey's capital	**Trenton**
Pennsylvania winter base for the Continental Army in 1777–78	**Valley Forge**
home of the US Military Academy, in NY	**West Point**
West Virginia city with a powerful radio station	**Wheeling**
Massachusetts port and marine lab center	**Woods Hole**
site of the famed 1969 music festival, in NY	**Woodstock**

In the South

Robert E. Lee's Virginia home town	**Alexandria**
Virginia town where the Civil War ended	**Appomattox**
Thomas Wolfe's North Carolina home town	**Asheville**
home of the U. of Georgia	**Athens**
Georgia's capital, burned by Sherman	**Atlanta**
Louisiana's capital	**Baton Rouge**

Mississippi town to which Jefferson Davis retired	**Biloxi**
"Pittsburgh of the South" in Alabama	**Birmingham**
home of Western Kentucky U.	**Bowling Green**
Virginia site of major 1861 and 1862 battles	**Bull Run (Manassas)**
home of the U. of North Carolina	**Chapel Hill**
South Carolina port where the Civil War began	**Charleston**
West Virginia's capital	**Charleston**
Tennessee town famous in the "choo-choo" song	**Chattanooga**
Georgia site of a key 1863 battle	**Chickamauga**
South Carolina's capital	**Columbia**
Florida town famed for its auto speedway	**Daytona Beach**
North Carolina home of Duke U.	**Durham**
home of the U. of Arkansas	**Fayetteville**
no-blacks-wanted county near Atlanta, Georgia	**Forsythe**
Florida town popular with college students	**Fort Lauderdale**
Kentucky's capital	**Frankfort**
Virginia sites of major Civil War battles 1862–64	**Fredericksburg and Spotsylvania**
home of the U. of Florida	**Gainesville**
resort town in Tennessee's Great Smokies	**Gatlinburg**
South Carolina home of Bob Jones U.	**Greenville**
Virginia Chesapeake Bay port including Newport News, Norfolk, and Portsmouth	**Hampton Roads**
Kentucky county infamous for strike violence	**Harlan County**
1774 pioneer town in Kentucky	**Harrodsburg**
Florida town famed for thoroughbred racing	**Hialeah**
where Andrew Jackson defeated the Creeks in 1814	**Horseshoe Bend**
warm-water resort in Arkansas	**Hot Springs**
NASA space center in Alabama	**Huntsville**
capital of Mississippi, Eudora Welty's home	**Jackson**
Virginia town founded by English settlers in 1607	**Jamestown**
southernmost US city, in Florida	**Key West**
North Carolina sites linked with the Wright brothers	**Kitty Hawk** and **Kill Devil Hills**
1st capital of Tennessee	**Knoxville**

center of Kentucky's Blue Grass horse country	**Lexington**
site of Custer's "last stand," in Montana	**Little Big Horn**
capital of Arkansas	**Little Rock**
home of the Kentucky Derby's Churchill Downs	**Louisville**
key Confederate supply town, in Georgia	**Macon**
center of Virginia's "horse country"	**McLean**
Presley's Tennessee home, where King was shot	**Memphis**
Florida's main port, created by Henry Flagler	**Miami**
Alabama's port city	**Mobile**
capital of Alabama, site of a 1955 bus boycott	**Montgomery**
capital of Tennessee and country music	**Nashville**
trading town up-river from New Orleans	**Natchez**
Louisiana's oldest permanent settlement	**Natchitoches**
reconstructed Cherokee capital in Georgia	**New Echota**
Louisiana port city and jazz capital	**New Orleans**
Virginia home of a mariner's museum	**Newport News**
early uranium production site, in Tennessee	**Oak Ridge**
home of Walt Disney World, in Florida	**Orlando**
home of the U. of Mississippi	**Oxford**
rich resort area north of Miami Beach	**Palm Beach**
Mississippi resort savaged by a 1968 hurricane	**Pass Christian**
home of the US Naval Air Station, in Florida	**Pensacola**
where 3 civil rights workers were killed in 1964, in Mississippi	**Philadelphia (Neshoba County)**
North Carolina's capital	**Raleigh**
capital of Virginia and Civil War battle site	**Richmond**
site of a lost English settlement in Virginia	**Roanoke**
oldest town in the US, in Florida	**St. Augustine**
main towns on Florida's Gulf Coast	**St. Petersburg** and **Tampa**

Florida city linked with circuses	**Sarasota**
old Georgia port and fort	**Savannah**
site of some key civil rights marches, in Alabama	**Selma**
Tennessee site of a key 1862 Civil War battle	**Shiloh**
old "red light district" in New Orleans	**Storyville**
Florida's capital	**Tallahassee**
Florida town famed for its sponges	**Tarpon Springs**
Elvis Presley's Mississippi birthplace	**Tupelo**
home of the main U. of Alabama campus	**Tuscaloosa**
home of Booker T. Washington's Institute	**Tuskegee**
key Mississippi site taken by the Union in 1862	**Vicksburg**
Georgia place where Franklin Roosevelt died	**Warm Springs**
old, now-restored Virginia capital	**Williamsburg**
North Carolina tobacco center	**Winston-Salem**
Florida home of the Cypress Gardens	**Winter Haven**
the Virginia town where the British surrendered	**Yorktown**

In the Midwest and Far West

Kansas cow town, Eisenhower's home	**Abilene**
Ohio's "Rubber Capital," home of Goodyear	**Akron**
Iowa cooperative community, now manufacturer	**Amana**
Oklahoma's reconstructed Indian villages	**Anadarko**
Montana's copper city and would-be capital	**Anaconda**
home of the U. of Michigan	**Ann Arbor**
main ski towns in Colorado	**Aspen, Steamboat Springs, Telluride,** and **Vail**
Wisconsin home of the Ringling Brothers Circus	**Baraboo**
Michigan home of Kellogg and Post cereals	**Battle Creek**
Montana city near Custer's Last Stand	**Billings**
North Dakota's capital	**Bismarck**
home of Indiana U.	**Bloomington**
Idaho's capital	**Boise**

Colorado town watered by a glacier	**Boulder**
western Montana copper and silver town	**Butte**
Illinois site of the Hopewell Mounds	**Cahokia**
Illinois city where the Ohio and Mississippi join	**Cairo**
home of Southern Illinois U.	**Carbondale**
Wyoming town at an Oregon Trail ferry site	**Casper**
home of the U. of Illinois	**Champaign/Urbana**
Wyoming's capital	**Cheyenne**
Illinois's "Windy City," a Midwest hub	**Chicago**
1st capital of the NW Territory and of Ohio	**Chillicothe**
"Queen City of the West" on the Ohio River	**Cincinnati**
Ohio's largest city	**Cleveland**
Wyoming town founded by Buffalo Bill	**Cody**
Colorado resort below Pike's Peak	**Colorado Springs**
home of the U. of Missouri	**Columbia**
Ohio's capital	**Columbus**
Iowa pioneer and early trader meeting spot	**Council Bluffs**
Colorado mining town with violent strikes	**Cripple Creek**
Ohio city at the fork of the Great Miami River	**Dayton**
where Wild Bill Hickock was killed, in So. Dakota	**Deadwood**
Michigan home of the Ford Motor Co.	**Dearborn**
capital of Colorado, the "Mile High City"	**Denver**
Iowa's capital	**Des Moines**
Michigan's Motor City or Motown	**Detroit**
Kansas town guarded by Masterson and Earp	**Dodge City**
Minnesota port on Lake Superior	**Duluth**
Colorado home of the last narrow-gauge railroad	**Durango**
Ohio site where nuclear waste was dumped for years	**Fernald**
Arkansas gold rush supply center	**Fort Smith**
Indiana hot springs resort town	**French Lick**
Indiana town built by US Steel	**Gary**

Minnesota site where voyageurs crossed overland	**Grand Portage**
Michigan city of Gerald Ford and furniture	**Grand Rapids**
Mark Twain's Missouri home on the Mississippi	**Hannibal**
Montana's capital	**Helena**
Minnesota site of the largest open-air iron mine	**Hibbing**
Dutch-settled town in Michigan	**Holland**
Nebraska center of the 1860's free land offer	**Homestead**
Harry Truman's Missouri home town	**Independence**
capital of Indiana, famed for its "500"	**Indianapolis**
coldest city in the US, in Minnesota	**International Falls**
home of Iowa U.	**Iowa City**
Wyoming ski resort	**Jackson (Hole)**
Missouri's capital	**Jefferson City**
SW Michigan industrial city, "Boiling Water"	**Kalamazoo**
Kansas and Missouri cities with the same name	**Kansas City**
capital of Michigan and home of Michigan State U.	**Lansing**
home of the U. of Kansas	**Lawrence**
Oklahoma home of Fort Sill Military Reservation	**Lawton**
Colorado home of the Unsink-able Molly Brown	**Leadville**
Kansas town with a fort and federal penitentiary	**Leavenworth**
Nebraska's capital	**Lincoln**
Wisconsin's capital	**Madison**
home of Kansas State U.	**Manhattan**
Michigan town named for its missionary-founder	**Marquette**
Michigan home of Dow Chemical Co.	**Midland**
Wisconsin town made famous by beer	**Milwaukee**
Minnesota's main city, paired with St. Paul	**Minneapolis**
home of the U. of Montana	**Missoula**
Illinois town founded by Mormons	**Nauvoo**
Indiana town where Rappists and Robert Owen tried for Utopia	**New Harmony**
home of the U. of Oklahoma	**Norman**

Minnesota site of Jesse James's last raid	**Northfield**
Oklahoma's capital	**Oklahoma City**
Nebraska's largest city	**Omaha**
Wisconsin town on Lake Winnebago	**Oshkosh**
central Illinois city synonymous with mid-America	**Peoria**
South Dakota's capital	**Pierre**
home of Idaho State U.	**Pocatello**
Michigan town named for an Ottawa chief	**Pontiac**
Wisconsin town founded in 1673 on an Indian site	**Prairie du Chien**
home of Brigham Young U.	**Provo**
Colorado crossroads town	**Pueblo**
South Dakota home of Ellsworth Air Force Base	**Rapid City**
restoration of an Ohio canal town	**Roscoe Village**
Missouri starting point for the Pony Express	**St. Joseph**
Missouri town where Missouri and Mississippi join	**St. Louis**
Minnesota's capital	**St. Paul**
Ohio site of an 1850 women's suffrage convention	**Salem**
capital of Utah and the Mormons	**Salt Lake City**
Ohio resort town on Lake Erie	**Sandusky**
Sinclair Lewis's Minnesota home town	**Sauk Centre**
Missouri town where Joplin wrote *Maple Leaf Rag*	**Sedalia**
Wisconsin town for mentioning my name in	**Sheboygan**
western Iowa grain center	**Sioux City**
Illinois site of a controversial proposed 1978 neo-Nazi march	**Skokie**
home of Notre Dame U., in Indiana	**South Bend**
where Lincoln lived, Illinois's capital	**Springfield**
popular Idaho resort area	**Sun Valley**
Oklahoma Cherokee capital after the Trail of Tears	**Tahlequah**
Indiana home of Paul Dresser and Theodore Dreiser	**Terre Haute**
Ohio port on Lake Erie	**Toledo**
capital of Kansas	**Topeka**
Oklahoma's oil center and 2nd largest city	**Tulsa**

Montana gold rush city with restorations	**Virginia City**
Illinois home of the US Naval Training Center	**Waukegan**
Wisconsin mineral springs resort town	**Waukesha**
Wisconsin lumbering and then paper town	**Wausau**
largest city in Kansas	**Wichita**
South Dakota site of an 1890 massacre of he Sioux	**Wounded Knee**
Ohio steel town	**Youngstown**

In the Southwest

oldest inhabited village, in New Mexico	**Acoma Pueblo**
New Mexico site of the 1st atomic bomb blast	**Alamogordo**
home of the U. of New Mexico	**Albuquerque**
main town in Texas's Panhandle	**Amarillo**
capital of Texas	**Austin**
southernmost city in Texas	**Brownsville**
striking ruins of an Anasazi town in Arizona	**Canyon de Chelly**
New Mexico site of major Pueblo ruins	**Chaco Canyon**
Texas site of the US Naval Air Station	**Corpus Christi**
Texas city where John Kennedy was killed, "Big D"	**Dallas**
Rio Grande border town in far west Texas	**El Paso**
Arizona base for the Grand Canyon	**Flagstaff**
Texas home of the Kimbell and Amon Carter museums	**Fort Worth**
Texas port open to hurricanes	**Galveston**
oil town with the Astrodome	**Houston**
Texas home of Kennedy's successor	**Johnson City**
home of Texas A & M U. and the King Ranch	**Kingsville**
Arizona home of the old London Bridge	**Lake Havasu City**
once capital of the Republic of the Rio Grande	**Laredo**
Nevada's gambling capital	**Las Vegas**
near the Santa Fe Trail's Fort Union, New Mexico	**Las Vegas**

New Mexico's center for nuclear research	**Los Alamos**
Texas town where Jessica McClure fell into a well	**Midlands**
center of German settlement in Texas	**New Braunfels**
capital of Arizona and retirement town	**Phoenix**
Nevada's divorce capital	**Reno**
site of the Alamo, in Texas	**San Antonio**
where Texas won its independence, near Houston	**San Jacinto**
capital of modern and Spanish New Mexico	**Santa Fe**
Frank Lloyd Wright's Arizona winter headquarters	**Scottsdale**
old Indian town north of Santa Fe, New Mexico	**Taos Pueblo**
home of Arizona State U.	**Tempe**
Arizona site of Wyatt Earp's OK Corral shoot-out	**Tombstone**
Ralph Edwards's adopted home in New Mexico	**Truth or Consequences**
home of the U. of Arizona	**Tucson**
Nevada town built by the Comstock Lode	**Virginia City**
Texas home of Baylor U., on the Brazos River	**Waco**
historic Arizona site near a US army proving ground	**Yuma**

In the Pacific States

California home of Disneyland	**Anaheim**
Alaska's main southern city	**Anchorage**
U. of California town famous for '60's protests	**Berkeley**
California movie town with Wilshire Boulevard	**Beverly Hills**
California coast south of San Francisco	**Big Sur**
headquarters for the California missions	**Carmel**
home of the U. of Oregon	**Eugene**
central Alaska's main city	**Fairbanks**
Washington site of the nuclear plant like Chernobyl's	**Hanford**
Los Angeles region synonymous with movies	**Hollywood**
old whaling port, Hawaii's capital and resort town	**Honolulu**

Alaska's capital	**Juneau**
permanent California home of the *Queen Mary*	**Long Beach**
prime beach community near Los Angeles	**Malibu**
California's reconstructed New England fishing town	**Marina Del Rey**
Oregon's pear capital	**Medford**
capital of Spanish California	**Monterey**
gateway to California's wine country	**Napa**
main city in western Alaska	**Nome**
capital of Washington State	**Olympia**
southern California town with hot springs	**Palm Springs**
home of the Rose Bowl, in California	**Pasadena**
Hawaii port bombed in 1941 by the Japanese	**Pearl Harbor**
town where California's gold rush started	**Placerville**
northernmost US city, in Alaska	**Point Barrow**
Oregon's largest city	**Portland**
early gold rush center, now California capital	**Sacramento**
Oregon's capital	**Salem**
California home of John Steinbeck	**Salinas**
active California fault line	**San Andreas Fault**
home of California's 1st mission and Sea World	**San Diego**
California's Golden Gate, site of the 1906 and 1989 earthquakes	**San Francisco**
Washington's main city and 1962 World's Fair site	**Seattle**
capital of Russian America, as New Archangel	**Sitka**
gateway town for Alaska's 1890's gold rush	**Skagway**
end of the wagon part of the old Oregon Trail	**The Dalles**
southern Alaska city hit by a 1964 earthquake	**Valdez**
Washington site of an old Hudson's Bay Co. fort	**Vancouver**
old Washington fort site where 2 rivers meet	**Walla Walla**
Washington State's apple center	**Yakima**

Asia

China and nearby Central Aisa: Cities and Regions

Among cities and regions in China and nearby Central Asia, what is or was . . . ?

Cities

capital of the early Shang dynasty	**Anyang**
capital of China, "Northern Capital," once called Beiping or Beibing, "Northern Peace"	**Peking** or **Beijing**
China's main old southern port	**Canton (Guangzhou)**
capital of Szechuan province	**Chengdu**
WWI Chinese capital	**Chongqing (Chungking)**
old Chinese border town on the Silk Road	**Dunhuang (Tunhuang)**
major port south of Shanghai	**Hangzhou**
Manchurian refuge after Russia's 1917 Revolution	**Harbin**
old Mongol capital, known to the West as Xanadu	**Khanbaligh**
main city of the Yunnan region	**Kunming**
Tibet's capital	**Lhasa**
sometime capital and terminus of the Silk Road	**Luoyang**
one-time Russian city of Port Arthur	**Lushun**
capital under the early Ming and later Manchu	**Nanjing (Nanking)**
China's largest city, a business and fashion center	**Shanghai**
capital of Nationalist China, on Taiwan	**Taipei**
site of a devastating 1976 earthquake	**Tangshan**
international base during the 1900 Boxer war	**Tientsin**
Mongolia's capital	**Ulaan Baator**
capital of Xinjiang	**Ürümqi**
actual port serving Canton	**Whampoa**
main port on the middle Yangtze	**Wuhan**
old capital, burial site of the army of soldier-statues	**Xian (Sian)**

Regions

province at the eastern end of the old Silk Road	**Gansu (Kansu)**
province centered on Canton	**Guangdong (Kwangdong)**

British colony on China's south coast	**Hong Kong (Xianggang)**
province south of the mid-Yangtze, with spicy food	**Hunan**
China's Central Asia province	**Inner Mongolia**
peninsula off Hong Kong	**Kowloon**
Portuguese colony on China's south coast	**Macao (Aomen)**
region north of Peking, invaded by Japan in 1931	**Manchuria**
steppe region between USSR and China	**Mongolia**
SW stronghold during WWII, noted for spicy food	**Szechuan (Sichuan)**
Himalayan "Shangri-La" region now part of China	**Tibet (Xijang or Xizang)**
province bordering Burma	**Yunnan**
Central Asian region of Sinkiang, "New Dominion"	**Xinjiang**

Japan

(See also Islands in *Special Places*)

Among the cities and regions of Japan (Nippon), what is or was . . . ?

main port on Hokkaido Island	**Hakodate**
city in southern Honshu leveled by an atomic bomb in 1945	**Hiroshima**
12th–14th-c. A.D. capital	**Kamakura**
main cruise ship port on southern Honshu	**Kobe**
8th–12th-c. A.D. capital	**Kyoto**
city on Kyushu leveled by an atomic bomb in 1945	**Nagasaki**
cradle of Japanese civilization, its 1st capital	**Nara**
site of a modern US air force base	**Okinawa City (Koza)**
2nd largest city, on Honshu	**Osaka**
main city on Hokkaido island	**Sapporo**
capital from the early 17th-c., once called Edo	**Tokyo**
main cruise ship port, on Honshu near Tokyo	**Yokohama**

The Koreas

Among the cities and regions of North and South Korea, what is or was . . . ?

where US Marines were surrounded, and most died, in 1950	**Chosin**
heavily fortified border between the two Koreas	**DMZ (Demilitarized Zone)**
Seoul's port, where MacArthur landed in 1951	**Inchon**
Chinese-influenced northern region of old Korea	**Koguryo**
7th–10th-c. capital of old Korea	**Kyongju**
SW region of old Korea, which influenced Japan	**Paekche**
border city between North and South Korea	**Panmunjon**
port city on South Korea's southern coast	**Pusan**
capital of North Korea	**Pyongyang**
capital of South Korea	**Seoul**
central region of old Korea	**Silla**
alpine area near the DMZ	**Sorak**

The Near East

Among the cities and regions of the Near East, what is or was . . . ?

Cities

emirate and capital city in eastern Arabia	**Abu Dhabi**
Christian capital during the Crusades	**Acre (Akka)**
capital of Southern Yemen, once called Arabia Eudaemon, "Blessed Arabia"	**Aden (Al 'Aden)**
Syria's 2nd largest city, an old trading town	**Aleppo**
capital of Jordan	**Amman**
Turkey's capital, home of Angora cats	**Ankara (Ankyra)**
old trading crossroads and Crusaders' city, where a 526 A.D. earthquake killed 250,000 people	**Antioch (Antakya)**
key Jordanian port on the Red Sea	**Aqaba**

the site of the tower of Babel and the Hanging Gardens	**Babylon**
where Alexander married Roxanne	**Balkh (Bactra)**
capital of Iraq and of the medieval Abbasids	**Baghdad**
main port of Iraq on the Shatt al-Arab	**Basra**
main town in the Negev Desert	**Beersheba**
embattled Lebanese capital, with many hostages	**Beirut**
where Jesus raised Lazarus from the dead	**Bethany**
Jesus's birthplace	**Bethlehem**
where the Bible got its name	**Byblos (Gebal)**
Anatolian town dating to 7000 B.C.	**Catal-Hüyük**
old crossroads city near Baghdad and Babylon	**Ctesiphon**
capital of Syria and of the medieval Umayyads	**Damascus**
Syrian city to which Armenian survivors were driven and many killed in WWI by the Turks	**Deir el-Zur**
site of a 1947 Jewish massacre of Palestinian Arabs	**Deir Yassin**
Qatar's capital	**Doha**
Roman border trading town on the Euphrates	**Dura-Europos**
old Aegean port in Turkey, linked with Artemis	**Ephesus (Efes** near Selçuk)
Turkisk site of a failed 1915–16 Allied offensive	**Gallipoli (Gelibolu)**
where Alexander cut a knot, showing he would rule Asia	**Gordion (Yassıhöyük** near Polatli)
Israeli port and Bahai center	**Halfa**
the site of the orig. Mausoleum (Tomb of King Mausolus)	**Halicarnassus**
pre-1300 B.C. Hittite capital in Turkey	**Hattushash**
burial place of Abraham	**Hebron**
old Mediterranean port serving Antioch	**Iskanderun (Alexandretta)**
Turkey's main city, once Byzantion (-ium) and Constantinople	**Istanbul (Stamboul)**
where Alexander defeated the Persians in 333 B.C.	**Issus (Dörtyol)**
old port south of Tel Aviv	**Jaffa**

perhaps the oldest city, linked with Joshua	**Jericho**
capital of Israel, sacred to 3 religions	**Jerusalem**
Saudi Arabia's main Red Sea port, near Mecca	**Jiddah**
old capital of the Afghan region	**Kandahar**
key Iranian port city on the Shatt al-Arab	**Khorramshahr**
Seljuk capital in Turkey, where St. Paul preached	**Konya**
site where Jews died, not to surrender, in 73 A.D.	**Massada**
Mohammed's birth place, which all Moslems are supposed to visit	**Mecca**
Mohammed's home and burialplace	**Medina**
old Aegean port in Turkey, early Ionian home	**Miletos (Milet)**
Iraq's 2nd-largest city	**Mosul**
10th-c. B.C. Israeli capital, as Shechem	**Nablus**
Jesus's Galilee home	**Nazareth**
Israeli city famed for Jewish-Arab coexistence	**Neve Shalom (Oasis of Peace)**
Turkish site of the 325 A.D. council on heresy	**Nicaea (Iznik)**
site of the Assyrian king Ashurnasirpals's palace	**Nimrud (Calah)**
ruined capital of ancient Assyria, near Mosul	**Nineveh**
Roman era crossroads city-state in Syria, the biblical Tadmor	**Palmyra**
home of the ancient Greek Asklepios medicine cult	**Pergamon (Bergama)**
old Persian summer capital, destroyed by Alexander	**Persepolis**
old trading city of rose-red rock "half as old as time"	**Petra**
Saudi Arabia's capital	**Riyadh**
Palestinian refugee camps where hundreds were massacred in 1982	**Sabra** and **Shatilla**
capital of North Yemen	**Sanaa**
western end of the Persian Royal Road, in Turkey	**Sardis (-es)**
where Florence Nightingale revolutionized nursing, an Asian district of Istanbul	**Scutari (Üsküdar)**

Neanderthal site where flower pollen was found in graves	**Shanidar**
old Phoenician port, now Saida, in Lebanon	**Sidon**
old port, a post-WWI Greek-Turkish battlefield	**Smyrna (Izmir)**
Biblical towns destroyed for depravity	**Sodom** and **Gomorrah**
eastern end of the old Persian Royal Road	**Susa**
capital of Iran	**Teheran**
Israel's diplomatic capital, on the Mediterranean	**Tel Aviv**
old Turkish Black Sea port and site of a 1988 earthquake	**Trabzon (Trebizond)**
old port north of Beirut, in Lebanon	**Tripoli**
town of the *Iliad*, rediscovered by Schliemann	**Troy (Truva)**
old home port of the Phoenicians, in Israel	**Tyre**
home of the Sumerians, who invented writing	**Ur**

Regions

huge Asian peninsula occupied by Turkey	**Anatolia**
shifting homeland of Christians in a Moslem world	**Armenia**
biblical name for the region of Israel	**Canaan**
region in southern Turkey where a 1268 earthquake killed 60,000 people	**Cilicia (Kilikia)**
region in northern Israel	**Galilee**
disputed borderland between Egypt and Israel	**Gaza Strip**
disputed hilly region in NE Israel facing Syria	**Golan Heights**
southern coastal strip of the Arabian peninsula	**Hadramaut**
western strip of the Arabian Peninsula	**Hejaz**
country ruled by shah, then ayatollah	**Iran (Persia)**
country in the 1980s war with Iran	**Iraq**
Jewish homeland formed in 1948 from Palestine	**Israel**
old names for what is now southern Israel	**Judah** or **Judea**, later **Palestine**

capital of Afghanistan	**Kabul**
oil-rich Iranian province disputed with Iraq	**Khuzistan**
area of SE Turkey and NW Iran seeking independence	**Kurdistan**
oil-rich pocket state, and its capital city	**Kuwait**
sultanate on the SE coast of Arabia	**Oman**
Holy Land of the Bible	**Palestine**
emirate on a peninsula in the Persian Gulf	**Qatar**
where the Dead Sea Scrolls were found	**Qumran**
ancient region south of Galilee	**Samaria**
nation occupying most of the Arabian Peninsula	**Saudi Arabia**
mostly desert land between Iraq and Lebanon	**Syria**
federation of 7 emirates in eastern Arabia	**United Arab Emirates**
disputed uplands west of the Jordan River	**West Bank**
southwestern strip of the Arabian Peninsula	**Yemen**

Southeast Asia and the Pacific Islands

(See also Islands in *Special Places*)

Among the cities and regions of Southeast Asia and the Pacific islands, what is . . . ?

Cities

capital of Commonwealth-linked Western Samoa	**Apia**
14th–18th-c. Thai capital	**Ayuthaya**
important archaeological site in Thailand	**Ban Chiang**
Brunei's capital	**Bandar Seri Begawan**
capital of Thailand, once called Krung Thep	**Bangkok**
beach resort on Penang Island	**Batu Ferringhi**
1st colonial capital of the Philippines	**Cebu City**
Thailand's northern capital, the City of Roses	**Chiang Mai**
where France lost their Vietnam war	**Dien Bien Phu**
port for Hanoi, ancient Cattigara	**Haiphong**

North Vietnam capital	**Hanoi**
South Vietnam capital once called Saigon	**Ho Chi Minh City**
Vietnam city central to the 1968 Tet Offensive	**Hué**
Indonesia's capital, main industrial city	**Jakarta**
site of the POW's bridge over Thailand's River Kwai	**Kanchanaburi**
US Marine base near Laos in the Vietnam War	**Khe Sanh**
Malaysian town where the Japanese landed in 1941	**Kota Bharu**
Malaysia's capital	**Kuala Lumpur**
north Burmese city celebrated in song	**Mandalay**
capital of the Philippines, on Luzon Island	**Manila**
site of a notorious massacre of civilians in Vietnam	**My Lai**
center of an old Indian kingdom in Thailand	**Nakhon Pathom**
medieval capital on Burma's Irrawaddy	**Pagan**
US Samoa's capital	**Pago Pago**
capital of Kampuchea (Cambodia)	**Phnom Penh**
main port on SW New Guinea	**Port Moresby**
site of a key 1972 Vietnam War battle	**Quang Tri**
key town near Manila, on Luzon Island	**Quezon City**
Burma's capital	**Rangoon**
important pottery site in Thailand	**Sawankhalok**
capital of Laos on the Thai border	**Vientiane**
capital of Vanuatu (formerly New Hebrides)	**Vila**
cultural capital of Indonesia, on Java	**Yogyakarta**

Regions

east-central region in Vietnam	**Annam**
peninsula near Manila, site of WWII Death March	**Bataan**
small, very rich country on Borneo	**Brunei**
traditional name of Myanmar	**Burma!**
main opium area in Burma, Thailand, and Laos	**Golden Triangle**

island nation including Java, Bali, and Sumatra	**Indonesia**
the Indonesian part of New Guinea	**Irian Jaya**
Viet Cong guerrilla base just north of Saigon	**Iron Triangle**
troubled region once called Cambodia	**Kampuchea**
nation of Micronesian islands near the International Date Line	**Kiribati**
landlocked nation west of Vietnam	**Laos**
Thai area with medieval Khmer Buddhist temples	**Lop Buri**
old Portuguese colony near Hong Kong	**Macao or Macau**
peninsula now part of Malaysia	**Malaya**
nation formed by Malaya, Singapore, Sabah, and Sarawak in 1963	**Malaysia**
name of Burma, from 1989	**Myanmar**
nation on the east half of New Guinea island	**Papua New Guinea**
nation with over 7,000 islands	**Philippines**
Thai region, once center of a Khmer empire	**Phimai**
former British colonies on Borneo, now part of Malaysia	**Sabah** and **Sarawak**
once-British colony founded by Sir Thomas Raffles	**Singapore**
country once called Siam	**Thailand (Prathet Thai)**
country where US soldiers fought in the 1960's	**Vietnam**

The Subcontinent

Among the lands of Asia's Subcontinent, what is or was . . . ?

Cities

home of the Taj Mahal, Babur's 16th-c. capital	**Agra**
old pilgrimage town with the Undying Banyan	**Allahabad (Prayag)**
sacred Sikh city in India's Punjab	**Amritsar**
site of the terrible Union Carbide gas leak in 1984	**Bhopal**
"Cathedral City of India," in Orissa	**Bhubaneswar**
terracotta capital in West Bengal	**Bishnupur**

India's 2nd largest city	**Bombay**
sacred Hindu city linked with Krishna's appearance	**Brindaban**
India's largest city, in the NE	**Calcutta**
capital of the Punjab region	**Chandrigarh**
Bangladesh's 2nd largest city	**Chittagong**
SE Indian ports called "Venice of the East"	**Cochin** and **Quilon**
Sri Lanka's capital	**Colombo**
Jewish town in India, destroyed by the early Portuguese	**Cranganore**
old Moghul capital	**Delhi**
capital of Bangladesh	**Dhaka**
site of the Aga Khan's palace	**East Kirkee**
main city of India's central Deccan	**Hyderabad**
Pakistan's capital	**Islamabad**
capital of India's Rajasthan region	**Jaipur**
largest city in Pakistan	**Karachi**
Nepal's capital	**Kathmandu**
temple-filled early Hindu city in central India	**Khajuraho**
Pakistan's 2nd largest city	**Lahore**
old crossroads town high in Kashmir	**Leh (Ladakh)**
"city of gardens" in central India	**Lucknow**
Nepal's jumping-off point for Everest attempts	**Lukla**
Buddha's birthplace, in Nepal	**Lumbini**
Indian city famed for its printed cottons	**Madras**
capital of the Maldives	**Male**
birthplace of Krishna, in India	**Mathura**
site of the 1857 Sepoy Mutiny	**Meerut**
modern India's capital	**New Delhi**
center for India's Jains	**Palitana**
capital of Bihar, once of India as Pataliputra	**Patna**
old trading city east of the Khyber Pass	**Peshawar**
major center for Buddhist sculpture	**Sanchi**
where Buddha preached his 1st sermon	**Sarnath**
site of Mahatma Gandhi's ashram	**Sevagram**
once the Indian viceroy's summer capital	**Simla**
Kashmir's capital	**Srinigar**

| Bhutan's capital | **Thimphu** |
| the Hindu Mecca, in Uttar Pradesh | **Varanasi (Benares)** |

Regions

NE mountain state of India	**Assam**
Hindu's name for their homeland, India	**Bharat**
land east of India, formerly East Pakistan	**Bangladesh**
region now split between India and Bangladesh	**Bengal**
small kingdom in NE subcontinent	**Bhutan**
the Indian state bordering on Nepal	**Bihar**
plateau region of central India	**Deccan**
former Portuguese colony on India's west coast	**Goa**
old trading region, a peninsula in NW India	**Gujarat**
peninsula in NW Sri Lanka, a Tamil stronghold	**Jaffna**
mountainous, Moslem region of NW India	**Kashmir**
SE region of India, with Jewish settlements B.C.	**Kerala**
state centered on Bombay	**Maharashtra**
SW coast of India, where Da Gama landed	**Malabar**
island republic SW of India	**Maldives**
nation in the Himalayas between Tibet and India	**Nepal**
NW region, center of the Sikh religion, now split between India and Pakistan	**Punjab**
a once British protectorate, now part of India	**Sikkim**
island nation south of India, once Ceylon	**Sri Lanka**
region centered on the Ganges River	**Uttar Pradesh**

Australia and New Zealand

Cities and Regions

(See also Islands in *Special Places*)

Among the cities and regions of Australia and New Zealand, what is . . : ?

main city in south Australia	**Adelaide**
central Australia town, in Nevil Shute's book	**Alice Springs**
largest city in New Zealand	**Auckland**
capital of Queensland, Australia	**Brisbane**
gateway to Australia's Great Barrier Reef	**Cairns**
capital of Australia	**Canberra**
3rd largest city in New Zealand	**Christchurch**
main city of Australia's Northern Territory	**Darwin**
capital of Tasmania	**Hobart**
Australia's 2nd largest city	**Melbourne**
large Australian province around Sydney	**New South Wales**
main city in SW Australia	**Perth**
New Zealand's jurisdiction over Antarctica	**Ross Dependency**
huge NE region of Australia	**Queensland**
area of Melbourne much frequented by artists	**St. Kilda (Esplanade)**
Australia's largest city, with a famed opera house	**Sydney**
Australia's SE province around Melbourne	**Victoria**
capital of New Zealand	**Wellington**

Europe

Belgium

Among the cities and regions of Belgium, what is . . . ?

major port city and medieval diamond center	**Antwerp (Métropole)**
wooded, hilly plateau region important in WWII	**Ardennes (Haut Plateau Ardennais)**
site of WWII's Battle of the Bulge, in the Ardennes	**Bastogne**

medieval commercial center, shot through with canals	**Bruges (Brugge)**
home of the European Community, in Belgium	**Brussels**
cloth-making region of northern Belgium	**Flanders**
city long dedicated to caring for the insane	**Gheel** or **Geel**
city of flowers, a trading center on the Schelde	**Ghent**
canal-filled center of Wallonia on the Meuse	**Liège**
main boat-train link with Dover, England	**Oostend**
major WWI battlefield near Ypres	**Paschendaele (Passendale)**
site of healing springs since Roman times	**Spa**
French-speaking southern region	**Wallonia**
where Wellington defeated Napoleon in 1815	**Waterloo**
Flemish cloth center, site of WWI battles	**Ypres (Ieper)**
Bruges's port, site of the 1987 British ferry disaster	**Zeebrugge**

Eastern Europe

Among the cities and regions of Eastern Europe, what is or was . . . ?

Cities

Nazi concentration camp near Cracow, Poland	**Auschwitz (O'swiecim)**
capital of Yugoslavia	**Belgrade (Beograd)**
home of the bialy, a roll with baked onion	**Bialystok**
capital of Slovakia, once called Pressburg	**Bratislava (Pozsony)**
capital of Moravia	**Brno**
capital of Romania	**Bucharest**
Hungary's capital on the Danube, 2 cities in 1	**Budapest**
where the Orient Express once ended, in Romania	**Constanza (Toma)**
once Poland's royal seat, Pope John II's home	**Cracow**
home of the "Black Madonna," in Poland	**Czestochowa**
Adriatic port in Yugoslavia, old Ragusa	**Dubrovnik**

where St. John the Evangelist died	**Ephesus**
now part of Yugoslavia, but claimed in the early 20th c. by Italy	**Fiume**
Polish city where Solidarity was formed	**Gdansk (Danzig)**
Czechoslovakian spa once called Karlsbad	**Karlovy Vary**
Polish coal-mining center, active in strikes	**Katowicz**
Bulgarian site of a great 1389 Turkish victory	**Kosovo**
Czech town destroyed in a 1942 Nazi retaliation	**Lidice**
main cultural center of eastern Poland	**Lublin**
main city of the Slovenians	**Ljubljana**
Nazi concentration camp near Lublin, Poland	**Majdenek**
Czechoslovakian spa once called Marienbad	**Mariánské Lázne**
Bulgaria's capital before Sofia	**Plovdiv**
capital of Czechoslovakia, Bohemian royal seat	**Prague**
where Archduke Franz Ferdinand was killed in 1914, now in Yugoslavia	**Sarajevo**
capital of Bulgaria	**Sofia**
Polish port active in strikes	**Szczecin (Stettin)**
Nazi concentration camp in Czechoslovakia	**Theresienstadt**
capital of Albania	**Tirana**
other large Nazi concentration camps in Poland	**Treblinka** and **Sobibor**
Pope John Paul II's (Carol Wojtyla's) birthplace	**Wadowice**
Poland's capital, home of the Chopin competition	**Warsaw**
capital of lower Silesia, home of Jerzy Grotowski	**Wroclaw**
where the Allies made post-WWII plans	**Yalta**
Yugoslavia's 2nd largest city	**Zagreb**

Regions

SW corner of Romania, on the Danube	**Banat**
region in western Czechoslovakia	**Bohemia**
regions combined in the Yugoslav federation	**Bosnia** and **Herzegovina**

once-independent Adriatic region in Yugoslavia	**Croatia**
region of Croatia along the Adriatic	**Dalmatia**
Romanian Black Sea coastal strip	**Dobrudja**
Central European area north of the Carpathians	**Galicia**
peninsula south of Trieste, in NW Yugoslavia	**Istria**
homeland of Alexander the Great, now split among Greece, Bulgaria, and Yugoslavia	**Macedonia**
region in NE Romania	**Moldavia**
mountainous, isolated region in Yugoslavia	**Montenegro**
region in central Czechoslovakia	**Moravia**
Vistula Valley, Poland's long-disputed route to the sea	**Polish Corridor**
main Polish city between Warsaw and Berlin	**Posnan** or **Poznan**
militaristic region now split among Germany, Poland, and the USSR	**Prussia**
once-independent region in eastern Yugoslavia	**Serbia**
industrial and mining region, once German, now mostly Polish	**Silesia (Schlesien)**
region centered on Ljubljana, now in Yugoslavia	**Slovenia**
Czechoslovakian region Hitler annexed in 1938	**Sudetenland**
region east of Macedonia, now split among Greece, Bulgaria, and Turkey	**Thrace**
central Romanian region linked with Dracula	**Transylvania**
region in central Romania	**Wallachia (Valahia)**
federated republic of Balkan states	**Yugoslavia**

France

(See also Caves and Grottoes in *Special Places*)

Among the cities and regions of France, what is or was … ?

Cities

Provence town favored by Cézanne	**Aix-en-Provence**
Alpine town famed for its thermal baths	**Aix-les-Bains**
birthplace of Napoleon, on Corsica	**Ajaccio**

basilica town, birthplace of Toulouse-Lautrec	**Albi**
site of a WWI battle and a fine Gothic cathedral	**Amiens**
Charente city much disputed in religious wars	**Angoulême**
Riviera resort with a Picasso museum, old Antipolis	**Antibes**
Provence town favored by Romans and Van Gogh	**Arles**
WWI battle site in France's Flanders region	**Arras**
tapestry-weaving center near Limoges	**Aubusson**
home of the 14th-c. French popes	**Avignon**
Corsica's largest port, on the NE coast	**Bastia**
town whose tapestry portrays the 1066 Norman invasion of Britain	**Bayeux**
major port of the Basque country	**Bayonne**
Burgundy's wine-making center	**Beaune**
capital of the Franche-Comté region	**Besançon**
jet-set resort on the Biscay shore	**Biarritz**
Corsica's main southern port	**Bonifacio**
Julius Caesar's port for an attack on England	**Boulogne**
cathedral town and old capital of Berri	**Bourges**
upper Normandy capital, known for its stone	**Caen**
longtime coastal port connection with Dover	**Calais**
Corsica's chic northeast coastal resort	**Calvi**
site of a WWII massacre in Artois	**Cambrai**
Riviera city famed for its film festival	**Cannes**
medieval pilgrimage center on the Garonne	**Carcassone**
birthplace of revolutionary Jean Jaurès, with a Goya museum	**Castres**
Normandy port nicknamed Port de la Libération in WWII	**Cherbourg**
site of Joan of Arc's vision, on the Loire	**Chinon**

home of Michelin and focus of Ophuls's *The Sorrow and the Pity*	**Clermont-Ferrand**
site linked to the Cistercian religious order	**Clairvaux**
home and headquarters of the Benedictines	**Cluny**
town where the WWI armistice was signed	**Compiègne**
popular 19th-c. seaside resorts in Normandy	**Deauville** and **Trouville**
Normandy site of a disastrous WWII landing	**Dieppe**
town famous for its white wine mustard	**Dijon**
town where Joan of Arc was born	**Domrémy**
port from which WWII Allies fled to England in 1940	**Dunkerque (Dunkirk)**
champagne center, home of Moët	**Epernay**
place most associated with Monet	**Giverny**
Normandy site where the British built a temporary harbor after D-Day	**Gold Beach**
sports capital of the Alps, a university town	**Grenoble**
main modern trans-Atlantic port	**Le Havre**
Normandy site where Canada's D-Day forces landed	**Juno Beach**
old Huguenot port on the Bay of Biscay	**La Rochelle**
site of the Grand Prix auto race	**Le Mans**
mineral spring spa high in the Massif Central	**Le Mont Dore**
Auvergne cathedral town and pilgrimage site	**Le Puy**
porcelain capital, in central France	**Limoges**
Gascony site of Bernadette Soubirous's vision	**Lourdes**
France's 2nd capital, once a silk and trade center	**Lyon**
picturesque and tough old southern port	**Marseilles**
health spa and retirement resort east of Monaco	**Menton**
cathedral town and WWII German stronghold	**Metz**
old university town on the Riviera	**Montpellier**

old capital of the Bourbon dynasty	**Moulins**
longtime capital of Lorraine	**Nancy**
main port on the lower Loire River	**Nantes**
Riviera resort with Matisse and Chagall museums	**Nice**
old Roman town, which gave its name to denim	**Nîmes (de Nîmes)**
D-Day's US landing beaches on Normandy	**Omaha** and **Utah**
Provence site of a well-preserved Roman theater	**Orange**
city Joan of Arc delivered from the English	**Orléans**
capital of once-Spanish Roussillon in the south	**Perpignan**
capital of the Champagne region	**Reims**
capital of lower Normandy, where Joan of Arc burned	**Rouen**
Breton port from which early explorers sailed	**St-Malo**
town the D-Day forces wanted to take first	**Ste-Mère-Eglise**
Basque medieval pilgrim stop on the route to Santiago de Compostela	**St-Jean-Pied-de-Port**
yacht-filled Riviera port and resort	**St. Tropez**
where the Prussians defeated France in 1870	**Sedan**
on the Franco-German Alsace border, on the Rhine	**Strasbourg**
British landing site during the Normandy invasion	**Sword Beach**
naval port on the Riviera near Marseilles	**Toulon**
center of the wine-rich Languedoc region	**Toulouse**
Loire pilgrimage town, near where Charles Martel turned back the Moors	**Tours**
ancient capital of Champagne	**Troyes**
jet-set resort with year-round Alpine skiing	**Val d'Isère**
WWI battlefield on the Meuse where hundreds of thousands died	**Verdun**
old pilgrim center, and traditional burial site for Mary Magdalene's bones	**Vézelay**

watering spot and home of the WWII puppet government	**Vichy**
ridge near Arras where many WWI Canadians died	**Vimy Ridge**

Regions

disputed region, home of the Hohenstaufens	**Alsace**
old province in western France	**Anjou**
historic region south of the Garonne River	**Aquitaine**
area famous for Monet and asparagus	**Argenteuil**
NW area famed for its brandy	**Armagnac**
region between Picardie and Flandre	**Artois**
rugged farming country of the Massif Central	**Auvergne**
region around Bourges	**Berri**
major port region on the Garonne River	**Bordeaux**
peninsula dotted with Celtic megalithic circles	**Brittany (Bretagne)**
wine-making region joined to France in 1477	**Burgundy (Bourgogne)**
wild marshlands west of the Rhône River	**Camargue**
old Alpine home of the dukes of Savoy	**Chambéry**
home of France's ski and mountain-climbing schools	**Chamonix**
home region of France's famed bubbly wine	**Champagne**
wine-making area, home of the grands crus	**Côte d'Or**
peninsula west of the Normandy D-Day beaches	**Cotentin**
Flemish region, in the north	**Flandre (Flanders)**
region stretched along the Jura Mountains	**Franche-Comté**
SW region from Biscay to the central Pyrénées	**Gascony (Gascogne)**
wine-growing region around Toulouse	**Languedoc**
region centered on Limoges	**Limousin**
Joan of Arc's home province	**Lorraine (Lotharingia)**
region around Toulouse	**Midi-Pyrénées**
NW region where the Allies landed in 1944	**Normandy**
SW region along the Pyrénées	**Pays Basque (Euskadi)**
region around the Loire Valley	**Pays de le Loire**

region in central France, once called Guyenne	**Périgord-Quercy**
battle-scarred region along the Somme	**Picardie (Picardy)**
Roman-influenced southern coastal strip	**Provence**
coastal strip from western France to NW Italy	**Riviera** or **Côte d'Azur**
once-Spanish region in the eastern Pyrénées	**Roussillon**
France's SE Alpine region	**Savoie (Savoy)- Dauphiné**

The Germanies and Austria

Among the cities and regions of Germany (Deutschland) and Austria (Österreich), what is or was . . . ?

Cities

Charlemagne's 9th-c. capital, a WWII battle site	**Aachen (Aix-la-Chappelle)**
home of the Nürburgring car and cycle track	**Ahr**
trading city where peace was made in 1555	**Augsburg**
town where Napoleon defeated Austria in 1805	**Austerlitz**
Austria's old spa town, also a German region near the French border	**Baden**
German spa town, near the French border	**Baden Baden**
Austrian site of Franz Josef's summer court	**Bad Ischl**
Franconian city famed for its 11th-c. cathedral	**Bamberg**
site of the annual Wagner festival	**Bayreuth**
Nazi concentration camp on Lüneburg Heath	**Bergen-Belsen**
capital of Hitler's Germany, long a divided city	**Berlin**
West German capital and Beethoven's birthplace	**Bonn**
great emigrant port on the Weser River	**Bremen (Bremerhaven)**
Nazi concentration camp near Weimar	**Buchenwald**
old Roman capital near Vienna	**Carnuntum**
largest city on the Rhine, famed for toilet water	**Cologne (Köln)**
site of the Nazi concentration camp near Munich	**Dachau**

known for its china and a WWII firestorm	**Dresden**
industrial north city linked with Schumann	**Düsseldorf**
Bach's birthplace, where Luther translated the New Testament into German	**Eisenach**
home of the Esterhazys, where Haydn stayed	**Eisenstadt**
home of the hot dog and the international book fair	**Frankfurt-am-Main**
capital of Germany's Black Forest region	**Freiburg**
German town with an historical clock museum	**Furtwangen**
old university town in Saxony	**Göttingen**
main city in Styria, southern Austria	**Graz**
Handel's birthplace	**Halle**
key prehistoric lake-dwelling site in Austria	**Hallstatt**
great emigrant port on the Elbe, Germany's media center and home of the 'burger	**Hamburg**
home of the Pied Piper	**Hamelin (Hameln)**
industrial center in Saxony	**Hannover**
city with Germany's oldest university	**Heidelberg**
capital of the Austrian Tyrol	**Innsbruck**
German city built in the shape of a fan	**Karlsruhe**
where German sailors mutinied in 1919	**Kiel**
center of the mid-Rhine	**Koblenz**
on the Bodensee (Lake Constance)	**Konstanz**
old trading town, linked with Wagner and Bach	**Leipzig**
Austrian home of Bruckner and a tasty torte	**Linz**
"Queen of the Hansa," famed for marzipan	**Lübeck**
home of Johann Gutenberg and modern printing	**Mainz**
Nazi concentration camp in Austria	**Mauthausen**
famed for its porcelain, near Dresden	**Meissen**
capital of Bavaria (Bayern)	**Munich (München)**
site of the post-WWII trials, home of Dürer	**Nuremberg (Nürnberg)**

where the Passion Play is given every 10 years	**Oberammergau**
where Gruber wrote *Silent Night, Holy Night*	**Oberndorf**
historic city where the Inn joins the Danube	**Passau**
linked with V1 and V2 rockets, in East Germany	**Peenemünde**
where the Allies signed a key 1945 accord	**Potsdam**
Nazi concentration camps in Germany	**Ravensbruck** and **Oranienburg**
Bavarian town with a Celtic and Roman past	**Regensburg**
on the Rhine, with a famed WWII bridge	**Remagen**
East German port and old Hanseatic power	**Rostock**
Mozart's birthplace, in Austria	**Salzburg**
German city famed for its swords and cutlery	**Solingen**
in SW Germany, home of Mercedes cars	**Stuttgart**
beach resort near Lübeck	**Travemünde**
Germany's oldest city, a Roman northern capital	**Trier**
on the Danube, has a fine 14th-c. cathedral	**Ulm**
Germany's lock center, with a lock museum	**Velbert**
capital of Austria, the Romans called Vindobona	**Vienna (Wien)**
old artistic and intellectual center in East Germany	**Weimar**
"Queen of Spas," near Frankfurt	**Wiesbaden**
where Luther nailed up his 95 theses	**Wittenberg**
city where Luther was condemned in 1531	**Worms**
city with a fine clock museum	**Wuppertal**
ancient city in western Franconia	**Würzburg**

Regions

German region nearest Austria	**Bavaria**
home base of the Hohenzollern rulers	**Brandenburg**
home of Prince Albert's Saxe-Coburg-Gotha family	**Coburg**
German region between Bavaria and East Germany	**Franconia**

spa region and home of soldiers in America's Revolutionary War	**Hesse**
Rhine region from which many immigrants came to the US	**Palatinate**
disputed industrial province, joined to West Germany in 1957	**Saarland**
German region around Bremen	**Saxony**
north German province, once part of Denmark	**Schleswig Holstein**
home of a 1648 peace treaty and a popular ham	**Westphalia**
German region around the upper Danube	**Württemburg**

Great Britain

Among the cities and regions of Great Britain (except Northern Ireland), what is . . . ?

Cities

Scottish city near the North Sea oil rigs	**Aberdeen**
Welsh university town and resort on Cardigan Bay	**Aberystwyth**
SE town where Benjamin Britten lived	**Aldeburgh**
focus of peace marches in the 1960s	**Aldermaston**
Lake District town north of Windermere	**Ambleside**
fashionable horse racing site near London	**Ascot**
Hertfordshire town where Shaw lived	**Ayot St. Lawrence**
where Robert the Bruce defeated the British in 1314	**Bannockburn**
Welsh resort that inspired Tennyson's *Crossing the Bar*	**Barmouth**
popular watering place from the Romans to Jane Austen	**Bath (Aquae Sulis)**
NE entrance to Snowdonia National Park	**Betws-y-coed**
major industrial city in the West Midlands	**Birmingham**
long-popular Lancashire seaside resort	**Blackpool**
Leicestershire field where Henry Tudor (VII) defeated Richard III in 1485	**Bosworth**

SW port from which early explorers sailed, home town of William Penn	**Bristol**
burial place of the 9th-c. sainted Angle king	**Bury St. Edmunds**
supposed site of King Arthur's castle, Camelot	**Cadbury**
old university town in watery East Anglia	**Cambridge**
where Thomas à Becket was killed, in Kent	**Canterbury**
Wales's main commercial and industrial city	**Cardiff**
old NW border town, Bonnie Prince Charlie's HQ	**Carlisle**
Wiltshire village where *The Story of Dr. Doolittle* was filmed	**Castle Combe**
Buckinghamshire town where Milton wrote *Paradise Lost*	**Chalfont St. Giles**
Hampshire town where Jane Austen lived	**Chawton**
spa and retirement town in the Cotswolds	**Cheltenham**
old Roman town, capital of Cheshire	**Chester**
most popular of the Cotswolds' stone villages	**Chipping Camden**
hub of old Roman roads in the Cotswolds	**Cirencester**
NE town linked with Captain James Cook	**Cleveland**
Lake District birthplace of Wordsworth	**Cockermouth**
Roman capital in East Anglia's Essex	**Colchester**
Midlands cathedral town heavily bombed in WWII, home of Lady Godiva	**Coventry**
yachting regatta center on the Hampshire coast	**Cowes**
Scottish place where Bonnie Prince Charlie was defeated in 1746	**Culloden**
Devon port where the *Mayflower* was repaired	**Dartmouth**
real Casterbridge, from Hardy's book	**Dorchester**
main crossing point to Europe, in Kent	**Dover**
near Loch Ness, favored by "Nessie" hopefuls	**Drumnadrochit**

Scottish town linked with Robert the Bruce and Andrew Carnegie	**Dunfermline**
Suffolk town mostly destroyed by the sea	**Dunwich**
NE cathedral town on the Wear River	**Durham**
Suffolk birthplace of John Constable	**East Bergholt**
Scotland's main city, once "Auld Reekie"	**Edinburgh**
cathedral town on a marshy rise in Cambridgeshire	**Ely**
site of Britain's Derby	**Epsom**
main town of Devon, with a cathedral	**Exeter**
where Mary Queen of Scots was executed	**Fotheringay**
main industrial city of Scotland	**Glasgow**
supposed burial place of King Arthur	**Glastonbury**
where the Campbells slew the MacDonalds in a 1692 massacre	**Glencoe**
cathedral town in the heart of the Cotswolds	**Gloucester**
Lincolnshire town famed for its old inns	**Grantham**
Lake district village where Wordsworth lived	**Grasmere**
nuclear base and site of anti-nuclear protests	**Greenham Common**
Thames home of the *Cutty Sark* and "mean time"	**Greenwich**
long-popular "marrying town" north of the border	**Gretna Green**
ferry port of Suffolk	**Harwich**
site of William the Conqueror's great battle	**Hastings**
home of the Brontës, in Yorkshire	**Haworth**
town full of bookshops, on the Welsh border	**Hay-on-Wye**
Thameside town famed for its royal regatta	**Henley**
cathedral town and region on the Welsh border	**Hereford**
holiday resort in NW Wales	**Holyhead**
popular fort on Hadrian's Wall	**Housesteads**
great old port of NE England, on the Humber	**Hull**

Scottish city on Moray Firth	**Inverness**
main town of Suffolk county, Wolsey's birthplace	**Ipswich**
Buckinghamsire village where the *Mayflower*'s timbers are preserved	**Jordans**
where William Morris and Rossetti worked	**Kelmscott**
Lake District town linked with Coleridge	**Keswick**
old North Sea port in Norfolk	**King's Lynn**
capital of the Orkneys	**Kirkwall**
city that hosts the English National Opera	**Leeds**
old Roman town with the Jewry Wall	**Leicester**
Staffordshire birthplace of Dr. Johnson	**Lichfield**
main western port, home of the Beatles	**Liverpool**
Wale's main seaside resort	**Llandudno**
Leicestershire town of bells and steam trains	**Loughborough**
Dorset setting of *The French Lieutenant's Woman*	**Lyme Regis**
city home of Rolls Royce and much other industry	**Manchester**
Hereford site of a key 15th-c. War of the Roses battle	**Mortimer's Cross**
NE shipbuilding center on the Tyne	**Newcastle**
Cornwall's largest sea resort	**Newquay**
East Anglia's main town, with cathedral	**Norwich**
place where the Yorkists took Henry VI	**Northampton**
Samuel Taylor Coleridge's Devon home town	**Ottery St. Mary**
old university town on the Thames	**Oxford**
Cornish port of Gilbert and Sullivan's pirates	**Penzance**
Cambridgeshire cathedral town near Ely	**Peterborough**
site of a Scottish summer theater festival	**Pitlochry**
Devon port from which the Pilgrims' *Mayflower* sailed	**Plymouth**
Dorset home of fine stone	**Portland**
main port on Scotland's island of Skye	**Portree**

Hampshire coastal town with a D-Day Museum and the Tudor ship *Mary Rose*	**Portsmouth**
once-royal residential area up-river from London	**Richmond**
where King John signed the Magna Carta in 1215	**Runnymede**
cathedral town in Wiltshire, with a copy of the Magna Carta	**Salisbury**
old settlement north of Salisbury	**Sarum (Old Sarum)**
Hertfordshire town the Romans called Verulamium	**St. Albans**
place where golf was born, in Scotland	**St. Andrews**
capital of the Channel island of Jersey	**St. Helier**
popular Cornish resort, an old fishing port	**St. Ives**
main town and capital of the island of Guernsey	**St. Peter Port**
Orkney naval base where the German fleet was scuttled in 1919	**Scapa Flow**
Yorkshire coast town linked with Alan Ayckbourn	**Scarborough**
where Scottish kings were crowned	**Scone**
Hardy's Shaston, a Dorset town	**Shaftesbury**
Staffordshire town linked with Izaak Walton	**Shallowford**
Yorkshire town linked with cutlery and steel	**Sheffield**
main town of Shropshire	**Shrewsbury**
Stone Age settlement on the Orkneys	**Skara Brae**
Britain's main ocean-liner port, in the south	**Southampton**
site of a major English sailor's revolt in 1797	**Spithead**
ferry port on the Hebrides's island of Lewis	**Stornoway**
Shakespeare's birthplace, home of the Royal Shakespeare Company	**Stratford-upon-Avon**
Gainsborough's Suffolk birthplace	**Sudbury**
Welsh port on the Bristol Channel	**Swansea**
supposed birthplace of King Arthur	**Tintagel**
main town on Scotland's island of Mull	**Tobermory**

Isle of Wight town where Dickens wrote *David Copperfield*	**Ventnor**
where Alfred made peace with the Danes, in Somerset	**Wedmore**
cathedral town in Somerset	**Wells**
Dorset resort and Channel Island port	**Weymouth**
Yorkshire coast town where Stoker wrote *Dracula*	**Whitby**
Hampshire cathedral town, Alfred's capital	**Winchester**
main town and lake of the Lake District	**Windermere**
site of long-denied 1957 nuclear accident	**Windscale** (now **Sellafield**)
Severnold cathedral city on the Severn River	**Worcester**
NE cathedral city famed for its mystery plays	**York**

Regions

recently created SW county around Bath	**Avon**
low-lying region of SE Scotland	**Border Country**
dairy farming country west of Derbyshire	**Cheshire**
tin-rich peninsula in far SW Britain	**Cornwall**
west-central area of villages with thatched houses	**Cotswolds**
lake-filled far NW region of England	**Cumbria**
Devon region of Conan Doyle's *The Hound of the Baskervilles*	**Dartmoor**
county famed for its cloth trades and its peaks	**Derbyshire**
large SW county between Cornwall and Somerset	**Devon**
Thomas Hardy country, in SW England	**Dorset**
SW Scottish region, facing Northern Ireland	**Dumfries & Galloway**
industrial town NE of Edinburgh	**Dundee**
great bulge of land NE of London	**East Anglia**
Constable country, just NE of London	**Essex**
wild Lorna Doone country in Somerset and Devon	**Exmoor**
watery, canal-drained, flat region in East Anglia	**The Fens**

Scottish region just north of the Forth	**Fife**
region on the coast, west of Sussex	**Hampshire**
western mountain-and-loch country of Scotland	**Highlands**
orchard-rich region SE of London	**Kent**
hilly NW region beloved of Wordsworth	**Lake District**
coal county of NW England	**Lancashire**
county in the central Midlands	**Leicestershire**
tulip-and-fen country of the north Midlands	**Lincolnshire**
Scottish region just south of the Forth	**Lothian**
eastern Scotland's hilly, populated region	**Lowlands**
Welsh border country, formerly	**The Marches**
county that was once London's suburb, now part of Greater London	**Middlesex**
England's heartland, the central counties	**Midlands**
largest county in East Anglia, north of Suffolk	**Norfolk**
region north of the Humber River	**Northumbria**
county linked with Robin Hood	**Nottinghamshire**
eastern end of Leicestershire, once separate	**Rutland**
open, rolling region where Stonehenge sits	**Salisbury Plain**
Celtic region north of England	**Scotland**
Midlands region linked with A. E. Housman and early industrialization	**Shropshire**
SW region between Devon and Dorset	**Somerset**
potteries region in England's Midlands	**Staffordshire**
Burns country near Glasgow	**Strathclyde**
Constable country just north of Essex	**Suffolk**
Britain's south-central resort coast	**Sussex**
"Home County" on the Downs south of London	**Surrey**
Scottish region south of the Dee	**Tayside**
resort area in South Devon, the "English Riviera"	**Torbay**
Celtic region west of the Midlands	**Wales**

region of Stonehenge and the carved white horses	**Wiltshire**
Brontë and Herriot moor and dale country in NE England	**Yorkshire**

Greece

(See also Islands in *Special Places*)

Among the cities and regions of Greece, what is or was . . . ?

Peloponnesus region settled by ancient refugees	**Achaea**
hilly, supposedly idyllic, Peloponnesus region	**Arcadia (Arkadia)**
the main city-state of old Greece and its capital	**Athens (Athína)**
mountainous region around Athens	**Attica**
city guarding an old isthmus crossing, now a canal	**Corinth (Kórinthos)**
site of a famed oracle	**Delphi**
NW, hilly region of Greece	**Epirus ('Ypiros)**
site of the c. 1500 B.C. Palace of Minos on Crete	**Knossos**
homeland of Alexander the Great	**Macedonia**
site of a 490 B.C. battle and a race to tell the news	**Marathon**
where Byron died during Greek's 19th-c. war for independence	**Missolonghi**
main Greek city in around 1400 B.C.	**Mycenae**
site of the Olympic games and temple of Zeus	**Olympia**
many-fingered peninsula off southern Greece	**Peloponnesus (Pelopónissos)**
where Brutus and Cassius were beaten by Mark Antony and Octavian in 42 B.C.	**Phillippi**
port of Athens, used by many immigrants	**Piraeus (Piréas)**
Nestor's probable home, where Linear B tablets were found	**Pylos**
Athens' main military rival in Greece	**Sparta**
town supposedly founded by Cadmus	**Thebes**
Greece's 2nd largest city, with many Jews before WWII	**Thessalonica (-niki) (Salonica)**
region in central Greece	**Thessaly**

The Irelands

Among the cities and regions of Eire and Northern Ireland, which is . . . ?

northeasternmost county, in Northern Ireland	**Antrim**
west of Down, in Northern Ireland	**Armagh**
main city of Northern Ireland	**Belfast**
south of Kildare, in Mid-Eire	**Carlow**
south of Monaghan, in Eire	**Cavan**
south of Galway, on the Atlantic, in Eire	**Clare**
Ireland's west country, 1 of 4 old main regions	**Connaught (Connacht)**
southernmost county in Eire and an emigrant port	**Cork**
between Antrim and Donegal, in Northern Ireland	**Derry** or **Londonderry**
known for its tweeds, in NE Eire	**Donegal**
region just south of Belfast	**Down**
capital of Eire	**Dublin (Baile Átha Cliath)**
Wexford home of the US Kennedy ancestors	**Dunganstown**
known for its china and lakes, in Northern Ireland	**Fermanagh**
south of Mayo, on the Atlantic, in Eire	**Galway**
NW of Dublin, known for its medieval books	**Kells**
west of Limerick and Cork, on the Atlantic, in Eire	**Kerry**
known for its pewter, west of Dublin, in Eire	**Kildare**
south of Laois, in Eire, the "Marble City," also a county	**Kilkenny**
south of Offaly, in Eire	**Laois**
SE Ireland, 1 of 4 old main regions	**Leinster**
west of Fermanagh, in Eire	**Leitrim**
south of Clare, in SW Eire	**Limerick**
south of Cavan and Leitrim, in Eire	**Longford**
south of Armagh, in Eire	**Louth**
west of Sligo, on the Atlantic, in Eire	**Mayo**
north of Dublin, in Eire	**Meath**
between and south of Armagh and Fermanagh, in Eire	**Monaghan**

SW Ireland, 1 of 4 old main regions	**Munster**
south of Westmeath, in Eire	**Offaly**
south of Sligo, in Eire	**Roscommon**
near Limerick, site of an international airport	**Shannon**
west of Louth, in Eire	**Sligo**
on the Boyne, linked with Ireland's High Kings	**Tara**
west of Kilkenny, in Eire, prime dairy country	**Tipperary**
south of Derry, in Northern Ireland	**Tyrone**
1 of 4 old Irish regions, the 6 counties in the NE	**Ulster**
famed for its cut glass, in SE Eire	**Waterford**
south of Longford, in Eire	**Westmeath**
south of Wicklow, in Eire	**Wexford**
south of Dublin	**Wicklow**

Italy

(See also Islands in *Special Places*)

Among Italy's cities and regions, what is . . . ?

Cities

Allies' 1944 landing site south of Rome	**Anzio**
old Roman city on the Gulf of Venice	**Aquileia**
birthplace of St. Francis	**Assisi**
port city and capital of Puglia	**Bari**
city of the 1980 railroad station bombing	**Bologna**
NE city with the summer piano competition	**Bolzano**
port and eastern end of the old Appian Way	**Brindisi**
lace-making and fishing village near Venice	**Burano**
Sardinia's capital, main port, and largest city	**Cagliari**
violin-making city of Stradivari and Guarneri	**Cremona**
8th-c. Greek colony near Naples	**Cumae**
city SW of Venice, setting of *The Garden of the Finzi-Continis*	**Ferrara**
favorite hill-top town near Florence	**Fiesole**

city once dominated by the Medicis	**Florence (Firenze)**
city that was Christopher Columbus's home	**Genoa (Genova)**
city that was the home of Amerigo Vespucci	**Livorno (Leghorn)**
city once dominated by the Gonzagas	**Mantua (Mantova)**
main port city of Sicily	**Messina**
banking and fashion center in Lombardy	**Milan (Milano)**
SW port, the Greeks' Neapolis	**Naples**
main port on NE Sardinia	**Olbia**
ancient Rome's port	**Ostia Antica**
town SE of Venice, setting for *The Taming of the Shrew*	**Padua (Padova)**
7th-c. B.C. Greek site south of Salerno	**Paestum**
capital of Sicily	**Palermo**
famous for parmesan cheese, home of Verdi	**Parma**
chocolate center in the Umbrian hills	**Perugia**
city famous for its leaning tower	**Pisa**
two cities buried by Vesuvius in 79 A.D.	**Pompeii** and **Herculaneum (Ercolano)**
yacht-filled Riviera town east of Genoa	**Portofino**
capital of the Western Empire of Justinian	**Ravenna**
tourist resort on the Adriatic	**Rimini**
home of Europe's oldest medical school	**Salerno**
now-faded Riviera city east of Monaco	**San Remo**
city famed for its horse race, the Palio	**Siena**
cliffside city south of Naples where the Sirens supposedly tempted Odysseus	**Sorrento**
city famed for its summer music festival	**Spoleto**
once-powerful 8th-c. Greek city on Sicily	**Syracuse**
Sicilian coastal city backed by Mt. Etna	**Taormina**
naval port in the instep of Italy's "boot"	**Taranto**
NE city famed for a 16th-c. Catholic reform council	**Trent (Trento** or **Trient)**

once-disputed NE city on the Gulf of Venice	**Trieste**
Piedmont's main city, with a controversial shroud	**Turin (Torino)**
west of Venice, the setting for *Romeo and Juliet*	**Verona**

Regions

rugged region in the central Appenines	**Abruzzi**
mountainous coast south of Naples	**Amalfi Coast**
region that forms the toe of Italy's "boot"	**Calabria**
hilly plateau near Rome, in old Latium	**Campagna**
SW region around Naples and Salerno	**Campania**
region famous for its marble	**Carrara**
Sardinian coastline above Olbia	**Costa Smeralda (Emerald Coast)**
region south of the Po, centered on Bologna	**Emilia-Romagna**
reigning region in NW Italy before Rome	**Etruria**
region around Rome, once called Latium	**Lazio**
narrow strip of beach between Venice and the Adriatic, setting for *Death in Venice*	**Lido**
beach serving Rome at nearby Ostia Antica	**Lido di Ostia**
coastal strip on the Mediterranean in NW Italy	**Liguria** or the **Italian Riviera**
NW region centering on Milan	**Lombardy (Lombardia)**
Italy's agrarian south	**Mezzogiorno**
NW region around Turin, home of the Savoys	**Piedmont (Piemonte)**
region that forms the heel of Italy's "boot"	**Puglia**
SE of Genoa, lit. the coast of the rising sun	**Riviera di Levante**
NW of Genoa, lit. the coast of the setting sun	**Riviera di Ponente**
NE region, with mixed Italian and German culture and history	**Trentino-Südtirol/Alto Adige**
region centered on the Arno and Florence	**Tuscany (Toscana)**
hilly region NE of Rome	**Umbria**
Italian side of the Alps, centered on Aosta	**Valle d'Aosta**

city of the gondoliers and canals	**Venice**
NE region centering on Venice	**Veneto**

The Netherlands: Cities and Regions

Among the cities and regions of The Netherlands, what is or are . . . ?

capital and modern diamond center	**Amsterdam**
garden city of central Holland	**Appeldoorn**
sites of major battles in WWII, near the German border	**Arnhem** and **Nijmegen**
Catholic region bordering on Belgium	**Brabant**
pottery town, home of Jan Vermeer	**Delft**
shipbuilding and yachting port near Amsterdam	**Dordrecht**
watery, low-lying northernmost province	**Friesland**
home town of Frans Hals, with his museum	**Haarlem**
capital of old Holland and now The Netherlands	**The Hague (Den Haag)**
old central province of The Netherlands	**Holland**
home port of many early Dutch explorers	**Hoorn**
site of the World Music Festival every 4 years	**Kerkrade**
town famous for fine glassware	**Leerdam**
town that first voted to recognize the US, in 1782	**Leeuwarden**
old artistic and intellectual city south of Amsterdam	**Leiden**
southernmost province, famous for its cheese	**Limburg**
land drained and reclaimed from the Zuider Zee	**Polders**
burial place for many WWII Allied soldiers	**Rhenen**
main international port, a modern tile center	**Rotterdam**
seaside resort near The Hague	**Scheveningen**
Dutch silverworking center	**Utrecht**
towns famous for keeping traditional costume	**Volendam** and **Marken**
Nazi concentration camp in Holland	**Vught**

seaside resort south of Amsterdam	**Zandvoort**
island beaches of the SW Netherlands	**Zeeland Riviera**

Portugal: Cities and Regions

Among the cities and regions of Portugal, what is . . . ?

largest province, in central Portugal	**Alentejo**
southernmost province, on the sea	**Algarve**
region north of Lisbon	**Estremadura**
capital, wracked by a 1755 earthquake	**Lisbon (Olisipo)**
lively northern province	**Minho**
fishing village noted for its colorful dress	**Nazaré**
home of port wine	**Oporto**
bull-fighting region NE of Lisbon	**Ribatejo**
site of Henry the Navigator's navigation center	**Sagres**
wine-making peninsula near Lisbon	**Setúbal**
bull-fighting capital of Portugal	**Vila Franco de Xira**

Scandinavia: Cities and Regions

Among Scandinavian cities and regions, what is . . . ?

Denmark's 2nd largest city, on Jutland	**Århus**
Norway's Hanseatic port facing west	**Bergen**
Denmark's major port city, facing Sweden	**Copenhagen**
northern Norway, "Land of the Midnight Sun"	**Finnmark**
Sweden's old main emigrant port	**Göteborg (Gothenburg)**
Denmark's North Atlantic island colony	**Greenland (Grønland or Kalaallit Numaat)**
Denmark town linked with Hamlet and Sound dues	**Helsingør**
capital of Finland	**Helsinki (Helsingfors)**
mainland part of Denmark, a peninsula	**Jutland**
Arctic part of the Scandinavian Peninsula	**Lappland**
university town near Mälmo, founded by Canute	**Lund**

Swedish city across from Copenhagen	**Mälmo**
main town in Arctic Norway	**Narvik**
capital of Greenland	**Nuuk (Gothab)**
Norway's capital	**Oslo**
Finnish region from which many immigrants left	**Oulu**
capital of Iceland, site of the 1987 summit	**Reykjavik**
Sweden's southern region, facing Denmark	**Skåne**
SE Swedish region from which many immigrants left	**Småland**
Norway's main southern port and oil center	**Stavanger**
Sweden's capital, the "Venice of the North"	**Stockholm**
Norway region linked with skiing	**Telemark**
region around Norway's Trondheim	**Tröndelag**
early capital in Viking times	**Trondheim**
Finland's old capital	**Turku (Åbo)**
Swedish university town north of Stockholm	**Uppsala**
Finland's main west-facing port	**Vaasa**

Spain

Among the cities and regions of Spain, what is . . . ?

old Greek and Roman city on the NE coast	**Ampurias (Emporiae)**
SW region around Seville, once Rome's granary	**Andalusia**
old region facing the central Pyrénées	**Aragon**
old Carthaginian port, and Spain's 2nd city	**Barcelona**
largest city of northern Spain's Basque country	**Bilbao**
site of a 12th-c. High Gothic Cathedral	**Burgos**
Atlantic port founded by Phoenicians	**Cádiz (old Gadir or Gades)**
old city founded as Carthago Nova (New Carthage)	**Cartagena**
main central region	**Castile**
NW coastal region around Barcelona	**Catalonia**
Moslem capital, famed for its mosque and leather	**Córdoba (Cordova)**

popular coast of NE Spain	**Costa Brava**
dry SW region	**Extremadura**
wet NW region	**Galicia**
city and coastal area longest in Moorish hands	**Granada**
city bombed by Franco and painted by Picasso	**Guernica**
peninsula including both Spain and Portugal	**Iberia**
city that gave its name to sherry	**Jerez**
city and region in NW Spain	**Léon**
capital of Spain, also a province	**Madrid**
old Phoenician port in Granada facing Africa	**Málaga**
old Roman city in Extremadura	**Médira**
region facing France's SW Pyrénées	**Navarre**
Basque country near the Pyrénées	**Pais Vasco**
city famous for the "running of the bulls"	**Pamplona**
pilgrimage shrine, supposed site of St. James's (Iago's) bones	**Santiago de Compostela**
capital of 12th-c. Christian Spain	**Saragossa (Zaragoza)**
city near the remains of a Roman aqueduct	**Segovia**
southern city with a great Moorish heritage	**Seville**
city painted by El Greco	**Toledo**
city and region along the central coast	**Valencia**

Switzerland

Among the cities and regions of Switzerland, what is . . . ?

commercial center on the Rhine	**Basel (Basle)**
capital of Switzerland	**Bern**
resort region around Interlaken	**Bernese Oberland**
international capital, as of the UN in Europe	**Geneva**
resort region around St. Moritz	**Graubünden**
jumping-off point for Jungfrau climbers	**Interlaken**
main city on Lac Léman's north shore	**Lausanne**
where the Swiss confederation was born	**Luzern (Lucerne)**
resort town at Lac Léman's eastern end	**Montreux**

resort capital and 1928 and 1948 Olympics home	**St. Moritz**
Switzerland's largest city	**Zurich**

The Pocket and Island Countries

(See also Islands in *Special Places*)

Among the cities and regions of Europe's pocket and island countries, what is . . . ?

capital of Andorra, the tiny principality between France and Spain	**Andorra la Vella**
principality between Austria and Switzerland	**Liechtenstein**
duchy in western Europe, and its capital city	**Luxembourg**
island nation in the Narrows of the Mediterranean	**Malta**
principality tucked into the French Riviera	**Monaco**
capital of Monaco	**Monaco-Ville**
casino and resort town in Monaco	**Monte Carlo**
capital of Cyprus	**Nicosia**
in north-central Italy, founded the 4th c.	**San Marino**
capital of Liechtenstein	**Vaduz**
Malta's capital	**Valletta**
Catholic Church's city-state in Rome	**Vatican City**

Union of Soviet Socialist Republics (USSR)

Among the USSR's cities and regions, what is . . . ?

Cities

capital of the Kazakh SSR	**Alma Ata**
White Sea port where 16th-c. Britons traded	**Archangel**
capital of the Turkmen SSR	**Ashkhabad**
Caspian port, capital of a medieval Jewish state	**Astrakhan**
site of an infamous Nazi massacre of Jews	**Babi Yar**
Azerbaijan's oil-rich capital on the Caspian	**Baku**
capital of the Adzhar SSR on the Black Sea	**Batumi**
site of a major WWI treaty, on the Polish border	**Brest**

10th-c. capital of the Saminids, in Turkmenistan	**Bukhara**
site of a major 1989 railroad accident	**Chelyabinsk**
site of the massive 1986 nuclear accident	**Chernobyl**
main port on the Kara Sea	**Dickson**
capital of the Tadzhik SSR	**Dushanbe**
where Nicholas II and his family were killed	**Ekaterinburg** (now **Sverdlosk**)
capital of Armenia	**Erevan**
capital of the Kirghiz SSR	**Frunze**
city for internal exiles, as of Sakharov	**Gorky**
hub of south-central Siberia	**Irkutsk**
old capital of East Prussia, as Königsberg	**Kaliningrad**
inter-war capital of Lithuania	**Kuanas**
capital of a khanate from the 16th–20th c.	**Khiva**
old capital of Viking Russia and modern Urkaine	**Kiev**
capital of the Moldavian SSR, site of early-20th-c. anti-Jewish pogroms	**Kishinev**
Tchaikovsky's hometown	**Klin**
home of the "heavenly horses" that attracted 1st-c. B.C. Chinese	**Kokand**
site of a long-denied 1957–58 nuclear accident	**Kyshtym**
main Armenian cities devastated in the 1988 earthquake	**Leninakan** and **Spitak**
port on the Gulf of Finland, once St. Petersburg	**Leningrad**
main city in the western Ukraine	**Lvov** or **Lemberg**
capital of the Byelorussian SSR	**Minsk**
modern Russian capital	**Moscow**
northern port for Allied convoys in WWII	**Murmansk**
main port on the Laptev Sea	**Nordvik**
main trading center of Viking Russia	**Novgorod**
prime Black Sea port and resort	**Odessa**
linked with Turgenev	**Orel**
Pacific port on Kamchatka Peninsula	**Petropavlosk (Peter and Paul)**
capital of the Latvian SSR, a Baltic port	**Riga**
in Turkmenistan, that Alexander called Maracanda	**Samarkand**

main city on the Crimea	**Sebastopol (Seva-)**
city almost taken by the Germans in WWII	**Stalingrad**
capital of the Estonian SSR, on the Gulf of Finland	**Tallinn**
capital of the Uzbek SSR, an old trading city	**Tashkent**
capital of the Georgian SSR, south of the Caucasus	**Tbilsi (Tiflis)**
capital of the Lithuanian SSR	**Vilnius (Vilna)**
southeasternmost Russian port, on the Japan Sea	**Vladivostok**
hub of Siberia	**Yakutsk**
Crimean site of a key WWII Allies meeting	**Yalta**
capital of the Armenian SSR	**Yerevan**

Regions

southernmost small republic on the Black Sea	**Adzhar**
region seeking to annex land from Azerbaijan	**Armenia**
region from which some Armenians seek independence	**Azerbaijan**
once-independent region in Moldavia	**Besserabia**
region whose name means "White Russia"	**Byelorussia**
region between the Caspian and China	**Central Asia** or **Turkmenistan**
northeasternmost peninsula	**Chukchi** or **Chukot**
peninsula jutting into the northern Black Sea	**Crimea**
Baltic region pointing toward Finland	**Estonia**
important old silk trading region in Turkmenistan	**Ferghana**
Caucasus region linked with long life	**Georgia (Gruzia** or **Sakartvelo)**
peninsula jutting from NE Russia	**Kamchatka**
huge Central Asian province	**Kazakhstan**
region between Kazakhstan and China	**Kirghizstan**
Baltic region between Lithuania and Estonia	**Latvia**
region bordering the Baltic and Poland	**Lithuania**
region bordering on Romania	**Moldavia**
largely Armenian region of Azerbaijan	**Ngorno-Kharabakh**

resource-rich frozen NE region of labor camps **Siberia**

region bordering on China and Afghanistan **Tadzhikstan**

republic bordering Iran and the Caspian Sea **Turkmenistan**

breadbasket region centered on Kiev **Ukraine**

rich republic SE of the Aral Sea **Uzbekistan**